VOICES
of
WAR

VOICES *of* WAR

STORIES FROM THE AUSTRALIANS AT WAR FILM ARCHIVE

EDITED BY MICHAEL CAULFIELD

HODDER

Australian Government

Department of Veterans' Affairs

The Australians at War Film Archive was funded by the Australian Government. Full transcripts of interviews can be found at:
http://www.australiansatwarfilmarchive.gov.au

The stories presented in this book are drawn from the Australians at War Film Archive, commissioned by the Department of Veterans' Affairs for the Australian Government. The intent of the archive is to record Australians' experiences of war and its enduring impact on their lives and on Australian society. Some of the stories may not be historically accurate, given the passage of time since the events being recalled. Some aspects may be distressing to readers, while some of the stories may contain offensive language, depictions of sexual matters or negative stereotypes reflecting the culture or language of a period or place. These stories are the memories and reflections of the people who were interviewed for the film archive and do not reflect the views of the Department of Veterans' Affairs.

HODDER AUSTRALIA

Published in Australia and New Zealand in 2006
by Hodder Australia
(An imprint of Hachette Livre Australia Pty Limited)
Level 17, 207 Kent Street, Sydney NSW 2000
Website: www.hachette.com.au

National Library of Australia
Cataloguing-in-Publication data

Voices of war : stories from the Australians at War Film Archive.

ISBN 0 7336 2050 7.

1. Australians at War Film Archive. 2. Australia - History, Military - 20th century. 3. Australia - Armed Forces - Biography. I. Caulfield, Michael.

355.0994

Text design and typesetting by Bookhouse, Sydney
Jacket design by Nada Backovic
Printed in Australia by Griffin Press, Adelaide

*To all who have contributed
to the Archive—and all the others
whose stories are yet to be told.*

CONTENTS

Introduction   *ix*
Note to the Reader   *xvii*

Patrick Toovey   1
Arpad 'Paddy' Bacskai   29
Dulcie Toohey   55
Peter Warfe   77
Arthur 'Nat' Gould   103
Iris Roser   135
Frank McGovern   161
Barry Seeley   191
Dr Geoff Cornish   220
Ted Kenna, VC   242
Norman Cameron   260
Wendy Trevor   278
Walter Wallace   302
Keith Payne, VC   329
Paul Couvret   355
John Fraser   372
Noel 'Peter' Medcalf   402
Adele Manchoulas   430
Salvatore Andaloro   454
Garth Fitzgerald   490
Ted Smout   511

Index   529
Credits   538

INTRODUCTION

In a temperature-controlled vault somewhere in Sydney, row after row of boxes sit neatly stored on shelves—thousands of them, each one named and numbered. They contain the most unique and valuable collection in this country—not art, or jewellery or wine, but something paradoxically both ephemeral and enduring. They represent years of work by hundreds of people and contain, among many things, a great measure of generosity from two thousand and five Australians who gave a large part of themselves to their country for safekeeping. The boxes hold the images and sound of interviews, twelve thousand hours of interviews in total, and they tell the story of this country and its wars in a way not seen before: not dry history, but flesh and blood; not the movements of armies or the piece-by-piece reconstruction of a particular battle, but the stories of our countrymen and women as they faced the greatest challenge of their lives and lived through a time they cannot forget. In those cool, quiet rooms, a long journey has come to an end.

It began in the year 2000, with the production of the television series, 'Australians at War'. Eight hours long, the series was commissioned by the Department of Veterans' Affairs on behalf of the Australian Government, as a gift to the nation for the Centenary of Federation. I was the series producer. To tell the story of over a hundred years of our wartime history, 'Australians at War' used archival footage, newly filmed material, letters and diaries, and, of course, interviews with veterans, for nothing can substitute for the power and worth of the memories of those who were there.

We interviewed about sixty of them, from World War I to the UN mission in East Timor, their ages ranging from a brash, confident twenty-two-year-old to a wonderfully active one hundred and five. But it was a World War II veteran, a rifleman from the New Guinea campaign, whom I could not forget. I was sitting alone in a darkened room, watching interview tapes, a daily task, when he came on screen and I found myself shifting between tears and wonder at the sadness and heroism he was so quietly revealing on camera. He spoke tellingly of his wartime experiences, but I wanted to know so much more— where did he grow up? What were his parents like? What was his *whole* life like? It was frustrating. I left the room and returned to my desk in the production office to be told that we had just received a message from his family that he had died, two days after our interview.

They were grateful that we had spoken with him and so, of course, was I. But I was also distressed and, in truth, angry. Angry that because of the demands of television, we would only be able to use a fraction of his story and that even if we could use it all, it wasn't complete, and angry that we couldn't do more than we were doing. It didn't last of course; an eight-hour television series is a demanding animal, and the job went on.

But in the downtime that inevitably arrives after a major project, producer Liz Butler and I returned to it and investigated what other possibilities lay out there. The answer was disappointing. There were various interviews with veterans being collected but they were small in size, restricted in their reach and often based on nothing more than a view that if 'it's from the war then it must be valuable'. It wasn't nearly good enough and we felt compelled to try. But time was short—the WWII generation was passing quickly. And whatever we thought we could do, we had to do it now.

The Archive we proposed would film interviews with Australians from all our wars, conflicts and peacekeeping missions from WWI up to the present day. It would encompass the battlefront, the home front, media and entertainment, children, teachers, wives, workers and clerics. From signaller to Spitfire pilot, from SAS soldier to stoker, even to those who fought with us and those who fought against us; as long as they were Australians, then *everyone* who was in any way involved should be represented. Two thousand people in fact, from every state and territory of this country.

We took the proposal to the DVA, to the Commemorations Branch, and, to their lasting credit, they did not blanch, faint or laugh. They may well have swallowed hard but with the approval of the then Minister, the Hon. Bruce Scott, we began a year-long path that saw the project progress through a pilot study, financial projections and workshops. Then, on 11 November 2002, the then Minister for Veterans' Affairs, the Hon. Danna Vale, announced the project's commencement and the real work began. Finally, in 2005, the last interview was filmed, the last box of treasure placed in the vault. The Australians at War Film Archive interviewed over two thousand Australians who had participated in WWI, WWII, the Occupation of Japan, the Korean War, the Malayan Emergency, Indonesian Confrontasi, the Vietnam War, Gulf War 1, the War against Terror and Gulf War 2. We interviewed men and women who had seen service in UN and other operations in places such as the Sinai, Israel, Kashmir, Cambodia, Rwanda, Somalia, Bougainville and East Timor, along with Defence Force operations after the Rabaul tidal wave and the bombing in Bali.

We have spoken with people for whom the war ended eighty-six years ago and those who came home from *their* war fourteen days before their interview. Apart from the stories contained in this book, among our interviewees are a Lancaster pilot in Bomber Command who was shot down over France and spent the remainder of the war committing acts of sabotage alongside the French Resistance. There is a POW from the Thai–Burma Railway who upon his liberation after three long years of brutal captivity lay on a beach in Singapore, looked up at the stars . . . and realised it was his eighteenth birthday; and a rifleman from the 6th Division, who enlisted in 1939 and finally returned home to Balmain, six long years later, never to be the same man again. There's a male nurse from the astonishing 'guinea pig unit' in England, a revolutionary clinic for the treatment of burns caused by plane crashes in WWII, a Catholic priest from Vietnam, and the gay saxophone player from the concert parties in New Guinea. Among our last interviewees, men and women serving in the Australian Defence Force, were a major who, as a twenty-three-year-old lieutenant in 1994, had to defend the Australian medical team in a camp called Kibeho in Rwanda as men, women and children were massacred not twenty feet away from his horrified soldiers; a young aircraftswoman from the RAAF who flew into Denpasar on Operation Bali Assist in October 2002 and tended to the damaged and the dying on the long flight home to Darwin; and a Black Hawk chopper pilot, who flew the SAS into Afghanistan at the beginning of the War Against Terror.

None of these interviews were accidents. They were researched, located (often through a chase that would do credit to a detective novel) and, in some cases, then had to be convinced by us to overcome their natural modesty. We looked always for people that not only had a story, but could *tell* it, and the selection process for our final two thousand and five interviews involved the researching and pre-interviewing of over five thousand veterans. The Archive had the benefit of a consultant group of historians who helped us conceive and establish the collection's aims. We wanted diversity and depth, and our interviewees are divided into more than two hundred categories, ranging across all battlefronts, services and home front activities. So, there are separate categories for, say, Tobruk, or the RAN in the Mediterranean, just as there are categories for entertainers in Vietnam or POWs in Korea. Wherever it was possible we attempted to find and interview ten individuals in every category. Ultimately, this means ten separate and uniquely individual views of battles, campaigns and events.

Our interview teams were composed of two people, both of whom interviewed and operated camera and sound. The interviews, for the most part, were conducted in veterans' homes, where we knew they would feel more comfortable and relaxed with the process. This decision proved to be a mixed blessing. While it's certainly true that the teams reaped the benefits of relaxed interviewees, they also consumed a mountain of scones and fruit cake, a lake of tea and coffee and now know more about the care of roses and the value of Wedgwood figurines than they ever really wanted to. At any one time, there were ten teams on the road, in state capitals, regional cities and out in the bush.

The interviews were conducted across the landscape of an individual's entire life. We had always taken the view that the war experience must be seen in context, and so each interview begins with early childhood, growing up and life till the war, then the wartime period itself and around ten to fifteen years postwar. The brief for the interviewers was simple—detail, always detail. That meant not only details of training and battles, but details of home life, of meals, of social behaviour and relationships. We took the view that the particulars of, say, farm life in Gippsland in the 1930s were as important as that country boy's first impressions of jungle warfare. That how men were dealt with after death on a battlefield was as important as how they died. The interviewers would 'tag team' the veteran, taking it in turns to gently lead them back over matters that had already been spoken of, to elicit further and deeper understanding. This has led to unexpected benefits. The Australians at War Film Archive is now also a remarkable resource of Australian social and cultural life from about 1914 till 2004. Our material on the Depression, post-WWII Australia, the '50s, '60s and so on continues to surprise and delight us. If you want to know what kinds of games children played during the twentieth century, or what they ate and how it was prepared, or how you asked a girl to go out or what you did in the almost complete absence of sex education to improve your knowledge ... look to these interviews. They are frank, discursive and revelatory. We kept to our principal goal—that the Archive was not cut-and-dried history, the result of careful study and conclusion, but a repository of memory, with all the idiosyncrasies that can mean.

This project has, unquestionably, left its mark on everyone who has had the privilege of being involved. We recently received an email from one of our female interviewers, Naomi Homel, who, having finished her time with us, felt compelled to tell us what it had been like for her. Most of our interviewers were aged under forty and Naomi was in her twenties. She said, in part:

I've seen so much of the country, slept in countless hotel beds, been given a sapphire, homemade wine, recipes for lemonade, scones and jam. I've had to tell an eighty-year-old nudist that he'll have to pop a shirt on otherwise I'd have to clip his microphone to his nipple. I have been hit on more times by veterans than I have by my contemporaries and we all know that all it takes to make me blush is to be snogged by an eighty-five-year-old who thinks I'm 'a bit of a line' and wants to go where no veteran has gone before.

I have drunk endless cups of tea and coffee, discussed the housing market to death and even had to smile and nod when Pauline Hanson was referred to as Australia's Nelson Mandela.

I have finally figured out that a beaufighter is a plane and a bofors is a gun to shoot down planes. As most of my friends well know I can discuss a couple of wars at length and in detail and get quite excited about it!

More importantly I have walked through 121 normal screen doors and I have walked into 121 different worlds. These veterans have taken me on a journey that I could never have mapped. They have taught me lessons about my country, about men and the bonds of friendship, about war and about myself. They have quietened me down and I think made me look at things a bit more deeply, to not stand in positions of judgement, by all means to make your own opinions and stick by them, but to never assume your own superiority or moral high ground. I think this comes from a realisation of the importance of the individual. That two

men can stand next to each other in a battle and each have
completely different experiences and reactions.
   I have loved this job and I will miss it.

   Naomi.

I cannot allow this opportunity to pass without praising our interview teams. They worked impossibly long hours, often under difficult physical conditions, for base-line salaries. They were compassionate, insightful and caring to such a degree that they would often be found in a veteran's home hours after a day-long interview had concluded, still listening, still involved. They have contributed to their country's heritage in an enduring and meaningful way. God bless them all.

Without the confidence and guidance we received from the Commemorations Branch of the Department of Veterans' Affairs, we may well have stumbled or lost our way along this journey. Of many, I must particularly thank Kerry Blackburn and Cathy Moore, whose contribution to this project is beyond any measure.

I've never made a film that is anything like this epic, and I never will. The only similarity between my past work and the Archive is an unrepayable debt to my producer partner, Liz Butler. Liz was responsible for the entire administration of the project, every nut and bolt. Let me illustrate with the process of just one interview. The veteran was called by one of the six researchers to determine their potential for the Archive. The name of that veteran may have come from a service association, or an RSL, or another veteran, from our own searches, or from the veteran themselves. If all went well, the researcher continued the telephone interview for a couple of hours, gathering the basic biographical material that would form the core of the brief for the interview team. After passing through another filtering assessment with me and the other researchers, the name was passed to Liz and the production staff. That veteran could be in any state or territory in Australia, they could live at home or in a nursing facility or in a hospital. They might have medical needs that needed to be taken into consideration, or they may even have not spoken with anyone for the last three months. Whatever their situation, it had been decided that we wanted them and it was Liz's task to fit them into the schedule, ensure that they received regular contact with our office, that they understood the process and that the interview team could reach them. We had ten interview teams on the road anywhere in Australia at any one time, interviewing fifty people each week and sending back hundreds of hours of digital video tape, each one so valuable it was a constant fear that they would go astray. (They never did, not one.) The tapes from this veteran's interview were then copied and sent to one of the forty transcribers who needed to be trained, checked and managed. The text of the interview then went to a transcription editor, who checked for inaccuracies and added explanations of military terms, acronyms and outdated slang, and then to a supervising editor for final assessment. At last, it would be uploaded to the website. That process happened two thousand and five times. It was a ridiculously challenging task that Liz met head on with meticulous planning, endurance and a humour and optimism that kept the rest of us afloat. As one of our vets said, 'That woman could run a war!' He's right, she could.

Film is the people's medium, the storytelling mechanism of contemporary choice, and here, in this Archive, the thousands of men and women we interviewed are the gatekeepers of the stories that filmmakers want to tell and people want to read and see. It will always be important to remember that the Australians at War Film Archive is not distilled, proven history. That is the task of historians. It is rather the memories and reflections of our countrymen and women, their lives, their thoughts, their disappointments, tragedies and occasional triumphs. I cannot know what each of you will bring to this book, what memories, or prejudices or desires. What I do know is that you will never look at war the same way again.

Michael Caulfield

NOTE TO THE READER

I have selected segments from twenty-one interviews that I hope represent the breadth and depth of the Archive, though not necessarily of our entire military involvement over the years. Because the methodology of the interviews was to circle back over stories during the course of a day, the interviewees often spoke in further detail about matters they had mentioned hours earlier. What I have done is to select those sections and pull them together, whether they were paragraphs or sentences. I have not changed or added to the words that were spoken in interview, simply joined like with like. I have also been careful not to change the sense of what was said, nor its intent. Wherever separate sections are found together, a series of dots indicates there was a break of time between the two passages. As well, wherever it seemed necessary, I have explained acronyms or unfamiliar terminology inside square brackets. All italics are also mine. If you wish to find further information concerning particular units, squadrons or ships associated with the interviewees, I would refer you to the original transcripts which can be found in their entirety on the Archive website: http://www.australiansatwarfilmarchive.gov.au

PATRICK TOOVEY

El Alamein
Prisoner of the Italians
Prisoner of the Germans
World War II

1929 came, the big Depression, and everything changed then. It was very, very hard going. It affected us a great deal because at that time things were starting to become available, for instance motor cars and tractors for the farm and other stationary engines and things like that. With the Depression it was so bad and so severe that we weren't able to afford those sorts of things. Things really became very stagnant in the 1930s. In any case in those days, establishing a farm meant clearing land, putting in fences, sinking dams, putting in crops, taking them off. It's all just manual work.

... The members of the family were expected to contribute. In fact that's the only way you could survive in those days. One of the things I've often said, I was too young to remember when I didn't have a whole heap of jobs to do. That was all a part of life, even when you're two or three or four. Even at three or four years old you could help herd the sheep or carry things, run messages and do things. You can imagine, for instance, my mother having seven children, apart from the fact of illness and a couple of operations, she had to have the actual going away, and having more babies meant that my older sister really, for quite a lot of the time, was looking after the rest of the family when she was only probably fourteen of fifteen. That includes everything, housework and cooking and everything, a lot of responsibility. That's what people were expected to do in those days.

... The farm life in many ways is good and I shouldn't paint too dismal a picture because we had for instance everything there by way of food ... we had a ten-acre orchard and a big vegetable garden and the chooks and the meat of course with sheep and cattle and the dairying so that's milk and cream and all that sort of thing. We probably lived pretty well. The main problem was no cash, no money. To get anywhere for clothing and joining things and travelling a bit for sport and whatever else, you really needed cash money so it was very, very difficult in that respect. Also transport was a big problem from a family point of view. For instance, we went in a sulky to school. It was eight miles and that's a fairly long trip. That was about an hour and a quarter. That's an open sulky so it's summer and winter and you know, that's pretty hard going. In many ways it sounds a bit romantic and quite pleasant but there's some hard times.

... There was a little one-teacher, one-room school at this place, Tenterden, and so I went there for my primary years starting in 1927 when I was six. I went through there until 1934 and then the government had a scheme going because things were so hard, to try and get some kids scholarships to go away to school. A scholarship meant you got it for free. That was the burning question in those days. I sat for a scholarship in 1934 and passed satisfactorily and I got two years at the Narrogin School of Agriculture.

... My first teacher, and I had him for about my first five years, he was a Gallipoli veteran. He lost a leg at Gallipoli and he'd been re-trained as a school teacher and he was a fantastic bloke. With my involvement later on with the army and other things that was a good grounding because he told hundreds of yarns about Gallipoli and his war experiences and all those sort of things and I used to enjoy that more than say, nature study. One element of this country life and farm life, we were a Catholic family. I only mention that, it's nothing to do with religion, it's just simply a story within a story. The Catholic organisation during the holidays when I was a young bloke gathered up all the disadvantaged ones of the Catholic Church faith and brought them in to the convents in Albany and Katanning for the holidays, for what became dubbed as 'the bushie school'. You learnt a bit of religious instruction, that was a bit by the way but that was my first trip to Albany as well when I was about eight or something like that. Going down to the ocean, you go swimming at Middleton Beach and all those sorts of things, absolutely fantastic... Perth wasn't a big city then but it was a marvellous town. It was wonderful old buildings and good sporting facilities for the times and of course you could soon learn your way around. It was like a big village really.

* * *

When things went wrong you couldn't get a mechanic or electrician or what have you, so we all had to know something about everything. A cousin of my father's, a farmer, lived sixteen miles away from us. They were starting shearing and they couldn't get their shearing plant to start ... so they were going mad and they got a message through to us to see whether we could help them because we had a shearing plant and I had a little bit of experience with stationary engines and also because it was a part of the curriculum at the agricultural school so that my father just assumed that I knew a bit. When they said they couldn't get their plant started my father said, 'How about you hop on your pony and go out and see if you can help them?'

They were sixteen miles away and on a pony you get that exhausted if you go more than about three miles an hour so it's about a five-hour trip or so out there. Anyway all I did was to clean out all the petrol pipes, clean the spark plug and everything was loose, tighten it all up and what have you, turned the handle and away it went. I was sixteen at that time and I thought I'd done a big job, I was looking for a bit of kudos but the motor started and the dogs started barking and the farmer started shouting and the two shearers grabbed a sheep and started shearing and I was completely ignored. The shearing had started now, there was no room for me so I rode home the sixteen miles and I was telling my dad what had happened but he reckoned that was just normal so I had to accept that. That's just the experiences of human relationships you know.

... I'd been at boarding school and then I'd got this bit of a start so I was looking round for something else and actually I got a job... in the shearing season. So I was working in shearing sheds. I liked this, this really was my thing. There's farmers and the sheep and the dogs and the shearers and the wool bales, all that sorts of thing. There's pressing the wool and the classer was there classing the wool. It really is quite an interesting exercise and I liked it. I was what they called a roustabout. You did bits of everything, putting the sheep in, clearing the board for the shearers, picking the wool up off the floor and throwing it on to the table where the classers would come round and class it and then herding sheep in and then branding them afterwards... The shearers are notorious characters, yarns, and of course they worked the eight-hour day and then there's meals but in those days there was no television... and practically nobody had radios and if they did have one it was only in the house anyway, so there's lots of big gaps of time for yarning and other things like playing cards.

I learnt to play cards of all sorts but bridge in particular when I was very young and by the time I was twelve, you have to have four for a game of bridge you know, two pairs of two partners and frequently I was required to make up a four in bridge. So because of the sport and the cards, bridge and things like that I spent a huge amount of time with adults like these shearers, land-clearers and all those sorts of people filling in this time at night playing cards... One chap down there was a remittance man. Remittance men in Western Australia in those days were usually ones who were illegitimate offspring of some royalty or something, or they were some social misfit like a communist or something. Now, a communist is not a misfit in my language but they were in those days in England. So this chap had been educated in Oxford, a wonderful upper-class English accent, but he'd been banished out to Western Australia and he received his remittance. Now the remittance was a legal agreement whereby whoever was sending you out, such as the father or whoever, the agreement was you'd receive a certain amount of money and you'd sign a document you'd stay away, you know. So this money would come out every three months. There were trustees would receive the money, sign for everything and send the documents back and this chap Lou was a remittance man. He was a son of somebody fairly famous over there but I don't know exactly who, and he'd been mixed up with communists and making trouble for the establishment in London so he'd been sent out here. He was a wonderfully educated chap, a wonderful conversationalist and I could sit and listen to him for hours and hours. So these sorts of characters you meet along the road and they have an influence.

I think it was 1934 when we got our first wireless. This wireless was a big cabinet-type thing with a wet cell to drive it, like a car battery, similar sort of thing, and two dry cells and the wet cell'd need pumping up now and again. The dry cells would eventually run out and you had to get new ones. It had two wires, the aerial wire and an earth wire which you had to bury. You couldn't get reception unless you had a decent aerial so we used to get thin poles and tie them together until you got to about forty or fifty feet, sink a very deep hole and put the aerial pole in that and of course fill it in and then have guy wires to keep it upright. The aerial wire from the wireless went to the top of that pole, that's how you got your reception. I'll tell you what, the first time we heard that wireless coming over we couldn't believe it, fantastic. Of course I'm mad on sport but there were other programs for instance *Dad and Dave*... that was a great one. They're the ones I remember. The first time I heard the cricket coming over the radio, because I'm mad on cricket, was absolutely fantastic. So these things were happening through my life.

* * *

Even though I wasn't a great scholar I learnt to read at a very young age and used to pore over the newspapers, particularly the sporting part, cut out the cricket scores and averages and paste them in a scrapbook. We were much more aware, it's surprising really because another thing in those days of lots of time and a slower pace, there was a lot of yarning went on, a lot of conversation. Instead of half the people being at takeaways or the TV or whatever, all those old houses had a big table and everybody just sat around the table and talked and the kids'd butt in and make themselves heard. So leading up to the war, we probably knew a fair bit about it. They used to get very irate about things happening to people in Europe. For instance back in that time there was a big furore going on, the Middle East is always in the news even now, there was a big furore about a shipload of Jews that had been banished from Europe and were trying to find some place where they would be taken and they ended up in the Middle East in Palestine . . . but being turned away. Those sorts of things just like today we have issues to carry on about, well people used to write to the papers and get worked up about this sort of thing. Because of this we knew a fair bit of what was going on.

. . . I don't think it's any good saying I joined up through a lot of patriotism or anything like that although in those days we were very strictly a part of the British Empire. In fact in my education, I learnt all about England and going right back about the royal families and that sort of stuff . . . Robert Menzies was the Prime Minister when the war broke out and I still remember his words, he wouldn't get away with it today, he said that, 'Because England is at war, Australia is at war.'

There was no question about should be there or shouldn't be there. Of course this is something which my father didn't agree with by any means, that's why I've always had the two sides of the argument . . . we have always been Labor supporters so that we've been a bit anti-establishment all along the line. My father was very much anti-war. Not so much anti-war but what I mean is he liked to look at all these things and not accept them. Anyway, when the war came I wanted to be in it anyway. That's the short answer. There's a certain amount of patriotism. We were very close to Britain in those days. Practically everything that we've got or we had in those days was manufactured in Britain and brought out here by ship to Australia. Of course all the people, we were surrounded by English people coming out here as migrants. So I wanted to be in it early.

* * *

I had rather a mixed-up time early in the war because I went and enlisted in the air force. I passed through the qualifications and the very strict medical and all the rest of it but I was never called up. I wrote to them a couple of times whether they had enough or were they only calling up the ones who had put down unemployed and unfortunately I put down farmer or something which didn't help in those days. So I was never called up and time went on so I just got sick of it in the end and I joined the AIF [Australian Imperial Force] as a volunteer.

... The camp at Gaza was quite good actually ... Ultimately there was about a hundred thousand AIF in Palestine and these huge camps. Some were smallish but some were up to twenty thousand. They were set up very well like little cities, with main streets and streets going off and tents for the troops and doctors and the RAP [Regimental Aid Post] outposts to tend to the sick and a big parade ground and a big training place which was quite organised in as much as there was rifle training, machine-gun training, mortars, hand grenades and so on so you'd pass through these sections in the training. That was very good.

In those days lots of route marches, route marches up to thirty miles and things like this ... The British had full control of Palestine in those days. It wasn't exactly a part of the British Empire but it was virtually. They just said what they wanted. So if we wanted space for camps and for training and for parade grounds they just took it. That doesn't mean to say we kicked people out. We went to vacant spaces and just built. See, in the army in those days you could go to a big bare piece of land and you could start from scratch with the tents and build up a city in a matter of days and put in ablution blocks, parade grounds, training facilities, hospitals and everything. Quite remarkable it was. That camp at Gaza, that first one I was in was said to be about twenty thousand people. There was wet canteens and dry canteens and when I say that, booze, and the dry canteen was just cigarettes and chocolates and all those sort of things and a big marquee, a huge marquee for visiting entertainers and for film shows and things like that.

... I was just a driver in a big pool so it could be anything. I got all sorts of jobs and in fact later on one of our divisions came home and that's about sixteen, eighteen thousand people came home in one hit and I was in a group that helped to ferry them and clean up the big mess that they left behind. One of the things I found fantastically interesting was trips back across to the Suez Canal. I'd already seen it coming so I wanted to see more of it. In between Palestine, Gaza where I was, and the Suez Canal, is that Sinai Peninsula which is very notorious. That's a part of Egypt you know. I got lots of trips across there because we had people coming in and going out, messages to be sent and pays to be taken over and all sorts of things like that. So I got lots of trips over to the Suez Canal. I came from inland in Western Australia, a bushie from inland, not on the coast and so this activity over on the Suez Canal was great, I was fascinated by it, of great interest to me. All ships and boats and barges and canoes and of course going over the Suez Canal they were putting down pontoons, driving vehicles across and taking them up and all that sort of thing. There was seamen from all over the world, Chinese and Indians and all sorts coming and going in teeming millions, well, teeming thousands anyway. I always volunteered for the jobs going over the Suez Canal.

* * *

Stopping the Axis [Germany and its allies] at El Alamein was very, very important. You can't put enough importance on it. Both sides knew this and that's why that fighting, particularly in that first month or so, it was savage and unrelenting. It was in full swing when I arrived there and the first thing I noticed, you couldn't help but notice, was the terrific noises. The machine guns, aircraft flying everywhere, dive-bombing, the incessant bombing, the mortars exploding in every direction and the Axis forces were trying to get through the Allied line so they're attacking in big numbers here and two or three other places and then shifting to see if they can find a weaker spot to attack and we found ourselves in the same sort of situation where we kept shifting all the time to block up this spot and block up that... the smoke and dust, you couldn't see your nose really. Smoke and dust, noise, the heat and the flies, so that's what the impression was, chaos. They called it 'the fog of war' I think, but chaos and of course, we were just new into it... I got a job there early on in the piece being a runner. These days you'd use your mobiles and that see, but a runner's doing it on foot taking messages from here to there. Nobody knew where anybody was, it was no good asking questions and that was a nightmarish job.

... El Alamein was one of the historic battles of the Second World War. Very significant historically, strategically and every other way. A huge amount has been written about it, lots of books and accounts of all various sorts but they vary a lot from the story of an ordinary private soldier on the ground and that's what I was. My story really doesn't fit in to the official accounts. If somebody read the history of the El Alamein campaign they probably wouldn't make any sense of what I'm saying but that's what it was like on the ground for a twenty-year-old private.

... We'd just come up not very long into the front line and on the very first day we started to have casualties. This has a huge effect, the bonding effect of being in a battalion, even being in the division and then in a battalion and then in a platoon and then down to a section, which is about eight or nine in a section with a corporal in charge. You become very close and also we've all got our duties, say two on a machine gun, all riflemen of course, but say two on the machine gun, two on the mortar and all with their duties, but all this flies out the window if you start having casualties and not only wounded and killed but in no time quite a few got sick. The conditions were horrendous. Of course there's millions of flies so there's no hope of keeping food clean or your hands clean, the water, the eternal thirst, water's very short. Everything had to come up by truck from behind but then the truck would be bombed and machine-gunned and all the rest of it. So apart from whatever else that might do to you, missing meals and not having enough water it also meant that a lot got sick. Stomach problems, desert sores, sore eyes and all those sorts of things. As a young soldier this is what I saw around me, immediate casualties.

One was killed almost the first day...one killed and three or four wounded. Two or three had to go off on sick [leave] and then we didn't see them, they sent them off to somewhere, hospital. And so in no time all our plans have gone out the window and even our officer, you have one officer to a platoon, he was wounded on the second or third day I think, so he's gone, you've got three corporals, one for each section, two of those were wounded and gone and so everything's in turmoil after a while but you find others taking over and it's amazing how you can make adjustments.

... The terrain, it's desert but in that particular area at Alamein you only had about four or five inches of soil on top that you could dig in to. Of course we used to carry the little spades for digging trenches for protection of yourself, but we could only dig about five or six inches down and then you struck hard rock and couldn't go any further. To add to our burdens we had to carry sandbags, and our digging, in would be mainly filling sandbags and putting them around to make some sort of shelter. That terrain had quite a big bearing on the casualties and certainly on how secure or insecure you might feel.

... In the army they might do it these days with all the psychologists and that around, you never got to be taught how to handle the psychological aspect of things. That is, the noises...the German machine guns, they were very advanced, particularly in those early years of the war... Their 88-millimetre all-purpose machine guns were much advanced to ours and they had a technique...they advanced the fuse on the shells so the shells could come over above us and burst before they hit the ground, they'd burst say twenty or thirty feet above us and shower out metal. So this was a terrible thing to the troops on the ground, a frightening business from that point of view and also inflicted lots of casualties...and then the dive-bombers. You have to really experience them to know what you feel like. The bombers come over and instead of just dropping their bombs . . . as soon as they turned to come down they'd start screeching and then they'd come low swooping over us and drop their bombs from pretty close. Apart from the bombs you had this terrible noise going on.

. . . It's an eerie thing. Everything seems to be magnified. Your hearing becomes very intense, your sight, watching, you're on the alert all the time but it's an eerie feeling. It's hard to describe the feeling but you're very conscious of being out there and being vulnerable and really you're not, being all up to yourself really. It's quite a remarkable experience actually . . . I was taken in a group which was to go out through the German lines . . . the intention as far as I know was to spike some guns. In this little group . . . there's an officer, a captain, and a lieutenant and a sergeant, a couple of others who were specialists for finding directions and myself. I was the donkey in this. I carried all the extra water and I carried a Tommy gun apart from my usual gear and in addition to that what we call sticky bombs. Now the sticky bombs are bombs which are magnetised · and you can just put them near a metal object and the magnetism draws them on to the metal object. So you can put them on a tank or a gun . . . So I had these sticky bombs and there was an amount you were supposed to not carry above, you know, so many pounds and nobody ever weighed us I'll tell you, I was loaded down like a donkey . . . I was pleased when some of the water was drunk because that narrowed the load down a little bit. We went out through our own lines, through no-man's-land, through the German lines and went out trying to find this thing. In addition to trying to spike a gun I'm sure they were also noting everything they could see with regard to intelligence, what was out there, how deep they were and where things were. I didn't have very much to do with all that but I do know we were away about four days and four nights and it seemed a lifetime.

You just hunkered down on the ground. Actually you'd be surprised how good you become at this. You can lie down on the desert and put your tin hat under your head and go to sleep. It doesn't sound very comfortable but when you're tired it's very comfortable . . . Here again I emphasise the one private soldier on the ground and those sorts of things which happened become lifetime memories. They're very significant in the life of one person even though they're insignificant in the overall scheme of things. I remember every step of that. The desert you know is a bad enemy in itself, you can see for miles. There's little undulations in the desert so if you're in them, when you're down in an ebb, the bottom part, you can walk on not too bad, pretty safe, but when you're up, when we were on the top of the undulations we had to virtually crawl, wriggle on our bellies you know otherwise you're a target . . . What the officer in charge of the party found out and what he recorded and what he reported I really don't know but what I do know is we were challenged along the line and it was probably the German observation post and this is where the Tommy gun, I was carrying the Tommy gun slung over my shoulders with about fifty rounds I think from memory, just pulled the trigger, that's all you do and run for your life.

* * *

I didn't get any mail at Alamein. It would have come through I think, had I survived there for say three or four months, because in previous campaigns I had heard that they'd received mail but certainly not immediately. They wouldn't have bothered with it; it would have been all banked up. The situation was too dire, too pressing at that stage for them to waste manpower on mail and that. You're cut off; you just had this job to do. You are out there and even though you're getting orders to do this and do that and going along with the battalion there is that feeling that you're on your own, you know, you've got to keep your end up and do whatever your job is. This applies to senior officers. There are generals who fell by the wayside, got sacked and got sent back to England as well, so each one of us in our own role with your own sort of pride and self-respect, it was very important that you kept going and did your job.

In those days mateship was an unspoken thing. Whether we took it for granted or not I don't know. It existed all right, the mates were good, this particularly came out if anybody was sick or wounded. It's an important aspect of it but things get a bit callous. After you start getting casualties and the ranks are thinning, there's a lot of things to be done, you also have to protect yourself that you don't overdo it and spend too much energy on something else rather than sort of looking after yourself. That's fairly hard, that's a big psychological question that, isn't it? I think for instance it's very, very important to have people around you that you know and trust and you're friends with. I think that more or less answers it. When you're feeling a bit off, a person is feeling a bit ruffled by the situation, these friends around were a reassuring aspect, there's no doubt about that. As a matter of fact we were more likely to tell each other what was going on and what we felt rather than say go to an officer or something like that.

. . . Any conversations that we have today are vastly different than what they were, this is over sixty years ago, you know. Because people are generally better educated and educated more in scientific areas; these conversations might take place today but in those days they still took place, but in a totally different form, 'How are you, mate? Hang in there, stick with it. Can I give you a hand?' And that sort of thing. Of course a lot of things just by looking at each other, they're unspoken things, just a hand on the shoulder. I remember when we got on in the prisoner of war camps, when I'd been sick, because that's a different situation altogether, I was getting a little bit, probably depressed I suppose, but I remember standing out in the compound by myself, just thinking about things, about my family back home and things like that and suddenly an arm comes round my shoulder. That's conversation.

* * *

The 2/28th Battalion were given this job of attacking and taking this strategic position known as Ruin Ridge. There were other plans of course. If we successfully took the ridge a tank formation was going to come up in support and then there was another infantry formation which was going to play a part and then of course, the supports of ammunition and food and water and all that to come up. In the long run the infantry formations and the tanks never got there; they were beaten off by the enemy but we actually took the position and held it for a few hours.

... This area all through there was heavily mined, thousands of mines, there were our own mines, the Germans had put in mines, the Italians had put in mines. Our engineers were very good. They had the job of making a passageway through the mines and putting a long tape which we would follow in our attack going in, but unfortunately on the way in we were attacked savagely with bombing and shelling and quite a lot of our trucks, we had about forty vehicles all together apart from Bren carriers and armoured cars, they'd been hit and they'd run into mines and they were all alight. So we were supposed to be in the dark but actually were lit up with all these burning vehicles, it was lit up like daylight. So we suffered heavy casualties on the way in but we got into Ruin Ridge. There was hand-to-hand fighting but we took it and were holding it next morning.

The overall intention was to take this position and when the other formations came in we were going to form a little army and go another forty miles behind the lines and take a place called El Daba, a strategic place ... That didn't come about. The other formations were beaten off and we were in there by ourselves and no extra ammunition or medical support or food or water had come up or could come up. By this time all the minefields were all closed and there was no way of getting through. So we were there high and dry by ourselves and when we run out of ammunition there was not much we could do anyway. Then a formation of German tanks came in and attacked us and surrounded us.

We were just an infantry battalion. We had no hope in there and then we'd lost communications eventually. There had been communications and we'd asked for ammunition and reinforcements and what's happened to everybody else and all the rest of it, but we'd lost communications completely. Once the situation became regarded as being hopeless our commanding officer surrendered the battalion and declared, 'every man for himself'. That was that. Very quickly we were surrounded by Germans with tanks and submachine guns and all sorts of other weapons and we were all prisoners of war.

... They arranged for the wounded to be carried forward and they put them all on trucks and they were taken away and the officers they split off and this was the normal procedure, to take the officers, and they took them somewhere to a fairly close airfield and flew them over to Europe. They were regarded as more valuable so they would fly them over under escort. So the wounded are gone and the officers are gone and the rest of us were marched a long way, right back as far as we could go before we were all knocked up and there's probably a bit of sense in that too, because that would avoid people wanting to escape, they wouldn't be so keen on escaping because we were exhausted ... The procedure on the enemy side was that all these administrative things were done by the Italians. They had the fleet and they had the ports, they had all the big truck convoys and so the Germans that afternoon or next day, anyway, fairly soon, they handed us over to the Italians and then went back to their front line.

... You feel ashamed and you feel guilty and then you're wondering what people will think of you back at home. You're not trained to become a prisoner of war, that's the very last thing so there's all sorts of thoughts rush through your mind and of course it's a very depressing, miserable event in a person's life, probably the worst experience. I didn't have fear so much as just frightened of what people would think and let the team down and all those sorts of things. All these things happen but you never think they're going to happen to you. I was surprised all right, yes. Because you know in this case we didn't have a build-up to it. In some other cases we had formations that got cut off and then hung on in an isolated area, there's six of them or something and they knew that unless something happened they were done for, but this wasn't that situation. We had taken the objective, we were there, we'd done the job, we didn't think that this was going to go wrong.

When the order, 'every man for himself' is given, you can escape if you can and you're not classified as a deserter, that's a legal requirement of the army. So at that minute when the sergeant major said that the OC [Officer Commanding] had surrendered us with every man for himself, if I could have I would have run for it and got out but in actual fact there was no hope. The Germans were around us in a very, very short time, in fact in a matter of minutes, seconds even. In addition to that we were always very conscious of these minefields. Unless you've got away through these minefields there was a huge risk so there was that factor and all these experienced soldiers, we didn't get any advice that if you try this or try that you'll get out; it was a no-hope situation. We were way out past no-man's-land behind enemy lines.

The tanks had been creeping in on us all the time and they were all around, German tanks and then the trucks full of soldiers were behind them . . . they seemed to have a hundred guns each but they've got about six or eight pointing at us, and the German soldiers with their submachine guns were in among us in a matter of seconds, and of course, if you don't drop your own weapons and come out of dugouts, well you can be shot, that's the risk. I must have made a decision that this was it. I feared for my safety from then on until I got back to England three years later. There's all these other emotions of feeling ashamed that we'd messed it up and now being a prisoner of war, see the Germans speak a bit of English they say, 'For you the war is over.'

And just round us up pointing their guns. There's all sorts of mixed emotions for sure. It's a terrible time, I can tell you. It's an indescribable experience. We didn't say too much to each other, we just had to accept what we were doing. Nobody wanted to talk about it too much I can tell you that. Then of course it dawned on us later on, pretty quickly rather, like in my case I realised that I was hungry and thirsty and dirty and tired and wondering what the heck was going to happen next. I certainly didn't think it was going to be three years before I got out of that, three more years.

It's a pretty international language, pointing a gun. There were a few could speak English and so there were some orders given to the senior ones and that sort of thing. We were just herded together back behind and marched in a big column.

* * *

Eventually we got to Benghazi and this was a famous camp called 'The Palms'. There must have been a couple of palms there somewhere. It was about a two-acre lot fenced in with barbed wire, no latrine arrangements and it was just full of vermin and lice and that sort of thing, a terrible place. From there, you can imagine what that was like and with my bad back I had to rest a lot on the ground and of course it was terrible and I got very sick there. I got eventually dysentery and other things and I was taken to an Italian hospital in Benghazi.

... I didn't strike anybody there who could speak English except I eventually found this one Aussie, and I couldn't speak Italian of course, so communication was nil, so I couldn't tell them what was ailing me or anything so it was just a matter of time improving me. It's a very harrowing experience not to be able to communicate, that was a terrible time. Eventually they just put me on a truck and took me to another camp. Another aspect of all of this was that in the meantime I'd lost everything, my water bottle, my tin hat and anything else which I may have had so I just had ragged shorts and a shirt, a pair of boots and socks, everything else was worn out and so it dawned on me that apart from everything else, I didn't have any possessions at all. We usually have so many possessions around us, we keep our things, but I had nothing. I was taken back to this other camp which wasn't much better, there was certainly no protection, no huts or anything like that, we were just out in the open. This friend and I decided that we would try and hang in, in the hope that our troops would come and eventually be relieved so we changed names with two South Africans. Why we changed names, the policy of the Italians was to take all the Australians and New Zealanders off as soon as they had a boat, take them over to Italy. They didn't like Aussies and New Zealanders. Because they'd given them such a hard time in the wars. They knew them too well.

... The idea of changing names and hanging in there almost worked. It seems silly that the Italians bothered about us, they just could have let us go. Anyway, they didn't ... it was just hopeless. We were marched down to a boat in the Tripoli harbour and taken across to Italy and we arrived at Naples.

* * *

As it turned out for several weeks we were just shifted from one staging place to another ... but after a time, I don't know how long it was, we were taken to a permanent camp in north-east Italy. The town was called Udine and the camp was called Gruppignano PG57. The PG stands for *'prigioniero di guerrais'*, prisoner of war in Italian, so PG57. This became a notorious camp. There were thousands there, mainly Australians and New Zealanders.

... The Red Cross had also reached us with some sporting gear for various things like cricket and then of course cards and chess, although lots of times we made our own cards or chess sets and this made things a bit better. One of the great things in these camps was some who'd been involved in entertainment, so singers or played musical instruments or could entertain in any way at all would go from hut to hut and put on little shows and these were wonderful, and also it was organised that volunteers give little talks on whatever they were doing. Some might just give talks on the political system in New Zealand or if somebody worked in a newspaper, how a newspaper operated. In my case I got roped in ... all the officers had been taken and so the senior ones were the warrant officers, in other words sergeant majors ... I was trying to teach three blokes how to play bridge so they could make up a four with me. These two sergeant majors were walking around because they were the senior ones there then and just seeing how everything was going and they had been organising these things like the musical and the lectures or talks you might call them. They struck me showing this bridge. They asked what was going on so I explained it. Anyway, they said, 'You'll be our bridge instructor from now on.'

In no time I had about fifty pupils.

I played thousands of hours of chess and bridge and other cards and teaching people how to play and making up little competitions even if you only get four teams you could make up a competition. Competition makes people try a bit harder. So I played thousands and thousands of hours of that and that helped a lot. Anything else that was going on like, for instance, making things, I wasn't much good at that and for a long time I wasn't fit, I was just simply intent on just getting my health back actually. But people were doing all sorts of things. They were making all types of things . . . they made packs of cards out of cardboard and chess sets and these little things, the tins in the Red Cross parcels, you couldn't make fires but they used to make these little gadgets like the old-fashioned forge and made little bellows and a string, I don't know what they call the darned things, pulleys to run the bellows around and blow and a little place at the back and put little bits of wood in and you could boil water and make a cup of tea off that.

. . . I think the army discipline, and the British are very good at this, they're better than the Aussies really, the army discipline probably saved us. They used to say when we got there, 'Never mind about Hitler. This is a bit of England and we're going to carry on just like we're in England here.'

And so their discipline was good. They were particularly good on things like keeping the very best hygiene you possibly could and going round seeing if anybody was lying around too much and trying to encourage them to get up and have exercise and all those sorts of things.

* * *

In 1943 Italy capitulated and withdrew from the war, in September 1943. The arrangement from England, the original arrangement, was that they were to guard us until the British got there to take us home but there's a whole mix up like there always is and that wasn't followed and when Italy capitulated, when we thought we might be out, the Germans were already there. They surrounded our camps and they took us, in my case into Austria through the Alps, through the Brenner Pass and into Austria.

... I was registered as a prisoner of war and given a number which I've got at home, and a plaque, square thing with a number on it and name which I had to wear all the time. Then they were vetting through the privates so I had to go out and work. I was put on a work party and sent out to a city called Graz. My first job with this group was building air-raid shelters. This was very, very hard work. The old-fashioned business of mixing the sand in the cement, six times each way, then in a wheelbarrow wheeling it around, digging the holes and other holes underneath, tunnels underneath for the air-raid shelters and wheeling the cement around. I tried to stay out there because I thought staying out there to work, you'd pick up and get in better condition but I started having fainting fits and falling over on the job and that... Anyway I ended up in a hospital there in Graz and that wasn't too bad. The conditions weren't much better in the hospital than anywhere else because there were still shortages of food and all that sort of thing.

... From the hospital I went back to the stalag again and then went out and I was put into a group which was doing all various jobs and taken all over the place. I got really a tour of Germany and Austria out of that. The bombing had all started now and that bombing changed everything for them and for us as well. These jobs included going out and shovelling the snow off the railway lines and the marshalling yards at the stations, repairing after the bombing and clearing away in front of facilities like hospitals, schools, railway stations and all those sorts of things and then hopping on a train and going somewhere else because another train had been caught up with the snow and ice, shovelling that off and it might only last a few hours and we were on the train again. I got another experience with a German hospital where they took us and by this time the German casualties from the Russian Front, were coming through now and it turned out, they admitted to us through our interpreter, there was this sort of secretive place where they were sending us rather than their own civilians because they wanted to keep from their civilian population the extent of the casualties happening in Russia... When the trains came from Russia we went on board with civilians to help carry off the wounded. They weren't only wounded; some of them had lost their feet and toes and fingers to frostbite and that, terrible conditions there.

* * *

We had our escape plan made... we planned our route and this George MacDonald, he'd been on two previous escapes but I wasn't interested in that. I'd had a lot of bad health as a prisoner of war and I'd just got into good health and I wasn't going to risk it again out there for nothing. So I saved up everything for one big effort at the end of the war. This is where all the rumours and talk came in again. There was all these millions there and with all the refugees coming, all the millions being killed, bombed, and all the rest of it, we didn't know what was going to happen to us, we didn't know whether they'd just simply shoot us all towards the end because they had nothing to lose, did they? We didn't know whether all the food would cut out and parcels would cut out, because towards the end they got less and less and less and we'd starve to death or whether, and we saw a lot of this, whether the angry civilians from all the bombing would turn on us and shoot us. We made a general plan that we'd try and assess when the war had possibly two or three months to go and then we'd leave... what spurred us on is that we had a lot of prisoners of war over in eastern Europe, right over in Poland, working in coal mines and all that sort of thing. When the Russians started to advance the Germans started marching them away from that eastern area into the middle of Germany, to central Germany. They marched through the winter... they were marching them out in the open, they marched them a thousand kilometres in the middle of winter and just dossing down in the open night and all that sort of thing.

... Part of the plan was to get disguised. We all got disguised, the four of us. My disguise was a local hat, all traded from cigarettes and stuff, the Tyrolean I think they called it and I had to give up my British greatcoat for a local, long coat which went almost down to my boots, and a scarf. You could put the long coat on over the top of my uniform and the scarf on and then I had a bottom of a pair of old pants which I sewed on to my uniform pants up above my overcoat, that was my disguise. Then we'd acquired a wire brush, also from trading, which we scuffed up our army issue boots and put axlegrease on them and just made them look like old working boots you know. Eventually after nearly three years of all of this we left from this working camp and set off.

... I was the navigator and George MacDonald was the interpreter and the boss, the leader, and the other two just to do other things and other things were important too, because of scrounging and keeping guard at night because these people were refugees, ex-prisoners and forced labourers all sorts of people, been there for years and food getting short and dangers everywhere so you had to be very careful somebody didn't just knock you off for anything, for a crust of bread. So we always posted a guard when we were out.

... We'd made a couple of haversacks out of an old blanket and the cigarettes came in fifty tins and we made up a sort of a pudding to put in these fifty tins out of chocolate and raisins and cereal-type stuff, made it into a sort of a pudding, melted the chocolate and put it in the tins. We had quite a few of those tins to carry with us as our food. Then of course there was water everywhere so there was no shortage there and we took cigarettes which we could buy bread with you see. We travelled quite a long way on foot, keeping out of the road and posting guards at night and all that sort of thing. Eventually we were getting tired and we thought there might be a faster way of making it so Mac bought four tickets for us at a railway station and we took the risk and we boarded a train. We went quite a long way because those trains travel pretty fast there, probably travelled as much as we would do in three or four weeks on that train trip, but we got scared. Everybody seemed to be looking at us; everybody seemed to be a Gestapo or something you know. So we thought we'd bucked our luck far enough so we got off the train and proceeded on foot. I don't know how far we went and I don't even know where we got to because we weren't going into cities. I knew Salzburg and Munich but after that I didn't know that part at all so I don't know exactly where we were except we were about in the middle of Germany and our food was running out and we were getting sick of that stuff anyway.

We were going to go into a house and try and see if we could buy something for a few cigarettes or something, but just as we got there, a carload of German officers came in front of us. They got out of the car and just left the key in the ignition and went in to the house so we said, 'Oh blow it, we'll take the car.'

So we hopped in the car and off, and we went in that car hours, probably going at fifty miles an hour we probably covered a hundred, two hundred miles or something. We had to slow down at times and watch out, we were still careful but we might have covered a hundred and fifty, two hundred miles and then we got bailed up at a roadblock. We were taken from there and interrogated by a German officer and when they found out who we were they put us in a barbed-wire enclosure . . . they put us in there with a guard on and we were there for a while and some more started coming in, two or three more prisoners of war and then we just thought, 'We'll have a go at trying to get through here.'

We've used this bribery and trading and that all the way through so eventually with Mac doing all the talking and over a period of two or three days a German major made us a pass through the German lines. That's what it says, it's got our names there, 'These English prisoners of war named so and so and so and so have got permission to pass through the German lines this day.'

We gave him fifty cigarettes. We were getting pretty low on cigarettes by this time. Fifty cigarettes we gave him, a German major.

. . . So we thought we were through but we weren't through. We were in no-man's-land between the Americans and the Germans, so we hunkered down in a shell hole and within a couple of days the American foot soldiers came over the top of us. And then they weren't that easy to convince either, interrogated us but eventually when they were satisfied about it that was good, and so now we were out, we'd escaped, we'd got out. They just thought we just looked like anybody else you know. We were lucky we didn't get shot there. Nobody was worrying too much about who they shot in those days.

We didn't do much celebrating. We're not out yet, we're still in the middle of Germany. We were so set on getting to England and getting right the hell and gone out of it, we didn't think of anything else. Anyway at least we had a couple of good meals there. They had things which I'd never seen before, they had those ration packs you know, one pack a day. It's got everything in it, fantastic things. They had biscuits and they had dried eggs and all sorts of things, just boil them up and you've got scrambled eggs and soups. They had everything in those ration packs

... The Americans must have just simply communicated with the British because a couple of bombers came in. It was getting towards the end of the war; within a few days was the end of the war. A couple of bombers came in and they just opened their big bomb hatches at the back and we just piled in, twenty in each and they flew us to Brussels in Belgium. Belgium was under the control of the British there... When we got to Brussels we got deloused straightaway. They wouldn't have us anywhere near anything till we got deloused. They had these things like bellows you know, poking down there and up there and in there, puffing away with this chemical of some sort but anyway there we got treated well by the British. We had to shed our uniforms and everything we had on and put on new clothes and the British battledress. So that was in Brussels... I even got a bit of pay there and had a couple of beers for the first time for about four years or so.

* * *

There was a reception centre for the AIF prisoners of war at Eastbourne and at Brighton, a bit further along the coast; there was a reception centre for the air force prisoners of war, ex-prisoners of war now. There were I think four thousand of us processed through, they called it Gowrie House, but we were given good treatment there of course and they put us through medicals and all those sorts of things. We were able to write home and received pay and so it was great ... we started gathering possessions together again ... one of the things was to draw some pay, so I've got this in my hand and so okay, I go and buy a wallet, so I put some in my wallet and put it in my pocket, that was a big deal, having my own money in a wallet and I can pull it out and spend it ... One of the chaps when he got into freedom he couldn't help himself from pinching a tin of sardines and putting it in his pocket. So that sort of thing took time to get over that and to get normal again.

... And then they gave us a leave pass to anywhere in England. It's a free leave pass right up to the very north of Scotland and all ports between so you could travel anywhere in England free. There was a few good things happened. They had a big reception or big thing on Hyde Park with all the royal family, Winston Churchill and all those there, millions milling around. The royal family were very noticeable, coming out to everything that was on. The present Queen now, she was nineteen then, and Princess Margaret was sixteen I think. They were out with their parents all the time, everything that was on, showing the flag you know. This was the end of the six-year war don't forget. As a matter of fact, the lights had just been switched on after six years of blackouts in England so the mood was like that.

... It's an interesting thing about prisoners of war and women, perfectly understandable I reckon ... Coming to England and hearing the women's voices, the lighter voices and that sort of thing, it was hard to get used to and often hard to understand. It didn't take very long to adjust but it was something you wouldn't realise you'd get out of touch with it ... Surprising about the weight, you put it back on fairly quickly. I used to be about twelve stone and I was probably down to about seven stone when I got out and I probably got up to say ten within a matter of a month or so. It doesn't take long to put it back on although you're pretty flabby, you've got to get back in nick again. That was an important thing about getting condition back on again as well, very important. That was a long time to be out of condition.

... I got news from home. I hadn't had anything from home for a long time in fact I don't remember getting any mail when I was a prisoner of war. I moved around so much, it never caught up with me. In England I did find it and one of my brothers was a prisoner of war with the Japanese. At that time he was in Changi camp. Another brother was in North Borneo still, that was the last campaign in the Pacific that we were in. So there was two brothers away. The family were pretty spread out. We were a bunch of orphans you see. It was pretty hard to find out and it wasn't necessarily that good a news really. Also of course even though the war in Europe was over the war in the Pacific wasn't over and I was still in the army so as far as we were concerned, they said that those who were checked and were fit could still have to serve at the time.

＊

I sort of had relapses. I had to have two operations. I spent time in Hollywood Hospital in Perth. Being an orphan; I didn't have a home or a job or really a stable family. I had a family but they were all over the place so it wasn't quite the same as it was for certain other people. There'd be others in my boat as well. It took longer to adjust. Eventually I got into the Commonwealth Public Service ... I didn't want to go back to the country. Now I like the country and I go back frequently now, I like country people and all that sort of thing but I never, ever fitted in there. My main experiences were the Depression years so I had a bad impression. I didn't want to go back to that again. I was determined to make a different life.

... It was hard. It was a lot harder than a lot of people imagined. As a matter of fact even the repatriation authorities after the war didn't have a clue really of what all this was about. They have now. Things are a lot different now, a lot better educated people. This is why I mention psychology and that all the time. They treated the wound, the lame leg or whatever it was but they never treated us up here. I think that was a big mistake. As a matter of fact way back, I've worked a lot with the ex-services organisations and been on committees and that for years and I wrote sixty pages to the Repatriation Department about forgetting—look after all the wounds, limps and all that sort of thing but talk to these people, have a look, see if they've got any problems inside their head ... What I observed around is that half the marriages weren't working to start with; any sort of relationships weren't working. They'd work for a little while and there's no counselling or even the recognition that your problems might be because you've had a hard time, we'll try to help you get on your feet again and try that. So there's nothing. We were very ignorant back then of these sorts of things. Mind you, the government didn't want to get too involved because if they got too many on their books under the repatriation system it would have cost a lot of money I suppose.

... I actually got some treatment. I had insulin shock treatment in Hollywood Hospital. That was the first year after the war, when I first came back from England. I was only ever diagnosed as having 'war neurosis'. That sort of covers a wide range of things. See I'm pretty good now and have been for years and years. I was fairly shaky and even walking and that, a little bit hesitant for a good while ... There were wards of us down there getting various treatments including electric shock, a lot of electric shock but I didn't have that. I was in another ward with this insulin shock treatment ... I could observe from where I was what was going on in the electric shock area and apparently they were wiring them all up in batches and then when they put the switch on, all their bodies would go up in a big 'whoof', up into the air like that and back onto the bed. They'd rise two or three feet above the bed when the switch was on. Seemed pretty cruel to me ... I didn't like the idea of it but then I didn't really know what I was up for. I was only young then and inexperienced and I had no experience in that area. Hadn't even talked to anybody about it so I really didn't know, had to trust ... We wanted to try and find out what was going on and it seemed as though they were electrocuting them. You know, you think the worst. We just wanted to find out what it was all about and what they expected to achieve and the difference between insulin shock and electric shock. We didn't find out very much and nobody seemed to know although the ones doing the treatment, you would have thought they knew.

The staff were always good. You're dealing mainly with nurses and there were no male nurses at that time, they were all female nurses and they're always good. They've got a wonderful reputation right through, for the most part, certainly in treating people. As far as the doctors were concerned, those old-fashioned doctors, they were probably under too much pressure, they were very distant. They never explained anything to you, they never consulted you, they said what was needed and they'd go ahead and do it, you know. My opinion is in these areas of medicine, particularly the more specialist ones and psychologists and psychiatry and those sorts of things, we've advanced leaps and bounds since then.

* * *

The hardest thing about being a POW was the loss of your freedom. It was a degrading situation really. People say it wasn't, it's just what happens in war, but at the time when you're young you didn't know that and so we suffered from this sort of guilt and embarrassment and all those sorts of things. Everybody did, very common. I don't worry about it now and haven't done for many years. I went out there at a fairly early stage and offered my services and did the best I could, I don't worry about that but see these effects on your mind and body came about by those experiences then.

... There is a school of thought that we ought to put that all in the past, get on with what's in the present and the future but I've got a different view, I think that our present is what it is because of our past. If we understand where we came from, this is all hackneyed a bit, but in my opinion it's quite true, if we understand where we come from we've got a better understanding of where we're going.

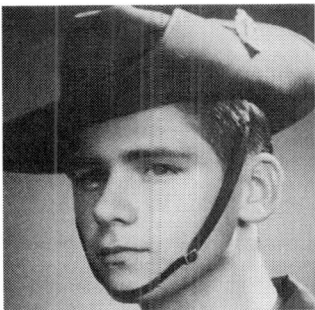

ARPAD 'PADDY' BACSKAI

Refugee
World War II

Rifleman
Malayan Emergency SAS
Vietnam

Where it all came about was prior to Christmas '44. The Soviets had already besieged Budapest and were starting to make forays south-east... the Germans of course, were coming up... Hungary had the pleasure of being occupied by both the Soviets and the Germans. One was an enemy, one was an ally. But nothing seemed to matter very much; you were the meat in the sandwich. You were the populace and all of a sudden you had not one, you had two occupiers... and we became part of the front line... and that particular day... the Germans came into our house, they told us to be quiet, very politely. They stuck the old machine gun over the sink. The linked ammunition rattled in the sink. Later on I was to handle heaps of linked ammunition in combat. I just find it strange.

... One came in with a crowbar and one came in with a huge sledgehammer. If you can imagine, the sink was facing this way towards the Soviets and over here they started to knock a huge hole in the kitchen wall. You can imagine how that impressed Mum and old Granny. The house was pretty shaky from the bombing as it was... obviously they were going to use the street as a front line, as a defence position.

... Just before Christmas it is so cold in Hungary. I mean the snow is often two metres deep. The Siberian wind blew in. We were pretty chilly beforehand from emotion, but all of a sudden the cold wind blew in, and my God... And then we were surrounded by these young SS troopers, forget about them being brutal or anything, they might have been down the line, but these were kids... with the camouflage gear and the old potato masher grenade in their boots. And they were winking at me and perving at my Mum's bum, and my Auntie Clary was there, too. And it was a sort of organised chaos, which the Krauts are very good at. Anyhow, the next minute the shooting started, the MG [machine gun] let go with a good burst... It was to become so familiar to me later on. They started firing... sustained bursts obviously to keep someone at bay. And then the shelling started. I don't know if it was the Germans that fired a salvo first... The German artillery started to rip into the Soviets, then the Soviets replied with a twenty per cent increase and those Katyusha rockets. I don't know if you've ever seen them in the movies... They'd come in, they'd whine in, they'd scream in, that instrument of the devil. I've been in mortar attacks, close artillery. And I've never experienced, even with the section to section rockets in Vietnam... These Katyusha things... If you were at the wrong end of them...

And this thing went on and on and on. And the troops started to stage through the hole, and pass you. And some were pale. Christ knows what I must have looked like. But when you're a kid all you do is take your fear from the adults. That's all. And it's like a dog, it's palpable. Fear is palpable. And you can't avoid it. But when group fear grips, you can cut it with a knife. And sometimes, when I say 'the poor old Germans', they were just a soldier like anybody else. When they came through and especially when some of the barrages got heavier, and everything shook and everything was dust, and everything was flying shrapnel, and people were praying and people were groaning... they weren't screaming, because everybody had a certain military discipline by then. I screamed, I let go a few good ones. By the way, this is not new stuff; it had gone on before, but this front line! Oh Jesus Christ . . . anyhow, Mum . . . the bombing started . . . Mum lost it, totally lost it. She became zombified. We prepared for an evacuation; we had our suitcase packed, like any normal person does. But I knew she was zombified because she didn't take her suitcase. She had fur coats in the cupboard and she threw a couple on, didn't take the suitcase, perhaps took her purse, this was mid-winter mind you, and walked out on me and Granny. Walked out, abandoned us, just like that . . . if it wasn't for Granny then later getting hold of me and a suitcase and trudging through the snow to try and catch up with her, which was by a fluke that we did, I would not be sitting here now.

We had a rough idea where she was going because she was an aluminium worker, and the aluminium boss could sort of see it coming and said all the important workers—aluminium was a very important substance in armaments—and he said he had made the evacuation plan and he had created an RV [rendezvous] point. What we also didn't know was that he was my mum's lover and she was torn between all kinds of emotion. Like, 'Am I going to . . . this is my kid, and this is my mum, but this is my lover, and the world is really turning to shit.' And unless you're really there in real life and experience it, never judge anyone. I've long since given it a miss about who is a coward and who is a hero. There's a thin, fine line between the two. The only one I will call a coward is the one who deliberately leaves his mates behind, that is a no-no.

And we struggled through the two metre snow, Granny was a little fat thing, I think the snow was higher than she was. It was nearly to her shoulders, and we were dragging this big bloody case. And there was another bombing raid while we were walking; a small one. It was a pitiful thing. She was never meant to be a refugee, nor was I. We didn't use the word, please believe me. I think we caught up with Mum who was hiding in a derelict building to avoid the second bombing raid, then somehow or other in a heated exchange between daughter and mum, about, 'leaving your kid', and all of this, then Mum managed to convince Granny to become a refugee and the three of us headed for the RV point.

That was the beginning of the end for her. When I confronted Mum later on as a more mature person, she looked me in the eye, she never dodged it. She said, 'Son, at that very moment I couldn't care about my country, my family, my home, or you or anyone, I just had to get out of the place.'

She looked me in the eye, that was good. If she had of looked away I wouldn't have liked it... She lost it. 'Shell shock' it was called. In later wars that I was involved in, we used to call it 'bottle fatigue'. Because the more you were under stress, the more you drank.

* * *

We were shipped over to a place called Berchtesgaden, oh Jesus Christ it was chaos... we were quite innocent at this point, we were heading for an assembly point but we didn't know. Anyhow, there was a German officer. He had one arm, one arm and two suitcases. And Mum being Mum and young and fit and strong, and he was trying to get on the train, she grabbed his suitcase and put it on the train with him. And he was very grateful and he was talking to her in German.

'Where are you from, *fraulein*?'

And she said the place where she comes from...

'Oh Hungary,' he says, 'Beautiful ladies, beautiful wine.'

Crap, crap all this kind of thing.

'By the way,' he said, 'Where are you going?'

And he leant over and he read her tag. Well, he just shut up... and by that time you were like a jungle animal. You sensed every change in mood. You sniffed it. And Mum could see straightaway that something was wrong. Anyhow, she said to him, 'What is wrong?'

And he said, 'Nothing.'

But she was insistent, and this took place in a few seconds...

He said, 'Look, *fraulein*, how many of you are there?'

And she said seventy-five, whatever there was in the big group, and he said, 'No, I'm talking about you and your immediate kin.'

She said, 'Just me, my boy and Granny.'

* * *

Granny was sitting on the suitcase. The suitcase incidentally had been marked, slashed with paint. Tagged, everybody tagged.

He said, 'I can tell you something; those things are for the concentration camp. You will be shunted further down the line to the assembly point where you will be met and sorted out.'

And Mum started with, 'But we're not Jews.'

And he said, 'No, relax. Even some of my relatives are there.' He said, 'Anybody.' He said, 'Today, see the chaos on the platform?' He said, 'Today, the Soviets had crossed the river. There is panic in Germany now. The Soviets have crossed onto German soil.'

He said, 'Get your mum and your boy. Get out of the station any way you can. Rip those tags off, hide and go catch any train back the way you came.'

Mum again crapped herself. Mum was very brave, but these situations just never stopped. They were just an endless thing. Anyhow, he could see that we're a bit stunned for a minute. He said, 'First of all go and get your mother.'

She got Granny.

He said, 'Rip the tags off.'

We were frightened, terrified of ever doing anything against authority. By that time, we were programmed like lemmings. That's what happens in war, in occupation, you become a lemming.

She said to him, 'Can you buy some tickets back?'

He said to her, 'Now you are thinking.'

He actually went to the ticket box and got three tickets for us, and because Mum wasn't handling the shock too well, and I don't know how you would handle it if you were told that you were going to the concentration camp . . . how do you think you would be?

. . . He not only bought our tickets but he escorted us out of the station, past the old train conductor and the soldiers standing around and said, 'Lose yourself in the town until dark.'

And he saluted with his cane and we watched him go. And all of a sudden we were absconders in a very harsh system. Very lonely. I seem to remember that instead of waiting for a train, we tried to hail down a hay cart with a draughthorse. I've got a recollection of sitting beside this bloke. And as we drove towards the Germany–Austria border in this hay cart, I think—poor old Granny was just—she was at sea with all of this. Mum lost her nerve.

'How are we going to get across the border? Is there barbed wire? Are there mines? Are we going to be shot?'

There wasn't. And I reckon we could have got over easily. Anyhow, I think, as a result we hid there. We got off the hay cart and hid there. But then towards evening we went back into the station. Of course, we had tickets so we were right, we had no tags, we looked like we were average flotsam and jetsam that went around the place, and we got on the train and went back exactly the way that we had come and we got off. And we were absolutely petrified as to what punishment we were going to get. But when we got to . . . it was either Vocklabruch or Schwanenstadt and got off and handed ourselves into the authorities under some guise, we must have made up a story of some sort, that's when they took us and allocated us to Castle Lager Mittleberg Eins . . . But this is how it was. There were always choices. Every time was choices. And the main choice was, 'Do you want to croak it or do you want to stagger on?'

* * *

We were smack dab in the middle between the Yanks and the Soviets by then . . . the Soviets were thirty kilometres this way, we were here, and the Americans were thirty kilometres this way. And they were both racing towards us, and we were praying that the Yanks would reach us first. There was a lot of talk in the cookhouses, where us kids went, and the washhouses and all of this, and there was quite a lot of fascist, communist-type, refugee displaced person talk. A few of them wanted the Soviets to win, or a few, they thought the Yanks would betray them, that kind of stuff. Anyhow, all of a sudden there was the mighty German Army, or parts of it, and horses everywhere because petrol was almost impossible to get. I remember these Lipizzaner horses, one German soldier was riding and leading about six or seven—for a young kid that was so magic. And then you saw them limping without shoes, and you know how the Germans were always immaculate ... they are really great people, honestly. If they had of been better led, they would be the salt of the earth. And equally, if they're led the wrong way, they go wrong. Blokes with Iron Crosses, bandages, crutches, horse-drawn carts with bodies piled on them to buggery, like wounded dead, I couldn't tell. Heaps of them, heaps of them walking ... I think they were going west, east, I'm not sure. And this was a huge parade of this beaten army. Of course you still see the odd fancy staff car with a flag and they looked all right, but the average bloke there was so ratshit ... anyhow, we thought, 'It's getting close.'

... The Yanks overran our area first. It was unbelievable. Once again we ran down from the castle to the road and the scene couldn't have been any more different. Jeeps by the galore. The typical Yankee GI chewing gum, reading a book ... slack as shit, half of them ... and us kids, with our hand out screaming out for something, anything. And they were chucking off these little chewing-gum dispensers. Little plastic things, this square, like a cigarette lighter, and every time you clicked one down, a little square chewy would come out. And they came in convoys of powerful trucks. You know nothing like the poor old Kraut army looked like. Equal and opposite. And laying back and reading a stick book, Dick Tracy, or Christ knows whatever they were reading, and giving the odd wave, but really looking at you half-interested ... but they got the idea, and look, they must have been sick and tired of it. We threw our rations out in Vietnam to the locals. And funny enough, in our convoys in Vietnam, and the kids used to be there like that, and we looked down, we had the same American stuff, I could see myself. In actual fact, I saw two or three Vietnamese urchins with their arms out to me like that looked like me, physically. And it tugged at my heart. Actually, I feel so strange about it, I still do.

* * *

We became displaced persons all of a sudden, but it was good because we got a status. Before, we had no status, we had no work, we had really nothing ... we were nothing. And all of a sudden, this new piece of paperwork and this change of administration, a lifting of the servitude burden, if you want to call it that, with it the fear. There is still a bit of anxiety, but this anxiety was the sort of normal anxiety you might have about meeting your bills at the end of the month, which is not so good, but it's all right. Better than the anxiety of walking around the corner and being searched, punched down and perhaps never seen again ... we were almost proud of it. We fitted in somewhere. And also they allowed you to work, to keep the money. They allowed you free accommodation, be it just an extension of what you had before.

... All of a sudden, one family is saying, 'We're off to America.' Off to South Africa, off to Canada ... Australia was hardly ever mentioned, except the very near and dear group we made friends with, they were off to Australia. That was the first we ever heard about Australia. Bit by bit, these people who helped you survive all these years were going and being replaced by these political refugee types, and we started to feel almost unpleasant at the castle. Anyhow, every year you would have to front up to the German administration and they would give you a work leave pass. Like when a Brit comes here and has to have a certificate to work. And anyhow, this year we fronted up full of steam and things were different, because by this time Mum had my sister, and this was worrying the Austrian authorities, because all of a sudden they almost had a citizen on their hands ... and this worried the hell out of them because they would have to be responsible for education and they said, 'You've got one hour to make up your mind whether you're going to America or to Australia. Take your boy down to the local village and buy him a lemonade and tell us whether you are going to America or Australia.'

We were astounded—gobsmacked the word is now. My mum said, 'We're not going anywhere. We're not going anywhere at all. We're staying here. We like it.'

They said, 'No, you're not.'

This was after they interviewed us about my young sister, who was virtually a babe, and where she was born and all that ...

They said, 'No, you're not. If you don't take our options. It's your choice. We're very kind. We're giving you back to the Russians.'

That's all they had to say to my mum, 'Give you back to the Ruskies.' She dropped a bundle... She couldn't believe it, she absolutely couldn't believe it. She said, 'Are there any gangsters in America?'

I said, 'Yes.' Because I distinctly remember the photos of the black cars with the Tommy guns. I said, 'Oh yeah, Al Capone, Bugsy Siegel.' All these.

'God,' she says, 'We better not go there. We better go to Australia.'

I thought for a minute and I said, 'Where is it?'

She said, 'Near America, down a bit.'

Anyhow, we sort of mulled over it and we went back to the Austrian UN Aid fellow in his gleaming white shirt, it nearly knocked the socks off us, I don't know what kind of washing powder he used. Anyhow, he wouldn't let us back in the building. We said to him, 'We've made up our mind, we're going to Australia.'

He put his arms around Mum and said, 'Good choice. Just like Austria.'

Anyhow, on the strength of that we were processed through three or four other camps in Northern Germany... and from there put on a ship for Australia.

* * *

The differences were astounding. From memory, we landed here in the onslaught of summer. The bushfires to begin with. The foliage, the blackboys, the long trip... I mean, four and a half weeks on a boat to the other side of the world, in '50... The only way you can say its equivalent is the astronauts now landing on the moon. Actually, I would say that people would accept astronauts landing on the moon now, more humdrum and mundane than it was in those days to go from Europe to Australia. And the thing was, you knew you couldn't go back. You could, but when? I knew how the old, original Brits must have felt who sailed out on the original fleet and were landed here. There is a way back, you can become a ticket-of-leave man, but when are you going to become a ticket-of-leave man?

And the locals were so different, and so strange. When we pulled into Fremantle, perhaps it was a Sunday, but there was nobody there at all. When we landed, the entire population of West Australia was 300 000. Three MCGs worth lived in the state. On a grand final day that is, three MCGs on grand final day, that was the entire population. I said to our escort officer, Major Day, 'Where is every bastard?'

He said, 'This is it. That's why you're here, son.'

I should have got the message then. He gave a wonderful speech before we got off the boat, it was marvellous ... about landing in a new land and the opportunities. And how we were like the second wave or third wave of pioneers ... It was an absolutely marvellous speech. 'Go and make a name for yourself,' and all of this ... it was absolutely beautiful and perfect. He pointed us in the right direction. How we had to behave ... in other words, the chances were in your hands to go and get them. Most of us did.

* * *

Four thousand of us were at Northam Migrant Camp. The flies from the shit pans, the military dunnies—the food was unbelievable. We'd never seen food like it. The abundance of it. We couldn't believe it. We thought this was a trick. We never believed there could be so much food. A lot of the people began to dig into the sugar bowls and filled their pockets with sugar, because it's got to be a trick, and as soon as we're marched out, everything will come down, it will be back to normal, you will be back into the prison camp. So people would walk out of that mess hall ... filling their pockets with sugar for the next day when the reality will start to bite. Things like that. The food there ... it made such a big impact on me. And the flies ... if you were a doctor, you got a job as an orderly in the camp hospital. If you were an engineer, you got a job as a truck driver. If you were a carpenter, you got the job of hosing out the shit buckets. If you were anything below that you went into the kitchen and washed the plates, and this was how the jobs were allocated. You probably had a heart surgeon pushing you around on the trolley. They all made it.

... Everything was foreign. Nowadays, you can jump on a plane and go to Singapore, go to the USA, go to Los Angeles, anywhere.

And the mode of dress, the mode of furniture, the mode of handling climatic conditions are the same. But in those days, everything was different. Your mode of dress. We had urchin-style haircuts, which were like Mick Jagger—urchin or pageboy, which looked like a Beatle. The Northam kids had short back and sides style. The Northam kids were well fed, brown, everyone was brown as a berry, we were pale. If we wore the old shorts we wore leather shorts. We were used to everything being enclosed, even the dunnies being enclosed. All of a sudden we were in an environment where everything was open. Like one step back from outdoor camping. The spiders, the willy-willys, sandstorms, the bushfires, the funny sounding names . . . real funny sounding names . . . as far as being a cultural shock, it was immense.

. . . There were tragedies that resulted from what went on in the huts. Like, you know, mum finds a new lover; the new lover liked the mum, but just didn't like the kids and didn't want to start a fight. We would often be sent out on search parties to look for kids to come to class. I won't say it was that common, you would find them in the dunnies and they'd hung themselves with a skipping rope. They used to issue us with a skipping rope and some of the kids used to use that to hang themselves. I'm talking ten year olds. I don't know how many of the old camp administrators are left, but if they are dinkum and they've got any balls, they will back my story up. For what it's worth, I don't care what they do. It was happening, it was happening. There were quite a few homos in the camp, so just like the old times in Austria; we younger boys had to run around well and truly keeping our bums against the wall. And there was one very close to us, and by that I mean in the system. In the system. And the staff used to change girlfriends every time a new consignment came in. It wasn't a pit of sin, but it was certainly a pit of humanity and—raw human—it couldn't be any other way. Because all of a sudden you've been transplanted into a foreign environment where you desperately have to make a new go of it or otherwise you are not going to survive and so this puts humanity to what it is. It was no different. It was a more modern, Westernised version of what went on in the camps over there. That's all. More civilised but the same. Human nature is the same. Human nature hasn't changed.

* * *

I just couldn't wait to join the military. I did my exams when I was still sixteen virtually and come seventeen, at Subiaco, I was waiting at the bus stop with the rolled-up towel and the toothbrush and all that, and then an amusing thing happened. While I was waiting at the bus stop...and I always wanted to go to the SAS, always, that was an ambition, and an SAS Jeep broke down in front of the bus stop...and of course my eyes are agog; these are the killers from the sky, or whatever, my ultimate goal. And there they were trying to work out what was wrong with the Jeep. Kicking the tyres in and the usual garbage, and I thought, 'Do I have enough guts to say anything? Bugger it!'

And I walked up to the leader, and I know who he is now, because he later came back as a regimental sergeant major of ours. And I said to him, 'Hey, I'm joining the army,' and I'm expecting, 'Well done, son' or something like that.

And he said, 'Get out of it while you bloody can.'

And then while my jaw was still hanging down, I jumped on the bus and out to command personnel depot. But that was 1957... And then they sort of get hold of you, and you go off to Kapooka, in New South Wales... This time I was entering a camp of my free will, full of enthusiasm and looking forward to an absolutely wonderful life of adventure. Barely seventeen.

* * *

During the Malayan Emergency I was an infantry soldier. Deep penetration patrols. We had a wonderful system, we didn't like it because it worked us to death, we were all like marathon runners almost...a patrol would last between twenty-eight and thirty days, then you would come and do five-days refit or you got five days, which was either five days Penang, five days Ipoh...and this was an endless cycle. It never varied, at least while I was there. It was twenty-eight or thirty days, and I did two end-on-end, sixty days.

Now I have no idea if you've ever spent sixty days under the canopy, because in the jungle, you've got a canopy virtually. Everything strives to go upwards, to try and get a bit of light, competing with each other, and eventually a canopy is formed under which you lived, patrolled, did everything. There is the odd bit of sunlight, but there is a dimness in everything about us. There is a netherworld of leeches, spiders, snakes, call it whatever you like, all this sludge in the netherworld that you walk through, sleep on, etc. We slept off the ground if we could, mainly because of the parasites and everything that were almost a greater danger to you than one of the communists shooting you in an ambush. There was hookworms, there was heartworms. There was rats' excreta and urine, which would give you things like leptospirosis. Malaria was common; I got it twice in spite of the Atebrin tablets you had to take.

. . . Say you were laying an ambush onto . . . a high-priority target, that would mean twenty-four hours a day, rain, hail or shine, bucketing down, you would just be there . . . You would get relief from your base camp, which was set up at a considerable distance, or a good enough distance away not to give anything away, and there you would be twenty-four hours a day in ambush position. It wasn't the most dangerous war that I was in, far from it, but it was by far the hardest work I've ever done in a combat situation, bar none. We carried ten days' rations. What would that weigh? Sixty pounds, I suppose. A full complement of ammunition. And every ten days, weather permitting, we would get an airdrop to keep you going. To walk into an area, the border area, would take ten days. So sometimes you would walk in ten days, because you didn't get a helicopter ride . . . If you got a helicopter ride to it, it was only twenty minutes . . . Ten hard slogging days.

It's an eerie world living under the jungle, under the canopy. Anything that can pull, pulls, anything that can jab you, jabs you, anything that can bite you, bites you. You can't see from here to there, you don't know from one minute to the next what's behind.

. . . You went as light as you could. You virtually had what you had on you and a dry set to change into at night-time. Because everything was damp all the time. And if you were in the rainy season, you've never seen rain like it. Because when you're sitting in the rain, or standing in the rain in Australia, it falls on you. But there in the jungle, it doesn't only come down, it's draining towards you from every leaf, every bush . . . it's like mini-waterfalls at times. It's like living in a mini-waterfall. And in some of the highland areas, where it's very high, I don't know ten thousand feet, twelve thousand feet, I'll you what, it got bloody cold when it shouldn't have got cold. And on that ridge it took seven hundred hours of patrol before you had a contact or incident with one of the communist terrorists, who of course did their work whenever they wanted to, because you were after them. And yes, if they came after you, you knew all about it. But they would do their job of sabotage or propaganda or collecting debts or whatever, at whim, whenever they wanted. But you had to head down, bum up, to counteract them and do them some damage.

* * *

You never saw much more than the man in front of you, and one or two men behind until you harboured up, until you came together for the harbour in the evening, when you got your permission ready for standing to and all of this kind of stuff. That is just the way that environment was. So even though you were working with twenty-five, thirty blokes, most of the day you hardly ever saw them. You knew they were there, and the signals came and went up and down the rank. Sometimes you could hear them, but then the platoon sergeant would demand a bit more silence. But really, honestly, patrolling was magnificent. You learnt how to sway your body to go through the bush rather than bash your way, brush aside rather than bash away . . . Everything was done with field signals. We used to call it a jungle sway, with a pack on your back, to get around the obstacles. Yeah, patrolling was top class. Stood us in perfect stead for Vietnam later on, perfect stead. I'd like to think a lot of Australians are safe and sound in their homes tonight, because of what us older Malaya and Borneo fellows managed to pass onto them about how to patrol in these jungles. I really believe that. It was really an invaluable experience.

* * *

Paddy left the infantry and joined the SAS. He was posted to Vietnam to begin the patrol work that characterised SAS operations in Vietnam.

You were generally landed to do a specific job . . . the thing was, you were not to be discovered . . . you went towards your objective, which was a camp or a suspected site or a track where you were perhaps to lay an ambush on or just count them walking past, or whatever the task was. Now towards the end of your patrol after you more or less did your intelligence task, you could request that you engage them. Now you either got a request, or you sometimes got your request granted before you went out. This will be a reconnaissance, or whatever, but you can have an ambush phase if the target warrants it. So I have been on quite a few where we were told to just do the intelligence and that's it, avoid contact at all costs. You're there, but you are a phantom. And often those are a lot harder . . . because the minute you do have your contact, or you lay an ambush, they know you are there . . . and it's always hairy, five of you, four of you against a platoon or whatever . . . The bits and pieces are falling off the trees and the lead is flying past. But then you break contact and you escape, you got to one side, they were onto you.

The only thing that ever used to pause them, we knew it from the prisoners, is because our weapons were automatic, they were confused. See there is a ratio in most armies. A section consists of around nine men; you can have more or less. But always the main firepower is a machine gun. So all the other soldiers count how many there are by the machine guns. If you hear one machine gun, if you hear two machine guns, you know there are about eighteen blokes. You hear three machine guns, you say thirty. But all of a sudden you're hearing five going off in session. And quite apart from that is a lot of firepower coming in towards you, and even though you're a fanatic you don't really want to die . . . [the Viet Cong] were very brave and very dedicated but they came to a grinding halt when they were greeted by the firepower of five automatic weapons. It confused them. To hear five automatic weapons, that would mean about a hundred people as far as they were concerned. A company, they were striking a company. They'd think, 'Shit, we better ease up on this, we're going up against a company of a hundred blokes.' But it wasn't, there was only five of us. And by the time they sort of got it sorted out, we were gone like a rocket. You can imagine us. It gave us that breathing space to break contact, to go off on our flank, outflank and then, as soon as we could, ask for the helicopters to come and take us out. Because to stay there was suicide, absolute suicide.

... We used to get them in every kind of position. Like on the bog house, making love ... sometimes we'd shoot them, sometimes we didn't. It depended on the job. It was just unbelievable stuff. It was very normal then but looking back on it now; it wasn't quite the norm I suppose. They hated us, they absolutely hated us. We were their number three hate. Number one was B52 [bomber] strike, number two hate was H & I fire, which was harass and intermittent fire, which later on was called A & I fire, acquired and intelligence target, most of the intelligence targets came from us. We would plot their camps and then gunners back at Nui Dat would plot in whatever the Task Force told them for that night, and then at one o'clock in the morning, two o'clock in the morning, they would just roll out of bed and fire a salvo. At the other end, the Viet Cong would be nice and asleep and the next minute they were under this huge barrage, out of nowhere. That is harassing and intermittent fire or acquired intelligence target fire. And they do it intermittently, anytime they like. And according to the prisoners, it had such an effect that they started to sleep without their mosquito nets. And their rate of malaria went sky high. Things like that. And we were number three; according to this lady who used to come on that we called 'Hanoi Hanna' [communist propaganda radio broadcaster]. We would 'jump out of the bushes and stab their honourable men in the back'. The price on our heads, if we were to believe it, was more than a helicopter ... fifteen thousand piastres, that is their local currency, fifteen thousand piastres, and we were guaranteed a trip to Hanoi for interrogation. And they tried a few times to put us in the bag; to capture us rather and take us in ... fifteen thousand piastres for them was a lot of money. More than a year's wage... They had called us *Ma Rung*. Phantoms of the jungle.

And there is another thing we didn't realise. When we shot them or whatever, what appeared to aggrieve them was that we left the bodies laying face down, some of them. We just left them as they were. This was combat, right. So we get in there and we realised they thought we did it deliberately, because apparently you are meant to roll the body over so that the soul can get to heaven. And they thought that we deliberately left them lying face down. And we never had the faintest idea about that. It's amazing what you learn from the enemy. They were scared of us; they didn't like us, that was obvious. You didn't have to be a Rhodes scholar to work that out. They reckoned we were brave, that was okay.

... Helicopters would always be governed by an Albatross leader, as we called it. A high helicopter that had a greater picture of the thing, rather than the helicopters down at tree level, who were going to do the operation and pluck you up. And he would command wherever they needed a strike first, to neutralise the enemy around us... But to attract their attention we would hit them with a mirror, we had a mirror... Then they would talk to you... they would ask you to throw smoke, but you didn't tell them what colour. They would look around, because the Viet Cong if they were around, they would throw smoke, too, and the chopper would ask you what colour yours was. It was a bad mistake for the other blokes if they had another colour, because then they used to use that as a marker and absolutely demolish them. That's like marking your own positions... And this is how an extraction took place. It was either the decision of the Albatross lead, because by that time he was in charge and you were just a package. He would let the gunships well and truly neutralise the ground, strafing, or have the gunships standing by. Have the slick ship come and pick you up first and respond. And they used to do all sorts of cover and deception, criss-cross patterns and whatever. But the minute you were lifted, they would saturate the area. Absolutely saturate it.

* * *

I would have to assume it was day one or day two of this patrol. We always used to sleep close to the track, because you learnt a lot by people walking past. It depended on the tactical situation. Sometimes you got right away, but generally, you were within cooee. Which had its advantages and disadvantages. Advantages that you got warning about movement and stuff, disadvantage in that if they sprung you they could line up on it and use it as a start line and finish you off. Anyhow, we were relatively close to this one . . . and we were actually awoken by their signals shots. Because they were short of radios they used to signal each other with different guns at topographical points, 'all clear' or whatever it was.

Anyhow, we were woken by that and by blokes patrolling past. So we got ourselves together, that was the only time you took your gear off, was at night. And even then you slept on it. You just never took your gear off, you might unloosen your belt at midday, but that's it. You had to have it on you ready for an instant. We decided to move position across to the other side of the track and then we patrolled towards where these Viet Cong had patrolled. So that went okay for a while, then we looked up and there was this bloke bearing down, stalking us . . . from where I was on the flank I had a wonderful view of the men stalking us. There was a tall one and a short one, and the short one was very, very small. Anyhow, when he got to the point where—because we were quite prepared with our job to let him pass. But once somebody is stalking you it is pretty hard to break contact and get out of his way, but we were hoping against hope. So we let him come, from me, two metres, three metres. Incidentally, in both my tours, I think the furthest I ever got at a bloke was two or three metres. It was always that close. No way in the world was it something like fifty, or forty or thirty. It was always two or three metres when we engaged.

So this was it, we engaged the bloke with the crossbow and we well and truly drilled him. And I still remember movement behind and I give it a bit of spray or whatever. Anyhow, part of the job was . . . them not having the administrative system we did, they carried the gear on them, so paybooks and things were always in their packs.

Valuable intelligence, right. Often signals movements. So our job immediately always was when we got one of them was to cut off the equipment and we would carry it all back and give it to the intelligence people. So that always means somebody does the searching. So the boss yelled out, 'Paddy, search the bodies!'

No problem. We put a lot of bullets into this man, because he was coming into a half circle almost of us. By this time we were all pretty hardened, but his back was so riddled that I said to the boss, 'We're not going to turn him over, are we? Because the other side is always worse.'

He said, 'No, no. Cut the gear off him and let's get out of here.'

So I'm running forward with my knife when all of a sudden the smaller one runs out, who happened to be a kid. And a head wound, bleeds like mad. You cut your head and ... well, it was a horrific sight. He would have been a boy of about nine, like I was after the Second [World] War. He yelled out, '*Uc da loi, Uc da loi!*', which means 'Australian' and comes running towards me, and I'm there cutting the gear off this fellow. And I don't know if he grabbed hold of me or if he cuddled me, I just can't remember that bit ... I really can't. But anyhow, that was a shock, that was an absolute shock. And of course, the people who had earlier fired the shot on the track had gone ahead of us and heard this shooting, and now they were all turning around and coming back towards us. So there we were, with this dreadful situation, this young kid, who had obviously been wounded in the head, we got some intelligence, we were doing our job and of course the bad guys are bearing down on us like steam. So, the boss said, 'Paddy, shoot the kid.'

Now whether he meant it or not, I don't have a clue. By rights, that's it. Because there's only five of us and we were outnumbered. I said, 'No way in the world, you do it.'

And he said to the 2IC of the patrol ... not because we were cruel or any damn thing, this was a pretty desperate situation. Any minute ... if you delay much more, you are going to be dead as a maggot, these are the decisions and the choices that you have got. Anyhow, he said to the patrol 2IC, 'You shoot the kid.'

And he says to the boss, 'Go and get stuffed!'

There was this big argument with the whole enemy bearing down on us, and there we are having an argument about a humanitarian issue. Anyhow, Maller solved it. He ran forward, grabbed the kid and then we peeled off. We had a drill. Firing and peeling off . . . there we are running through the scrub like mad things, in a line, control, with a kid under the arm. I remember the old signaller who at this particular point in time hadn't been able to do his stuff, I mean we had to be able to get away and get into some sort of a safe, calm situation and send a code word to say, 'Come and get us.' I remember . . . he sort of had the crossbow at the ready as well. As soon as we could we sent the code word and we said, 'There are too many of them.'

Then of course, over comes the bird, the Albatross one, but mind you, it took forty minutes. So we had to hide away and avoid for forty minutes. And the kid was extremely well trained, and I mean trained like a soldier. When we went into all round defence he took his part, he went down in a fire position. He had no rifle. And even though we were gunning against his people. When we gave him a drink of water, because we knew he must have been in some kind of state of shock, he didn't just scull it, he sniffed it. He put it in his mouth, swilled it around, spat it out, decided it was all right, then had a drink. We're talking about a nine-year-old kid here. When we gave him a chocolate bar, he smelled that. He didn't gobble it down; he put it in his pocket for later.

Anyhow, when the Viet Cong pressure came on, he started to gibber a bit, maybe even calling out to them, we said, 'Shut up!' he shut up immediately. He followed every order exactly like a trained soldier. We were amazingly impressed. Anyway we managed to get the signal up and over came the bird, after a while, it was an agonising long wait. And this comes back from an Albatross, he said, 'No good, I can't get you out of there. No good.' He said, 'This is what I want you to do. I want you to get in line; I'm giving you a compass bearing. Your last man puts the red panel over his pack. But don't deviate. And when I say go I want you to run on that compass bearing.'

Which was all right up there in a cool aircraft, but down below... The bloke holding the compass' hand was like that. He had us all very worried.

When he said, 'Go!' We did, we ran on that bearing as best we could, keeping in mind the logs and the trees and everything. And you wouldn't believe it, he had a gunship on either side of us, he formed a tunnel. And we were running and to be on the wrong end of there, to be down at ground level with the gunships, and they've got mini guns on either side, six thousand rounds per minute... which is pretty flaming fierce I think. And the crescendo down at this level was just unbelievable. So there we were running in a tunnel...we were very frightened of deviating off it now with all these hornet things coming on either side. He got them to fire a nice path for us through, until we got to another clearing and then he said, 'That's it, stop there!'

That's the bloke controlling it up there; it was out of our control by then. And we propped and then he said, 'Now throw smoke,' which we did. He said, 'That's funny, we've got two of them. What colour is yours?'

Now I can't tell if ours is the same as theirs, but it didn't matter, he very quickly sorted out, with our mirror or our panel, and plus the fact that they were looking at us as we were running, and within minutes that other smoke was pulverised. Forget it. Absolutely pulverised. And the next minute the pick-up ship flared... You know how a helicopter loses speed by flaring, like a big dragonfly and virtually dropped into our lap and we just all ran on. I can't remember if it was one or two. As we lifted, the door gunners just opened up and let it rip. I think we also shot out. And that was when the kid lost it and started to cry. That was the only time he lost it, but I mean that was such a...unless you were used to that sort of stuff, it was real traumatic stuff.

Anyhow, the bottom line is this. His dad was the guerrilla leader for the area, and he was with him when he was shot the week before.

The person who was with him was his uncle, and he was on patrol with his uncle. His mum was sick and tired of the guerrilla life ... I can't remember the unit or whatever, and she had in actual fact surrendered to the nearest ARVN [Army of the Republic of Vietnam] unit, and gave herself up. However, they being what they are made her an agent and sent her back, and said, 'You've got to stay.' They probably blackmailed her ... said they would tell the rest of them that she was an agent provocateur or whatever ... and in the meantime, of course, this kid is going out on patrol with all his relatives, which the security forces are killing in front of him. Anyhow, the upshot of the whole thing is that when we got him back to the Task Force, we got a voice aircraft up from the intelligence people. I forget her name, Mrs Wi, and the voice aircraft flew over the area, it was pinpointed by then, and said, 'Mrs Wi, we have your son. Please come out of the jungle immediately.'

By that afternoon she was out, we put him in the orphanage, and by that afternoon she was out and rejoined with her boy at the orphanage. Because afterwards we used to send money ... and she just gave us bundles of intelligence, just an absolute bundle of intelligence. It's a classical example of how an extraction can happen. But the forty minutes it took, that's a long forty minutes.

* * *

We got to the point where we were confident enough because we had some armoured personnel carriers nearby, where we could attempt a snatch. To attempt a snatch, to take a prisoner ... prisoners generally happened rather than you deliberately snatching them. Like, we did try all kinds of things, like using gas or whatever ... and we did take prisoners, but as I say, more often than not it was a happening rather than a deliberate snatch where you had to take a man. But on this occasion, I decided with the situation as it was, and I only had a few minutes to make up my mind, I was either going to shoot him dead on the spot or take him.

... This fellow was a very big man for a Vietnamese, authoritative; he had a proper uniform and all this kind of stuff. But I couldn't see his AK47 so I thought, 'Unarmed,' you know. I can't remember the second bloke. I remember him, I can see him, but I don't know, I couldn't see a weapon on him. If I had seen a weapon on either of them I would have just dropped them like a hot potato and that's the end of the story. Anyhow, a rush of blood to the head. I let him come up to about two metres away, and then I said really loud, '*Dung loi!*' which is 'give up' or 'hands up'. And he did, they were rooted to the spot. But the thing was he couldn't see me. He heard the voice, but I was in the bush and so was the other bloke, the rest of them were way back, there was only two of us. And he just didn't realise that I would have to get up, stand up to my full height and confront him and I did. I bore down on him, I looked him in the eye and I said, '*Dung loi!*' I thought, 'We've got this fellow, he's going to do what he's told.' No way in the world.

What I didn't realise was his AK was tucked here and in a flash he had it out and he was firing about here. Blasted past my right-hand side, ruffled my hair like that and by that time I had hit him two or three times here, spun him around, and then my other mate just went, *thrum*, and drove him back with his burst—I'm not going to go into it, but buckets of blood came out of the person. He dropped his weapon, and I could see the rest of his mob coming up behind me. So I suppressed that and of course by that time my other mates were coming down and joining in. By that time we were up and we moved forward to the bend, around the bend, and I don't know how the other blokes felt, but every time I had to get up when I felt somebody had me, it's quite a feeling. That's when you've got good discipline. You've either got it or you haven't. Your legs are rubbery.

* * *

To go back to Australia between tours . . . you weren't really disengaged. I reckon from 1966 through to '71, when I think I came home from my second tour, perhaps up to '72, you're not really disengaged. All right, you come home to your family and all right, you might be away from the location, but you are not away from the job. And you are getting briefed every day. There was briefing every day because you don't know when you are going to be on a plane back again, and you were training the new blokes. So what I virtually did between tours was I trained the next batch of blokes. And I was away from home. I can't remember the time, but I was very seldom here. I would say that I would be...in the twelve months between the tours, I would have spent at least eight not home, training the next lot of blokes intensely for the job. And I mean intensely. You had to impart everything to keep them alive.

And the most gratifying thing I can recall is a young fellow, because we used to keep off the tracks, we weren't in a position to be bold enough to use them because the tracks were their highways, right. So we used to reach a track and we had a track-crossing drill. Where you put out your flankers and so on... My phrase for teaching them was that when you stepped on the track, be prepared to kill your mother. I said, 'That's it. When you step on a track, you be prepared to kill your mother.' I used to drum it into them, drum it into them. I said, 'Because it happens so fast...' And anyhow, I went up and joined 3 Squadron for a while. And he came up and he shook my hand and he said, 'Paddy, I want to thank you very, very much.'

I said, 'Why is that?'

He said, 'First track we ever come to, first patrol, your words came to me. 'When you step on the track, be prepared to kill your mother.'

He said he got on a track, Charlie [the enemy] put two rounds through his sleeve and he dropped a man and got over the other side. And he thanked me, and I felt so great. I felt so great. He got on the track and Charlie put two in his sleeve. Now that's getting close, isn't it? But he got the upper hand.

* * *

For the first time in the second tour I got R&R home, ever. A big mistake. I really don't believe you should be allowed to come home. It sounds fine, it sounds great, but when you go back after actually coming back to the unreality...you say the reality of home, but the unreality ... because by that time, what went on *there* was real and this was unreal. And I mean when you land back, in your defence position, after you've been home seeing your wife, seeing your kids, five days only ... I don't know how the other blokes reacted to it, but it sort of took the momentum or the wind out of your sails. Like my sons, if they go into a situation like that, I've got three sons, tomorrow, I would say to them, 'For Christ's sake, don't come home. Go to Hong Kong, go anywhere, get pissed, play up with the women, do whatever you like. But for Christ's sake ...'

* * *

Because you go back and you just can't ... And the minute the fire in the belly dies remotely you are up for getting that third eye, in my opinion. Bad mistake.

* * *

I was sitting in my lounge room, had the next-door neighbours there and she called me a killer. The next-door neighbour! It was a very bad atmosphere. I never got pelted with tomatoes like some of the blokes definitely did. We used to sneak into the airports, not like chest out, although we carried ourselves that way. It used to be almost like trying to hide you away. There you are, fighting for your country, upholding the pride of your nation and when you come back from doing exactly that, what do they do? They try and sneak you in the back door. No, it was a very bad atmosphere.

Full uniform with my ribbons on, I wasn't allowed into an RSL at all. I was stopped by the bouncer at the door. I said to him, 'Listen, all these civvies are going in. There I am in full uniform, I'm transiting from R&R Perth back to Nui Dat and you're not allowing me to come in for a drink!'

He said, 'I'm sorry, mate, I'd like you to, but it's my instructions from the president of the RSL.'

I said, 'Okay, can I please speak to the president of the RSL?'

So the president came outside, wouldn't even go inside the doorway, this was the Sydney RSL, I said the same thing, 'Look, I just come from a war zone and I'm going back to a war zone. I just saw my family in Perth, I'm transiting, I'm in the camp, I've just popped down here for a drink and there's your bouncer on the door not letting me in.'

He said, 'Oh, you Vietnam vets are a bundle of trouble. You all just want to cause trouble.' He said, 'That's my instructions.'

I don't want to tell the camera what I told him . . . pissweak, bloody idiot. I mean, can you imagine how I felt? Anyhow, I said, 'Well, go and get stuffed!'

I was pretty aggro. And I suppose I was playing up to what he was saying about us Vietnam veterans getting angry and all that. Anyhow, he stormed off inside and the bouncer says, 'Come here.' He said, 'Listen, mate, your mates are not here. They're around the corner at such and such a pub.' He said, 'Just go . . .'

So anyhow, I went there and walked in and it was like a Nui Dat job, all the vets were there, getting drunk, and I was home again. This is how it was. Now isn't that a bit of a disgrace?

* * *

I wouldn't have missed it for quids. It was a life's experience. I mean . . . if you were to ask me what was the greatest experience of my life, not the most pleasant but the greatest . . . Chris would probably say our marriage, but look, I'm very sorry, but Vietnam and the two tours I got were by far the thing that I will live with to the day I die. I'm not sorry that I went. Would I do it again tomorrow if I was as young as that? Probably. But no, it was an unbelievable time in our period of history, our world history. It was an unbelievable opportunity to contribute. I was an anti-communist in the worst possible way. They were communists; they wanted to bring about a regime which I didn't want to be a part of. I loved my country, that's it, into it. No questions asked.

DULCIE TOOHEY

Child
Farm Worker
World War II

'Sunnyside' was about a hundred and sixty acres. The house there was much like any other house in Ipswich—veranda on the front, with a hallway through, and a very large kitchen. There was the boys' bedroom added on the back. There was a wide set of stairs where my father would sit and smoke a pipe after tea ... and think about things.

... There were four boys and four girls plus myself. Charlie, Elsie, Percy, Louie, Rosie, Mabel, Edna, Vince and me ... I was really more or less adopted into the family. One of my older sisters was really my mother ... Rosie was my birth mother, really. It's a strange case, because I now know who my father was. I have no wish to ... well, he's gone, anyway. See, if anyone wanted a helping hand, then it was Rosie that would help out. So if this man's wife was going to have a baby in Murgon, then Rosie would be sent to do the milking and help with the housework, and ... let's just say that he assumed that she was there for other purposes as well. I know what we class it as today ... I never spoke with her about it at all. I've spoken about it with my stepfather and with cousins. It was a strange situation. My grandparents wanted to adopt me legally but they were too old at the time. So I think they did a bit of social service themselves and through the church. They did a little ceremony and I joined the family as the little sister. I can remember when I was told about all this, which is rather strange. I was seventeen and my grandfather—who I called Dad—he was in hospital, dying. And my grandmother and Rosie came home, and my grandmother said, 'Sit down. We've got something to tell you. Rosie isn't your sister, she's your mother. But it's always going to stay the same as it's been, so don't worry about it.'

...Everybody knew—well, not everybody knew...one of my cousins told me that his parents knew, and it seems that most knew. But I was never made to feel any different, and I think it was pretty courageous of the family. Usually the girls were just sent away back then and that was that. And it was in the Depression also, so an extra mouth to feed was not all that welcome.

... We were a pretty lively sort of family—very talkative. Most of our time was spent in the kitchen, around the kitchen table. It was a very big one. We all had our certain place where we sat. Charlie was always beside the teapot—a huge one. Dad sat at the end with Mum on his left, and the girls lined up on one side and the boys on the other... You were always talking over each other. I've heard from people who later visited that it was very confusing because you didn't know who to listen into. There were so many of them going on at the same time, and they marvelled at how my father could keep track of the lot, and put a spoke into each of the conversations...my father would chip into whatever conversation he was tuned into at the time...whatever was going on in the farm, that was discussed. Politics, they were greatly into that. They were the only Labor voting family in a strongly National Party area. I think because my father's side of the family had come from the north of Germany. They were more liberal in their outlook than my mother's side of the family, which came from the south of Germany where they were more conservative...we didn't really talk about why they came here. We only knew that they came because they'd had enough of war...they were very anti-war. War was the reason they came out...in the 1860s, the original families that settled around here.

After tea—that's what we called it then—Dad always sat right beside the wireless. He was partially deaf. But he'd sit right beside the wireless and listen to whatever programs were on; the ABC, that was his after-tea ritual. The rest of us would just be chattering away . . . We very often had visitors. There were a number of cousins around there . . . we were in and out of each others' houses quite normally. So there was never any lack of things to do or people to listen to. And I think because I was so much younger . . . as kids watch TV today and soak up stuff, that's what I did. That was my sort of entertainment; listening to all these conversations going on around me.

I don't remember it being the Depression years at all. In fact, I'm amazed when people come on television programs and say, 'But we were so poor; we had nothing!'

And I think, 'Well, we didn't have much either.'

* * *

Our house was very basic and we didn't have refrigeration. We had wireless. That was the thing we valued most. A number of people did not have wirelesses in those days, and we'd have neighbours come down to listen to the cricket, especially when the Australians were playing the English over in England. It would be a cold winter's night and the kitchen would be full of people from the neighbourhood who'd come over to listen to the cricket. And of course we all thought it was absolutely genuine when we heard the bat hit the ball—but it wasn't at all, was it?

Washing for nine people was a fairly big task. The boiler had to be got ready the night before, and the tubs all put out, and the work clothes soaked in. Then next day there were three girls all lined up with a tub each—one for the washing, one for the rinsing, and one for the blueing. My mother would be there at the boiler with a stick, prodding the things that had to be boiled up. Tuesday was ironing day, and Wednesday was baking day. On top of the dresser that we had in the kitchen was a line of cake tins, and those were filled every week with cakes and biscuits—enough to last us for a week. Every afternoon we'd have afternoon tea and those were what was on the table for afternoon tea . . . breakfast would be on once all the farm jobs had been completed. It was mostly eggs and something... eggs and bacon, or egg-over-meat which was the remains of the corned round. Or there was eggs done like an omelette, or just fried, or poached. It nearly always included eggs.

The work was very evenly divided into male and female occupations. The women did the housework and the laundry, and the men did the farm work. They crossed over in milking—both sexes would do the milking, of course. Minding the cows—which we often had to do in the drought years. We had to keep them in a special section of the paddock where they would eat. It might not be fenced off, and we'd have to stop them from getting into a cultivated area. We all did that as girls. I remember that my sister Edna knitted two dresses whilst sitting on a horse, minding cows.

... Being on my own a lot as a child, I played a lot on my own. I think I had the most dolls of any girls in the district... I played at dressing them more than mothering them. Rosie was very good with the sewing machine—she was an accomplished sewer. She'd have been a designer in today's world. So I always had lots of dresses for these dolls. I'd change them and play with them, and I'd push them around and things like that. And I had a cat, which I could also dress up and push around in a pram. It didn't protest... the cat would sit there and I'd go through the process of playing school with it. Stick horses—we had horses of our own, but stick horses were still okay. You galloped around on a stick with string through a hole that someone had bored for you. Cob horses was another one. When corn was threshed, the interior of the dry cobs was really very colourful. It could range from quite a deep reddish colour through to a pale, pinkie colour. This was common amongst all the children—we'd have our own teams of cob horses. We'd link them together with string, and then put another string on them, and we'd drive them. We gave them all names, usually the names of the horses that were on the farm.

... We used to visit each other on Saturdays. We'd play dolls, ride horses, and also take part in whatever was going on at the farm at the time. Later on we realised that it was really work that we were doing, but at the time we thought we were having fun and playing. We were dipping cattle, and some of the harvesting. It wasn't until the war came that we 'had' to do it. When the war came, then we really had to do those jobs, and to do more of them.

* * *

Dad was a great listener . . . and he was a very fair man. I can remember him being visited by an uncle. And Uncle Guy was sitting at the table and Sam Chambers—he was an Aborigine who was a drover—he used to go around when a dairy farmer wanted to sell off an odd cow or two that was past their prime and Sam would go out and collect them from all the farms. We were sitting at the dinner table—it must have been a Saturday because I was there—and Charlie looked out of the window and said, 'There's Sam.' and he called out, 'Hey, Sam, you're just in time for dinner!'

And Uncle Guy said to Dad, he said, 'He's not going to eat with us, is he?'

And Dad said, 'Of course he is; he's a friend.'

He was very tolerant of the Aborigines. At that time the Act that confined Aborigines to the reserves was not being enforced. It had been passed, but it wasn't yet enforced. They would come from the Aboriginal settlement near Murgon—it was called Cherbourg—and do some work for the farmers around the place. Very often it was clearing away undergrowth in the scrubby areas that were still left on the farm, or they might do a bit of digging for fence posts and that type of thing. But the women, they always camped in our scrub. We had a patch of scrub that my father insisted should never be cleared—he said it was shelter for the animals, both the native animals and the cattle as well. When it was cold or there was a storm, then they could get into the scrub. So they used to camp in there too. I can remember playing with their kids. They were always very welcome . . . my mother, too, she was also very tolerant of them. I can remember when they enforced the Act and the women came out to the farm and they'd never come into the house yard that was fenced off from the farm. They wouldn't do that; they'd only come to the fence or the gate. But I can remember this woman coming to the fence and throwing her arms around my mother and saying, 'We can't come here anymore.' And the two of them just cried. They had been coming for so many years and camping in our scrub. We got quite involved with them, but now they wouldn't be able to do that anymore.

* * *

The shows were the great event of the year. Our family was very heavily involved in them. Dad was on the Show Society committee; and my mother was involved in the catering part of it. All the older members of the family worked on it in some way—they were stewards in the cattle section; Louie was a steward in the ring; Mabel was a steward in the fancy needlework section; and Rosie was in the catering with my mother. I can't remember what Edna did, but I think she had something to do with it as well. It was the most exciting event of the year, of course. We would live from one show to the next, and we'd enter items from our school work, and also from the farm. I can remember getting a calf ready to show. And also, my father had a little bit of a bent for breeding Orpington poultry, and so we'd pen up a few hens—feed them up and get them ready to look really nice so they'd put on a good show.

The first day would always be judging day, which was a bit of a non-show day, really. There'd just be the few people who had to go in for that. Then Friday would be the main show day when everybody went. We'd let the cows go in, in the evening. But all the displays seemed to me to be so wonderful. You look at them now and they pale in comparison to that stage of my life. You'd look at all the big farm pumpkins and vegetables, and all those things were very interesting to a kid on the farm who knew how these things grew and developed. Of course, for days before the girls would be busy making cakes for things they were going to enter...and the car would be loaded up on a Thursday morning with all these cakes to enter; and corn, and heavens knows what—there'd be a chook in the boot, probably. So you had to go round then, and see what prizes

you'd won; and whether you'd won anything in the schools section.
That was exciting.

And of course, the sideshows—they were something unbelievable.
I had a postcard for years with a picture of a Saint Bernard dog on
it. I'd visited that sideshow about three times . . . I was pretty good
at working the system then, because all the other members of the
family were installed in various parts of the showground, and I knew
that I could find Louie at the ring, and Percy in the chook pavilion,
along with Dad. I knew I could find my mother in the catering
pavilion . . . I knew where all of them were. So I used to go around
and con them all for a shilling every now and then so that I could
go into all these sideshows—two or three times. They were always
good for a shilling . . . There would always be the fat lady; and the
boxing tent, and the ring of death where the bikes went round and
round. There were rides, but I wasn't a daring rider on any of them.
I only went on a few of those . . . the merry-go-round and the chair-
o-plane, as they called it, which was like plough seats attached to
chains which whirled around . . . I think there were little trains also;
and one year there were little boats you could go round on.

They used to bring [the Aborigines] into the show. They'd be
standing like sardines in the back of a truck when they arrived. These
trucks would bring them in from Cherbourg. They would be
everywhere. They really liked the show, too; and they always came
to the pavilion where you could have a proper lunch, a two-course
proper lunch. And there was a little window at the back where my
mother served made-up sandwiches, and the Aborigines always came
to that window. She knew them all, and they knew her from show
to show. They'd come up and say, 'This is the baby I had this year,
missus.'

And she'd compliment them on it. And they'd all be sitting around
having their picnic-style lunch on one side and all the whites would
be having their sit-down meals at tables on the other side.

But it was a wonderful day. Then at night they began to have
fireworks . . . and there'd be the Show Ball on the Friday night. We
all had new, long frocks to wear to the Show Ball, and the fellas of

course would wear their suits. And there used to be a travelling show come, before the war. It was called Thorley's. It was a stage show, like a revue type thing. My father was very interested in that. He and Mother and I would go to that, while the others went to the ball and danced. I think I picked up a bit of a love of theatre because of that. For a country kid it was a great experience.

War broke out and we didn't have shows for a few years.

* * *

I think it was at night when we first heard the news—when it was announced that Britain was at war and that we were at war, too. I can remember the dead silence in the room, and I can remember my father looking up with this worried look on his face that I'd never seen before. It was tea time—news time—and as I said before, we always had all this chatter going on around the table, but this night there was just dead silence. We all just sat there waiting for the repetition of the broadcast from London on the radio. Then the next day, I had a little nook, a little place near the boundary fence and the road. It was just one of those lovely little places where there were shrubby trees and womba vines and little birds that would flit in and out. Sometimes there might be a little bird's nest in there somewhere. It was a place where I often used to go and just sit by myself there, and think about things. And this day, I had this feeling that I'd better go back to the house because horrible men might be coming—and soon. That was the feeling I had, but then nothing happened. I sort of expected that something was going to happen in the war, immediately.

After war broke out, the debate suddenly shifted . . . there were a number of us from German descent, and others who were not German descendants. This is something that not many people realise. We talk about the postwar migration but at Wellwood School at that time there were families of German descent and a family of Italian origin, and one of Dutch origin, and one of Chinese origin, and a couple of English . . . Suddenly, the school was split in two. It was pro and anti-German. And we didn't know what Germany was, having left it about four generations ago. We had no ties with Germany whatsoever.

But that went on. One of the English men in the district actually proposed to the parliament that German descendants should leave their farms. They were proposing that we should become more or less employees, and not be owners anymore...there was a distinct feeling of a split in the community. I think that mellowed after Japan came into the war. Then the division disappeared.

... We had a big map up on the wall, and every morning the teacher used to ask the bigger children to pinpoint where the war was at that stage and what was going on. They went through the quick advance of the Germans across Poland and whatever. So we knew that something was going on over there. The men who left from our district, they went to North Africa. So we followed the 9th Division, we followed them there on the map. But apart from that we didn't take too much notice of what was going on. My father continued to listen to the [short wave] news from Germany and we were worried that this would lead him into an internment camp but he refused to listen to us and kept on doing it. But my mother was still scared of the fact that he did this.

In World War I a number of the Lutheran pastors had been interned, so we knew of that situation. Our pastor's wife was of German origin. She had migrated with her husband when she married. Their family was very much afraid that their mother might be taken and interned. So we sort of had an idea of being shut up with barbed wire around us. But by the time Christmas came, things had sort of settled down, and the 1940 Christmas I can remember vividly. It was one that never happened that way again. In a small town, everyone knew what everyone else was doing; it was common knowledge. Our family had always celebrated Christmas, sometimes at our place, sometimes at another uncle's. This year it was at Uncle Carl's. So that was where all the preparation went on; all the families contributed something, and it was a great day for eating and meeting everyone. And at that time, the only late-night shopping that was allowed was on Christmas Eve. So it was very exciting to go to town and have a few drinks and buy the last Christmas presents, and so on.

... I'd sold a calf for ten shillings prior to Christmas, and that ten shillings was to buy presents for the family. So I went to Coles and bought presents for everyone, and debated how much I was going to spend on everyone ... In the morning, you wouldn't have known that it was Christmas Day, because we all had to go and do the milking. I wasn't milking regularly at that stage, but was doing the other little jobs. So we came in and had our breakfast, and then all of us—I don't know how we did it—but we managed to bathe and get into our semi-good clothes; and then we opened our presents at home, before we left to go to uncle's place. Of course, at uncle's place there was a crowd. Everybody was there and we were welcomed in.

One guest who was there that day was a fellow named Billy Needy ... he had a little sulky. It was polished up beautifully and was drawn by two little grey ponies named Jack and Jill. All the leathers on the sulky were red, and it was absolutely beautiful. Sometimes, he would give us rides in it. Not often though; because Billy was very shrewd, and if he gave a ride to *this* person, and didn't give a ride to *that* person, then he was in trouble. But I can remember on that Christmas at Uncle Carl's, he gave rides to all the kids. And we loved it.

And we had this huge table set up on the veranda with thirty people plus. There was duck and goose and chicken—'chook' as we called it—and all the vegetables we had fresh from the farm. We had a lot of China Flat peaches that grew on Uncle Carl's tree just near the kitchen window and there were lollies and nuts that the grocer had given us with our order—he always included those, free. So we had a wonderful day, finished off with plum pudding and custard and fruit salad. After that, we kids used to disappear for a while. That was because we didn't like the fetching and carrying and cleaning up after the big feast. The women, of course, had to do that. The men stayed on the veranda and talked. That was their privilege.

After the cleaning up was all done ... I don't know what we all did—sang a few carols, I think. And then there was the obligatory cricket match, where everyone joined in—even the aunts, they were all in. The pitch was bounded on one side by the barn and by the house on the other; and we played. And it was probably hot. We also had this dog that had been given to us by some people from Wondai. It was a town dog and not a country dog, but he was a very faithful dog and he could catch cricket balls. So we didn't have to do too much running after cricket balls—'Rob' brought them all back. Then after that we had afternoon tea—Christmas cake, biscuits, the lot. And then we went home to milk. Everything seemed quite happy. We had good rain; everything was fine—1940 Christmas. It was a sort of really carefree Christmas the likes of which I don't think I've ever experienced since.

* * *

In 1940 they'd started to take an interest in training Australian men for military purposes. Men had to register and be medically examined and so on. The letters came, saying that one of the men had passed A1, and my mother would tense up, thinking that he was going to go tomorrow. So, throughout that year they came and went. It was quite fun really because we went to see them off at the station, and we went to meet them when they came home. So it was just like having Christmases one after the other, as they came and went.

I don't think [my brothers] worried a great deal about it, and they really enjoyed their three-month training camps. When they were called up, I had this vision in my head of my older sister Edna going for the mail, and finding in it a brown envelope with OHMS [On His Majesty's Service] on it, addressed to one of the brothers, and throwing it down on the kitchen table in front of Mother, and saying, 'He's going off for three months to Brisbane, where he can go to the pictures, and to dances, and eat chocolate...'

When was she ever going to get a chance to do that? That was her reaction to it. But the boys really enjoyed their training... But everybody of course—from all around the district—there was a couple of them like that from every family. So we were partying from one day to the next, with send-offs and homecomings. But then, when Pearl Harbor was bombed and the call-up came, Jack went and Louie went—he was the one who wanted to be a policeman—and so he was quite happy to go into the army. Suddenly, the dads in the district were doing what I call 'cow sums'—'Right, that's fifty cows between five milkers; that's ten each. And fifty cows with three milkers, then that's a bit of a problem.'

... They all went at different times. They didn't all go together. It was one week, and then another week, one at a time. It was different to waving them off when they just went to training camp. After Pearl Harbor you knew that even if you did see them come home again, it might be the last time before they went somewhere else.

* * *

You were allowed one man per farm. My father had only one kidney, so he applied to have his youngest son—Vince—exempted. But they didn't take into account his state of health, so Vince went all the same. But he didn't join the AIF [Australian Imperial Force]. He remained with the CMF [Citizens Military Force], but still served in Bougainville. Of the other two who joined the AIF, Percy ferried ammunition to ships in Brisbane, and Louie helped to build the Mount Isa to Darwin road. He was stationed in Mount Isa. So the two who were prepared to go overseas stayed in Australia; and the one who was digging his heels in a bit, he went to Bougainville. But that's bureaucracy at its... well, maybe I shouldn't be expressing opinions, but that was the situation as I saw it.

All around the district these young girls were coming to replace the male teachers. Teachers at that time were quite high up on the social calendar, and one of the ladies in the district, her husband went off to meet the replacement teacher. I can remember her grilling him about how he must behave and how his manners must be perfect and how he must wear his suit; and he must call her 'Miss' all the time. Her name was Betty Eagle. So he went and met her at the station and welcomed her, saying, 'You must come and live with us, Miss Hawk.' And he called her Miss Hawk all the way home. Betty laughed about it later. So they made their homes with us, these young teaching girls.

The first thing that we really noticed was the shortage of elastic. That was a big thing. And also the shortage of materials fit to be made into underwear. You could buy singlets at the counter, but you couldn't buy children's knickers ... because all the mums made them—they just bought the soft materials and made them. The store that we supported got in a large bolt of yellow head cloth—pretty stiff, cotton material. My mother and one of the other mothers bought yards of it, and they managed to get some elastic—it used to be put away under the counter—and she'd say, 'Psst, I've a bit of elastic in this week; you can have three yards.'

And the ladies would say,

'Oh yes please, that'd be good!'

So Kathleen [a friend] and I had these horrible bright yellow bloomers. And because of that, we couldn't have a swing for the entire duration of the war, because if our dresses blew up, we'd be showing these horrible yellow ... by the end of the war they were just about worn out!

I can remember, too, getting extra coupons for being an outsized child—I was a fairly early developer, and was over five foot tall. If you were over five foot you could get extra coupons. Well, I was five foot tall at age twelve—and I never grew after that. But these were the sorts of things that were done at school—Ruth, our teacher, had to measure us and send away whatever sort of application form was required. And she had to do surveys for possible evacuation of city children—all our houses had to be measured: the number of rooms, the size of the rooms; estimates of how many people we could bed down, and all of this. It caused quite a stir because some of the women said things like, 'I told my brother that if it got bad in Brisbane I'd take in his wife and kids. I don't want these other people.'

So that exercise was not very popular.

[The 'Brisbane Line'] was another bone of contention in the district—were we going to be above it or below it? And would it be a straight line, or would it follow lines of ranges and rivers. It was a very worrying sort of proposition for our people ... another thing, at that time the city schools, they had to dig slit trenches and that sort of thing. They'd been doing that for some time. Anyway, they decided that all schools had to have slit trenches, so the committee met one afternoon under the pepperina tree at the school—I think one of them brought a shovel—and it was black clay soil around the school. He put the shovel in and said, 'This is a waste of time. What'll we do about it?'

But there was a gully that ran across the corner of the school yard and one of the Dutch dads—Bill Bligh—he said, 'No, they can go in the gully! What's the use of trying to dig anything out?'

So they gave it away; went and had a yarn under the school, then went home.

There was no indication of what would happen to us. That's what caused most consternation, because we didn't really know what our position was, and we didn't know what would be expected of us. We were doing these surveys to take evacuees, but we didn't know whether we were safe or not . . . there was a 'Dad's Army'. A couple of the farmers; most of the ones of English descent went into that. There wasn't much interest in it from the others. They were a bit of a joke really, I think . . . 'Broomstick Warriors' they were.

* * *

In the early 1940s there were a number of staging camps in the Murgon–Wondai districts. There was an air force camp at Kingaroy and army camps around Murgon and Wondai. The ladies in town decided that these poor boys are so far away from home—they were from Victoria and New South Wales—and they couldn't get home on leave because they were so far away—and so we should introduce hospitality Sundays. So everybody in the district lined up to take two of these fellows on a Sunday. And they'd come along in a military vehicle, a truck or whatever, and they'd be dropped off at the gate— two of them. So we got to know quite a few of these locally established young men. One night, my father was sitting on the steps puffing away at his pipe, as he usually did, and he said, 'There's a light out there.'

We were all blacked out, and to be in the country when it was all blacked out, well, it was really dark. And we watched it for while; we all went over to the door and we watched it. It was going to the right and to the left, and then suddenly it disappeared; and then we saw a flash of light on the dairy. And we could hear a truck or car, and then the next minute they pulled up at the back gate. So that was the first of it. They would get a truck and some of their mates and come around to our place, where there were four girls and lots to eat.

After that they came regularly of an evening, to play monopoly and cards and singing; and to have a good feed for supper. And they wanted us—the girls—to go to the local dances and pictures with them. But we didn't have enough petrol. Petrol rationing was very strict. And so they talked it over with Dad and they said, 'Will the girls be able to go if we can get some petrol?'

And I remember now that army petrol was a bit different from normal petrol. It was a different colour. But by that time we had a tractor. It was powered by kerosene, but it was started with petrol. So they worked out that if anyone queried it, they'd say it was the ration of petrol for starting the tractor. And my mother walked out to the shed one day and said, 'There's an extra drum of petrol out there.'

And Dad said, 'Yes,'

And she said, 'Where did it come from?'

And Dad said, 'It's for the tractor.'

He knew perfectly well it was pinched petrol and that it was going to be used in a car to give the girls the opportunity to go to dances and the pictures with these young men who'd been visiting us.

They got quite close ... One of my sisters, I think she really lost her heart to one of them. She wrote to him but we heard no more of him. I think he might have been killed, because we heard no more of George. And of course his people—goodness knows where they were in New South Wales—it was like being on the moon in those days; so she went through a rather sad time and never looked at another after that. But we wrote to them all. We did a lot of letter writing, both to our brothers and to these young fellows that we'd got to know...every night we wrote letters.

...We kept track of the war every morning early, and we started war-savings stamps and we had a chart on the wall with our targets. We had a list of all the fellows from the army who were in the war, up on the wall—where they were, as far as we knew; it was only generalised because you could get censored for that. But that was part of it. And of course, letters that you'd get would be censored heavily—you know, they'd say, 'I'm well...' and then there'd be big pieces cut out of them. They might as well have written seven words and been done with it...that was especially from Vince, when he was in Bougainville. There was no indication of where he was or what he was doing...the local blokes were involved in the Shaggy Ridge campaign. There's a picture of one in jungle warfare gear, and so they had a really torrid time.

* * *

Bill [Eisenmonger] was killed at Salamaua, before the Milne Bay offensive I think. He was a sergeant, and his officers had been killed. There weren't too many of them left, and he rallied them, and they captured a Japanese machine-gun post; but he was killed in the process. That was the detail they gave to his parents later... It was one afternoon. We were doing afternoon things...mostly writing; Ruth was reading to the younger ones. A car went down the road by the side of the school, and heads popped up. Then another car went down; and there were whispers around...'Who's going to town today?' 'Were you going to town today?' We were all absolutely puzzled, because we all knew what everyone else was doing. If we went to town, we sort of put the hat around in case anyone needed anything that we could bring out. So we were puzzled for a while. Then there was a knock on the door. It was Charlie, actually; and Ruth went out to the door, and they talked for a bit. Then she beckoned to the two older boys who were on flag duty that week, to run the flag up. By that time we were all craning our necks out of the back window towards the flagpole. They ran the flag up, and then lowered it to half-mast; then she came back in and said, 'Stand up all those of you who are related to Bill Eisenmonger.'

I suppose about fourteen of us stood up. Then she said, 'I have to tell you that Bill was killed at Salamaua.'

And that . . . well that brought the war right home . . . right home. And everybody in the district—some of them were related, but all of them had gone round to Uncle George and Aunt Margaret's . . . and she went from being just the jolliest aunty, who you went round and made biscuits with, to . . . she became very different, for quite a long time. She set up on her sideboard sort of like a shrine, with all photos of Bill growing up, and she had flowers and . . . I don't think she really got over it till after the war. She and Uncle George went to New Guinea to see his grave. Whether it was his grave or not, that's debatable too, but she was satisfied after that. It made a big difference to her.

I've got a photo of a cousin's wedding, and when you look at it you can see that there's all these uncles and aunts, and a group of kids, but nobody in between. See, when the girls went to dances it was the fellows who were stationed in the area that they danced with—all the locals were gone. And then, as things started to get worse, they started to go. It just drained the whole male population in that age group.

. . . Mum was always looking for the mail, and I think when the telephone rang—we were on a party line . . . you had several subscribers on the one line, and each one of them is given a Morse code signal for their own particular call. We were 65B, so we had a long and three shorts—which is 'B' in Morse code. If it was just a local call you didn't have to go through the exchange. You just rang each other on the line. And if Mum got the feeling that there was a phone call, not just someone on the line—but from further away, she'd get a bit jittery because she was expecting it might be a telegram. I suppose we all sort of lived with the apprehension that something could happen. But we knew that Percy and Louie were up in Australia, so it didn't really hit us like it did other people whose sons were overseas.

My cousin Myrtle, her husband, he had a three-day leave; and he came home one day, and the wedding was the next day, and they both went back the next day. We saw them off at the station for their one-night honeymoon. He went off on a ship to New Guinea, and she came home on a train. I felt that, more than I felt for my brothers, because I was quite close to her. I knew that she was very sad and apprehensive.

It was a country wedding so the reception was held in a barn. It was late winter, and everything left in the barn that had to be fed to the animals, the farmers took home and brought back. I think Rosie did most of directing the catering for it. Mabel and Edna also. Work was just sort of dropped for a few days and they prepared for the wedding. There was the usual sort of Sunday dinner menu for the wedding—geese and ducks and hens and chooks and vegetables from the farm. Plum puddings and fruit cakes... They were very good at making plum puddings. There was an iced wedding cake in three tiers—one to be eaten, and one to be sent away to people you liked; and one to be kept for the christening later on, when the child arrived. That was the usual thing. But Myrtle didn't have what you'd describe as a wedding dress. She wore what, up till then, had been called the 'travelling' dress. Every bride had to have two outfits—the white outfit with the veil and whatever, and then a travelling outfit to change into: a smart dress, hat, gloves, handbag and shoes to wear when they set out on their honeymoon. But she and a number of others made that concession—the travelling dress became the wedding dress. And there's two pictures—one of my sister-in-law... and Myrtle, both in the same colour pink travelling dress. They had the handbag, with the posy attached, and a smart hat and gloves. So this was how a wedding went off. But the photo reveals that there were older people there—uncles, aunts, and children—but no one much in between.

... Every man had a three-piece suit that he wore to church and to dances and if he was going out anywhere. Sometimes my father would wear his three-piece suit just to go to town. They were tailor-made; you didn't buy suits 'off the hook' in those days. On the farm the men usually wore what they called 'cotton twist'. It was not quite like denim, more a cross between denim and chino; that sort of casual material you see today. Dark coloured shirts, too. We used to be regularly visited by travellers from places like McDonald & East, and from Bayard's. That's where most of the ordinary, everyday clothing came from. A big van used to pull up and they'd open up the sides of it, and there would be all the things that you wanted.

Dresses were all homemade. Nobody bought a dress. And there were no dresses off the peg. Everything was homemade, out of good material. So we were always very well dressed. I used to love it when the traveller came, because at the end of it he'd give me a little book of samples. If there was something that you particularly liked and it was not on his van. They were in a little stack and stapled onto a card. He'd give me one of those I'd flick through it, and dream of things. And I can remember my father buying a new hat. He always wore a ... I can't think of the name of it ... like an Akubra, that sort of hat. He said they were useful for belting a bull over the nose with, or you could have a drink of water out of them, or fan himself on a hot day. Gradually it would get to the floppy stage, and then he'd sacrifice it for a new one. But it was always bought from the traveller.

Up till the war the girls farmed in dresses. You had your good Sunday dress, and when that was a season or so old, it would become your second dress—like the one you wore when you came in from doing the milking. We didn't have a bathroom in the house, we just brought one of the big tubs into the bedroom and had a bath there—provided there was enough water around—otherwise you just got by with a lick and a promise. We'd change into clean clothes anyway, just to have tea at night. And those were the sorts of things we wore on a Sunday, or to go and visit cousins and the like. Then, when those were beginning to get daggy, then they became work clothes. You'd wear them for your work around the place. And even for the everyday clothes, we always wore a black apron over the top. That was no doubt to help with the washing, to help keep everything clean. And the girls wore stockings too—lisle stockings, a cotton mixture. And garters. They were always crinkly, and they were always pulling them up. When the boys left, Edna, the most outspoken of the sisters said, 'Well, if I'm going to be a farmhand, then I'm not going to do it in a dress.'

She said to Mum, 'You can get some material and Rosie can make us some shorts.' There was a great furore over that. Mum wouldn't have it. She said, 'That's *fast*; only *fast* girls wear shorts!'

But Edna stuck to her guns and some navy head cloth was bought in reams, and Rosie sewed shorts and overalls for us—the overalls for the winter and the shorts for the summer.

* * *

It was the day that the grammar school bell rang for the first time in five years. And we could hear music in the distance because the Boys' Grammar cadet band had marched from their school across to our school and were coming in the gate. We were having a Latin lesson with my original Latin teacher, and she wasn't going to be swayed by any bell or band or anything like that; so she struggled on for another five minutes until the boys were in the courtyard and everyone had become very restless. So she picked up her books and went. And so did we. We just went out and followed the band down to Brisbane Street and Nicholas Street, which was just absolutely crowded with people. We danced and we sang, and somehow or other I must have gone home and changed out of my school uniform— I can't remember how. But I can remember being there until very late in the evening, still dancing and singing and carrying on like an idiot. And none of us were high on drugs or anything either! Celebration. Nobody thought about what was going to happen afterwards.

I think it took a while for it to sink in . . . a couple of years; because they had to bring these men home from all over the world. My husband came home in 1946, so that was quite a long time after the fifteenth of August, 1945. They had to bring them all home, and they had to get them all into occupations, and I don't really know . . . Most people thought, 'Right, I'm going to go back into the slot where I came from.' But they didn't realise that that slot was no longer there. On the farms it was sort of like that. But the men were not happy with that slot either. My brother Percy . . . didn't come back to the farm. Louie came back—but he sort of wanted more say in how things were done and run. When my father died he actually took over his share in the farm with my mother, so that he could do some of the management. He actually had to do all the management, really.

. . . Most farms were just subsistence level up until World War II. We were always well dressed and well fed, and had money to spend when there was something on; but as for people being paid a wage, well, there was no such thing. People in town were paid wages. They got wages every week, but we didn't. We just sold our produce and paid our bills, and whatever was left over we just shared amongst us. It was really just subsistence farming. And after the war, all that changed. The men had got wider horizons and had different experiences. Even if they didn't go overseas they were still looking toward things being different. It took the old people some time to realise that that was the way things were going to go.

. . . They came back in dribs and drabs, and I think this is something that may have been blown out of proportion. I think there may have been parades in Sydney or somewhere that I saw on TV, but nothing strikes my memory here for Ipswich or Brisbane—nobody turned out to welcome anyone because they came back in such an erratic fashion. Like, Jim was a navigator in the RAAF and he just came back with a bunch of other people and went to a staging camp. So did Morris— he was invalided back from New Guinea and went to a staging camp at Redbank, and then went home. The fact that there was no welcome homes and no saying thank you, is something I think that has been blown out of proportion.

When they left, I was a child; and I regarded them from that light. They were the 'big blokes' and they teased me and bought me things, and sometimes they'd give me a shilling, but afterwards I'd grown up, and I suppose I'd grown away from them. And they'd grown away from the old style of the family as well. They weren't going to be told what to do anymore.

* * *

First of all, it was rather exciting; different from the usual. And then after that, after realising what war was really all about—which occurred when Bill was killed at Salamaua, and with what happened afterwards—then the war just seemed a bit of a waste; a waste of six years of people's lives. Some of the changes were for the good, of course. The women I think gained something for having worked in that time but . . . you don't sort of . . . when you're living . . . I don't know how young people think today . . . but you thought at the time, that your times are [not] any different from what's gone before, or what you expect to follow. It's only when you get to be . . . when you get to the end of the scale that you look back and think, 'Well, that was a waste of time.' But then, we got contacts with a lot of people that we wouldn't have met otherwise. We exchanged views with them. It was good for mixing social attitudes, but we still all went on living. It wasn't an entire interruption of our lives—we just went on living.

PETER WARFE

Commander
Second Australian Contingent to Rwanda
Force Medical Officer
UN Assistance Mission, Rwanda

My father joined the army in World War II as an officer, and went overseas to Greece and the islands. He was a particularly successful infantry company commander. He was one of Australia's leading combat soldiers at that time ... My mother was brought up as a bookkeeper and they were married just after the end of the war, and she basically had a more traditional role as a mother and wife looking after a house and helping us to get through school. They both died relatively young. I was nineteen when my mother died, and about twenty-three when my father died. So that's quite some time ago now. They were a traditional, conservative middle-class Australian family. Hard working, bringing up the kids, get a good education, that sort of focus in life. It was very hard for that generation of Australians. There were not a lot of opportunities for higher education. They were brought up through the Depression. When things were getting better, in a sense, Australia had been smashed to pieces by World War I, we lost a whole generation of people, and then the Depression and then when things were getting better World War II came along—difficult days. They didn't meet until after the war, but obviously the country was trying to get back on its feet for a long time.

My father was unsettled after the war. He tried to go back into private business after the war, as a carpenter, but he missed the military, he missed the camaraderie and, I think in retrospect, he had some difficulty coming to grips with peacetime life again after five or six years of war...he had a lot of difficulty settling down. In retrospect he was drinking too much and he was probably suffering some elements of post-traumatic stress disorder, which he would never admit to, or his whole generation wouldn't admit to at the time... He had an exaggerated startle reflex. He used to have nightmares all the time. He was frequently screaming out in the middle of the night. He was an introspective, quiet sort of a person. He refused to mix with the veterans after some time. He wouldn't get involved in Anzac Day. He was a member of the RSL [Returned Services League] but he wouldn't go there. He resented people talking about the war, particularly those who were talking about it with bravado or inflating their own role in it. He didn't like it. And he was a pretty blunt sort of a guy. He made it fairly clear to people if he didn't like it. He was a pretty tough guy. He used to intimidate a lot of people. I guess that's why he was a particularly successful commander... Like most people, he would only talk about the funny occasions. He would never really, in any detail, describe the combat, the privations, the horror of it, the loneliness or the fear. He would only talk about the funny occasions with his friends, or when they'd chased the Italians down the waddies in Europe to capture a wine cellar. He would describe events like that rather than the actual combat scenes. Yeah, like most people he wouldn't discuss it very much, other than the humorous incidents, or perhaps the feats that others achieved... Mother was basically at home. They weren't particularly happy together, but people stuck together for the sake of the family. That's a pretty long time ago now.

* * *

My school was pretty tough. It was a conservative Presbyterian school. At the time they were interested in the First Eighteen Football Team and how many kids could get honours and get into university and that was it. In retrospect, I can say it now, they recognised that the world was a competitive place, and they were preparing us to take our place in it, and hopefully to lead in it. But at the time, it was pretty tough. There was a lot of work, you had to play sports, you had to join the school cadets, you had to do this, you had to do that. There was a lot of discipline, there was corporal punishment, there was Saturday detentions, they were thrown around like confetti, chapel and all the rest of it. Yeah, they were a conservative, God-fearing, rigid, authoritative group of people that ran that school, but it provided an excellent education. I know, it's an ambivalent answer, I know, but it did, it provided an excellent education in terms of a broad-based education, and the technical competencies that a person like me needed to get into university to study medicine. On the other hand, it taught us virtually nothing about our country, nothing about our culture, it excluded us from access to girls because that was considered no good and you should play football and have cold showers. So it didn't really prepare us for the day-to-day social interactions in our society. It also taught us everything about England and nothing about Australia. It taught us to be grateful for what we had, rather than analysing what was going on and questioning whether there was a better way. Well, that's the way it seemed to me. Maybe it was because I was studying sciences, and there were problems and there were solutions and that was it. It was only later in day-to-day life that I realised that there is very little black and white, that most things are grey.

* * *

I was a third-year medical student and there wasn't any money around in those days, and there was little part-time work available. I was working one afternoon a week and Saturday mornings in a grog shop, and working over Christmas holidays demolishing houses and working in warehouses and things like that, trying to get some money to live on. I had been called up, I was called up when I turned twenty, halfway through my third year of medicine and I knew I was going into the army anyway. The army had an undergraduate scholarship available, which paid your tuition . . . so I applied for that scholarship and there were entry things, psychological and medical entry tests, interviews, and I was successful in those and I was awarded an army scholarship. That allowed me to continue my medical studies for the next three years, but then after the compulsory residency training, I had to come into the army for four years. So that was the deal ... I guess I was a bit of an economic conscript and I had been conscripted into the military. They were two compelling reason to take it on. And yeah, I was criticised by a lot of people for doing it, for selling my soul and for joining the military. And a lot of those were living in forty-square houses down by the bay with extremely wealthy parents who were rolling them through and giving them sports cars for their eighteenth birthday. Their circumstances were slightly different. So yeah, I pretty well kept it to myself rather than getting the criticism. But the dynamics were like that. I didn't tell people I was a medical student. We rarely did, we were criticised too much for being silvertails and privileged and ridiculed socially. And I didn't tell people I was in the army. I got tired of justifying it and the arguments and the criticisms. I just kept it to myself.

Peter rose through army ranks, taking on some of the service's most challenging medical tasks, until finally he was chosen to command the mission to Rwanda. Rwanda is one of the smallest countries in Central Africa, with just seven million people and two main ethnic groups, the Hutu and the Tutsi. The Rwandan Genocide saw the slaughter of approximately one million Tutsis and moderate Hutus, mostly carried out by extremist Hutu militia during a period of one hundred days in 1994. The United Nations (UN) had a peacekeeping operation in Rwanda at the time but the UN peacekeepers on the ground were forbidden from engaging the militias or even discharging their weapons. The genocide was brought to an end only when the Tutsi-dominated expatriate rebel movement known as the Rwandese Patriotic Front (RPF, sometimes referred to as the Rwandan Patriotic Front) overthrew the Hutu government and seized power.

The United Nations had been involved in Rwanda before the genocide of 1994 ... they'd had a small presence there, and they could see a genocide was going to occur, but there was resistance from the UN to reinforce the UN group there, and I think . . . undoubtedly there was American ambivalence, they were stunned at what had happened to them in Somalia and they were loathe to get involved in another African adventure . . . So, there were about two hundred and fifty United Nations' people there when the genocide occurred in April 1994, when up to about a million people were killed, and about half-a-million to a million went over the border into refugee camps, or stayed in Rwanda, or stayed within Rwanda in internally displaced people camps. So after the genocide . . . it seems a bit late, doesn't it? But afterwards, the former Rwandan Patriotic Front (RPF), who had been refugees in Uganda, swept from the north down through Rwanda and captured the country and took it over. And, of course, the place had just been wrecked, it was absolutely destroyed. There was no power, there was no food supply, there was no police, no transport, no fuel. It was just wrecked. So the United Nations decided to assist Rwanda in rebuilding and to establish a peace presence in which the country would have a chance to rebuild. So that was the central thrust of the United Nations Assistance Mission in Rwanda, (UNAMIR). And our role in it, in total it was about three-and-a-half thousand soldiers, mostly African infantry battalions, but our role in that was to provide the level two and level three, the evacuation and hospital support to the UN force. And, from within spare capacity, to provide humanitarian relief to the Rwandan people.

. . . There had been a contingent of about three hundred Australians there for about four months. I'd been told I would be commanding the second contingent, so I went for a reconnaissance in late 1994, October or November. Flew in, there was a C130, an air force flight . . . we landed at Kigali, I was met by Wayne Ramsey, who was my predecessor in Rwanda, stayed with him for three or four days, visited the UN headquarters, visited the Australian hospital in Kigali, visited one of the refugee camps and had a good look around there. It was interesting. The place was wrecked, and I had never really seen anything like that before, and there was still a lot of violence. In fact, we stopped at a town called Butare and I checked with the guard about taking a photo of a destroyed building and he agreed.

I took the photo, but his mate didn't like it and tried to take the camera, and there was a bit of trouble and they shot up our car. It was a bit of a difficult day, actually. I had no doubt about the place and what was going on there. I knew it was going to be quite a challenge to come back, but we had a couple of weeks training in Townsville in January/February 1995, then I went there for about six or seven months throughout 1995.

* * *

You never have enough resources to do everything you want to do, but when we were there we were providing at least a third of all the primary health care of the country. At least a third, initially, when the place was wrecked. We had the only diagnostic service in the country, X-ray and pathology, we had the only safe source of blood in the country, we had the best operating facilities in the country, the only physio service, we had the only health surveillance medicine capacity that was able to get out and monitor the provision of safe water, and control the tropical disease vectors and scanners and things, so we were able to do an awful lot. If we had more we could have done more, but we were able to achieve the mission of providing good quality health support to the United Nations force, and we were able to provide health support to a large part of the Rwandan population from within the spare capacity of the group as well. So the simple answer is, we had enough, but we could have done more, with more.

* * *

The situation in Rwanda was that the government and their army, the Rwandan Patriotic Army [RPA], had been refugees in Uganda until about a year before, so they had come in and now they were the legitimate army and government of the country of Rwanda. There was still a lot of the former government people and the perpetrators of the genocide were still largely inside Rwanda, and they were still fighting each other. There was lawlessness, there was no police force, there was a lot of random killing, a lot of hijacking of vehicles, a lot of assault. The jails were chock-a-block with supposed criminals.

There was a lot of violence in the refugee camps and it was difficult. On top of that, the UN was there trying to provide a security presence, and then there were about three thousand non-government organisations that were helping people, largely in the internally displaced people's camps. And the problem here was there was tension between all the different players. The government didn't want the UN there, because they couldn't assert their authority and reassure the population that they were in charge of the country, because if that were the case, why would you need the UN? The UN military was there with a view that the RPA [Rwandan Patriotic Army], the army of the legitimate government was the enemy, the United Nations civilians that were there didn't give a damn about anything except for their income because they were on UN tax-free dollars, and they certainly weren't interested in the United Nations Force at all. They were only interested in themselves. The non-government organisations were looking after the people in the internally displaced people's camps, who the government regarded as the perpetrators of the genocide. So nobody trusted each other and everybody else was a bad guy. It's a fundamental paradox of humanitarian operations that this is what happens. That the non-government organisations end up propping up people that the rest of the population hates and would like to kill. So the non-government organisations and the UN are hated by the legitimate government of the country, it's complicated. So there was this seething tension all the time. Most of the government of Rwanda, half of their people had been killed in the genocide. The same with the Rwandan Patriotic Army, so they hated all the people in the refugee camps, they thought they were criminals and they deserved the most severe punishments. They said they weren't bloodthirsty, they only wanted to execute six or eight hundred criminals that had perpetrated the genocide. That was their view—that wasn't many people. That wasn't my view. They were trying to create an atmosphere of reconciliation, but in doing it the RPA was virtually lawless. I mean, they were killing all over the place.

* * *

... The African view about European involvement was that there was no oil in Rwanda. That there was no interest for Americans and Europeans being involved in Rwanda. There were no riches to be gained from it. I'm not saying that was the case, but that was the Rwandan view. The other view of Africa was, at this stage, all the fighting and the huge UN force build-up in Yugoslavia had occurred, so the Africans had a strongly racist view that the Americans and the Europeans were only interested in white man's wars, and didn't care about blacks killing each other, and they used to state that frequently, the Africans. I don't think that's true either, but that was their perception. The next thing was when the images, the stark images of the genocide actually came to air. I think there was disbelief. It is just hard to understand when you're sitting in your lounge room that tens of thousands of people are being killed everyday, by people who know each other. I think they were just stunned, I mean, 'What can you do about this?' I think there was a reluctance by UN member states to, one, believe it; two, they had already talked themselves out of any effective intervention for what they considered to be effective reasons; and, three, now it was getting worse. 'What can we do about it? Um, um, um.' So sadly I think, once again, we saw this genocide on a huge scale, like Cambodia, or Europe in World War II and nobody does anything. And that was certainly the view of the Rwandan government afterwards. You can imagine their view, the United Nations stood by while all this killing occurred. And then the UN goes in to build-up the force and support the NGOs [Non-government Organisations] largely looking after the people that the Rwandan government had thought committed the genocide. A lot of tension. A lot of tension. And so it was in that sort of seething background that the seeds for the Kibeho massacre were sown.

* * *

There were a lot of displaced people's camps, all around Rwanda, that were being supported by UNICEF [United Nations Children's Fund], Oxfam [British relief agency] and other non-government organisations, and it had been going on and on for ages, and the government was furious that these camps were still in existence, they wanted to get the people home, and try to get normality back to the country. The trouble is when the people left the camps and went home, there were property disputes. There were disputes because of the people who had lived in the houses in the villages immediately before the genocide, and then these refugees from Uganda had come back in. They had been in Uganda for a generation, for twenty years. So they came back in and said, 'My family used to live there twenty years ago, that is my house.' So there was killing and dispute and there was no legal system to resolve it. There was talk about getting ID cards, but that didn't help, because of the original split of the nation's population into Hutus and Tutsis had been done by taking photographs of people. And a lot of people thought that those photographs had caused the unequal division and the selection of people for extermination later. So it was really hard to get the people out of those camps where they were being fed and watered better than the basic population.

* * *

The Rwandan government and the Rwandan Patriotic Army were sick and tired of the internally displaced people's camps, where they thought the perpetrators of the genocide and perhaps former government forces were hiding. They were forcibly closing the camps ... the camps largely coalesced, the smaller displaced ones coalesced into bigger camps. So where there were originally camps of a thousand people here, or five thousand there, they gradually coalesced into bigger ones, and when the smaller ones were forcibly closed by the RPA, some people went back to their original homes, but others went to the larger camps, so Kibeho camp was getting bigger. When I first went there, there were thirty thousand people there, in about October 1994. By April 1995, when the massacre occurred, there were a hundred and twenty thousand there. It was getting bigger as time went on, and that was infuriating the RPA further and further and further. It was straining the government politically, it was an embarrassment. They were trying to put forward the view that they were an effective government of the country, that they were rebuilding the country, that they were in charge of law and order, that they were restoring power and water and training police and all the rest of it. It's a bit hard to say that you are in charge of your own country when it is full of internally displaced people's camps. And there was a lot of hatred of these people there . . . they were seen as the enemy. So they were very upset that these people were being fed by the non-government organisations and ostensibly being fed by the United Nations. Although the UN wasn't really protecting them, they were just trying to provide a security presence in the country, in the absence of any police force or any other body that could effectively establish security.

. . . Kibeho had been going on for so long, it had become an entrenched little community. They were running a market in there, there were some people baking bread, there were traders, there were woodcarvers selling things, it had developed a micro economy of its own. And in that there were crooks, there were stand-over merchants, there were people controlling the marketplace. It had its own hierarchy of authority in there that involved former government officials, former soldiers, people who had been involved in the genocide. So it was not the sort of picture that you would expect to see, of people sitting on the ground starving. No. Not at all. People had been in Kibeho for over a year . . . They had, they call them 'blidis'. Little huts, largely provided by UNICEF [United Nations Children's Fund]. Almost like little igloos, but with blue UN plastic sheeting over the top to provide protection from the rain. And little fires, cooking fires here and there. There were cooking pots and food distribution centres and a lot of reticulated water, huge water storage tanks and distribution systems. Our environmental health people were looking after the quality of the water of the place . . . These people, I mean the people were putting on weight! They were looking healthier than the people who were living in the villages of Rwanda.

* * *

We knew that there was going to be a lot of people killed at Kibeho, the United Nations knew that. And we were working very hard with the RPA and the NGOs to try and get the people out of Kibeho. Unfortunately, different people have got different goals. The NGOs, their role was to give the people food and water, that was keeping them in the internally displaced people's camp. They were living relatively comfortably there, because of NGO effort, and that was great. But that effort was infuriating the government. The government was becoming more foolhardy, trying to close the camps. It was grossly impatient that these camps were there and it was being shown on the international news that the camp was there.

. . . There were attempts to move it out and we were organising transport to move the people out, to encourage them to leave. We were going to provide things like trucks with food on them, and say, 'Get in the truck and have something to eat.' But the Rwandan Patriotic Army wanted to move it along faster. In April 1995, they put two battalions, about six hundred soldiers around Kibeho . . . we thought that there was going to be trouble, because there just didn't seem to be a way to get the people out. And with that sort of simmering hatred, and that situation, there were a lot of armed soldiers dealing with people who they thought had killed their families and former soldiers, at the very least there was going to be an accident, there was going to be a flare up. At the very worst there was going to be a total camp extermination. I don't think any of us thought that was going to occur. I don't think any of us thought that there would be a massacre as large as there was. But we knew that there was going to be trouble, that there was going to be killing, and we were trying to get UN transport together and NGO transport together, to get the people out of there after the RPA had moved in. But the NGOs wouldn't help us, because they had been directed by their headquarters' largely in Europe, not to get involved in a forcible camp closure. So the very time that we needed the NGO resources, like the trucks and vehicles that they had, to get the people out, they wouldn't allow them to be used. It seems ludicrous in retrospect, that the very time that the NGO resources could have been put to good use, they refused to do it. And that was because of the politics ... Many of the NGOs see their roles as being totally apolitical, and taking neither side, which is sensible and right, so when a forcible camp closure occurs, that is seen as a political act and they mustn't be involved.

... But they knew it all right. I'd been to Kibeho, just before the massacre with the deputy force commander and the colonel of operations, and there were a lot of dead people around and we could see what was happening, and we went and got some of the NGO leadership and we flew them to Kibeho in our helicopters to show them what was going on. They were saying, 'We're not allowed to intervene in a forced closure.' I said, 'Well, you're going to be involved in a massacre.' And then they spoke to their headquarters and nearly all of them did assist, then, at that time to get the people out, but we had lost about thirty-six hours and then the massacre occurred about thirty-six hours after that.

* * *

The RPA started firing in the air. And they got a bit carried away and they fired into the crowd a bit, and there were some people killed, and there was a stampede and about ten people were killed. I visited then and I remember the ten bodies were laying out there, and I said to the Rwandan battalion commander to bury the bodies because they posed a disease threat ... I didn't think they really did, but it was ... everybody was so agitated. So this went on over two or three days, this sporadic shooting and firing at night, and there would have been some firing from the crowd at the soldiers as well. And machete attacks, and the next day there was a stampede and about another fifty people were killed, and there was more firing, and then they just went berserk and opened up and fired into the crowd for about an hour, with rifles and machine guns and rocket-propelled grenades. And it had been difficult. There had been no food, no water for a few days, people hadn't been sleeping, there was a rainstorm, people panicked, the Rwandan soldiers saw it as a breakout attempt. So they fired into the crowd and they killed another couple of hundred people. And it went on like that, all afternoon, backwards and forwards.

* * *

The Kibeho area was built along a ridge line, and this hundred and twenty thousand people was largely congregated along the ridge line, which was about twice the size of an AFL [Australian Football League] football ground. It was about three to five hundred metres long and about a hundred and fifty metres wide. And the Zambian company was in the buildings in the centre of the area there, and the Australian Medical Support Group of about thirty-three people was there as well. So the killing occurred around them, when people were trying to break out of the area, the RPA had surrounded the area and were firing on them then . . . I mean they were right next to each other. They were right in the middle of it. There was a lot of shooting. It was fortunate that none of our people were injured. There were bullets everywhere. There was plenty of lead in the air, but nobody was injured, fortunately. They were in the buildings and they were wearing protective equipment, and a lot of them were in bunkers. The medical personnel were treating people while all of this was going on. But when the shooting got so heavy, they went into the bunkers. They were all wearing Kevlar jackets and Kevlar helmets to protect them as well. And the killing was occurring in waves. Initially it was for an hour, and later it was for twenty minutes and then it was a ten-minute episode, and then it was sporadic shooting all through the night. Our people withdrew during the night and then came back to provide health support the next morning.

* * *

They wouldn't let any UN people in to control it. There were some UN people there at the time, there was a Zambian company of soldiers, and we had about thirty people providing medical support to the Zambians and also the Rwandan group. The shooting and firing went on all day . . . it was just repeated and random shooting. Some of it was directly targeted. Some people were arrested by the RPA and marched off as though they were going to be incarcerated, but they were taken around the side of the hill and shot. There were an awful lot of children killed, which was very, very upsetting to our soldiers. And the women in the camp were heard saying to the children, When the shooting starts, run to the white men. And the kids did, and they hid in the wheel arches of the United Nation's vehicles, and a number of them survived that way. But I've got photos of the Zambian soldiers carrying dead children out of the place, and that was very upsetting for a lot of people. Particularly those of us who had children ourselves. Yeah, it was difficult.

... There was plenty of lead in the air to make it seem like it wasn't peacekeeping to me. But there is a hierarchy of the way people look at things. Like the World War II veterans thought Korea was a joke, Korea thought Vietnam was a joke. The Vietnam veterans think peacekeeping isn't real military operations. And that might be right, but I tell you what, when you're actually there it can be pretty startling stuff. And it doesn't matter how an operation has been categorised in New York or Canberra, killing is killing.

At one stage, a Rwandan platoon, about thirty soldiers, came out of a church mission on a hill, and they marched down the hill singing, and everybody used to like their singing, and they used to go running around the streets in Kigali singing, but we didn't know that they were singing, 'We kill the Hutu, who will we kill next?' And this platoon marched down the hill and stopped at an Australian bunker and they turned towards it and cocked their weapons and there were about ten Australian soldiers in it, and the young section commander, a nineteen-year-old Australian, he ordered his section to fix bayonets. In fact, they didn't fire at the Australians, they started firing into the crowd. But it was interesting, I was lecturing at a Law Of Armed Conflict meeting some years later, and a lawyer said that the legal procession can't wait for the first poor bastard that gets his soldiers to fire when they shouldn't. And I explained this incident to them. I said, 'This nineteen-year-old man had thirty soldiers in front of him, cocking their weapons and pointing them at him. He had the presence and the control and the intelligence to get his soldiers to fix bayonets, that is to make an aggressive action, but not to cock their weapons.' I'm not sure that fixing the bayonets stopped them firing, but he maintained the discipline and cohesion of his group by putting the bayonets on and they felt that they were doing something threatening and they deterred from going further. Now in that half a second that he had to make that decision, he could have easily told them to load their weapons, and if one rifle had gone off accidentally, as they do, those ten guys would have been dead in fifteen seconds. So I pointed this out to this lawyer who was looking for some poor bastard who had fired at the wrong time, and he had the grace to apologise actually, and felt that he had been misquoted and it wasn't that sort of incident that he had been referring to.

It is an awful lot of responsibility to put on the shoulders of a young man, in a situation like that. And he acted brilliantly. And it is at a time exactly like that, that the military training and their experience and skills and their knowledge and their working together, allows a person like that to make the right decision at the right time, the critical decision . . . He knew what the extent of his authority was, what the orders for opening fire were and what the risks were and he made the right decision. I'm sure there were a number of circumstances like that. Where a person was in an isolated situation, he's in that position of command, or she, because of their training, their intelligence and their ability to motivate and lead others and they have to assess the situation rapidly and make a decision. And it comes back to our training. The military training of our commanders, our junior commanders in particular, is outstanding. Their selection and their training is outstanding. And it is for that very reason, so that those people do the right thing during an extraordinarily difficult time.

* * *

. . . The United Nations peacekeeping mandate expressly prohibited intervening in these sort of activities. Our force commander at the time was directly ordered by New York [UN Headquarters] not to get involved if there was a forcible camp closure. He was directly and clearly ordered not to be involved. And there were even questions why there were Zambians and Australians there at the time that it occurred.

Well, in fact, the Zambian company was there to provide security within the camp, because the people inside the camp were fighting with each other, and we were there to supply health support because the place was falling apart. There was a lot of illness and there were a lot of people dying regularly, because of the conditions in the camp. But we were expressly forbidden to be involved. And a lot of people would say, 'Well, there was an infantry company of Zambians, why didn't they do anything about it?' Well, there were two infantry battalions of RPA. There were a hundred Zambians, and six hundred RPA. If they intervened, I think the RPA would have killed them all. And they had a track record for doing that. Don't forget that just before the genocide started, the former government captured twelve Belgian soldiers and they were ordered by New York to hand over their weapons. And the head of peacekeeping in New York at the time was a man called Kofi Annan. And he gave the order for the Belgians to hand over their weapons and all twelve of them were killed within a minute. So there was no doubt about what these people would do to UN Forces if they retaliated. Quite simply, they were outgunned.

. . . Our people had been well briefed on the rules of engagement, and the legal authority for the force, and the legal authority for them to open fire or not. And they knew they could be prosecuted if they fired, if people were killed or injured as a result of a breach of those orders for opening fire. They had no doubts about the limit of their authority and the limits of the action that they could take and I had no doubt about the limits that I had as a commander. It didn't mean we liked it, but we had no doubts about what our orders were and what we could do and what we couldn't do. And I had no doubt about what the risks were either. These were dangerous and unpredictable people, that were quite used to killing and did it without blinking, without a moment's hesitation, and often enjoying it. I saw a soldier kill a woman and he smiled. He was smiling because he demonstrated his power to just kill somebody else, and that was all that was in it. Like Bill Clinton, he did it because he could. Same thing, the ultimate abuse of authority, doing something because you can.

* * *

At the end of it, there was a dispute about how many people had been killed, but we counted, one of my warrant officers counted, physically, with a counter, over four thousand bodies. And we evacuated three hundred people that day to a hospital nearby. About a third with gunshot wounds, a third with machete wounds, a third with gunshot and machete wounds. And as you can imagine, there was a fair bit of emotion around at the time, because as soon as the killing started the NGOs left, all the United Nations civilian groups left there, largely because they had been told by their bosses in Geneva not to get involved in a forcible camp closure. So at the very time the people actually needed the external support, everyone was leaving, other than the military. So that was difficult. And there was a lot of accusation and counter accusation and blaming later.

* * *

. . . The bodies were cleared up very quickly. In a day and a half nearly all the bodies were gone. A lot were buried in the sewers around there, or were very quickly buried. A lot were transported out and burned in a nearby town. Those who were still alive, many dispersed the camp very rapidly. And a lot concentrated in an area in the centre of Kibeho camp, where the old Catholic mission station had been, and there were about five hundred there for another week or so, surrounded by the RPA. We went down there trying to get the people out on several occasions, and we did get some people out. And it was a disgusting scene because there were five hundred people in there and it was a cross between a garbage dump and a mortuary and sewer, because there was nothing, there was just all these people living in an area half as big as a football field. And they still had some weapons in there, and they were firing occasionally, and the RPA were still killing them. And it was getting international attention. There had been this massacre. There was a lot more international press there, and we took them down in the helicopters to film all this, because the RPA were going to violently terminate the incident, they were going to blow the place to bits. They were setting up anti-armour weapons and they were just going to smash down the buildings and slaughter the whole crowd. There was talk about an armed intervention, about attacking the RPA with infantry forces, and it was planned about how it could be done, but it was realised that the RPA would have reinforced it and that the UN would have all been killed. There would have been retaliation against all the UN throughout the country, and therefore a total disruption of any sort of security force being present. So, in fact, what we did was we took about thirty members of the media with all their TV cameras down there and filmed the whole thing. And the RPA couldn't afford to smash the place to bits under those circumstances, so then they organised some transport and got the people out and took the credit for a peaceful settlement of the whole issue. So they weren't primitive people, they knew how to play their PR [public relations] game quite effectively. But at least the final sad chapter was resolved peacefully. I thought they were all going to be killed. It was going on too long, there was too much violence, too much hatred. Too much room for a mistake. People were tired, accidental discharge of a weapon, somebody doing the wrong thing, just complete mayhem. But it didn't end that way, I was wrong on that count, fortunately.

* * *

The RPA tried to say that there had only been a couple of hundred killed, but in fact they had buried a lot of the bodies and they organised some contract transport to cart all the bodies out to a nearby town where they were cremated by another contractor. Which puts another light on contract services to the military, doesn't it? The Rwandan government, they downplayed it, they disputed . . . it became very silly, it became a concentration on body counts. How many people were killed, how many were not. And that became an argument. The Rwandans very effectively diverted the argument from whether this was a legal or illegal activity, to whether three hundred or three thousand people had been killed. And of course whereas that is sad, that wasn't the point. The point was whether it was legal or illegal. And if it were illegal, what action would be taken. The United Nations point of view was, of course, the same thing. 'Here we go again, there's been this massive disaster, we couldn't prevent it and we couldn't stop it.' So they wanted the discussion about the matter over as soon as possible. But there was an external commission that came and reviewed everything, and found everybody accountable and nobody responsible. There were no charges ... I think the RPA battalion commander was probably relieved of command, but there was no investigation into it, in the sense that we would understand it. No proper legal process.

The camp sort of closed about a week later. And I remember speaking to the Minister of Health, he had been a doctor in Uganda, and the principal medical officer during the civil war, then became the Minister of Health ... I said, 'This business in Kibeho was pretty grim.' He said, 'Oh look, beforehand so many people were dying of starvation and disease, there was about twenty dying a day, so we had to do something about it.' So he sort of saw this intervention as a public health measure, which was putting an interesting spin on it. And the Rwandan government never really understood what the to-do was about. To them it was a drop in the bucket ... A lot of their foreign aid was suspended immediately, which hurt them like hell, and that was largely due to the presence of the free international press that reported it, and a lot of very brave journalists who filmed this stuff and wrote it down and got the information out. And that hit them hard. That hit them in the order of hundreds of millions of dollars of US aid. And there was no more of that heavy-handed tactic again. So that was the message that I had for our troops. In fact, I tried to change the focus and put it within the context of the overall horror of the country, and, in fact, that their presence had done a lot of good, rather than the awful results that they had seen.

... Our soldiers were horrified and I guess devastated, and we all felt guilty, that it should have been preventable, that we should have been able to do something about it. They were pretty angry. And I was trying to calm them down because I was afraid that people would start taking the law into their own hands, as it were, and might try to beat up a couple of Rwandan soldiers, which would have created ... we would have had a lot of trouble. We had had confrontation with them, with soldiers cocking rifles and things before. These people had done an awful lot of killing, and a few more wasn't going to bother them at all. And I didn't think it was worth spilling any Australian blood having a dispute with these guys. I tried to stress to them, that I thought their very presence at Kibeho had actually diverted a disaster. As bad as it was, I think it was well within the capacity of the RPA to kill the whole hundred and twenty thousand people that were there. Now that might sound a bit like an exaggeration, but don't forget it was only a year ago that they had been involved with killing more than a million of each other, and they thought that these people were the ones that had killed and murdered and raped their relatives and mothers and children, and they were going to give them a fair whack. And if the UN hadn't been there, I think they would have exterminated the whole camp. And certainly they weren't able to do that. They didn't try any more forcible camp closures like that in the future.

* * *

The reactions were varied. Some were stunned, and they were working almost like automatons, they were just going about their day-to-day work without thinking very much. They were exhausted. They were emotionally drained. Some were very angry. You know, shouting, furious about what they had seen, and threatening to take action against the RPA . . . Some were shouting, 'This is terrible,' . . . there was still RPA around then, they were shouting at them that they were child-killers . . . I was concerned. There was a lot of tension and I was afraid that there could be significant conflict between the RPA and the Australian soldiers that were there . . . It was an extremely explosive situation. And emotionally charged, and people were tired and upset and angry, and you get a mixture of adrenaline and testosterone and fear and firearms, you have potentially got trouble on your hands. It takes a lot of control, a lot of control. People talk about control and command in the military a lot, and everybody knows what command is, 'I'm the boss, you do this,' but not too many know what control is, you know that effort laterally to have people working together and to be holding the line, and that is not easy, but it is critical.

... Some were emotionally blunt, empty, tearful and non-communicative. Most were pretty worn out, and upset by what they had seen, but still functioning pretty well. I, in fact, relieved them all and replaced them with others, that is standard military procedure after people have been through a particularly demanding or gruelling incident, and they're tired and worn out, you would normally relieve them and get another group in to continue the work, that was normal. And some of them were a bit upset about that, they thought that they had done a good job and they thought that they were being taken away because they hadn't done a good job. I had to explain to them that it was normal standard operating procedure to do that. They had worked very hard for a few days, they were exhausted, it had been tough stuff and it was time for them to have a break, for other people to shoulder-up and do the work. It shows their spirit tremendously well, doesn't it? That they wanted to carry out the work and perhaps misunderstood the intention initially, but were quite happy once it was explained to them afterwards.

* * *

I felt the same as everybody else. Horror, disgust, revulsion, lack of understanding, disbelief. But once again, within the context, it was consistent with the very sad, long history of that part of the world, and the way that they treated each other. And in my, I suppose, relatively long life now, we've seen a lot of pockets of mass murder and genocide around the world. Whereas we don't like it, and we have trouble understanding, we know that it does occur. We wonder about the reasons, as a preventive medicine physician, I like to think how we can stop this sort of thing in the future, and I'm sure so do all like-minded people. But these are extraordinarily complicated issues. Generations old. Hate, prejudice, get even, payback, resources, wealth, power, authority, blame, superstition. Very, very complicated.

* * *

... After a disaster, and not just a massacre ... people are initially stunned. They can't contemplate what has occurred. They can't analyse that information in an effective, logical and useful manner. They are overwhelmed ... The first thing was people ... would normally get their 'buddy aid' to look after each other for the first twenty-four hours after a stressful incident. And to try to digest it a bit. At twenty-four hours afterwards, the commanders, the padres, the doctors and psychologists were offering individual and group counselling. I personally spoke to all the people involved, in groups, tried to set up that contextual framework once again, of not trying to focus on the body count, but on the overall horror of Rwanda and the fact that their presence there had saved a lot more people from being killed. I tried to give them a more acceptable framework upon which to organise their memories and understand the event. But the counselling was made available to everybody then. They weren't forced to undertake it ... as groups, we did it. We made everybody attend in groups. It was offered to people as individuals, many of them attended as individuals.

... There were a number of us who really had nowhere to go. The chief padre had nowhere really to go and I really didn't have anybody to go to and ... although we discussed it and things. I'm not suffering post-traumatic stress disorder, but I will never forget the events at all either. And sometimes, even in an interview like this, I think, 'Well, why won't these people let me forget about it? Rather than have to?' Because as you can imagine coming back from that peacekeeping mission, I was virtually on the lecture circuit for two years, describing these events to people, and quite commonly it becomes upsetting, recounting those events but it's important to share those experiences with people. To assist those who went through it at the time, to inform others who don't understand it and hopefully shape thinking so that steps can be taken to prevent those sort of awful incidents again in the future.

... Before we went home there was group debriefing and opportunities for individual counselling again. There were follow-up letters on return to Australia, at the six, twelve-month mark. There have been highly publicised Defence initiatives, and Veterans' Affairs initiatives of providing counselling service and opportunities for people to seek help. Those that were still in the military, either within the military or confidential support arrangements outside of the military if they feel that it is going to jeopardise their career. So overall I think a good responsive, supportive framework was put into place, in the short and medium and long term.

The problem, of course, is that after something like that, a lot of people leave the military, either because they feel that that was the only likely deployment that they were going to have, or they didn't like it and they wanted to get out, or it was time to move on anyway. More people get positive outcomes, I think, from serving on peacekeeping missions than negative outcomes, but they start leaving quickly. And it is very hard to trace them afterwards, to keep in contact with them. That has been one of the problems, tracing people and trying to extend that support to them effectively. But Defence and DVA [Department of Veterans' Affairs], to their credit, have tried to do that.

The ones that left first of all might have been the ones that had the biggest problems. So that is a worry, yeah. Certainly some of those suffering... Unfortunately, a lot of our people who were involved there, and it wasn't just for the massacre, we had a hundred people working around Kibeho over two or three months and they saw a lot of death and a lot of sadness in that time. Unfortunately, a lot of them have had trouble coming to grips with it. I know we've had a lot of people suffering post-traumatic stress disorder. A lot of them have left the military.

I believe about seventy or eighty of the six or seven hundred people who served there in a year are receiving Department of Veterans' Affairs pensions for stress-related problems now. That's a fair bit, that is ten per cent. It is nearly ten years, but it is still increasing. The US Army experience in Vietnam of PTSD [post-traumatic stress disorder] was ten to twenty per cent maybe twenty years later, so it is getting up there. There is a price to pay for all of this, these peacekeeping operations... I know that some of those who were involved in the massacre and were having difficulties in the immediate aftermath have gone on to suffer quite badly, and they're on full permanently incapacitated pensions now, unable to work again.

* * *

Command is a very personal thing. Everybody brings different experiences, different outlook, different training, different views and judgements to it. The environment is constantly changing, it's dangerous, it is unpredictable, there are political considerations, there are UN considerations, there are force considerations, there is direction from Australia about what is going on and what shouldn't be going on, it's not easy, it is a lot of work. If you look at the outcomes, the hard outcomes, good health support was provided to the force, a lot of people were treated effectively, efficiently. The UN Force health was largely good. There were deaths, there were deaths through AIDS, through motor vehicle accidents and through gunshot wounds. There were no Australian lives lost, that is a pretty significant and good outcome. We got everybody back and all the equipment back. We left with a good reputation in Rwanda, and in the United Nations. Good outcomes. Our work was appreciated by the Australian population. We received the RSL Anzac Peace Prize. A number of members of both contingents received honours and awards, recognising the service of their contingents. I think our work was respected by the Australian people.

. . . I think the Australian contribution to UN operations over the years has been tremendous. We haven't been involved with all of them, but many, many of them, including Korea and Yugoslavia and Somalia and other places, and generally our troops have provided technical expertise. There are a couple of hundred nations that can provide infantry battalions, but there are not that many nations that can provide communications networks, deployable field hospitals, things like that, technical capabilities, the airlift capability, avionics, that sort of thing. So normally we've made those sort of contributions and they've been effective contributions to UN Forces. They've generally been effective in doing their job, in accomplishing the Australian mission and certainly assisting the United Nations in accomplishing their missions. The success of the communications outfit in Cambodia is a great example as well, I think. So Australia can be largely proud, our military and our general population and our government can be proud of the Australian contribution that has been made over the years, and undoubtedly will be made in the future.

* * *

Fortunately Australia and Australians are in a privileged position, to be able to have the opportunity to assist others to get onto their feet, improve their life and their societies. And it is a privilege to be able to have that ability and capacity to be able to do that. That is the first thing. And I would hate to think that we as a country would ever turn our back on that sort of approach to helping other nations. I would hope that we would never develop a, 'I've got it, you try and get it attitude,' like some other countries. The second thing is to be assisting other countries is to do it in a cooperative manner, not in a unilateral manner. You need to engage with the people, seek their goals, work with them, to get the outcomes, the shared goals and the shared outcomes. You can't impose value systems or culture or outcomes or goals which fit in with our society. We need to work together to establish goals that they want, that are achievable and particularly important, that are sustainable. There is no use intervening or assisting with something that is going to fall over when you go away. The goal has got to be helping these people to take control of their destiny and their future, and get on top of where they are going, rather than treating them as a parent treats a small child.

On a day-to-day basis, it is a matter of fostering and helping them to develop, to get on and be able to do it themselves. It sounds easy, but it needs sensitivity, cultural sensitivity and patience, and respect. It is not just money and influence and power and authority, it needs sensitive and genuine mutual respect and cooperation, understanding, discussion, negotiation, the diplomatic arts. Even for military forces that are doing this, they require a large degree of diplomatic skill rather than just the force of arms.

The next thing that I think is important, is that the approach must be reasonable. It must be achievable and realistic. It is not a matter of going into a country and trying to create a mini-Australia there. It is, what is this country capable of creating and sustaining? That is what needs to be done. Realistic goals need to be developed early, rather than simply replicating in another country what seems to work well here.

... The other thing about it is that the benefits to our country can be varied and many, and it is not just financial, or political or having greater influence, it can be the intangible benefits of enriching our society by what it is doing, for enlightening our society to be helpful, by educating the next generation of Australians that we behave in a decent way, and that we believe in the force of law and decency and honesty and courage to do the right thing. These sorts of values can only be instilled by repeatedly demonstrating it to people... And perhaps in the very long run, with that sort of approach, eventually that is going to be the solution to the War on Terror, something like that. A cooperative, holistic, genuine, international approach that is going to iron out the inequities and trample on the prejudice and bigotry and hatred to stop this awful ongoing payback, this never ending payback...

Now that might be a little airy-fairy and perhaps a little impractical, but we're not going to win the War on Terror by bombing people who live in holes in the ground, or exploiting them for their oil reserves. That is not going to work, because the fundamental roots of terrorism are based on the way that people think and the way that they learn and the way that they live. It's not just a group of fanatics who want to kill people... It's easy to say, 'What are we doing in Africa? It's got nothing to do with us.' But if we are serious about being a player in the world, in the big world, why not Africa? It just doesn't have to be Papua New Guinea or the Solomons, in our backyard and our region. Why not anywhere? If we're a serious world player, we're going to have to put up our hand and play anywhere in the world that there is problems where we can assist.

ARTHUR 'NAT' GOULD

Fighter Pilot
United Kingdom
Russia
Milne Bay
Royal Navy Fleet Air Arm
World War II

I was about fourteen or fifteen and I used to go to Archerfield Aerodrome. I'd ride my bicycle out there and peer over the fence and watch them all ... they had Gypsy Moths. I remember there was a wonderful aeroplane there ... it was a rotary engine plane. The cylinders all went round, the whole engine went round, the propeller was fastened onto the cylinders, a most astonishing thing ... Mum and Dad were immigrants. Dad worked for Queensland Railways. It was in the Depression years when I was growing up. There were five children. I had two elder sisters and two younger brothers. We weren't poor, we weren't desperate, but there was no way they could pay money for me to learn to fly.

One of the things I did to get a few dollars before I started work while I was still at school, I used to go round the paddocks in Ashford where we lived, collecting cow manure, which I used to sell to the local gardeners, one and six a bag. Also I'd get up early and go and get mushrooms which we'd sell to the local pubs. I can't remember how much we got for those. When I got 10 shillings or 15 shillings, on my bike out to the airport and got myself a half hour of flying.

In fact it was such a success that by the time I was seventeen I got a pilot's licence, just on cow manure and mushrooms.

. . . The first dual flight was absolutely great. I had no idea where I was or what I was doing, but it was absolutely what I expected of it. I remember taking off on my first flight in the back seat of this Gypsy Moth. The pilot took off and he did a bank to the left and I looked down and there was a little cemetery there, which I thought rather interesting. I remember that quite vividly. All these people had been killed flying aeroplanes. Apart from that I don't remember much about it. Just the sheer joy, everything I expected.

* * *

I suppose I was in the CMF [Citizen Military Force] as they call it, from whatever age I was allowed in, seventeen to nineteen, until the war broke out in December '39. Now, I must admit I was one of the few people who was absolutely overjoyed, because I knew I was going to get some adventure and I could see myself joining up. I didn't think I'd get into the air force straightaway, but I said, 'Hey, this is where I'm gonna get some fun.' I was living in Brisbane and there was very little chance of travelling. I was certainly aware of geography around the world, but not so much politics. History I knew a bit about. This was going to be that opportunity and I had to be very careful. Everybody else was terrified of the fact we were at war and thought we were going to get killed. I was quite happy . . . Mother of course knew that I was going to go and probably that my brothers would go. Like all mothers she was, I wouldn't say terrified, but she was concerned about it all. I suppose reading the media in those days . . . Hitler was marching across Europe and knocking over Czechoslovakia and Poland and Holland on the way and was at the door of Paris. It was quite terrifying. It really was. But not to me. My hope was they wouldn't finish the war until I got there . . . I can almost remember Menzies' words. 'It's my melancholy duty . . .' I think was the words. 'To inform you that we are at war.' Yes. I do. I was out on the veranda at our place at Ashgrove and I was chuckling to myself. I really had quite a laugh. I had to pull a long face when I talked to Mum about it, but I was happy.

... Can I say quite clearly and categorically, in those days the cause was just. We had none of these hesitations that people have now, you read about the Iraqi War and so on, the nation's fairly divided on that. All of us were quite convinced that this was a battle for our future. I don't suppose we could have put it into words like I am now, but we were right. Hitler was a threat and our way of life was under threat. Particularly when the Japanese came in. There was absolutely no doubt.

* * *

We reported out to Archerfield and . . . there were cadets going through who were going to be cadet officers and they were going to be commissioned. We went in; they didn't know what we were. We had no rank, we had no uniform. We were given long blue overalls and a beret. They called us 'Mister' and we ate in the cadets' mess. The troops used to salute us, but we had no rank at all. We didn't know what we were. It was a pretty tough life. We didn't have beds or anything. We had palliasses on the floor. We had to get up at five o'clock and go and have cold showers and the cadets were making sure we had them. Then we'd go flying and do ground school. The flying was great. I took to it, I loved it. We did it in Tiger Moths. I had a civil aero class instructor. He wasn't very good frankly, as I learnt many years later when I was instructing myself. God knows how I ever learnt to fly with that bloke. However, I passed and I came out round about mid-1940.

... We had a strict thing that we were taught, straight and level, and you were taught turns and climbing turns and descending turns. Then you went on a bit, to steep turns and aerobatics, which most of the civil instructors weren't very good at. They didn't like being upside down. I used to love it. It was the only way to go. I really took to aerobatics. Loops and rolls and spins and all that.

... We went straight onto Wirraways and the others went onto Avro Ansons. Then, remembering how brash and overconfident I was, the air force hadn't had Wirraways all that long a time. The instructors didn't know much about them either. I had an instructor, who shall remain nameless, he'd sit in the back seat and I'd sit in the front seat. So we'd go and fly. It was a piece of cake I reckoned. Mind you it's an enormous jump from the Tiger Moth to Wirraway, because you had, amongst other things, two or three times the speed, you had all sorts of other things, you had variable pitch propellers, you had a retractable undercarriage, you had flaps which you could put up and down and all sorts of other things in it. Half your time was worrying about the cockpit checks and so on. But I remember my instructor was very nervous and they used to do the take-off. I used to teach him how to do some of the flying in the Wirraway . . . I was overconfident. I think one of the reasons I left was that I wasn't at all concerned about it. We did night-flying for the first time, which was terrifying. We did basic strafing and dive-bombing. It was very basic. Then we got our wings. You were qualified. They put your wings on your left breast. I've got my original ones up there.

. . . Night-flying we did at Wagga where it was very black. Black night. The problems are you lose most of your references. It's hard to explain, when you fly normally, under what you call visual flight rules, VFR, you orient everything by the horizon, the ground and the sky, you know where they are. You know if you're that way or this way. At night, and this was a very clear horizon, it can be very deceptive, sounds silly, but you can get the stars and the ground lights mixed up. Not quite, but if you're not careful. You have very good instruments in the air force and what you've got to learn to do, as I learnt many years after as an instrument-flying instructor, God didn't make a very good job of us as far as our reactions and our orientation. For example, normally you know where you are relative to everything else, by sight. You've got verticals and horizontals and things to refer to. You've also got muscles that tell you when you move and so on . . . so when you get up in an aircraft, all sorts of movements, those things, particularly your visuals, you could lose them. So you have to trust your instruments. Sometimes it's very difficult to do. Your body's telling you to turn to the left and your instrument is saying, 'Shut up, you're straight and level.' You've got to do that. So that takes an enormous amount of discipline. You have to overcome all your normal reactions and believe it.

The other most worrying thing is coming in to land, particularly in an aeroplane like the Wirraway with a long nose and propeller in front of you. You had a flare path, ordinary kerosene flares each side of the runway. When you're doing final approach, remember to put your wheels down. One of our fellows got killed doing the wrong thing. He meant to put his wheels down and put his flaps down and finished straight into the ground. That was one of my first solos when I saw that. What you do, as you're coming in to land and you see the flare path and it changes orientation. One moment it looks flat and next it's like that. So you have to find it, and it takes a little bit of getting used to.

. . . Two Ansons collided in midair. Quite incredible. This bloke, they were on cross-country training. The Anson was a twin engine aeroplane, originally a bomber . . . It was a beautiful day, not a cloud in the sky and their paths crossed and one flew into the other and they got jammed in midair together. The bottom fellow bailed out. The fellow in the top, he landed them both stuck together. Rather rude actually. He landed this thing. Rather tragic end to that. He passed and went over to England and became a bomber pilot. He did a full tour in bombers, came back to Australia and was riding a bicycle and got hit by a car and was killed.

. . . You develop a strange attitude to deaths. It sounds a bit stupid I suppose now, in the cold light of day, but it's not you, it's him. You're all right. You become a little bit cold-blooded about it all. Somebody's got to write to his wife or his parents and tell them, but it's not you. You don't have to do it. I wonder if he's got any clean shirts, I'm running out. That sort of thing. And you do. After we were in England, one of the chaps got shot down flying Hurricanes over the Channel. In those days of clothes rationing and no laundries, we all used to run out of clothes, we didn't take any of his money or photographs or anything, but all his underclothes and socks were pinched. Keep us going. Bloke turned up about three days later and he demanded all his clothes back.

* * *

Things were going very badly in the UK. The Battle of Britain was well and truly on. I remember hearing about it all the time. So there was a bit of a desperate hurry to get people over there. I think we had ten days' leave from memory. I came back up to Brisbane. Then we sailed from Sydney on the 10th December 1940 . . . we went via South Africa, down the west coast into Freetown and halfway to Bermuda. We came right round up the north and into Scotland over the top of Ireland, round over the back into Glasgow. We took about six or seven weeks to get there.

. . . Sutton Bridge is a pretty gloomy sort of place. It's out in the fen district in England and flat country, lousy weather and it was January. It was a bad time. I hadn't flown for two and a half to three months. We got there and the Hurricane was a quantum leap from a Wirraway and my instructor had been shot down a couple of times and he was very twitchy. He took me over to a Hurricane. He gave me one typewritten sheet about all the cockpit checks and all the speeds and all the clever stuff. Gave me a quick check in a trainer called a Harvard, we did a couple of circuits and he went off. I climbed into this aeroplane and took off.

By the time I got my wheels up I was in cloud. One of the funny things about transferring from Australia to England, amongst other funny things, is their maps and the countryside. In Australia, when we learnt to navigate at a place like Wagga, you had maps that were fifteen miles to an inch for example, on scale. Got to England and it was four miles to an inch. So you had to make that enormous jump. Plus the fact that flying in a place like Wagga, if you were map reading and you saw a railway line, there was only one railway line, and there was only one road that crossed it. So you knew where you were if you found that place. In England there were railway lines and rivers and bridges and things and flying down very low in a fast aeroplane, which you're unaccustomed to anyway, you didn't know where you were. I had no idea where I was most of the time.

A couple of strange things happened. You always flew these aeroplanes, even the first time when you were only learning to fly them; you always had your guns fully loaded because you were just as likely to have anything happen. Intersect an aeroplane on attack, after you got airborne. A friend of mine, Nolly Clarke, did his first solo and he came in to land and as he landed he pulled the stick back and he was kangarooing as they called it. The gun button was just a little thing you pressed with your thumb. Every time he pressed his thumb on it, eight machine guns spraying all over the airfield. Everybody ran into cover as he did his first landing.

. . . Another time I got lost soon after. It shows you how stupid we were in those days. I took off, ran into cloud, by the time I shut everything off, wheels up, flaps, tidied everything up, I was well above the cloud, but I had no idea where I was. My radio wasn't working. We weren't used to radio. We didn't have them in the Wirraway. I didn't know what to do for a while. I saw an aircraft and I said, 'That's a Blenheim bomber. I'll formate on him and he will show me the way to some aerodrome.'

Because there were plenty of aerodromes in England. I couldn't catch him. I got up close to him. The faster I went the faster he went. So I was getting a bit low in fuel and I thought I should go. I very cleverly worked out, now that's the North Sea, there's no mountains or hills out there, if I get out over the North Sea and down through the cloud, I shouldn't run into anything. So I did exactly that. It was very clever of me. I came out over the North Sea and flew due west and found my way home and landed at Sutton Bridge. The blokes said, 'Good on you, mate.'

I said, 'What for?'

They said, 'You chased that JU88.'

What happened, while I was airborne trying to formate on this, it was a German JU88, a bomber. I didn't get close enough to see the bloke's red crosses on him. He'd just bombed the airfield. Here's brave old me on one of my first trips chasing this German.

* * *

I got posted to a famous squadron called Number 17 Squadron Royal Air Force, just had the rugged old Battle of Britain. They lost lots and lots of blokes. They shot down 170 aircraft, so they had a pretty good tally. But they'd lost fellows and they needed some new ones. So our people, two of us got sent to 17 Squadron. By the time I joined them, we took a bit of leave first, went to London to the best spots, and so on. A bit naughty. We stayed a bit longer than we should have. We finally got to the squadron. By that time it was up in Scotland. A place called Castleton. You can't go any further north. We joined them up there.

What you did in those days, when the squadron was on readiness, they usually had you on readiness for four hours, or relief for twenty-four hours. When we were on readiness you have maybe four aircraft. You go out to your aircraft when you're due to go on. You do all the cockpit checks ready for take-off. You set your rudder trims, your fuel, you put your helmet on the gun sight with connect to your radio and oxygen. Your parachute would be in the seat with the straps to one side. Then you would go back and sit outside or inside the disposal hut with Mae Wests on, flying boots and gun strapped to your shoulder all this. Maps stuck in your flying boots. You'd sit there trying to read or play cards, twitching like mad, waiting for the call. They'd phone eventually and say, 'Scramble all directions!' Scramble meant get airborne. You'd race out to your aircraft, it wasn't very far away. By that time the ground mechanic had started it for you, so the prop was going and it was warmed up. You'd leap in ready for take-off and put your parachute on, helmet and everything on, while you're pulling your wheels up. So by the time they said, 'Scramble!' you'd be airborne in three minutes and off on the intercept. You wouldn't know until you got your radio and helmet and everything on and warmed up, usually two of you at a time, maybe four. The ground control would vector you. They'd say, 'Steer 180, angle 30.' Thirty thousand feet was what that was. So off you go on this thing and they changed as the raid came in. They'd say, 'Steer 160,' or whatever. They give you bearings and distances until you'd gotten to your intercept and they'd say, 'Bogeys!'

Bogey was the word for if they weren't sure if it was a friendly or baddie. Bogey was unidentified. So, 'Bogeys at twelve o'clock above you or below, or three o'clock.' When they were positively identified they'd say, 'Bandits three o'clock!' and you'd say, 'Jesus!' That's when your tummy turned over.

... I had a pretty unpleasant thing. There's an airfield called Alden, which is just near Inverness. We were supposed to be rested, but we had a couple on night-readiness. I got scrambled and Aberdeen was being bombed. Oh God it was a black night. In a Hurricane at night the exhaust, you looked out of the cockpit and the exhaust was just streams coming past. You couldn't see through it. Just streams of orange and red coming through. You got on your instruments and you were being vectored. I'll never forget this. They started off, they vectored me to chase a JU88 that was bombing Aberdeen and he was heading out over the North Sea. So they give you all sorts of things like, 'Buster, buster!' which is, 'Faster, faster.' 'Gate' means, 'Go right through.' They gave me a gate and said, 'He's twelve o'clock, same level.' So I was just up his backside. Suddenly the whole of Aberdeen ground defence opened up on me. They had anti-aircraft guns. They were supposed to be aiming at him, but I was copping the lot. I had red and yellow and greens going all over the cockpit. Quite frightening. So I said a few rude words over the radio to tell these blokes to stop. I was the goodie and not the baddie. He got away and I didn't get a shot at him because by this time I couldn't see anything because of all this stuff going on.

* * *

We went up to Shetland. Next stop was the North Pole. You've got to remember you wanted to go, you wanted to be in the action. The big war was on in the Middle East. That's where 3 Squadron [RAAF] was and all the action was. So I applied for a posting. I said, 'I want to go to the Middle East.' ... The Russians came into the war round about this time. I'm talking towards the middle of '41 ... They were having a rough time. Stalingrad was coming up, the worst of it. So Stalin was jumping up and down and asking for help, Churchill decided to send some fighter aircraft to Russia. I didn't know that at the time. So when I applied for a posting, wanting to go to the Middle East, it was all, 'Okay, off you go.' Half the squadron was sent to somewhere in Yorkshire.

They started issuing us with big woolly leather jackets and neck-to-knee underclothes and three pairs of gloves, silks, woollens, leathers and so on. It didn't sound like the Middle East to me, but no one knew where it was, we weren't told. Then we went and caught a big transport aircraft and went up to Glasgow and joined an aircraft carrier... After we'd been aboard for a little while they told us where we were going.

The idea was to teach the Russians, we weren't supposed to necessarily go there fighting, we were supposed to teach the Russians how to fly the Hurricane. But more importantly how to maintain them, look after them, because it was a big jump from the agricultural aeroplanes they had. Rolls Royce engine and all this sort of stuff, lots of guns. So that was the whole idea. I think we had twenty-four aircraft in HMS *Argus*. The *Argus* was not much of a ship. I think she could do about twenty-two knots an hour. We'd never been on an aircraft carrier. We had no idea what carriers were like. We were in fog, out of fog and in the fog again. We got spotted by a German reconnaissance aeroplane that went around and around telling everybody where we were. Back into fog again. Finally we decided we'd fly off. There was no wind speed, so no wind at all, very little wind speed over the deck. So it meant our take-off was very critical.

... What they said was, 'You take off in this thing and fly to port. We lined the destroyer up on the starboard beam, that's about there, so many miles away, and fly over the aircraft carrier and over the destroyer and pull your direction gyro out and you're heading south. You fly on that course for twenty minutes or half an hour and you'll hit Russia. It's a big country, you can't miss it. You won't go over it or anything. When you hit it, turn right and after a certain time you'll find a big river. Fly down that river and after a certain time, on the left you'll find a little village and that's where you're going.'

We did that.

... Strange thing about this *Argus*, it had a little ramp like a ski jump out on the bow. Rather interesting ... the whole idea was they were supposed to send you off. On the first trip they hit it and broke their undercarriage. So they had to prang in Russia. That was rather nice. First aeroplanes into Russia. I got away with it somehow. I didn't break mine ... I've got my vision still of that. You put the brakes on, full throttle and off you went. Hope for the best. 'Our father, which art in heaven, hallowed be thy name.' The other unpleasant thing about it was that if you ditch, too bad, we can't pick you up. Too many submarines around. Not only that, you weren't going to last long in that bloody water up there. So that was a nice thought.

... None of us had ever been on a ship, never tried this before. We were briefed by some of the fleet air arm pilots. I've still got the instructions here of exactly what happened. They push you as far aft as possible. I think we had three aeroplanes at a time take off. The rest were down on the hangar. So you could have maximum flight deck take-off. I think the ship was at the most six hundred feet, if that, long. Usually, in taking off from a ship, the two things that happened is the ship always steams into wind because the total of the ship's speed and the wind across the deck reduces your take-off run. We had no wind over the deck. We're talking about this foggy place. So what we were told to do, they pushed us right aft, we hopped in, ran up the aeroplane full bore, feet on the brakes, holding the brakes on, you had ten brakes. The brakes full on and the bloke waved a green flag and you tried to keep on the central line, otherwise you'd hit something over the side. The ramp went up in front, pull the pole back and hoped you got airborne.

... We were there supposedly to teach them to fly these things, not to go to war. and the Germans, I learnt this later on, they had one of their biggest divisions trying to take Murmansk where we were, because it was a warm water port. They wanted it badly and they put everything into it. When we landed and got into our little huts and things we could hear gunfire only just up the road. It might have been twenty to thirty miles away, but you could hear the guns.

So the ground war was close to us, which we didn't like very much. The other thing which was disconcerting, the Russians had no worthwhile radar... so the first thing you knew about a raid was when the anti-aircraft guns on the airfield opened up, or the bombs dropped on the airfield. So we'd take off between the bomb bursts. We'd be on readiness and sitting in the freezing bloody snow. The bomb burst would go and off you'd go. We shot down I think about sixteen confirmed aircraft. We shot down a lot more than that, but the Russians were strange people. They were loath to give us any real success. We never quite understood why, but we think that it was a sort of national pride; they were going to shoot down the German aeroplanes, not these bloody English.

... One of the most absurd things, and I give you my word of honour this is completely true, the Russians had one of their destroyers up in one of the fjords, right on the front line, providing naval gunfire support... So we sent one of our flights, that's about six aeroplanes, over to fly escort around the destroyer to keep the German bombers away from it. The Russians then sent over three bombers from our airfield to dive-bomb the German troops... It was a beautiful day, not a cloud in the sky, see for miles. We got over this fjord and we were at about fifteen to twenty thousand feet. Suddenly the lead Russian dive-bomber peeled off and dive-bombed the Russian destroyer. Word of honour. Dropped his bombs on the Russian destroyer. The Russian destroyer opened up and shot the Russian lead bomber out of the sky. We were scratching our heads, metaphorically.

'What the bloody hell's going on here?'

For one awful moment we thought, 'Maybe they're not our Hurricanes, maybe they're somebody else's Hurricanes.'

It was very confusing. I'd love to tell the story and say the Hurricanes had a go at each other, but they didn't. The Russian crew bailed out of there. I think we watched them flutter down, I don't know what happened to them. Couldn't care less by this time.

... Because of the conditions and the snow and so on, we had semi dugouts for the aircraft. They were almost underground, but not quite, with a roof over the top. So we were down there. When the bombs started dropping you sat in your aeroplane, opened throttle and got up, climbed up the hill and onto the airfield. The Hurricane was very nose heavy. So what you always had to do was taxi, particularly in snow or mud and so on, a couple of airmen would sit on the tail and lean over the rudder fin like that to keep your tail down, otherwise you'd tip up. Then you got up the ramp and you stopped and they got off and you took off. I was coming out of my little ramp and our flight commander . . . had his two airmen on. Bombs are dropping and guns are going off. He climbed up the ramp and opened his throttle and didn't let the blokes get off. I watched in horror, I stopped and watched. I saw this Hurricane going across, tail going down like this, full throttle trying to get off. All these heavy blokes were not only keeping the tail down, but they were blocking the airflow of the elevator, so the thing didn't work. He finally staggered into the air like that. It was awful to watch. He got up about a hundred feet and was absolutely vertical, and he catapulted down like that, cartwheeled like that and the two little airmen were flying from the sky. Not much left of them. Not much left of him either. The aeroplane was in a mess. So we took off and came back. We couldn't understand why these two blokes didn't get off. So we tried. You can't. If you're sitting on the tail of the plane and you've got the fin coming up like that, and the fellow's got full throttle, you're pinned with the slipstream. You can't get off. So that was terrible to watch.

. . . They called it lack of moral fibre, LMF, which I suppose is a polite word for saying coward. 'He's not with us; he doesn't want to be in this anymore.' I think it happened more with the bomber boys. I would have hated that. I think you did twenty missions over Europe before you had a rest. At one stage there the fatality rate was shocking. I think with the fighter blokes, I think too many sorties and the blokes would start to say, 'Hey, this can't go on. I can't keep it up.'

I knew one chap in 17 Squadron when I joined it that was shot down twice in one day. Had to bail out twice. The second time, he got a good rest the second time, 'cause he got badly burned, the aeroplane was on fire. To this day he's got what looks like an oxygen mask, because where he had his mask wasn't burnt; the rest of his face was where the helmet wasn't. It looks like he's got a pair of white gloves on, 'cause he wasn't wearing gloves. So all his skin was badly burned. Some blokes had enough. I can understand. I came close to it myself saying, 'Hey, can I get out of this for a little while? Just rough weather. I'd like a bit of a good rest.'

Some squadrons they didn't get a chance. Particularly in the Middle East. It was far worse than we had. I knew one chap in the Middle East. He got shot down and he bailed out in the middle of a tank battle in the desert. He landed next to some of the German tanks. They were trying to depress their machine guns to shoot him and he was running along the side of the tank keeping as close as he could so they couldn't shoot him. He lived to tell his tale. He didn't fly for a long while after that. That would be dreadful.

* * *

I enjoyed London in those days. It was being blitzed but the people had a wonderful spirit. There were blackouts, which were unpleasant. It was Christmas time so it was foggy. They had fogs in London. There was plenty for us. They had lots of dances and parties going in clubs and so on, which we belonged to. We were quite well paid relatively to everybody else. So you can stop at a decent hotel. Stopped at one right in Piccadilly. Had nice young ladies around. It was good, particularly after Russia, it was great to have a good time even though it was dark and blackout and blitzes and so on. It was pretty good.

... 134 Squadron was the number of our squadron then, we were to re-form and re-equip, 'cause we left all our equipment behind as a lot of blokes were posted. So we were moved to Northern Ireland, just outside of Londonderry to re-form. We re-formed from Hurricanes to Spitfires. It was a rest area. There was no real war going on. A little bit, but not much... We used to go and escort the convoys coming in across the Atlantic. Meet them a hundred miles out or something, just make sure nothing ever happened.

... I loved the Spitfires. It's hard to describe what it was like to fly one. It was absolutely beautiful. I describe it rather like a ballerina.

It was delightful to fly . . . the aeroplane did it for you, but not quite. It had no vices except it was very fragile. Couldn't take much punishment either on air or land. It had a little dainty undercarriage that would collapse. Just for pure flying it was delightful. It really was lovely. Good to go to war in too, in Europe. I would sooner have been in the Spitfire than the Hurricane.

* * *

We had four Australians then in the squadron. Pearl Harbor happened on the way home, so we're talking February '42 and all we wanted to do was come home. 'King and Country', now it's 'Australia and Country'. We wanted to get home. Things were grim. Singapore had either fallen or was about to fall. I can't remember now, but the Japs were well and truly knocking everybody over. So we wanted to come home. We all put in for a posting home.

. . . I can tell you a lot about Americans on the troopship when we came over. They were the most uninformed people I've ever met in my life. They were absolutely, completely uninformed. There'd been no war as far as Europe was concerned. That was somebody else's war, couldn't work out why and what we were doing over there. That sort of thing. This was officers too. Not just the old Joe in the street, senior officers would say, 'Hey, do people speak English like you in Australia?' And 'How many white people? Are you outnumbered by the blacks? What sort of money do you use? Do you have trains? Transport?'

These were senior officers. They were absolutely uninformed. So we had to give them lectures on this sort of thing. We used to pull their leg a bit. We'd come up with all sorts of lies about it. We got so angry about it, we'd say, 'No, very few people speak English like we do. Might find one or two, but only the very senior people speak English.' We pulled their legs.

* * *

We got back in May '42. Things were very bad out here then of course. The Battle of New Guinea and in the Pacific islands was pretty bad. I think I had about ten days leave up in Brisbane. Then we were rushed off to Kingaroy where a squadron called 75 RAAF Squadron, was re-forming. They were the famous squadron in Moresby who got shot down almost to the last aeroplane and lost most of their pilots, which is not a very well-told story, the Battle of Moresby, 75 Squadron. The survivors were there at Kingaroy and you had P40 Kittyhawks, which was an American aeroplane.

There were quite a few of us back from Europe. We were looked upon by the New Guinea pilots with suspicion. They thought we'd had too good a war, we had lovely messes over there and nice pubs down on the corner of the street and a pretty good war and they'd been slumming it up in Port Moresby and so on. It had a bit of ill feeling to start with. Didn't last long.

Our first impression of Kittyhawks was not very good...we described it as a bulldozer. It was a great big heavy aeroplane. Not as nice to fly as any of the others I've flown, but it's pretty reliable. Hefty and strong. Could take a real belting. Thank goodness it could, 'cause after we'd fought up there a little while we got sent up to Milne Bay with a sister squadron called 76. I was in 75. That was one of the worst wars I've ever been to. Russia was a picnic compared to Milne Bay. Milne Bay was bloody awful. Never stopped raining. The mountains came straight up from the strip. The strip was just mud with steel planking on it... Spitfires wouldn't have lasted... When you landed it was an up and down ride. It was carved out of a coconut plantation, so if you went off the runway, which you did, you ran into a coconut tree, which didn't do the aircraft much good.

... We all had malaria and dysentery. I had both at one stage. Just unpleasant. Our living conditions were so squalid. We had six in a little bloody tent and a little bit of timber on the floor, but mostly it was mud. I had malaria...the doctor would come in and tell you to stay in bed and the squadron commander would come and say, 'Get airborne!' What else could you do? You didn't have enough pilots. We didn't have pilots. We had no reserve. We had no fat as they called it. We had nobody spare. No pilots coming through the pipeline at that time to replace you, so that was it. You flew until the whole squadron was relieved...and you'd go out, have a little vomit on the tail wheel, get in the cockpit. I'm not exaggerating this, truly, and you'd get airborne . . . you take your oxygen mask off and have a vomit all over the place and put it back on again. You'd have diarrhoea and it'd be seeping down the back of your legs into your flying boots. You had another hour and a half to sit up there in all this. That was unpleasant.

. . . And the food! Baked beans, bully beef. We were lucky. The only time we ever got a cup of tea was when the Salvation Army came in. They were up the front line. They'd give us a cup of tea and cigarettes. The food was dreadful. We couldn't even light a fire most of the time, it just rained and rained and rained . . . so we just didn't, there was nobody there to light a fire. As for bars and things like that, we never ever had one. We all grew beards because we couldn't shave. The physical demands . . . I don't know how to describe it.

* * *

We were raided quite a few times by the Japanese who came over from Rabaul. They sent over dive-bombers escorted by Zeros. We had quite a few fights and lost quite a few blokes and we shot down quite a few. One of the most important things that happened up there, I believe it was a turning point, the Battle of Milne Bay was a turning point like the Kokoda Track thing. Perhaps more so at Milne Bay. We got the word one day that there was a Jap invasion fleet coming to land at Milne Bay, because the Jap strategy was to take Milne Bay and they could then take the rest around to Moresby over the Kokoda Track and up that way. When this Japanese fleet was coming in, for some reason we couldn't get the American heavy aircraft bombers to go out, so we were given the job in single seat Kittyhawks to go out and attack the fleet, which we weren't designed for. We were fighter aircraft. We could carry two 500-pound bombs and we went out.

I'll never forget it because it was a typical New Guinea day. Low cloud, pouring with rain and we weaved our way out of the rain and we sighted this fleet. It was terrifying because it was escorted by Japanese ships, destroyers, a cruiser or two and some gunships. Our briefing was, 'Forget the naval ships, go for the troopships. Knock off the troops before they land.'

We went out there and we tried our best. I happened to be a very good dive-bomber. I selected a troopship, came at it, very low clouds. The Japanese were firing everything at us. The flak was quite enormous. I didn't stay too long. I aimed at the troopship, dropped my bombs and got back up into the clouds where it was fairly safe. We finally got back to Milne Bay, to our landing strip and the wing commander, Peter Turnbull, came over to me and said, 'Well done, lad.'

I said, 'What for?'

He said, 'You sunk the gunboat, the flagship.'

I said, 'I did not.'

He said, 'Yes, you did. You were flying so and so?'

I said, 'Yeah.'

'I watched you.'

I said 'I wasn't aiming at that, I was aiming at the troopship.'

Anyway, I got a flagship gunboat confirmed.

The Japanese landed and that was very unpleasant because the strip we were on went into the bay itself. The Japs landed and in the end they took one end of the strip and we had the other. So we'd take off over them, crouch down under the armoured plating. They shot at you when you pulled your wheels up, which is not recommended. One of the satisfactions I had, again please put this in the context that we were in a war and hated the Japanese very much, I was leading a couple of fellows round to where they'd landed some barges. They were up on one of the beaches there and they were waving at us. We found out afterwards that they were told that there were no Allied aircraft there; any aircraft they saw were theirs. So they could feel quite safe. They were waving at me, so I pulled the boys in astern and we went down and strafed them. I regret to say it, but we killed many, many, many of them. Rather an amazing sight when you hit fellows, the Kittyhawk had six guns. When you hit them you could see they were just like little rag dolls jumping up in the air. I wasn't upset at all. I was happy to kill so many.

... Our main job then was strafing. It's well documented that it's one of the reasons the army won the war, because of our strafing the Japs, making them keep their heads down. It was difficult strafing targets there because it was thick canopy jungle. Absolutely thick. On one side were these very high mountains, I don't know how high they were, they certainly went up in the clouds. So it was only a narrow strip between the sea and the mountains. There was thick jungle and the Japs were advancing towards us and towards the army. We couldn't see anything when we strafed. So what we were told to do was the army would fire up through the canopy ... a green Verey [flare], so that's our front line. Then a number of white Verey lights for every hundred yards in front of the green to strafe. The problem with that was you were doing a couple of hundred miles an hour round and round in low cloud, dodging the cloud and watching the mountain on that side and so on. When the green came up you'd see it, but how the devil could you pinpoint exactly where it was in the canopy when the jungle on the top was the same? So you tried very hard to make sure you weren't strafing your own fellows, you went well past them. We couldn't see the Japs, but we knew they were there, so we just strafed and came back and landed. We were only airborne about ten minutes and back and landed and had a quick feed and got back in the aeroplane and did it again. You strafed and strafed and strafed and in the end there we were. You have to know a bit about ballistics to realise how many rounds we fired. For example, the ammunition was so organised in the aircraft that we had tracer, which was a light sort of thing at the end of the belt. That was to tell you, you were running out of ammunition so you may as well go home, it wasn't there to help you.

   ... Some of the fellows got shot down and walked back. They found their way. The natives walked them back. One bloke got shot down at the end of the islands. He got brought back in a dugout canoe by some native. They were very good ... Very much on our side. They didn't like 'Japan man' very much. Evidently there were a few atrocities committed around the place. No, they were intensely loyal, at Milne Bay anyway, I don't know about the other places, but yes, they were. I don't think they ever were tempted to turn us in. I don't think that opportunity arose as such. Whenever our blokes got shot down they'd bring them back. Time and time again they brought them back. Might be a couple of weeks along, but they'd bring them back.

... The army was incredible up there. Bloody hand to hand. The army used to brief us every morning. The general, whoever he was, would come and talk about where we were. You could almost hear the gunfire at the end of the strip. I'm glad I wasn't in the army then.

I'll give you a funny story. The army wanted intelligence. They always do. Everybody wanted to know what's going on, what's the strength of the enemy and where he's located and what sort of weapons he's got and so on. We shot down a Jap, a dive-bomber thing. He crash-landed on the beach, well away from us. The natives got him and brought him in for interrogation. We found out he was a Jap officer.

I was at the strip at the opposite end. They walked this bloke in. They had him like a pig. They had a pole on the shoulder of this fellow and another fellow, another Kanaka [Papuan] up in front. They had this thing like a stuck pig. His wrists and his ankles on this thing. His wrists were nearly cut through from the vines. They dumped him with the army. They took the thing off him. He was on the ground there and they were going to talk to him. And an air force cook came up and said, 'My first bloody Jap!'

And pulled out his gun and shot him. There and then. Whatever happened to the cook, he was in serious trouble after that. He was going to kill a Jap before he finished the war.

* * *

When you weren't flying you went in one of the gun pits with the army, the anti-aircraft people, because their recognition wasn't very good and they were just as likely to fire at a Kittyhawk as they would a Zero. Not deliberately. Only that it was low cloud and they're going very fast. I mean, an aeroplane was an aeroplane to them. It all used to happen so very quickly. I was in this gun pit at the end of the strip and Zeros were coming in to dive-bomb us and so on. I saw one of our Kittyhawks running, with a Jap right up its backside and it was very low, well below clouds. The Jap shot this fellow, shot the aircraft and it started to catch fire and Kingston was the fellow, I knew him quite well. He bailed out just up there, I watched him, and his chute was streaming as he hit the ground. He was dead of course. Another couple of seconds and the chute would have filled, but it was streaming. I watched another, I don't think it was the same day; it was another day I think in the gun pit. I saw another fellow called Stuart Munro come screaming out of the clouds with two Zeros up his backside. He didn't seem to get shot down, but he went over there somewhere and we heard the gunfire and they disappeared into the clouds and that was Stuart. I don't think we ever found him. The jungle up there was very fierce. If you went down in it, the canopy just closed up over you. They're still finding aircraft up there now that got lost. I don't know how long we were there. I know we got out by Christmas.

* * *

Morale was the worst I've ever seen it. We were all pretty sick and fed up. The conditions, after being in the UK and even Russia, at least you had reasonable quarters, you had a bed and so on. We had a stinky stretcher and a muddy tent. The Japs had landed and you knew they were around you and so on. We had to move our tents to the other side to get where the army were . . . The sister squadron, 76, their squadron commander was a chap named Peter Turnbull. I was telling you about the Japs had one end of the strip. He got shot down on take-off from the ground. He was pulling his wheels up and they shot him out of the sky. That was the end of him. It doesn't make you feel very good when that happens on take-off.

Then a very famous bloke took over from Peter called Bluey Truscott, who was a very great chum of mine. Bluey was good for morale, particularly how good he was. He was a wonderful bloke. We got the order to evacuate all the pilots. Those who had an aeroplane flew it back to Moresby and the rest were going to walk. Blue was ordered to fly back. He was a squadron commander and very valuable. He told them all to go and jump in the lake. He handed his aeroplane over to a sergeant and got himself a .303 rifle and got in the trench with his troops. He was going to fight the Japs on the ground. That's the sort of bloke he was. That was very good for morale. Most of the time we were glad to get out of it.

... We drew lots to see who would fly back and who'd walk back. If you look at the map, there's a long walk from Milne Bay to Moresby. I drew the short straw so I had to walk back. Supposedly. So I took all my possessions, which was my log book and a Rolls razor I had and my gun and started to walk off leading a whole bunch of the ground troops, the airmen. We were about to go, and in came a Lockheed Hudson. He came in and landed. The Japs were on the other end of the strip and he said, 'Come on, hop in' so we all filed in. I don't know how many we got in this Hudson, but I know I was up in the bomb-aimer's position, lying flat on my belly with two fellows on top of me. I could see where we were taking off in this thing and we hit a coconut tree on take-off. Blew the tree apart, but we got airborne.

... We were relieved eventually just before Christmas, by an American squadron of Air Cobras. They weren't very good at all. They were full of talk. Anyway, the war was over when they got there. That part of the war.

* * *

I had two weeks leave in Brisbane. Then I was posted to Mildura where they were just really getting going on the Fighter School. They called it an operational training unit. That was an interesting thing... Mildura was where the fellows got their wings coming through the pipelines, just got their wings on Wirraways. Then they came to us for six weeks. In six weeks we had to convert them to their fighter aircraft, which in those days was a Spitfire, Kittyhawk or a thing called a Boomerang. We had to convert them and then teach them the art of fighter pilots, which was teaching them to fly in battle formation, air to air gunnery, strafing, dive-bombing, whatever. Which was rather difficult for us, we went there as instructors, none of us were instructors. We hadn't instructed people flying aeroplanes. We were supposed to instruct them in fighter work. Some of these kids only really just got their wings and they weren't very good at all.

. . . That was where we really killed people. We killed more people there. They called it 'the killer school'. The day I arrived they killed four. In one day. The day I arrived! It was six weeks before they went to the war. You have to do everything in the six weeks and convert to a new aeroplane. They didn't have many hours up. So dreadful things went on. Just an example. We were trying to teach them dive-bombing in a Kittyhawk. There was a dive-bombing range. You could almost see it from the airfield.

We'd be standing out on the tarmac and somebody'd say, 'Hey, telltale wisp of black smoke.'

You'd see the smoke coming up. Somebody else had gone in. What was happening was that in the dive-bomb, you'd tell them whatever angle to dive on, say it was forty degrees, and you get up to whatever speed it was and you release your bomb at whatever height it was, let's say it was two thousand feet, and pull out. There were some dreadful navigating results. Nowhere near the target. So we worked it out that they'd gone from the Wirraway to this other aeroplane, the Kittyhawk was much, much faster, so the closing speed was much greater. Not only that, the Kittyhawk had this terrible thing, wanting to roll and yaw. If you let your bomb go and the aeroplane's not pointing at the target, the bomb will go anywhere.

. . . The other place where we killed a lot was Lake Victoria, which was this great big lake there. We used to teach this deflection shooting, how you've got to aim well ahead of the target to make sure your bullets and aeroplane coincide. It was what you call shadow-shooting. You put an aeroplane up and it flew across the water with the sun, made sure the sun was up there, so the shadow was on the water. So as you flew your shadow was there. The kid would dive down and have a shot at the shadow that was moving. But again they'd forget to pull out of it. I remember I was flying some aeroplane, I think it was a Boomerang. Put my shadow on the water and said, 'Come on,' calling him up and saying, 'Come on.' I looked over my shoulder and there was a God-awful splash in the water as he went in. He was trying to get the shadow.

You have to appreciate in those days you didn't have time to do all these things and people got killed. I did my time there. This was how I got to the navy. Because I got so, what's the word? We all thought it was too bloody dangerous to fly at the school; we'd sooner go back to the war. Every Friday we used to go up before the group captain who I knew very well and say, 'Hey, what about a squadron posting?'

He'd say, 'You've had three or four.'

I'd had all my ops. There were too many blokes wanted to go to the war and I'd had a lot. There was nothing to do.

'You're staying here.'

So I didn't like that very much.

... Instructors were coming from all over the place then. A lot of Middle East fellows were coming back. A lot of English blokes from the European theatre. As a result of the Japs coming into the war they were getting our own people back and they were coming from all over the place. There used to be a little bit of friendly rivalry. The desert blokes, we used to tell them they had too much sand in their shoes. The fighter boys from England were too much with Piccadilly naughties and so on. I was pretty good. I was amongst them all. We were what they called the jungle blokes. It was a big school. A very big school then. I suppose we would have had three or four thousand people on the base. Including the airmen and all the rest of the blokes. It was a pretty big place. A lovely little town Mildura.

* * *

I had one of my more unpleasant prangs up in Darwin. We were operating from a small strip cut in amongst the gum trees at a place called Livingstone; it was the name of the strip. It was just a bitumen strip and beside it was the main north–south road, beside that was the main water pipeline, supplying all of Darwin. A great big concrete thing. Twelve-inch pipe. I was taking off there and I had a number two. We used to take off in close formation, 'cause it was only a narrow strip. I had this bright young bloke tucked in beside me. Wings almost touching. Taking off and I was edging away from him, he was getting a bit bloody close. I hit one of the flare paths, which was a big cone-shape thing providing the light for night-flying. This was daylight, not night. I hit this thing just before I got airborne and my number two got airborne. He pulled the stick and climbed up over me. I veered off the thing and I should tell you prior to this, because the road was right beside the strip we had a sentry at each end with one of these boom gates to stop traffic. Because when we were taking off you were likely to do some damage. A truck was coming up there with a young pilot officer in it and a driver. The sentry stopped them at the boom gate and this officer pulled his rank and said, 'I'm on urgent business, I've gotta get up to Darwin'

And so the officer told him to go. He got halfway up the strip and he stopped to watch the Spitties take off. I veered this thing off the runway and straight through this truck, hit the bloody water pipe and I finished up, the engine fell off, the wings fell off and I was upside down in the little box, just the cockpit. Very shaken. The ambulance came racing up. It was always right beside the strip. The ambulance came up and a doctor called Des, peers up at me, I'm upside down in my straps in this thing. He said, 'You all right?'

I said 'I think so, but look, I just hit a truck.'

He said 'Don't worry about them, they're dead.'

I just killed a couple of blokes. Didn't make me feel very good. They gingerly lowered me down, the aeroplane didn't catch fire. There wasn't much of it left there when it was finished. So that was that. That was one of my more unpleasant actions . . . I was a reasonable pilot, I really was, but those sorts of things are not pilot errors so much, as I suppose I made a bad judgment. I don't know what I can do. The young kid was pushing me over. He didn't mean to, but he was just being very keen.

* * *

By this time, gearing up for the war had started to move up to the home islands of Japan. The Allies were gearing up to attack on the mainland . . . so the Royal Navy, whilst they had all these aeroplanes, they could do with some more pilots. Experienced pilots. The RAAF had them coming out of their ears by now. The war from the RAAF's point of view had gone so far north that the Americans couldn't be bothered with our logistic supplies and looking after them, and they had enough anyway. So nearly everybody was getting out of work. So the two governments talked to each other and the British Government said, 'How about we have some of your fellows?' The Australian Government said 'Okay.'

So one day a signal came round to us to all the air bases, all the front bases, saying, 'Who would like to join the fleet air arm?'

A lot of blokes like me, all the fellows who wanted to go back to the war, put their hands up. So after a lot of interviews they took twelve of us. One day I was a flight lieutenant and the next day I was a lieutenant in the Royal Australian Navy Volunteer Reserve.

. . . That night in the mess, it came through that I was going to the navy, and I had a great big walrus fighter-pilot moustache. We decided to lose my moustache. Couldn't have one in the navy. The blokes started wielding shaving sticks and blokes had razors, the blokes were going to take it off, we were all fairly sloshed by this time. I got a bit terrified about this. Finally I let the doctor do it. What they did, they took off one side completely. So I was walking around with one half of a big moustache.

So we went and joined the navy. I was RAN VR on loan to the Royal Navy. Got new uniforms and so on, navy uniforms and went to Schofield just outside Sydney. It was a very big Royal Navy base then. I went to a squadron called 801. There were twelve Australians went to the squadron. We ranged from lieutenant to sublieutenant, some were very junior, but we all were quite experienced in flying aeroplanes. I joined Squadron 801 and it had twenty-four aeroplanes and thirty-six pilots. Huge amount. I was made senior pilot. I had been in the navy half a dog watch and I was made senior pilot of a fleet air arm squadron. It was rather good. So we could fly the aeroplanes. They were Seafires, which was the naval version of Spitfires. We'd spent hundreds of hours flying, so we had no trouble flying them.

... They had a hook on a bit of string for deck landings and so on. What we had to learn was how to do a deck landing. So we did what they called aerodrome dummy deck landing. We fly around and around Schofield, and to air force pilots everything else was right until the approach. You had to rely on a batman [deck flight director] giving you signals up and down, too fast, too slow, turn left, turn right. So we had to learn all of that. The most frightening thing was flying the aeroplane at a very low speed on the approach. You got right down to just a few knots, stalling speed, which we weren't used to. When you look at the air speed indicator and it's getting near the stall pin you start to get a bit concerned. But you had to do that to get down to minimum speed and the art of deck landings was to have a very nose-up attitude, lots of power on and you were sort of holding the aeroplane in the air on its propeller and you just went to stall. So when the batman went 'Cut', you pull off your throttle and you fell out of the sky. That was the theory and the practice. You caught the wire.

So after these dummy deck landings, which we finally got to do, we got out and did our first deck landings off the coast of Sydney here in a ship called [HMS] *Indomitable*. Most of us got away with it, but one young bloke, Charlie, came in to land and there were two signals that were executive signals from the batman. One was 'Cut' and you had to pull out your throttle and the other was 'Go round again' and you'd made a mess of it and go round. Poor old Charlie. He came in, it was a pretty calm day, the sea was steady. He really made a mess of this thing. He was really committed to the deck and he got a wave off. He tried to take it and he stalled, went into the water just beside the ship. We were all watching. It went straight down. Getting out of the cockpit of a Seafire, would have been pretty difficult, because you've got your straps, you've got your parachute harness, you're hooked up to your radio and your oxygen. So you've got to get all these things undone. The cockpit of a Seafire was terribly tiny. You've got your shoulders against it. We all waved goodbye to Charlie and miles astern we saw a little yellow figure bob up. He came up. The destroyer, we had a tracer destroyer for that reason. Pick up when people went over the side. They picked up Charlie and he never flew again. I've seen him since, but that was it for Charlie. He didn't want to fly anymore. He reckoned he got down so far he burst his eardrum. So we did our DLs [deck landings] and were now qualified fleet air arm pilots.

* * *

The war ended and on the 4th of May I was going to be a civilian. It's a terrifying thought after you'd been in the womb since you were seventeen or eighteen. I'd been a good staff officer. I'd been taught how to analyse problems and look at all the courses of action and so on. So I sat down, I had plenty of time to do this, with a pencil and paper and said, 'Okay, what are you going to do? What do you want to do? What are your qualifications?'

Didn't take long to work out the only thing I really knew anything about was aeroplanes. So I said, 'Okay, now what can you do as a civilian with aeroplanes? You can go and fly for Mr Qantas, or Mr Ansett, you can be a flying instructor at a civilian school. Not much else you can do. Do you want to do it?'

I thought flying in an aeroplane Sydney–Melbourne, Sydney–Melbourne, Sydney–Melbourne. Like driving a bus. No.

... I'd been flying since I was a small boy, I'd had a few accidents, I had been damned lucky I was still alive. I just thought I'd be pushing the luck to start flying aeroplanes again. My hearing was starting to go, bloody jet engines screaming in my ears, and my eyesight wasn't as good as it should be. I said, 'I can sell them. What could I sell and who could I sell and how would I go about selling?'

I talked to another chum of mine who I knew quite well that was in the air force, he finished up a wing commander and fighter pilot. Famous fighter pilot, his name was Dick Creswell. He said, 'What are you going to do? Why don't you come and work for our company?'

I said, 'That's a good idea.'

Hawker DeHavilland down at Bankstown. Big aircraft company. I had a lot to learn. I didn't even know things like what an invoice was. I had no idea what commercial life was like. I had to learn very fast. Fortunately, most of the stuff I was trying to market was military equipment and so I soon worked out quite a good system, which I think they use today. I did some staff work and realised that if you're going to sell some equipment or market some equipment, you've got to make sure the right people know about it. You've got to make sure that other people that'll be on the fringe of it, for example, if you want to sell the air force an aeroplane, the army wants to know what it's going to do for them. The navy wants to know, 'What can it do for me?' Defence and Foreign Affairs, Foreign Affairs particularly will say, 'We've gotta be careful what Indonesia are gonna think about this.'

Not only that, I knew all the people in Canberra, they were all buddies of mine and they had all become fairly senior by now and so I could go and talk to them. One of the things I must say about defence lobbying, people have said, 'It's a business; you're using all your old mates.'

The first thing I say is, 'You will never sell the services anything; they'll buy something off you if it's what they want.'

What you've got to find out is what they *really* want. Is the company you represent, have they got something that can do that? If it can't, can it be altered to do it? Or can you talk to the service and say, 'Hey wait a minute, there's something better coming off the drawing board, which will do more what you're asking for.'

So it's a sort of liaison, you interpret.

... You had to talk the language. People say, defence salesmen, gunrunners, arms salesmen, 'Why don't you employ an ordinary civilian to do it, not a warrior?' Well, he doesn't talk the language of these people. You can talk to them. You know what they're talking about. A civilian wouldn't. I would be quite honest with them and say, 'We're not going to meet, we'll fall short here and so and so.' 'Okay,' they'd say and we won't be in that competition. So it becomes a trust with you and the military ... You get a credibility factor. They

132 • Voices of War

know your history, most of them do, some of them fought with you and so on. The politicians don't know that.

* * *

I welcomed the war because it gave me everything I wanted, that was flying and travel and everything. How did it change me? I suppose I became more worldwide in my knowledge of international politics for one thing. I learnt a lot of lessons. My geography's very good now. I can draw you a map of the world without any help. I think the most important thing it really taught me was ... I know it's a bit trite to talk about mateship. In the defence forces in the war you really do become absolutely reliant on your mates, on your friends. They protect your tail when you're flying.

... I think it's character building, the services. I do, I know this is almost an old-fashioned word, like discipline. I do believe discipline is still part of your life even if you're not in the services. You drive on the left-hand side of the road; you're not going to drive on the right-hand side of the road. That's an absurd example, but you learn you've got to perform certain things and in the military you learn to do it. There are a lot of misunderstandings about the service life, I was taught, before you can give orders and tell people what to do, you've got to learn to take them yourself. Always somebody senior to you. So I don't mean without question. There's nothing to stop you saying, 'Aye, aye, Sir, but what about so and so?'

... I think there are people who take to service life more than others. It's not a matter of a killer instinct or anything like that, it's a matter of there's a special camaraderie in the services that you don't get anywhere else. Don't get it in companies. It can be a fascinating job, but I don't care if you're flying an aeroplane or driving a tank or whatever, it can be challenging and the pay is very good these days by the way. Very good. Some people are more, not warriors, but more inclined to like it, like the idea of war rather than others who don't. One of the things I still can't come to grips with completely is the number of females in the service now. I read a debate the other day about now putting them in the front line, in the infantry. I have reservations about that. I welcome them aboard big ships and so on, not so sure about on the submarines, but if you've got a woman in the front line I wonder about her colleagues, male soldiers, whether they wouldn't be wanting to be a bit more protective than if it's another chap. Whether they could rely on her when, and I don't want to be anti-feminist, but what happens when a fellow comes at her with a bayonet for example? I'm just not qualified to talk about it, but I just have reservations about it all. It is a different Defence Force, different than those days of course. I think some of the women officers that I've met, and I've met quite a few of them, I was down at Nowra not so long ago, and my old flying squadron, the engineer officer was a female. She was engineer officer of the whole damn squadron. One of the senior helicopter pilots is a woman, flying big Sea King helicopters. When they had a ceremonial march-past, carrying rifles and so on, pretty little girls. Just a different service. I don't object to it. It seems to be working all right, but I just have one or two reservations about where you can deploy them, that's all.

. . . Staying alive, getting through it all was my biggest achievement. When I think of whatever it was, all those years, and the few prangs I had and so on, I suppose it's an achievement getting through it all. That's not the answer you want I suppose, I can't think of any other one. Getting promoted was pretty good . . . It was ninety per cent luck, ten per cent perhaps skill. There's a lot to do with being in the right place at the right time too. The worst thing is people were killed in the wrong place at the wrong time. I lost a whole lot of pilot chums in the war. Lots and lots of them. Some very close friends, some just other squadron chaps. I've seen so many, actually watched people get killed. Strangely enough it didn't move me one little bit. I watched for example, this is in Ireland, I'm standing out on the tarmac and there's a Spitfire came into circuit. He's about eight hundred feet just up there. He was doing barrel rolls. Right in front of me he got himself into a flat spin and the aeroplane just went like that, went like that, went like that and he almost got out of it and it burst into flames and he was killed. On a slow motion like that. That's just one example. I can give you lots and lots of these things. 'Oh dear, poor chap.' That's it. You don't go to mourning... I'm not insensitive, but having seen so many blokes killed, I just shrug myself. I don't say I was rare, but most people didn't feel like me. Most people were more sensitive and used to, not get up their nose, but some people overdo it. 'Let's have two minutes' silence for Joe.' Bloody hell, he's dead, that's it. Having two minutes' silence is not going to do him any good. I just don't go with it. I think not all of us, but a lot of us were like that. You had to. You weren't going to last very long if you were going to get upset about people being killed.

... I don't get the dream of being in a burning aeroplane now. I'm often flying, but that one I had a lot after the war. I remember Mum and Dad used to come and wake me up on one of my few days of leave, I'd be screaming. What I could see in my mind was being upside down on the ground and on fire. They can't get you out... I haven't had that for years. Now and then I get, I think it's as I get older and lose my hearing and eyesight and so on, I have this bloody awful dream. I'm in a strange aeroplane. I don't recognise the cockpit, everything's all over the place. All these millions of dials and I don't know what they are and I can't find anything. I've got my glasses; I take them on and have a look. It's pitch-black night, I can't hear what they're telling me on the radio and I've got to take-off. I wake up absolutely sweating. It's a silly dream, but that's more terrifying than being burned.

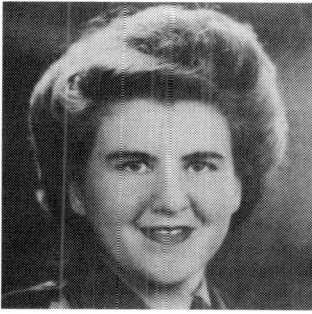

IRIS ROSER

Australian Women's Land Army
World War II

Civilian Medical Aid
Vietnam War

I was born in Tenterfield, seventy-seven years ago. And I have been very fortunate to do many things, meet many people, learn many things and, I guess, enjoy a very full lifetime. Seeing as we only get one. I suppose my first adventure away from home was joining the Australian Women's Land Army, during World War II of course.

I started off on a tomato farm. And from early morning to late afternoon, we picked tomatoes. When you start off of course you're so good, you're bending over, but by the end of the afternoon you're sliding along your backside, your back is so sore . . . but when it came to pulling turnips and they were in ground that was like cement, that was hard. We lived in tin sheds, and there were, I think, about sixty of us. Can you imagine sixty girls in tin sheds? Very noisy at times. I had carried my mandolin with me. I played mandolin, so about all we had for entertainment was to play the mandolin and sing songs, and wish we were home.

The Land Army, we used to get about thirty shillings a week, and about fifteen of that we had to pay for board, so everything else, our toothpaste and all that sort of thing, we had to purchase from what was left. And there were times that you didn't even have the tuppence that was needed to buy a newspaper. I'm just saying, it was a fun time as well because I was generally the one who was allocated to snitch a newspaper that somebody had left on a seat... It was a very different world to nowadays. Let's take the word 'sex'. Nobody would even think of saying that word. Nobody would even think of the things that go on today, definitely not. I'm not saying we were all pure. I don't know who was pure or otherwise, but I think the majority of us was as naive as I was. I've learnt a lot since. Too much, perhaps.

* * *

My marriage wasn't working all that well. I don't know why my husband ever married me, actually. He didn't seem to have much time for me. Nor did I spend that much time with him. But we had different interests. He was very much occupied with sporting things, and I had never been sports-minded. So it was obvious the marriage was breaking down, and at that particular time, the Vietnam War was happening, and a local doctor had been working in Vietnam up in the mountains, with the mountain people, and he wrote in the local paper how they badly needed a secretary. So I thought this would be a good thing to do. And I wrote to him, and he wrote to America. It was an American-sponsored program called Project Concern. And within a very, very short time, I got a letter back from America that said, 'Yes please. When can you leave?' Now it wasn't easy to just take yourself off to Vietnam where a war was raging. But I had the assistance of the local Member of Parliament, Mr Reg Schwartz. And Paul Hasluck, who was the Minister for Immigration, or something. So between them they managed to get me a permit to enter Vietnam. And then, I suppose, really starts the story of the great deal of the rest of my life. And, of course, it made me feel quite different about many, many things.

* * *

All hell broke loose in Saigon, because of the Tet offensive. That was in February 1968. And whereas it had been planned that I was to go in by plane, that held things up for perhaps two or three weeks, before I could get a permit to travel. Going in, the plane was full of

American soldiers, who had just been on R&R in Hong Kong. And talking to them, and them asking me why I was going in, they thought I was crazy. Because, why would anybody want to go in there? Anyhow, I got to Tan Son Nhut, the Saigon airport. Meanwhile, a friend in Hong Kong had explained to me that he had been there. He was also a volunteer with Project Concern, and he says, 'Now, watch out for taxi cabs. They'll want to charge you twice as much as they really need, because you're new.'

But when I got there, I could hear bombs going off; the place was full of guns and tanks, and all sorts of things. I had my luggage, and yes, I did eventually find a taxidriver, and I would have given him everything that I had, just to get out of the place.

I walked over to an office, and there was a black American in charge. He looked at me, sort of did a double-flip, and I said, 'Can you tell me how I can get to Da Lat?'

He gave me a very nasty look, and said, 'Go sit over there and I'll see what I can do.'

So I went over and sat on a bench, and I sat there and I sat there, and of course, here I was, a white, not-so-young woman sitting on my own, surrounded by a couple of suitcases, and everybody who came past me seemed to look at me as if I was a unique exhibition, which of course I was. And I sat and I sat and I sat, and eventually ... I was called back to this little office thing, and he said, 'If you go over there ...' and so forth, 'You can get on a plane to Da Lat.'

... I got on, if I remember correctly, it was about a six-seater plane, and they helped me on, and as we flew into Da Lat, the pilot said, 'Look what they did on that last bombing raid.'

So we looked down. And he said to me, 'If you look down at that pile of ashes,' he says, 'That's where the Project Concern townhouse was last week.

So that wasn't very encouraging, either.

And then they came and told me there was a helicopter, a gunship, taking off to strafe a village. They said if you like they can continue on a bit further and put you down at the hospital. I said that was fine, that was great, I was getting there. And on a gunship, there were guns on either side of this big helicopter; they sat me in the middle, and of course, they didn't give me anything for my ears. So it wasn't particularly pleasant with these two guns spraying out hundreds of bullets, on either side. And along with that the feeling of, okay, down there they're killing people. That wasn't very pleasant at all. Also, it was scary. Then they flew me into the hospital, and of course, the hospital had a pad, because often they put patients down there. When I got out of the helicopter, I could barely stand up. My legs had decided they were too scared to want to stand up. But anyhow, people came running out of the hospital and they welcomed me. So that, sort of, was fine. I had arrived. I had actually arrived.

We went down to the hospital, and from a person coming where hospitals were hygienically clean, and smelled nicely, looked nice and white, it was a physical and very much a mental shock. The floor was cement, of course. The beds were iron beds, with the wire mattresses and a mat over them, a cane mat. The beds were full of people. In Vietnam, when somebody went to hospital, somebody went along with them, generally, to take care of them. And of course if they had children, they couldn't leave those at home, so they take the children along, too. So all the beds were covered with bodies. The clothing they were in was possibly the only clothing they ever had, so there was no things such as pretty pink pyjamas. The colour of most of our premises in the Project hospital was brown. Not brown paint, but brown of the earth over a lot of time. I'm not saying it was dirty. I later learnt that it was relatively clean, by comparison. But the people were all happy, they were asleep, they were being taken care of. We had two doctors. These two doctors . . . they were Chinese. And with the uprising there in China, they had swum the river, so they were actually refugees from China. They were wonderful men. They were really, really wonderful doctors.

* * *

The people were Montagnards. Montagnards means 'hill people.' They were very different to Vietnamese people. They rarely mixed and they didn't inter-marry. They were the farmers. They grew their own rice, and they lived on what they grew themselves, and fish from the river . . . Most of these Montagnard people hadn't travelled any more than a day's walk from their village. They knew nothing about the outside of their villages.

The women controlled the land. They controlled the money . . . but then again, they also did the work. It would come to rice-growing time and . . . the women would do all the hoeing. Whereas the men would poke the holes to put the seeds in, the women bent over to put in the seeds. But the husband would always carry the hoes home. Wasn't that good of him? You would see the women walking home, and the husband carrying the hoe. But they were happy people. They loved their children. An interesting factor was if a [child's parents were] killed or anything ever happened to a child—a child was never an orphan. That child was taken in by the family who had the least children. So they really had some interwoven, good qualities. We loved them.

I'll never forget one day I went into a Montagnard house . . . and Dorothy, a friend of mine was there with a camera and we saw this lady, sitting, she had the loom on the floor. And Dorothy said, 'Take her photo,' and she knew what we meant. She said just a minute sort of thing. She had one tooth. She was sitting there, topless, with two sorts of flaps of breasts hanging down. She said, 'Just a minute.' And she went inside and combed her hair. Now, women all over the world, if you want to take their photograph, what do they do? They comb their hair. And she came and sat down with a big smile, and Dorothy had her photo. There are always these beautiful little snippets of things to keep you smiling.

We had a volunteer who was a dentist from Massachusetts. And he came across to pull teeth, to do dentistry . . . we sent out word that we would be coming into the villages to pull teeth. And we got in there, and I went with him. And they used to have long wooden seats. So we would line up the people that wanted their teeth looked at. And he had the means of numbing the gum and for pulling teeth, but it used to distress him very much he couldn't do anything about fillings or things like that. And he would put in these syringes, then that person would go to the end of the line and one would move up. By the time we got to the end of the line, it was time for them to go up and...as he pulled the teeth, and we'd do what looked like hundreds in a day, he'd just go 'one, two', over his left-hand shoulder. And by the time we left that village of an afternoon, there would be a whole mass of teeth on the ground. But it wasn't much fun. If you look into the mouth, repeatedly, of someone who's never seen a toothbrush, it took a very sort of dedicated person to do that. We went to village after village, and the people sort of knew we were coming, and this ended one day when we were pulling teeth and all of a sudden a little boy came around the corner and he said, 'Viet Cong come get you!'

So, we used to use an old Jeep, and we just threw everything in that old Jeep and took off across country. And we didn't go back again; we thought that was enough, because we had almost covered the whole area anyhow. He went home to America and ended up the mayor of a city, or something like that. But he came to pull teeth and that's what he did. He pulled teeth.

A man used to come on a bicycle, and he had a huge basket on the back of the bike, and used to carry these beautiful loaves of long, crusty French bread. That was the nicest thing we had to eat. He came every morning, and I used to get up early, and I'd go to see that he had porridge, and a cup of coffee...and one morning I decided, while he was having his porridge, I'd take some of the bread in for him. I looked at the bread, thought to myself, 'Why take in one or two loaves when I can carry the whole lot?'

I went to pick up the basket and I couldn't budge it. And I realised that he was carrying ammunition. He was an ammunition carrier for the Viet Cong. And I thought, 'Oh my God! What do I do?'

So I decided to do nothing. In-between time he saw me lift it and he came out and panicked. But I made out I hadn't seen anything. I went in and sat down with him, and had some porridge with him. Because I was afraid he wouldn't come. And that French bread was the only thing we had worthwhile eating. And not so long after that,

I heard a banging on the door of my room one morning, and went out and there he was, and he was sort of throwing his arms around and trying to say something, which I couldn't understand. So I got an interpreter up, and the interpreter says, 'This man says you no go to town today. You no go to town today.'

Because it was my go to town, for market day.

And I said, 'Why?'

And he said, 'Viet Cong.'

They had bombed some bridge. So they had actually put bombs on the bridge to take me out that morning. So it saved my life. By not reporting this little man, for his gun carrying. So that was a good thing, wasn't it? I wouldn't be here.

* * *

One village was being bombed. After it was over, a girl was brought in screaming, she was a beautiful girl. And we couldn't stop her screaming . . . because she had been going out with an ARVN soldier [Army of the Republic of Vietnam—the South], the Viet Cong had tied her to a chair and made her sit and watch while they cut the throats of her parents. So you can imagine that was something that stayed with us. We couldn't stop her screaming. And they brought her to the hospital, and we tried to quieten her down. But even with what we had, we couldn't stop her crying. And eventually she went home. But she took her own life. And that's understandable, too, isn't it?

We saw quite a few drastic things like that. The Viet Cong would come into the villages, and harass the villagers. For example, one day, the medic I was travelling with in the vehicle, he saved my life, because we were going through a village, and as we got into the middle of the street, there was a body of a man laying, his body here and his head unattached and cut off. My immediate reaction was to cover this so the children of the village wouldn't see. And I was halfway out the door of the Jeep when the medic dragged me back. He said, 'No, no, no. That is the way the Viet Cong control the village. You will do what we ask you to do or we will cut your head off, too!'

And he said if I covered that head, the Viet Cong would have gone after me. So that's the sort of thing that was happening you had to learn to live with. And of course, it worked. Then they would go into a village and they would harass the village and eat all the rice. And meanwhile, they were burrowing under the village. And they would take out enough, and they would build a cavity under the village for themselves to live. And they would come out at night, and harass the people in the surrounding areas. In one village close to us, the village chief used to ask us to buy them rice, and we would bring it home, and they would come to the hospital and fill their pockets and things like that, and take it back. Just to feed themselves. And in one place, the Viet Cong came out and they did a most unforgivable thing. They wrecked the only sewing machine in the village. That was too much. They reported them as being there.

We used to get all these donations from America, they used to come in with all sorts of things . . . and the headquarters would send me out with X boxes, of distributions for people, But I never knew what I was going to get when I opened a box. At one time we had a group of people in from a very mountainous area. The women were topless; the men wore just a little thing. But they were topless, with a sarong from the waist down. And one day I was doing one of these distributions, and I opened up a box and this box was crammed with red brassieres. Now this really created a stir. The women loved them, and from then on you could pick out that particular tribe, because the women were wearing red bras. You could pick them from a mile away.

Another distribution was people had knitted woollen bedsocks. Now, these people had never had anything by the way of footwear in their lives. So, why people would even not . . . sort of say, 'Well, what do they need?' Didn't matter. But anyhow I had these bedsocks. I thought to myself, 'What do I do? What do I do?' So I put one on my head. And they loved caps, because they believed the heat of your body goes out through your head. So once again, I had a whole tribe running around with bedsocks on their head, right? But the worst one was the day I opened a box, put my hand in and came out with a handful of condoms. 'Oh my God! What do I do with these?' So I put one on my finger and as they filed forward I gave them one. I don't know how long they stayed on, but we had all these people running around with condoms on their fingers. They were quite happy . . . they were grateful, for whatever they got, regardless of what it was, they were grateful. What affected me most was their serenity, their acceptance of their situations.

* * *

I was pretty worn out. And in a place like that you live on your nerves all the time. A couple of times I had to evacuate the hospital, because . . . almost every week we'd have a letter from the Viet Cong saying 'We're coming to get you next Friday.'

. . . and all of these things, even if you don't want to let them, they get on your nerves. So I decided it was time to, at least, have a holiday and they had extra people to come in from the States, so I decided to go home . . . I would leave, I would go home and I would think about this. And that actually was towards the end of 1968, so that's a little bit about one year. I had been away from home a year. And a year of entirely different functioning, thinking factor, and I was realising already I wasn't fitting in very well where I'd left. And I realised there was a lot to be done with the Vietnamese people, so it didn't really take much thought.

After a couple of months I was on the plane again and went back, and that was another different experience altogether. Well, my sons didn't seem to be missing me all that much. No mother to nag at them. 'Don't do this, don't do that.' I was concerned, I did feel there were things I could do, that were more humane, necessary than at home. So I did what I had to do at home, like there's all these things to arrange and bills to pay and things like that. And got myself back there.

* * *

I was a Welfare Advisor for Region 3. Region 3 was around Saigon . . .
I was in charge of all the orphanages. I had about thirty orphanages,
I forget how many children. I was supposed to survey; see that they
had food, that they were being looked after and that sort of thing . . .
many of the children in the orphanages were not orphans. I one time
went to President Thieu and I said, 'Would you please designate for
me, give me some sort of direction on what comprises an orphan?'

He says, 'In Vietnam, all children are orphans.'

And the mothers, a lot of them, their husbands were away in the
army. They were working. The women did everything over there.
They built the roads, they did all the jobs. There were no men around
to do them. So they put their children in orphanages. And of course,
in orphanages they got a good education, and a lot of the orphanages
were well run . . . Unfortunately, as happens with so many things, so
many of the orphanages for the people that ran them were a way of
making money. They had all these thousands of American troops
there, who were very generous.

One of the orphanages for example, on the way to one of the
military bases, used to make it possible for the men going past in
the trucks to see their little children. Some would have singlets on
and no pants; some would have pants on and no singlets. And of
course, the boys would see this and they'd pull up and they'd say,
'This can't happen.' And they would write home to get their parents
to send them singlets or whatever. And that was because the nun
said they couldn't afford to have them all fully clothed. This was a
typical way they had of making money, because what came back
would go on the black market, and the children would continue to
run around like that . . . so when the soldiers would take the singlets
in, they'd probably take a whole lot of other goodies as well, and
continue to do that. That was done in many forms.

Most of them wore religious gowns, but there was nothing to say
that any of them were ordained priests or nuns. The Vietnamese men
and others, some worked as spies, and some worked off in the army,
they wore the nuns' habits, so you never really knew who you were
talking to. I discovered that at other places, the nuns were getting

medical attention. Each unit of men, air force and army, that were based there, they had a medical team that used to take the medicines to the villages and to the people, and they used to go the orphanages and whoever was in charge would trot out all these little children, with their ailments, and the medical team would give them medicine and care, and I took my interpreter one time, I had a beautiful interpreter, to watch one of these medical visits. And she came to me and she said, 'All these little children are all saying the same ailments. And I met a nun and she was telling them all what to say.'

So in other words, these children were getting medicines that they didn't really need. And we found at this particular place, we had three medical teams going there in the same week, so if the children were actually getting injections or whatever, they could be getting three injections a week, which was detrimental.

And another one was when a man had a big sign saying, 'Come and support this orphanage.' And to get there you had to go down this small lane. And somebody said there was something funny about it, so I went to have a look myself. And I found that when I got in the beginning of the lane, a loud whistle blew. And then a lady came out and kept you there talking for a while. What was happening was the man in charge of this so-called orphanage used to blow this whistle, and all the little kids of the community would run around and pretend to be orphans. So we called him 'The Whistleblower', but that's how he got his children. You never failed to be amazed at the things they would think up to get money from the troops. So you had to try and be one step ahead of these people all the time.

* * *

We had lots of problems with the graft and corruption. America sent in a tremendous lot of food, food aid, and each welfare office was supposed to get a certain amount. I found that they were bringing in, say, twenty ton of rice, and signing it off as eighteen and they would keep the rest for themselves. So I threatened to go to the source, to expose what they were doing. We had the welfare chief, and she said, 'If you do this, you won't get back to Saigon alive.'

... I went back to the office one day and my counterpart, the welfare officer, was in a great state of affairs, because a priest had been in to tell her that he had overheard they were putting a bomb in the old car I used. And he was frantic that I would get in the car, before he could tell me. Fortunately, or I wouldn't be here, he caught my interpreter and told her not to use the car. So we called over one of these bomb experts, and yes, the bomb was there ... in a war zone you've got to expect these things to happen. You walked around; you knew it was always there. People ask, was I afraid? I guess the adrenaline was working all the time. But actual fear, I suppose like everything else, you get used to it, in the back of your head. You just wouldn't carry on if you went around crazy and afraid all the time.

... You sort of had to learn that when you walked into an orphanage, the little children and babies would be lying in their cots. And whereas we sort of wrap babies up in swaddling clothes, these little babies would be lying there, and admittedly, it was quite warm. But they wouldn't have any clothes on at all. But the bottom of the cot had slats, so if their bowels or anything moved, it went straight through, didn't it? Onto the floor, which was simple. Because it was just as easy to clean up the floor as to wash nappies, and they couldn't afford nappies anyhow, right? But you had to learn all these things and look at them in a factual sort of a way. To me that was a much easier way than washing a hundred nappies. And the floors were hosed out. So they were kept nice and clean. And there were just so many things ... And, of course, with the troops ... there was a lot of them that would take toys to the children, and they would take lollies, other sorts of food. I had a lot of trouble with milk. In Vietnam the children don't have cows' milk, no cows. But they have a rice milk. It's milk made by boiling and boiling rice. But of course the American troops would bring in all these gallons of milk. And the next thing I would have a whole orphanage with all the kids with diarrhoea. And that was very difficult to explain to the troops.

'No, they don't have milk.'

There was this orphanage and TB centre and aged people's centre. It was three storeys. The little children were down below, then we had the people with ˉB . . . but these aged people and the sick people, they were on beds possibly two foot wide. This whole dormitory of these people lying, just lying on these beds. And I looked at it, and thought, 'Oh my God, imagine having nothing to do except lay there, waiting to die.'

And in my Western imagination, I decided I've got to do something about this. So I went and I rounded up a whole bunch of television sets, card games, radios. I was so proud of myself. I would give them something to look at, something to do, all this sort of thing. I was so proud of myself, and I had all these things. And I went to the lady manager of this, and I said, 'I have this for you, I have TV sets for all your people to watch.'

And this and that and that.

'Ba Rose,' she said. 'I know you like us very much, and we appreciate all the things that you do for us. But thank you, no.'

'What?'

She said, 'If I have a TV set on, for some it is too loud, some can't see, some will want a different program. If I have a radio it is just the same. Some people will turn it down, some people will want it turned up. If I give them card games, they are great gamblers. Whereas now they get a little money every week. Somebody would end up with all of that money.'

She said, 'I'm just here working it out on my electricity bill. Even those small things would add to this bill which I find very difficult to pay.'

So there I learnt to stop thinking with my great western mind. And from then on I sent the things to other places, but we gathered together pretty picture books, and some pretty bed coverings, and we worked on an entirely different happening for that place. The civic action guys, they decided instead of seeing all these women washing by hand, they would buy them washing machines. But there wasn't enough water. You know how it puts the water through and it runs away? There wasn't enough water. And a sister said there wasn't enough electricity. So last thing seen by me, those washing machines were still sitting there, serving as a cupboard. So, as I said, that was one of my great lessons. To never think with my mind, to ask the people first if they wanted to.

* * *

I had another favourite orphanage. It was a little one in the country. Father Tean came to me and he said they'd received a rocket through the roof, and six children had been killed, and please could we get someone to repair the roof? Which I was able to do, because the air force, the American Air Force, the civic action, came and did it for them . . . It came Christmas time, and Father Tean came and brought me an invitation out to have a Christmas meal with them. I went out of course, and the children all sang little Christmas songs for me. And Father said, 'We're going to eat now.'

And we went in, and on my plate were two church sparrows. You think of a little sparrow, and the feathers have been plucked off him, and he's been cooked, he's very small. There were actually four of them on the plate. Father said, 'You know we're very poor. But we feel this is something special for you.'

I thanked him. I'll never forget this thing. I sat down, and I said, 'Oh my goodness. We've got one each.'

So there we were, all nibbling on these tiny little sparrow bones.

And after the meal, Father said, 'We also have a present for you.'

And I said, 'Yes, what is that?'

And he said, 'Come with me.'

And I walked out. And in the courtyard of this orphanage, they had this real old monkey. And every time when I'd been there I'd went out and said a few words to the monkey and gave him a little pat. Father Tean said, 'We know that each time you've come here, you go and you look and you like our monkey. So we have decided to give you our monkey for yourself.'

Fourteen years ago, the Father and his nuns had walked, all the way from Hanoi, to build that orphanage, and they had brought the monkey with them. I had to do a quick flip, and I said, 'I have no place. But I love my monkey, would you keep him here for me?'

And everybody smiled again . . . some years later, Father came to my office. He refused to speak to the manager of the office; he just wanted to see me personally. And eventually he caught me. He said, 'I have just come to ask you what I have to do.'

I said, 'What do you mean, Father?'

He said, 'Your monkey.'

I said, 'Is my monkey well?'

He said, 'Yes, he's just become a father. And we would like to ask you, what would you like to do with the monkey's son?'

I said I was very excited; to have the second monkey, but once again please keep him for me. So that was Father Tean and his children.

I owned two monkeys in Vietnam . . . but the first one, he was a great delight to me. He lived out in the back. I guess he was everybody's monkey. But he lived out on a tree, near the back door of the office. And he was very cheeky. He absolutely disliked dogs. And if a dog came past him he would jump down out of his tree and get on its back, until the dog threw him off, screaming its head off. And he also disliked some of the staff. Don't ask me why. Perhaps they tormented him, but when they walked past he would spit on them. He was his own monkey. And then one time we evacuated the hospital, we went back, and he'd gone. Some Vietnamese people take monkeys, take the top off their heads and eat the brains.

* * *

In the orphanages, particularly the ones in the country, they had no medical help, really. So I found that quite a number of them had what they called a 'dying room' . . . and they just put the child in there to die. And I found this room in this orphanage and this little child was very close to death, and the manager didn't want me to take her, but I insisted on taking her. I took her home, found a lady to care for her, got her the medicine, and she was doing quite well. I called her Small One. I was actually thinking about seeing if I could adopt her. But one day to my desk came a young American soldier, who asked for me. He explained how his buddy, a Vietnamese soldier, used to take him home. And he used to play with this man's child. This fellow, this American had come back from America. And he promised this Vietnamese soldier that he would take care of this child. Well, the Vietnamese man got killed. And the wife, because she couldn't take care of the child, put her into this orphanage. And this American managed to get himself back to Vietnam, as a civilian, to get this child. But of course when he arrived there, the child was not there. So the lady in charge she sent him to me, and this little child, she would never smile. You could never get her to smile ... and he walked in, and she got the most beautiful smile. And she recognised him and he took her back to America. So it was quite a story, wasn't it?

* * *

I was sitting on the front porch one afternoon, actually I was sitting there and I was watching a B-52 raid in the distance. But a little man came around the corner of the house, and he said, 'Viet Cong come get you, five o' clock.'

And I said, 'Yes.'

But then I saw from the next village, the people all moving past. People laden up with all their goods and chattels, everything they could carry. Every man, woman and child were carrying something and going slowly down the road. And when they sent for an interpreter, he said they had been warned that the Viet Cong were coming into the hospital at five o' clock, and they would come through this village to get to us. So they were moving in. Now, it was sort of getting on about three or four o' clock in the afternoon, so I sent around to all the staff to be ready, to do the moving, and the patients that could went off to live in the woods somewhere.

And when I looked to our staff, to say, 'Well, what are we going to do? Are we going to stay here or move or whatever?', we found we didn't have a vehicle. One of our vehicles was in Da Lat with mechanical problems. And it was Unkar, our maintenance man; it was his day off to get high, really, and he was away. So we didn't have a vehicle ... and we were just about getting ready to walk, and

Unkar and the old vehicle came around the corner. We dashed down to the gate, with all we could carry. We all jumped on, I think there were about thirteen of us, got into that old vehicle and turned around and went back along the road. When we got to the American outpost, I said to them 'Look, drop me off here. Then I can wait and see what happens, and I can listen to what the soldiers say. And if nothing happens I'll be close to go back. But you go on into Da Lat.'

And I'd rang ahead and I asked the Americans in there could they find a place where the staff could stay...now, that was a very memorable night. I don't know if it was fear or what it was. But I had dinner with the men, then they'd allocated me one of the rooms they kept for the occasional guest. But all of a sudden, that was it. Was I sick! I had diarrhoea one way and vomiting the other way. And there I was. And the latrines on a men's outpost were not exactly meant for privacy. And what could I do? I'd go in and get out as quick as I could. Or I'd be in there throwing up or something and a soldier would say, 'What the hell are you doing in here?'

'I'm thinking of dying in here.'

Anyhow, I had just got back to bed and the bombs started falling. The incoming rockets started falling on the outpost. And the colonel was running around, 'Get yourself in the bunker! What are you doing in here?'

'Well, Sir, I've got a problem here.'

'What's your problem?'

'I've got diarrhoea, Sir.'

That was one of my most embarrassing nights, let's put it that way.

* * *

There was some ten thousand Vietnamese from the Tet offensive, living in all sorts of buildings made out of cardboard and all sorts of things, on the Saigon River. Now, the American Government, they decided to move those people...to build a village for them at the sea end of the river, even though the place was predominantly mud. First of all they were given money to make a cement floor...I controlled the money by the way, it sounds ridiculous. But then we gave them money to build the walls. Then, from the Australian Government we got roofing iron ... So all this happened over a great period of time. But they had footpaths that were sort of up in the mud, they put areas up so that you could walk a little bit higher. But I could never manage to walk on those mud footpaths without falling over, and the whole village used to turn out to watch me fall in the mud. Which I did frequently. Nevertheless, there came the day when people moved into their house. Even though there might be water running underneath their beds or something, they had a house. And they were celebrating now that everybody had a tin roof, so of course, I had to be there.

There were all of these people who hadn't had a home for a couple of years, all of a sudden had a home. They were fed, they were happy. And it was going to be, and it is now, a very prosperous village, fishing conglomeration. They make their money fishing and apparently it's flourishing ... And they had a table set out the front, and I was asked to sit down at that table. And I wanted to wash my hands. And I knew there was a drum at the back of what was supposed to be this restaurant, so I thought I'd walk around the back, quickly wash my hands. And I got around there, and I saw a man with some meat. I said, 'Oh, what are we having for lunch?'

And he held up a dog, a skinned dog, he had just cut a slice off its hip, and its little black feet ... Anyhow, that was it. I made a point of always eating what they gave me ... time went on and we had a couple of rice beers, and everything, and I forget what else they gave me to eat. A sweet potato sort of thing. And they then, *lad de dah de dah*!! And they brought me in to eat the first meal. It was heart, a dog heart. I had to eat the heart of a dog. That adds to my list of snakes, and sorts of other things that I'd eaten. But I ate it, and I kept it down ... actually, it tasted quite nice. If it hadn't been dog, I would have enjoyed it. And then the men, of course, ate the entrails of the dog. Yes, I've had some fierce meals ... We had a special meal with the people I was travelling with. And it was most unusual. A bit tough. And I said to the people, 'That was very nice. Do you mind telling me what it is?'

And they said, 'It was specially for you today, we are serving penis of the ox.'

There isn't much I haven't eaten, somewhere along the line... Oh dear. Then we come to the toilets... a lot of them are over water. And generally, in the water they're growing fish. I was never happy about eating the fish. And of course, it was up on stilts, and you walked in, and if you were lucky there was a bit of drape of some sort down the front, and you just do what you have to do. Funnily enough, the whole village would come out to watch. If anybody was standing around it was like you were putting on a show. They'd come and watch... Oh dear.

* * *

I used to have to deliver the dead, in the old van. Back into the villages. Because it was very important that the person was buried in their own area. And we didn't have any elaborate sort of special covers or anything. We just had the thick paper sheets. So you would roll them up like a cocoon, and tie it at both ends of this paper sheet. And then we'd put them onto a stretcher in the back of the old ambulance, and I'd drive off to the village. And that was a fantastic experience also. Because remember there was no telephone, but they had a very sort of wonderful bush telegraph factor. Because I would perhaps be two miles from that village and I would start to hear keening. Keening is their wailing. And it gets louder and louder and louder, until I got to the village. But I don't know how they knew I was coming. Anyhow, mostly there was a bed ready... to put this body on.

But this day I went into the village with this old fellow. And it was apparently a Viet Cong occupied village... if the Viet Cong controlled the village, they'd be afraid to talk to me, in case they got into trouble. So they would all disappear. They would leave a bed out, and they would all disappear. Now, normally, there would be somebody there to help me off with the body. This day I was left with it on my own. Fortunately he was just a little fellow. I picked him up as best as I can, like that, but the paper burst open, and he burst open

I was just . . . covered in fluid, stinking fluid, round all the way . . . I put him on the bed, jumped in the car, and drove back because I had seen a creek. I stopped the car and I ran down to the creek and I was washing myself off, and a little voice came out of the woods and said, 'There are Viet Cong here, go, go!'

I didn't care. I didn't care who was there. I just had to get out of it and get washed.

Another day, with a dead body, I had to get it to a village. Because the village chief had died and I had to get it there. And it was way up in the boonies. And I rang through to request a helicopter. And the colonel said, 'Look, you're asking a lot. We've got a battle going on out there, you know!'

I said, 'I appreciate that Sir, but if you could just detour I'd be most gracious.'

He said, 'Is it a matter of life or death?'

I said, 'Yes.' I said, 'It has to go back to the village, for, you know the reasons.'

And he said, 'I'll have a chopper there in ten minutes, it will set down for five minutes, and then it's gone. So whatever you have, get it there.'

So we had this dead fellow. The boys were halfway through making a coffin, a wooden coffin, out of thick planks. So I said don't do the nails, because they put in all his chattels. When a Montagnard man dies, he has to have all his gourds and all that sort of thing, along with him. And let's get it out to the pad. So we put it in the back of the old van, and we took the boys along with us. He had two of his rellies along with us. So we had it all there. By the time that chopper set down, we had it all ready to just slide off into the chopper. Which we did. With the boards just sitting on top. And we practically flew his rellies in on top of it. And I said to the chopper pilot, 'The colonel said life or death. He's dead.'

A long time before they'd speak to me, after that one. That really did get me into trouble. But it got him home.

And then another time when we were ferrying a guy to hospital because he didn't have anybody to claim him. The medics went over and they dug a hole for the coffin on the side of the hill, made the coffin, then about four or five of them carried it across and the coffin wouldn't fit in the hole. So I thought they would take spades and just make it a little big bigger. But they didn't. They set it as neatly as they could on top of the hole, and then there was some sort of signal I didn't get, they all jumped on the top of it. And forced it down ... and I said a few of the words I could remember of the service, and he was gone.

* * *

Vietnamese wives absolutely amazed me. They had the art of being able to twist their husbands around their little finger without him knowing it ... I used to watch them and think 'Wow!'. The women were incredible people, are incredible people. For example, they would be working on the roads, or they would be working in garbage or anything, but they would wear hats in the sun, they would have long gloves. Their face would be part-covered if they were working outdoors. And they would work in these really dirty jobs. But come home at night, they would be impeccable—like their hands and everything. They were working on the roads, the dirty roads, and they'd come home and they would look as if they just sort of stepped out of a shop or something. They're able to do this.

The *ao dai*, you know, is a beautiful garment. It not only looks good, but they worked at never getting dirty. They would carry a little handkerchief thing with them. Now, if we sat down on a seat, they would first of all wipe the seat, and then flip the *ao dai* up the back, it was a double back, before they sat down, so the *ao dai* never got dirty. And if it was raining they would pull it up over their head. But it really is a very versatile garment. We would go out on a day, working, and they would come with me on the planes, on the helicopters, on the gunships, wherever. They would come with me. And they would step out neat and tidy at the end. They never showed any fear. But they came with me, wherever I went, they would come with me. And this was incredible, I learnt a lot from them. I was very lucky.

I always had one or two Vietnamese women working with me. And I would get a message to say something like: 'Tomorrow will be a windy day, and windy wind makes me feel ill, so I can't come in.'

It was because she had her periods coming. Nothing to do with the wind at all. But they had all these beautiful little excuses, rather than say what was happening. They would put it more nicely to you . . . you would see these little shoes lined up on a bridge and I was horrified when my interpreter says, 'She's jumped in the water to drown.'

And I said, 'Oh dear, can we do something?'

And she said, 'Not to worry.' She said, 'She won't jump until she sees somebody there to rescue her.' I said, 'Why does she do it?'

She said, 'Well, that's what you do.'

Perhaps she had had an argument and her boyfriend had left her. So she is supposed to be very sad, and do something drastic. Well, she'd attempted it and done the right thing, hadn't she? Whether she survived, didn't matter. But she had done the right thing, by proclaiming her grief or anger or whatever it was, by doing the accepted thing of suicide. I have never heard of any of them that didn't get someone there to pull them out. But it was an accepted thing. It comes back once again to the little quirks in our culture, doesn't it? They wouldn't tell you anything that was really sad. They would concoct some other little story that was much nicer listening to for me, than the real story.

* * *

A village was built as to what the location provided. A village would have a school, the normal little plank desks, a typical thatched roof or whatever they could get on it. It would have had as much land as they could get, that was growing rice. And remember, in these villages there are very few men. For example, if you went into a village and there were no men, but a couple of dozen pregnant women, you would know that there was a high possibility that it could be NVA [North Vietnamese Army]. That is, a North Vietnamese village. And the men were hiding. Or it could be that they were

Viet Cong, and they came home often. Like they had to come home sometime, didn't they? To get the women pregnant.

There was no such thing as a typical village. The people all very much cared for and looked after one another. They were not bright places. You know what I mean? You go into a little community here, somebody grows flowers . . . at one time, often, the village chief used to ask me for more of the food. The American food. And I'd say things like, 'No, this is all I have. This is a ration that I have at this particular time.' Because it was so much per person per village.

'But how would you like me to bring you out some vegetable seeds? You have the land, you have a river there, you have so much water. And you can grow this. I've got seeds for whatever you want. So all you've got to do is ask me for seeds, and I will see that you get seeds, that you can plant and grow your own food.'

Not one village asked me. Not one village really wanted the seeds, to plant their own crops.

The practical thing was to do nothing. The sensible thing was to do nothing. There was one village, my interpreter had a rellie in this village . . . Once again, this was an all-women village, and they grew tea and they produced quite a lot in that village . . . we used to go in because her grandmother used to give me tea, she used to grow tea. And I said, 'How do you dry it?'

And she showed me how she put it out the front on a flat mat until the sun dried it.

I said, 'But how did you get it crushed up into little pieces?'

She said, 'Very simple. I put the mat out when the children are coming home from school. And as they walk past, they all go crunch, crunch, crunch, with their feet. And that makes the tea all chomped up.'

I lost the feeling for her tea that she gave me and passed it on to somebody else. But that was a very happy village.

* * *

An American would go into a village where they wanted to do something; he would tell them what they were to do. I would go in and ask them what they thought about this, and what they had heard about this, what's your idea? So I got on, and I could get it done. So I was able to get things done, that they were not able to do. When I left, of course, they put on a great do, and they gave me the meritorious honour, and apologised because the medal couldn't be of a higher quality, because once again getting back to the fact that I was a 'Third Country National'. So that was the best that they could do. So I was given a great deal of assistance. I think there was some sort of an impression that I was quite crazy. My what-the-hell attitude. They were not quite sure about that.

I went to see my interpreter one evening. And her husband was home. He was an officer in the South Vietnamese Army. And he had a friend there, a cousin, or something, who was an officer in the South Vietnamese Air Force. And they decided they would walk home with me, better to walk home with me, make sure that I got home safely. And we sat down in a marketplace to have a bowl of soup. You didn't have a cup of coffee; you had a bowl of soup in Vietnam. And we started talking, and they said how difficult it was. They said in Vietnam there were the NVA, the North Vietnamese soldiers and Viet Cong...but as one said, 'What we're being asked to do is to go out there and kill. But we don't know if we're killing our cousin, the man down the street, or who. Because we never know.'

And we never knew what side—they could work for you in the office during the day, and be Viet Cong at night. They said, 'We repeatedly hear of the Americans pulling out, which we know is going to happen not too far off. Where are we then? Are they taking their money with them? Does that mean we won't have any gas for our aeroplanes? Does this mean we won't have this, we won't have that? Are they taking with them the guns? What are we going to be left with, if anything? We're criticised,' which they were repeatedly, 'as being lazy and not being good soldiers. But mostly our criticism comes from soldiers who are very well-fed. Who have the very best equipment.' He said, 'Our meals, if we're out away from a normal place. We carry two pocketfuls of rice and a tin of fish.' He said 'That's our meals.'

See, some of the Americans in the field used to have their hot meals delivered. It sounds ridiculous, but it's true. And they had this beautiful tinned food. And the Vietnamese lived on pocketfuls of rice.

'So they're criticising us from their full bellies. That gives them increased energy.'

And we had no means of answering this. And they went on to tell me their side of the story. And I often said to myself, 'If I was a Vietnamese, would I be Viet Cong, or would I not?'

I honestly thought that many times I would be a Viet Cong, because they were fighting directly for their families. It was a very, very complicated war.

I was walking out of the office, and walking back to the chopper pad, to get back to Bien Hoa, and I walked past six dead Vietnamese war-wounded men, lying on a pallet, ready to be picked up I guess, and taken back. And it didn't mean a thing. I walked past them as if I'd been walking past a stack of wood. I said to myself, 'It's time you went home.'

You know, I had so completely lost compassion, I looked at those and it didn't mean anything. So that's when I made the very positive decision 'It's time you left here.' Yes.

* * *

It was harder to come home than it was to leave. Because I'd been out of the world for four years. Out of the world. And of course, the friends that I had before I went away . . . I was a different person. I am a different person. But they had stayed in the same town, and they were all talking to the same people, and they were all looking at the same TV shows. With a lot of people in those days, if you get together and you're talking to them, they relate to the latest football, or the latest *This Is Our Lives,* or something like that. Of course, I couldn't join in those conversations, could I? I went into Hong Kong at one time, to a ladies' meeting, where they were discussing reporting to a cosmetics company that the lip rouge didn't quite match the lipstick. And my friend quickly got me away, before I blew my top. I don't know that I've ever really got back into this world.

But there were so many things like that. And you never really come home. A lot of these Vietnam veterans, you never really come home. You certainly don't come home the same person. Because you've seen a totally different aspect of life. But yes, it was hard. It was hard... I've never had the courage to ask my two sons what they thought of me going to Vietnam. I've never had the courage to ask them. Now they're both in their fifties, perhaps... perhaps they'd give me an honest answer. Well, they've always had a weird mother. Their mother was always doing different things.

I had two jobs then. I was matron at two geriatric hospitals. That took six years. After I left those, I was coordinator of the first women's shelter. I worked there, all these jobs were twenty-four-hour jobs. I worked there for four and a half years, at the shelter. Then I thought I'd retire and get a little old lady's sort of tea and scone shop. And I did that. And I made the scones and I made the pikelets. But of course the people that I'd helped during my term at the shelter; they all came to visit, didn't they? And I didn't charge them, did I? And my sons called it Mother's Soup Kitchen... the business was good. Except I gave away the profit. Anyhow, that wasn't working all that well. And one day, a young American came in, he actually came in to see me, because he had heard that I had done things and I could possibly tell him things he could do as a volunteer. So we got to talking, and I told him what he could do. And he said, 'What would you like to do next?'

I said, 'I would like to put a welfare program into a leprosy hospital in India.'

He said, 'Have you got a pencil and paper?'

I gave him a pencil and paper. He wrote this and that down, and he says, 'My uncle runs one.'

His uncle. His uncle was running a leprosy hospital in West Bengal. So I wrote to his uncle, who was a priest by the way, Father Kent. And his uncle wrote back and he said, 'I have been praying for seventeen years for somebody to ask me that question.'

So I closed up my shop, and went to India for a year.

FRANK McGOVERN

Sailor
Prisoner of the Japanese

The Battle of Sunda Strait opened up at about eleven o'clock and only lasted about an hour to an hour and a half; we were engaging what turned out to be the Japanese western invasion fleet of Java.

At one stage . . . we could see the Jap gunners from about three thousand yards away. They opened up with their searchlights on us and we put those out with our short-range weapons but then according to Jap sources they fired eighty-seven torpedoes at the two ships, [USS] *Houston* and [HMAS] *Perth*, so they had to hit a few of them, which they did. We were out of ammunition at that time, this was signalled to the skipper . . . and then he decided to head the ship through the Strait. We had just picked up speed of about thirty knots, almost full speed, when the first torpedo hit the starboard boiler room, the forward boiler room and wiped out all the crew there. And it almost lifted the ship out of the water; we're doing thirty knots, 7000-ton ship and the force of that torpedo! I was on the upper deck and I was thrown off my feet and a few of the others were too. It lifted the ship up momentarily and as it settled back again and the heat from the torpedo blast was like opening a furnace door as it swept down the upper deck. Well that reduced speed to about ten knots and after that it was just a matter of time. The second torpedo hit up forward, we got numerous hits from the shellfire, I think the forward stack was knocked out and from the shrapnel there a lot of the fellas on the signal deck were killed or

wounded. The starboard pom-pom had received a direct hit and also
A turret, and then after the second torpedo hit, the order came
through to abandon ship. It was useless and then another torpedo
hit on the port side. I went down to the quarterdeck to go over. I
had a pair of sandals on, it was just instinctive, I just kicked them
off you know, take your boots or shoes off when you go into the
water and as I was doing that the fella next to me said, 'Aren't you
going over?'

There were still shells coming over and explosions in the water
and I said, 'Yeah, as soon as I kick these off'.

I had my Mae West slightly on; the Mae West, you might have
heard of it, it was a life jacket that you partially blew up, fitted
across your chest, and it was named after that buxom actress, Mae
West. As I went over the side I thought, 'I'm clear of everything,
clear of the fellas in the water.'

The next minute I was sucked under the ship because one of the
screws was still slowly turning and as I came down under the stern
of the ship, I could see these huge blades coming down, lit up by
the phosphorous in the water, and I said my last prayer there I think,
and then the next one up, heard the swish as it went down, then I
was dragged in and tumbled around, like in a giant washing machine,
and then shot aft, terrific speed from that slowly turning propeller,
and I ended up surfacing about two hundred yards from the ship,
almost out of the water, so I looked back and saw the ship just
drifting away and a few other blokes in the water and I called out,
so we got on to a Carley float from our ship, the Carley float was
damaged by shellfire in one corner but it was still okay, still floatable,
there might have been about a dozen of us on that.

From there we floated around for a while trying to dodge the Jap
destroyers that we heard chugging up and down the Strait and then
from there we got on to a lifeboat which was almost under water,
it was off one of the Jap transports and we bailed that out and got
into that. But the *Perth* by that time was lit by the searchlights from
the Jap destroyers and was just slowly sinking by the bow, as she
went down, gathered speed and just went beneath the water, you

know, you looked at it and that was your home for so long, and I thought, jeez, it was like what you might call a sinking feeling as you saw it go down.

Anyway the water wasn't cold; it was warm in the water. We got into this lifeboat, covered in oil fuel. We headed towards what we thought was the coastline, it was still just early morning, pre-dawn, and still with the current so strong we weren't making much headway. There was a tattered sail in the boat that we saw and we thought that might be handy, we had great thoughts about we sail this and make our way to Australia but this didn't happen. About midmorning, it was coming up pretty hot by that time, the shoreline was still quite a distance away and we were rowing a bit and we were pretty tired by this time and exhausted after two or three days closed up at action stations, so we were still making progress a little bit, a little bit at a time and there was a Jap destroyer on the other side of the Strait which was just patrolling up and down and we saw it peel off and head towards us and I thought, 'Oh yes, we'll keep rowing anyway.'

As it moved nearer to us, a few hundred yards away, the skipper came down on the fc'c'sle through a loud hailer and yelled out to stop in English. I thought, 'Oh bugger you, you know, we'll keep going.'

So we kept rowing. With the shoreline a few hundred yards away, a Jap destroyer a few hundred yards that way, so we kept rowing. Then they trained a forward gun on us, it was a 5.9 you know. So looking down the barrel from about five hundred yards away or less, at that 5' gun, there wasn't much future in that, so the order came through to stop, so we were cowards, we stopped.

They took us on board, had to discard all our clothing, it was covered in oil fuel, but they were all right on the destroyer, they gave us kerosene, cotton waste, to clear the oil fuel out of our eyes and ears, some of the fellows were blinded by it, the hair was matted, we were just like painted you know, we were black. And then they picked up a few more of the fellows floating around on bits of planks or whatever, they were exhausted too, so we dragged them on board and the destroyer then gave us water and explained the situation with regard to their rationing of water. These fellows were British trained originally, the navy, the Jap Navy, whereas the army I think was German trained. Anyway they were quite okay on the destroyer. Then from there they took us to a transport, Japanese transport, *Somdong Maru* and there were a few Yanks there off the *Houston* and thirty or forty of us I think off the *Perth* and we were on there for about a week. We were not treated too badly there and then we were taken ashore. I think the Jap destroyer captain spoke fairly good English and said that you would now be handed over as prisoners of war, I would say to the Japanese Imperial Army, more or less apologising that we were going to be handed over to the Jap Army as prisoners of war. So as it was we were taken ashore at a place called Merak in Western Java and it was an embarkation point for the ferry service over to Sumatra. So we just had Jap g-strings on, underpants at that time, a bit of string and a piece of cloth about that long and about that wide which you put underneath and lapped it over, like a lap-lap, so that's all we had for the next six weeks.

* * *

We were brought ashore, lined up in front of this waiting shed, made to squat down, and as we looked up there was a Jap Army officer with two machine guns in the enfilade position on either side just pointing at us, and he explained to us that we were POWs in broken English and, 'If you try to escape you will be shot.'

Oh yeah, what chance have we got of escaping? . . . So we were there for about an hour or so squatting in the sun while they made up their minds what to do with us and I just glanced around the waiting shed . . . I thought—what did I see? So I looked again. There was a poster stuck to the wall of the waiting shed, pretty big poster, and it had a painting or a photo of the Three Sisters in the Blue Mountains so I said 'Jeez!' and in a caption in Dutch and also in Indonesian and English it said, '*Come to sunny New South Wales*'. I thought, 'Oh jeez, wouldn't I like to be there now!'

So we weren't allowed to speak to one another so I just nudged the bloke next to me. I just indicated, 'Have a look at this.' When he looked at it he couldn't believe his eyes—'*Come to sunny New South Wales*'—oh it can't be true.

From there we were just loaded into trucks and taken off to this place, Serang I think the natives called it, a native village. That was a dreadful place, we were stuck in the local cinema that they used just to house the prisoners, and there were hundreds in there already taken prisoner when we got there. It was like a tile floor, no seats, and you just had to squat one behind the other down the main aisle leading down on either side, we were in rows with Jap machine guns on either side of the projection room, and the guards on either door and at the entrance and we soon learnt there that we had to salute the Japanese, from the officer right down to the lowest private, and very forcibly we were told we had to salute and if we didn't we just got a bashing, be it with a rifle butt or with the fist.

We were there for about six weeks and our meal in the morning, we thought these Japs only have two meals a day, so we had a tenko in the morning; a tenko is the muster and they're hopeless at counting, they were just hopeless, they would come down and this row they'd number, '*Ichi ni san chi*,' then the next row, the next row, right down to the stage and then they'd do it for the other side. That might go on for an hour or an hour and a half. There we are crossed-legged just sitting there. A bowl of rice cooked by the natives was left outside in the hot sun in these little tin plates while this tenko went on, and then when it was brought in with this pinch of salt on the top, probably myriads of flies had descended on them. We'd have that rice in the morning and then anything from say eight o'clock to ten o'clock at night we'd get a small bun, be about that big. If you chewed your food thirty-two times as you are supposed to chew each mouthful. I used to chew that sixty-four times till there was nothing left in your mouth, you know it would just melt.

So after about a week of eating this stuff, caked hard on top so you could just eat it with your fingers, dirty, filthy and most of the blokes had dysentery after about a week or two. The latrine outside was just a pit, dug probably about eight foot by six foot . . . with a few branches across to squat on and . . . every afternoon you'd get a heavy downpour of rain midafternoon, consequently there were hundreds of blokes with dysentery and the rainwater filling this latrine up, it was getting pretty full and when we stood up we'd have a blackout because we were weak. So this afternoon just after a heavy downpour of rain, this fellow stood up and he swayed a bit and had a bit of a blackout and wanted to go to the toilet, so out past the guard, gave him a bow, went to the latrine, had a bit of a giddy turn while he was there, put his hand—there was a tree there— near the end of the latrine, he put his hand against it, the tree trunk was all wet from the shower of rain and his hand slipped off and he took a header into this mess and all you could see were his feet and his ankles, so the blokes that were there dragged him out and everything went crazy. So the Jap he sort of, 'What was going on?' took him into the street and threw him into the river, the muddy river and cleaned him up. That poor bugger, he went a bit bonkers for a couple of days I think.

A Jap officer used to come in every day or every second day and he would be all dressed up, they were all smartly dressed, he'd come in, and you'd know when he was coming and the Jap guards would '*Squatski*!' they'd yell out which was 'attention' and he'd just stand there and look down at us filthy, dirty, mass of humanity, you know, he'd just look at us as if we were not worth looking at see, and he'd pull his Luger out of his holster and there was deathly silence in the theatre. Hundreds of us there, not a word.

* * *

We were there for about six months I think in Java, working parties each day, organised down to the wharves, loading ships...barrels of oil, pushing them along, stacking them up and all these kerosene tins, I can remember all these kerosene tins coming off the assembly line, all nice, brand new, shiny, neat, we had to stack them all up, the Nips were taking them somewhere. So one of the fellows got a piece of iron, sharpened piece of iron metal, so he said, 'See what we can do with some of these tins.'

So we said right, so as we passed them along the line this sharp piece went into the bottom of each tin as it went up to be stacked up, so that was our bit of sabotage for the tins. Anything we could do, we did. Now there were big crates of machinery, huge crates of machinery and in the top of them, we prised the lid off when the Jap guards weren't looking and we saw all the instructions written out there and you know, what to do, so we just got those and just ripped them up and put the lid back on. Whether it did any damage, any good or not. But we tried everything, we did all that.

* * *

From Java, the Australian prisoners were taken through Thailand and began forced labour on the infamous Burma Railway.

During the wet season, blokes were dying like flies, with dysentery, malaria, beri-beri. With the beri-beri, your feet, ankles and face would swell up, it would be like puffy, like a mound of dough, and your hands would be puffed up, and you would put your finger in and push the flesh in like that and the hole would stay there like that for a couple of minutes until it gradually moved out. You know some blokes died through drowning in their own water, into their lungs and that, they'd fill them up with water, they could hardly see out of their eyes sometimes, they were just slits and puffed up. But with a combination of beri-beri and malaria more or less that was it.

And then the ulcers, they were shockers. You would only have to have a scratch. If you were ballasting and one of the stones hit your leg and you just cut it or scratched it, after a few days that would fester and it would grow bigger and you could see it growing bigger day by day and then it would be an ugly, horrible sore and it would go in deep, and . . . the doctors used to try to gouge it out with a spoon because they had nothing. Sulphanilamide would have cleared it up I believe, but they didn't even get basic medicine. They cleared it out like that. They called one of the camps there, the hut, the Ulcer Ward. Well, you'd go in there and the stench—rotten flesh and that. With some fellas maybe it would start at the ankle and it would go right up to the knee and the whole sinew would be exposed and the bone it would be that deep, this rotten flesh. Poor fellows had legs amputated with primitive equipment, but they did the job and they came through all right. They'd beg some of the doctors to take their leg off, the pain was absolutely shocking. But quite a few died from the ulcers and subsequent disease, malnutrition, malaria, dysentery . . . well you've heard all that anyway. Some of our fellas did get cholera but died through it. But not too many, we were given injections by the Nips, I think I've still got the mark on my arm where the blunt needle went in after about a thousand blokes had been given this needle, you know. Got a bit blunt.

* * *

Some of the Jap guards or Korean guards along the line, we called them by names, the ones we didn't like, there was one bloke called 'Holy Joe' who used to come along to our church services, he was a Christian, he'd be at the back, he wouldn't join in, he wasn't a bad Nip, but there was another fellow, we called him 'George'. He was trying to learn English; he came to me one day and said pointing to the sky, 'sly'? Couldn't say k, 'sly?'

'No, George, sky.'

'Oh.'

You could imagine him behind a plough you know, a peasant.

'All right, George.'

'Berry difficult.'

I said it was.

'Berry difficult, George, almost bloody impossible, you know, buddy.'

But some of the fellows taught them to swear, it was the worst thing they could do because if one of our blokes had got into a bit of trouble and swore at a Nip, this Nip got on to it and one bloke had a terrific bashing one day for swearing at this Nip engineer and he was led out. We were all made to sit down, we were all out on the line, sit down, the Jap engineer called the guard, this fellow was led out into the jungle with the Jap guard after he'd been bashed, and he told us afterwards what happened. The Jap guard loaded his rifle and made the fellow walk ten paces and the engineer made him turn with his back to the rifle and he thought this is it, anyhow they fired a shot but it was flying over his head, just to intimidate him. They broke his jaw and he had to get a couple of teeth out and his jaw had to be wired. See the swearing, they had got on to it. It was pretty silly—things like that.

The Korean guards were as bad as the Nips, because they were treated by the Japs as second-class citizens; Japan had occupied Korea for umpteen years . . . and consequently they used to take it out on us—they were bigger than the Japs, bigger blokes, and they packed a lot. We had one fellow called 'The Storm Trooper', he would have been about six feet and he was like a boofhead bloke and he'd wear these jackboots and plod through the camp and he'd have a length of bamboo, be about that thick and he'd belt hell out of you with this length of bamboo, if you were doing something that he thought was wrong, he'd just give you a whack with this. Crikey, he'd belt hell out of you.

One night we were having a bit of a singsong and we were singing, what was it, 'Road to Gundagai', or something like that or 'Irish Eyes Are Smiling'—'you could hear the angels sing' . . . So 'Boofhead', as we called him, this 'Storm Trooper', called the camp interpreter who was Captain Drouer, . . . Englishman—a real good bloke—he survived the war, I saw him a couple of years back. He spoke fluent Japanese so he was called out by 'Boofhead' this time who wanted to know what we were singing, so we were all lined up like . . . the six of us, so the interpreter had to tell him what we were singing. And just prior to that the first air raids were happening on Bangkok . . . So when we came to the words, 'you can hear the angels sing,' 'Boofhead' said we are signalling to, you wouldn't believe this, we are signalling to the bombers.

He said, 'You are not to sing anymore, no more singing!'

With that he bashed the six of us and that was it, no more singing. Captain Drouer, by the way, later on along the line, must have upset the camp commandant because they made him dig a foxhole and they filled it with water after they had bashed him and they made him stand outside the guardhouse for twenty-four hours, and he had to stand in that water-filled hole for two days—they kept filling it up with water and they made a mess of him, he can't use his right hand too well, so he shakes hands with his left, so he survived and he got back, but things like that, they were bad wretches some of them.

* * *

As the war worsened for the Japanese, they began to ship POWs to Japan to utilise them as slave labour. Frank and his mates began their journey.

So we marched through the jungle for a day or two and then we came across some of these temples that had been there for hundreds of years covered with vines and monkeys clambering all over them and we went through there and we slept that night at a rail station I think it was, slept there for the night and then the following day took us through to Saigon. Now Saigon, or Indochina, was occupied by the Japs, I don't think the French fought them, I'm not too sure, but I think it was just occupied so it wasn't like Malaya or Java, it was a different set up. We could sense it and we were a bedraggled looking lot of blokes you know that had been through the jungle, marching through the jungle and on trains, in cattle trucks, so we're a pretty dirty, dishevelled looking lot and we're marching through the streets of Saigon with Jap guards on either side, so we see these French people and a couple of the French girls riding pushbikes. We hadn't seen a white woman for two years so our eyes were sticking out a bit so, 'Look at these . . . !' it was beaut, they were good sorts you know. Anybody would have been a good sort by then.

As we came through the town we smartened our step up instead of dragging ourselves along and the French people came out of their houses . . . and they were giving us the V for victory sign and putting their hands up when the Jap guards weren't looking. So we started to pick our feet up and march a bit better and some of the blokes who had good voices started to sing songs. So one of the blokes knew a bit of the French 'Marseillaise' and so he started singing this, so we know a bit of the tune . . . we picked our step up and the Nips guards saying shut up, you know telling us to keep quiet. Didn't mean a thing, we kept going you see. So more French people came out, probably the Japs knew the French 'Marseillaise', the national song. So we kept singing and then said, 'Okay they don't know who we are, what about "Waltzing Matilda"?'

So we started to sing 'Waltzing Matilda'. And that went pretty well. So we were still singing this as we marched into the camp.

* * *

Thirteen hundred POWs were loaded onto a cargo ship, one of many taking prisoners to Japan. But to American submarines, every Japanese flag on the ocean was a target.

We were shoved down into the hold of this bloody transport, standing-room only in the hold, it was a narrow gangway coming down into the hold and only one could fit down at a time and we were standing there all that day, no air, it was fetid and blokes with dysentery too and the perspiration was just running off you and forming a puddle down the bottom of your feet and blokes were just keeling over left, right and centre and the Jap guard up top was using his rifle butt, nobody up, until we're carting blokes up that had flaked out and finally the Jap, the lieutenant, he could see what was going on and allowed a few up on the deck. We put the salt-water hose on them you know, to bring them to. After that a few were let up on deck providing we behaved ourselves, this was the proviso.

. . . We headed out from Singapore with a few other ships and a few more ships from the Philippines joined us and it was a pretty big convoy, about a dozen more ships, escort on either side and up the forward part and just before dawn on the fifth day out . . . two tankers were hit, they just burst into flames ahead of us. I was on the upper deck at the time forward of the bridge, blokes were sleeping all over the hatch covers and that and then we thought, 'It's on!' and then we heard the Nips clattering across the upper deck in the clogs and I thought, 'Yeah this is it,' and the torpedo hit us midships.

And the Nips in their panic, lowered some of the lifeboats straightaway, and a few minutes after another torpedo hit right up in the forward, right up in the bows, and the geyser of water from that was like a waterfall. Tons of water went up into the air and came down on to us and flattened us through the deck, it was that heavy, and a tidal wave of water swept down over the fo'c'sle and fellas were being swept off their feet you know, they'd come to their feet and swept off their feet, a tremendous amount of water.

So a lot of the blokes went overboard straightaway and some of the 2/2nd Pioneer blokes, the army blokes, they got stuck into the Nips and as they came up from below they were hitting them with these bits of timber, giving it to them... one of the fellows, he was a big bloke, he did a bit of boxing, Frank McGrath, a big tough rooster, he pushed a couple of the Nips under the water and stood on them and kept them under there, drowned them. He did two over and then... he grabbed the Nip officer to take him too, but the Nip officer was pretty strong and he'd already done two over this fellow, they both went down, and that's what happened to them. I didn't sight them after.

... We went down to try to get to the galley, but that was under water, we were looking for food, so I went down aft where the Nips used to have some of the comfort women there, they carried their own women with them, and they'd taken them all off except one who was sitting there on this gangway leading up to the deck, crying her eyes out, seeing us all dishevelled-looking POWs, what was going to happen to her, we weren't interested in her very much... and then the ship started to creak, started to move a little bit, creaking and groaning. I thought, 'I had better get up out of this.'

... By this time a few of our fellows were trying to lower a boat down which the Japs, in their panic, had jammed in the davits. We eventually got it free... We said to the Nip lass, 'Do you want to get into the boat?' indicating the boat, so we tied a rope around her middle and lowered her into the boat and as we lowered her down on to the water, a lot of the blokes were in the water, piled into the boat and I'm on the upper deck with my mate and we don't even have to get our feet wet, we slid down the rope but you couldn't get into the boat because it was packed, there must have been about a hundred on there. Two inches of freeboard, so we hung on to the side of the boat . . . and our blokes were in the water everywhere and the Nips had pulled off about a quarter of a mile in their lifeboats and that ship floated all that day until about dusk.

My mate Jerry Parkes who was with me, he said a couple of blokes swam back to the ship to look for food or whatever, so he said, 'I'm going back to see.'

I said, 'I think I'll stay here, Jerry, I'll hang on here.'

So he swum back to the ship and that was the last I saw of him. That afternoon two destroyers came up, Jap destroyers and the sea was getting a bit choppy by this time, picked up all their own crowd . . . we told the Japs in the boats that there was a Nip woman on board and one of them yelled out, we indicated a woman in Japanese, he said, '*Mati presento presento.*' 'You can have her, we don't want her, she's taking up room in the boat.'

I'm hanging on the side in the water you know. They came over eventually took her, they had side bayonets, took her and also a keg of water that we had managed to put on board and there was another keg of water, so I said to the blokes to cover it up with your feet and with your legs, which they did. Anyhow they took the keg of water and took the girl so I managed to get into the stern sheets at that time on the boat and floated around all that day.

Two Nip destroyers came up that afternoon, picked up all their crowd . . . and we thought, 'Oh yeah, what are they going to do?' because it was pretty choppy water by this time and the skies were lowering and coming up like a storm, and finally they turned, slowly turned, and started to head away and we thought, that's good and a Nip officer came down on to the quarterdeck and through a loud hailer, waved to us and said, 'Goodbye, goodbye.'

So we gave him a sailor's farewell and let him have it we said, 'Hope the bloody Yankee subs send a torpedo to you and sends you to the bottom!' you know. Anyway they just shoved off and left us. So all the lifeboats that were around, our blokes got into them.

This lifeboat came alongside, nosed into me and a few of the *Perth* survivors were on there, I'm in the stern sheets this time, not knowing anybody and Frank Ritchie, one of the *Perth* survivors was standing up steering this other boat, and he saw me and said, 'Oh Mac, we can take two more.'

So I said, 'Righto, Ritch.'

And I stood up to step into the boat and two squaddies, soldier diggers, stepped into it from the middle of our boat at midships and he said, 'I got the two now, Mac.'

So I said, 'Okay, Ritch, see you later.'

That lifeboat headed towards the Philippines and was never sighted again. Somebody's looking after you, you know, up top. We offloaded some of our crew into the other three boatloads, there must have been about thirty-odd to a boatload so we had bit of a council and, 'What are we going to do, where are we heading?'

And we said, 'We'll head towards China, we must be up there near China somewhere.'

So being five days out from Singapore heading up to Japan we decided to head west, nor'west to China. And the one that went to the Philippines was never sighted again and the other six boatloads, six of them, with Brigadier Varley and all that crowd headed in a more northerly direction I think and we did hear, and never sighted them again that day, until the following day we heard machine-gun fire, it was heavier than machine gun, naval pom pom gun, heard naval 2' shells, pom poms going off, we didn't sight anything, we just heard it, because sound travels over the water as you know, and we never sighted those six boatloads either from that day.

We four boatloads headed towards China as we thought, what was that song 'Slow Boat to China', which it was. So we did that the following day and we had one keg of water and in the bottom of the boat we found a cigarette tin . . . so we used to eke out a couple of mouthfuls of water from that every afternoon at dusk, and drink that, each one of us. If there was a squall of water, we'd suck the water off our arms and dunk ourselves over the side during the middle of the day, keep a watch out for sharks, while we still had the strength to cool ourselves off and get back into the boat, but we thought, 'How long does it take us to get to China?'

Maybe we had enough water to last maybe to last eight or nine days, so on the morning of the third day we're doing the drill, the same drill again, that night there was the tail end of a typhoon I believe, and a pretty heavy following sea and we thought we made good pace that night with the following sea, good way, but whether we did or not I don't know. But on the morning of the third day a recce plane came over, it would have been a Jap, and later on that morning we saw smoke on the horizon astern of us and two Jap frigates, they were in sight, about midday I think it would have been and we thought, 'Oh yeah, see what's going to happen to us.'

We could see the Jap gunners manning the guns as they came close in and there was a more humane skipper on this one. One boat astern of us with Rowley Richards, Doc Richards on it, they took them on board and came in and nosed in alongside us and bumped us as they nosed in, and we swung alongside and they had a scrambling net down, a scrambling net, which Big Doug and I hung on to, all the crew got up and then we got on board . . . and we explained to them about the other boats, the captain more or less explained that the other boats would pick them up. They were never picked up.

* * *

Ultimately, Frank was taken to a prisoner of war camp in Yokohama, an industrial port city, thirty kilometres from Tokyo.

It was pretty dreadful up there you know, drab, horrible, and as the winter came on, strike me, it was that cold, it was a shocker. The thin pieces of cloth we had on us, we used to wear everything to bed, the clothes you wore to work you just stayed in them, even the cap, you put that on of a night-time just to get warm and we used to sleep together, there would be two or three sleeping. They had blankets but they were heavy that's all, there was not warmth in them, and the work in the factory wasn't arduous just a drab, drab existence, on a rice diet or a rice and millet diet and we worked probably an eight or nine hour day and the tenkos, the mustering, morning and night, lights out...and all the signs around the place, 'work cheerfully,' oh you know...

So the fumen [probably a shortening or alternative Japanese expression for guard or sentry] who were in charge of us, they were like a quasi-military lot in a nondescript uniform with badges, they went for badges a lot and we called them fumen and they were a bad lot of wretches. Watanabi was one bloke, he was the first Leutenant, horrible looking wretch, and a horrible so and so besides, sadistic, the head fumen, he was a sadistic brute...if he was bashing anybody, his face would drain of colour, just get embroiled into it, and they used to have those long pogo sticks, as long as a billiard cue, and they'd have sharp edges on them like a hexagonal and they would use those to give you a bash on either sensitive parts or on your elbows where they'd hit most, or on your head.

So that went on day after day. Some small misdemeanour they'd get you for. It was getting that cold that we used to sleep in all our gear to try to get warm and sometimes the guards, they'd be out with a brazier in front of them at night in the guardhouse, outside in the compound. Some of the blokes who had committed a misdemeanour, some slight thing, they'd be standing outside to attention for up to six hours at a time, outside the guardhouse just away from the braziers so that they wouldn't get any warmth, kept on the side and if they moved a bit, the change of guard would give them a bit of a bash as they went through. They'd be like blocks of ice when they'd come in. It went on all the time and as the air raids started, it got worse, you know, they took it out on us. My mate Keithy Mills, yeah, we would get in after walking through the snow and all that, just in the water troughs, wash our feet hands and face, we almost stopped doing that. We'd go into this platformed area and we'd have a piece of soap which was about an inch or so long and the towel would be a piece of cotton cloth about so big, you'd have to wring it out every time you tried to dry yourself. So it was that cold this day, I said to Keith, 'Wait till I soap up, mate.'

Which I did and I got a bit of soap, was shivering like blazes and I said, 'Righto, throw the bucket of water over.'

Which he did and this day it had a thin sheeting of ice on it and he threw it over me and I nearly froze to death. So I said to Keith, 'No more, no more, finish!'

So we had no baths after that for about three weeks. So we must have been about that high that even the Japs probably thought they'd do something about this, so they piped some hot water though into this big tank and we soaped ourselves in that, which was good.

We were a pretty filthy looking lot, scabby sores on us and that, horrible, I won't go into that, and one day Pat Major was working on the guillotine, it was a pretty big guillotine about eight or nine feet long, cutting up huge pieces of steel, and on there one day he saw four fingers which had been lopped off by one of the Jap workmen and he got a piece of cloth and put the fingers on it and took it over to the foreman, the Jap foreman. He just looked at it, he couldn't bear to look at them, he was nearly physically sick you know. So one of our fellows walking past said, 'What have you got there Pat, don't throw them away, don't waste them, bring them back to the camp and put them into the soup in the camp.'

He said, 'Righto.'

This Jap foreman in charge of our section, the arc welding, he wasn't a bad Nip. Even the coldest weather, he was a fairly old bloke, a couple of teeth missing and gold teeth and that, in the coldest weather he'd be going around in clogs, biting cold winds you know, how does he do it? Anyway, he wasn't a bad Nip . . . and the ordinary Jap that you worked with, they were okay, they were under the thumb of the military. Give you an instance. We were marching two to three kilometres to the factory during the peak hour, we'd come to an intersection, hundreds of Nips going to work too, a lot of them riding pushbikes, so we're going across this intersection, come to a halt, so probably this fellow on his pushbike was getting a bit anxious to get to work, rode through our ranks, so they chased him, the guards, in full view of us and the population, used these pogo sticks, knocked him off his bike and kicked hell out of him, just left him lying in the gutter. I said to my mate, 'What chance have we got if they do that to their own?'

* * *

By 1945 US bombing of Japan had become intense and the entire city of Yokohama was burnt to the ground by repeated raids.

That night those flyers were still going, and hundreds of these B-29s came over and after they had been going for about an hour, we were preparing to evacuate the camp because it was getting closer and closer and as we came out of the stockade gates to this narrow street, you looked down to the end of the street and fire towers everywhere, and all you could see from one side of the street to the other was this mass of flames, like it was rolling, an army of fire just rolling up the street, you could hardly breathe, it was taking all the air away and you were finding it hard to breathe and it was a residential area where we were and it was just exploding as the fire came up, so we doubled away with the guards as far as we could, and we were going along this narrow street and women and kids, women with babies strapped to their backs, kiddies running alongside them trying to escape the flames, pretty impossible, and they were all heading down towards the Sumida River, trying to get down there.

This plane was coming over, we know we won't survive this one, this won't be far away, and he dropped this load of incendiaries, it was like a firework exploding a few hundred feet up. We crouched down beside one of the low brick walls and this street going away from us is jam-packed with women, kids, civilians, as this lot came down. As we crouched down we just looked, and the whole street, the whole lot just erupted in flames, the whole bloody lot.

'Gee,' we said, 'Let's get going before the next lot comes over!'

So we ran and caught up with the main bunch, and came to an intersection, like a Y intersection in the road and there were a lot of Nip civilians there and in the glare of the fire you could see their faces, they were contorted in hatred, they wanted to get at us, well, we were burning their place down, killing them. So the Nip sergeant,

Sergeant Hino, out comes the sword, holds it aloft, and you could see it burnished against the flame, and he speaks to them for about five minutes and goes on in Jap at them, shows you how powerful the military was, we're standing there—what's going on—they're wanting to get at us, and the guards had their fixed bayonets. After he had finished speaking, they fell back on either side. Through we went, except one bloke at the back, he dropped off a little bit. I don't know whether he had a crook foot or not and they fell on him and gave him the works, they gave it to him.

We're going across this vacant allotment away from the flames and silhouetted against the people in front of us the fellows are bending down and getting up and we thought, 'What's going on here?' and then we could smell onions, and we thought, 'Onions!' and we were going across a field of onions. Here we are grabbing these onions and devouring them as we went over this paddock of onions. It looked as though a team of locusts had gone over that the following day. It was denuded.

That raid went on for possibly four hours. We were led back the following day through it all. As far as we could see it was just burnt, sixteen square miles, can you imagine sixteen square miles? Say from here to Coogee to Maroubra. Nothing except, have you seen photos of the atomic bomb on Nagasaki? Like that. A few concrete buildings that's all, the rest burnt. A few dark, drunken, scarred telegraph posts to show where the roads were, you couldn't tell where the roads were, deep in ashes and we had to walk through this . . . the bodies, as they were coming out some of the buildings collapsed and they were piled on top of one another and through the heat, the intense heat, they were welded together, the bodies were just melted together. They wouldn't know how many were killed. It was man's inhumanity to man—it was a shocker.

Anyway that was in March, April and we were moved out of that camp, actually it was burnt, to the factory area. Put in a disused building, one-storey building near the factories, there were factories all around us, and the raids were then changed from incendiaries to the heavy stuff, thousand-pounders, so we thought, 'Strike me, it won't be long now,' because they were doing pattern bombing coming over in hundreds, the B-29s—they'd do that area over one night and that area over another, saturation bombing, they were getting closer to where we were . . .

This night the air raid had been going for about an hour and I was talking to Keithy Mills, me mate, he was standing next to me and I was sitting on the shelving where we slept, timber shelving, and he said to me, 'Mac, what do you reckon we go up to the air-raid shelter?'

Well, the air-raid shelters were only a few sandbags piled together and if you dug down any further than a foot or two it was water, saturated ground, you'd strike water and the camp or the hut, the building was built over a reservoir of water. So as he stood there and was speaking to me about going up to the air-raid shelter, I said, 'Oh no what would be the use of going up there?'

And this bomber came over and there was this roaring, crashing sound like an express train and a sticker bomb went right through the place and blew it apart. I rolled over on to my stomach and the next minute I'm up in the air going over and over, somersaulting, a queer feeling, like being in slow motion, up and over, up and over, and then falling, fortunately feet first. When I landed I was in water up to my chin. I thought, 'Where the hell am I?' Didn't know where I was, thought I had been blown out into the bay because we were only a hundred yards from the bay. When my head came up I hit something and I could see flames, fire and shadowy figures and I thought, 'Bloody hell, what's going on here?'

So I put my hands up and held on to something and it was the timber roofing, the place had been blown apart, and all the timber had come down across the crater where I was. I held up with my hands, I could breathe because the water was up to there, I saw the shadowy figures silhouetted against the flames and it looked like *Dante's Inferno* I should imagine, a scene from that, and then I felt nothing from there down. And then I thought, 'Oh God!' so I held on with one arm and I felt down and that leg was there and I did it with the other arm and felt that leg there see. Then I felt this terrific pain in my back and I thought, 'My spine's gone.'

As it turned out it was a compression fracture of the vertebrae in the lumbar. I learnt later. I was paralysed from there down. So I just hung on and then I saw a bloke coming across and it turned out to be Mike Palmer, he lived in the US, he was a US Navy man who'd been taken prisoner in the Aleutians and brought down to Tokyo. I formed a good friendship with him over the years and he said, he sort of looked down; I could see him looking down and sort of heard my voice, because I yelled out and he said, 'Is that you, Mac?'

I said, 'Yes, is that you, Mike?'

And he said yes.

I said, 'Will you help me out?'

He said, 'I can't get you out of there. There's a hole further down and you'll have to go under.'

So I said righto, down under the water line, hang on and finally I got to the surface and he dragged me out. Only the rubble of the building, that's all that was left, only two ends standing. Took me out of the compound and laid me alongside a lot of other blokes lying there. There were yells and screams and fire so he said, 'I'll have to leave you here, Mac, I'm going back in to help some of the others.'

So I said, 'Okay, Mike.'

He laid me down, and I was like being in a straightjacket, all the mud and that had come up under my jacket, and it was in my ears and my face was cut and I was out like this and I couldn't move, and then they put another bloke alongside me and then another bloke and then they evacuated the camp, they moved away to a bombed-out area because the Nips had figured it out that they wouldn't bomb that again. So they stayed there all night and I'm lying there and the fires are going around me, yells and screams had died down and the drone of the planes had faded into the distance and I turned my head to this bloke and spoke to him and he didn't answer—he was dead. So I spoke to the bloke next to me on the other side, no answer, so I'm just lying there in amongst all these dead ones, so I thought, 'Oh well, you know.' I think I said a few prayers. Then it started to rain, gentle rain and it helped put the fires out and I thought to myself, 'What's going on?'—that was the loneliest night I had ever spent I think.

Anyway the fires subsided, the rain stopped and the sky was beginning to lighten, dawn was breaking and then I heard voices in the distance, they were coming back to the camp. Then they started to sort everything out, the dead 'uns, the injured blokes, and they washed me down and scrubbed all the dirt and rubbish off me and loaded me on the back of a truck with some other blokes, they were in a pretty bad way some of them with shrap wounds, there were a couple of Dutch fellows with huge chunks out of their legs which necessitated amputation later. Anyway we're on the back of this truck, about twelve of us, and they set off, it must have taken half the night, I don't know how long, I think I had passed out with the pain till we got to the Shibauru Hospital because they were going over rubble-strewn roads and into craters and my back was aching like blazes.

They had a SBA in charge of us in the hospital, a Yankee SBA [sick bay attendant], Buck Barlow, I remember his name, and they put the fellows with the bad wounds in bed and put me on a stretcher, I was just lying on a stretcher. A couple of Nip doctors came over and a nurse and looked down on me and said something to one another, and I just lay there, the nurse took my footwear off and I said, '*Arigato*,' thank you, and they operated on the two fellows who had these bad shrap wounds I think, and they were coming good, they did a good job on them. I'm lying there, it must be two or three days, I can't move, I've had it, and the pain, and that night I said to the sick bay bloke I said, 'Buck, can you give me something, can you give me a shot?'

He said, 'No, Mac.' He said, 'I haven't got anything to give you. We're in hospital and they haven't got anything to give you, not even an aspirin.'

So I said, 'Okay, mate.'

He said, 'There's other blokes pretty crook too.'

So I said, 'Yeah all right.' I got the message.

We sweated that out and about three days later one of the fellows that had his leg amputated, they took him into the operating theatre and about an hour or so later they wheeled him out and Buck came over to me and said, so and so's dead. I'm looking up on my back, so I said, 'Dead!' I said, 'He was coming good.'

'Yeah,' he said. 'The so-and-sos had cut an artery in the groin and had drained all the blood out of him, they wanted the blood, see they murdered him.'

I said, 'Strike me this doesn't sound too good.'

And I'm lying down there and I thought jeez. So next day they started to wheel the other bloke in, that had had his leg amputated and the SBA fellow said to me, 'I'm going in this time.'

Just like that. When he got to the operating theatre door, there were two guards there, sentries, and they shoved him off back to the ward. They wheeled the other fellow out and he was dead too. Cut the artery in the groin. So I said, 'Buck, help me up.'

It was a great incentive to get up, so with his help he got me up and I could just shuffle my feet a bit and the next day I did the same. I said, 'Leave me, mate, I think I can do it,' just a few yards and back.

So I was on my feet but I think we were there about ten days and the Nip officer came in one day all spruced up and spic and span as they usually do and he said, in English, very briskly, 'All walking wounded outside!'

I looked at Buck and said, 'That's me, outside, I want to get out.'

So I hobbled out along with about six others. The officer said this way, so I'm on the veranda and went to this courtyard where there were some Nip soldiers with their rifles standing in a group. It was an enclosed area with a brick building around. So with his sword scabbard he drew a line in the dirt and we had to toe that line and he paced off to where the Nip soldiers were about ten to fifteen paces, they'd all come to attention. I looked at the bloke near me and said, 'This doesn't look too good, mate.'

He drew another line and he said, pointing with his sword scabbard at the end of the line, 'You walk.'

So we thought, oh we've just got to do a sort of a trial run for him, and then next bloke, next bloke, next bloke and then he came to me and I said oh gee, and then I walked fifteen paces, I'm going to do it, so real parade-ground style, stiff, I got up and got to it and then I couldn't do an about turn because I think I would have fallen over so I did a quarter turn, quarter turn, and got back to the other lines—I'd made it. The sweat was pouring off me by this time. We were all loaded on to a transport truck and taken back to where the fellows were building a new camp away from the factory area

* * *

Hope was a big thing for us because we thought we'd never get beaten. That was our thought, we'd never get beaten. And hope, probably a bit of hate kept you going, we hated the swines, we probably thought that too but you can't, you can't keep hating forever, it would just rebound on yourself. But I think hope, and faith for me particularly, and some of the other blokes too. When you say it was hopeless, well there was a particularly bad day during the winter months, I'd been caught up in the bashing business and I felt pretty lousy, couldn't see out of my eyes, all black and that, and it was snowing like a bad day at the office, and cold and miserable, hungry, dirty, filthy and you'd be getting back to the camp and you didn't feel like talking to anyone you know, and it was getting to me, and I thought, this grey day, grey skies, smog, and the sun had only come up a little while and gone down again, and this smoggy atmosphere and it was something just inside me, I don't know what it was, this particular day I just simply said, I was down you know, I just said, 'God. How long ... how long?' But it just lasted a few seconds, I just cried out, 'How long?' Had to keep going.

* * *

1945, August 15, about midday, we were all herded into the air raid shelters and we learnt later that Emperor Hirohito was to speak to the people but we as *horihos*, despised prisoners, we were not allowed to listen to the divine emperor, so we were put in the air-raid shelter and we thought there must be an invasion on or something, you could tell by the body language and by the way they were going on, the Nips. Anyway an hour later we get out of the air-raid shelters, they've doubled the guards and instead of the fumen they've got regular army blokes too, they've doubled them all. So away we marched out of the factory back to the camp but we go back by a different route and as we came over one of the last bridges remaining there, this old crone, she was just standing there, woman with thin bony hands and face, and tears streaming down her face and she was screaming and she was wanting to get to us to tear us to bits. The Jap guards just pushed her aside. Came back to the camp, locked the gates on us and afterwards the camp commandant came out and through the interpreter said peace negotiations were going on between Allies and Nippon. But Nippon is still strong. We thought, 'Oh yeah, Nippon is still strong.' We thought, 'Yeah not very strong, I don't think.' Vic Duncan, a mate of mine, he died a few years back, said, 'Mac, I think it's over.'

I said, 'I don't believe it's over until those air raids stop and the sirens stop.'

So that night the sirens started, so I said, 'There you go, mate, there go the bloody sirens again.'

So the following day about midday sirens went again, but it was only a recce plane going over and the next day word came through that we had to paint on the roof of the hut 'PW' in white, in thirty-foot letters, so we then knew that this was it. There was no rejoicing or jumping in the air like that, we just accepted because we thought of the blokes that had just been killed and we thought how close it was until they changed the guards, took out all the fumen and put English-speaking guards only with side arms, no rifles. They tried fraternising with us, sat down on the bench with us, say, 'Have a cigarette,' you know, 'Where are you from? Australia, oh yeah.'

So one bloke squatted one day next to me, one of the Nips and he said smoking a cigarette, he looked at me and said, 'You very hoppy,' very happy, couldn't say it, very hoppy.

'Yeah,' I said, 'I'm very hoppy.' Very happy and he said, 'Nippon very sad.'

I said, 'Oh well, time marches on and it's your turn now.'

* * *

The B-29s, came over the following day, the bombers that did all the damage, they were huge planes, four-engine jobs and coming over the camp dropping food parcels. The first one that came over was a fighter plane off one of the carriers I think, he zoomed over the camp, pretty low altitude, and did a victory roll, circled round and he was about a couple of hundred feet up and dropped a food parcel out, just dropped it into the compound and it had a note on it, 'Chin up, beer and steaks for everyone in a few days.' Pilot officer, forget his name, but he was from Milwaukee, I remember this quite well, so he did another victory roll and away he went. Anyway the next day another plane came over and opened these bomb bays and dropped these huge parcels, they must have been about twelve-foot long and a couple of feet square, in different coloured parachutes, hundreds of them coming down, they were at pretty low altitude and some of the parachutes didn't open so they went through the roof of the hut, one bloke ended up with a broken arm and I said, 'I'm not going to wait to be killed by a food parcel I'm going up the air-raid shelter.'

Which I did, then they dropped hundreds of these things, one outside the camp went through the roof of a house and it killed this Jap who was lying down I think at the time. Just went straight through and flattened him and you know the families were there, the wife and that, crying. We got a medico to go out there and see if he could help them but it was too late, he was squashed, he was dead.

Anyway we had enough chewing gum, cigarettes and KD rations [emergency rations packs], as they called them, for a thousand blokes, there were only three hundred in the camp. Boots, they were piled high in one of the rooms as high as you could jump over you know, a thousand boots... So Mick and I, we were told we had to stay in camp, we said, 'Oh no, we'll be right.'

And we went out, took some food in a food parcel, because we knew the Japs and civilians were pretty well starving too, they were rationed pretty solid, they didn't have much food, so we went out and went into a couple of the places, we could see the situation there, a wife and a bloke there and a photo of one of their sons with black around it, explained killed in the war and all this, the same thing, so we left a couple of tins there for them and went somewhere else and fed up a few more. One little kid was running around and I gave him some chewing gum, his eyes wide open, 'Chew it see, don't swallow it, spit it out.'

Anyhow he ran home, told his mother and she came running out and we gave her some food parcels too.

It was about a week or so after that we were told to get ready and we would be taken by trucks down to Tokyo Bay. By this time after a couple of weeks of good food we were feeling all right and we said, 'No, we don't want trucks; we want to go down in buses.'

So we got a little bit uppity about it, we wanted to do it in style. So they said okay and put the buses on. For miles we went down through this devastated area, factories just obliterated, the whole area was just flattened, miles upon miles where factories were, the industrial area, all wrecked until we eventually got down to Tokyo Bay and all the Yanks were there and the sergeant who was in charge of our camp, Sergeant Hino, he came down too. You can't understand the Jap way of thinking; we'd been with them for three and a half years. He just stood there on the parapet, and as we got into the landing barge to take us out to the hospital ship, the Yanks were taking us out there, he was standing there with a handkerchief, he took a handkerchief out and waving us goodbye you know. I said to Big Duncan, 'Can you work them out?'

He said, 'No, I think he's really emotional about it you know.'

There he was waving this handkerchief goodbye, we said, 'Hooroo, we're glad to see the last of you.'

Anyhow they took us on board the *Benevolence* the USS *Benevolence*, the hospital ship and we, dirty, scabby looking lot, all the nurses were there you know, and they said, 'Right, strip off and into the hot showers!'

And we thought, 'Yeah, you've got to be joking.'

We got into the shower – 'Throw all your clothes out here; we're coming to get rid of all those filthy clothes.' We had a decent scrub up, hot shower and we got out of each cubicle, there must have been half-a-dozen cubicles there, was this underwear—underpants, singlet, gob's [soldier's] outfit, shoes, we had to work the size out, and a gob's cap so we had to dress up as US soldiers, it was terrific. That night they bedded us down on the *Benevolence* in stretchers and blankets and the whole works. And halfway through the night I woke up, there was a fellow coming around with a blanket, putting another blanket on us, tucked us in and all that, couldn't do enough for us. It was unbelievable. So we were all there for about a week I think, and word comes in that we were to be taken to Manila in the Philippines.

* * *

It took eleven hours from Manila to Darwin and when we got to Darwin I kissed the tarmac and thought, 'You beaut Aussie, we're here!' and the following day after they had fixed the engine up, put us on board and came in over Sydney Harbour, a beautiful spring morning it was, September 17th, it took eleven hours direct flight to get from Darwin to Sydney. So the captain of the crew said, 'Fellows I've got permission to circle the Harbour,' so he said, 'Just keep to one side of the plane, don't all race to one side, we'll have to keep it on an even keel.'

So we said all right, and he said, 'I'll go back the other way too.'

We circled the Harbour, over the northern beaches, Manly, all that area over the Harbour Bridge, straight over the city, Watsons Bay, back through the Heads, and then did it the other way. It was terrific . . . You were just there, you were home, you were in Australia, you were there. Oh such a relief. The relief was fantastic. And then the sight of Sydney Harbour, coming over on that clear spring day on the plane, you just looked down and oh gee, you'd just look at it, you just couldn't absorb it all, just looking at it, you were thinking,

'Oh jeez, no place like home.' It's well said that old song, *'no place like home.'* Who wrote those few words? *'Be there a man never so dead, be there a man ever so dead, never said to himself this is my home, my native land.'* It's quiet true, yeah it's quite true, home sweet home.

. . . Anyhow we got back home, met everybody, met up with Merle eventually and quite a few others, so that was it, settled back into civvy life. It took a while though. Very difficult. I said to one of the fellows they should have locked us up for six months after we got back. People were not supposed to talk to us about the war. They thought we were all a bit stupid, I think we were a bit stir happy. I remember one night going out on a tram to Bondi, to meet Merle one night, and still in uniform and we were in a Dreadnought type of tram, open at the back, you know that type of tram, and there was only another bloke sitting in the corner and I was sitting there, in uniform, and as we came around from Queen Street into Edgecliff Road one of the fuses blew out and it just went bang! I ended up under the seat opposite, straight under, and I was in uniform and God I was feeling stupid and the bloke sitting down there, a digger who'd been to war, he just looked at me and said, 'Son, it's going to take you a while to get used to it.'

I just shook my head and said, 'Yeah.'

* * *

Things like that, you're bomb happy, you might read about it, but it really happened.

We were in a pub there one day, a few of us, and one of the fellows who had been with us, a POW, we were talking to two other blokes that hadn't been POW and this fellow came around and saw us over there and yelled out *'Squatski!'* which means attention in Jap. The two of us, I dropped my glass, I had half a glass of beer, I just dropped it and came to attention. Immediately I knew so I stopped, so the other bloke did the same, that was a couple of months after we got out. It was imbued into us, it was there. We gave him a right shellacking, it was all right afterwards. These other two blokes just looked at us and said, 'What's going on, these blokes are stupid?'

Which we were I think. Things like that, people couldn't understand. Very, very hard to get it through to them and we would maybe go along and talk to some of the fellows who had been in the army or navy but weren't POWs, we'd have a drink with them, we might be there for a while, and we'd be having a conversation and they'd be talking about things that we didn't know anything about. It seemed as though for those three and a half years the world had just passed us by you know. We then went and saw our own mates who had been POWs, that's what we did, we were on common ground when we talked to one another but it took a long time, a hell of a while.

And I don't know, people didn't talk about it much and I used to wonder at times, and I believe they were told not to talk too much about it with us, we might just go off the deep end or something like that. I don't know, I don't think we would have, we might of. Some blokes couldn't cope with it. See I wasn't married at the time, some blokes came back to broken homes, the wives had gone off with somebody else, a Yank or somebody, because of course they didn't know what had happened to them, three and a half years, so they thought, *'posted as missing presumed killed'*, so there it was and a couple of blokes committed suicide, they couldn't cope, one bloke put his head in a gas oven, another bloke threw himself under a train, things like that you know, none of our fellows. But most of us settled down to civvy life. Pretty tough but we did it.

BARRY SEELEY

Infantryman
Malaya
Borneo
Vietnam

On the Isle of Wight they use to have dummy ships built out of concrete around the island and of course we used to go down and play on these . . . a Messerschmitt had crashed on a hill and there was a bit of the tail of this Messerschmitt up in the tree. As kids, every weekend we'd go sit under this tree and look up because it had the old black-and-white cross that used to be on the tail of their planes. I always remember my grandmother telling me, they were farming and she was out in the paddock one day and she was so used to seeing the Spitfires going over to France or Germany, she used to wave to the pilots and they used to dip their wings. One day this plane came over and she waves to it and it dipped its wings and it wasn't until it had gone and came back that she saw it was a Messerschmitt and the German pilot had actually dipped its wing to my grandmother. It seemed so strange because you'd hear stories of the different things that happened during the war, it was quite possible that he could have machine-gunned my grandmother, you just don't know. My mother she was in the Land Army, but she also used to work in a laundry place and they use to sew rank on military uniforms and she was telling me how the young pilots used to come in with their rank to be sewn on and they never came back to pick up their uniforms. She'd tell you how she felt about it; you'd see these young pilots knowing full well if they didn't come back it was because they might have lost their lives on bombing missions or whatever over Germany.

... I had seen a couple of shows on TV about Australia and I had read some magazines, particularly about sheep farms, you have sheep farms in England but they are very small, and you'd see the big properties in Australia. One day there was a big article in one of the Sunday papers saying 'come to Australia, immigrate to Australia', so I wrote for the information and I started the ball rolling from there ... We left Southampton on the SS *Oriana*, it was her second voyage ... and we went ashore at Naples and had a look at everything there. You could imagine to me, the furthest I had been in my life was to London and here I was standing in Naples, different people with different cultures, the climate. The same when we went through the Suez Canal, I just couldn't believe it. We went through the Suez and then we called into Colombo, again I've never seen anything like that, the little kids and beggars in the street in India. I had never been exposed to anything like that in my whole life. Not even on TV in England at that stage, it just didn't happen, we didn't know anything about that. It was a real eye-opener just the trip that far.

... We went down to Melbourne ... from there around to Sydney ... and I came by train from Sydney up to Brisbane ... and the next day a guy called Mr Sentanella came up from Redbank plains and introduced himself. Said that the YMCA had contacted him and how I would be employed by him. I said 'Okay,' and I threw all of my gear on the back of the ute and he put me in the back of the ute. I had never been in the back of a ute in my life and here we were going down the Ipswich Road to Redbank to work. That's how the trip started and ended.

... I was reading a paper and it said, 'Join the army and see Malaya,' and there used to be only three battalions in the regiment there and if you signed on for six years you were guaranteed two years in Malaya. I had itchy feet and I was a bit adventurous, my brother was in the British Army and we were writing and he was telling me about the British Army, and my sister being in the RAF,

I thought that I might have a change, a different direction. That's what I decided ... When you were brought up in England you have these two different classes of people, there are people who serve and the people who have been served. We were the people to serve and I just always had the feeling that that was my thing in life. I think it was probably from my grandparents and my father who had a military background. It was just the impression that I had in life that it was my part to serve.

* * *

On the train to Kapooka, this was when the area got to me, how big Australia was. To get on a train up here and I forget how many hours it took us, but it seemed to take us forever and a day ... the Riverina area down there, the open area, it was unbelievable and the different types of country you went through from dry to greenery, opened to closed ... It was the first place where I had ever struck Australian mateship, real mateship as we understand it today. It was hard but everyone pushed for each other to get through, to get through the training so that we all remained together in a military career. There were areas where you could get back-squadded if you couldn't do press-ups or push-ups, ropes, but everyone gave everyone encouragement.

... Everything was going along so fast, they took us to one area and gave us boots, hats, greatcoats, pants, the guy would just look at you and say, 'They'll fit.' We'd all go back to our huts and we'd all have to swap and mix and match to make our uniforms fit. Our hats were over our eyes, it was just a mad rush. We had to get our uniforms and get our inoculations, you'd have rows of guys and of course guys were fainting getting their needles. We had to go and have psychological tests, but it was generally the first couple of days you doubled and ran everywhere, the instructors used to hassle you. I think it was their way of breaking you down to see what you could do, whether you were going to retaliate against what you were going to do. Later on I became an instructor in the army so I knew exactly what they were doing to us because we used to do exactly the same thing to people. It was the way of finding who the people are you need to watch or look after.

... You keep people on the go, they haven't got time to think, to miss home, maybe they might be missing their parents or their girlfriends, don't give them time to think about that, just keep them moving and on the go. Getting them thinking military, 'Yes Sir, no Sir, three bags full Sir.' First they make sure their gear is right, their clothing is right, their beds are made right, lockers are right, they know what the ranks are and who they have got to call Sir and who they don't call Sir, all this type of thing. Usually you can see the pecking order within the platoon, you can work out who is going to be the leader in the platoon and who is going to be a follower, you might see a weakness there that you might pick up on ... you might have a situation where someone has got a problem. That they are in the army and they do not really want to be in the army. Some of the regular soldiers didn't really want to be in the army, maybe through family or even the court system giving them the opportunity to, 'join the army or the other'.

... The first grenades we had, had a detonator and it came separate from the grenade. They would put you in one bay and you had to take the detonator out of the box and actually put it into the grenade and screw the base plate of the grenade in. Imagining all these thoughts of this grenade going off, they were perfectly safe, but initially as a recruit! Later on when I was an instructor I used to watch recruits and people do it and see them shaking to put the detonator in or the primer. They were completely safe and then we'd go into another bay and pull the pin out and prepare to throw them. But the instructor would hold you up until they said 'Down!' A lot of people used to throw it and straight down behind the wall because they were frightened it was going to go off straightaway. I remember a couple of the big burly sergeants would just hold you there and they seemed to have it right down to the last second, because they'd say 'Down!' and just when your head and your helmet seemed to get below the brick wall, the grenade would go off. It was very interesting.

... The infantry soldier is the best of the best; he is the guy who can adapt to any situation that you throw at him. He's a guy who can laugh, cry, he is physically very fit, he's a good mate. He can do almost the impossible and he's always there. He is the type of guy that you can rely on, he's the type of guy that never bludges on his mates... He is the front-line man, he is the guy who closes with and destroys the enemy, that is what he does. He lives under all conditions and all terrains, all weathers, eats all types of food; he is the salt of the earth. Regardless of what type of warfare that you'll ever have, whether it would be nuclear warfare or whatever, the infantry guy would still have to go in after it is all over to clean it up. It wouldn't matter what computers or what systems you've got or electronic warfare, the infantry guy would always be the guy who has got to go and do that, the hard yards at the end of it.

* * *

Our idea was to train and get to Malaya; we wanted to go to Malaya and to be a part of it... the instructors, the way they spoke about it, we just wanted to be a part of it. Policies, treaty organisations or the politics of the thing didn't even enter into it. We just wanted to be a part of the Royal Australian Regiment; we wanted to be part of the battalion in Malaya as mates in the platoon... We would be doing exercises; we would be mixing with the local people. We were told more about the way of our behaviour with the local people. We are Australians and we are representing Australia and our country and they would judge Australia by our conduct. We would go over there and there would be a Kiwi and British battalion with us, and that's about it, that was virtually what we were told. We would go over there and do exercises in Malaya and we may go up into the Thai border and if need be we would go to Borneo.

... We knew the Indonesians were coming across the border, and we also knew there would be a requirement for us to go across their border, although it was totally illegal. This has only just come to light because it's the thirty-year period so we can talk about it. We certainly went across the border and we were told there would be a requirement for us to go across the border... There were contacts but my company didn't have any contacts. Charlie Company had a contact and they lost a couple of the guys up on the border, they had a couple of guys wounded but they got a few of the Indonesians. We lost another guy over there, he went out on sentry... he went in front of the machine gun. While he was out the sentry behind him changed and he didn't know he was over there and he walked back in and the guy that got shot was slightly deaf, the guy behind him challenged him but he didn't hear it and naturally once you are challenged and you don't stop, then they open fire and they killed him straight through the heart.

... It would be about eight hundred to one thousand metres to the border. There were tracks going up but it was up to us whether we used them or whether we went through the jungle, it just depended on the situation. We had two Iban scouts with us, they are the guys that have tattoos on their necks and they have tattoos all over their bodies. They were the original headhunters from over there; they had tattoos on their ears. Some of them had teeth but their teeth were all gold. Where their teeth were they'd cut it and put a coloured stone where the hole was. We had two with the platoon and they used to carry shotguns, they'd carry virtually no food at all, just a bit of rice. They'd find the food and they introduced us to all sorts of things, we weren't sure if we were eating fungus or mushrooms. They'd go off and come back with leaves or stuff off the bark of trees. Even with water, if we were short of water they used to find water. The strange thing about them was we thought they had permanent malaria because we used to take tablets for malaria, they seemed to be born with it and that it was a permanent thing. Very, very nice people but again different, the difference between these people, the Ibans and the Dyaks. The Dyaks are the actual village people in the kampong and the way that they treated us was completely different to the way that the village people in Vietnam treated us.

The things that they used to do for us in Borneo, they'd give us fruit, they were always happy to see us, we used to give the kids chocolates and things like that... A couple of the villages that we went into up onto the border and all the girls were bare-breasted in the rivers washing, but there weren't any smart remarks on our side, they felt comfortable with us. We could sit down and have a brew and they would continue on with their work. I can remember one local village we went into the old headhunter there and they were telling us about their fingers, didn't have a couple of fingers, down to the tips. He explained to us that if you chopped off so many heads then they'd take so many of your knuckle fingers off, so anyone looking at your hand knew you had cut so many people's heads off, particularly with the Chinese and the Japanese during the Second World War. To prove a point he took us into his old hut and in the loft of the hut there were actual skulls there of Japanese, incredible. It was a real eye-opener. These people again were so good to us; you just had a feeling that you could trust them. If you were in the area and the Indonesians were coming in, they wouldn't tell the Indonesians, they would be more inclined to tell us, and it proved so time and time again... They were very onside with us, a bit different from other areas like in Vietnam.

... You get a lot closer to the other guys because you know that you are watching out for each other's backs all the time. Just the simple thing of actually stopping for a smoke stop, if a guy is told that he's the sentry it would be deadly serious. When you are on exercise in Australia and you're put on sentry you know that nobody is going to hurt you, it doesn't matter what training you do, there is nothing that can hurt you in Australia, but over there you realise that that guy is your ears and eyes when you are at rest. The respect we had for each other knowing full well that we were going to do the right thing by each other. We kept our weapons clean to make sure that if we did get into a situation they did work. We carried the right amount of ammunition. You carried the right amount of medical supplies to look after each other. Everything revolved around the team effort that we were going to look after each other; we couldn't do it by ourselves. It was an ongoing thing, the commitment to each other never ever wavered, it never ever stopped, even back at camp in a relaxed type of atmosphere, there was even commitment there that if something could happen in our base camps, anything could have happened. The Indonesians could have gotten a bigger force, we don't know, but our commitment to each other never wavered. Even when we went back to Malaya and I think we then became the band of brothers.

* * *

Just outside of the camp area we used to have the main gate and the Malaysian police used to do all the security on the main gate. Then about two kilometres down from the main gate there was another gate and that's where all the bars used to be. There used to be the Sydney Bar, Sheraton Bar, Cyrano's I think it was, they were the main bars. You had the British and the New Zealanders there, the Kiwis would take over one bar, the British would take over another and the Australians would have another bar and of course if you go into one another's there'd be fights and things like that, but that's just natural, that's just part of life. The girls were very nice, very well educated and a lot of them were only bar girls to help their families. We used to have good times in the bars particularly after we came back from Borneo, because we had had a fairly rugged sort of a time. We spent nearly all our spare time in the bars. As I said we were single and we didn't really worry about saving money. There were guys that didn't even leave town the whole time they were over there because they just stayed in camp and went to the movies, they had the pub there. They saved their money, they came back and bought houses, we came back and probably bought a pushbike . . . We had a great time, we'd go to the bars and the girls would look after us, they are very honest, there was no taking of your money . . . They would feed us, a couple of the guys married a couple of the girls in the bars and they still live here in Brisbane and they are great. The girls, after a while they started looking after you. Especially if you were drinking and you weren't eating they'd say, 'Make sure you have something to eat!' and this type of thing. They were very nice people.

I took one girl out and her name was Shirley and we had a relationship, no different to a relationship that you would have in

Australia, we used to go to the movies. I used to go to the Buddhist temple, I'm not a Buddhist but she was a Buddhist and she'd take me to the temple and burn the sticks. I'd go around to her family's place and we'd go down to the market and buy the veggies and they'd cook it all up. It was a pretty good friendship . . . Her family, she was Chinese but the Chinese family are so close-knit. Things that I couldn't understand was if you went for a meal all the elders would eat first, when they finished then the next lot would eat and then the kiddies, it wasn't that everyone sat together. Whether it was a Chinese tradition I'm not too sure but that struck me as different. The prices, if I wanted to buy a shirt then Shirley would go and buy the shirt because she would get it at her price.

* * *

The war in Borneo hadn't been going on for so many years, and it wasn't a constant thing, it had only just sort of started. The fact that the Ibans and the Dyaks didn't trust the Indonesians; they didn't have any time for the Indonesians plus the way that the Indonesians used to treat them. They knew the British forces were there to help them, and they did, they gave them certain things. The British and the Australian engineers actually built roads into the area so they could get out of their area to go to other areas. They built different things like water tanks. All their 'hearts and minds' were spot on in Borneo, really spot on. The way that the Australians conducted themselves too in Borneo. I never ever saw anything that would suggest any other way, that everything was straight down the line, nothing said or done wrong to the village people at all.

* * *

At this stage Vietnam was the buzz. 1RAR were over there, we were hearing a lot about it because everyone was talking about Vietnam. The 1st Battalion had been committed, but not only that the first people that were killed in Vietnam were actually buried in Malaya . . . Because we were the Australian battalion there we used to be the burial parties, as well as doing all the patrols we'd provide burial parties. It started to come home to us about Vietnam because a lot of the people that we buried we actually knew. I don't know if you have ever been to a military funeral, they play 'The Last Post' and you fire your weapons up in the air, it is very sad. Funerals are sad at the best of times but a military one is very different from a civilian-type funeral. It certainly brought Vietnam home to us, a bit of a clout because we were actually burying some friends that actually got killed in Vietnam. It definitely was the buzz, it was again another adventure, we had been to Borneo and we were fairly fit. We had given the Indonesians a bloody nose, so to speak, nothing particularly worried us. We were very well trained and we were ready to go.

* * *

We got over to Vung Tau, from there we got sent up to Nui Dat and that's when our tour started. I arrived at Nui Dat, completely different from Malaya, very open, a different type of smell, a smell of dead vegetation. You imagine a compost heap; well that's what Vietnam smelled like. The country, the dirt was all red, dust, the heat was no worries because of being in Borneo and Malaya, the heat was no worries at all.

We then got trucks up to the tents where we lived in at Nui Dat, they were a bit of a shock to us. They were old tents and they didn't look well prepared or anything, there were sandbags but the sandbags were broken. The whole camp area didn't seem to be well organised at all. A bit of a downfall after being in Borneo where everything was underground. If you thought you were going to get overrun in Borneo you felt safe because you had bunkers, in Nui Dat your tents were all above ground and you had sandbags around them. From there we initially started training, getting the troops acclimatised. It didn't worry us so much, the guys who had come back from Borneo... the countryside was slightly different but we were still on the same sort of mission. The guys who were first-time overseas particularly from the national service, you could see, looking at these guys you could see, 'What the hell am I doing here? What the hell am I in for? Oh, am I going to sleep *there*? Oh, have I got to carry this? Are we going to go out where? Oh my God look at the barbed wire!'

Things like that. The guns going off at night firing in support of somebody already out on patrol, 'What's that noise?' We had been exposed to it so it didn't worry the experienced guys. It wasn't just the national service guys, it was the regular guys that had never been overseas, never exposed to something like that but all of a sudden you have live ammunition, these guys probably never carried live ammunition in their lives. The only time they had carried live ammunition was on the ranges where it's so controlled, after the practice every round is counted. There, all your ammunition was left on your sandbags, your grenades were there, you slept with your ammunition, Claymores were left, your grenades were left up on your sandbags. Bands of ammunition from machine guns, your machine gun, rocket-launchers, were all on your sandbags, laying there by your bed.

I don't think these people came to grips with it. Not only that a lot of them felt the heat, they found it very hard. Particularly when we started our first patrols, the equipment, they used to carry a lot of equipment; I think we carried a lot more equipment in Vietnam than we did in Borneo. The weight ration, you carried more ammunition, you carried rocket-launchers, M79 grenade-launchers, multiple Claymores, multiple rations, grenades and any other equipment that was needed to be carried, plus all your water bottles. In the dry season you didn't get water out of the creeks because there wasn't any, so you had to get it choppered in. In the wet season it was all right because there was plenty of water there. In the wet season it used to rain every afternoon at the same time without fail, so you'd get wet. When you put your tent up at the night-time you'd put your water bottles down and the water used to run down into your water bottles. These guys, even in training in Australia weren't exposed to the humidity. The guys that went to Canungra [the Jungle Training Centre] were never exposed to what Vietnam the country was going to be like. The smell of it, the vegetation, the humidity, the heat.

... Canungra was a training system, it didn't really prepare you for Vietnam, it sort of put the icing on the cake before you went over. I think it was for the government's benefit so that if anyone, especially national service guys got killed, they could turn around and say, 'We provided the best training in Australia before we sent them to war.'

That was the only reason we all went to Canungra. I don't think there was any need for us to go to Canungra, I think we could have done all the training within our own battalion and still got the same benefit. The reason we did that was the government was able to cover their backside.

Things like mine incidents; you can't explain a mine incident to anyone. They used to go through the actions down in Canungra. With a mine incident it's the smell, the noise and the burnt flesh and you can't explain that to anyone and it's not until these guys have been exposed to it that they can realise what it was all about. You can prepare them for someone shooting at you, to get into a fire position and return fire, you can show them how to navigate on a map or how to get on and off a helicopter, how to shoot a weapon. It's the things that happen, the casualties, to see someone actually shot or wounded, to be able to prepare them for exactly what does happen. I don't think they would ever be prepared for that. The way that the village people used to treat them or look at them, you could never prepare them for that. You couldn't show them anything in Australia that was like it.

* * *

The first operation was a sort of shakedown operation; we went out and just did a couple of days patrol to get the feel of the jungle and the land. Get people to know how their sections worked under those conditions. To hone in on the finer points that they had learnt in Australia and had learnt in Borneo. Get people comfortable wearing their equipment. Even down to wearing your equipment to make sure that your water bottles are in the right place, because the belt on your hips would rub you raw, knowing where to put your equipment. Exactly what to take into the field with you, some people were ridiculous. You put extra rations in, extra ammunition and what you really needed. The first couple of days were to get the finer points in the patrolling techniques and your equipment. How to make sure you know how to call in dust-off helicopters and the artillery.

We had various incidents in my first tour; I had five minor incidents at different times on the tour ... The very first incident, one of my friends, a guy who been in Borneo with me in the same section, he actually trod on a mine and he lost a leg and we had a couple of guys wounded ... It happened so quick, and we went up to where Tim was, it was fairly obvious that Tim had lost his leg, you just go into a reaction of medical aid, fixing the people up and get them on a helicopter and just getting them away. Because you are on patrols or operations there is not a lot of time to reflect. You are saying to yourself, 'It's a shocking thing but thank God it wasn't me.' It's happened but you can't do anything about it, but you are still all right. It was a shocking thing for Tim and I didn't see Tim until after we got back from Vietnam.

The good thing about it was that Tim did survive ... I'd say within twenty minutes of the action happening, Tim was on the operating theatre in Vung Tau ... if one good thing came out of Vietnam it was the medivac helicopter system that could get guys onto the operating table probably far quicker than even in Australia. I think if you walked out to the front of this building and got hit by a bus I still don't think you'd be able to get on an operating theatre as quick as what the guys could have done in Vietnam ... As soon as we had a minor incident like that we would call up for dust-off helicopters. The first tour, the dust-off helicopters were American helicopters and those guys are very experienced. We had the Australian pilots but they weren't really as experienced as the Americans. I've seen American dust-off helicopters come in and across the top of the jungle with their rotor blades and cut the branches off, small twigs, so they could come down, you'd never see an Australian pilot do that. In a dust-off situation if you were still taking fire, they are still firing at you, the VC, usually the pilots wouldn't come in but the American pilots would. Australian pilots would ask, 'Are you taking ground fire?' and if you say yes they would hover off and wait for the action to die down. Where I've seen American pilots where it doesn't matter if there was fire or not, they'd bring the choppers in to get the guys out.

* * *

The second one was a mine incident in a place called the Long Green; it's on the coastal area of Vietnam. In that incident we had contacted the VC and we did a follow-up of a blood trail, the blood of the VC that was on the ground. We stopped at a mine sign; it was a skull and crossbones, that was the way that the VC marked their mines. We stopped and the next day they brought in the Australian tracker dogs, the Labradors, and we patrolled onwards with the dogs going in front. We came across a junction and there was another mine sign on one junction and none on the others. The patrol then went up the left-hand side one and the platoon commander trod on a mine. That platoon commander I think lost both legs and a couple of other guys were wounded again with that one and we had to call in the dust-off helicopters.

Days after that we were actually on a patrol and one of the VC that was a part of that mining, he was the guy that we found alongside the track, he had been shot in the foot or something had happened and it had all maggots in it. We were leaving to patrol that particular day and it would have been easy for us to have killed that guy, but for some reason we didn't kill him. Nothing would have been said if we had shot him, for some reason he was just laying there, just in the jungle laying on his back and his foot was all maggot eating and the look in this guy's eyes. My machine gunner was there and I was standing there and we were looking down at this guy and in a second I could have said, 'Kill him.' After what had happened to the platoon commander a lot of people and even when we got back to camp said, 'How could you have done that, why didn't you kill him?'

It was very strange, for some reason just in that fraction of a second we could see the look in his eyes, he was a soldier and we were soldiers, for some reason we didn't do it.

They brought a helicopter in to take him away and we had a captain, 2IC of the company, he was Australian and he came up to take the prisoner and put him on the helicopter and the way that he treated him, just threw him in the helicopter. The guys in the section were very, very upset about that, the fact that they had the courage not to shoot this guy and to let him live. I will always remember that day because it was my dad's birthday, the 10th of August. Within a day they took photos of him and took them over the province and dropped the photos over the province with a note on the leaflets saying that this guy had been captured by the Australians and he was being looked after in an Australian hospital and that the Australians don't treat the wounded badly and things like that. He came out of it all right but looking back on it now, after this horrendous mine incident and then a few days later to have this guy there, a lot of people said that it could have been a revenge killing or something like that and you say, 'No.' Even today I often wonder where that guy is, you could go back to Vietnam and maybe if he was still alive you could say, 'Do you remember that day?' just in the one second it was the difference between life and death for that guy.

... We were still at the Long Green and they put us in the back of APCs, the armoured personnel carriers. The APC that we were in went over a mine and blew the track off the APC. But the most frightening thing of that one was they told us to get out of the back of the APC. There was the thought of, 'A mine has gone off there must be more around!' For a fraction of a second you say, 'Oh my God I can't do it!' and everything takes over and you go out.

You are sitting there and the explosion has gone and the APC is shaking and with a mine it has a distinct smell like gunpowder, a distinct smell. We knew the track had been blown off and the commander just pulled the back down and said 'Everyone off!' There is the chance that maybe something bigger is going to happen to the APC. You have a choice of staying with the APC and getting completely blown up or get off the APC and get yourself into another position. It is the thought of putting your first foot down on the track. Usually where there is one mine there is another mine, which happened.

The Long Green, just the name of the Long Green was a terrifying experience. After all those experiences we had, every time they mentioned Long Green for operation guys would think, 'Why do I have to go out on operations?' because we knew that going to the Long Green meant we were going to have mine incidents. It was a beautiful place, there were no hills and no jungle but it was open, it was just like being at the open area of the coast and there were a couple of graveyards there and a few other things. It was easy to operate in because you could see everything but there was the thought of the mines in the sand.

There is just an explosion and everyone freezes, no one moves, they know what it is and they just freeze. As you get experience, as soon as it happens you initially freeze, but then you'd move to the side and someone has to take over control of the situation, you can't just stop . . . we were going down this track and there was a hunk of bamboo about that thick across the track. Everyone else stood over the top of that bamboo, he trod on that bamboo and that triggered the mine. That happened right in the centre of the patrol. Usually mine incidents happen at the front of the patrol where the first people go, but this guy actually trod on it and he was in the centre of the patrol.

. . . Someone then has to completely take control and say, 'This is what you have got to do.' It's usually down to the commander, on this particular occasion it was me because I was in the centre of the patrol. The forward element of the platoon went forward, the rear element went back and then I remained in the area where the mines were with a couple of other guys and we did our thing. What you normally do is with your bayonet you prod around the wounded person to make sure there were no more mines. You actually put your bayonets into the ground to make sure you don't feel any mines, on your hands and knees and you prod into that area until you get to your wounded guys, then you take it from there. In that particular case there were two guys, the guy that got the mine was completely cut in half. The guy that was behind him had previously been a forward scout; the forward scout was always the first one into an area. This particular guy just had the feeling that something was going to happen to him as a forward scout so he volunteered to be the guy who carried the sig [signals] set and the guy with the sig set is always in the middle of the patrol, you'd think it would be the safest place in the world. But in this case it wasn't the safest place in the world and he lost one leg I think. He is still alive and everything is all right, we did get him out through helicopters otherwise he wouldn't have survived. The other guy didn't survive but that wasn't a very nice scene. Again, someone has got to make the initial decision, 'What are we going to do?' You have got to realise once that happens the quicker you can get to those guys, the chances of survival, there's no point freezing like animals and saying, 'Oh my God I can't do anything, let's run!'

M16 mines they jump out of the ground. When you tread on a mine it detonates and the mine actually comes up, it jumps, they are called 'Jumping Jacks'. When the blast happens it usually gets the rest of your body like this, the top or the middle of your body. If it doesn't jump clear it will just take your legs off or your foot. In the case of the last mine incident when the young guy got it, his body was actually cut in half so his top body was like that but his legs were up where his shoulders were, it was if you had folded the body in half. In the other incident where the platoon commanders got badly wounded, the engineer who was there he was dead and he didn't have a mark on him, and we couldn't find a mark anywhere. We put him on the helicopter and we couldn't work out why he had died until he got to hospital. He had a bit of shrapnel no bigger than that big and it was right under his heart, it had gone straight into his heart and killed him, but not another mark on his body. It's a horrific thing mines, you can imagine what any explosion can do to a body, it's just horrific.

The problem we had there, because most of the mine incidents in Vietnam were our own mines. They had built a minefield outside a place called Dat Do, between Dat Do and Horseshoe; it was an Australian commander who made the decision to build a minefield. They put thousands and thousand of mines into the ground and put barbed wire and everything up. One of the principles of a minefield is you must have it covered by fire all the time, someone protecting the minefield to make sure that no one gets into it but they didn't have that. The VC went in there every night and just took the mines out, they lost people doing it but for every one person that they lost they probably got fifty or sixty mines.

... I don't think you ever forget about mine incidents because there is nothing you can do. If you get fired on you can fire back but with mine incidents it's very hard for the morale of the troops, to get them motivated to want to continue on. Once you are in a minefield or anything like that or in that situation, to get people to keep going forward. The smell of a mine going off, especially when it involves someone is a smell that you will never forget. It's a real putrid smell, you have got the thud of the explosion, the smell of the burning flesh and the smell of the explosive, it's unbelievable. I think most Vietnam veterans will tell you that the most feared thing and probably in other wars too, is the mines.

* * *

We would go in very early in the morning, we'd put a cordon around a village. It might take one battalion to cordon the whole village because the villages are fairly big. They would then send over the voice aircraft, the voice aircraft tells the village that they are now surrounded; this is what is going to happen to you. They were moved to the end of the village and then another battalion would go in and they would do the search. They would cordon everyone off, everyone in the village would have to go down to one end of the village and they'd put barbed-wire barricades and they would then herd those people into the barricades. They would have water and everything there for them because they'd be there for most of the day. In that area there they would have the local police and the local forces and they would then start going through everyone. They would look for draft dodgers from the military, VC suspects and they would look after that. We would not have anything to do with talking or interrogating the locals. They would go in there and then we'd sit down and go through every hut or every building and search it, like tunnels or anything like that.

... With a hut, a couple of us would go inside and the rest would remain outside, looking into the hut but facing out from the hut and then we'd take it from there. If we weren't sure of anything at all, say there was a booby trap; we'd call up the engineers. If we did find a weapon and we thought it was booby-trapped, again we'd get the engineers up. If we didn't have to move it, we would put a rope on it and go out of the hut and give it a quick pull and hoped it didn't go bang ... the guys knew too to be very wary of things like that, particularly in VC camps. Say there was a VC flag up, no one would ever go near the flag because that was bound to be booby-trapped. Common things, things that guys would want to take as a souvenir, like a flag, anything that could be souvenirs would straightaway be suspect that it had been booby-trapped.

If we found anything suspect we'd call the interpreters over and they'd find out who owned that particular hut, while we were still there they would bring that person up to justify it ... You'd go through the whole village until it was over and we let them all go back in. I never ever saw any looting at all from any of the Australian troops. There was one village down on the coast, it was a fairly big village with an old French hotel in there and it had a camera shop. Again when we went through those I never ever saw any looting or anything like that ... They were a big experience the village searches, because that was probably the only time you got very, very close to the local people and found out exactly the way that they lived. Could you imagine if you had a house in Australia and say German soldiers came into your home? You're not there; you would feel that your whole life has been raped. It would be like someone breaking into your house, after it has happened you feel shocking that someone has been into my house. So you can imagine how these people felt with us going through all their possessions, everything that they owned in their life, to check them out ... A lot of personal stuff, like personal photos, letters, a lot of jewellery, watches. A lot of things that probably meant nothing to us but it meant the world to the people. It might just be their feeding bowls, but again it means nothing to us to see a feeding bowl but to those people it might be the only feeding bowl that they had. A lot of Buddha-type things, a lot of things; if they had lost their family during the Vietnam War they'd have pictures above a little altar in the house with the Buddha sticks burning, and fruit that they had actually left for Buddha. But again with that kind of thing none of the guys ever touched any of the fruit; it was there. At a lot of times it would have been a great temptation if you saw a nice banana there especially when you were on ration packs and you hadn't seen fruit for a long time but nothing ever happened. They would always respect the dead.

. . . I understand now why the Vietnamese people treated us like that because we didn't realise the history of what they went through. It would be the same if another country came to Australia and we were villagers and we had been at war for thirty or forty years, we would treat troops with contempt I'm sure. Straight contempt and being very arrogant with you. The kids weren't too bad because I don't think they understood anything and plus if you give a kid a bar of chocolate or some biscuits you've won them, sort of 'hearts and minds'. But certainly the older people, the way that they looked at you and everything that you did, they weren't sure whether to trust you or not . . . We did that to six or seven villages on the first trip in Vietnam . . . It didn't particularly worry me at that time because again it was a thing that we were doing, I didn't have any particular feelings for it. I felt sorry, particularly for the older people, because I think anybody who has got a mother and father, and you'd see they had family . . . I don't feel any shame of actually going through the huts or the buildings; it was a job that we had to do. Reflecting on it now I've got a different idea of that and I think I'd find it difficult now to have to do that sort of thing.

. . . I think in Vietnam where the difference was, the Vietnam War had been going on for so long and the people, they had the French, the Americans, they had us and I think always, we didn't understand what they had gone through. We didn't understand, to us the war would be over in twelve months or two years, if you went back for a second tour. But for the people in Vietnam it had been going on for years and they had seen it all before, had seen troops before and we didn't know what they had gone through before, that was the difference. Maybe if we were told a bit more of what they had gone through and understood the complete history of the Vietnam War and particularly the villagers, what the particular villages had gone through I think it might have been a bit different.

* * *

Initially over in Vietnam it was all about body counts, how many people you killed and all this sort of thing and it sort of became a competition between each platoon ... When they did have a kill in an ambush, whether they had equipment on them that you could use as souvenirs, like watches and money, it went on; you have to be honest about it ... It was a way for the platoon and the sections to prove that they were the better section or the better platoon. I know it's hard to say but it would be a bit like sport, who scores the first try. It's a bit of an ego-thing maybe, I'm not quite sure, but it was a way of probably letting off steam a bit, letting off your emotions once the first kill has happened or the first contact and it's not so bad after that. In a lot of cases, a lot of diggers went through Vietnam and never seen a VC or ever fired a shot in anger. I reckon their twelve months must have been hell for them, because they never had the chance to let everything out. Once you get into a contact situation, particularly in a big contact situation, I've seen and heard guys laughing when they were firing their weapons and really getting involved in it, it's relieved like a steam pressure; it's as if you have taken something off and everything has come out. You see a difference in guys after they have been in a big contact, they are like a mob of budgies and they get together and they can't stop talking, but the pressure is off for the time being. As I said the guys that have never-ever experienced that must have gone through about twelve months of hell.

... The second tour, the commanders were more or less after prisoners to get information and that would encourage you to get prisoners and get some information, they'd sooner have that than to kill someone. Having said that a lot of people thought the other way too, once you had got a prisoner they held you up a bit, stopped your patrol and you were tied up with getting choppers in to get the prisoners out. Whereas if someone was shot in a contact it was just a matter of actually burying them and just send the contact report away. Again there was a difference on the first and second tour, the first tour you could have contacts and you could have bodies and you just buried them. On the second tour they used to fly in a camera and you'd have to take a photo of them, to verify that you actually had the bodies and if their face was still intact they could take a photo of the face and put it in a museum.

... I don't ever remember discussing how the war was going at all; it was a day-to-day thing over there. I think if you got through the day and survived I think you were happy. If we got into a contact situation and we came out on top it was like a game of sport, you survived and everything is going all right. I don't think we ever sat down and said 'Jeez, I hope next week they are signing a peace treaty.'

It was never like that at all. We had a job to do at the time, at the end of the day, and after our patrol, if it was successful and everything was right and we are all still alive. We'd have a smoke, have a brew and go to bed and get up and have your piquet of a night-time, that was your daily routine. I don't think we got into conversations of how the war was going or who was winning or losing. The conversation revolved around sport, who was going on R&R next, leave and that type of thing. Maybe your family at home, other soldiers or contacts or other companies you had in your battalion and that type of thing, that was the general conversation during the day.

* * *

There was one operation and I'm not sure if it was *Santa Fe* or *Finnaroo* but there was one operation where we were actually sprayed with pesticide, of course we didn't know what it was at that stage. Our gear was as if someone had thrown kerosene over you, we stayed like that I think for most of the day and then they had to get new gear into us so we could change out of it... We believe now it was Agent Orange but then we didn't have a clue what it was, the aircraft went over and that was it... We had been through areas that had been defoliated... everything was just dead, what I would imagine the moon would look like. There were no birds, nothing, we'd come out of some areas that were thick jungle and then all of a sudden it was as if you were in another world. All silence, not a bird, nothing on the ground, no flies, no insects, everything was completely dead.

* * *

Everything the Americans did, they did by numbers, they made a lot of noise. Our idea was when we were out on patrol we sort of got into the jungle and melted into the jungle and there was no noise or anything. The Americans tended to just drive into the jungle and make a hell of a lot of noise, 'clear by fire' as if they wanted everyone to know that they were there. Whereas the Australians were completely different, straight in and you virtually became the phantoms of the jungle and you take ownership of the jungle. In some areas it wasn't bad showing strength like that, say in a village-type situation and you are going to take a village back, then showing your strength in numbers or your firepower. With the Australian Army, because we were so small we could never accept casualties like the Americans could. If we lost one guy it would shatter us, whereas the Americans if they lost a few, fifteen or twenty it was just part of the battle. I think if the Australians ever lost twenty or thirty in a battle, I don't think Australia would have been in Vietnam long, I think we would have got pulled out. I think the Americans accepted that more than we did as Australians.

Initially rules of engagement were very strange, particularly with the younger soldiers... one of our first contacts there was a female from the VC group and the young soldier who was the forward scout he could have shot her, but the first thing he said to his commander was, 'Do we shoot women?'

He wasn't sure of the rules of engagement. The fear that you were going to kill someone that you shouldn't kill because of the rules of engagement... We used to have a curfew of a night-time... they used to fire flares into the air and the locals in the paddy fields, they used to see the flares because they didn't have watches, they were given a certain amount of time to get back to the village. If they didn't get back in that time then it was open slather, there was always that doubt that someone might have been working that hard they didn't see the flare. They used to call them in Vietnam, 'Free Fire Zones', that meant if we had our orders read and they said we were going to a Free Fire Zone, anyone in that fire zone and it didn't matter who it was, it was open season. You could shoot them; you wouldn't have to challenge them, you wouldn't have to do anything.

... I don't think the Americans really had rules of engagement as it was spelled out for the Australians quite clearly, of what you could and couldn't do. I'm sure the situations that the Australians got themselves into, if they had any doubt they wouldn't shoot, whereas I think the Americans would have, that was it, there would have been no sort of grey areas, they would have done it... The Phuoc Tuy province was always known as the Australian province, I think we controlled that fairly well, it became virtually our own province whereas the Americans had all the other provinces. I don't think their 'hearts and mind' things were the same as ours. I think if we had killed a couple of civilians in the Phuoc Tuy province it would have probably put us back so many months or years with the 'hearts and mind' thing.

... But in those days I didn't particularly worry about what everyone else was doing, all you were worried about was what your troops were doing and if you were doing the right thing so that was all you were worried about. You probably had enough on your mind with your guys that you couldn't worry about what everybody else was doing; it was just the way of life. It was slightly different when we did a patrol up in Nui Dinh with a Vietnamese platoon and there were four Australians and we took this Vietnamese platoon up to Nui Dinh. The conditions that those guys lived under was a bit strange, there was a platoon commander and he'd sleep in a hammock and his batman, the guy who looked after all his food, he would sleep underneath it. We would actually see this platoon commander beating his batman with a hunk of bamboo. That was their way of life, and they accepted that but it was hard in those days, the four of us used to sit there knowing full well we couldn't say anything. The guy was getting beaten and he didn't worry about it, he expected it, he did something wrong and it was the punishment... The same when they took prisoners, I've seen some incidents where some bodies of the VCs have been dragged behind the APCs and again you don't say anything because that was their way of life, it was completely different from the way that we operated. I think they see in our way a weakness that the Australians do these things that you are not tough enough, if you are going to really put your story home to someone that you are really serious then you have got to hurt them, and that's the way that they see it.

... I think what the other countries respect about the Australians is an Australian calls a spade a spade and he would tell you as he sees it. If he sees that something is wrong, say I was a platoon sergeant and my platoon commander made a decision that I didn't agree with, I would say to him, 'Don't do that, I don't think that is right, I don't think it's proven that we do it that way.'

... I don't think they do it that way in any of the other armies. If a platoon commander makes a decision because he is seen to be educated and he's done all the right things in life, then he makes the decision. Whereas in the Australian Army it's not that way and particularly in Vietnam I think a lot of the platoon commanders took a lot of advice from the senior NCOs and I think other armies could see that and got a lot of respect for the Australian soldiers for that. The willingness of the Australian soldier to do anything and to look after each other. Particularly looking after each other in all sorts of areas, not just in combat areas but socially, after hours, looking after each other's back and this type of thing. Sticking up for each other, sticking up for each other's rights, very evident in the Australian Army compared to other armies in the world. I think that's why we didn't have and particularly in Vietnam where a lot of the American forces had a lot of problems with officers getting shot, grenades thrown at them and this type of thing.

* * *

With an ambush, we would go in late in the afternoon and have a recce of the area; we usually ambush a known track that could be on the outside of a village, or a watercourse from a river. The VC camps had to be near water somewhere, so they could come down and get water. We would go in late in the afternoon and put the ambush position in; in different areas we'd have the sentries out, the early-warning systems. We'd put all the Claymore mines out and you'd have banks of Claymore mines, you might have twenty-five Claymore mines out. You'd have your machine guns staked and ready to go, you'd have your rear protection party for the ambush. The ambush would go in complete silence, no eating at all, no smoking, nothing to give smells away, eating Minties or anything like that. Sometimes we wouldn't shave when we went into those areas because of the smell of the soap. We could be in there for twenty-four to forty-eight hours and then we'd just wait until someone came into the ambush. They weren't always sprung; you would just take a chance on that area that they might come along. If they were sprung we usually activated the Claymores first, it's quite possible that you could do a hollow ambush, blowing your Claymore mines and not opening small arms fire. By doing that if other VC people hear it they might think it's just a mine incident and there's no one there, but as soon as you open up with your small arms fire they would know that you are there. So you could do it either way.

Within an ambush the most time that you get on edge is when you do have a successful one and you'd go out and check for bodies. Particularly if this is in the night, you have to got to decide whether to go out at night to check the bodies or wait until first light of the morning. There was one incident with a Kiwi platoon commander and they had an ambush and the Claymore mines set off a fire with the grass. When they went out one of the Claymore mines hadn't gone off and he actually walked in front of where the mines were and the fire set the Claymore mine off and he got caught in his own ambush. There are all those sort of things that you have got to consider, if you are actually going to go out there and check for bodies. The ideal situation is to have the ambush in the day, do whatever you have got to do with the bodies, get the information and then clear out straightaway so you don't become a target for their mortars.

... We used to go in early; we would have a feed and go in early. In the ambush position ... there would be no cooking, nothing like that at all. All your food would be eaten dry, no cooking whatsoever, no cups of coffee, no shaving ... you'd be in pairs or in threes on the actual killing ground and one of you would be awake the whole time. The way that we contacted the sentries on each point, say there was a track coming down that way there would be a sentry on each end. If this sentry saw somebody coming down we'd have bits of rope and we would just pull the thing to say that someone was coming ... you'd have it tied somewhere around his body and give it a tug to let you know that somebody was coming ... if you just wanted to urinate you'd roll over but if you wanted to go the other then you'd have to get relief. There would be two or three of you in little groups then one of you could sleep and the other guy would stay awake. When the other guy felt that he was going off he'd give you a nudge and then you'd wake up. You knew very well that it was life and death and that if you all went to sleep then you were all dead, no doubt about it and if they knew that you were there.

... Once a dust-off came in and we got the person out, if the person was wounded and you fixed them up and you knew they were going to survive there was no problem. It's a bit different when someone dies in action, particularly with the guys who were very close to that person, it's a bit different. The other way around with the VC there was no reaction at all. I've actually seen guys with dead bodies of VC sitting there having breakfast the next morning and the bodies just to one side, no feeling because they didn't mean anything to those guys, it was just a body, it was just nothing. Some of the guys might have felt something but I never had any guy come up to me and say, 'Barry, I feel sorry for that guy.'

There were cases where you were taking things off these people and you actually saw photos of their families but again there was no time to start thinking about that type of thing. I think about it now looking back, but certainly in those days it didn't worry me in the least, and I'm sure it didn't worry the soldiers.

* * *

We went back to Townsville, we were lucky going to Townsville because the people of Townsville weren't exposed to too much military and they opened their arms to us. The locals were good to us and we only ever had one incident in Townsville prior to going to Vietnam on the second trip. We had the university next to the camp up there and there was a huge big rock at Laverack Barracks, as you drive into Laverack Barracks and someone painted 'Death 2RAR' on it . . . the guys rightly or wrongly believed it was the students. A couple of guys retaliated with paint and they went up to the car park and painted all the students' cars. There was never anything in the paper about it, no publicity; they wanted to keep it quite. The deans of the university got together with the COs and they came to some sort of agreement, from then on we had sort of a good working relationship with the students. I still believe it was the students; it was certainly our guys who painted the cars I've got no doubt about that. But that incident maybe brought everything to a head and the students got invited down to our sport events and we got invited up to their sport events, and people got together and they realised that we were doing what we were told to do by the government, whether we wanted to go it was immaterial, we had no choice in going. I think it worked their way too, we understood the way they felt, that they had freedom of speech to do things, but to do things the right way. Protest against something but don't protest directly to the soldiers.

* * *

As a commander it has certainly taught me to look at myself, what I do, how I do things, how you treat people. Not to ever expect anyone to do anything that you won't do yourself. Always lead by example, don't be too critical of anyone, and always look at their side ... The best thing is mateship, the mateship of the guys, the funny times, the good and bad times. Even during the bad times it always brings the best out of people and you look back on those. In the twenty-two years in the army I had some fantastic experiences you can never buy, even the bad ones, there were so many good ones too, it was great. I could never have had a better life; I could never have had the life that I wanted outside of what I've done in the last twenty-two years in the military or the twenty years I've been in this service. I could never have sat down and said 'This is what I want to do.' Everything in life has come to me whether it's been good or bad, and at the end of it everything has come out good. Initially as I said before when we first came back from Vietnam there were very bad periods, but now my life is complete.

... You think about it now and naturally there are times when your mind goes back to Vietnam. Those people had families exactly the same as us and they were soldiers. I've learnt a lot more about Vietnam probably in the last four or five years than I ever knew, I've read a lot more about not so much our side of it but the other side of it. There are a lot of documents out written by the other side about different things and you tend to have a completely different idea about Vietnam, what you were fighting. Some of those people must have had a hell of a life. There is no way in the world we would have lived the way they had lived and they were constantly doing it. The superpower of the world, against all the modern equipment and to still come out of those holes and fight and in the end win the Vietnam War, whether they won it completely or whether it was handed to them by the politicians, what they went through is unbelievable, they have all my respect.

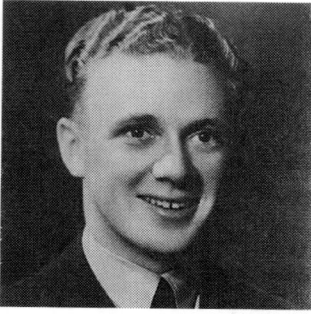

DR GEOFF CORNISH

Pilot
Bomber Command
Prisoner of the Germans
World War II

My job when I left school...was the cadet in the chemistry department at the University of Western Australia on seven and six a week. I found out that cadet was a very fancy name for the cleaner... I had only just started by about a month when the RAF advertised in all of the Australian newspapers for Australians aged seventeen and half to twenty-five to apply for a short service commission as pilots with the RAF. The reason was that a few years previously, about 1935, when Hitler started to rise, they knew that they had to build a powerful Royal Air Force capable of opposing him. But how to do it quickly and pay for it was another matter. So the application was for a short service commission, in other words you were an officer, they gave you a commission straightaway, but after six years serving as a pilot anywhere, they paid your fare back to Australia and gave you five hundred sterling gratuity. Now that would have bought Mum and Dad's home and it would have been a wonderful leg up for me to do honours and start my science degree...but of course you were on the reserve, if there was an emergency and you were on the reserve you could be called up immediately. Now that gave them a very big reserve of highly skilled pilots not on the government payroll. We were all earning our own living as soon as we finished our six years, but we were obliged to come in, in case of an emergency. So that enabled the RAF to successfully oppose Hitler and win the Battle of Britain. It is not known very much but that is actually what happened.

So twenty-two of us left Australia, I was selected from Perth on the *Orana* that was an Orient cruise liner, and she picked us up, the boys from Brisbane, Sydney, so on around the coast, and we were halfway to England, past Colombo and almost to Aden when war was declared. So all of our lovely peacetime plans of six years serving somewhere in the world, gone. And when we reached England on the 13th of October '39, only five weeks after war started of course, there was pandemonium. We were put straight into training.

When we went onto the squadron our expectation of life, this was October 1940, was six weeks. When you're nineteen and you have six weeks to live on average, we were a pretty wild bunch. You name it, we did it, we had no future and we were determined to have at least a brief experience of what life was all about ... the moment you got weekend's leave you shot down to London and did a round of the pubs and the RAF Club and that sort of thing, saw a show, met as many girls as you could of course. Because at eighteen, nineteen, well, we had been at school virtually the whole time so that you had no money to take girls out up until then, but by gee you wanted to.

* * *

It was on, I think, my eighteenth raid, that I was caught over Holland. Up until then the German searchlights had been what they call sonar-controlled, that's a big sound bell that follows you like a pair of ears does, if you have got two ears like this you can say, 'Well, that is where the sound is coming from, over there,' and the searchlights were trained to follow that, but this night that we went over, the Germans had put radar control on the searchlights for the first time and that was very accurate. And the night that we crossed the Dutch coast and were heading to Düsseldorf to bomb it, there was something not right, you could tell something was wrong. There were no searchlights, there was no anti-aircraft fire, and you couldn't see any nightfighter machine-gun fire, because they had tracer in it you see, and you would see this burst of tracer as they tried to hit somebody in the sky, there was none of that at all, so it was eerie.

And then all of a sudden, when I was just south of Eindhoven in Holland, a terribly bright, pale-blue searchlight came on flat on the ground going exactly along my track . . . and then he brought the beam up until you just couldn't see, it was very bright. And then as soon as he got me, about three hundred searchlights were given a height to cone on, and I was sitting in amongst these searchlights. Just like the star on a Christmas tree. Whatever you did, wherever you went, whether you dived, climbed, went sideways, combined all three, you were going straight into two or three searchlights and they could hold you . . . and the first thing I knew having been caught in the searchlights was this tremendous roar and damning thud as heavy cannons from the Messerschmitts, they were the twin-engine ones, 110s, who were above us, they came screaming down, firing as they went. The leader hit my armour plate that is up behind the skipper's seat. And of course that's like being run into by a car from behind and about five hundred miles per hour, it's a terrible job. And as he pulled away he hit my starboard motor on the right side and set that on fire. And he also got the intercom, the microphone that I talked to each of my crew members with. So I couldn't communicate . . . and then, just after he pulled out, another one came in, but then your second pilot is sitting down in the nose of the aircraft, in front, at the bottom corner of that box, because he is the navigator and front gunner as well. And there were standard drills for everything, so should we lose our intercom, which we had done, and he wanted to communicate with me he had to stand up, turn around and he could then see the soles of my feet on the rudder bar and he had to tap the sole of my right foot and I knew straightaway to bend down and there would be a message there, his message pad was there. And when I pulled it up, there was just a lot of splattered blood on it and the message, 'He's got me.' And I had just barely read it when slam! The next guy came in and the one after that. So I was just dropping, because both hit me and I was losing a bit more control every time, a bit more of the controls were damaged, it was like being in a running accident, you lost a little bit more control of your vehicle... I thought, 'Well, if they have hit my armour plate and they have hit me, they have gone right through the wireless op behind me and/or the rear gunner.'

And I turned around and they were both slumped unconscious in their seats. So I thought, 'Well, there is no point in pushing on, I have got a dead crew and an aircraft that is crippled, I am over Holland, I have got to jettison my bombs safe.'

Because Holland was of course a friendly country, and there is a toggle, very much like a rifle bolt on the side, and you have to pick it up in your hand like that and push it forward and lock it down in place and that opens the bomb doors and allows the bombs to fall away safely. As I reached for the toggle it disappeared, the next guy had arrived and he shot away that side of the aircraft, another half a second sooner I would have lost my right hand. You don't dwell on that thought, it is happening so fast.

I think about the fourth guy, it is very difficult to keep it serially related, but he shot away the canopy that you pull back so that you could get in or out of the aircraft, because it is minus twenty degrees at that height. And of course when you shut it there is nice silence in the cockpit and you can hear what you're thinking about. But that was just blown off completely...just after that all I can remember is that it was as if we just, all of a sudden all of the controls went, they were just floppy and useless and we were just tumbling through, like a paper bag in the sky. Not like a paper bag because there was weight in it, but you were just tumbling out of control through the sky. Apparently, they did, they got all of the controls, but then the next guy who came in, I suppose was most junior in the fighter squadron and he got so excited about pressing his cannon he forgot to pull out and so he slammed into me at full throttle, in a dive at a huge speed, and of course when he hit me his petrol just went right through my aircraft apparently, and the starboard engine is on fire. So the next thing, you have just got two hollow aluminium cans and bang! They exploded, and that apparently blew me out into the air, because there was no cover over me to keep me in, that must have happened. Of course I was concussed; I have no recollection of that at all. But I came to freezing because, as I say, minus twenty degrees and my parachute was open and I was picking up my levels of consciousness wondering what had happened. But I realised my parachute was open and found that the rip cord was still in my hand. So it shows you how thorough the RAF training was, that even when you were unconscious you could carry out automatically the training that you were supposed to have done. And of course that saved my life.

I was just seeing what was happening when I saw the same searchlight catch my best friend, Dave Powell. I took off and he took off, same squadron, thirty seconds after me going to the same target. And I saw him caught in the searchlights and of course by this time I must have been some thousand feet below him dangling on a parachute and I was yelling out to him, 'Dave, look out for the bloody 110s! Look out for the 110s!'

And then I saw them come in screaming and catch him and I saw him catch fire and start to fall and he was shot down also. Then, of course when you're drifting through like that it is completely silent and after the roar and bang of battle and the explosions and things, you're wondering if you're still alive and you're floating down to heaven instead of up to heaven. You're just completely bewildered and then you get your senses back again and I thought, 'I have got to land this parachute.'

And as I dropped towards the ground in Holland I could see that I was over a very big forest that had a canal running through it, and right next to one bank of the canal there was a little cleared bit of land. So I had to aim my rigging lines and try to land in that. Otherwise you land in a tree or a canal, neither of which was a very tempting prospect under those circumstances. The one great difficulty of course, was at night you cannot judge how far away the ground is because it is pitch-dark. You do not know if the ground is one centimetre away or one hundred metres, so you hit at full speed coming down, thump! And that once again just winded me completely. I think I passed out for a while, I am not sure.

I came to and I was aching all over in every joint and every muscle . . . the little bit of cleared land turned out to be a farmyard. So of course the dogs started to bark as soon as they saw and heard this strange vision arriving, and it woke all of the fowls up and they were clucking and squawking all over the place. And then a young boy came out, remember at that stage I was nineteen, this boy was about eighteen. He came and unlocked the farmyard gate and he sort of helped and half dragged me and lifted me up and I got to his father's house which was not far away. His father was the local schoolmaster and when they took me into the lounge room it was full of kids, apparently they had thirteen kids and they were all there to see this airman who had been shot down. Seventeen-year-old girl was Wilhelmina . . . and she was slim and dark . . . and spoke perfect English, so she is telling me how they watched the whole event taking place, so they knew virtually who I was and where I had come from. They didn't know my name but about everything else they knew. And she is saying unfortunately, because of the fact it was a new weapon they put on, the Germans were expecting to catch somebody.

As I say, they got four of us in fact in ten minutes, and she said, 'They heard the dogs and all of the noise and they are doing a house-to-house search now.'

And I don't think she had finished speaking when the door was just blown open and in walked the Germans and I had a loaded revolver pointed at my head, put onto full cock and the German officer saying, 'For you, the war is over.'

And I remember thinking at the time, 'I hope it is just the war,' because you don't know whether he was going to pull the trigger, that wasn't a thrilling moment either.

But he didn't, and I was marched off to a car outside and taken away up to Amsterdam, and that was Easter Thursday 1941, and I spent Easter Thursday in gaol in Amsterdam . . . the next morning when they let me out of gaol for exercise out come three other airmen who I recognised as Dave's crew, the three of them and the only one that was missing was Dave Powell. Now there was thirty seconds between us, otherwise everything was identical, all of my crew were killed and I was alive. And in his plane all of his crew were alive and he was the only one killed. I was pretty fatalistic after that for a long time. I believed that if your number was on it well . . . and if your number was not on it then you were lucky. He was a very nice, quiet bloke, Dave, it was a bad blow.

We were interrogated for about four or five days and then a batch of us, about twelve of us who had been shot down over those two or three nights went by train up to Stalag Luft 1 . . . and we spent one year there. There were three or four huts, very few of us, bitterly cold, but then it was inadequate and they had constructed Stalag Luft 3 south-east of Berlin, between Berlin and Breslau at a place called Sagan, It is still there and it is now in Poland. This one they said was to be escape-proof, and they transferred us all by train down to there in April 1942, into East Camp. And a year later they had finished the big camp which was North Camp and we were moved there the day that it was open. And that was the one from which we dug the Great Escape tunnels.

* * *

There was very little food, we were starving hungry. Because in the air force in our mess, in aircrew, you had everything in the way of food. Everything. It was nothing for us to fly an aircraft up to Scotland to pick up some salmon, from Oxford say in the middle of England, or over to Northern Ireland to pick up some beef or butter or something like that, which were heavily rationed in England. Because you had to flight test your aircraft before you went on operations somewhere, so you took it to somewhere where you could come back laden with beautiful food and so we didn't really want for anything. And to give them their credit, the air force made sure that their aircrew did have the best of food. But the Germans weren't so thoughtful and it was stinking cabbage, sauerkraut, rotten potatoes and horse flesh occasionally. Which I never really enjoyed. But when you got into a room and the cook produced lunch you were so ravenous you ate it, and after a while you adapted to it and you learnt, your stomach definitely shrank, because we had been overeating far too much. In ordinary life if you are hungry you can always go to a cupboard and get something. There was absolutely nothing. And of course, every book that you picked up to read to take your mind off where you were would describe the most magnificent banquet that the hero or heroine were just sitting down to. You would think, 'Oh, not another one,' and change to another book. But after a while you ate everything that was given you.

If a new boy who had just been shot down came into the room and said, 'Oh, I don't eat that, I couldn't eat that.' Whip, he didn't get a second chance to say he wouldn't like it, it was divided up amongst the other guys and it was gone, and he soon found after a few days that he suddenly had a great liking for this particular food.

We had eight in a room and we finished up with eighteen, six three-tier bunks in exactly the same space. And the feeling of being hemmed in by people was huge. You wanted to bust a chap's nose in just because he was there and he was too close to you. As they say, 'invading your space' is the term now. You knew it was no good losing your temper or picking a fight or something like that because you had to live with him twenty-four hours a day. Okay, there were some minor scuffles in the first week or so. But people soon learnt to control their temper and to control their attitude and to be more thoughtful of others. In that way it was wonderful discipline, you had to pull together as a unit and you did.

It was like an RAF station and the biggest sub-organisation if you like was the escape committee. And they coordinated all escape activities, everything to do with escaping. And that was headed by Roger Bushell and he was in our room. So a lot of the planning and a lot of the detail was done in our room. And Roger was a very great friend, he was a South African, brilliant lawyer, and a top barrister and he was working in London in the top law branches there. He spoke fluent German, he was brave and he was cunning. He was the ideal type, and he loathed the Germans. Absolutely and utterly. Underneath the sub-committee of the escape committee there was the security commission, who made sure that nobody talked carelessly and gave away anything. They made sure that people didn't glance the wrong way because they knew that some activity was going on. And if a lot of people glanced sideways at a certain spot the Germans would know there was something there. So all of those fine details were taken care of in security.

And then underneath, we had the German bribery department, that was about five of us, German speakers, and it was our job to get in contraband like special paper for the documents, photographs, whatever we needed. Radio valves, because we had our own wireless set and we had to keep that operating. There was a mapmaking department, forgery department, the tunnel planning department, carpentry, metal work, to name a few . . . in the German bribery department you had guards with a family and they had no scruples about providing us with contraband things providing they got one of the four main articles which came in our Red Cross parcels: chocolate, Nescafé, soap and cigarettes. Those four items, any of them on the black market was worth a fortune . . . so when one of your guards was going on leave, if you were in the bribery department you would say to him, 'Look, we're not all terror fliers,' *terror fliegen* they used to call us. Terror fliers . . . 'We're not that at all, here is some soap for your wife and some chocolate for your kids and some cigarettes for you, have a good leave.'

When they came back they had had a wonderful leave and perhaps six months later they would be going on leave, and they would just say to you, 'I am going on leave next week.'

And expect to be given all of these things, see? And we might give them to them the second time too. But on the third occasion, might be a year later, we worked very patiently, we would say, 'No, they are in short supply.'

Well, straightaway he knew the children would be whining and whingeing, and his wife would be the same and he wouldn't have any cigarettes to smoke either, so we could say, 'We do have a few on the condition that you could bring back this or that.'

'Couldn't possibly, no, I would never do that.'

'Please yourself.'

But I remember saying to one guy, 'You know I am studying science here?'

And he said, 'Yes.'

And I said, 'I need a magnet because I am studying magnetism and electricity.'

Well, that made sense to him, he knew it wasn't true but it was enough logic that he could say, 'Well, he told me that.' So I said, 'Get me a small magnet, it doesn't have to be anything.' Of course that was used for making a compass.

* * *

The only absolute mandatory obligation was if the Germans said, 'roll call' you had to get out onto the parade ground, which was just a flat open area of semi-grass, semi-sand. And we were drawn up in columns of three or five and counted. And if they thought that somebody was trying to escape and might be down a tunnel, they would call a snap roll call and, of course, you would have to get the guys out of the tunnel on the double, up from down below and washed so that they didn't have sand all over them and dried and on parade in a couple of minutes. So that's the way they would try and trick us and try and see if we were running a tunnel, and if so they could try and locate it to a certain hut. Apart from that, their only obligation was to make sure that we didn't get out, and apart from that they didn't interfere internally at all. It was just extra work for them; they had no hope of being able to get us on side or to co-operate with them so you had all day to fill in, in fact it was the sheer boredom did drive some of the guys a bit stir happy, a bit crazy. But to combat that the senior officers in the camp used to organise classes, and there were always elementary German classes, middle German classes or advanced German classes. Or French. It didn't matter what you wanted to do, there was somebody in that camp. Remembering there were about two and a half thousand people who had either finished their tertiary education, or were into it before they joined up. If you wanted to learn photography, if you wanted to learn to make wine or distil spirits, there was somebody who would do it for you. If you wanted to learn Mandarin-Chinese, Squadron Leader Murray had been in Hong Kong, in the Far East for twelve years, and he spoke fluent Chinese. You could learn Japanese, Russian was a very popular choice. A lot of people learnt French while they were there. I mean, I had the science master from Edinburgh University giving me one-on-one tutorials in chemistry and physics. He was delighted, it kept him interested and occupied and it was great tuition for me.

* * *

Not long after we had moved into North Compound we had the radio going secretly at night and took the BBC news so that we were informed of what was going on in the outside world. But by detection . . . the Germans worked out that there was a radio somewhere in our hut. Then Jimmy Higgins . . . our code name for the man in charge of all the guards . . . who was supposed to be keeping us in and responsible for all of this, but was in our pay, came in.

He said, 'Tonight at three o'clock in the morning there is going to be a secret Gestapo search of this hut because we think there is a radio here. They must not find anything or *phht* for me!'

We said, 'Relax, Jimmy, they won't find anything.'

Sure enough, three o'clock in the morning *tramp, tramp, tramp, tramp* and there are thirty guards surrounding just our hut so it is absolutely isolated. They keep the far door locked and open this big one at the end of the corridor and in came two funny looking, little, weaselly Gestapo men in civilian clothes. You would swear that Hollywood had done them up as Gestapo men, they were so typical. They put a small table like a kid's school desk in the centre of the corridor and we had to file past them, one on this side and one on this side and be strip-searched as you went past, and they did a pretty thorough search and anything they found they dumped on the table. It was a very hot night as well and after a while they got so hot, because they were working furiously to get through this hut, they took their coats off and hung them somewhere safe where we couldn't get at them and went on searching. And they soon built up quite a big mound of old maps and bits of compasses and things that we didn't particularly want. And they were feeling quite pleased with themselves.

But there was some stuff that we did want to get out, including the radio. And different guys had different bits of it secreted on their person. So we called in Bush Parker, our Queensland stage magician, and when one of the Gestapo was searching Bush he dropped a small round compass onto the floor, grabbed it and the Gestapo man said, '*Geben Sie mir.*' 'Give it to me.' And Bush, who spoke perfect German, pretended he didn't understand. The Gestapo man started to prise his fingers open and when he got it open there was nothing there.

Bush looked at it, 'Oh, here it is, up here,' and produced it out of his hair. So the Gestapo man grabbed his hand and of course the same thing happened, by the time he got that prised open it had gone again. And then he is trying to search him. Bush pretended he was violently ticklish, so the Gestapo man is trying to search him and Bush is finally lying on the floor thrashing around being tickled by this Gestapo guy everywhere. And of course he wouldn't stop, so the Gestapo man said to his mate, 'He has got a compass, come over and give me a hand.'

So finally they got the little compass and stood up in absolute triumph, only to find that there was nobody left in the hut at all. While they were fighting with Bush on the floor everybody with all of the contraband has gone out the other side and they cleared out everything that had been confiscated and reconfiscated it in our own name and the table was bare. They were livid with rage.

So they turned around and put on their coats to go out and complain to the commandant. He had told them before they went in, 'Now for heavens sake, be very cautious, they are cunning and will do anything and they will set traps.'

'We are the Gestapo, stand aside.'

So the Commandant and the officers were then as much on our side as we could have them. They hated the Gestapo also. So the Commandant more or less said, 'Well, I have warned you.'

And then they had to put their coats on and come out to the gate to come out. Of course they had to produce their pass to get out of the camp and when they went into their pockets there is no pass there. Nor is the Gestapo identity badge in there, we had pinched that as well. And when they said to the guard, 'Open the gate, we are the Gestapo.'

He said, 'No, you pull these tricks continually, I know you are not Gestapo. You can stay there.'

'Ring the Commandant, he will come immediately.'

'I will not ring the Commandant at four in the morning. I will ring the Commandant when he has had his breakfast at six o'clock.'

And he refused to budge. So these little guys have got to walk all around, they were prisoners, inside the warning wire, very disgruntled and from our huts of course the German speakers were calling out to them, 'You're going to be executed for this aren't you?' 'You're Gestapo; you've shamed them and let them down.'

We could see them swallowing hard and we were hitting home quite desperately. And we kept that up non-stop the whole time until the Commandant came up, cigar on, and they raced up to him and blabbered away this whole story.

'Hmm,' he said. 'Yes, I will retrieve that for you, we know where they hide those things.'

And he walked into the hut and through to another hut and of course we gave it all back to him, so he was able to go back to them and give them their wallets with their passes to get out of the camp and their Gestapo identity cards.

But when they got to the gate to show them and opened their ID card, they looked rather like our letters; we were allowed to write three letters a month and two postcards. And each one, of course, was read by the Germans and then marked with a great big stamp, '*Geprüfft*' which means approved, 'by the German censors Stalag Luft 3' in a great big letters, with a swastika and a German eagle on top of it. And when they opened their Gestapo passes there was a great big black rubber stamp, which we had made from the heel of a flying boot with RAF wings and the RAF crest and the crown on top. And in English underneath, 'Approved by the RAF censors Stalag Luft 3'. And there was no way out of it, the German

Commandant could not take the smile off his face, and he said, 'Well, there are your passes, we won't be seeing you again, will we?'

And they knew they were probably, certainly a long custodial sentence as they say. And we never saw the Gestapo again for the rest of the war.

* * *

[There was a doctor for the camp and] we met, quite casually, he was a friendly man. I can't remember our first contact, probably I reported to sick bay with a sore hand or something like that. But he was always interested in everybody in the camp, as a doctor should be, we were his patients and he was very professional, in who we were, what we were doing, what our interests were. So I probably confided in him that I one day wanted to be a doctor too . . . and then he would come in and just sit down at a table with me, and he had been trained at the Middlesex Hospital in London and he had been through his exams about three years before when he joined the army and got posted to France and got caught at Dunkirk when the British Army retreated from France and the Germans pushed them out of Europe. So he was not that much older than we were. And, as I say, because nobody else in the camp wanted to talk medicine we gravitated together because I just loved hour after hour of medical talk where I was picking up and I was learning well, private lectures instead of being in a class of a hundred, it was one on one with a wonderful teacher. So it fostered and we became very, very good friends.

His name was Norman Montennuis. He used to say, 'It is tennis with a U-I-S.' It was Spanish, he had quite an olive complexion and he used to say his ancestors probably came across with the Spanish Armada and that could well have been so too, he looked Spanish but he was very English and very proper because he had, of course, many generations in England. He had just graduated so he hadn't had time to specialise in anything, but . . . Middlesex still is a wonderful teaching hospital. And he had been well taught there.

One day he said, 'They are transferring me to this camp where all of the new people are going and I will be the only doctor there and I want you to come with me.'

... I moved into the hospital, I think about October, November '43 and the Great Escape was March '44 ... it was a difficult decision to make, once you had made it, it became clear that that was obviously the only decision to have made looking back on it, but looking forward and trying to work your way through it, it was a hard one, I must admit. But I know I made the right one. The escape committee said I couldn't do it; I couldn't pull out unless I had somebody else capable of taking the photographs for the forged passports and documents. And that's when I found Charles Hall who had done his full apprenticeship in the RAF as a photographer and then got onto photographic reconnaissance on the Spitfires ... he was much more professional than I was ... and that was when Roger Bushell said, 'You can go.' Oh, he told me I was mad, Charles Hall said, 'You're crazy, you're giving away this opportunity?'

I said, 'Yes and I am not changing my mind, I am off, this is all yours.'

And he couldn't believe his luck. Well, he hadn't had to do anything at all for it.

Dr Montennuis and I shared a room and of course that was a relief in itself rather than being one of eighteen, that's what I was trying to study under. But then just sharing with the doctor I could be tutored privately non-stop as long as I wanted to, in the hospital on nothing but medicine. That was just a utopia, that was just an upward move that was beyond, I just couldn't believe it ... and that's where he started to teach me as much as he could, doing things like how to bandage properly, what ointments to use on what simple stitching, how to put in a local anaesthetic. How to work with simple aseptic techniques so that you didn't contaminate anything with your fingers. General, the same treatment you would get in a casualty department, virtually identical.

We never had any serious illnesses. A couple of suspected meningitises, which didn't turn out to be so. We did have one guy, an American, Lowen Delp. He did contract meningitis and he was slammed straight into a single ward in isolation and I volunteered and went in to sleep and nurse him and be with him. Of course I ran the risk of meningitis but it was better for me to do it than the doctor to do it . . . it was to be my life and somebody had to do it. I was just in the spot and I regarded it as my job. What do I do? Stand back and say, 'No I don't want to do that.' And let somebody else do it? I volunteered, I had agreed to go and join him, I had agreed to do what he asked, he didn't have to ask me that, I said, 'I will do it.' Somebody had to do it because it couldn't be him, because if he caught it the whole camp was in trouble. So you have got to sort through it and as they say, the buck stops with you. Luckily it didn't stop permanently.

It was the opportunity I had been asking for. To be able to do medicine, that's why I joined the air force in the first place, the end picture that I never lost sight of. And here was a huge step forward closer towards it, actually being as close to a real medical school as I could get. And I learnt a tremendous amount in that year with him. A tremendous amount. I just thought it was the most wonderful challenge and the most wonderful vocation or profession to be involved in, and to be able to do it and above all to be able to do it well. And to have the opportunity to do it, I couldn't ask any more in life. No, I didn't ask any more in life, because it fulfilled everything, it gave you a hobby, it gave you a focus, it gave you hope and you were looking towards your own future as well and helping in the present. I think I was very fortunate to be in that position.

***

They told us at roll call . . . that last night seventy-six prisoners had got out and we were elated. And then ten days later the German captain came in and said seventy-three of the prisoners have been shot evading capture. And the senior British officer said, 'How many were wounded?'

And he said, 'None.'

'In other words,' he said, 'You murdered them.'

And the German just hung his head in shame, didn't answer and walked off because that *is* what had happened. They said they were shot trying to avoid recapture which was absolute rubbish, they were executed. So there was elation for a couple of weeks and then very deep gloom after that for quite a long time from which we never really recovered throughout the war.

[Charles Hall] was one of the ones they executed. So yep. Once again, if your name is on it, it is on it. And he was an only son and I could not go back after the war and visit his parents, ninety-nine per cent of me said that I wanted to, but what could I do? It was four years since it happened, no, it was eighteen months later that I got back to England, they were probably just over most of their grief and what was I going to do? Knock on their door and say, 'Here I am, I am the lucky one, I am so sorry that Charles was killed and I wasn't.'

I couldn't say that, that was a lie, I wasn't. It was a lose-lose-lose situation. So I just said, 'I will let this one go quietly.' It has troubled me a bit since then but I still don't see that I could do anything else. Sometimes you get decisions that are not clear cut and never will be. But almost it becomes philosophy then rather than a reasoned approach.

* * *

From somewhere the Germans got a load of filthy, old, cattle trucks and loaded all of these boys on stretchers two deep into those and loaded us on the train right through the night clear across Germany ... to Nuremberg, and I was the doctor on that train looking after them all. And then when I got to Nuremberg, we weren't there very long before Patton crossed the Rhine and advanced straight to Nuremberg and they picked us all up and force marched us back towards Munich, and I had about two and a half thousand, only two hundred RAF, but the rest were United States aircrew boys and I was the doctor for the whole column ... at the end of the day you had to patch them all up, twisted ankles, because if you didn't march you fell by the wayside and we knew that the SS was twenty-four hours behind and anybody that they found was shot. So there was a great onus on the doctor to keep the boys marching and a great willingness on theirs to overcome a lot of pain and keep going too, because it was that or nothing. And then at the end of patching up my mates, in would come the guards to see *Herr Doktor*. And when I had shot of them in came the townsfolk to see *Herr Doktor*. Because they didn't have a doctor in these little villages, and I had the medical supplies from the Red Cross, and I could speak it, so I was treating them as well. That's the meaning of the Hippocratic oath, it doesn't matter who comes to you for medical help, whoever they are, whatever their colour or their creed you help them, and there was a bloke, if I had tried to escape he would have shot me but that's the way it was.

And then we got word from the German guards that the next step was to take the two hundred RAF and march just us to Berchtesgaden, to Hitler's secret hideout in the Austrian mountains. And we were to be held there as hostages. It didn't take more than a few seconds to work out that that would be the end of us. If we weren't bombed, because they couldn't bomb Berchtesgaden and not bomb us if we were going to be held inside it, and so we thought, 'We are either going to be killed by friendly fire, or the Germans will shoot us, they're never going to let us, they are not going to die themselves and let us go free.'

So that was when we really bribed some guards and a couple of the guys got into Munich itself and knocked a couple of heads in, people unconscious and got into the German radio station and broadcast a message to England saying they were going to march us to Berchtesgaden as hostages. That night the RAF sent over Mosquitoes, very low level, a lot of them and when we awoke in the morning those A5 white leaflets were like snow right through the camp and all around it. And it said:

Attention. [in German of course] *Any man or woman in the armed forces or civilian who moves or causes to be moved or takes part in the moving of any prisoner of war from here to anywhere else will be held guilty. Be charged with a war crime. Upon liberation you will be tried by court martial on the spot, the penalty is death and the sentence will be carried out immediately. Signed Harry Truman, Winston Churchill, Josef Stalin.*

We didn't move ... and we were liberated only a few days after that, Patton came in himself, and twenty minutes after the tanks had come in and bashed down the gates, the guards had disappeared of course, they heard the tanks coming and just vanished. Twenty minutes later they had a doughnut van and we were eating hot doughnuts and were as sick as dogs. After our food to rich American sweet doughnuts and we were scoffing them you know, gutsing them, you can't call it anything else.

* * *

It is funny how your past catches up with you. Sydney was on the short list for the 2000 Olympic Games with Manchester, Sydney or Beijing. And each nation had an International Olympic Commissioner, the IOC, and they would ask three or four, they would ask them to come out ... and I was contacted by the RAAF headquarters in Sydney to say did I remember a man, a prisoner of war from that camp whose name was 'Jarbloff' or something or other. And I said, 'Spell it.' And he said, 'S-T-A-U B-O.' I said, 'Jani Staubo, I sure do remember him! He was part of my digging team and a wonderful guy.'

'Oh, thank heavens for that. He is Norway's International Olympic Commissioner.'

Before the war he had been in their Davis Cup squad. And he was a champion cross-country snow skier and a wonderful sportsman right up to virtually Olympic standard. But when he was shot down, when Norway fell, like the Vikings, a few of them just pushed a boat out into the sea and like the Vikings, just managed to sail across to England. And land in England and join the RAF and be retrained and get back into combat. Then he got shot down again and captured. And he got away and they recaptured him and he got away again. And when they recaptured him again the next time they had him in manacles with a length of chain in between. And he was being brought to the main camp by train and he was sitting next to the window there with a German armed guard there and a German armed guard there by that window. And I don't know who was in the fourth seat, but there he was and he waited until the train got up a lot of speed . . . and it was rocking around the bend like that and then when it started to sway the other way he just went, 'Phew!' And being an ex-Olympic guy, he was tall, about six-three, he just shoulder-butted and flat on his back and he was just off, running like only he could run. Straight down the train. Now those trains, rather like the trains here, they have a sliding door between each compartment and he ran through it, tried to shut it behind him to be able to get to the end of the train to be able to jump off and get free. Well, he almost got there when they went around a bend the wrong way and he was pinned half through a doorway and with his manacles he just couldn't, and a guard was after him. He said, '*Hande hoch!*' which means, 'Put your hands up!' So Jan had his back to him, the German guard was behind him and he didn't know where he was. But there was a rifle there somewhere of course so he just pretended he was going to put his hands up like that but as he brought them up he had a double length of chain between them and swung around and was going to kill him and the German fired his rifle almost touching his chest. I have seen the burn.

Well, of course he was straight off to hospital and very ill for quite a long time and eventually came to our camp into our hospital for final rehabilitation. And that's where I met him. He was very keen to get involved in the escaping and that's where we became closely associated, but we were separated at the end of the war when I stayed in the hospital and he went out, being marched away in the snow with the rest of the camp and I lost contact with him.

His letter said he was coming out to inspect Sydney for the Olympics and while here he would love to catch up with some of his old ex-Aussie POW mates and that's where the lives started to intersect again. And they flew me down to Sydney for a meeting. They gave us a two-hour briefing, first the Sydney Olympic Committee on Homebush, they had a model four metres by four metres I suppose, and you had to try and memorise everything that was there so that you could explain all of the virtues of it to the visiting delegates. And then they said, 'You have got a lunch with Jan Staubo at the

Oxford Military Barracks.' The old barracks in Sydney. 'You have got four hours to convince him that Sydney is the place.'

So when I went to the Oxford Barracks they picked us up by car and he was being introduced to the guys as they came past, shaking his hands, and he caught sight of me and he just ran straight to me and he said, 'Geoff, I would like you to sit next to me, please?'

And I said, 'I would very much like to, Jan.'

And so I sat next to him and it was on. And I said, 'If you can, when you're finished with Sydney, come back and have a couple of weeks on the Gold Coast with me and we will have a real...'

'Oh,' he said. 'I would like that but I think they have got me on a tight schedule, I have got to get up to Beijing yet.'

And next thing I got a letter from Oslo saying he was sorry he couldn't get the time in. 'Anyway I hope courtesy of QANTAS to be back one day and I will see you again in Sydney.'

Now he did not mention the Olympic Games but we knew damned well that he was voting for Sydney and that was the deciding vote. There was 34 all and Stabo made it 35 to 33. And Sydney got the Olympic Games just through a chance association that I picked up his name. It is true, absolutely true.

* * *

I would say the single most outstanding thing that I found was that I don't think before I was in the height of war I had ever had to trust the man on the left side of me and the man this side of me and the man behind me, with my life. Know that he would defend it with his own. And then knowing that I would give my life to save his if necessary. In other words a team spirit under threat of death in war and that is what I think makes an army, and by army I don't just mean land army, I mean air force, navy, fighting armed forces. I think it is that. It is the absolute need to have complete and absolute confident trust, not just half-trust, 'I hope he looks after me and is prepared to do what he should do.' No, you learnt that the only way through it was a complete sense of unity, a complete sense of purpose and absolutely one hundred per cent loyalty to the death.

And I think that helps mould your character and your thoughts and the way that you handle a lot of the rest of your life. You learn to trust other people, depending on them, but not a one-way dependence. You are not depending on them saying, 'Well, he is not going to repay me.' You know he might start to depend, but then you will be doing the repaying.

TED KENNA, VC

Infantry
New Guinea
World War II

Well I have a lot of fond memories of Hamilton, all fond memories actually but—you know how they operate. Boys do certain things and the girls do certain things. But I went to school. I wasn't much of a scholar. Done reasonably well. Got merits . . . reading and writing and arithmetic, and that was about it . . . if you passed those three, oh, a bit of geography and English, yeah English was the main and that was of course the big thing at my age, if you got merits you could get in the bank or get in the police force and all the rest of it.

We went rabbiting after school. We knocked off at a quarter to four and went rabbiting. We'd walk out, had to walk of course, you could walk out to about six mile, five mile, and you could start catching rabbits then . . . and then the weekends of course was rabbiting again, we had to keep on rabbiting otherwise we wouldn't have had much on the table I don't think, because Dad was only on the railways and their wages wasn't so hot. Well, none of our wages was hot then anyhow and the few bob we got for the skins . . . shooting them, catching them, digging them out—any way we could get them. We skinned 'em, hung 'em out to dry, would take about a week, then take them down to the skin-buyer. There was about three here then and see which one was the honest one and which one tried to cheat you penny or twopence and sell them the best price you could get for them and that was it.

Socially I done all right because Nell, the younger sister, she took it on herself to learn me to dance. I took till after I was married before I learnt to dance, so she had to keep me informed...all the old-time stuff you know, barn dance all that. I never had a go at the other. That was too reckless for me... Hopalong Cassidy and Tom Mix. Do you know Tom Mix? Oh should have, you were born too late; you should have seen Tom Mix. He was a great cowboy. Tom Mix and Hoppy. Oh yeah I used to never miss a movie, never miss a cowboy. They were good.

... The first job I ever had was after school—a couple of bob for running a water boy. Know what a water boy was in that day? Well, I'll tell you what a water boy is...the sewerage was going in here then and some of the trenches were down sixteen feet and some of them were even deeper than that...and you had jokers digging... digger here and then a digger there and in between was the same distance and they tunnelled, both of them tunnelled in till they met— and I was the water boy and that meant when some joker got thirsty or something like that he said, 'Water, water, water!'

And I had to run down with a bucket, fill it up and drop it down to him and he would have a drink see, out of me bucket—and they were drinking out of that and put it over his head or something and off I would go to the next one and the next one and the next one. You'd be going like a yoyo—I got a few bob out of it. Anyhow that come to a sorry end. This joker was singing out for water, water, water and I was a bit late, I was hung up somewhere and was doing the best I could and he started abusing me for not carrying the water. He had to wait for water so he started abusing me.

I said, 'What are you abusing me for? I've done the best I can.'

And he said, 'Well when I sing out for water I want water!'

So I had me bucket here that I used to fill out and I said, 'Do you want water here?'

And he said, 'Yeah!'

Whoosh! That was the end of the water boy.

* * *

They signed us in down in a shop down in Grey Street. They bundled us off to Geelong and we were at Geelong, oh, a few months, and all we done was gun training, marching and learnt to blow up a few trees. Had a cocky [a farmer] there, I think he must have had something to do with the army somehow because he let the army in to demonstrate to us how to blow these trees or bridges or whatever we had to do and of course I'll always remember him. Whitnall was his name—and he always used to say whatever you do—so forth and so forth, one there and one there. Stack it up with jelly [gelignite] but he always said, 'Take the majority—and add to that to make certain.'

We blew up this tree down on some property near Drysdale somewhere and we blew it up and up it went. It went that high I thought it was a kite. He put far too much in it and blew it and pieces were going everywhere—anyhow but that was his argument, add more. So we did and blew it all right. I wouldn't like to do the same thing now and I think the same gentleman, I don't know but I think it caught up to him too. I think he blew his hand off in the finish poor fellow.

* * *

After serving in Darwin, Ted became a replacement for the 2/4th Battalion. Their next stop was New Guinea.

City of Mexico. Oh, that was a lovely ship. I really had a good time. They lined us up, well, some had half a deck each. It was a lovely layout you could lay anywhere... but I had a bit more trouble than a lot of them too. I happened to have seasickness hit me as soon as I stepped on deck and the boat wasn't even going and I felt myself going and I was really—I was going, the ship wasn't going and when the ship was going I was going.

... And every time dinner companies used to line up... and had to go down 1, 2, 3, 4 passageways, the line was going down and around this passageway to the kitchen where I believe, I don't know if this is true or not, where I believe they handed out your tea, your spuds, and whatever there. But I never got there. I had to leave—upside down and outside every time. Anyhow when they said—I think a couple of nights out—someone said, 'I hope they don't come and sink us.'

I said, 'I hope they do, it would have been a blessing.'

...That's how I felt about our lovely boat that took us to New Guinea so if it had of went down...and I can't swim either at the time. I can't swim, I would have been thankful. So that was me trip.

* * *

Well, it's a funny thing actually. You kind of want to go very much but then you think about all the rest of it and then you have your doubts and then one thing and another, what you'll do and how you'll perform. The greatest battle I think the soldier has to perform is actually waiting to go. It's a queer thing to say, but the thing that's always in the soldier's mind is how will I go and it doesn't matter where or how or what distance in between actions, it always comes back to the night before—the first shot, how will they go in this, will they stand up or will they do something silly or something like that? Let your mate down or something. You don't know and that's always in the soldier's mind, I think, and it's a question that every soldier, big, small, indifferent, has to answer. And he can't answer that until he fronts up. He can't say I proved meself there or I proved meself there. He can't prove himself until the time comes and it's always in the back of his head is that question, how will I go and that's it. And you don't know until you've been through it I'm afraid. And then he says I didn't go so hot—could have done more but you only get once chance and that's it.

A lot of times that I've spoken to a higher up, like say a captain or lieut or something like that and told him in certain terms that what he was doing wouldn't win the war at all, but when I look back at it now everything I done and everything I was going to do and failed like they told me, and I went against it to me own stupid mind... And how many times the lieut told me that or a private or a corporal and at the time of the moment I'd forgotten, it didn't register or something or whatever. They're trying in the best of their minds to try and teach you something that you should know probably but don't.

We learnt, which I had a fair idea of anyhow, learnt the way to treat a jungle and the way the jungle treats those that is kind to them somehow. And the way to walk and the way to move in the jungle. It might only be walking from here to there but you've got to move with certain care or certain respect I'll put it that way, and that's how it is. If you do it the other way you run into trouble—if trouble's there of course... But in war of course all these things add up. They're not written on a book, they're in your mind and they've got to come out. Your mind tells you that's how it is, I suppose.

... Well myself, I had the Bren for a start, and that was what, thirty-two pound, I think, and on top of that I had magazines, about four or five magazines and then some more bullets—and then me gear and that, and all the rest of it. I don't know what we carried, seventy pounds or so. Well, I'll tell you what it wasn't cold. Yes it was very hot. It's a different heat. It was no use changing your shirt or anything like that, it was wet again in two seconds so it didn't make any difference. That's how hot it was... muddy and slippery and nice cursing weather.

* * *

Wewak was a funny place. It was kept as storage... and they had Wewak tunnelled right through. Not one tunnel, like tunnelled right through, and they had a kind of store of everything there, stores and ammo the whole lot, everything was there... there was supposed to be a Japanese general was shot in one of the tunnels and our section got the nice little job of going in and bringing him out, which was—well a job I'll never forget, I don't think, ever. You couldn't see and you were feeling your way up till you got a bit of light; they had light and that coming in at certain places—and all the rest of it. Anyhow we got this chappie after a while and then we had to try and get him out and he had shot himself of course I might add. He shot himself. Anyhow we got him out with all his gear and I heard later, I don't know whether that was right—they got valuable information out of him but it was pretty tricky because we had a fair few Japs still in the caves and it wasn't my idea of cricket, actually... but even at night you couldn't rest or anything like that because you didn't know when one of them would take a go to get out or something like that and a couple of times they did too, you could hear them.

At times I think the Japanese was a good soldier, a very good soldier, but other times he seemed to go walkabout in lots of ways. You'd come across him at times in a position where he looked to be pretty well set in and take a lot of moving and half the time he'd up and leave then when you attacked. He'd fight for a while and then he would retreat back again. He would leave a good position and go back further which seemed to me like a roundabout way. In other positions you reckoned he'd lay down quite easy, and he'd fight and he would fight to the last man and you had to kill him, simple ... I don't know, he was hard to understand and that but he was a good fighter ... I think for the simple reason that you didn't know what he was going to do. I don't think so anyhow. It's confusing, not stand up and fight or anything like that.

... One of our boys was shot—and they couldn't do anything about it at the time and they had to leave him there. I think there were several there till things got organised, but they were still out in the bush in front of the company and anyhow when we did finally overtake it, and killed the ones that were there, when we held the position, they found several of the Nips had the muscles of this chappie in their containers. Not cooked or anything, but just say the muscle of a leg there, cut off, and had them in their containers. So that laid down the message that they were doing it, that some of them were hungry ... I thought it was a bit hard, I suppose, but then again, when you're soldiering and when you're doing things that actually you shouldn't be doing in the first place, at times, what goes on to carry out and carry on doing those things that this rule has got to be broken and of course they were probably in that position that they had to break it ... but I suppose the poor joker that got shot didn't mind it and, put it round the other way, the poor joker who shot him, he didn't mind it either, so there you are that's war. We don't want to get into it—but it's war.

... When men were shot they were shot ... It's happened but like it's a quick, evil thing and he's fighting and shooting and you're shooting and he gets it, well you haven't got time to knock off shooting and just know he's gone and you keep going. You don't realise it till after that you were next to him—just go, that's it. That's the way it is. Just go. If you stop too long in a certain position in places like that, well you're kind of asking for it.

We'd call first aid and then the first-aid people would get him and if it wasn't the doc, just corporals and privates in the first aid, they'd probably bandage him up or something and put him on the stretcher and then carry him back, which happened to our first one that died. He got shot and we got him onto the stretcher but by the time we got him out from where he was, by the time we could get him, he'd lost too much blood. He was shot through the leg here somewhere and by the time we got the others around him and got him so that we could handle him and got him onto the stretcher, but before the doctor could do much he had died. A lot of cases like that happened where you just couldn't get to the person at the time and you just had to let him go until you'd done what you had to do and if the stretcher-bearer couldn't get to him well that was just too bad, that's what happens . . . like even your best mate, once he goes down and sometimes you've got time to do something and sometimes you haven't even got time to do something, you've got to keep going and if you've got time to do something you're only there for a few minutes anyhow, to put a field-dressing on him or something like that, and then you're off again because there's two reasons for that. One is, of course, your own survival. You're sitting there just where he is and he got shot there, well the law of war says he can shoot there again. He mightn't be there, but nine times out of ten he's going to have another shot and you're going to be the next one. So if you don't pull him aside or under protection you're doing the wrong thing by doing anything for him. So you've got to have the protection before you start thinking of it. It's one of the horrors of war because at times that's how it happens and sometimes you've got to do it that way.

* * *

Our company crossed this river at four o'clock in the morning and one chap was crossing it—all quiet, the less noise you can make—and he was taking it very easy. He pulled out his pipe, put the pipe in his mouth and was trying to light it—in the wind you know, and the matches were going out and flames going everywhere in the middle of the river but the poor fellow, he was making noises and singing out and that—they got him to the other side, the side where we were going and then that's the last I seen of him. Just one case where it was just too much—big joker, tall, he was six foot, quiet, just couldn't help themselves.

All the time in New Guinea, well every day was a day of war, but you can't say, 'I'm not in New Guinea.' You can get shot at any time and, as I said, on lots of occasions too, you hear some soldiers here of my age say that, 'Oh I was in the thick of a certain area.' I don't know but war isn't an area of numbers. You're in war in a country. In the Second World War, when they went over to France... and war could be a little patrol. One men, two men, three men on patrol and you get shot, well that war is the biggest war he's ever been in—only a handful of men. It's not the number of shots that counted—well real hits, I suppose—but that's the biggest war he's ever been in and if you call them big, in my book the small little patrol could be the biggest war of the lot. But you hear some chappies skiting about, 'Oh I was in that big war—lost so many men,' and all the rest of it but it doesn't take men, it doesn't take anything. It's one life as far as they're concerned and that's the big war. That's my idea of war. You can't tell me that war is something like taking Wewak or the Kokoda Trail where they stopped the Nips coming out, that's no bigger than the others... Now they might have been a better unit than ours and they lost less men on the Kokoda Trail than we—we had more killed and wounded on the Aitape, down in the Wewak area, and yet they say Kokoda was the bigger, the big war. It's the same in Vietnam and all the rest of it. There's no such thing as big war. It's a one-man job and that's it.

* * *

We went back for a spell for a week or so after nine weeks of fighting I think. We went back to rest up, supposed to rest up back a few mile and we had duties where they kept us right on our toes of course, drill and that—biscuit patrol as they called it. Biscuit patrol, which was the Fuzzy Wuzzies carrying all our gear into the main fighting areas... We were guarding them but a couple of times we did fire a few shots here and there to keep the Japs off. They didn't mind bully beef either so they wanted their share of it too but we denied them that little pleasure. It was good there. It put a bit of humour back into it and gives you a break from war. You're actually in war but it was actually a break from war, a different thing and you're guarding them. I used to smoke and smoke fairly heavy and when we were marching, at ten minutes to the hour, break for a smoko if you wanted or whatever and at every smoko a little fellow that I was guarding... he used to always find his way next to me. Every time I sat down and was resting he'd be sitting there and I used to give him a smoke of course and he used to smoke this smoke and really love it and everywhere I went he kept at me, all the time I was there. I would just roll this smoke and just started it up and just enjoying it and here he would be sitting next to me, grinning all over his face. So I would give him a smoke and he'd be happy as hell so away he went again and the next spell, didn't matter where we were, he'd be there again for his smoke. Didn't miss a trick. They were good fellows... they could move in the jungle a lot better than we could, the boys, as I found out when I got wounded when they carried me back. It was downhill and up dale and all the rest of it and you'd hardly know you were moving actually but it took eight to carry one so I had four men, four on each side with the pole—but when they come to change, even downhill, they'd walk under and you wouldn't know the ones that take the weight and the others that walk out beside it, you wouldn't know you were moving. They were great.

* * *

Ted Kenna was awarded a Victoria Cross. His commendation read:

> *In an engagement with the enemy two sections attacked but were halted by intense fire after several men were hit. Kenna, in the support section, endeavoured to bring his gun to bear on the bunker, but was unable to because of the nature of the ground.*

Without orders, and on his own initiative, he immediately stood up in full view of the Japanese and engaged the bunker with a Bren gun, then a rifle and then a Bren gun again. The enemy machine-gunners were only 50 metres away from him and their fire was so accurate that bullets passed between his arms and body but miraculously did not hit him. The remaining post was then knocked out by a tank and the attack was successfully concluded; many enemy were killed and several automatic weapons were captured.

This is Ted's telling of that day.

They had a gun up near Wirui Mission, up on the hill. They fired down into the swamp so it wasn't too comfortable there for a while but they brought a tank up then and got rid of the machine gun and of course we just went up and wiped out the few Nips that was visible and then formed our own defence across it ... it was pretty rugged, like even when they say it was flat it wasn't mountainy but it wasn't flat either. You were walking up hills and down dale all the time and we went up the track, but we had the tank, which cut out more or less, we were behind the tank guarding the tank so that they couldn't attack the tank ... Anyhow, just before the Wirui Mission the tank couldn't go any further. The tank was stranded up on the hill there and we had to go forward on our own to take the Wirui Mission ... a few bullets were flying around but nothing much. Then when we really got inside of it they opened up completely there and we went to ground of course. There was a kind of a mound, bit of a mound, a hill, and they were dug in and had the machine gun halfway up but when we went down of course it was close enough to them but the ground was that hilly and rough that you couldn't see anything. You're kind of looking at nothing.

... And anyhow this machine gun opened up ... and that's when I got up. I couldn't see down below, I got up and opened fire, three shots and was a bit lucky there and a couple got in the road of a couple of bullets. But then ... when I was doing that, the second bunker opened up on me and that's when I put that out of action too, with a bit of luck ... I couldn't get at it properly with the Bren so I called for a rifle which one of the boys threw up from the grass and I happened to get hit there so I was all right ... we didn't know anything about that bunker at all until it opened up and then that's when I got me good shirt ruined I might add.

Three weeks later, Ted was badly wounded in another action.

[The officer] said, 'Private Kenna, your job is to attack and capture this position.' I thought, 'It's a bit hard.' I said, 'I can't do that, Sir,' and he said, 'Why?' I said, 'I haven't got any authority. You took that lance corporal job off me,' and he said, 'That's all right.' He said, 'We'll make you a corporal in the field.' I said, 'That will be good.' So I went back and told the boys, had a good jaw and I don't think they were too keen on it. Anyhow I explained the position to them and as I said that you could walk around here safe as anything but as soon as you were out in the open and there was one tree—and this is where I made the blue of me life, one tree and a big one. It had fallen down across, in between me and them ... and I thought if I get me gun set up there I might be able to do something. So I took off. I got there. Plonked down—gun in front of me and I suddenly seen something out of the corner of me eye—and swung me gun around but I was too late. Of course it hit me here and the next thing Lieutenant Whitehead lobbed down beside me and he said, 'Are you hit?'

And I mumbled something—but he couldn't understand me and he said, 'We'll get out ...'

You might have thought it would knock me out but it didn't. It gave me a bit of a headache for a while. Me mouth was all shot away. Me tongue was all right but I couldn't get anything out. I thought it was all right ... as I got halfway down I heard another shot and didn't know it at the time but poor old Whitehead, he got hit through the side of the head and anyhow I got down and they pulled me down and put a couple of field-dressings on here.

There was only a great gap—and they put this field-dressing on, two of them, and gave me a drink and so forth and then I had to walk back, I don't know how far, I had to walk back to the doctors where he was operating on a couple of jokers that got hit and I laid down there and he just come along and had a look at this. He said, 'Oh yeah that's all right.'

And then he must have spotted some more blood here or something . . . Anyhow he found out then that there were two holes here and the blood was pumping out the hole—shooting it out. That was the main danger I think in the first place. He said, 'This is going to hurt.'

And he sewed those two holes up—stung a bit but not much. Anyhow he said, 'I don't know about that, it will have to be a hospital job.'

I said, 'Will I make it all right?' I tried to say that.

He said, 'You'll make it. You're all right.'

And anyhow I got two days ride with the Fuzzy Wuzzies and me brother of course, he was down the coast with malaria and he heard that A Company got done over and he said, 'Damn Ted!' and he borrowed boots and he borrowed a shirt and borrowed this and that and dumped his uniform and went out to the track and he hitchhiked a ride up to where I was at the tent on the beach . . . he was sitting on the stone outside the hospital when they carried me out. But I couldn't speak to him of course but that's how it was. That's a bit of connection of brotherly love I suppose. He knew it straightaway, so that's how it was.

You haven't got that much time. You know, you say you're thinking of this and thinking of that, well you do too, but actually when the time comes you're thinking of yourself and that fellow up there. I would say it was—I think—because we were pretty good pals pretty good mates. But I think too—the whole thing, the whole war, that not only brothers—but you're all kind of brothers in a way, and to miss them is something. Hearing they got killed or seeing them get killed or hearing them get killed. It's a hard thing and you've got that close feeling right through the army so there might be one or two in C Company you get along well with and really well and B Company and C Company, you know, it's all kind of scattered. Very hard, very hard. If you stop and think that, the idea as they say, is not to think, but that's the way it goes, mate . . . What is mateship, how do you get this and the answer is still the same. For me to try and tell anyone what mateship really is I'm stretching it. I can't put words to it. I think it's something that grows there. Well, that's it. I don't know. I'm damned if I know.

So that was it. I don't think I was scared. I don't think I had time to be scared. I wouldn't know ... I suppose every man's scared. I suppose every soldier I think is scared—but that's it ... It's just one of those things that you do, I suppose. It's hard to say. I think anyone would have done the same thing in the same position because, well it's no good laying down there and doing nothing. You had to do something and I don't think the Nips would have brought tea or dinner for me so I had to get up and do something and I honestly think that any soldier would have done the same thing.

* * *

The old doc and the priest came around the next morning at the hospital where the Fuzzy Wuzzies dumped me and the priest said to the doc ... 'What's he got and what chance has he?'

And he said, '40/60 against.'

I said, 'Pigs. I'm the other way, don't you worry.'

I couldn't say it but that's what I was thinking—don't you worry and that's the last I seen of him. Then we went further up to another hospital ... it was a car ride and aeroplane ride. I forget the morning now. I wouldn't have a clue but they got me up one morning from that hospital, drove me for a day in the jungle track up to another hospital. I didn't know, just an overnight stop, there was some of me mates there and some of the enemies too, some Japanese and some Australians and I stopped there overnight and then got on the plane the next morning and landed on top of Australia, I've forgotten now, the big airbase up there. Townsville ... and stopped there for a day or two, a day I think. I think they were all overnight stops then from Townsville to Brisbane to Melbourne and it might have been a day or two days I don't know. I was a bit hazy at times. And lobbed at Melbourne ... the bandage was still on, that my mates had put on when I first got wounded ... and of course Sister Scully had to clean me up a bit. Not that I thought I needed it but anyhow.

Marj, who later married Ted, was a nurse in that ward. This is how she remembers it:

It was pretty dramatic, really, because you know I was only a young twenty-year-old and put into one of the worst wards there, I'd say, and he arrived in with this bandage on and the sister called me in to help and clean him up and took it off and well just about rocking on our toes I think from the smell of it. All this was blown away and all this had a hole. They said, 'Put your hand in here.'

And the sister said at one stage 'Go and get him a cup of tea.'

And he drank the tea and it all just poured out the hole. That was a very bad sight actually. I hadn't quite got used to it either because there were lots of bad sights there. And yeah that was the first introduction. And we cleaned him up and put him in the ward and from then on I was assigned to sort of look after him a little bit.

For Ted, a long and painful period in hospital was about to begin.

Well they had to heal this up first and then they had to get two pieces of jaw, a piece had shot right out of it and then they had to cut my golden hair off and put a plastic ornament around it just like a bike riding cap, or it was exactly the same but in plaster. Like bike-riding equipment to hold the seat of your bike steady when you're racing, to hold it steady on the bar ... Well, they had one of those and they hooked it in the plaster here and that was sticking out here. Quite an experience this was and then they cut me jaw there and they bored through the bone and hooked some barbed wire or something on that and hooked it onto the bike-riding tool here so they could keep that level.

They put bone from my hip in my jaw which he done by cutting the top where the hip is you know, the hip comes to a bit of a point ... they cut that off, the whole thing off, and then they sliced it up like a loaf of bread, the bone, cut up singly and then jammed the two bones together and tightened it and kept tightening it with this here till it knitted and then when that knitted I was right. I was ready to go home but that took, oh it took a fair while to heal for a start because they found in the neck here there was two little bits of cartridges we didn't know about and they kept expelling stuff out and I said to Doctor Rankin at the time I said, 'Sister Scully still can't fix that up. It's still weeping.'

Anyhow I opened my big mouth; I shouldn't have in front of the doctor. I said, 'It's got something in it, doctor.'

He said, 'How do you know?'

I said, 'I can feel it.' You could too.

He said, 'You're right there.'

And they stuck it in the hole and pulled it out and there was a bit of a shell. So he pulled that one out and it was a bit of casing shell of some kind I suppose from a faulty bullet or something like that and they got that out and it was the size of me nail on my little finger I suppose and they tried to heal it again and it wouldn't heal, still wouldn't heal, and I said to the doc next time he come around 'There's still something in it.'

And he said, 'Are you sure?'

And I said, 'Yeah.'

He mucked around and pulled another bit out about the same size and everything was perfect then. They healed it all up. Me hip healed up and anyhow I said to the doctor next time 'Well right. I'm ready to go home. I'm finished.'

And he said, 'Well in a fortnight you'll be right.'

And I said, 'Why?'

And he said—you see the jaw never sank in quite far enough and that's when I first done it—he said, 'What I want to do now is open it up and shave the bone inside and to heal it up again.'

And he said, 'Are you right, Ted?'

I said, 'No, Doc, I'm finished thanks.'

And with that I was discharged from hospital.

* * *

Marj's memory:

He explained about his operation but he didn't explain why he'd lost weight, because when they did the bone graft they had to keep their jaws locked, so their jaws were locked with a lead substance and they left one little hole on the right side where they could put a glass tube down. So all these boys that had jaw trouble, had locked jaws, and Ted had to be fed by tube so that meant they could only have soup or Bournevita and they lived on that for about nine or twelve months or whatever it was they were there. So that's why they lost weight. Ted used to come out to the kitchen sometimes and soak some toast in butter and then put that down the hole a little bit but not much. So that's why they lost weight. At one stage, oh I think Ted was anointed [given the Last Rites] about three times, once on the beach and then back at the hospital they thought no, he wasn't going to make it and the problem was that because of that blood being pumped out he'd lost a lot of blood and then the shock set in so he was put into a private ward and I used to feed him with a glass tube and so forth. And then we progressed from there.

He was talking once he had the bone graft and sort of muffled, through the locked jaw. About three weeks after he had been out to it at one stage he looked up and he said, 'Oh I think I'm going to marry you.'

Oh yeah that's a joke you know, and so this went on a bit longer and eventually, he used to walk me down to the sleeping quarters where we slept. We were only allowed to a certain stage. Actually they weren't supposed to be down there at all but they weren't allowed to step over the mark. I used to wheel the boys down to the theatre, to the pictures and so forth. They talked about it, they reckoned it was the talk of the duckboards, the romance of the duckboards, but I didn't even get a kiss goodnight because his jaws were locked anyway. I don't know whether it was a romance or what.

... The day before he'd had an x-ray on his chest because they thought the bullet might have hit the lung and so of course when this mate came rushing down and said, 'You're wanted urgently up in the ward. Quick, come up in the ward!'

And she told them all, 'I know where he is, he's under the shower.'

So of course we rushed Ted straight back and I worried all night. I thought, oh well, it looks like the bullet has hit the lung or something . . . I didn't know what it was all about till the next morning and there was people everywhere and photographers and women, the girls and women all sitting around the bed. I didn't even realise the extent of what it meant until after that. I mean you read about these things but it doesn't register till it happens. I don't think Ted even realised himself what it all meant till later on when it hit him.

* * *

I heard a voice—'Ted, Ted, where are you?' and I recognised the voice. It was one of me mates in hospital in the ward and I said to Marj, 'I've got to go.'

He said, 'You're wanted back in hospital straightaway. They're looking everywhere for you.'

And I said, 'Well this is strange.'

And it appears that the adjutant that rang up and wanted to see me, talk to me and of course there was no Ted Kenna in the ward. Anyhow Sister Scullion said, 'Oh he's in the shower, we'll get him.'

And everyone's out looking for me and Bernie knew where I was and he came and got me. He said, 'You're wanted on the phone.'

He rang up and he said, 'Congratulations, Private Kenna, you've been awarded the Victoria Cross.'

And I said, 'Oh that's a strange thing, you know, at this time of the day.'

He said, 'Yeah we'll be out straightaway more or less.'

And I said, 'That's fair enough, I suppose.'

Anyhow he came out and told me all about it and everything, that I had won the Victoria Cross but I couldn't work out why or when. And then he told me and I said, 'Oh that's it.' I don't know. So I was very happy of course, but didn't know what to say. Anyhow he reckoned it was true so that was it. I got it in Melbourne actually, Government House, by the Duke of Gloucester and Lady Gloucester. Mum was still here and Mum was an old-timer, you know, and she said she wasn't coming down to see it and I was engaged to Marj then . . . and Marj come, and we went out to Government House and they presented it out there. That was a big day and a big day for Marj too. Then we got married on 2nd June '47.

* * *

I can go into a company of young men which I've done a lot of times and given out trophies for the best rifle shot and the best that and the best this and mix with the young soldiers of the day, the up-and-coming ones at their walking-out parades and all the rest of it. I go there and I can stop into a club now and I can close me eyes actually and listen to them talk to one another and you can go back to me talking to one of me mates. You can hear them say that, but to tell them this is very, very hard for me to explain to them what happens to a soldier. It's like many have asked me how would the younger generation soldiers of the day operate in the same position I was in. Now to me this is quite easy to answer that, because you've only got to put yourself in an old man's position and try and think what the young one would do. Well, the young ones would be a lot better soldiers than we were. They've got to be because they've got a better education for a start. They're more knowledgeable. They've got better weapons and they're better trained. All they've got to do is to like the job. If they don't like it they can still be a good soldier but just not too often. So I say this and I'll say it to the day I die, that the younger generation must be a better soldier than we were, they must be.

Well, it wasn't my first choice in the world but I suppose I liked it, yeah. Liked it enough up to a certain thing but I don't think I'd ever make a general. Well, I liked being a soldier. It was all right but they had some fancy ideas that you had to march properly and all the rest of it which is a good thing. They all looked good and all the rest of it but somehow that kind of thing didn't impress me a great deal. But put me out in the bush and that's a different thing altogether and that is the life. We'll leave it at that. I'll be getting in trouble here.

NORMAN CAMERON

Dog Handler
Vietnam War

When we were young in Kingston and Mum and Dad were just coming out of the Depression, we had absolutely nothing. Mum and Dad and there was five children ... we lived with Dad's uncle and they got thrown out from there and we went to live with Mum's sister ... and it was too inconvenient from there, so they found some old tents that they patched together and we lived in tents under pine trees for about two years, where we used to walk to people's places ... to go to the toilet and have a shower ... and the local doctor recommended us for a Housing Commission home ...

Dad never ever drove in his life. He worked on the highways and his fortnightly wage was thirty-five pound a fortnight and until all the children were at school, Mum then left and got a job at the local hotel and she did the washing and laundry. She worked there for about twenty years and retired there before they moved to live in Adelaide. So financially wise we had nothing and we never went around asking for anything and we were happy just to have a close-knit family.

Most of the town where we came from were, in those days, related to someone and some had businesses there and some were like us. We just worked for the normal wage and got by on that and never complained. There wasn't any time that we didn't have a good meal on the table and that today is the main thing and the whole lot of us there together ... There was two local teams and believe it or not, with a family of five brothers . . . some of us played for the opposition. We played against each other and in those days it became fist-fights in the house against each other and sometimes one of my brothers would move out. And some of the businesses were run by people on opposite sides in the competition and some of them used to travel sixty to seventy miles to another town to do business rather than shop with the people in the same town, because they wouldn't patronise them during the football season. And that's just the attitude that we had and that's how we were bought up and how we played and that's how it was. You just don't mix.

* * *

I probably thought about it and looked at the town, and if you didn't work in the railways, or the council, or the highways, or on the boats as a fisherman, well, you could stop school at grade seven and go into those jobs anyhow because you didn't need anything. But looking at your future outside of those and you used to say, 'What am I going to do? There's nothing here.'

And when I got a job at the hardware I said, 'Where do I go from here? Selling nuts and bolts and earning five pound a week!' I said, 'You'd never afford nothing.'

[When I enlisted] . . . and first hitting New South Wales and finding that you've got hotels open after dark, this was unheard of. This was in the day when everything was closed by six and that's how we lived. Here we are in a place in Sydney where the lights and everything seem to go for—it doesn't close down. And you've got people coming from all different sorts of walks of life and it just blinds and boggles you, just mind boggles you and all this exists outside of your little town. There was a lot of adapting to do . . . and the Vietnam War was just virtually getting going in those days and down there we didn't see, or we didn't really know what was happening over there compared to in the city because they had TVs and we never, so they could see what was going on. But they didn't care, they were all for it.

[Communism] . . . was something that we just didn't agree with and as far as we were concerned we would stop that and we didn't want it and for that to get to here that was something that we just wouldn't have, and it was a no-no as far as we were concerned. And looking at communism, we thought if we could stop them there we were doing a good thing and we didn't want it here, and if we had to go there to stop it, so be it, and that's what we were led to believe, or that's what we ended up thinking, stop it there—it wasn't a good thing.

* * *

When we finished the corps training we were put into our battalions and to wait our turn to go to Vietnam, but when I applied I was only eighteen and a half and too young if the battalion was called to go overseas straightaway, I wouldn't have been able to go, so they sent me to a tracking team, a place called tracking team where they send all the young diggers that were too young to go to battalions. So I went there much to my disgust and learnt how to become a dog handler . . . and I was given a dog straightaway, once I said, 'I'll be a dog handler,' and someone else had it [the dog] and left and I took it, and I had it for about a month and it just liked chasing kangaroos that one, so I used to be chasing kangaroos instead of people, so they chose to get rid of him . . . see we used to go bush on Monday and come back Friday and just lay tracks for each other and teach our dogs how to track, and you might have a half-a-mile one, or you might have five-mile tracks you'd follow, and mine, if there was a kangaroo around he'd just take off and I'd end up miles from where I was supposed to be and only learning it, you wouldn't know the difference, but I hardly ever found the bloke at the end of the track, so we got rid of him.

I didn't have a dog and then I was a duty dog handler the weekend the RSM [Regimental Sergeant Major] rang up and said, 'Someone's got a dog for you, go and get it'.

So two of us went and picked up a dog, fatter than a pig, that round, had to lift him on the back of the Rover and let him out of the back of the Rover, and he nearly broke his neck jumping out. He took off from us, ran ten feet and collapsed and the next morning the boss came in and said, 'Hear you've got a new dog? Just picked up another dog?'

I said, 'Yeah, it's good for nothing.'

He said, 'Why?'

I said, 'It's too fat and it won't work.'

He said, 'Well that's your problem, boy, 'cause that's your dog now.'

And I said, 'Oh!'

And they all laughed, big, fat dog that couldn't walk ten yards and anyway off we went and I thought, 'Well if he's going to be mine, I'd better do something about it.'

So every morning, every afternoon, we built up to a five k jog, morning, afternoon, and being a seeing-eye dog I didn't have to teach him much obedience. He was smarter than the other dogs, so we had one thing up on them as they were still trying to teach their dogs to sit, stand, down, come, and my little fellow did everything because he'd been trained as a seeing-eye dog, but he was too boisterous . . . A month went by and we had this lovely dog, fit as a fiddle, as strong as an ox, going past all the dogs that had been there for six months, seven months, twelve months, just going past them gradually, bypassing them in fitness, bypassed them in tracking length, tracking distance . . . and that was mine, Cassius . . . the whole training wing used Roman emperors' names, all Roman names, Cassius, Caesar, Justin, Brutus, all Romans.

When we initially started them to learn to track we give them a bit of a biscuit at the end but not when they got working, otherwise if you start doing small tracks, say two hundred yards, when you're learning them and you give them a biscuit at the end, a lot of them would think, 'When I get to two hundred yards I should be getting a biscuit,' and pack it in. 'I'm not going to keep on going if you're not going to give me a biscuit when I've done me two hundred yards.'

So you had to cut that reward out pretty early because some of them would say, 'That's it.' So you had to be as smart as them. As dumb as they are, they're smart, that's why you had to learn to be a team, work around them and I learnt how he worked and he had to learn how I worked and it was just something that you just can't pick up and give to someone. But doing it, you're learning, man it's absolutely fantastic that you've got something there and something you learn to love and trust and he does the same for you.

An Aboriginal is a visual tracker. He doesn't go on the scent or whatever but they work on ageing. They can pick the ageing of the rocks being turned, the sand being scooped, twigs being broken and everything that we cause on our path to somewhere. See . . . they're looking for that broken twig, they're looking for the turning rock, they're looking for anything, where all those things create a scent of their own, which moulds up into the scent that you give off and that is what the dogs follow . . .

How we did that initial training was our instructor would get us to harness a dog up and by this time I'd built a relationship with my dog, and then I'd give the dog to the instructor, and I'd run away from my dog, yelling and screaming at him and getting him all excited so all he wanted to do was be with you anyhow, and then he'd turn him away and face him in a different direction and then I'd take off and I'd hide in the bushes somewhere. And then he'd turn around while I was down and all the dog wanted to do was find me anyhow, and once he learnt, 'Oops, where did he go?'

The only way he could find me was he had to smell and every time he found me scent, there I was at the end and then we'd change it over and probably after three or four times, someone else would do it and he got to know and he'd see no one and it got to the stage that this harness meant it was tracking, and we'd do that for probably two weeks at base before we went out scrub, laying tracks and that for them, bigger ones. We'd work from one-minute-old tracks while they were learning, up to probably five-minute-old tracks so someone would sit there for five minutes. And at that stage, that was when the initial scent would start, he had to try to learn how to point and that but he was just like a bull at a gate, just wanted to get to there . . . he found something that he loved to do and he did it good and all he wanted to do was work, work, work and this is why he would just punish himself, and he'd literally track himself into exhaustion every time, literally collapse . . . and to have someone that really worked their guts out for me and got the results that he did for me I was happy as anything. It was all right here when we were playing games, but as we were getting readier for where the big things are, it's going to be different for the both of us.

* * *

I was chosen to be the first one out with a dog to go to Vietnam and join the battalion . . . and they said, 'You're going through Canungra.'

Which I hadn't done and everyone has to go through Canungra [Jungle Training Centre] before they can go overseas. And I thought, 'Oh,' and everyone laughed at me, because here was a new soldier, never been in a battalion, didn't know the goings or ins and outs . . . and off I go to Canungra for three weeks before I join the battalion up north. That was all right and the next day they came and said, 'Righto give us your dog. We're going to put him in a kennel for three weeks while you go to Canungra.'

I said, 'No, he comes with me.'

They said, 'No, we're throwing him in a kennel.'

And I said, 'No, I'm going nowhere. I'm going to Vietnam in two months' time and I'm not taking a dog that's not fully fit or up on his training, so forget it.' And they said, 'Don't you tell us what to do!'

And I said, 'Get me the highest person that you can get and I don't care where they are, I want to speak to them.'

And I ended up getting onto the adjutant general in Victoria and I spoke to him for half an hour and the next morning I was on the train going north to join the battalion.

I said, 'I'm not going. They want to kennel my dog for three weeks and we're going to Vietnam.'

I said, 'My dog will be six months behind in his training.' And I said, 'And I've got my life and people's lives at stake and what's it worth? Me spending three weeks in Canungra?'

He said, 'Don't worry, we'll get a course for you somewhere.'

So I joined the battalion up north and, 'What are you doing here?' And I explained to my commander and it was then that I was introduced to the battalion commander and the RSM of the battalion and they said, 'Don't get as fat as your dog, off you go.'

That was my introduction to my battalion commander and the RSM. The next morning, still not used to what goes on, the battalion has enemies [troops dressed as enemy soldiers] and all that up there working with them . . . and the next thing, I'm taking my dog for a walk and 'Bang!' and the RSM comes up, 'You're dead.'

And I said, 'What?'

He said, 'You're dead, you're shot, a grenade went off.'

I said, 'Where?'

And he said, 'We're in war times up here fella, you don't know nothing, get your dog and get out.'

Three days and I was banished back into nothing, and I said, 'Can't I walk my dog?'

And he said, 'Get your dog out!'

So I said, 'This is going to be a lovely twelve months in the battalion.'

So I did my three days out and came back and they said, 'Get the dog squad out of here.'

So me and my twelve mates were just told to get away from the battalion and work on our own, so we worked the dogs for three weeks on our own, just keeping the dogs going . . . We didn't have anything to do with the battalion, no ongoing events up there. We just did our own work. We just laid tracks and worked with the dogs and field tracking for three weeks. They didn't want us. I said, 'Here's twelve months in Vietnam sitting on our arse, walking the dogs around the block.'

. . . And that was my introduction to the battalion with my little dog and what made it worse was 'Private Cassius', everyone laughed. This was what the RSM had on his roll call and everyone laughed because they knew it was my dog and no one answered and then someone went, 'Woof woof' in the background and that made the

RSM look a goose and no one makes an RSM look like a goose, so we become a bigger outcast

* * *

Vietnam blowed me out of my mind. You've just got no perception of what it is, what you're coming into and it doesn't matter what they tell you or what you do unless you're actually there, goodness me. You've got all these people running around in little go-carts and in their dress and the language; you've just got no perception of just what it is. You know that people talk different and you've seen them but you're just thrown in and that's where it all happens, and there were about four of us in Vung Tau and all it was Americans and Vietnamese. And of course we called in and had a couple of drinks at the bar before we went out there and just different altogether. No bottled beer and it was all rubbish, to our taste anyway, but later on you'd probably drink it anyhow, but the whole thing was just strange.

It was probably intimidating first off. 'This is it, we're here amongst it.' But what are we amongst? Because we're in a town with these people and these are people that we're helping or are we going to shoot? Who is it because they're the same, everything's the same, everyone's the same and how are we ever going to tell the difference in these people? And let's get out and be with our own, nothing against the people but that's just how you feel. We got off the plane and we were there and driving around in Vung Tau itself and, 'How can we be here and fighting them and we're driving around in the midst of it? There's a war here and yet we're driving around in amongst people and who are they?'

We don't know and yet the town's full of both Vietnamese and Viet Cong. Well, they tell you that, just watch out because there's Viet Cong with them and you say, 'Who's going to shoot, who's going to do what?'

You've got no idea.

* * *

The first operation that we went on, Operation Lismore, the battalion went out and they took the [visual] tracking team but they said, 'The dogs are not going.'

So we straightaway said, 'There we go, we're forgotten in the first operation.' But . . . we had our radio there which was kept on standby and we'd listen to it when the battalion was out and we could hear what was going on all the time and I think, probably the second day the battalion was out and we were ready to go to tea and the next thing, *bang*, a call for us. And Blackie [the other handler] and myself were picked up by helicopter, so we were close to the airstrip and straight out to the airstrip and picked up a helicopter and out to A Company. When we got to A Company we learnt the reason we got called out was because a very good soldier in Reggie Parker, he used to be part of the tracking before, there was an altercation where they'd had a contact and the enemy got away. And he said, 'Well why don't we try the dogs?' He said, 'I've seen them work.'

So they experimented and said, 'Why not?'

And we were called in and I put my dog on and five minutes later, contact. Oh, we followed the blood trail where they'd had their contact and Cass kept on tracking on and the next thing coming around the corner and coming into this big bamboo, and the next thing all we could hear was this screaming. And I grabbed my dog back, dragged him back and A Company, the platoon behind us, opened fire and we ended up getting a lady out of there anyhow and the other couple got away out the back. It was just getting on dusk so we didn't continue, but we had our first, that was our first kill there, with A Company and by the time we got the girl and I said, 'Let's have a look at her.'

And I took my dog around and I let him have a good sniff and show him. Because this is a blood trail, this is the first time he'd ever had a blood trail, normally it's just scent but this time he's got scent with actual blood there, and I give him a smell and give the other dog a good smell around. And so we went back and spent the night with A Company inside the perimeter and the next day, everyone wanted us. A Company got the first kill and all the other battalions said, 'Well if they can, we're going to get the dogs too.'

So for the next week or so everyone wanted the dogs. They'd call us here and the track's a week old and there's no one been here, and just everyone wanted to use us. But the best thing, in between that, was the following day the battalion commander and RSM flew in a Bell chopper and they came over and seen us and congratulated us and from then on they had a different outlook for the whole twelve months with us and they were just different people towards us.

* * *

We were sent in that week, the battalion commander said they got caught and they were hit, Alpha Company was hit again, and he said, 'I want you two in again.'

So in I go in a chopper, in a Bell . . . a Bell chopper is the one with the glass front, just two of us can fit in and we were coming in there and they were still having the contact and then they started shooting up our helicopter.

The pilot said, 'I'm out of here!'

And I said, 'No, let me out of here.'

So he got me and I jumped ten or fifteen feet into the mud and slush with my dog. I said, 'I'm getting out of here too.'

. . . And Cassius, for the first time in his life, indicated. He indicated from about fifty metres and I said, 'What are you doing?'

He stopped, looked and pointed straight over there on top of this ridge and I thought, 'Oh,' so I stopped and I said, 'What's he done?'

Went through the normal drill and said, 'My dog has indicated over there,' I said, 'He's never indicated before in his life but I'm going on taking his trust that he's stopped and he's pointed on that hill.'

So they said, 'All right, we'll just sweep around a bit and have a look.'

So as soon as we started sweeping around, they shot down along where we were, and had he not indicated we would have walked straight smack-bang into a big ambush and his indication saved our platoon from walking into an ambush by a gun post up the hill there.

* * *

To be honest, it's the old saying, 'If shits were trumps, they'd be trumps,' if you know what I mean? And to be out there . . . our thinking was not if we would find something but it's a matter of when, and being out there it's quite scary, and at the same time you know this is your job and you've got to keep pushing in and pushing in and just keep on going. And sometimes it come to something and sometimes it come to nothing...it was quite nervy and I'd be lying if I said I wasn't scared, because no one in their own mind would say that they wouldn't be, and nearly every time you went to the front, you saddle up and away you go and think, 'Here we go again.' And most of the time you were tracking along, you forgot about being scared because you were too busy concentrating on watching your dog and trying to be as alert as possible...what made it a lot better is that I myself was happy that I had a machine gun right next to me, and the machine-gunner that I had he was a top gunner and that put me at ease, but being at ease doesn't take away being frightened or scared because no one wants to have any bullets whizzing around them or hitting them or whatever, and it was tension-filled when we were up the front and a bloody big relief when you changed dogs and you had to go to the back of the line and you'd say, 'It's not bad back here.'

And that's what it felt like...it's a tough thing to do and you can sit back today and you can go over your way of thinking and a lot of times I still think about it and dream about it over the years, because they turn out to be weird and wonderful dreams sometimes, where you wipe out people because you've dragged them in and taken them into situations and that was the worst part. Where was I going? Then you're terrified of it but today I wouldn't have cared a continental and if it was a matter of going and getting him, I would have gone in and got him out, even if it cost.

* * *

I started having some dreams and thinking, 'What am I going to lead someone into?' More than anything and we had quite a few hits in the first three weeks and so I just kept thinking, 'Am I going to lead someone into trouble or whatever?'

... But we continued to do our training with the dogs and so much so that the battalion commander came and said, 'How can we help you in getting your dogs to tiptop condition?'

PATRICK TOOVEY (*right*) with Ozzy Symond and Jim Maunsell, 1941.
'In those days mateship was an unspoken thing. Whether we took it for
granted or not I don't know.'

ARPAD 'PADDY' BACSKAI (*far right*) with his platoon on the Malay–Thai border in
1959. 'During the Malayan Emergency I was an Infantry soldier. Deep penetration patrols
[in the jungle] … There is the odd bit of sunlight, but there is a dimness in everything
about us. There is a netherworld of leeches, spiders, snakes … all this sludge … that you
walk through, sleep on, etc.'

DULCIE TOOHEY spent World War II on her family's farm in Ipswich, Queensland. 'We'd play dolls, ride horses, and also take part in whatever was going on at the farm … Later on we realised that it was really work we were doing, but at the time we thought we were having fun and playing. We were dipping cattle, and some of the harvesting … when the war came, then we really had to do those jobs …'

DULCIE TOOHEY (*middle row, second from right*) with her school mates at Melwood School. 'We had a big map up on the wall, and every morning the teacher used to ask the bigger children to pinpoint where the war was at that stage and what was going on.'

ARTHUR 'NAT' GOULD was in fighter command in World War II. 'I think there are people who take to service life more than others. It's not a matter of killer instinct or anything like that … there's a special camaraderie in the services that you don't get anywhere else.'

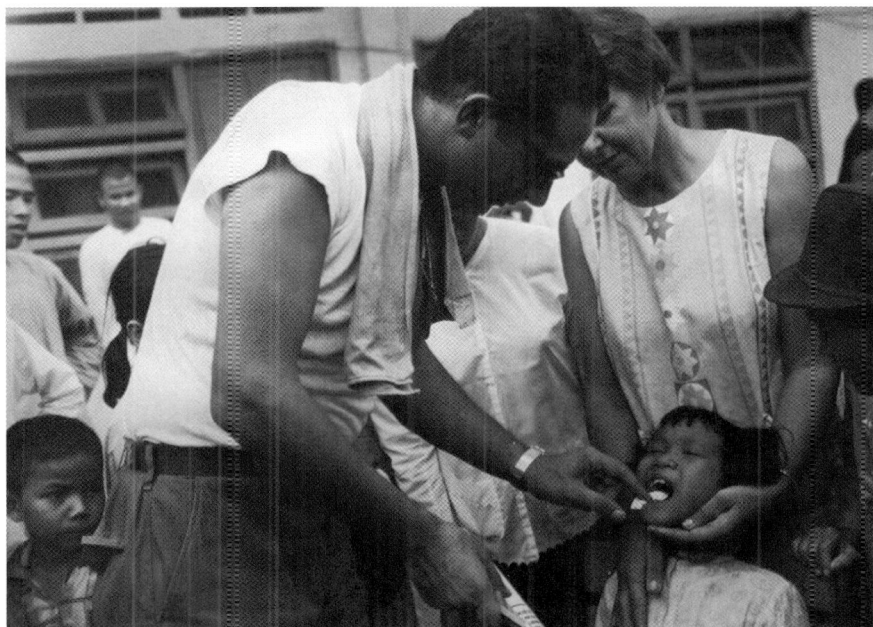

IRIS ROSER (right) helping a volunteer dentist in Da Lat, Vietnam. 'It was harder to come home than it was to leave. Because I'd been out of the world for four years … I was a different person. I am a different person.'

SERVICE DES PRISONERS DE GUERRE.

FROM P. O. W. No. *4059*
NAME *FRANCIS, JOSEPH Mc GOVERN.*
NATIONALITY *AUSTRALIAN.*
RANK *ABLE SEAMAN*
Camp: War Prisoners Camp,
Moulmein, BURMA.

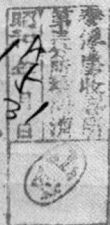

Mr. Mrs. JAMES, P. Mc GOVERN,
1 TAYLOR STREET,
PADDINGTON,
SYDNEY, NEW SOUTH WALES,
AUSTRALIA.

FRANK McGOVERN was a Prisoner of the Japanese in World War II. 'Anyhow we got back home, met everybody … settled back into civvy life. It took a while though. Very difficult. I said to one of the fellows they should have locked us up for six months after we got back.'

IMPERIAL JAPANESE ARMY.

I am still in a P. O. W. Camp near Moulmein, Burma. There are 20,000 Prisoners, being Australian, Dutch, English, and American. There are several camps of 2/3000 prisoners who work at settled labour daily.

We are quartered in very plain huts. The climate is good. Our life is now easier with regard to food, medicine and clothes. The Japanese Commander sincerely endeavours to treat prisoners kindly.

Officers' salary is based on salary of Japanese Officers of the same rank and every prisoner who performs labour or duty is given daily wages from 25 cents (minimum) to 45 cents, according to rank and work.

Canteens are established where we can buy some extra foods and smokes. By courtesy of the Japanese Commander we conduct concerts in the camps, and a limited number go to a picture show about once per month.

DEAR MUM AND DAD. AM IN BEST OF HEALTH. HOPE YOU ARE WELL. DON'T WORRY. PRAY AND TRUST IN GOD. LOVE TO YOU ALL FRANK

BARRY SEELEY on patrol in Vietnam, 1970 (*above*); in Nui Dat sleeping lines, 1970 (*below*). 'Initially over in Vietnam it was all about body counts, how many people you killed and all this sort of thing and it became a competition between each platoon.'

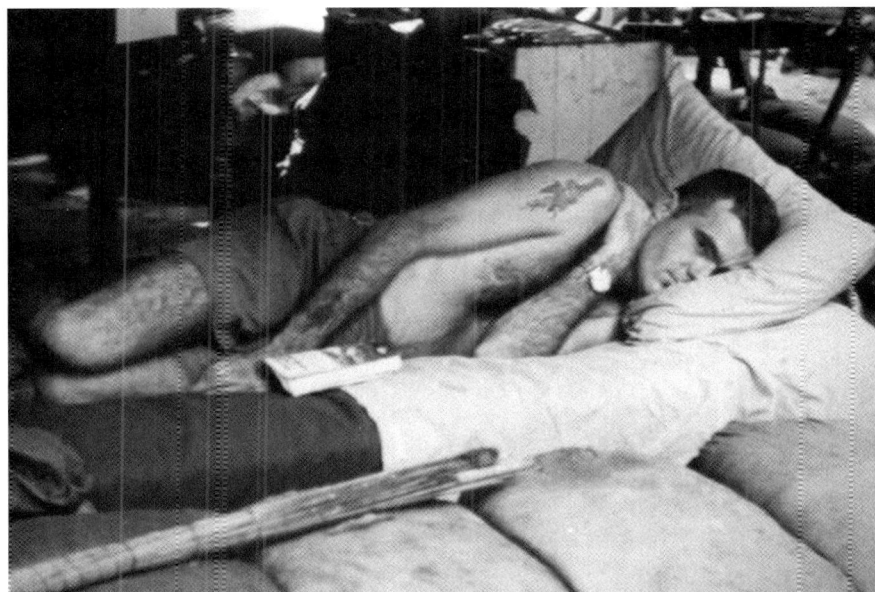

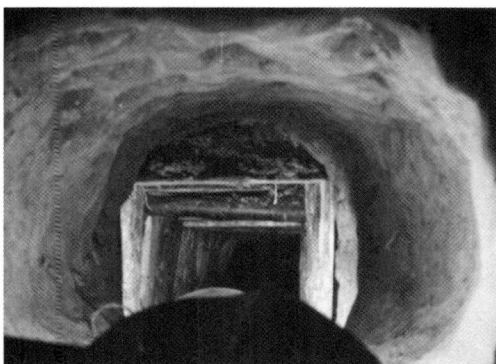

GEOFF CORNISH was a member of 50 Squadron RAF in November 1941 (*above*) and was later captured and became a German Prisoner of War. The photos *left* and *below* show a secret tunnel and room the prisoners had made under Stalag Luft 3, south-east of Berlin. 'You had to pull together as a unit and you did. It was like an RAF station and the biggest sub-organisation if you like was the escape committee.'

TED KENNA (*above middle*) with two other Victoria Cross recipients and (*below left*) with his wife Marjorie after receiving the Victoria Cross from the Duke and Duchess of Gloucester. 'I don't think I was scared [about going to war]. I don't think I had time to be scared. I wouldn't know … I suppose every man's scared … every soldier. It's just one of those things you do …'

NORM CAMERON with Cassius at the Vietnam Training Centre, 1966. 'I was chosen to be the first one out with a dog to go to Vietnam and join the battalion … Vietnam [blew] me out of my mind. You've just got no perception of what it is, what you are getting into …'

I said, 'We need somewhere where we can really work them.'

And he said, 'Go to Vung Tau where there's not so many people running around, where you can work them.'

So we went down to Vung Tau and the first day out, Cassius being Cassius, we were tracking over ninety-five per cent sand and he'd just go and go and go and go until such time as he just collapsed, and we were only close to the sea, only a hundred and fifty metres from the sea, but we took him and laid him in the sea and cooled him down and I put him on my shoulders and we carried him back to where we were staying there. And I went and seen the section commander, went and seen the transport people and said, 'We want transport at ten o'clock in the morning to get my dog to the vet.'

And half-past two, three o'clock a vehicle turns up and we were nearly five hours sitting there waiting for them to come and get a vehicle for us to get the dog to the vet, and by the time we got there and they got the proper treatment at the vet... he died within an hour of being there.

... Base wallahs and poofters, base wallahs and poofters, that's my attitude to them. People who sat back on their arse and did nothing. All they did was get a vehicle, transport, they're sitting there and that's why you hear a lot of them calling them base wallahs. I've got nothing against them. They've got a job to do, doesn't matter what it is but if they want that job they do it properly just like we had to, and it didn't take long to get a vehicle if you wanted it.

... He's someone I slept with, and someone—I ate out of the same bowls as him, I drank out of the same bowls as him. He was good enough to do that with and he was with me and sat with me on piquet and he did everything with me and never complained, and it can make you love them and probably later on, made me a lot more sadistic in a lot of things because I lost something I didn't want to in such a manner, and maybe it could have been stopped and I blame myself or whatever and it just made me cynical... Oh I had eighteen months next to him, just like one of my mates in the platoon and they felt it, the same thing. It cut the whole section in half that did, because he was bloody brilliant in more ways than one, he was, absolutely. And not just a good mate and a good worker and a bloody good friend to the other twelve. And he showed everyone how it could be done, he did...he was a soldier and he's been remembered as a soldier...his personality, he was a dog that wanted love. He had love where he come from before I got him and they absolutely adored him and you could say to Cassius, 'Sit Cass.' And he'd sit. And you'd say, 'Cass, do you love me?' And he'd howl. 'Cass, do you really love me?' And he'd roll on his back and he'd just howl his head off. And he could dive in water and he would swim under water for three or four minutes without coming up and we'd just sit there in awe of him. He was just quiet, loving and very strong, what I mean his strength...he was robust. I looked at him and how could he be robust, that big fat thing? But man, the strength that he had in those four legs was just astronomical and that's how he wanted to go, just go. That's why they couldn't have him as a seeing-eye dog. He used to keep pulling the people around but he loved doing it. He loved to please. That's all he wanted to do was please you, and if he had the track and it meant him dying to please you—that's what he did. It was not the first time he fell down in heat and exhaustion, it was the third time, and no inclination that he was getting tired or puffed, just bang, fall in a heap and that's all he wanted, he loved it...and he just wanted to do what he loved and love you.

* * *

I got another dog in two weeks time...I went and seen my company commander and I said, 'I lost my mate and I just won't feel right there no more.'

And he said, 'That's all right.'

And two weeks later he called me down and he said, 'We've got a dog, no handler and have a guess what? He's yours.'

Well, being fair I took him and probably took a couple of weeks before I could work with him and understandably, he wasn't in the same class as Cassius and the bitterness I still had from losing Cass and it took a month before I said, 'Well I've got another seven or eight months of this, so I'd better get used to it and work at it.'

Which I had a go at but he wasn't trained nowhere as much as all the other dogs. Fortunately we continued to work with and get on with him and we had a relationship and we did some good work with him. Tiber and me, like I said, it took a good month for me to soak it in because I was still hurt, sad and got to the stage of, 'That is it. No matter what you're going to do, I'm not going to get back into this.' But at the same time then in 7 [Battalion], I was the only one that really knew what was going on because I had done twelve to eighteen months training on it prior to any of these blokes and then I thought, 'Got to get back into it and get switched on because it's blokes' lives at risk.'

... He was more of a work-dog than a mate ... and I'm not saying ... I didn't dislike the dog; it was just that I had that bitterness there where I couldn't accept him as Cass, not Cass, and I couldn't get that, but we got through our tour with him, and like I said, he did some good tracks and stuff-ups and we had our good and bad times together but he ended up finding a home and like I said, he's still a soldier. He didn't choose to go there.

* * *

[When men died] ... oh we felt for them all because they were our mates, and no one would say you don't feel anything within the family or you get a small community and something happened there, but you don't feel it, but you're talking to him today and he goes out tomorrow and *bang*, dead, not real good. But at the same time tomorrow goes on and we were out again and nothing's going to change it. But how you felt about it, you felt sad and how do we convince ourselves? Have another beer, hoping it would go away, have another beer. How else are you going to do it? Otherwise you'd never go outside the fence ... it's just part of the thing that you have to learn to accept or not accept, and we accept it but we *don't* accept it. We accept it in the fact that we know it's going to happen but to a close mate you can't accept it, but you've still *got* to accept it. I don't know if you understand. I still don't understand myself. Sometimes even today you think, 'I couldn't care a shit if it was me then.'

Wouldn't have cared, but sometimes you say, 'Those poor buggers were better off than what we were.'

But they're not. There was no answer to it and never will be an answer to it, to someone sending someone to what is going to happen, to the day that this world blows up or whatever. There is going to be wars and people are going to die and we are not going to stop it. We've just got to accept it as something that's going to happen and it's going to be sad because it's someone's son that is dying, someone's mate that is dying, whether it be in a car or whatever. But this here, it's no different if he's signed up, it's the person's life and it's precious and you like your life and I love mine but they give it up and we accepted when we signed the line, we give it up for the country and that's the difference. Hard ah? But if we don't accept it we run away, and I'm bloody sure I wouldn't run away. No one would call me a traitor and you would too if you were in something that we learnt to believe in and that's what we were there for.

I've stood under rubber trees and bawled my head out and got on my hands and knees and cried out to get through the times because there was nothing else and I'd be lying if I said I had never, because I did. I didn't want to have my head blown off and like you said, I was too young; I had too much to live for, but tomorrow you'd still walk outside the fence and put yourself in the situation. But it doesn't hurt to cry out for help, or have a good cry, does it? Doesn't hurt, but that was the last, didn't cry for a long time then though.

* * *

[When we came home] we flew from Tan Son Nhut airport to Melbourne airport and no one met us there. Flew from there to Adelaide airport where my mother and Donald...come and picked me up and Mum had come up from the country town to Adelaide to meet me...oh I was drunk for most of it and they were probably looking at someone different that I couldn't understand until many years later...and then I had a month at home and then I left. I wouldn't go home for six years. One time I went home and me mother opened the door and she said, 'Yes, can I help you?'

And I just stood there and I said, 'It's your son.'

She'd seen me once in ten years, joined up and gone and come back and I just lost the track and I don't give a crap if they said anything. Up your bum.

... I used to drink a lot and go out and get drunk and go somewhere and end up somewhere and go back to my cousin's where I grew up. I'd stay home for a couple of hours and that with Mum, and I'm not saying that our relationship wasn't any good. Our mother loved us and it wasn't for many, many years that I ever said that to my mother ... but I just went in there and got drunk and didn't give a crap about anything and don't know why and couldn't wait to get back to, well I went back to another place anyhow, to the boys, and just got into drinking all the time ... I stayed in the army. I went back to Infantry Centre as an instructor. About eight-weeks leave before I went back and started again, so I went back up there and I started a new job. I went back as an instructor with the dogs for three and a half years then.

* * *

I knew a lot of diggers who had served wherever and a lot of people had got help and I could see where they were coming from in different things. There was people would talk about Vietnam and a lot of people would get up them and say, 'All he ever talks about is Vietnam.'

Not me, I'd say, 'Shut your mouth.' I said, 'That's the way this bloke releases himself.' I said, 'If he doesn't ...' I said, 'he'll go mad, so if you don't want to listen just let him go on ...'

And it wasn't until later that I'd see people and I didn't want people coming around home and then we had no one coming around. And if they come around home I wouldn't talk to them or I'd take off, or then they wouldn't come home because no one felt comfortable at home. And then years went by, and in my business people would come in and I'd start thinking, 'Shit I wish I could knock his neck off.'

It's not funny, and I thought, 'Oh what's this arsehole coming in for? Hey, I'm running a business and I've got to have people in here.'

And I'm not saying it to them.

I'd go and do my shopping and poor old people in there, I'd push them over or tell them to shut their neck and if they want to talk go somewhere else and talk and I'd bump into them and knock them arse over head going through with the trolleys and say, 'I've got stuff to do, out of my road.' And I said, 'Stuff this.'

And I knew another bloke and he said, 'You should be seeing someone.'

And I said, 'I don't think so, it's only you weak-gutted bastards that go looking for someone.'

And it got to that stage where I was down on me and I said, 'I'd better go and see someone.'

And I went and seen someone and I just broke down and I was crying my guts out and they said, 'What's wrong?'

And I said, 'I can't, I'm just crying and can't stop myself nowadays.' and I said, 'It's not me.'

And he ended up getting me onto someone and I see a psychologist and psychiatrist and doctors and started talking about things and I said, 'I don't talk to no one.'

But they tried to make me try and see how I feel and whatever. I had nightmares and I'd entertain them and it was just silly, but I got help and I'm still getting help and I feel like I've got a new lease of life and feeling a lot better by being smart enough to go and do something about it instead of waiting and wrecking my whole family's life and other people's lives too. That's what it would have been, and I don't know where I would be today if I'd never done that about seven years, eight years ago.

... I get pins and needles up my spine and in my head and my eye twitches a lot and my leg will vibrate a bit when I know that I'm getting stressed out a lot and I just turn and go and get away from the situation and don't worry, and get away out of that situation. I may be in shopping and I don't want to be in there today, or I'm going driving somewhere and I don't want to be there, or someone comes and I don't want to be here, so I just get out of the situation. Corrine knows and has been along to a lot of sessions with me and she knows where I'm at and she helps me out a lot. I like Corrine being here and she likes working and all that too, but all I do is walk around all day, wanting her to be here.

... Up until five years ago I never marched [on Anzac Day], didn't want to know nothing about it, but I believe now if we don't stand up and be counted and talk to people, our kids, or kids at school or wherever it is, the spirit of [an] Australian soldier is going to die, so it's up to us now whether we like it or not, to stand up and be counted. And the response the soldiers, sailors, airmen, whatever they are, that they are getting from the Australian public on Anzac Day in the last four to five years is something that just makes you proud to be part of it and you want to get out there and say, 'This is what we did it for, is all the young kids and we believe that we went there so that all the ones that are following us will have a good life and a safe life.'

And to see them coming in and taking Anzac Day by the throat, if they want to do that, we've got to learn how to get out there and give them something to be proud of.

WENDY TREVOR

WAAF
War Bride
World War II

We moved from Westminster to Upper Clapton because my mother had thought it would be safer out of the immediate environs of the city, because we were pretty sure that we would be bombed, that there would be air raids. They'd been digging air-raid shelters in London the year before in 1938. It was the worst move she could have made . . . during the Battle of Britain I can remember being in the air-raid shelter and looking out, this was a daytime raid of course, and I counted ninety German bombers going over. And they were going slowly and quite low because you could see their swastikas on their fuselages and everything, and you know they were so sure of themselves and then just a little while later, two Spitfires chasing after them. I mean what hope did they have, two against ninety?

. . . Anyhow, we'd had this air-raid shelter, an Anderson air-raid shelter, built in the back garden. It was built of, if I remember rightly, sort of corrugated iron, they didn't sink them very low into the ground because it was too wet and too many pipes around. I remember this particular night I went on night duty and I said goodbye to my mother who was in the house, and I said to her, 'You'd better get down the air-raid shelter soon, Mum.'

And she said, 'It's so cold down there, I'll wait a bit.'

. . . And apparently the house behind them . . . got a direct hit and she wasn't killed outright but she was taken to a hospital at Slough outside London and she died three days later... I came off duty in the morning and going home I couldn't get anywhere near and the police stopped me and they said, 'You can't go anywhere near there.'

And I said, 'But I live there.'

And they said, 'Oh, we'll let you go closer.'

So I went and there was nothing, nothing left, but two things I do remember was there was a park near us and the leaves of the trees were sort of stripped I suppose with the shock, I don't know, and I well remember there were toilet rolls hanging in the branches. I don't know where they'd come from, and the smell. The smell of plaster, nowadays you have plaster board, it's not the same thing but you smelled this plaster and for a long time afterwards, if I went anywhere and I smelled that it brought everything back to me.

... My only other relative was my 94-year-old grandmother in Somerset and she was deemed too old to have responsibility for a teenager so I became a ward of Chancery. And they thought, now what can we do with this girl... Anyway they decided that to get rid of me so to speak, they would allow me to join any of the forces that I wanted earlier than necessary. I went to the recruiting office... and they were recruiting for the army, navy and air force. And I looked at the army thing and I thought, 'No, I don't like the colour of that uniform and I don't like the funny little hats that the navy wear.'

And they had a big poster of a WAAF with a man in flying gear and it said, 'Join the WAAF with the men who fly'. So I joined and I went down to the depot where they sort of pulled you all into shape and issued you with kits... and I passed out trained, and I asked if I could go to the London area, which was 11 Group Fighter Command and I went to Hornchurch... a station near the mouth of the Thames. Very convenient for Jerry because he just swept up past Southend and followed the Thames and there he was. So, it was a very busy station.

* * *

The RAF bombers would come to a fiery death thousands of feet above the earth or they'd crash and mostly all would be killed or there would be just a few of them would become prisoners of war or something. Or they'd be struggling home and we'd get the plot, 'Bomber SOS signature 1 at 10' and the next plot you got would be 1 at 6, 1 at 2, it would be obviously coming down and you'd see where it was, in the middle of the North Sea. And you'd know the survival time in the North Sea was three minutes. And there'd be seven or eight men gone. The whole crew. We always hoped they'd manage to get to England, to at least Manston, which was the forward drome, which had everything for rescue work for the bombers that would come in. And you'd hope they'd make it but when you'd see it in your last plot it would fade. You'd see it would be in the middle of the North Sea and you'd know.

... And if you were in London ... you had the pilot-less planes, the V1s, the bombs that came over and in the night's sky the flame of them at the end would look like a huge Bunsen burner on its side, and when they ran out of fuel they'd just stop, the drone would stop and you'd wait, '*Bang!*'. If you heard the bang you were safe. Because you never knew where they would come down, they'd just glide. And towards the end of the war we got the V2s, they were the rockets. They were supersonic, you couldn't plot them. But if you were outside and you heard the bang you were safe because they'd already landed. And you know, I think back to those days—I mean that was a war.

Well we were there 'til 1943 and by that time they were starting to think of D-Day. And so we were all posted to Oxbridge, which was the headquarters and from there we plotted D-Day. And I can tell you D-Day was the best kept secret for a long, long time of anything, I think. We'd been plotting planes over the Continent, and France particularly, for weeks ahead. Sweeps they used to call them. And we went on duty this particular night and when we got to the ops room, I might tell you the Oxbridge was very heavily guarded. It was quite a way underground and it had levels of steps down to the ops room and it had guards on every level and you had a pass that you showed at every level ... and when we got to the ops room we knew it was on. I remember there was that much activity, we heard later that there were eleven thousand planes airborne and that's a hell of a lot of planes. We couldn't plot them individually; we plotted them mostly as blocks. But I remember they had two pink tapes from the coast and Southampton alone, and hour by hour they lengthened towards the French coast and between those two tapes was so many thousand craft . . . and I remember when those tapes were just off the French coast they knew there were thousands of men being killed at that time. And I know I said a prayer for them.

And of course they had terrible accidents sometimes with the bombers you know, if they veered off their runway. Say they were taking off and they were fully laden and they'd veer off and I mean with the rain and everything, except for the actual flight path it was soft ground. And if they veered off fully laden onto that, there were so many cases where they wouldn't even get off the ground. Blown up to smithereens, because you'd have the petrol on the plane and you'd have the bomb load, there'd be nothing left or very little. That was the way it was.

. . . Say it was a squadron based where you were, say Biggin Hill or somewhere like that, we probably would know them and they were all young men and everything and it seemed such a terrible, terrible waste to me. I mean they trained for that certainly and they knew that that was on the cards but it seemed such a terrible waste of young lives and everything. But that's war.

* * *

We went up to London of course, that was our Mecca when we were on leave pass . . . Covent Garden, the Opera House was one big dance hall, and we all went there. They'd taken all the seats out of course, and they had a double band on a revolving stage and it was marvellous. When you're young and you've got that much energy, just marvellous. And we met all sorts of service people there. I mean there were that many Allied and American and Free French, Free Dutch, Free whatever, service people, it was marvellous . . . You could always meet people there, or the Aussie Boomerang Club and you could get free seats for shows, I remember I went to the Windmill Theatre and I think the Windmill Theatre was synonymous for the nude in those days. Certainly the most popular one with the servicemen.

And we went to the Overseas League ... and there was a crowd of Aussies in there. And we liked the Aussies because they were more free and easy, they were rather like us. I wasn't keen on the Yanks at all. I knew the girls thought they were marvellous, you know, they got nylon stockings and goodness knows what, I just didn't like them. But I liked the Aussies ... oh well of course that blue orchid uniform, the colour of them stood them out ... they looked very good and they were all, I don't know sort of, more 'devil may care' than most of the others, you know.

Anyhow this particular Aussie, he was a big chap, air gunner, and he'd been watching me and apparently he said to one of the crowd that I was with, 'What gives with the WAAF over there drinking lime juice?'

And they said, 'Ah, she's all right, she's a good girl, she's on her own, Aussie, and don't you go for her, we'll find you if you do. Don't worry, we'll find you.'

And he was a bit intrigued so he came over and started speaking to me and we got along fine and we went to the Covent Garden Hall and that was fine too. And he told me he was with an Aussie squadron up in Lincolnshire and he was the tail gunner and so on. Well, that was all right, anyhow we sort of got together and we saw each other on a lot of passes and he knew my story, that I had no home and I might say that was a good thing ... whether we were very much away from home like the Australians were and New Zealanders or like us ... we were all away from home. So I didn't feel out of it. And anyway we seemed to get along all right and he said to me 'Ah, I have a farm back in Queensland where I come from, and look why don't we get engaged and then you know, we'll get married and you can come back and you can have a home?'

And I thought, 'Oh marvellous, marvellous. Okay he's a nice bloke, righto.'

So I said, 'Yes.'

So we got engaged and then as I say, he'd been a tail gunner and he'd done thirty-one ops. And it must have affected him in a lot of ways, and at the end of his tour he went to an American squadron as a gunnery officer. Well, no doubt he drank a lot, I don't know, but he had a stomach ulcer, which broke while he was at the American squadron and they kept him there for awhile and because he'd collapsed and hit his head they thought he was bleeding and he was going to die anyway, probably. And they didn't want him there so they send him to the RAF hospital in Rauceby, Lincolnshire. And I went up there to see him, they sent a signal down that he was very ill indeed and I was to get up there. So I went up and I stayed up there for a while, they had a place for relatives of men who were very sick. And I stayed there awhile and I said to him, 'Look, if you want to cancel out the engagement because you know, you don't know what's going to happen . . .'

And he said, 'Oh no, no, no, you better hurry up. I've had my banns called for the first time.'

Those days in England, if you were getting married in a church you had to have your banns called for three consecutive Sundays, and they used to say, 'I'm publishing the banns between so and so and so and so, which parish, and if anybody knows of any reason why they shouldn't be joined in matrimony you will have to state so now. This is the first, second or third time of calling the banns.'

I don't think they do that anymore. But they did in those days.

I went on the black market and got myself a wedding outfit. You could do that. There were lots of places in the East End, you know, factories where you could go and as I remember they charged you a shilling for each coupon, which was eighteen shillings for eighteen coupons and that was your whole lot for a year . . . it was a dusky pink suit, jacket and skirt with dark brown facings on it. And I had a little hat like a bird's nest; it was dark brown feathers, sort of worn a bit down on one side and that. And brown shoes and that was my wedding outfit. And I think I had a corsage of pink carnations, yes, I think I did.

So we were married with just our two witnesses, but the two people had told the local paper and the local paper turned up and took photographs, which went into the London papers. So when we went up to London for our honeymoon we met some of them up there, and they were all congratulating us because they said, 'Oh it was in the papers!'

Well, it was in the papers all right and it came out in the *Courier-Mail* and of course he hadn't told his parents. Well, he'd told them that he was engaged I think, but he hadn't said we were getting married, so that was strike one up against me before I even arrived out here—I was the harpy that had trapped sonny boy when he was overseas and sick.

. . . We'd been down in London on VE Day and I must say I don't think I will ever, well I'm sure I will never see again such a euphoric crowd as were there. We couldn't believe it. The war was over, at least our section, and to me personally I thought, 'Wow, there'll be no more killing, no more plotting the bombers strings out and know that so many of them wouldn't be returning to those friendly English skies . . . no more fighter boys with us at breakfast, dead by lunchtime.'

It was just, life was so cheap. And you were only sure from day to day so you lived life with an intensity, you were young, you were there. And life was so cheap.

We were given two bottles of beer by a Yank and we wandered around, the pubs had long gone dry because everybody drunk them dry. You know I remember the blackout was still on of course but the searchlights were coned on the gold cross on the top of St Paul's. And that to me was something so marvellous to think that the war was over, it was over.

* * *

. . . He was medically repatriated and like a lot of English brides, we tried to find a bit about where we were going but nobody sort of knew, or Australia House wasn't saying so we really didn't know . . . Anyhow he sailed, he went down to Brighton and he sailed for Australia and I think he got back sometime in June or July . . . As the Pacific War was still on, the war brides that came out then were sort of under secrecy. I remember I got my sailing orders with twenty-four hours to get myself demobilised from the air force and up to Liverpool.

... When we got to Liverpool they put us up in houses up there and I met the other war brides and we were billeted up for the night and the next day they took us down to the docks. And we saw the little ship that we were coming out on, it was the *Nestor*. I think she had one funnel, wasn't very big any ol' how. And we met to say that we were all the war brides and we didn't really know what we were coming out to. For example ... there was one girl, her family had bought her a fur coat, mind you England was very much still under rationing and she had this fur coat and they must have donated all their coupons for her and bought this fur coat. And she was so proud of it, she wore it to breakfast, she wore it everywhere and we'd say to each other, 'And where are you going?'

Well this particular girl, guess where she was going with her fur coat?—Thursday Island. I doubt if she'd need a fur coat at Thursday Island. So I hope she gave it to the chief, it would have put her in sweet with him. And there was another girl, she told us where she was going and we said, 'Oh that's a nice name of a place. You know, you can imagine trees and parks and that, pretty place.'

That was Birdsville. Imagine.

There were about fifty-odd brides on the ship, 'cause there were other people as well but the predominant lot were war brides. And it was very interesting to see the children, they had never seen or eaten bananas or oranges and they were given them on board ship you see, and they didn't know what to do with them, one kid was just stamping on his banana, no idea that you ate it because we hadn't had them.

* * *

The war ended when we were halfway across the Indian Ocean ... so that when we arrived in Fremantle, we were the first civilian ship to arrive, with war brides too. And they gave us a big coverage in the papers, I remember the headlines, '*All Young and Smartly Dressed, English War Brides Arrive*', da-de-da and all the photos of the Australian husbands meeting their wives and so on.

... We arrived in Fremantle ... and then we went to the zoo. I made a big faux pas, we were watching kangaroos and one of them was in his pouch with his legs sticking out and of course I wasn't used to that, and of course I found the keeper and I said to him this kangaroo had got a young in the pocket and it was suffocating, it was upside down. He rolled with laughter and he said, 'That's the way they usually are.'

... When we got to Sydney we got in quite early in the morning and I remember coming on deck. And the first thing I saw was, we weren't going under the bridge, and that face at Luna Park, you know the smiling face. I couldn't think what the devil it was, but still there we were and we docked in the wharves ... my husband was there to meet me, and that was marvellous, I'd come thirteen thousand miles and here he was. Well, we spent the night at the old Australia Hotel in Pitt Street and of all places where we went that night, we went to Luna Park. And I remember going on the dipper and going up and seeing the lights in the Harbour and then *vroom*, down the other side of the dipper. I nearly flew out of the contraption anyway when we got to the bottom I couldn't stand up, I remember that.

Well, then they arranged for us to go up to Queensland, now he was medically repatriated so he went up on the first division of the train, in a sleeper, but the bride sat up in the second division with the luggage. That's the first time I think I struck that sort of division between the men and the women, so to speak. Well, we got up to Roma Street and the same thing, he was in the sleeper and I was sitting up and we were going through the night and these tiny little places we'd stop at with extraordinary names, I remember one was called Bakingboard and I thought, 'Fancy calling a place Bakingboard!'

But you couldn't see much of them except invariably there was this big brick building and every little tiny place had this big brick building and right across the front of it was, 'School of Arts', and

I thought, 'Well, they must be a pretty cultured lot because there they are, even in these little places it was, School of Arts.'

They probably studied painting or something because I didn't realise until a long time later, that was the pub. No wonder it was the big brick building and probably very popular, School of Arts. Funny way Aussies have, of calling drinking an art, no doubt it was.

... And I remember the people that were in the carriage with me, I looked at them and I thought, 'Oh gee!' and then the thing that really shook me was there were blooming cockroaches running around, big cockroaches, 'cause everything in Queensland grows very big. And there were these cockroaches running around and I thought, 'Ah my God!' Anyhow we got into Roma; I remember it was the early hours of the morning. And I was on the second division so the first division had come and gone and I got off and there was nobody there to meet me at all, there was a crowd of people down the other end of the platform but there was nobody with me and I got out with the suitcases and I thought, 'Where's my husband gone? Oh,' you know, 'This is funny.'

And suddenly somebody from this crowd of people from the end of the platform, the other end of the platform must have realised, 'Aaaah ... didn't he have a bride, ah that must be her!'

And some of these people came up to say hello and look at me and sure enough I was the bride and here was my husband with all the crowd of people and I might tell you the thing that struck me on the journey up was the size of Australia. It was so enormous compared to England, I mean from Hyde Park Corner to Windsor on the old scale was just over eighteen miles and here it was hundreds. I think Roma is 350 miles due west of Brisbane. The sheer size is so overwhelming.

* * *

We got in the car, an old Pontiac I remember it was, and we seemed to be going and going and going ... and this country was so bare and so dry and the trees, oh! Coming from the green of England it was such a shock. Later I found they were in the middle of a seven-

year drought, three and a half years into the drought...we were
going to the in-laws place and their property was twenty-six miles
from Roma. And we got out and it was so bare, there was nothing,
just dirt on the ground...and this house, sort of up from the ground
as the Queenslanders are, it was the in-laws place and I thought, 'It's
a bit strange, sort of nothing around the house, no garden or trees.'

There was what they called the cultivation, which to me was
ploughed field...but, that's where I got initiated to the outback
dunny. Apparently there wasn't toilet paper as such; they used to
tear up the *Women's Weeklys*. Put them on a nail which was all right
if you started reading a story but then you lost it you see, 'cause the
other bits had been used so you missed out and they said to me,
'Just put some ashing on top.'

They had this kerosene tin full of ash from the fires and a dipper,
and you put the dipper in and threw the ash down but it was a good
way from the house. And I thought, 'Gee coming up here at night,
going to be a bit difficult.'

But however I said that to my husband and he said, 'Oh, don't
worry, just go outside.'

And I thought, 'Oh, things have really gone down the drain. I've
got to come down off the veranda and squat somewhere,' you know.

'Oh well, this is the outback.'

I was the son's wife so they sort of put up with me but I don't
think they ever really understood what we'd been through in England.
Certainly their son had been over there and he'd been flying and
everything but on a property, rationing really hadn't hit them, certainly
not the food rationing. They had milk and the thing that I'll never
forget was their meat. Now in England our rationing had been one
and tuppence worth of meat a week which was roughly a chop, that's
all. They had meat, chops or something for breakfast, the men came
home for lunch, meat again and meat at night. I just couldn't believe
it. And although they'd had clothing rationing certainly, I mean in
the country well, you don't exactly dress like a fashion plate at all.
And I found it so terrifically different, I mean my grandmother had
lived on a farm in Somerset and when he told me he had a farm I

equated a farm with the farm in Somerset. But this was so totally different. They had Hereford cattle and the poor cattle they would get so weak they'd just drop down, they couldn't get up they were so weak and they'd just go out with an axe and axe them in the head and leave them, I couldn't believe it. I mean, there were the dingoes and the crows, the crows, the first thing they did, the crows would peck their eyes out and to me, I mean all right I'd known killing you know, with people and that, but I hadn't associated killing with cattle or horses at all, this was the new dimension of killing as far as I was concerned.

... We'd had electricity for example in England, electricity was taken for granted, there was no electricity up there. The water was bore water which was full of minerals and my neck swelled out as though I'd got mumps and they choofed me into a doctor at Roma and he just looked at me and he said, 'You're not used to the bore water are you?'

And I said, 'No.'

'Ah you'll be right in a few weeks' time.'

And I was, but it has a terrible taste to it, awful ... But it was a totally, totally different life ... my mother in law thought she was completely modern because she had one of the old Silent Knight kerosene refrigerators. And I remember they had a long brush, it had a pipe around the back and you had to get up on the chair and push this brush down to clean the pipe periodically, it would smoke like anything.

... Two of his sisters they were still there and I used to get around with them and they were quite okay to me, they weren't abusive or anything, and he had a young brother and I used to feel very sorry for this young brother because he might as well not have been there, everything was for my husband, the young boy just didn't figure at all. And when we did eventually get in our own home, Gordon his name was, the young boy, he had a passion for fried onions and nobody would ever cook him fried onions so he would come over to me and ask me if I'd do him some fried onions and I'd do a big pan of fried onions, used to smell terrible but he loved them. And he'd eat them all and he was so pleased that somebody would cook him fried onions. Poor kid, I mean, such a simple thing.

... They thought, which was perfectly true, that I just wasn't suited for the life, I'd never even been brought up in it or anything and it was too great a distance but I think the girls at least, they put up with me, and at times they could be quite nice to me and certainly the young son, poor thing, he was really happy because I was the first one that had ever taken much notice of him I think. But you could never get, at least I couldn't, you couldn't get close to them. You see, there again there was nothing in common, like they couldn't think what an air raid was and certainly they couldn't think what he had gone through flying, that was another thing they didn't realise at all.

* * *

The funny thing was bath night. There was no bathroom as such with a bath or shower, no, nothing like that. There was a room and I suppose like Victorian times with the wash basin and jug and a big tin bath. Well, they'd heat up water in the empty kerosene tins, heat them up on the stove, carry them out to this bath, plonk them in the bath and the baths were taken in strict sort of rotation, first of all mother-in-law, then me, then the eldest girl and then the youngest girl. Same water 'cause water's very precious you know, then they'd take that out and empty it on any tree that might be living at the time and start over again with the men, and there'd be father-in-law, my husband and the young boy. But the young boy never took very long at all and we sort of wondered why until one day they found out he just used to slosh himself over, never got in the thing or sat in the thing, because they found he never took his boots off. Somebody got him to take his boots off one day and his feet were absolutely black and there was a tide mark around his ankle, he'd wash down to the boots and that was it. It was a real funny family.

And, of course, I hadn't been used to snakes or redback spiders or anything like that and I remember the first thing that I saw was a big goanna... Now the nearest thing I'd seen to that was in the British

National History Museum in London and that was a skeleton of a dinosaur called a diplodocus. And here was this living dinosaur crawling across the cultivation and I called out, 'Ah there's a dinosaur, aye.'

And they went, 'Ah no, that's only a goanna.'

Well I'd never seen anything like that before. And then the snakes, *ahhh*. They said to me, 'A snake will never come in the house.'

And one afternoon I could hear this frog going, croaking like anything and I tracked it and I went out and they had this water tank . . . up on the level with the house on the veranda, and here was this green frog, it was turning purple because coiled around it was this snake and the snake had bitten this frog and was just waiting for the frog to die I suppose, before it swallowed it. And I thought, 'They said snakes never come in the house and here's this one up under the water tank!'

Well, that wasn't the only snake. When we used to go for the mail. I might tell you the mail and groceries and everything came out once a week, the mailman bought it out. And he never brought it up to the house, he left it on the letterbox, you had to ride four miles . . . they'd say, 'Whose turn is it to get the mail?'

And if it was my turn they'd say, 'Oh well, we'll come back for afternoon tea.'

'Cause they knew it would take me all day to get there, practically and a long time back, whereas the girls that could ride, no problem at all, they'd just ride and back. Anyway they'd say to me, 'When you get to the tin,' which was the mailbox, 'Don't put your hand in because death adders like to get in there because they're out of the sun and they're warm.'

. . . I had never struck such heat. I mean in the old scale it was 112, 114 degrees and you got up at four o'clock in the morning, very early, did what you had to, because by nine o'clock for me at least it was too hot, I had to come into the house, and spend the rest of the day in there. In fact I spent a good deal of the day in the house and certainly the heat of the day with a wet towel around my shoulders because it was so darn hot. Anyway they were never really happy with me, I'm sure of it. I'll just give you one instance how different we were. In the evenings they had one big Tilley lamp they used to put in the middle of the table and you all sat around the table and did whatever, you either read a book, the girls did what they called fancy work or you wrote a letter or whatever. And I remember this particular night the wind was howling around the place and I said, 'Hark at that wind.'

And there was dead silence. And then one of the girls said, 'What did you say?'

And I said, 'Hark at that wind.'

They said, 'Oh isn't she funny, you know, she speaks like the hens, "Hark the herald angels sing".'

* * *

We were there for a while then we got on to our own property. But looking back, had we lived in Roma for a while we would have been together, I could have found my legs so to speak and then I could have ventured out but I was thrown in the deep end and it was just a terrible thing . . . When I got to our own place, there was this little humpy of a house made of round timber. And it was wallpapered inside completely with newspapers. And I thought, 'Ah my God, with the cockroaches and the spiders around here, I'll have to get rid of that.'

And I started pulling it down, mind you it was very interesting 'cause the newspapers went back to about 1921, very interesting, but when I got it all down I realised why it was up in the first place. Because it was round timber and the wind plus the rain just used to blow through . . . And of course when my husband went to work in the morning he'd saddle up and go off doing whatever he was doing and I was on my own. There was nobody around at all, but I might add that even in that heat, the only heating you had was the wood stove, the old Crown stove. And you'd have to light the stove first thing in the morning before you could heat anything for breakfast or ironing. Now ironing, I had the old Mrs Potts irons and I've seen them these days, sort of a metal sole plate and a wooden handle that you'd click on and I ironed with those.

... Somebody told me that if you hung meat out on the safe with holes, I think they're called the Coolgardie safe or something. If you hung that out on the veranda the flies wouldn't blow it, well they obviously hadn't met those flies. They blew it all right, blew through the holes, don't know how they did but they blew it. Other than that I had no refrigeration so the only fresh meat that we had was when the mailman came out, which was on a Friday, we had fresh meat on a Friday, the rest of the week we had silverside, corned beef. You know, boil it up and to this day I can't look at corned beef. I think, 'Oh God, I had you six days out of the seven, I can't.'

But at least it was meat, which was more than we got in England of course.

... And the thing was the loneliness of the place although when we did get this home, the saving grace was what we called the 'dah dah dit phone' and if you've ever seen it, it's quite a big contraption on the wall and in our case there were eighteen people on the one line and you were responsible for the line that ran along your property ... anyway it wasn't private at all because you each had a letter of the alphabet and the corresponding Morse code, so for example we were 18U and when the phone went you'd listen and hope that it was your 'dah dah dit' but it really didn't matter, because the thing with that phone was it was a party line, and you had a cut-out button on the top so you'd press the cut-out button and have a listen in to everybody's conversation, you know private calls it certainly wasn't, and particularly when the stud grazier there sold his cattle and they'd phone the prices up to him, I can remember I bet every grazier along the line would get on that phone with the cut-out button and I don't think he ever heard his prices clear and strong because they all listened in of course.

But the country, if it could only get a regular rainfall that country would be magnificent. I remember when the drought broke we were down in Brisbane at the time and we came back from the train and we were picked up and of course it was early morning, it wasn't quite light and I thought I'm hallucinating, I keep seeing lilies, and I thought I must be. And I said to them, 'Look, I'm seeing lilies.'

And they said, 'Well tell us when you see the next one and we'll stop.'

So I did and we got out and there were lilies, they were tall white lilies with a lot of flowers on the top. Now that country had been absolutely bare, we got the rain; lilies were growing, not to mention the grass came and another thing, we had a waterhole and during the drought they'd dug down six foot and there was nothing but sand, when they got the rain, that filled up and we could see fish in it and we couldn't believe it, fish! And we got little bent pins on twine and we went down and we caught these fish on little bits of nothing really, little bits of meat and things and we got enough of these little tiny fish, in England we'd call them tiddlers, you know about four or five inches long. And we got enough of them for a meal.

It's an extraordinary country up there. It really is. And you know I used to feel the age of it. In the very early morning you'd hear the dingoes howling on the ranges and you could feel the age of the country and coming from a country where it's green all the time, it's a country that's been fought over and fought on for hundreds of years and here is this country, this huge, I don't know, well it's empty sort of, but I used to feel that when you could hear the dingoes howling and everything, that it was a country that was saying old man didn't matter to it. And I used to feel that the country would be saying, 'Do what you like on the surface. Do what you can, but I will remain.'

It was so old.

The people on the next property... they had a generator so they had electricity 'cause they had a stud farm and they had thirty thousand acres and she was a champion cake-maker, always won every prize at the Roma Show but she was diabetic and couldn't eat cake, her husband didn't like cake and her cooking efforts were far too good for the riders, you know the ordinary roustabout. So she'd ring me up on our 'dah dah dit' phone and say, 'I'm baking tomorrow missus. Would you like to come over?'

Well of course. Would I what! So I'd get every empty cake tin and I'd get my old horse, and the horse was, well she would have been out in the knackery long enough ago I think ... because she had a dainty way of putting her front hooves down that half the time she fell over them. And that wasn't too good if you were riding her at the time. She was stone-deaf, but I'd saddle her up and put what they called a wallet over her, you know what a wallet is, you know, a hessian sack, and I'd put all these empty cake tins in it and of course I would have been lost going through the bush, I would have been lost completely except they sent a rider over with a tin of paint and they blazed a red dash of paint on every tree over, so all I had to do was to follow the red paint and I got over you see. Well, I'd go over and have lovely fill of all this prize cake and fill up all the cake tins.

Well the mouse plague came when the drought was over or finishing anyway and the farmers had sown their property with whatever they were putting in, wheat or maize or whatever ... that's when the mouse plague came. And they appeared from nowhere, I don't know where they came from, where they bred or what. They were in their millions, quite literally, you could go outside and the ground would sort of part in front of you, solid with mice. When I set my turkeys in the shed they'd eat their backs raw, 'cause the turkey wouldn't leave the eggs, neither would the mice leave them alone. And they stink. And the cats would be fed up with them, I mean the cat would catch a couple of mice and then *phew*, fed up, they wouldn't go for them ... if you'd saw a mouse or something in London, you called the local council and in those days they came out and completely sealed your house and fumigated it, you had to go out for the day sort of thing. Because, you know a mouse, oh dear, terrible. And cockroaches too, same thing. Well there, cockroaches bred up everywhere and those mice will eat anything. Like I say, they'd eat the leg stops out of the big watertanks, they'd eat the tops off the bullets, they'd eat anything.

The people that had been on the property before, the lady'd had turkeys you see and she'd build these wire nets, enclosures sort of thing and I thought, 'Well, that'd be a way for me to get a bit of pocket money.'

So I bought six hens off of her and they were duly delivered by the mailman and I got these hens all set up and they were all right but they'd get down in the dirt and they'd sit there real mopey and I thought, 'Oh, ticks that it, they've got ticks.'

So I phoned her up and I said to her, 'Look, those turkeys I bought off of you, they seem sick. I think they've got ticks or something. They're always just sitting down in the dust.' I said, 'They don't do anything.'

And she laughed, she said, 'You ain't kept turkeys before 'av you missus?'

And I said, 'No.' It was obvious I hadn't.

'Nothing wrong with them. They want the gobbler but you can't get one from round here 'cause it's related.' And she said, 'I'll tell you what, I'll send you one that's not related.'

So all right, out with the mailman came this big crate and he put a plank of wood from the tail of the ute down and opened this crate and out came this turkey and the hens were there as usual sitting in the dust. Well, he saw them and they saw him and the first thing they do is to gobble like mad, I suppose he was saying you know, 'the line forms from the right dears'. And they sprang to attention and I remember his fan came out and he slowly came down the wood and stood there and from then on everything was all right.

But when I sold them to a local hotel in Roma I said to the mailman, 'Tell her to clip their wings because they'll fly.'

And he said, 'Oh, all right, okay.'

So he did and when he came back with my money the next weekend he said to me, 'Oh missus, you should have been in Roma when I took them turkeys.'

I said, 'Why?'

He said, 'Well I told missus whatever her name was what you said.'

And I said, 'What did she say?'

He said, 'Do you want to know?'

I said, 'Yes.'

'Oh that stupid Pommy sheila, what does she know? Turkeys don't fly.'

Well come sundown of course they were looking for a tree, and there was no trees so they all flew up onto the roof of the pub and I believe all the drinkers inside came out and had a look because they couldn't believe it and the traffic which was slow in main street anyway just stopped because everybody was looking at these turkeys up on the roof.

* * *

Unfortunately my marriage didn't work out, I think they had wanted him, I found this out later, they wanted him to have psychiatric treatment in the RAF hospital at Rauceby where he'd been, but because he was an officer and a colonial as they said, they couldn't force him and he'd refuse and it was as though, I don't know, as though he was two people. I mean if we went to Roma, if we went to anything in there he'd be so nice and everything and I'd think, 'Oh, aren't I lucky to be married to him!'

But when we were back on our own, we would be sitting probably just having breakfast and I wouldn't have said a thing and he'd suddenly lean over and smack me around the face. He was a violent man, very, very violent. And I stood it for three years and three months and what could I do? I mean I was stuck, because the nearest town was twenty-six miles away, and if I wanted to leave where would I go, the only people that I really knew were down in Sydney and that was a girl that had come out with me and we had been able to correspond for a while but then no.

I can remember when they were burning off, you know in the trees and that sort of thing, they wouldn't have made a bushfire but at night there were dots of the fire all the way around and they looked like lights and I've gone and sat out on the veranda and looked at them and thought, 'Oh wouldn't that be nice if they were city lights.'

That's how far I think it was, the sheer loneliness of it too. I mean had he been all right I could have coped I'm sure, but with him as he was and where I was it was too much. Too much, coming straight from a war out to people who had never heard a shot fired in anger and certainly never had a blitz or bombing. It's probably, that was it, I don't know, anyway.

He would get my letters and everything. I knew I had to go but it was so difficult. See I had no money; I'd turned all my money over to him, the little that I had and the only way that I got any pocket money was to keep turkeys. I'd sold some turkeys in at Roma and I had a bit of money and he'd decided he'd go to the Roma Show and take his horses, because he had a horse stud. And he left me and I knew he'd be gone for three days and he didn't cut me any firewood or anything and his cousin who lived on the next property and his wife, he'd been in the Australian Army in the islands I think, anyway he'd been coming up to see him about something and seen him bashing me up on the veranda so he'd gone back home and told his wife and when he knew that he'd gone into Roma, he came down and said, 'Do you want any wood cut or anything, Wendy? You know, cut you some wood and that if you like?'

And I said, 'No, the train comes through tonight doesn't it?'

And he said, 'Yes.'

And I said, 'Would you put me on the train?'

He said, 'Yes, yes we will because I know what's been going on.'

So I collected all the little things that I could, I'd come out here with a good lot of things that I'd brought from England . . . I packed two suitcases with the things that sort of really mattered to me and I had two little cats and a dog out there and the cousin said he'd come and feed them for me until he came home. And they . . . took me down to the railway station and I just sat in the Jeep outside until the train came. And I got on the train with my suitcase and I left. It was the only thing I could do; it would never have worked out. I couldn't put up with the physical abuse and there was nothing like today. I mean, if people are bashed up they've got centres to go to but there's nothing like that then. And I was told that when he got back and they'd said that I'd gone to Brisbane he was so furious that I'd got away he went out and he shot my cats and the dog. So

I can only imagine that he would have had a go at me had I been there, or come back or something.

Anyhow I got on the train and I changed at Wallangarra and I went down to Sydney. Now remember I only knew two people in Sydney and I didn't know whether they'd have me or not. They lived at Warwick Farm and I left my two suitcases at Central Railway and I had five pounds and I took the train out to Liverpool and had to walk back to Warwick Farm and I remember I found where my friends lived in little fibro houses in those days, and I knocked on her door and she opened the door and she said, 'Oh, I've been expecting you for a long time.'

And they were the first really welcoming words I'd had in Australia. Because her husband had been in the RAF too, in the same squadron and he knew what he'd been like on the squadron which I didn't know, and so they knew that if I could, I'd get away.

* * *

I came back to Sydney . . . and I put an ad in a paper and I got lodgings at Drummoyne and I'd registered with the labour exchange, which had a section for ex-service people in those days. And they sent me a telegram to report so I did and they said that 2GB . . . wanted a telephonist so I went up there, fortunately for me the personnel officer had been in the RAF so he employed me and that was my first real job and I was there for eight and a half years.

I couldn't apply for divorce because I left him, I was the guilty party right, and then he went to Greenslopes Hospital and he met a nurse who was also a society girl but he still had to wait for the three years before he could apply and then I remember the private eye came down to 2GB and he had a photo of me and he served the papers on me and there was a forces legal aid section here and they just replied for me, and when the case was heard, you had to wait another six months before they finalised, and when it finalised he remarried. I didn't remarry for another six years.

I got myself a little sort of flatette as they had in those days on Cook Road, Centennial Park. It was one of the big houses and you all had little rooms or flatettes or whatever . . . further down the road apparently was living a police constable and he'd seen me but I hadn't seen him and he was on duty at the school crossing . . . and I was crossing with an old neighbour of mine and he stopped the traffic for us and afterwards he came across and started talking and my old neighbour said, 'Oh do you know him?'

And I said, 'No.'

And she said, 'He's talking as if he knows you.'

And I said, 'Well I've never seen him I don't think, only on duty probably.'

Anyhow he found out where I worked and he phoned me up and said would I like to go to the Traffic Office Ball with him. They used to have the old Trocadero going for balls and things in those days and I said, oh yes, and I did and we got friendly and started going out together and I might tell you in those days there was quite a stigma attached to you if you'd been divorced. Most definitely so, nowadays it's so common, in fact they don't even bother to get married so why worry, but in those days it was very different. And I thought, 'Oh well, you know he's a career bloke, he's just friendly and that's that.'

And I was very surprised when, in the typical down-to-earth police way, he picked me up from the *Herald* one New Year's Eve and we went back to my place and toasted the New Year in, I remember at that time I thought I'd go to America . . . and I was all set more or less . . . and I remember I said to him, 'Next Christmas I'll probably be in America.'

And he said, 'No, America's not the right place for you, Wendy, you're not commercialised enough for the Americans. Why don't you stay here and marry me? I can go a long way in the job but I must have a wife and a home.'

I mean it wasn't what you might call very romantic. But we married and it did work out very well and we were married for eighteen years and he went to get the Sunday papers one morning and had a massive heart attack and dropped dead in the street at the age of fifty-two, which was a complete shock. But he had done well, he was a one-striped constable when we married and when he died he was a second-class inspector. So it was true, it was quite true, he could go a long way in the job provided he had a wife and a home and I had provided that for him.

WALTER WALLACE

Infantry
Tobruk
El Alamein
Huon Peninsula
New Guinea
World War II

Well for me I suppose, I don't know if you call it patriotism or what, but I just felt you needed to be part of your country's defence. And at that time see, war was coming on, and I suppose like so many others I thought it was a bloody great adventure that was going to happen and I was going to be in it. Because while patriotism is definitely mixed up in it, the fact that it was the biggest thing going around the place at the time and you could be in it with a hell of a lot of other blokes your own age, nothing beats it. And of course there were times when you wished to Christ you'd never joined up too. But you get over that, I think, the first time a shot flies past your head you get over the fear of dying because you know it can happen and you see other blokes it happens to. And you just think right, you're lucky, you take it a day at a time sort of thing. Any bloke that tells you he wasn't frightened is a bloody liar, or he's a bloody fool one or the other because it's natural enough to be frightened, but you overcome that because you know you've got a job to do and on top of that, there's no way on God's earth you're going to shame yourself by showing fear in front of anybody else. And so you get on with the job and it becomes part of your life and particularly when you're in it for years, it's just a natural way of life.

. . . Other blokes trust you and you develop a mateship that, I don't know how you describe it but well, you know damn well that you're going to tell somebody to do something and they're going to do it, you know you've been trained and they've been trained to do as you're told, when you're told, 'cause otherwise it might mean your life. And strangely enough as much as the histories always said the Australians are, what shall I say, rebellious or not obedient, don't believe it . . . well they might be when they're on leave, but when it's down to earth and you're fighting for your life it's a different matter, as far as I'm concerned there's no troops in the world bloody any better than them, and they're better than most. And it's just something; it becomes part of your life.

* * *

The 6th Division had cleaned up the Ities in the desert and we thought, well that's over and finished with and we were on our way to Europe . . . but then eventually of course we realised when we got to Colombo and had to get onto this smaller ship, where we were going. But nobody at that time had a clue that the Germans were even thinking of coming into the desert, we thought we were going over to relieve the 6th Division and they'll go somewhere or other, the Germans were moving up above Greece then, but we went up to the desert.

. . . It was completely alien to anything we'd ever seen before, and the canal was a marvellous feat of engineering but miles of sand either side and you'd see the wogs, the Arabs, in these long dresses and we didn't have a clue what they were called at that stage. And also the wedding-ring bombers, now this was a bomber with a delousing arrangement right round the wing, this great circle and we were anchored while they flew up and down the canal to cause magnetic mines to rise and then they could be destroyed. The wedding-ring bombers we used to call them . . . there was *ack ack*, the first time we'd seen hostile fire I suppose, not against us but against enemy planes coming over. And then we were disembarked there and into these trains and on our way.

... We could march well, we could use a rifle, we could shoot quite well with a rifle, we weren't too bad with the Lewis guns, we'd thrown grenades. We'd done a few manoeuvres but nothing sort of to prepare us, well we were taught obedience and things like that, discipline, which probably is the greatest factor.

* * *

After their early successes against the Italians, the Australians and their allies were pushed back across the desert by Rommel and the Afrika Corps. Only one thing lay between them and full-blown retreat to Cairo—the port fortress of Tobruk. Around 14 000 Australians would end up behind its defences.

It was the early hours of the morning, two or three o'clock in the morning and we could see this big shape up ahead of us, big dark shape and Cobby said to Don, 'Slow down, Don, might I tell you turn round and go for your bloody life,' he said. 'That's a bloody tank up there.'

Well, we just got half-turned around and the next thing there's bayonets in the side of the truck and a foreign language, and I thought, 'Jesus Christ we're bloody prisoners!'

'Cause I didn't know German from Japanese sort of thing as far as the language went. And the next thing along comes a Pommy colonel, 'By Jove what have we here?'

I've never been so pleased to see a bloody Pommy colonel in all my life; we'd been taken prisoner by an Indian Regiment. So anyhow we ended up being damn near the last into Tobruk.

... While this was going on our battalion came to a spot on the coast road where there was a diversion through the desert ... and there was a British MP [Military Police], a 'Red Cap' there, and he was directing them into the desert until somebody woke up that his jersey had a bullet hole with blood round it right in the centre of his chest. And they pulled up and he went back and he spoke to an officer about it and this officer came forward and they challenged this bloke and he was a Jerry, they'd killed the British MP and dressed this bloke up as an MP and directed our troops into the desert. Well, 187 of our battalion got taken prisoner; they went into the desert and the Jerries were waiting there with tanks. The rest of them then went round the coast way when they found out about this and they eventually got through to Tobruk. But the CO [Commanding Officer], the 2IC [Second in Command], the adjutant, most of our senior officers, headquarters, all most all of Headquarters Company were taken prisoner.

... Tobruk was an Italian fortress originally, that was taken by the 6th Division. It's mainly desert country right down to the water because Tobruk is on a harbour; it's a typical Italian-style town, flat roofs, concrete places but not a big place. And of course, when we got there it was deserted. The perimeter, the Tobruk perimeter which runs for some forty-odd miles has concrete posts and we dug in between them, intermediate posts we called them. And we held the front... the posts themselves were concrete with an *ack ack* pit on one end which was probably three feet deep I suppose, quite a circular thing, fifteen feet or so across, we used to call it the tennis court in my platoon.

... As you came out of the line for a rest, you went back working all day on pick and shovel and wiring all that, it was no rest but you weren't under constant fire. And you were getting better; you were getting a hot meal whereas up in the line it was bully beef and biscuits all the time. And our refrigerator was probably a half an acre wide and about ten cases high, of bully beef out in the sun and night whatever. And if I remember correctly it was mainly Fray Bentos, the Argentinean bully beef and these terrifically hard biscuits. But you had... what they called 'Happy Valley', where you could, if you were lucky and you got out of the line, you could go for a swim in the sea. But when you were there of course, nine times out of ten you were machine-gunned by the Stukas [German dive-bombers] ... they used to come over, bomb Tobruk and then machine gun hell out of us on the way back, or come up and bomb us.

... I can remember an English battery sergeant major standing there with his arm almost shot off at the shoulder by machine-gun fire still giving fire orders. And we were in front of them, they were firing directly over our heads and then the infantry came in with the tanks we had engaged ... and we bought home the first lot of prisoners. From there we went up to the line to do a counter-attack in an area that the Germans had taken ... and when we got there Jerry was pulling out. So there was a German truck there with the flaps down and I can remember we'd gone though, cleaned the trenches out and cleaned the Jerries out but we walked over, well somebody walked over to this truck, climbed up on the back step and lifted the flap, put the flap down and came back and never said a word. And then somebody said, 'What's in the truck?'

He said, 'Nothing.'

So somebody else went over and had a look and they came back.

'What's in the truck?'

'Nothing.'

So a couple of us went over to have a look and we lifted the flap and the first thing was a fist, stiff with rigor mortis, in our face, and the back of the truck was full of dead Germans. This was the first really close-hand experience we'd had of dead enemy.

... Most action or most war is ten per cent action and ninety per cent sheer bloody boredom. You know it's on and it's on quick-smart and you think your whole life's taken place in that few hours or couple of days whatever, and then you get down to living and every day is a bonus. But oh, I have terrific admiration for the British troops, a lot of people like to say the British aren't good, but believe me there's no better troops anywhere. They were well disciplined and if they were told say, to go to the back door and dig in, that's where they'd go, whereas our mob, they'd get to the back door and they'd think, 'Oh, we could go down to the back fence.' And they'd go to the back fence and quite often you'd find yourself with enemy on three sides. On odd occasions our blokes put themselves in positions like that but they extricated themselves just as well too. But it's as I say, that's war, and you get on with the business of doing what you're supposed to be doing, that's what you're being paid that magnificent five bob a day for.

... My mate and I, Roy Parker, were going through the trenches and we had been warned that the Germans were dropping booby traps such as thermos flasks, pens and cakes of soap. And the idea when they were dropped, the thermos flask had a propeller on them which spun down and then that armed the thing when the propeller came off, and it was armed when it hit the ground, if you picked it up, up it went. Anyhow we came across this good-looking black pen on the bottom of the German trenches and Roy looked at me and I looked at him and we got a big rock and dropped it on top of it, we thought, 'Oh it's probably a booby trap.'

Well, about 30 seconds later Jack Anderson came through and said, 'Anyone see a black fountain pen?'

Roy got killed at El Alamein but I never told Jack until we came back to Australia because he'd have murdered us on the spot and it was a pen his mother had sent to him, we didn't know.

* * *

... When Jerry launched his big attack on 'the Salient', and this was the closest he got to getting Tobruk while we were there, he hit the 24th Battalion, which was alongside me, and they were almost wiped out...a tank came...with flamethrower equipment...and they were coming for our post but we had a dummy minefield of old Itie aerial bombs with the noses showing out of the ground and they weren't game to come across it, and they wouldn't have gone off it you'd hit them with a bloody hammer, and it was bluff. But they turned on the 24th; well we couldn't do anything to assist them except fire at the Germans as they were coming. But oh, all through the night the flamethrowers were into these poor buggers and about two o'clock in the morning a young stretcher-bearer came down from the 24th to my post looking for extra medical supplies, which we didn't have a lot of but we gave him what we had. I said to him, 'Don't go back, son.'

He said, 'I've got to go back.' And he went back.

The next morning we saw probably a dozen at the most come out of that post as prisoners and the Germans moved into 'the Salient'. We were in 10 Post, we were opposite the Jerries, they were probably a hundred yards away I suppose... and the first morning we were there, about five o'clock in the morning, one of my blokes, Jimmy Arnold, came to me and said, 'Come and have a look at this.'

And at that time I was a corporal platoon commander because we were disorganised and things hadn't settled down. And I went and had a look and here's the Jerries in the half-dark shaking out blankets, having a wee, all this sort of thing, wandering about and Jimmy said to me, 'What are we going to do?' and I said, 'Nothing today but we'll be up bloody early tomorrow morning.'

So the next morning we were waiting for them and it was sheer bloody murder of course, when you think about it now, they didn't have a bloody clue and we got stuck into them and we must have killed a heck of a lot. Because from then on it got so vicious in that particular area... Later on, I met this sergeant that I'd taken over from, he took over from me again some time later and I met him when I was on leave and he said to me, 'What the bloody hell did you blokes do up there?'

I said, 'What do you mean?'

'Jesus Christ we couldn't bloody move!'

I said, 'I thought that was the name of the game, killing Germans.'

* * *

... We dug dugouts, we went back and got a couple of sheets of iron to put over the top of them and we covered that with dirt and whatever, camel bush and stuff like that and we would lie there that day and then attack up 'the Salient' the next night... and on our way back... I saw this flash under the boot of the bloke behind me and while it registered on my mind that he had stood on a booby trap, at that particular time there was the explosion of the booby trap and I couldn't make up my mind whether it was a booby trap or a mortar and I didn't know whether to hit the ground, to kneel down or to stand up, because normally if Jerry sent over a mortar when it exploded he'd machine gun the spot, just on the off-chance of getting people moving. And anyhow I realised it had been a booby trap and I said, 'Anybody wounded?'

... And Keith said, 'Yeah I'm wounded; I'm hit in the back of the head.'

And I crawled over him, he wasn't badly wounded, to the next bloke who was Harry, and Harry was gone, his head and shoulders blown off, Keith had stood on the booby trap, a jumping jack, and it had jumped up and exploded on Harry's chest. Behind him was my mate Roy Parker and Roy had been wounded and a couple of blokes behind them were okay. I'd been splattered in the back of the head with a bit of light shrapnel from the booby trap, but nothing much. And I yelled out to the two blokes back in the post to bring up what bandages they had, which was only field dressings, and I left them to look after the blokes there and I went forward looking for stretcher-bearers.

Well, I crawled forward because I thought well, booby traps, this hasn't been cleared and they say a coward dies a thousand deaths a hero dies but once. I'm crawling forward feeling for these three prongs of booby traps and what was known as 'camel bush' is a little bush that grows oh so high, prickly sort of a thing, every time I touched it I bloody near died with fright, expecting a booby trap. But anyhow eventually, and I'm thinking to meself, 'If I get one I'll mark it with my handkerchief.' And I'm thinking 'I've only got one handkerchief!'

Anyhow I eventually got through and got onto stretcher-bearers and we made it back and got the wounded fixed up . . . we went back into these trenches, put the iron over the top of them and laid there all the next day and roasted in these shallow bloody trenches with the iron over the top of them. And then the next night we were told it was off, we were dragged out of there, thank God.

* * *

When you patrol no-man's-land, in every company front there'd be a break in the wire that you could pull apart, so you could get out through it and you'd have a path through the minefield so as you could go out without stepping on your own stuff, and of course, when you went out you closed the wire behind you. Well, if you went out on a fighting patrol you'd probably go out in platoon strength, thirty-odd blokes, and you went out on compass bearings to where you reckoned you were going to launch an attack on the enemy line. And you made your way there in the dark, and believe me you can see by starlight because over there there's no lights to distract you, and the stars are that bright, you can see by starlight. But you've got to be careful, the Germans have this habit of firing on fixed lines, so they've got machine guns sort of crisscrossing their fronts and you never know when they're going to fire, but they are a methodical sort of people and they tend to fire more in a fixed time sort of thing, so that we got to know where the fixed lines were. So you'd move up to that position, you'd wait for them to fire and as soon as they'd stopped you'd move across onto the next position, that sort of thing. Then if you got into Jerry's line you had to try and get through the wire and into their lines. But they were like us; they'd have an outpost with a couple of blokes in to give warning of this. And then on their wire, the same as we did, you'd have jam tins or anything with a couple of stones in so that if anybody moved the wire they'd rattle and you know it wouldn't be cattle or anything coming through, it had to be blokes.

But if you went on just a normal listening patrol you went out a certain distance in front of your posts, you spread out and you lay there watching and listening for German patrols, they used to come out and they'd be on working patrols, you might go out near their lines where they were digging, enlarging their trenches or doing wiring work and sometimes you could capture prisoners like that. You'd go out there waiting on their working party and grab a bloke and rip him out of it and take him back with you.

When you went out through your lines you had a set time to come in so that when you came back, you had a password of course, they would be looking for you to come back. And if a blue went on out the front unexpectedly, well you would attempt to get a runner back to tell what was going on. At one stage I nearly became the most infamous bloke in our battalion. We were on a listening patrol one night and we saw what was obviously a fighting patrol loom up out of the dust sort of thing and they went to ground not far in front of us, and you could see who was obviously the commander and his sergeant get together and speak and they posted a sentry on four corners. And then they both disappeared and I thought, 'Oh, this is a Jerry fighting patrol.'

I had no word of any fighting patrol out. So I sent a bloke named Jack Anderson back to tell Don Parker that if you heard a blue going on we were stuck into a German patrol and I'd instructed my blokes, two grenades each into them and follow it in with the bayonet and I had a Thompson gun and whatever we had. Anyhow we heard this bloke coming back from our lines and we rolled over, I had the Thompson, Jimmy Arnold's got the rifle and bayonet and he just jammed the butt on the ground, the bayonet was pointing back that way and this fellow almost run onto it and he said, 'Jesus Christ!'

And I said, 'Who's that?'

And he said, 'Col O'Brien.'

I said, 'What the bloody hell are you doing here?'

He was a sergeant or a corporal from C Company I think, he said, 'We're on a bloody fighting patrol and we got lost.'

I said, 'Is that your mob in front of us?'

He said, 'Yes.'

I said, 'Jesus Christ!' I said, 'We were about to get stuck into them!' I said, 'If it had of been Jack Anderson come back instead of you, we'd have been right into them.'

'Oh bullshit!' he said.

I said, 'Well go and tell your officer where we are,' I said. 'We were going to put a couple of grenades into youse and get into youse.'

Anyway he went and told his officer and the officer told him, bloody rot, it's not there and Col yelled out, 'Gordon, stand up!'

And we were well within grenade range . . . We might have committed an awful bloody crime, well I don't suppose it's a crime, it was an accident but you'd have never lived it down. And it shocked hell out of me, but how do you, there's no way you can determine who they are, you see a mob of blokes come up, light machine guns over their shoulder, you can't see them, they're in the dusty sort of atmosphere and you just see them go to ground and as far as you know, your information, you've had no information about a patrol going out. And it's a touchy business, but we got to the stage where we thought we were pretty good at patrolling until you got out there and you felt a hand feeling over your shoulder for your Australia badges and that was the bloody Ghurkhas, and you hadn't heard them or seen them and you had a good chance of getting a kukri across your throat and cutting your head off, and because they were fantastic at moving through the night.

We communicated generally by hand, when you're going out, say you're going out on a compass bearing, you've got one bloke on the compass there's another bloke counting paces, 'cause you might be going out say on a hundred degrees for a hundred and fifty paces and then you might be turning to eighty degrees for two or three hundred paces and you've got one bloke counting. Then you've got to reverse that coming home. But in Tobruk in one way it was reasonably simple coming home providing the night was clear, because where we have the Southern Cross here as our dominant sort of formation in the sky, over there it was the North Star. And we had to get used to the fact that when you looked up the Southern Cross wasn't there, it was all northern stars. Well, the North Star hung over Tobruk more or less, and if you headed for that you were coming home. But luckily in B Company we had a bloke named Ted Donkin from Innisfail who played the saxophone; he used to be in an orchestra before the war and at night-time Ted did the playing and most of the patrols would home in onto Ted, and one of the things he used to play quite often which got to be a favourite of mine was 'Little Star', and he'd be playing this and we'd know we were going in the right direction.

... You go out on working patrols to lift mines, you know, you go out to Jerry's lines, into his minefield and you're lifting his mines so that if you need be you can go into his mines at a later time ...

normally they were an anti-tank mine and they've got a detonator on top, a heavy brass arrangement and it's got a sort of a key piece on top that you can use a screwdriver or a coin or something and you turn that from white to red which is armed, turn it from red back to white and it's safe. But when they realised we were lifting them, then they would attach a detonator to the bottom of the mine so that after a couple of blokes had got caught, then you started to dig round, feeling. And it ended up at the end there'd be about five different detonators attached to the one mine and you were digging around in the dirt with your hands, softening it up with the point of your bayonet so that you could dig the dirt out, feeling around for these detonators. And ninety per cent of them have got a little hole where you can stick a nail or something through so that if it fires it can't hit the detonator. Well we used to carry nails in our matchboxes or things like that and you'd feel round, you'd slip a nail through them, and then you'd cut the wire, whatever it was attached to. Sometimes they'd have trip wires and you'd hit the wire and that would detonate it, but they did all sorts of things to try and prevent you from lifting the mines, and that was a risk you had to take, if you were going out lifting mines.

When the Poles came into Tobruk the only thing they wanted to know was where were the Germans, and I had a couple of them sent to me in my section and one big bloke was like a big dog, he'd go out there and you'd be going to lift mines and he'd be in there digging, pelting dirt hell, left and right. And I used to tell him to bugger off because he was going to blow himself to hell and everybody else near him, he was dangerous. Oh they were just dead keen to get to grips with the Germans, we never had the same reasons that they had, they definitely had reasons, we were only there because we were supposedly stickybeaks and thought there was going to be a big show on and we wanted to be part of it.

... Depending on the night, generally you walk upright, you're watching for the fixed lines and things like that. If they sent up flares you either hit the dirt or you stopped dead still, and if you're not moving it's hard to pick men up at night, even with the flares.

Sometimes if you got close or you're near their wire and that, you'd be down on your hands and knees, or you'd crawl forward. It's amazing how a tin hat and a bit of camel bush on a little bit of sand makes you feel bullet-proof, if they're firing at you, you're lying behind it. I suppose it's a false sense of security but that's the attitude you get, you think you're under a bit of cover . . . I suppose for me ninety per cent was trust in God, the other part you trust your luck and of course you trust to your mates, they warn you of danger, or they protect you in case of danger. There's more decorations won that are never awarded than ever are awarded because it happens so bloody often. A bloke might see something fire and you're not looking in that direction and he'll push you over, or he'll say, 'Look out, get down, there's something coming!'

He's heard it and you haven't. No, you look out for one another plus you look out for yourself of course.

. . . You get into trouble naturally, if you're lucky you get away with it. For instance Jerry hears you and they fire on you and if you're lucky you don't get hurt and you learn something, you learn where they are and where their machine-gun post is. And you get to know, oh I suppose you get to know how close you are to their lines and you start to get very cautious then and you get in as close as you can and you start to learn the areas that you're particularly stationed in. I suppose it becomes force of habit, you're watching, you're using your eyes and your ears, your eyes aren't a lot of good to you at night over there but your ears are. And that is one of the reasons that we didn't wear tin hats or felt hats out on patrol, you had a knitted beanie because the wind, any wind blowing through them made a noise and you couldn't hear, whereas with a knitted beanie you didn't get any noise. And the tin hats rattled like bloody hell and probably in lots of cases give your position away. Not only that they're bloody uncomfortable, if you're getting barrage you'd probably have a tin hat on but most of them stuck to their felt hats. It's like everything else, it's on-the-job training and you learn to do it.

* * *

You'd come back and you'd go to your platoon commander and give him a report on what you'd seen or what you'd done. The blokes would come back, they'd probably have a drink of tea, they'd put their weapons away and get into bed if they could or if necessary you might bring some bloke that's seen something particular, get him to tell what he'd seen and that ... You'd settle down and you'd be coming onto daylight because all your patrols were done at night and you'd just smoke, clean weapons, load magazines, sleep, read, play cards. As I say, it was sheer boredom for ninety per cent of the time. I always reckon that after I left Tobruk I'd never play cards again, if it wasn't poker it was bridge and soon as you sat down to have a meal it was a bloody resume of what had gone on at the bridge, 'What did you play that for?'

And you got that damn bored with playing cards I reckon I'd never play cards again. Anything to pass the time to stop you going crackers ... Through the day you'd sleep, flies and dust and heat ... you never got an overdose of it because there was always explosions, you were being shelled or bombed or machine-gunned, some other damn thing. And there was always somebody putting up a racket of some sort or other, that you got what sleep you could, just sort of par for the course.

... Humour is the only thing that keeps you sane, oh there's some funny buggers amongst them believe me, there are some funny bloody men. This is a funny thing to say about the Pommies, they all tend to run the Pommies down a bit, but with the Australians we were the most untalented bloody mob you'd ever meet, you get three Pommies together and you've got a bloody concert party, they can sing, they can dance, they can play some instrument and they were fantastic, and it's a fact, you get three Pommies together and you've got a concert party. And our blokes, oh Christ, odd ones of them can sing but they tell yarns, lot of them write poetry or they say poetry, they read but as far as artists go, well our mob weren't ... anyhow, no way.

... We got relieved in this particular position by the 43rd Battalion, early hours of the morning. And this particular joker was coming up and we said, 'Who are you?'

'We're the f****** 43rd.'

And he said, 'Who are *you*?'

And from our place a very, very tired voice said, 'We're the f****** 15th.'

... In the trenches we'd talk about everything, in those days of course you must realise that the average Australian bloke was pretty naive, what I mean is we weren't up on sex or anything like that, like the kids are nowadays, probably what we learnt we learnt from watching animals, nobody taught you anything like that. We didn't race around with photos of half-nude sheilas all over the place, there might be odd ones and that but generally speaking you had photos of your family or your girlfriend in your wallet. You would show them to one another, if mail came in normally speaking you'd get the news from everybody, somebody from a different town to yours would say, 'Oh such and such happened.'

'What's that?'

And they'd tell you all about it. You'd talk about different places and of course you knew blokes from different towns, some of us came from the same towns, but then you got to meet blokes from all over and you heard a lot.

* * *

We came out of Tobruk on the HMS *Abdiel,* it was the latest thing in the British fleet, fastest thing in the navy, thirty-four knots, it was a mine-layer. And the most marvellous thing about it they had fresh water and they cooked their own bread on board and I can remember standing under the showers and drinking it because our drinking water was about thirty-three per cent salt. And eating fresh bread and butter was absolutely marvellous ... you know the old saying the navy is here, well thank Christ they were because without them we wouldn't have lasted in Tobruk. They supplied us, ammunition and food and they bought in reinforcements and took wounded and that away, and without the navy I can image Tobruk would have been a very short siege.

* * *

We moved down . . . to El Alamein . . . and Jerry wasn't really set up there at that stage, he was pushing our blokes back, the British had these big shells, they hadn't exploded there and I thought to myself, 'Jesus Christ, they're not fooling this time.'

They were big. And so anyhow we get dug in there and from then on things proceeded. People forget that we were there for months, everybody thinks about the Battle of El Alamein as the 23rd of October but they forget we were down there in June and blokes were getting killed and wounded every day, and we were still carrying out our normal duties, patrol work and that.

. . . The 23rd October and we went up that night. At that stage it was the biggest barrage that had ever taken place . . . they had a Bofors gun firing on our line of advance, tracers so that you could follow, they had those old white torches in beer cans facing back our way on stakes, green and red on either side to show you where the minefield had been cleared so you could walk up. And the artillery behind us, there was thirty miles of guns wheel to wheel and when they let go . . . the whole horizon was lit up and these bloody shells going over the top and I thought to myself, 'Thank Christ they're going the other way.'

Of course they started to come back too when Jerry got back into it.

. . . Flashes of light, explosions, you can see material flying up, you can see tanks on fire where they'd been hit and on fire. You can hear people yelling that have been hurt, wounded, or you can hear fire orders being given and directions of where to fire and that sort of thing. You are looking all the time, watching for Jerries coming in to attack, or if you're in attack of course you're looking for the Jerry that you're going onto. But it's just terrifically confused; oh I don't know how to say it, a terrific mess of flashes and explosions and men walking, you see them silhouetted, you see silhouettes of men behind machine guns, it's a really confused business. But you have a rough idea of where you're supposed to be going...and you realise by how the battle is going forward if you're gaining ground, that you're getting to your objective. And then the firing will die down, when you've sort of taken your objective and firing gets desultory, you know you get the odd shot...because your enemy is withdrawing, he's attending to his wounded, getting his equipment out and you can't see him, it's dark, when you're in close contact you can of course but once he starts to withdraw. You're busy attending to your wounded, you're trying to dig into new defensive positions, get rid of any mines or stuff or whatever might be left there, you're trying to put up wire and reports have got to come in from every section and platoon and that. So as you're trying then to reorganise your front until the next stage, which could be the next night or might be the night after or whatever, how the action develops.

But it's total confusion really; you often wonder how the hell you know what's going to happen, because you can imagine, you get into the middle of a trench of Germans and a mob of opposition troops and you're killing one another, or trying to. And they realise they're overdone, well they're trying to get out of it and you've got to be careful that you're shooting at the right blokes because it's quite easy, you can have one section of yours get ahead and you could think, 'Oh that's not my mob.' And it could happen. It's confusing and you've got to wait then till you're reorganised, until you settle down, then you walk round your guns or your platoons to check out how they're going. For instance we did one show one night and I had my guns in and then early the next morning I went round to check on them and I'm walking across from one gun position to the other and it's just on dawn and I saw this body on the ground and it sort of flashed through my mind, 'Another Jerry.' And as I'd glanced down it was a bloke I'd been on leave with, not long before we went up there, and you know, it stops you in your tracks, he'd been killed through the night.

... My battalion took all their objectives in every attack we went into. I don't know whether we were lucky or what because some of the battalions got a fearful hiding a couple of times and we had to go back in, whether we were lucky or not. But anyhow we were there from go to whoa and eventually we drove forward and then swung towards the coast and that was to try and encircle the Germans. And when the Jerries decided to run I was sent up . . . with four guns to straddle the coast road behind the Germans to catch them as they were withdrawing. But they didn't, they withdrew through the desert and left the Italians behind and took most of the transport for themselves. By the same token during the different battles that took place we took hundreds of prisoners actually and I took a hundred and seventy two back to Alexandria, to the cages back there at one stage during the show with my platoon. And we put them into this cage outside Alex and we spent the night in the Egyptian Army trenches there, got a chance to wash our clothes. We hung them out on the barbed wire and then somebody yelled out, 'The wogs are pinching our clothes!'

So they got the Bren gun out and dropped a burst alongside them and every time they dropped a burst they dropped some more of our clothes, so over a period of about a hundred yards we got all our gear back. But we went down that evening to these German prisoners and we went to put them in a cage with the Ities and the ranking bloke was a young corporal with these blokes, blond, typical Aryan youth, the ideal Aryan youth and anyhow he said, no they weren't going in with the Italians. Well we didn't give a bugger, there was another cage there so we bunged them into that one.

* * *

I was the only one awake just after dusk and I could hear these engines, I thought they were bloody tanks, and I was up on the flank of A Company. And I was going to wake the blokes and I thought, 'He changed gears!' and I thought, 'No it's not a tank, it's a truck'.

Anyhow he came over the top of this rise and when you've got an anti-tank gun you're usually set back from a rise so that when they come up you can get a shot underneath, as they come up over the rise. And this particular truck pulled up about, oh thirty yards away I suppose and he couldn't see me and I could see the truck because it was a mass, and I was just about to yell out, 'Hey Butch what the bloody hell do you think you're doing out there!'

Because I thought it was our ration truck had got lost. And two blokes got out of it and one bloke's walking towards me and he's saying 'Hello, hello.' I thought, 'Bloody Jerry!' I thought, 'This is lorried infantry!'

So I grabbed the batman, my officer had got knocked and I had his batman with me, and I grabbed his bloody rifle and typical batman's rifle, I drove three shots into these two blokes and the bloody magazine platform jammed down and I'm kicking Charlie around the bottom of the pit saying, 'Give us the Thompson quick!'

And I eventually got the Thompson and put a couple more into them and I yelled out to the section leader of the next section, 'Alec quick, Jerry!'

So I got stuck into the truck with the Thompson gun and my blokes woke up and they were stuck into it with rifles and we didn't use the anti-tank gun because it creates such a bloody flare that the Jerries are right on you and you want it when tanks are coming, you know, you want the surprise element. Anyhow the truck started to explode and I went out to this first bloke that had come out and he wasn't dead, he was screaming his head off and I went up to go through his papers and things like that. Anyhow I'm alongside him and the poor bugger is screaming his head out and he's dying and Blinko yelled out to me, 'Finish him off!'

And when he was up walking about it was okay but when he was on the ground, for me it was murder. And the bloody truck started to explode and I laid out there for two hours waiting for that bloody thing to explode over our heads, I thought we were going to be blown to bloody hell any minute, and how the Christ it didn't I don't know to this day. But it left the shell of the cab, left there, and this poor bugger eventually kicked his life out and the other fellow I must have killed outright. And then Jerry ranged onto that and he shelled Christ out of us, and from what we can gather it was a relief crew for an 88 mm gun, a German gun that we must have overrun during the night, either our battalion or somebody in that area, had overrun during the night and they were a relief crew and didn't know they'd been overrun, and he was lost. I suppose if I had have done the right thing I would have gone out and rounded him up but as soon as I saw him I thought, 'Lorried infantry, truck load of infantry, well, going out to round them up.' I wasn't going to take the whole bloody truckload on, and that poor bugger.

I've got his ribbons there somewhere and a photo of his wife and two twin girls and ... I lived with that bloke, I've lived with him ever since, for fourteen years he nearly drove me mad. I ended up writing a poem about him and it sort of got him a bit out of my mind but I've always had the feeling that I should have had enough courage to put the poor bugger out of his misery but I didn't, I didn't have enough guts to do it. But to me it was murder once he was down and I couldn't do much to revive him, to resuscitate him because he was too badly wounded. And I just had to lie there and listen to the poor bastard and I lived with him for so bloody long, I still do, I never ever forget him, that's one of the reasons I hate bloody war ... I don't know, it's upset me to buggery I can tell you, I don't think I ever recovered from him, and it's not as if he was the only one but under the circumstances it was a horrific way for some poor bugger to die.

I called it *Cairo*, it was written in 1959.

Cairo I once went there,
A young Aussie soldier for those who remember
You helped pay the fare,
The trip wasn't wasted after all we did win,
Or did we, I ponder.
It now seems a sin, to kill fellow humans,
Young boys, just as we,
There for the same purpose and maybe to kill me.

One face I remember, I dream,
He carried their photo, his wife and two girls,

God, they'd both be mothers and have boys of their own,
And I killed their father, how could I have known
My thinking would alter; I'd mellow with age,
How futile the practice, how stupid the rage,
We were both boys,
Who should have been friends and shared woe and joys,
Cairo, no thank you, the memory still stays,
I dream of the desert and those far off days,
I grieve for a German I killed as a boy
And memories are bitter, forgive me my friend . . .

And the bastard still gets at me.

* * *

The show didn't last for that long, from the 23rd October until about the 3rd of November, 4th of November I think it was, and it was over. And in that time two massive armies had engaged and one had been defeated over a great area of land. It was the first-ever victory, apart from Tobruk holding out, it was the first-ever victory over the Germans in the Second World War. And of course it made Montgomery's reputation.

. . . I was sent back to an anti-tank school and when I came back to the battalion they'd been withdrawn and were back in Palestine in camp and we were getting ready to come home . . . we embarked on the *Aquitania*, quite a big convoy . . . We knew the Japs had come into the war and naturally we were anxious and just incidentally some of our blokes got white feathers, not my battalion particularly, but white feathers were sent to some of our blokes in the Middle East because we weren't home defending Australia. They forgot we'd been there for over two years, the Japs weren't even thought of, well they might have been thought of but there was no menace. And anyhow we came home and we were definitely anxious, we heard that people were leaving the north and as far as we were concerned they were running away.

* * *

The Japs and the Germans were two different ends of the earth, like chalk and cheese to us. And I don't think we ever thought we couldn't beat the Japanese, you know, we were quite experienced troops, we were professionals by then and we had never been beaten and I suppose we were confident that we could do the job when it came to it, that they were just another enemy. But it meant having to learn to handle the jungle which was completely different, absolutely entirely different and I suppose we were as sure as we could be that we were all right. And it was the first sea landing since Gallipoli when we landed at Lae... there was practically no opposition, we were very lucky.

... Landing at Finschhafen... we had a bloke on our barge with a bulldozer and he'd been showing some pornographic photos that he'd been tied up with, with an air force bloke and some girls here in Brisbane, in colour. And they were in his wallet and he's showing them around and I just said to him, 'Are you taking those in with you?'

'Why?'

I said, 'If anything happens to you and your wallet gets sent home to your parents,' I said, 'You ever think about that?'

'Oh Christ!'

So then he was trying to give them away. But I give him his due though when we did land, and there was a little bit of opposition, he came ashore in this bulldozer, dropped his blade and ploughed the machine-gun post that was firing on us into the dirt. And I don't think he ever got a mention for it though, not that I know of, but he certainly had it where it was needed.

... In the jungle one thing we did suffer was this weeping tinea, so that at one stage I was covered from my waist to my feet, just this complete black scale. And you'd go down the RAP [Regimental Aid Post] and they'd paint you with Whitfield's Tinea Paint, a green thing which stung like hell. And you'd be standing there with your hat fanning yourself to try and cool it off. And it was taking some effect but not enough so the doctor said, 'I'm sending you down to B Echelon for a couple of days, get your clothes off, run round naked in the sun, sea and sun.' And in a matter of thirty-six hours the bloody stuff was falling off me.

... We took our turn going up the coast, at one stage I was the lead platoon and we hadn't seen many Japs but we smelled this fire, terrific fire. We're going up the track and I've got my platoon stretched out and we came across this Salvation Army bloke with a fuzzy wuzzy with a Jeep, and a big boiler boiling coffee, which he was going to hand out to the troops going past, and he was the forward troop for the whole division, and how the bloody hell the Japs didn't get him we don't bloody know. Because I was the leading platoon for the whole division and we come across him, how he got through our lines I don't know but here he was with the boiling coffee there to hand out to the blokes. That will tell you what the Salvos were like.

* * *

Not long after that, just around about Sio I got malaria bad and I was taken out, well I don't remember going out, I don't remember anything about five days after that because I came to in hospital... I went up to a place called Kokutai in the mountains outside Port Moresby, a convalescent depot, beautiful spot. And while I was there, I went up with a bloke from New South Wales called Ken Campbell and when we got up there all these blokes are running round with butterfly nets and Ken said, 'We've been sent to the bloody bomb happies!' [shell-shocked soldiers]

And then we realised what they were actually doing, they were catching these big Blue Emperor butterflies, putting them under a bit of Perspex or whatever and selling them to the Yanks for five quid. And Ken said to me, 'Christ!' he said, 'If I'd have known that I'd have pinched a bloody mosquito net before we left the hospital.'

... When I come out of hospital, or when I was walking, I went down to the theatre one evening with one of the sisters from the ward I was in and here was a young bloke about eighteen or nineteen standing on the corner of what they used to call 'the bomb happy ward', his hat on the ground, singing his heart out. And I was only twenty, and I'm thinking to meself, 'You poor, young bugger.'

I'm only a young bugger meself. But this is a boy there eighteen or nineteen and he's mentally affected, and he would have got a dishonourable discharge quite possibly. What they called lack of moral fibre, you were a coward. Christ, he was only doing the most natural thing in the world, he cracked up! It happens and you can do nothing about it, it's just something you've got to try and overcome and get back to living.

* * *

I was in Sydney on leave and we were in Hyde Park, it used to be a thing at lunchtime, all the clerical staff and shop assistants and that, Hyde Park was a place to go for your lunch, if it was good weather. And we were in Hyde Park, Don was seven months old and we heard that the war had ended and the bloody town filled up and people come out of shops and everything. And I'm standing there with my arms braced against a building and my back to the crowd trying to keep them off Else and the baby. But oh, it was marvellous. A couple of blokes were in the pool in Hyde Park, the memorial pool, they were swimming in there and people were just going mad, they were dancing they were cheering, the place was thick with people. And Sydney's a pretty town particularly when the plane trees are out, I love Sydney. But the place, just over a matter of minutes it just filled up with people, well I suppose they come out of the shops and everywhere, and it was marvellous.

* * *

It was difficult, difficult. I got into, oh what shall I say, a few altercations with people that hadn't been in the army when I got back to work. For instance one bloke, we were having dinner one night in the middle of a shift, this bloke's skiting about the number of cases of shirts and boots that he knocked off and of course I blew my top. I said, 'I was battling my bloody heart out trying to get shirts for my boys to wear! And you're pinching the bloody things!'

And things like that used to rattle you a bit, but you realise then it's over and you've just got to get on with living and let a certain amount of it pass overhead.

... I know my kids have got hidings, my eldest boys, that they should never have got because of my nervous condition, I expected that when I said, 'Jump' they would say, 'How high?' I'd been used to blokes doing as they were told for five and a half bloody years and I just expected things to be done as they were, and my first wife quite often said to me, 'You forget the boys haven't been in the army.'

But this is the thing that no one appreciates, these women that we married, what they put up with and how they supported you. What I mean, there's no use saying one thing and meaning another, we were pretty bloody hard to live with when we came back, you come back entirely different to what you went away, you've had experiences that have changed your life completely. And your whole being has got to have changed, and how do you, you don't come back and, for instance like when we came out of the army you were discharged, you walked away out of the army depot, you were expected to go and get a job, keep your wife and kids, or get married whatever and carry on as if nothing had happened. Well, how the bloody hell do you forget five and a half years of you being out there committing murder? Because after all if you get down to tin tacks, you're in the trench and you're shooting some poor bastard across the road, if you did it now, you'd be in gaol. And you've got to try and overcome it, nowadays they get counselling and all this assistance and those days they never expected, you were supposed to have nerves of steel and if a bloke's nerves went, a lot of them got committed to mental institutions, they never went into why it happened or how it was affecting the poor buggers.

... At the time it didn't worry me a great deal, I suppose, we'd done what we were supposed to do and we had to cop the flak back of course because we copped a lot of return, you couldn't move about at all, you had to be very careful. But oh I don't know you've got to live with it later on that's when it comes to you, you live with it, you think of the things you did, oh ... I don't know if you can say you're not very proud of it, it seems so senseless, when you think the fact that since then we've had so many migrants that have come out and they can be your next-door neighbour, they can be your fishing mate or whatever. And they're the same as us and they believed they were doing the right thing for their country, we thought we were doing the right thing for ours. And I suppose if the whole damn lot of the young people in the world said, 'No, we're not going,' there wouldn't be any wars. But that's not the way we're built I suppose, that's just what happens.

Australia was a wonderful place to live in, in those days, far ahead of what it is now. And we're doing such stupid things now, we're imprisoning people, women and children for no reason, what have they ever done, and all we're doing is breeding terrorists because they must hate our guts by now. They've been in there for years and for what? For wanting to get away from somebody, some despot and they've exchanged one type of imprisonment for another. No we don't know, we just haven't got a clue on how to deal with people.

With the war I was just glad it was over, when I went back to El Alamein the year before last and walked into that cemetery I just was in tears. I looked down and every name up come a face and a voice and they knew we were there, they knew we were there, there's no blue about that. And oh God, I thought, 'What a bloody waste' and we've had sixty years of living and being married and having children and those blokes never had the opportunity to enjoy and they should have done. It wasn't a fair go, that young men like that were denied the opportunity to fulfil their life. And for all you know we might have had the cure for cancer buried there, they could have been scientists or whatever, we just don't have enough sense to see that that's what we were doing, sending away our breeding stock and our people that can make a world of difference to the world in general.

Often times you'll hear someone saying, 'I remember when they used to call us "five bob a day murderers".'

But we were certainly not war-mongers, we might be patriotic but we don't believe in war. There's a rare bloke that you'd ever talk to, of our vintage, that would ever agree with war, it's so stupid and more particularly since we've had the opportunity to have migrants come in. Admittedly we resented some of them because we were

European stock and we had a different way of life to these people. But they're entitled to a way of life too and we've just got to learn to live with it and it's taken so long to learn the lessons and we still haven't learnt much. And then we have the audacity to think we're the only intelligent beings in the universe, God they've got to be joking, they've got to be joking. Intelligent? My God, we're too bloody silly to keep sending our kids away to get killed, I don't know.

KEITH PAYNE, VC

Child
World War II

Infantry
Korean War
Malayan Emergency
Indonesian Konfrontasi

The Australian Army Training Team Vietnam
Vietnam War

That radio. That Stromberg-Carlson radio, a little Bakelite, well, it was quite a big Bakelite piece of equipment that was put way up on a shelf because it was too high tech. Three knobs, one for adjusting, one for volume, I think, and one other, on-off switch. Three knobs. And it was put way up on a high shelf so Father could reach it. Mother couldn't even reach it. She wasn't high tech enough to turn this radio on, this magic piece of gear ... we used to sit there and listen to the old Don Bradman do all his things. And we got the news and the weather. And of course it was only to be used when Father was home. So we were pretty restricted in the listening period, though the girls later used to get up on stools and turn it on and used to get—What were they? – *Dad and Dave* and *Portia Faces Life* or something ... Yeah, we were pretty primitive. We had a copper boiler that we made out of a 44-gallon drum. I think every house in town had one of those, or if you were real fancy they made a brick concrete one and put the copper boiler in that. And they were mongrel things anyhow because you couldn't get the copper boiler out to clean it and that was the boys' job, clean the boiler and cut the wood and light the fire. And the girls had to help with the washing. And we did all the hard yakka and of course we had wood stoves in the house and they had to be fuelled, so every now and again, we had in those days an old T-model Ford. And I first started to drive on a T-model Ford when I could barely reach the pedals, all three of them . . . so we'd go out in the scrub with the crosscut saws and the axes and everything and load up with timber and come home and saw it all up and cut it all up and stack it all up and we'd cart it upstairs into there and the girls would burn it for us and we'd go crook at them quite often, you know, 'You're burning too much wood!'

And that was basically life, and life went on.

. . . We had a jolly time feeding the family during the war years while Father was away . . . we had a little BSA.22 that we were supposed to hand in. There was the .303 rifle that came out of the Boer War that we were supposed to hand in. Nobody was supposed to have weapons in those days, but we managed to forget about handing them in, and so we sustained the family with pigs, and a couple of shotguns, so with ducks and birds and all the rest of it we were doing quite all right . . . The only restriction we had at that time was ammunition for the weapons, but that problem was quickly overcome because the Americans were going backwards and forwards and they were camped just outside of Ingham, so we would negotiate with the Americans for some of our goodies for their ammunition . . . and pinch their pushbikes too, because we couldn't get rubber for our pushbikes so we used to pinch them, acquire, relocate all the tyres off the American pushbikes onto ours and away we'd go again. Yeah, it was pretty good times.

. . . Our own troops were all training up in the north in the Atherton Tablelands and all coming through Ingham and so the war was getting closer and closer to us at that particular time. And we had great times with the soldiers on the troop trains. We'd [have] fruit in season around the place, mangoes, pineapples, custard apples and all the tropical fruit, oranges and lemons and everything, we'd sell to the Yanks and half the time they never got their product. We'd take their money and say, 'The train's going'... and they never got their fruit. But we always gave to the diggers.

I remember a fellow we used to call Old Andy. Prior to the war, probably about 1938, 1939, when there was still swaggies on the line...walking around with a beard and everything, you know, and his swag. And we got to know him pretty well and he came back again the following year... and then the war broke out and of course the following year Andy never came and then it would have been a year or two after that, a troop train was coming through and all these diggers on board...and Old Andy as we used to call him, 'cause he used to always call us nippers: 'Come on nipper.' You know. And giving out a bit of fruit and this bloke says, 'Hey nipper, how are you going?'

And we're looking around, 'Who the bloody hell? That's Old Andy!'

So anyhow he said, 'I'm over here!'

And he was a bloody digger!... we never ever saw him again so we don't know what happened to Old Andy, but he wasn't real old anymore. He had a shave and his hair cut and he had a digger's hat on and he was only about twenty-two.

We did our air-raid drills and everything else like that and sang 'God Save the King' every morning and saluted the flag... very patriotic, which I think was a must during those war years, something to help hold the nation together and being patriotic was one way of doing it. And I think it was a lot of comfort to the younger generation, who were starting to realise what was happening around the place. It was strength in unity, but other than that we just got along with school work. There wasn't the sporting equipment because that was going to the army and a lot of things couldn't be obtained because the material to make them went into making other things, so we missed out on a lot of things, but we gained by improvisation. We became, well, if the rest of the nation followed Ingham, we became a nation of very good improvisers over those years, on fuel and everything, chook manure, driving motor cars with big gas tanks sitting up the back and boilers and, oh my God. The things we used to do to make a car go.

* * *

On completion of our recruit training we were then posted from Enoggera down to Puckapunyal to the 2nd Battalion, Royal Australian Regiment which was at that stage a training battalion that hadn't gone on active service for deployment to Korea. It was purely and simply a training battalion. Life had changed considerably from recruit training to corps training. Now you had a lot of live fire exercises and you had live ammunition going round you all the time and the training was very intense. The preparation for war was very much put to the fore and we were very, very well trained.

We were well briefed all the way through on what was occurring and who was in action, what units were in action, what was happening. And you had to have that so that you could build a pretty fair picture in your own mind. And all your training was virtually what happened in Korea today was happening to you in your training tomorrow sort of thing. You were living that experience of yesterday in Korea, today in Australia, so that when you got into Korea it wasn't a great shock. The only thing that became the shock was 'the two-way rifle range', you know—he was shooting at you and you were shooting at him...but on a couple of occasions we lost a few blokes in training through accidental fire from weapons and everything, giving overhead cover and things like that.

One of the accidents we had was brothers and they were firing a two-inch mortar. One elevated the barrel too much and the weapon hadn't been cleaned. The firing pin just engaged the cartridge and it just dribbled out the end of the barrel but enough to charge the bomb. And it landed just in front of them and exploded and one of the brothers was killed. The other one was wounded and a couple of other fellers were wounded as well... And another we had, he was hit crossing a rope on a creek. One of the instructors got a little bit overzealous and lifted the Owen gun a little bit too high and hit him across the legs. Another one drowned. He had all his equipment on, on a river crossing, and he couldn't get out of his equipment. There was no quick release on equipment in those days so he sank. And we tried to get him out but couldn't get him out and by the time we got him out, we were bashing him and everything. But nobody knew CPR [cardiopulmonary resuscitation] in those days, see. He probably would have been alive today if somebody had known a little bit about CPR. And there was another chap hit. We had a very low wire entanglement about a foot high, and the idea was you take your pack off and you crawl underneath it, pushing your pack and pulling your rifle underneath the wire. And a machine gun was shooting over the top of the wire and it was pretty dusty and everything and the fellow couldn't breathe properly so he lifted his head up through the wire and crack, crack, crack. He got it . . . I was about two behind him. He was in front of me and there was another bloke between him and I . . . we pulled him out of the wire. But he was gone. We knew he was gone. It didn't please us. We all had to go back and go under the wire again . . . to make sure that you wouldn't balk in future, you know . . . We thought that if they'd dusted it down, put water and stopped the dust and everything so you could breathe. But they said, 'Well that's not part of the training. You've just got to put up with the conditions that are there. Nobody's going to go and sprinkle the soil with water in a dusty area to let you through in action. You've just got to go.'

So you could see that. I mean it was nobody's fault, only the digger's fault.

. . . See we had a percentage of accepted casualties in place. We had a five per cent accepted casualty rating in training. And that particular training, we called that 'a battle inoculation training', so that was the last period of our training prior to going overseas . . . I went back to Sydney and was mustered at Marrickville and then flew out from Sydney to Port Moresby and then onto Okinawa. Okinawa to Iwo Jima to Kure and of course now I was in the big land of the oriental people.

Try and understand, we weren't kids anymore, you know. We'd grown up. We'd grown up fast, too fast I suppose. But we knew life.

We'd lived life, God, dear oh dear, and what grooming we never got on some aspects. Once we got to Japan we went through a whole heap of training again... We were there acclimatising... then land in Korea at Pusan and then a day and a half by train and it all started to come to pieces, that holiday you were having. It was no longer an adventure.

* * *

By June of 1952, we'd gone into a stabilised defensive position along the line and we were building up, fortified the defensive positions all along the line... We'd carry out fighting patrols, recce patrols. We'd go out and try and capture prisoners and everything else like this and we'd do a company attack on positions and on the enemy positions and he'd do them on us and we'd do them like that. Reciprocal, 'Your turn next buddy.' You know. So the first time I went out... we'd just started to get the first of the snow and I was bitterly cold... and I was forward scouting on this particular patrol and Charles [Charlie—the enemy] decided to take a few shots at us and I thought the whole bloody Chinese Army was shooting at me, you know. There was bits of snow going *poong*, *poong*, *poong*, all around me and I thought,

'My God! This is not supposed to happen!'

And I felt rather large. I felt like an elephant, you know. I thought, 'Jesus, I'm only a little bloke!' you know... that was pretty frightening to be in a situation where a couple of nights before we were getting artillery shells and everything. But that's not personalised. It's a very personal sort of thing when somebody's shooting at you. You're the target. It's quite different when there's a lot of ammunition coming in and it's impersonalised. It's going anywhere. But once you know that you're the target, it becomes a worry. In fact you say, 'I hope you keep missing me, you bugger.'

They weren't just shooting in your direction or shooting around the place. It wasn't just rounds going over your heads or anything. This was people actually trying to shoot and kill you and it got very personal and I got very angry about that too. I didn't like it at all and it's not a good feeling when you're selected as a target.

You engage them and the rest of the patrol comes up and joins in the firefight and then it becomes a little bit impersonal again, right, because everybody's shooting around the place and there's a lot of ammunition flying around and you can see people moving and you shoot in their direction, hoping that you'll hit them. You don't know if you do because everybody else is shooting anyhow. The adrenaline starts to pump and you start automatically carrying out the actions that you're trained to do. In other words I just returned fire, bugger it, you know. You've got to return fire and hopefully the other people come up alongside you and take over and get into the firefight with you.

[When it was over] you searched the bodies. You got what information you could and you left them there. Australians did that. If we had enemy casualties close in on our position we would retrieve and bury the bodies. In other words, we didn't allow him to come that close in and pick up the bodies and take them back. But if the bodies were halfway or closer to him we would leave the bodies, right, lay them out virtually, pretty dignified soldiers we were. And next morning they'd be gone and we knew that they'd come out and picked them up. They also knew that we would do the same thing and it was a gentlemen's agreement. We never ambushed, not like Vietnam. In Vietnam, you would ambush a body, waiting for somebody to come along and pick it up, right. Korea, we never did that. No, it was a very gentlemanly sort of an arrangement. He left us Christmas presents on our wire. We got pinged off about that. He'd come up and hang cards on our bloody front wire! We weren't very bloody considerate of that at all. Just bits of paper, you know, 'Merry Christmas', man with the big hat and the big bayonet. Yeah, 'Merry Christmas digger.' You know. And of course we reciprocated. We wouldn't let them bloody well get away with that antic without doing something, so we'd take, well I think we took them over a box of rations, American C rations and left it underneath their wire, so that they could have a Christmas feed...

The person in the line, the front line soldier was a different person to that person that was guarding prisoners at the back and I found that. I was escorting a prisoner out one day. I was going back for a twenty-four-hour rest. And we'd captured him the night before and brought him back and given him a feed and what have you and a smoke. He wasn't going anywhere. He was too bloody frightened to go anywhere anyhow and he was only a bloody kid. Well, I was only a kid too, and so I was one of the blokes escorting him out the next morning...and when we got back down to the Jeep and there was a provost down there and he grabbed and shoved an Owen gun in this bloke's back, 'Get up there!'

And I said to him, 'You're a big bloke, you are. You should have been out in the valley last night when he was shooting a bloody burp gun at us.' I said, 'And then you could poke your bloody Owen gun at him. Leave him alone.'

So he got in the Jeep and the provost jumped in the front and I give the kid a smoke, 'You're not supposed to do that. We've got to interrogate him.'

'Interrogate him?' I said, 'Bullshit, he don't know what's going on, he's that frightened.'

People back behind are different to line soldiers. Line soldiers have that respect for the enemy, you know that he's going to kill you if he gets the chance and you know you're going to kill him if you get the chance. But by the same token, you know that he's there under orders and you're there under orders.

We'd get anything up to 240, 280 shells on our position of a night-time, just a continual bombardment of artillery and the cold conditions, cold, cold, cold. And in summer time the bunkers all collapsed in and there were rats, rats like bandicoots. You wouldn't believe it. I used to lay there with a .45 and go *poong, poong* in my bunker shooting bloody rats, yeah...you were continually cold. You were never, never warm and you slept in a sleeping bag. You slept in your socks. You just put clothes on at the beginning of winter and you keep putting them on and they'd come up the line with the powder spray and get rid of all the lice and everything and two months later you can have a bath when you get out of the line. That's an experience. So you go down to the bath units and it's a big long tent arrangement and you come in one end. And in winter time obviously it's heated, summer time it's air-conned. And you peel off everything, get rid of everything. And good thing, at that stage you all stink the same and I mean you *do* stink. Your skin virtually rolls off like that because you've had clothes on and everything in winter, dreadful. And summer time it's just mud, mud, mud and you're sticking to your mud and you have a shower by getting out in the rain, if you can, if a gentleman doesn't throw some shells your way . . . So you go into the shower area and you strip off and then the next one in as you go into your shower itself and you're fumigated and you shower and gee that's bloody heavenly. It's absolute heavenly to have a shower. And then you go from there and you dry off. Then you go through to the doctor. The doctor checks you all out and everything and makes sure you haven't got too many sores and carbuncles and everything else like that and then you go into the Q [Quartermaster] store part of the area and you get a whole new outfit and you feel like a million bucks and you go out the other end and there's a pay bloke there, always a pay bloke, 'cause you never get any money in the line. What are you going to do with money? You have no money, right. But now you can go to the canteen so they probably give you ten quid or something . . . British Occupation Force money. So you go down, for twenty-four hours you just get on the booze, write yourself off and get back on the truck as a sick head, go back up the line again. But it's great.

* * *

You get snooty officers and you get soldiers' officers. Soldiers' officers don't worry too much about their career. They look after their men. They talk to their men and they invariably climb higher in rank than the snooties. Michael Jeffery, our present Governor-General, was a soldiers' officer. Sir Thomas Daly, who was a brigade commander in Korea when I was there, he was a soldiers' officer . . . They're good people, they're people that soldiers will follow, not because they're officers. But because they're the men they are and that makes a big difference.

... We were all in the same section, in the same platoon and you live together, you fight together, you're it. You're the family, like it or leave it, you're the family and you get to know everybody's little quirks and ways and everything and what to say and what not to say at the right time or the wrong time or anything. And soldiers are all very helpful to each other when you're in situations, always help each other. If you've got two bob, they got two bob, nobody's ever broke sort of thing. Old 'Benson & Hedges'. He was a skinny little runt and we'd been out on a fighting patrol and came back and one of the jobs you do, you count people as you come in to make sure you've got the right people and all this and of course you can sit down on the bloody trench and have a smoke then. But you can't take any smokes out with you. You can't take any paper, nothing. You're clean-skinned. All you've got is your dog tag, so when you get back in, the bloke that's there better have a smoke otherwise he's not real popular, right. And it must look like a cloud when the patrol comes in and they're all leaning back having a smoke in the trench. And 'Benson & Hedges' was on this night and I walked in. I said, 'Where's a damn smoke?' And his name was Benson, so he gets 'Benson & Hedges'.

'Give us a smoke, mate, give me a smoke!'

And he says, 'You owe me one now.'

And I says, 'Yeah, righto.'

Over the years, he's still alive too the bugger, over the years I must have given that bloke cartons of cigarettes for that one smoke. Every time he sees me he says, 'You owe me a smoke.'

Yeah.

* * *

The American soldier is a very brave soldier. There's nothing wrong with the courage of an American. And Vietnam was the same. It doesn't matter where he goes. He's got a force of numbers and his minor tactics on section level and platoon level aren't very brilliant.

They seem to cluster together and they operate from a platoon commander down and they operate more in the old British system of, 'Don't tell the soldiers anything and then they'll follow you because they don't know anything.'

And that's not a very brilliant way to work. Whereas the Australian military, God bless us, we have the 'must knows', 'should knows' and 'could knows'. You don't want to boggle the chain of command with giving them information that they don't need. If they need it, you give it to them. If it is information that is asked for, we give it, in our army. The Americans don't and nor do the Poms, though I believe the Poms are starting to wake up now and they're passing on information.

We give out information to our soldiers and question our soldiers on the orders that are given so that they fully understand them and they fully understand the task that they have to do. We also have an order of seniority within our own organisation so that if one goes down, the other bloke can take over. And I think it's something that you learn very, very early in your military career, that if you're to take over and lead, it is mostly done under active service conditions. The leader is down and you have to take over so you're taking over at the worst possible time. You're taking over in the middle of a firefight and you must know what's going on. Therefore in our army we pass down information so that whoever does have to take over, and any one of those private soldiers can take over at any time, and so they do.

* * *

Korea changed me in the aspect that I was to put all these lessons together, the things that I'd learnt. I was starting to become a professional soldier. Everything was starting to mesh together. Even though within your training you're learning all these sort of things, they haven't started to come together yet. In Korea, they started to come together and I'm saying started. They didn't all come together really until I started instructing. When I started instructing, because I had to now impart this knowledge, I had to know it in closer detail and how it all married and interlinked and everything else like that, to be able to pass the thing along. And that was when the true professionalism started to come, when you have to teach somebody else. It doesn't come necessarily with that first command decision that you have to make. The true professional, I feel, is when you have to impart knowledge to other people to keep them alive.

. . . So I ended up doing parachute courses, signals officers' course. I'm a qualified signal officer, regimental signal officers' course, mortar courses and courses, courses, courses, courses. And this rounded off the whole lot of our military training business, you know, and brought in true professionalism. We were able to see now how armoured married up with infantry, how tactical air married up with our whole tactical picture and how to employ it, the artillery and the mortars and everything, in the whole big concept. We just weren't infantrymen anymore. We were becoming very specialised people.

. . . A lot of us went on the warrant officers' course and qualified as warrant officers and were promoted to warrant officers and ended up at Scheyville, the Officer Training Unit training the young National Servicemen who were to become officers, who were to command and who we knew were going to command thirty men in action. So we knew that we had to make a damn fine job of these young men so that they could carry out their tasks and they could help to bring some young Australians home, so it was full-on. Five o'clock in the morning, ten o'clock at night, no problem, seven days a week. And those kids got trained and in a short period of time. In the short period that they were there, that's six months, they learnt to be a junior commander. They went into action and we eagerly awaited the reports from the commanding officers in Vietnam as to how our product was faring in country. And basically one line come back, 'Send us some more of this value.'

So we knew we'd done our job.

* * *

I'd start at five o'clock in the morning, knock off at ten o'clock at night, and I thought Flo was in bed all the time. I'd come home and go in and have a look at the kids and they were always asleep when I saw them and when I got up and at the start of an intake, I'd never see them for the first fortnight of the intake, I'd never see them, yeah. It was a hell of a job . . . the family never got much of our time at all and when we did have time off we were too damn tired to try and do anything . . . it wasn't a way to bring up a family. There wasn't very much quality time with the family. It wasn't family time and there was a lot of broken marriages and everything at that time. And of course within the married quarters there were those people, from different units and everything and they were away and infidelity was rife and, you know, not very nice in the services in those days.

. . . It was difficult. You were trying to support a family and we weren't getting paid a whole heap of money, support a family, try and be with the family. And Flo, God bless her, she looked after the family and she brought up the family. I did what I could when I was there, but I was never there. That's the service. You're just not there so it's very, very hard for the wives. Military life, especially the front-line units, you know, a regiment infantry battalion. They just never get home. They're copping it the same now, twelve months overseas, twelve months at home. When you're at home you're out on operations, you're rebuilding your unit. You're doing courses. And there's the family, but they come last . . . I'd come home and I'd be tired and Flo would say, 'Let's go for walk.'

And I'd say, 'Jeez, I just walked hundreds of miles with a pack on my back!'

It was hard. It was hard for both of us. But we made a go of it. You just make a go of it otherwise you give in.

It was pretty hard to get out of that unit and everybody was trying to escape. We had an escape committee going. Well, once you get into a position and you're instructors and everything, like National Service, they won't let you out, right . . . that's your job and you stay there and you do that. So the army bottles up its key people sort of thing and in this case nobody could move out of there unless the military secretary said so. But Vietnam was on. We *had* to go to Vietnam.

* * *

I'm a soldier, yeah. God if I hadn't have gone to Vietnam, if they wouldn't have let me go to Vietnam that would have been a disgrace to the nation and mother wouldn't have been able to live with me, no, that's a flaw in the character. Well, that was your duty, away we went. And having arrived in Vietnam . . . after having done my courses in Australia and I'd done a collateral language course down at Woodside, too, to learn to speak Vietnamese—don't know why. They'd have been better off teaching me French because I worked with the Montagnards and they could understand French and the Vietnamese could understand French. The Montagnards couldn't understand Vietnamese and they also had about 300 different dialects in their language, you know. Some of them couldn't speak to each other, let alone anything else.

Arrival in Vietnam was nothing dramatic. It was just receiving the smells of South-East Asia all over again. And the place had been pretty well bombed around all the airports and everything else like that . . . we were probably in phase two, leading into phase three. The terrorist war had finished . . . the NVA [North Vietnamese Army], North Vietnamese regular forces, had started to infiltrate the South so things were hotting up nicely. The oven was getting nice and hot and that was right throughout the country. The year before I arrived we'd had the Tet offensive. They were now rebuilding up because after the Tet offensive, though we had the Paris [Peace] Accord and all the rest of it. And the bombing was on and the bombing was off and the bombing was on and the bombing was off. And when it went off it would allow the enemy to build up and send more troops down south, do all the things, saying, 'Thank you very much; you've given us more time.'

And by the time I went there in '69, everything was percolating along very, very nicely in the kettle.

* * *

As part of the Australian Army Training Team Vietnam, Keith was assigned to a Vietnamese Special Forces unit, called a Mobile Strike Force. It was composed of soldiers from an indigenous people, the Montagnards. He was appointed as the Commander of 212 Company and told he would be taking them out on operations the following day.

And I hadn't seen any of my soldiers at this stage so I went over and the XO [Executive Officer], who was another [Australian] warrant officer, Warrant Officer Kev Latham, was fitting up the company ready for the operation the next morning, issuing ammunition, weapons, making sure they had all their gear and etcetera, etcetera. But no orders... I went down. I had a look at the soldiers and I thought, 'My God, this is what a Montagnard looks like. This is pretty good.'

Spoke to Kev. Kev seemed to be pretty switched on. He was an ex-SAS sergeant and was promoted to warrant officer so he appeared to be of pretty good value. Spoke to the [American] medic, Gerry Dellwo. Gerry was a 21-year-old, a volunteer, pretty highly trained in his medical field, had very little knowledge of infantry tactics or anything like that. They specialise and that was his MO [modus operandi] and Jack Clement who was an [American] radio man, knew his business. I was worried about the two Americans, I can tell you. I was very worried about them. Jack Clement had been around the traps a little bit longer than Gerry. Gerry, this was Gerry's first operation, my first operation there, his first operation. Kev had been on one, but not a heavy one ... and I was giving them problems and everything all the way through, being the old instructor, again, in the paddock.

So we left on the operation. We boarded the aircraft very early in the morning. We flew in and we didn't do a prep of the LZ [landing zone]. We flew straight into the LZ. By prep I mean we never had gunship fire onto the position and everything to make the LZ reasonably secure before we went in. We just took it in as a cold LZ, and bang, and in we went. The thought was that there were no enemy in the area or very limited. No enemy had been seen and it was supposed to be a shakedown operation for me anyhow... So Kev took the first bird in. Bird got on the deck and then the other two fluttered in alongside of him and they started to unload and next thing, *boong*, there's a red thing of smoke going up and I'm coming in on it. So we had a contact straight off and there was a lot of firing going on... I knew what I had to do. I had troops on the ground. I had to keep going in and I had to take command of the company and bring those other people in, make that ground secure for them to come in. And then the gunships came in then and rattled in all alongside of us and everything to keep the NVA reasonably busy while we got secure on the ground. Once we got secure on the ground, he beetled off. We went down and we found a blood trail, which we followed for quite some time until it run out on a stream and we just couldn't do it. And then I had to swing back and get into my own AO, area of operation.

... We had a peaceful day that day. That night was peaceful. The next morning we again saw signs of enemy and I went down off the ridge line and found an old village complex and we came back up onto the ridge line and it was reported there was NVA coming in our direction. We set up a hasty ambush. The ambush was sprung. There was a lot of firing and there was nobody hit. And I had a look at the ambush area after, and all our rounds were hitting high up in the trees so I had a big problem on my hands. The 'Yards' [Montagnards], needed training on how to keep their weaponry down and keep it down low to hit people in the knees and all the rest of it. So I knew then what half of my problem was. I had to do weapons training in a big hurry... the following day, we carried out a range practice. We just fired the weapons. I'd give them targets, then I'd put them down and I'd see who could hit the target and who couldn't hit the target. So I was sorting my people out and doing a bit of training on the operation. I was concerned about the standard of training of the company. I was very concerned about that, concerned not only for myself and my round-eyes [Westerners], I was concerned for the soldiers, they just weren't capable of hitting anything and doing damage to the enemy therefore they'd do damage to themselves. So it become a quick training course for the next two days. And then we were pulled out of that and went back to Pleiku . . . we were taken off operational duties for the next two weeks and we went into an intensive training program. At the end of the two weeks I was reasonably confident. I'd broken them down now. I created a killer group in each of the squads. In other words, it was either two or three men that could hit things, hit a target right, and they were the killers and I give them a little badge, you know. Anyhow it worked so they wouldn't just fire willy-nilly. They'd pick targets and do some knocking down and what the others knocked down, well that was just good luck.

* * *

Our next operation was straight up into the Bet Het area. It was good Indian [enemy] country. But he hadn't really come across the fence from Laos and Cambodia at that stage and this is in the Thai border area. We went down and we were patrolling along and two brothers were forward scouting. One went around one side of a bamboo into a little stream and his brother went around the other side and '*bup-bup-bup-bup-bup*', and he killed his brother. So we had to pull that operation up that afternoon and call LZ and get rid of the body and everything that afternoon. But I feel that that fire let the NVA know that we were in the area 'cause the following day, just after dusk, we run into a whole heap of problems. We had probably about a squad and a half of NVA fired on us from a ridge line. Fortunately they were on one ridge line and we were on the other . . . So we engaged them and then they broke the engagement.

. . . The next morning we were heading in a northerly direction. We had to check out an old French fort area. To do that we had to cross a bit of a stream and a pretty large, open plain area that used to be a couple of paddy fields. As we were starting to get down onto that and off the ridge line I picked up some corduroy across a swampy area. And corduroy is, you know, logs cut down and laid down and everything. And we followed that and I thought, 'Gee.' And I run into what I know was tank positions that had been dug into the side of hill and there was ammunition there, tank ammunition and everything like that . . . So I reported it, got the sig and we put a coded message through and I requested an air strike onto the whole thing. So I pulled back onto the ridge line and as I was pulling back onto the ridge line we bumped into a group of about four or five and I had one bloke wounded. And then we got the message that they were going to put in a B52 bomb raid on that particular area and for us to clear below the blue line, south of the blue line and I had to get down there before dark . . . it wasn't a very good tactical move. But we got down there carrying our wounded and I couldn't get right down below the blue line. But I got a pretty fair way down and the birds come over about two in the morning . . . we were in a real bad situation. As it was, the trees were all shaking and everything. So the next morning I was told to secure ground and I was airlifted out, so that was the end of that operation.

On the morning of 24 May 1969 Keith's Montagnard (Indigenous) battalion was operating close to the borders of Laos and Cambodia. There they came under fierce attack from the North Vietnamese Army and were forced to fall back. Despite being wounded Keith encouraged his men, throwing grenades and firing at the enemy. Indeed, in the next hours he worked tirelessly to provide cover for the battalion as it withdrew, reluctantly leaving numbers of men, including wounded, behind the enemy positions. As darkness fell on the battalion's new defensive line, Keith decided to go out, as his citation states, 'with complete disregard for his own life', and rescue the wounded. Over the next three hours, he located and assembled more than 40 wounded and missing men. His citation states: 'His conspicuous gallantry was in the highest traditions of the Australian Army.' He was awarded the Victoria Cross. This is how Keith tells it:

I received orders that I was to fly down to the 5th Battalion, who had been engaged by the enemy, and reinforce their position the next morning. The other two companies were to follow me in.

Try and understand now, at this stage the Mobile Strike Force was not designed to fight major battles. We were a reconnaissance outfit who could sneaky-ramp, push around the jungle, get information. We'd get into a firefight, then a heavy American unit, infantry units, used to come in and take over the firefight from us and we'd pull out because we weren't designed to fight heavy battles. Vietnamisation had now started [the handing over of military control to South Vietnam units]; therefore the heavy American units had gone off to the highlands and had now been taken over by a Republic of South Vietnam infantry division. They came in and they landed in a clear area about eight ks north of where we were. They took all the assets, all the guns and everything and ringed their position with fire and everything and left us pretty naked as far as artillery support and helicopter gunship support and everything like that. We invited them down to the firefight. They were supposed to come down. They would not come down to the party.

. . . So we kicked off and away we went. I had my company, left forward company. Monty was right forward. Tolley was bringing up the rear picking up weapons and everything from the day before and putting bodies in body bags and all the rest of it, and acting as a ready support element, to reinforce us if we got into trouble. We went down the ridge line, over the saddle and got up onto the main little feature. Just as we got onto the feature, there was a little knob on the end of it and we started to spread out and consolidate and the enemy opened up with three machine guns straight in front of us. Simultaneously, he started to mortar both our positions, mortar and rocket both our positions from the right and left flank. He then sent what was estimated as a company around into the low ground between Tolley and us and isolated Tolley's company from us. Tolley could shoot downhill at him. We couldn't shoot across it because Tolley would have copped our over-fire, so he was in a pretty safe position as far as we were concerned. He was in dead ground to us.

But not dead ground to Tolley. Montez was hit bad, real bad and we were starting to lose people and the NVA simultaneously attacked us from the front and two flanks at the same time. The Montagnards started to fall back after Montez was hit. I managed to stop them and keep them on line. My own people stayed on line all right, though they were getting panicky and they were shooting a lot of ammunition and they were taking a pretty fair toll of the enemy at this stage. Tolley's group had now moved back away from the firefight to form a firm base for us to break out...

The position became untenable and I knew that it was useless us trying to stay there and I also knew at this stage that he'd set up an annihilation ambush. He wanted us on that piece of ground. He wanted to kill us on that piece of ground and if we stayed there without any support, that's what was going to happen. So it was decided that the withdrawal take place. Montez's company started to break in some disorder. Again I managed to stop them for a bit and then I turned my attention back to my own people and we started to do a tactical withdrawal of some sort of a semblance, bringing out as many of the casualties as we could at that time...

It is now about just on dark. We formed a securer position on an intermediate ridge line and got our wounded up onto there and with the medics and everybody looking after the wounded. At this time I decided that somebody had to go and try and get some more of the wounded and everything off the position. It was no good me taking Montagnard because a) they were panicky anyhow and b) I couldn't talk to them. I couldn't communicate with them. And the medics, most of the other people had been wounded anyhow, around us. The only people who hadn't been wounded were Latham and Dellwo. The communications man from Montez's company was killed on the position. His medic came off the position. But he was severely wounded and he wasn't going anywhere. He'd lost half his buttock and had been wounded in the thigh as well so he wasn't going anywhere, and Montez had been severely wounded. He'd been hit in the face and all his jaw was blown away and so he was mortally wounded.

I then moved out and I'd only gone about fifty metres and I found the first group and I brought them back. And by now it was really starting to get dark down in the closed-in area down the bottom and there was a lot of smoke and flickering fire from the firefight and the explosions and everything that had taken place and it covered my movement pretty well. So I then moved about I suppose another two hundred metres, one fifty, two hundred metres, found another group, and then I found one more just forward of that and brought them back to a midway point and started to go back up again when I drew fire from a couple of the enemy. They missed and I fired . . . so I thought, 'Things are starting to get a bit dangerous now.'

'Cause the enemy knew that there was somebody on the position and coming back onto the position and he was starting to get himself organised. So I thought, 'Well, it's not the done thing to stay here any longer, best I get these other people back.'

So I came off the position, picked up the people that I'd left halfway, brought them back, right back on the old position, to find them all gone. Through the scrub and everything I saw phosphorus trail on the ground where they'd moved through, and I followed that and ultimately found the two medics . . . so we then moved off the ridge line. I started to go up the ridge line for a while because I thought Tolley might leave people secure up there on the ridge line. And then I heard firing start up on the ridge line. It was an AK47 and I knew that the enemy then had moved up along that ridge line, were probably moving up to engage anybody that was on the ridge line.

. . . I suppose we'd gone about two or three hundred metres, bad night, and then Gerry said that unless we get Monty out, he wasn't going to make it. We'd been crawling with him. He was a big man and we were crawling with him on our backs and trying to get him out, make him as comfortable as possible. Gerry had given him morphine so I propped and I radioed . . . to Special Forces, and they were going to send out a Charlie Charlie bird. That's a command and control helicopter, with Major Jagles, who was the commander of Mobile Strike Force. He was going to bring it out with a Maguiry, something you drop through and it's a clip-up thing and hoist people out of the jungle. He was inbound when Gerry said that Monty had passed away, yeah, so I cancelled the bird. We wrapped Monty and put him in alongside of a log to keep him.

So we knew pretty well where we were and then we took off . . . we got in onto the main position where the 5th Battalion was, about two o'clock in the morning. We secured the ground. We put our people around and we treated the wounded as much as we could that night. And the next morning we got helicopters in and everything and we got rid of our wounded and I went out myself because I'd been hit twice anyhow. I got hit earlier in the night and later again by rocket fire . . . All the wounded had gone and everything like that . . . and I was last out and I was pulling them out anyhow cause I was the senior Australian on the ground and I was pulling them out.

. . . I think it's personal, very, very personal, killing things and everything like that, people have got to realise that you're in action. You have a weapon. You're shooting at people and there's times when you know that you've taken people's lives and everything, and I think that they're personal sort of things, you know. They're the bad bits that you really don't want to talk about . . . I can say this to you, that soldiers in the field don't have a very dignified death. They die dirty. They're mostly unshaven, mud, dirt, dust, tired, hungry. They die, unless it's a fast one, they die very, very painfully and sometimes they die on their own. They die very lonely because of circumstances. Other times they will die and somebody, thankfully, is with them when they do go and they die in places that they never heard of, yeah. It's not a very dignified way of dying, a soldier's death in the field.

* * *

I went down to hospital. Then I went back to Mike Force and then I came home on leave and I was supposed to be going back on operation . . . and I was told I wasn't going back to Special Forces, that I was being reassigned to an ARVN [Army of the Republic of Vietnam—the South] unit in the north, up around Da Nang and I said, 'Oh well, so be it.'

That's what it was supposed to be. We were supposed to do six months tight and six months loose. Well, I'd done seven months or a bit more tight and now I'm going loose. But I'd been run down by then too, and I'd had a good set of ulcers and I was losing weight. I was about nine stone two. I was mentally and physically fatigued, mentally and physically. I'd had five really hard months of bashing jungle, living hard, making hard decisions, a lot of meal times without meals and seeing all this other bloody nonsense on top of it, five bad months, so I wasn't displeased in a way that I was leaving Special Forces, I can tell you. And then when I got my ulcers and everything and they sent me down to Vung Tau, to the hospital down at Vung Tau.

... The actual announcement of the award, when I went back off leave and I was being reassigned up north I got a real run around for a while and then I wasn't going anywhere. I had boarding passes to get on an aircraft here and I'd go out to the airport, 'No, you're not going on this one. You're going that way.'

And they sent me down to Vung Tau to talk to the soldiers and I thought, 'What the bloody hell am I going to talk about to the soldiers down at Vung Tau?'

The CO [Commanding Officer], R.D.F. Lloyd, Colonel Lloyd, was home on his ten days R&R and his position was being filled by Major Johnson, Frank Johnson. So I got a message to go and see him so I went and saw him in his office and he said, 'General Hay wants to see you.'

And he was the Commander of Australian Forces Vietnam and I said, 'Oh well.'

... So I went over to see General Hay and knocked on the door and, 'Enter.' I love that. I don't like senior officers and I don't like him and he wasn't my favourite officer. Good thing this will be all on tape when I'm all gone and he's all gone. And he just stood up from behind his desk and put out his hand and said, 'Allow me to be the first to congratulate you. The Queen has awarded you the Victoria Cross.'

And I went ... I can't do it on camera ... I just took a half pace back and said, 'Oh shit, Sir!'

'Cause I really didn't know what I was there for. And then we went down into the press room and it came across on the announcement ... and then we had a few beers all round and I was a bit confused for a while, you know, and Simmo [Ray Simpson] was there and Simmo's award had been announced just a fortnight before [also a VC]. And Simmo was there and after the announcement he'd go, 'Come and have a beer, mate.'

So we went and had a beer 'cause Simmo and I knew each other from Japan days and everywhere. We'd soldiered together long enough to be able to go aside and have a beer, yeah.

... And then they said, 'You're going home.'

And I said, 'Well, I'm not going to bitch about that. I've done my time, I'm away. I'm out of here.'

I would have liked to have finished my time. I had another three months to do, three, four months ... But I felt I'd done my bit and I was out and I wouldn't have been able to go operational anyhow. My physical condition wasn't there to allow me to do it and I was pleased to get home, you know. So I came home and they stuck me in hospital for some six-odd weeks, then posted me down to Duntroon in the middle of winter. Oh my God, I mean what a cultural shock that was. I'd been in South-East Asia, I'd been in the tropics for nearly nine years and then I'm down in Duntroon and oh my God, yeah. So fortunately I had a good commandant down there that I had served with in Korea. He was a major in Korea. He was now a major general and the commandant, Sandy Pearson, a hell of a fine officer, and 'cause it was just going into the winter and I was bloody cold and I had permission to wear greatcoats and winter dresses and everybody else was running around in summer gear and I'm freezing, yeah.

* * *

I'm tremendously proud to be able to wear the award for a lot of people. I also accept the responsibility that goes along with it, for the people in uniform of the nation, into the future, you know. To still be alive and to be able to go and speak to somebody, speak to cadets or school kids or something like that, to give the younger generation something to grab onto so that they can, throughout their life, have a look and say, 'Anything is achievable if you go about it the right way.'

And more importantly if they see it and read the history of it, and what you're doing on tape now, you're going to give to future generations, they will be able to say, 'Well this fellow is a normal Australian. He's not a Superman. He's not an Einstein. He's just an ordinary Australian who was caught in a very nasty position, recognised the responsibility that he was given of command and carried out the duties according to that responsibility to the best of his ability.'

Now if everybody in the nation sort of sees that and they say to themselves, 'Well, my responsibility . . .'

And I always give this to the children. 'What is your responsibility now? Well, your responsibility is to your family, isn't it? To your Mum and Dad, to your school, to the citizens in your own town, to your friends and to your nation.'

And it starts them thinking on a line of saying, 'Hey, I've got a part to play in this society.'

And if we can guide them in that light and make them probably have a look at the mistakes of the past, and I see today with the increase of interest amongst the younger generation of Australians, especially at the turn of the century, they were grasping out for something to guide them into the new century. They wanted a bridge to cover that gap from an old century to their responsibility that they will have to look after the nation in the new century and they wanted something to grab onto. If they wanted to use the award of the Victoria Cross as a prop to do that, if they want to use a footballer to do that, fair enough. As long as something motivated them to not give up and to push on and look after whatever they had to do and add up to their responsibility in the new century, in their life.

. . . I look back on it now and say, 'Well it was a happening in my life.'

I accepted my responsibilities for that phase of my life. I don't have any hang-ups about my life and as I say to Flo, when we go somewhere and we're mates and we're all gathering around and we're all talking and having a beer and everything and I meet people that I knew along the track in service and everything and there's always a good greeting and everything. And I say to Flo, 'That's what service is about. That's what it's about.'

You're recognised by your contemporaries, by your compatriots, that you did your job in service as well as they did and what better compliment could you have in life than a lot of friends, simple.

PAUL COUVRET

Dutch Fleet Air Arm
Prisoner of the Japanese
Survivor of Nagasaki
World War II

*In their relentless push through South-East Asia, the Japanese swept
everything before them, catching up in their net the many European
settlements that were outposts of colonialism*

I think generally speaking, the Dutch population in the Dutch East
Indies didn't pay much attention to a threat from Japan mainly
because of the Japanese we saw in Indonesia before the war, and
they had a lot of Japanese people who started businesses. Number
one, they had barber shops, Japanese barber shops, they had
photographic shops where you put your print and develop films and
it was all boxed cameras in those days, the 120 with eight exposures
on a film, and then they also had a number of shops where they had
cheap clothing and cheap toys, cheap bicycles and those sort of shops.
And most of those people . . . they were small, little Japanese with
heavy glasses and they didn't look like superheroes or supermen at
all. They were little in stature, very obliging and didn't have a high
profile at all; they just stayed in the background very much. So that
was the only contact we had with Japanese people. The equipment
they sold, the films, they did that all right, the barber, they gave you
a good haircut. The stuff you bought in the shops like the cotton
shirts and singlets and so on, they fell apart after a few washes. The

bicycles were very inferior, I had a Japanese bike one day and it just broke in half, so it all had a very poor reputation. And so we didn't think that the Japanese, we knew they had started a war in China, but it was a long way away. Later on we found that the Japanese people who ran those shops all came back to Indonesia in officers' uniforms.

* * *

When I went to war the whole school, our whole class, all the men in the class, because it was general mobilisation of all the able-bodied Dutch people, we were given an opportunity to go home and say goodbye to our parents, so I went to Sukabumi and spent the day with my parents. My mother was crying all the time and she wouldn't come to the station to wave me goodbye. So she gave me a little New Testament and in it, in the front page she had written, in Dutch of course, *'He that has a heart for God in light days will find the light of God in his heart in dark days.'*

And I thought that was very nice. And I never realised the truth of that, till a few months later when I was a POW. Anyway, my father he took me to the railway station and the last thing he said, 'I hope you'll never do anything I'll be ashamed of.'

So yeah, that was a bit emotional. Yeah, well, I don't think I've ever disappointed him. That was the last time I saw my parents...

* * *

They began to realise that Java was going to fall and a lot of, especially navy personnel, you know they had ships and motor torpedo boats and aeroplanes and they decided that they'd try and get out before; they couldn't do anything anymore there. There was no opportunity... a lot of ships were sunk and they tried to get away. And I think the Dutch Navy, the senior officers there played a very questionable role because instead of getting the fighting personnel to Australia so they could continue to fight against the Japanese, they chose to take their wives and children, and a lot of the Dorniers and Catalinas and Lockheed Lodestars were used to cart personnel to Darwin and Broome.

There were a number of ships and they went in three directions, some went straight for South Africa, others went for Ceylon and others went for Australia. And our captain decided to go for Fremantle...after two days at about eleven o'clock we were called on the foredeck and there was a speech from the bridge, it said, 'Men, if we make this day unhindered, we'll be in Fremantle in two days.'

And about two o'clock on the horizon appeared a Japanese float plane, which kept a safe distance, circled around us and then disappeared again. And two hours later we saw some white spots on the horizon and we thought, 'Hey, these are probably Indonesian perahu [boats].'

And as we were appearing and waiting we suddenly saw that the white had a centre in it and it happened to be the bow waves of cruisers and destroyers which were coming towards us at full speed. Well they surrounded us and with all the guns trained on our ship the captain decided not to give battle. We had one three-inch gun on the aft deck, but fortunately he didn't open fire, otherwise we would have been drilled into smithereens...the first thing they did was haul back the Dutch flag; hoisted the Japanese Rising Sun flag and they put a crew on board...so we were then landed a day later at Macassar.

* * *

Everybody had to stand on parade in one long line in front of the place where he slept...and we had to undress completely, stand naked, and along came a team of Japanese doctors, I presume they were doctors, they dressed in long white coats and they looked you over, what I remember well of that episode, that they were very keen on feeling your testicles, I think that was because they were all, had homosexual tendencies, I don't know what. Or whether our tools were bigger than they were used to, I don't know. But I remember that part, we were very insulted but nevertheless as they walked past and looked you over they every now and again said, 'One step forward.'

And you had to step forward and by the time they had a thousand of them the rest could go back. Now I was one of the blokes that had to step forward because, well I was in pretty good nick, from before the war, I was pretty athletic and very good in sport in gymnastics and swimming. So I apparently impressed the Japanese doctor with my physique at that time and so that's how I finished up getting that extra issue of clothing and finished up on board the *Azuma Maru*, a Japanese transport ship...and so in ten days we got to Nagasaki...and we were welcomed by the management of the Kama Minami Shipyard and they welcomed us as workers for the shipyard.

* * *

We were always looking for ways to sabotage but sabotage was very difficult on the shipyard...we built them on blocks you see, in big docks, and the docks were flooded and the ship pulled out and then it was finished on the quay and they put the engine room in it. And in the main bearings they have great big oil bars and I used to throw a handful of steel shavings in the oil bars hoping that that would do some damage later on. And another favourite trick of mine was to get a pocket full of cement, dry cement, undo a steam pipe in the engine room, fill it up with all that dry cement and then connect the pipe again and hoping that once they started running, that the cement would set and blow the pipe. Another favourite way of mine was the fact that we had so many bedbugs; we thought we should share them with the Japanese crew. So every now and again we had to work and clean up the cabins, which were the crew cabins on the ship...and you know the ordinary matchbox, a matchbox will hold about two hundred well-fed bedbugs, all swollen up with blood... and I had great delight in smuggling that in, put it in my pocket and take it to the shipyard and then when I was in the bunks of where the crew was going to work, I'd sprinkle a few bedbugs out of the box in each bunk. And once you get bedbugs in a bunk you can't get rid of it, so I thought as we had have all these bedbugs it was only fair to share it with the Japanese. Quite disgusting really when you look back at it, but that was another way of sabotaging and it made you feel reasonably good about it.

One way I earned extra rice and cigarettes was by drawing, see everybody had chalk in his pocket because whenever you had done something on the shipyard, you had to sign for that in chalk and so I signed it with my name in Japanese, and on an off day when there was nothing doing I'd draw a picture on the steel. They'd say, 'Oh, you can draw, oh good, draw me something else.'

And invariably . . . they wanted naked women of course and that attracted them very much. One day a Japanese came with a piece of paper and pencil and said, 'Come with me and draw me a picture of a naked woman.'

And he was standing guard and I was drawing a voluptuous blonde with big tits and all the details, no clothes on, and oh, that went around very quickly so I had a steady stream of customers and they always paid me for it and the more pornographic I made the picture, the more they liked it. And I didn't mind corrupting the Japanese morals at all. So that's how I made a bit of extra money. And I also, on a couple of occasions, Japanese guards they'd come into the room and say, 'Can anybody draw?' with the interpreter and, 'I want somebody to draw me.'

And they'd take you up to the guardhouse and they'd sit there looking very fierce you see, and then you made a portrait of them and that took several hours and whilst you were drawing that they'd give you the scraps of their meal, so that was very nice and I quickly learnt that what they really want you to do is make sure that they look very ferocious and give them a European nose. The Japanese were very sensitive about the flat noses and if you gave them a European nose that made them look much better and so I got a few free feeds out of that, till the CO decided that was too much fraternising and he stopped that sort of practice and I couldn't do it anymore.

* * *

The 9th of August was when the second atom bomb was detonated and that day was a nice sunny day and it was about eleven o'clock when a single B-29 dropped the atomic bomb over Nagasaki . . . now I was working in the bottom of a large dock where they built four 50 000 tonners at the same time and we had just finished the bottom of the ship . . . and the first indication we had that there was something unusual happening was we saw this bright flash as if somebody just took a picture of you with a camera . . . and it lit up everything and we looked around, 'Where in the hell did that light come from?'

And we looked up because the cranes which run across the dock . . . they had these short circuits on the bare wires which fed the power takeoff for the cranes. But the cranes were still going so we said, 'Now that's funny, what the heck is that?'

See, it took twelve seconds before the blast of the bomb . . . it was six kilometres away from us and it took about twelve seconds before the blast hit the buildings on the shipyard. And most of the buildings there consisted of very solid, big, concrete pillars with concrete floors and then in between the pillars they had built walls to make offices and storage places and all those walls, because of the blast, were blown out of the building and they came thundering down into the docks. So when we looked up we saw this avalanche of debris. You see there were five storeys of buildings alongside us. And we saw this avalanche come thundering down in the dock and we just had enough time because we were ten metres below the ground level, to dive underneath the blocks, in between the blocks, underneath the steel bottom of the ship. And all this debris thundered down at a tremendous rate and after about thirty seconds, it had all stopped falling. And our immediate reaction was we thought that the buildings had been hit by a row of bombs and that had blown the building apart. And our thought was that the aircraft would probably fly around and do a circuit and drop another row of bombs and if they hit the door at the end we would have a ten-metre high wave flooding the dock and we would all drown. So our immediate reaction was we must get out of this dock as quick as possible.

. . . So we climbed up these ten-metre high ladders and started running towards the shipyard air-raid shelters, which were tunnels in the rock face surrounding the camp on the one side. And, well, it was a 500-metre run and naturally we couldn't run too well. I'm seventy-five kilos now and I was only forty-four kilos then so you run out of puff fairly quickly and so as we slowed down and we looked over our shoulders still, because we were afraid that we might be strafed because that had happened before. An American aircraft had strafed the camp and then we had to seek shelter underneath steel plates and behind steel pillars to stop being shot at by our own people. But there were no aircraft and then as we looked around, we looked in the direction of Nagasaki and we saw this huge column of fire and smoke with the mushroom at the top, climbing in the sky at a tremendous rate, there was all this fire inside and it was absolutely amazing and we'd never seen anything like it . . . and everybody stopped running and the Japanese were looking too. And then the *kaiguns* came out, the Japanese guards came out, *'Kura kura buggaro!'*

That's Japanese swearing, and we had to get back to work as soon as possible. And the order came out; no POWs were allowed to work out in the open, so we all had to work inside buildings or below ground in the docks. But of course they couldn't stop us going to the toilets. So we went to the toilets, which are in different places around the camp, in threes, two cockatoos [look-outs] on the end of the toilet and then one by one we went in and stood on the seat and you peered through the ventilators in the direction of Nagasaki and the whole city had caught alight, everything was on fire and that big column in the centre had disappeared but the mushroom was still towering over the top of it all. So we could see there was a terrible fire had erupted in Nagasaki.

. . . That evening we marched back to the camp and we talked amongst one another, 'Where were you?' 'Did you see anything?'

And the boys that had been working out in the open actually had seen the bomb come down, because it dropped on three parachutes you see. The aircraft had to have time to be far enough away when the bomb was detonated, so that it wouldn't be torn apart . . . but they saw this come down and it had just disappeared behind the top of the hill because there's a hill between the shipyard and Nagasaki city, when it detonated. So they didn't see the thing explode...and we didn't know that it was a bomb and we didn't hear about that actually, it wasn't confirmed that it was a bomb till the 28th of August when we were visited by American aircraft, they were Mitchell Bombers, three American bombers, and we quickly rolled up blankets and made letters out of it on the parade ground...N-E-W-S?...with a question mark and they read that and one peeled off and circled around a few times and then he made a low run over the parade ground and dropped a packet of Chesterfields [cigarettes], and in the cellophane was a piece of paper out of his diary: *'War is over after Yanks dropped atomic bomb on Nagasaki, Godspeed home.'*

And that was the message and that's when we heard what it was actually and it confirmed that it was a bomb. Because the news that it was a bomb was kept away from the Japanese population too. And it's only later that we realised that, that moment we saw that flash, at that very moment seventy-four thousand Japanese men, women, children, babies, thousands of animals died instantly. And another nineteen thousand died a horrible death of radiation sickness in the next three months.

* * *

Now after the 9th, the following day, we still had to go to work because we were still POWs and there's normal routine, we went to work again but all the work on the shipyard had stopped and all the workers, the Japanese workers, were put into rescue teams and they were going into Nagasaki to see what they could do. The fire burned all night and the following day, it was a very big fire and we saw these blokes coming back at about five o'clock, bedraggled and full of ash and silt and they were really downhearted and they had seen a lot of horror there and you could see that something terrible had happened in Nagasaki...our job was cleaning and painting and repairing things, sweeping, to keep us busy but whenever there was an air raid we had to go into the shelters and we stood shoulder to shoulder with some of the victims they brought from Nagasaki into the dockyard because they had a little hospital there with about fifty beds ... there were no army people, just civilians who had been burned. And anyone, you could see their bare skin was all badly burned. A bloke had say his arms and his face was burned and his body was, not because of his shirt but wherever he had a big hole in his shirt, that's where there was a big burn. And so we thought these people had been caught in the fire itself but later on of course, we found it was the heat, that tremendous radiation heat from the bomb. We could feel that six kilometres away when the hot blast came and hit the buildings, we could feel this hot air rushing past us. And that was six kilometres away, so you can imagine how hot it was near the epicentre of the bomb.

One particular occasion ... is a picture I'll never forget, I'll have to take with me for the rest of my life. It was a woman, a Japanese woman, oh a little, you know, she was only about five foot four or something and obviously she had been leaning forward tending her garden and women in those days in Japan always carried their babies in a shawl on their back. And she had been carrying this little baby on her back but as she was bent forward, the baby was facing the direction of the bomb and the heat had burned off all her hair, her eyes were blind, her ears were burned off, her nose and lips were burned but the poor thing was still alive. And we felt so desperately sorry for this poor woman who was trying to shoosh her little baby and comfort the thing. All we were hoping is that the baby would soon die so that she would get out of her suffering ... and that's what happened to nineteen thousand Japanese afterwards. So it was a pretty grim picture.

* * *

That went on for the next three days and then suddenly on the fifteenth we didn't have to go to work. And we'd only had a day off about ten days before so we said, 'Hey, that's funny; we don't have to go to work.'

And the following day again no work and there were no more air raids, but there was just a single B-29 which kept flying, practically all the time, over Nagasaki taking photos, and reconnaissance and testing I suppose. And then on the 17th, we suddenly all got our Red

Cross parcels, which were stored there, and they were handing them out and we said, 'Hey, hey, hey, there's something happening here.'

And then finally you know we heard that the war was over and oh, I've never seen so many men cry when they heard.

'We made it.'

Yeah.

... Then our POWs in the camp decided to go searching for food ... and around Nagasaki are little farms, so they walked through Nagasaki to the farms and the farmers were terrified, they thought they'd come to kill them, rape their women and kill the children and that's what the farmers thought because the propaganda had told them that was going to happen. But of course all they wanted was a good feed so they were very relieved when the POWs went back after having a good feed. But these POWs came back with the stories of what they saw in Nagasaki. And the whole place was absolutely erased; everything was grey with a terrible stench hanging over it and that stench was still there on the 12th of October when I went through Nagasaki itself on our liberation ... there are little beaches around the bay of Nagasaki, little sandy beaches like we have around Sydney Harbour and the sand had fused into glass, sand is the raw material for glass and they brought back pieces, they'd broken off pieces of that big bit of sand which had fused into glass and they could sell it for two hundred dollars on Okinawa to souvenir hunters of the Americans ... wherever there had been heaps of bottles, stacked neatly, it was all melted into one big gooey mess of green glass, because of that heat of the bomb. So they came back with those stories. I didn't do that, I didn't walk around there because at that stage I had developed an abscess in my leg, I had beri-beri, which means your leg just swelled up that thick, and I had an abscess on one leg and I couldn't walk anymore. So I was cursing the fact that I couldn't go searching for food and going to the hills to get some extra food, but it turned out it probably saved my life because several of the boys who walked through Nagasaki in search of food, they died twenty years later of leukaemia and bone cancer. It was an epidemic among survivors both in Nagasaki and Hiroshima, twenty years later of people who died of leukaemia.

* * *

From the 29th of August things started to improve considerably because we then suddenly got the first aerial supplies from the Americans, who dropped food and clothing and medicine by parachute over the camp and on the island near the camp, there was an enormous amount of food they dropped there and oh, it almost killed some people you know, all this beautiful food and our stomachs couldn't handle that at all. And some people really almost killed themselves by overeating. There was one case of two blokes I well remember, the food came down in whole pallets with a parachute on top and they had a tin of dried, dehydrated rice with meat and it tasted so nice they ate it, they couldn't be bothered to cook it first and they ate it and got a terrible thirst of course, and they ate a fair bit of it, a terrible thirst, then they started to drink and then of course they began to swell up and I can't forget these blokes lying in the sickbay and they were looking like nine-month pregnant women and the sickbay attendant who had tried to push down on it, and they were screaming in the pain but they actually finally finished up forcing it through their system and they survived after a great deal of discomfort . . . we also found that fat food, if you took more than a teaspoon, a smooth teaspoon of butter it went straight through you like a laxative, our systems couldn't use any fat at all. And we had to very gradually work ourselves into normal eating and the doctors were warning us all the time about taking it very easy on the food, which we tried to do of course, but you know when you're very hungry you want to gorge yourself on all that good food. And it did a lot of damage because not always did the parachutes open and sometimes whole drums, they did everything in a big way; Americans do things in big ways. Cocoa powder came in 44-gallon drums. And I'll never forget there was one drum of cocoa powder landed on one of the Japanese barracks, three-storey barracks, it went through the roof, first floor, second floor and embedded itself in the concrete floor in the bottom, exploded and when you looked into that room everything was a beautiful even brown as if somebody had painted the whole place and it was all this cocoa powder, it was an amazing sight.

When they finally arrived, the Yanks sent...a landing craft to the camp and I'll never forget that, because the camp was on the seaside and they drove up and they landed, down came the front and out came these Americans sailors with a few petty officers, there were about twenty of them, all in beautiful, spotless, white outfits...and they came into the camp and they walked there with a spring in their steps and we then began to realise what we had changed into, we couldn't walk with a spring in our step anymore, we just shuffled along looking down, because you never looked up because then you might catch the eye of a Japanese and you'd attract attention so we used to walk with head bent and shuffle along...and that's when we realised how far we had, as human beings, we had actually sunk although they hadn't killed our spirits. And then the order came in, all POWs had to go back into their rooms because the Americans wanted to see what conditions we lived under. And so we were in the room and I'll never forget an American petty officer...opened the door, stuck his head into the door and he said, 'Goddamn! You guys stink!'

All the clothes that we were wearing went straight into an incinerator and naked we went into, it was a long twenty showers, fresh water, hot fresh water, well what a sensation that was. We hadn't had fresh water or a hot shower for all that time so that was a tremendous sensation. So you had to soap yourselves in and have a shower, soap yourselves in again and by the time you came to the end they gave you a towel and you had to dry yourself properly. And these beautiful white towels went straight into another incinerator and we thought, 'Oh, what a shame.'

And then we walked into the next team, still no clothes, all naked and there was a whole team of blokes standing there with shavers and they shaved, anybody who had a beard was shaved off, all the pubic hair was shaved off and underarm hair and if they had hairy chests, it was all shaved off and then the next team there were blokes with puffers and it was DDT powder and we came out all white looking like ghosts and then we got into a dressing-room and you got beautiful white underpants, a singlet, blue jeans, shoes with white socks and oh, what a sensation. And then when we came out there was a girl, a Red Cross girl waiting with an ice-cream and we hadn't had an ice-cream for all that time either and I'll never forget that ice-cream and it was absolutely marvellous and I've never enjoyed an ice-cream that much in my life.

* * *

When I arrived in Manila one of the first things I did was I went to the Red Cross missing persons you see, and I wanted to see whether they could find where my father and mother and my sister were. And I gave them the address, the last known address and to the credit of the Red Cross Missing Person's Bureau, they got my sister's address . . . she was liberated too, she was in a Japanese concentration camp in central Java with my mother and they found her, Red Cross, then gave her my address and I got a letter from Nell, a seventeen-page letter where she gave the whole history of what happened to my father and what happened to my mother and so I then heard that they had both perished during the war. My father died as a result of beatings he received in a Japanese prison, he got gangrene in his leg and that killed him. And my mother . . . died of starvation, a fortnight before the end of the war. Well, that really shattered me, that was the biggest blow I ever got in my life to hear that I suddenly had no father and mother anymore. And the tragic circumstances under which they had died. There was only Nell and myself left then.

* * *

When you are talking a shock, the only big shock I had I suppose was when we arrived in Melbourne. See, all the time since the war broke out we had been in the Dutch Navy and then into the Japanese prison camps . . . but we hadn't seen any normal life as we remembered it before the war. When we arrived in Melbourne on Christmas Eve we were in open trucks . . . and they took us to Melbourne first because we had to be processed and so on that trip back there we saw sights, well, it was just ordinary Australian life, you know, a park, you see a woman with a pram and two little children. We had forgotten completely what it looked like, it was such a shock there to see things, we had forgotten that they existed, like ordinary family life, shop windows with beautiful stuff in it, people standing on the footpaths laughing and talking to one another and nobody in a hurry and all the Christmas decorations outside Spencer Street, we went through, past Spencer Street Station in Melbourne and there were just thousands of people streaming out of Spencer Street Station and there was a Salvation Army band in front playing Christmas songs, Christmas carols and that was for us a tremendous shock actually to suddenly come back into normal life which we hadn't, we had been away from that for six years and to suddenly realise that that still existed and as you can see it was a shock to me because I still get emotional when I think about it.

* * *

It was mateship which helped you through, right throughout the prison camp actually it was your mates, if you felt down they'd talk to you and you'd talk to one another and cheered one another up and make sure that you get through it. Plus I haven't mentioned but religion really played a big part ... and I really found that when the days were very dark in the Jap prison camp every night I used to have a prayer and said, 'Look, I don't know what tomorrow will bring but will you please help me to get through it? And will you protect me?'

And it was always a great relief to know that you could turn and you felt also that the Lord was near you and I had some, you know most people in their lives have at one stage or more a mystic experience and the most mystic experience I ever had was in Nagasaki and that was Christmas in '44. It was a bloody awful day, it was freezing cold and as POWs we always saved some of our Red Cross parcels to eat at Christmas but we had no spare that day. The camp commander went to the Japanese camp commander ... and asked, 'Can we, it's Christmas, it's a big day for Europeans. Will you allow us to sing?'

And we weren't allowed to sing in the camp because you know, war was a terrible thing and so we weren't allowed to sing and anyone caught singing or humming was belted up. So when after several approaches the camp commander said, 'Yes, okay, I'll let you sing but you'll have to go outside on the parade ground.'

And he said, he thought to himself, 'They're not that foolish that they'd go out in the freezing cold.'

But there's a blizzard blowing and sleet and so the word spread around and it was eight o'clock and we were allowed out and much to the disgust of the Japanese guards who had to go out of the nice warm guardhouse, around the fire, they had to go out with overcoats and they went, they had to go with us to guard us because they thought somebody might run away and we all, practically everybody in the camp... we stood there together in the horrible weather, we stood like penguins, you know how penguins all stand together for mutual warmth and then we started singing Christmas songs, Christmas carols and we had some English Christmas carols and some American and then we all finished up with 'Silent Night'. And the atmosphere there was absolutely electric and I really felt that the Lord was with us and just stood there amongst us. And the funny thing about it the Japanese felt that too and the Japanese, who were swearing and that at us, they all got still, and they just stood there in silence listening to us and they could feel there was something happening there and I have never felt the presence of the Lord like that again. And it was absolutely unbelievable and we all felt that and we were greatly uplifted when we went back to sleep.

* * *

I believe in a golden thread which runs through your life and I'm not a pretty religious man, I don't go to church, if I got to a church once a month I'm doing well. I believe there's a golden thread which runs through your life and the good Lord is holding the thread in one hand and it's your choice to hold that golden thread. And I do believe that my time in prison camp was just a part of growing up and a huge learning experience. I got a very big insight in people and you can't judge people by what they look like. You learn to appreciate what they do and what they think. I've got a tremendous appreciation of the good things in life and when I say the good things in life, enough food, friendship, clean clothes and a nice home and a dry bed. The simple things, which we all take for granted, are the most valuable and I have also learnt what hunger is, for three years we went hungry every night and we always dreamed, we were dreaming of food. In prison camps nobody was talking about sex, we were impotent anyway, but we were always dreaming and talking about and exchanging recipes about nice dishes...and at night you were always dribbling, at night your pillow was wet because you'd been dribbling because you had been dreaming about food, to make glorious food, ice-cream and all sorts of lovely things, chocolate cake...and I'll never throw away any food. I can't stand people throwing away food because you get that appreciation of eating food which was thrown away from the Japanese kitchens. We used to crawl up behind the wall getting the crusts out of the big copper vats they used to cook the rice in, we'd pinch that and try to beat the dogs getting there, get it and take it with you and chew it up, and it was still food you see. So if you've been through all that, that I think has all been a tremendous learning experience and I felt that I came out much better equipped to cope with pressure and adversity.

* * *

In '93 I was asked to go to the world conference of Mayors for Peace. The Japanese every four years have a big conference in Hiroshima and Nagasaki and they invite mayors from all over the world to come to these cities, everything paid, you've got to pay your own passage but while you're there you are the guest of Hiroshima, Nagasaki and they had five hundred mayors from seventy countries and I was one of them and they had heard from my CV, which you've got to send prior, that I'd been a POW and even while I was still in Australia they rang me up...

'How come you were here in '42 till '45, what were you doing here?'

And I said, 'I was a *horyo*.'

'Oh, *horyo*.'

That means POW you see.

... While I was in Nagasaki, the reporters brought to me a woman, a Japanese woman and this woman said, 'You know, I was in that shipyard when you were there as a POW.'

You see all fourteen-year-old boys and girls were taken out of school and had to work. We as POWs felt sorry for these poor kids because they belted them up with baseball bats the same way, if they weren't working hard enough. And this girl had been working there and she said, 'Ever since I was there I have been feeling so guilty about what my people did to your people, the way you were treated, the cruelty, the rags you walked around in and I felt so sorry for you and I never had a chance to apologise, but today is the day.'

And then she stood in front of me and she bowed deeply and the only English word she knows, 'Sorry, sorry, sorry.'

And she bowed three times and said that. Now that really brought home to me, an apology that way is much better than an apology from a politician that means nothing. And then she walked away and she said, 'Could you wait a moment?'

I said, 'Oh dear.'

I said to myself, Japanese are very big in giving presents and I didn't have anything on me to give her you see but no, she did come back with a present, she come back with a little plate, two peaches, two pieces of apple, two cherries, everything, all the fruit they had, two of each and she said, 'You know, when I went to work every morning my mother used to give me more than I could eat.'

Like most mothers do, no matter where they come from, they give their children more to eat when they go to school. And they always bring something home and her mother did the same and she said, 'And I had so much, I knew how hungry you people were and I so much wanted to give it but I never dared.'

Because if they had been found to do so they would have been belted up mercilessly by the guards so she never had a chance and she said, 'But today my chance has come to share this, so let's eat this together.'

Well, so here we stood and I didn't know this woman from a bar of soap but I put my arms around her and we both stood there crying and I think any hatred, residue of hatred in my heart against the Japanese just melted.

JOHN FRASER

Infantry
UN Transitional Authority Cambodia

Black Hawk Loadmaster
East Timor

I had no doubts. I didn't want to be a doctor or lawyer or think of anything else. I just knew I wanted to be in the military. In fact I'd always go down and read up about World War I, World War II, look at weapons, just go through all the magazines. I was always going through the same books over and over again. It's funny, like, at twelve years old I was reading about weapons that I later on used, so I just always knew I wanted to be there.

... I left school after Grade Ten and obviously I had time to wait until I turned seventeen, so I just went off and became a horse strapper ... and got a bit of cash behind me too and got a bit of work. It was actually good. Sort of funny how being a horse strapper prepares you for the army, because you start at three o'clock in the morning and you work through to nine and then you start again at three o'clock in the afternoon and work until six. So when I went into the army, the army is renowned for starting early and when I first got there this big sergeant says, 'Yeah, there'll be no sleeping in here you bunch of poofters—you'll be getting up at 5.30 in the morning.' I'm going, 'Whoo, sleep-in!'

So I woke up bright and I was good to go, and everyone's going, 'Er, more sleep,' and I was powering. So I found Kapooka to be a blast. I had the best time of my life. In fact it was the most organised time in my life. Down there, routine is just the biggest word. You know what you're doing 24/7.

... You go in for a couple of interviews and the first interview is to have a chat with a nice recruit. He sits down and says, 'Well, this is the army. These are the different jobs and these are the processes.'

He makes it all sort of sound nice, all nice and airy-fairy and sort of, 'This is the life you want to lead, the good food and the good tucker.'

And *blah blah blah* and companionship and it's all sort of true in a way, and then you go away and think about it and you say, 'Okay, I'd like to do this,' and send in some more paperwork saying, 'I'm interested, I'd like to sort of join up.'

And then you come in the fourth time with your bags packed and get your photo taken and you're sworn-in to the military and you sign the dotted line and then off you go. From there they put you in a bus, take you to the airport and you're chaperoned usually by an NCO, by a corporal, and he'll basically take you all the way down to Kapooka. So we flew down and we spent something like eight hours at Melbourne airport waiting around which was actually good, your first taste of hurry up and wait within the military, and from there we went to Kapooka. Drove in the front gate and were met by a big burly MP sergeant and he said, 'Has anybody got weapons and stuff like that, knives?'

And this and that and *blah blah blah* and then we went off to our quarters and then we were just indoctrinated.

... Your locker is a work of art. You just don't fold it and put it in. Everything's folded and measured with a ruler, and your handkerchiefs are ironed in a certain way, and your socks have got to be folded so you've got the smiley face... but it's just a work of art. Your bed is made in a strict manner. You use your bayonet and ruler to measure it out and you've got to do the old coin-flip thing and if it's not good enough it's trashed and you have to do it again, and if your locker's not up to standard it's trashed and you do it again, and they're just teaching you discipline. They're teaching you

you've got to do things precise, and I can totally understand why, because when you join your units certain things, there is no room for error, so they're teaching you from day one to basically be precise with everything. It was sort of fun, I was having a good time, and you had to have your weapon clean, and every morning was a room inspection and you had to be standing out the hallway with both sheets over your shoulders. You couldn't cheat and sort of make your bed before you got up. You had to rip your bed apart and stand there with both sheets and they'd call, 'Hallway 11!' because we were 11 Platoon, so you'd race out and go 'Hallway 11!' and race out there and they'd come down and then you'd make your beds and they'd have a room inspection. So they built up from there.

. . . It bugs the hell out of my girlfriend. I mean in our relationship when my girlfriend comes over to stay I make the bed. She tries and, 'Leave it honey, I'll do it. Don't worry about it.'

It's just a waste of time, so I still keep my, I was about to say my locker, I still keep my wardrobe the same way. I think if you go to that much effort to iron your clothes, why scrunch it up? So everything's three-fingers apart and I've had people come over and they walk in and look at my wardrobes and go, 'Wow, that's beautiful!'

All my shoes are polished and stuff, because I just want to be able to come home and say, 'I'm going out,' just pick up the clothes I want.

. . . Nothing [in the army] is really called what it really is and if you get a nickname then no one knows who you are. They just know you are Bluey or Johnno or JJ or whatever. In fact it was always funny that when you got posted to your unit some people would call up for you, 'I'd like to speak to John Fraser please.'

'Who?'

'John Fraser.'

'Oh, you mean Mal, yeah; I'll go get him for you.'

In fact I remember one of my squadrons, I said to my troop sergeant, 'I'm just going to the bank with Roger.'

He goes, 'Who?'

I said, 'Roger.'

'Who?'

'Tommo.'

'Okay.'

He was the troop sergeant, he should know everybody. So yeah, the army is very big on nicknames and changing the names of things, what they are and what they really are ... I got Mal, because at the time the prime minister was Malcolm Fraser, so I thought, 'Oh yeah, just let it run.' ... if your name was Thompson or Thomson you were Tommo. If you had red hair you were Bluey. If your name was MacDonald or McKenzie you were Macca. So yeah, they shortened everything, so you just almost lost your identity, just about.

... Marching out parade was great, it was really good. Best drill I've ever done, because you practise again and again and it's your first formal marching-out parade and your family's there and your parents are there and everything and you just don't march on and do a few bits and pieces. You're marching on, you're sort of presenting arms, controlling arms, marching around in slow and quick time and doing all sorts of things, so it's quite a formal parade, and yeah, it was just a really great day. And the band is spectacular. I don't know the name of the tune but I've got the tune in my head. I just can't remember what it was. Yeah, and you get to practise with the band a couple of times. When you practise with the band the first time you think, 'Wow, this is pretty cool.'

That was a really big day because this is the day like, I'm now a soldier, well, a basic soldier, and you get sent off to your units. So yeah, that was a good day.

* * *

I wanted to go flying and especially when I saw the Black Hawks come in, 'Well, that's what I want to do. That's where I want to go.'

You know, sort of, I changed my hair so it was like Val Kilmer from *Top Gun* and I used to wear Raybans ... and I thought, 'That's where I want to go.'

So yeah, it was about '86, '87 it really kicked in and I was chasing it for a while and then I eventually got it.

... I was on exercise in Darwin in early '92 and I got a phone call from my squadron commander and he said, 'Have you got a girlfriend?' He said, 'Are you married at all?'

I said, 'No, Sir.'

'Have you got a girlfriend?'

'Oh, yeah.'

'Would that relationship stop you from going to Cam...?'

He didn't even get Cambodia out. I said, 'Yeah, I'll go.' Didn't even think about it, which is a bit sorry for the girl at the time, but operational service you don't turn down, and I said, 'This is great. I want to go, can't go fast enough.'

... We were explained that there were four warring factions or four competing factions within the Cambodian infrastructure. We had the government, the NADK [National Army of Democratic Kampuchea], the KPNLF [Khmer People's National Liberation Front] and the Khmer Rouge, and they were all basically vying for power. We were there to establish the elections, to put a government in power which had never been done before, and bring the peace and say, 'Hey, you know, we're just trying to get things settled,' and that we'd be providing communications for the UN electorates out in the middle of nowhere because there were no telephones, the internet wasn't thought of in those days, and the radios that the UN personnel had were only good for like local areas...so it all had to be done by military radio.

... When we got there we were issued more equipment. We had these big twenty by twenty tents and we got our magazines and ammunition and Kevlar helmets and Kevlar body armour and additional stuff we needed. It was just a great time in my life. I was taking photos of everything. I just got all my gear, piled it onto my stretcher and all the new equipment and other shit and had to take a photo of that, and it was like new backpacks and rifles and kitchen sinks and Swiss Army knives and that night everyone was just exhausted. We just all crashed out, like I think it was by six o'clock we were just unconscious, and the next day we got up and it started. We started getting lectures on first aid, on how to look after ourselves medically, the tablets, chloroquine and quinine, how to take that. Try and drink tonic water because it's got quinine in it so that's a good thing. We were also given lectures ... they used this theatre as a lecture hall, and it was good because we were told the price of a cab from the base to the city. We were told the price of jeans, we were told the price of Lacoste shirts because the locals knew we were there, knew we were cashed-up. They were going to try and take us for a ride. They said, 'No, no, no, this is the price,' and always haggle, haggling's fun, and they told us the rules of the streets and stuff. Stay away from the prostitutes unless you want something falling off in public when you get home. Yeah, it was almost like these are the rules of David Jones, but it was good, very, very good, well prepared ...

We were told we were just doing communications work over there. When we got over there and we started getting lessons, then we sort of, 'Okay, this is what we're *really* gonna be doing.'

And they said, 'You'll be going off to a village wherever, setting up with you and your communications team and just helping the elections for the country and you're working with the UN staff.'

They had UN civilians and they had UN police, and then they had us come in as well. We had infantry over there but they were Uruguayan infantry. I think we had some Cameroon infantry who were a joke. We had Pakistani police, very worrisome people, Indian police, even worse, had Sri Lankan doctors who really needed to take a shower. We had the French Foreign Legion there, they were great. They were very professional; they used to cruise around in the Land Rovers. They had a sniper, a machine-gunner and two riflemen. So they made a good little fire team ... and we had a few other countries over there as well.

But once we got there, we were two or three or weeks in Phnom Penh, got acclimatised, went through 'the Ho Chi Minh two step' phase where you got the shits and trots and you were sick as a dog for forty-eight hours. Everyone went through it, and then you got your equipment and you were deployed by a Russian helicopter ... Surprisingly like, if you do a comparison of the equipment that I would wear when I went to transfer to Black Hawks to what the Russian helicopter guys wear, it's vastly different. Like, we'd have boots and flight-suits and gloves and vests and helmets and all sorts. They wore thongs, stubbies and singlet and a bottle of vodka, but they did a really good job. They flew very well, they were safe, good guys to talk to and yeah, they were a blast. They were good fun.

. . . The Cambodians really know how to [have a] wedding. It's like a 48-hour thing, drinking and eating and dancing and then some more drinking and eating and a bit more dancing and drink and eat and if you're still standing you'll do some more dancing and things like that. We got invited to some lunches or dinners and the idea is to make you eat as much as humanly possible. You never look away from your plate because if you do the plate's taken away and replaced with more food. You've got to watch out for that one. They served up goat which is beautiful, it's like a roast. The food over there is fabulous. It's really, really nice. We got a lot of traditional food . . . they said be careful how you eat it, but really, you had no choice. We had rations with us but we had to mix it in with the local food and you had the Ho Chi Minh two step, so what can you do? There was a restaurant there that was run by one of the grandmas and she was a fabulous lady and she would cook this vegetable satay meal to die for. I mean, it was just so good, and then she would do this pork. I don't know how she did it but it was just so yummy, in a restaurant, loosely termed, with dirt floors, wooden benches and rats would run along the rafters but we didn't really care. And they always used to watch kung fu movies, these martial arts, all put the volume up way too loud and you're sitting there, 'Come on guys, give us a break!'

And that's how the kids learnt, and they did it pretty well actually. They'd watch TV and that's how they learnt. But the food was good and you didn't mind the rats, and they made enough money out of us to actually build a decent restaurant and it had lights and the fairylights and was all lit up and it was like, 'Wow, this is pretty cool.' . . . But it was great. We had a really good bonding with them.

... When we go to a country we don't try and take over. We like to establish ourselves with the locals. We establish a connection with the chieftains. We learn the language. We do hearts and minds and we do it very well. We don't try and take over. The Americans have got a bad habit of doing that. We got a compliment the other day from, I think it's General [Sir] Michael Rose who was in charge of the Bosnian peacekeepers, he said, 'The Australians are up there with the British as peacekeepers.'

So as far as I'm concerned from my experience the best peacekeepers in the world are us and the Brits. And we get a bond with them, like we play soccer with the local kids and we do medical work and we play cricket and we teach them things and we play games and speaking the language is a big thing. Once you learn the language you're halfway there. You've got everything sorted out. We would meet with the chief of the village and get to know him and bond with him and I used to sort of bribe him with some ration packs and say, 'We're here to do good.'

I'd go to the markets on a daily basis and say 'Hi!' to everybody, go around and sort of, 'Hi, how are you going? What's happening?'

I established a relationship with a couple of the traders there... They were impressed that we showed respect, that we weren't sort of belittling them and taking advantage of them, treating them like monkeys, because they were nice people.

... We had a maid... she was fabulous. She poisoned us. We had to get used to the local food and we had to actually teach her not to use so much cooking oil and the foods we sort of liked, and they put sugar on avocado of all things. It's very weird, and on their chips as well. I don't get that one. No, they like sour cream on their chips and mayonnaise. It's vile. But she was great, her name was Oon but we called her Baldrick from *Blackadder* and we actually told her that Baldrick was a sign of respect but she didn't know. But we looked after her very well. We paid her in American dollars. We were actually given an allowance to have maids. It was a good hearts and minds thing to bond with the local community and to boost up the village economy so to speak, and she would cook and clean for us and wash our clothes, which was good because we wanted to be able to do our jobs and wanted to alleviate a few of the menial tasks. And once she sort of cottoned-on how we wanted things, how to cook and that, it was great, and she wasn't backward in coming forward in playing tricks on us.

... I met the Khmer Rouge quite a few times and a lot of them were just misled soldiers. They didn't realise what they were doing. They were just like, 'Okay, we're soldiers. We'll just follow our orders and do our thing.'

And some of these guys were still in the jungle. I mean the atrocities that happened were long gone but these guys were still in the jungle awaiting orders to do whatever, and we told them, said, 'Hey guys, war's over. It's all gone.'

They said, 'Oh, oh, okay.'

So we convinced a few of them to hand themselves in and they got re-established, but I'm sure there were ones out there who were just like absolute bastards who did what the Germans did to the Jews in World War II, but a lot of them were just soldiers, just following orders and didn't realise, and they were following the propaganda and the rhetoric and they were just going, 'Okay, they're bad people, we'll kill them.'

They had no idea, and when we spoke to them it was like, 'Really? We probably shouldn't have been doing that.'

But some of the other Khmer Rouge we met were the full-on dudes. They were just, like, out for blood and wanted to kill us and there were a couple of standoffs which we managed to talk our way out of.

... There were eighteen million landmines still in the country and they've established a landmine clearing project. That's why we pretty much stuck to the village and the main roads. You just don't walk off the roads. As they say in the movie, *Apocalypse Now*, 'never get off the boat', well, don't get off the road ... There was an incident of a few people arrived in a helicopter and stepped off and didn't realise they were actually walking through a minefield and some mines can be a little bit itchy and the downward draft from a helicopter actually can set them off. Plus a lot of the landmines, some of them were French-made and they're called butterfly mines. They basically look like a butterfly, a green butterfly and they're deployed from a helicopter and they come out and spiral to the ground and just drop and then they're activated. So we'd had incidents of kids picking them up or people stepping on them and that sort of thing, and they're the worst kind because they're scattered. They're not marked in the areas. You can't mark them. If you throw them from a helicopter you don't know where they're going to land.

Normally when you set a minefield it's established and you've got a map of where every single mine is and there's patterns in the way you do certain things. I did an assault pioneer's course and we actually set out a proper minefield on a parade ground and we set the mines in the patterns and then we were actually blindfolded and told to walk through, and you couldn't walk through without tripping one. So those are the worst mines when they're deployed by aircraft because you don't know where they're going to go. You can't go and pick them back up. The kids think they're a toy because they look like a little mini Frisbee and they pick them up, throw it, their mate catches it and boom, there goes his hand. We saw a lot of that. Kids with no arms or legs or saw a lot of the adults missing a leg or two. That's why we did a lot of medical work in the last six months when I was in Krâchér. A lot of the patrols would go out and deal with medical stuff.

I met a little boy once and he had, you know the oil lanterns you get? And it dropped on top of him and all the hot oil and everything had gone down and burnt his back and his back caught on fire and he just came up and said, 'Can I get a bandaid?'

I said, 'Whoa, let's have a look at your back.'

I said, 'That's not good.'

And we had what we called the magic spray which is like, it's a very strong antiseptic, and this kid was so brave. I mean I'd actually used the stuff on myself and it stings like there's no tomorrow, and I cut off some of the dead flesh and cleaned his back up and put the spray on and cleaned it all up and he was incredibly brave and he shed a tear or two and then once the sting wore off he was okay, and I said, 'I'll be back in three days, come back and see me.'

Came back and it had all started to heal properly, but otherwise he would've been walking around forever and a day and would've got an infection for sure.

Another guy I worked on, we were doing like a clinic and we were just treating basic sort of cuts and abrasions or gashes that happens in normal everyday life. This guy had a boil or cyst the size of a golf ball down here on his leg, near his groin, and the local medic had just given him a bandage. He was just a Cambodian medic, said, 'Here's the bandage, off you go.'

I said, 'Hang on, what are you doing? What is it?'

And he took it off and like, 'Oh, that's interesting.' I said, 'I think I'll have a look at that.'

So I got him to lay down on a table and pulled out my kit and just lanced the cyst, boil, whatever you want to call it, and cleaned out all the pus and it was just, oh, it was just atrocious. It was just like, but oh yeah, whatever, I had my gloves and no big deal, and cleaned all the dead skin off, got all the pus and the blood, cleaned it up, used the magic spray and I was having a chat and said, 'Okay, try and be as careful as possible.'

It looked a lot better and I said, 'See you in three days, come back.'

He came back in three days, it was pink, it was healthy. It had gone down dramatically and dressed it again and that and came back a week later and you could still see, it was like he'd had it, but it was well and truly on the way out. So they have certain things they just deal with. They just walk around with these cuts and abrasions and burn marks and they just got no other choice but to have it there and they can't do anything about it.

... Some guys were counting down more than I was, but I wasn't keeping track as much as they were. I was having too good a time. In fact when I got home I was like, 'I wanna go back now.' It was very hard to get used to society again, very, very rare, 'cause here you go out, I've got my keys, my mobile phone, my wallet. Over there it's like, well I've got my rifle, my walkie-talkie, spare magazine. I'll go to the village and buy a loaf of bread, so it's a very different way of life... Took me a while to start wearing underwear again. That was the first thing they told us when we got over there. 'Got your underwear on?' Whoosh, lose it. The sweat and the tropical disease and the crutch rot and *blah blah blah*, it's not worth it. So it took me quite a while to get used to wearing underwear. It took me a while to stop wearing sarongs around the house and nothing else. Took me a while to get to the city and crowds. Yeah, you just had to slowly establish yourself. You were a bit blown away, it was almost like a sort of mild form of post-traumatic stress disorder 'cause, like, one minute you're in the village, the next day you're in Phnom Penh, the next day you're processed and you're back home again. The same thing, like, with East Timor, like one minute in a combat zone and the next minute we're back home again. It takes a while to adjust. It took me three or four months to even start to adjust.

* * *

Early Feb '94 I started my loadmaster's course down at the Australian Defence Force Helicopter School in Canberra... once you're qualified and know that you're not going to fail anything, it's like okay, now I can really enjoy it, and then you go off and you can have some fun, and especially with high-range training area, there's just so many places you can go to do your training. So many mountains you can fly around, waterfalls, that sort of thing. There's so many challenges. You can go out and do things, so then you can have a lot of fun. Even though some of the work is hard and it's challenging you're still having a lot of fun in the process because you've got your loadmaster wings and I've passed the course, now I'm part of the team and now okay, I can actually do this for real.

With a Black Hawk you've got a crew of four: pilot, co-pilot and you've got two loadmasters. Generally speaking the right-hand loadmaster is the senior loadmaster. Once you've got dressed, you've got your helmet, your flying gear, you go to the aircraft, you do your pre-flight, you check your equipment, be it the external load hook or the rescue hoist, check your seats, check all the equipment you may need for the sortie, whether it be external load gear, rescue equipment, that sort of thing. Then you go through your start-up procedures, all the equipment's checked, the engines are checked, the rotors are checked, that sort of thing. Then you take off.

As soon as you start taxiing you're actually giving clearances to the pilots, because the aircraft's quite long. The overall length is sixty-four feet ten inches and the rotor diameter is fifty-three feet eight inches. So it's quite a large aircraft, and when you're taxiing out you've got the tail kicking out wide, so you're letting the pilots know the tail's clear, right, and you clear the taxi forward left and clear the taxi forward right. Reason being is you're on a tarmac with other aircraft, so the last thing you want to do is plough into another aircraft while you're taxiing along. When you go to take off you're telling the pilots to clear up left and clear up right so you can actually lift off and roll away, because especially in airports there's always fixed-wing aircraft coming in, other helicopters, and in Townsville there's FA18s every now and then.

... With aircraft it's all weights and the fuel ratio. The aircraft weighs a certain amount and that allows you to have performance with the engines at a certain amount. It also allows you to lift a certain amount. The more fuel you burn off the lighter the aircraft becomes, the more you can lift, the higher you climb depending on the temperature and altitude, the faster you can go or the more you can lift or the less you can lift. So you have to take things into consideration, like the cooler it is the better it is. Like for every thousand feet you're climbing you lose two degrees, so once you're rolling away, you're doing up new performance charts because... the performances you have at sea level will be different at two thousand feet and different at four thousand feet. You start a fuel flow rate, so that way you're keeping track of how the fuel's going, make sure everything's in sync. That way if the controls start buggering up you can notify the pilots, 'Well we've been going for a while and we've only burnt up ten pounds, that can't be good.'

... If you're doing some basic work like, say, a tight [landing] pad, the job of the loadmasters is to inform the pilots. You're calling the run so when you're approaching into a pad you're telling the pilots, you run through checks at the back, you sit in the back, you say, 'Clear and left, clear and right.'

Which means he's clear into that pad. Then as you get to the area you're actually clear to come straight down, you say, 'Clear to the centre left, clear to the centre right.'

And you're telling the pilots the height from the aircraft to the ground or at some stage, you're calling distances, 'four hundred a run, forty below the aircraft to the ground or aircraft to the trees...'

If you're doing a sloped landing you've got to be allowing for the fact that the rotor will stay on an even plane, but the aircraft will tilt down the slope, especially if you land on some of the sloped landing pads that are on rocks. So you've got the wheels all touching at a different time, so as you come down, you say, 'One foot below the left, two feet below the right, four feet below the tail.'

And you sort of call it down bit by bit, and as long as the pilot's aware you can put the rotors, I think the closest I've put the rotors to the ground is two feet. That's on a sloped landing... You've got safety limits of ten feet from the rotors to an obstacle, be it a tree or a rock or whatever, so you're working fairly hard. You're the eyes and ears of the pilots.

If you're doing a hoist, you're operating the rescue hoist and practising deploying the sling down. Sometimes we take a jerry can to add weight to the sling itself because otherwise once it sort of comes out of the hoist itself it starts to spool around a bit and sort of fly all over the place and you may get it hooked in trees... If we're doing external load work we're managing the load, we change the performance figures of the aircraft and let the pilot know what the load is doing. Sometimes loads have a habit of becoming a problem. They did some flight tests on the cargo boxes that they use for the rotors for the Black Hawk to cart them around and they're going, 'Don't do this. This is not going to be good.'

And sure enough they took off and rolled away and the thing started to come out of control. It was just flying out of place so they just released it and punched it off and basically destroyed a $90 000 rotor. That was the loadmaster's call . . . he can release the load at any time if the aircraft comes in danger.

. . . If we're doing a medivac, if we're just picking up normal troops, if we're carrying stores, it's the loadmaster's job to ensure that everything is strapped down properly, both forward and aft and laterally. If you've got passengers make sure they're briefed, they're dressed properly, they're seated properly, they know escape procedures, safety procedure on the aircraft, and then it gets more complicated when you start doing work with the SAS or normal combat troops, but especially SAS and counter-terrorist work. Pretty much when you put on your helmet and plug into the intercom system you don't shut up from start to finish the whole time, when you're flying along and if you're doing air assaults, that sort of thing, you're just talking all the time, safety checks and formation information and it's like calling the aircraft into the target and it's just *blah blah blah blah blah*. If you sat in the back you'd think we were speaking Chinese because we were talking so fast.

. . . In two hours flying you're tired. When you get four, six, eight hours you're getting pretty shagged, especially in Timor because of the amount of equipment you're carrying. We have flying limits of ten hours a day, with night-vision goggles it's half because of the concentration and the fact that you're looking through a pair of optical tubes and you have no peripheral vision so what you see through those tubes is what you get, and you've got to be looking in a diamond shape the whole time. So you're looking forward, up, down this whole time. If you're doing a hoist it's even worse, because you've got to be watching what's happening on the hoist. You've got to have that really good situational awareness, and what they like to do is when you're doing a hoist and you're out with an instructor, he's already pre-arranged with the pilot certain code words to start moving the aircraft while you're focusing on something else. So you've got to be watching what the hoist is doing. You've got to have your reference points and all of a sudden you see the reference points are moving away or they're getting too close, oops. You've got to realise, you've got to pull these things up. So yeah, you can get quite tired.

... It's an element of the army that is flogged. There's not enough aircraft, not enough crews and the boys are just severely whipped and I bumped into one of the wives the other day who was up here and I asked her how things are going and she said, 'It's still tired.'

And they're just trying to do too much with too little, and people sort of question about the Black Hawk because of the crash the other day and is it a really good aircraft, but we've got thirty Black Hawks, not even that, for the entire Australian Defence Force. The Americans have got bases where they have a thousand Black Hawks on the base itself. So you just can't imagine that. And even within the Black Hawks, halve them because half of them are dedicated to the SAS alone.

So you've got guys who want the Black Hawks for infantry work or they want the Black Hawks to go and move artillery pieces or they want the Black Hawks to go and work with the navy or we've got to deploy them to East Timor or whatever... I think I've seen the squadron at full-strength for one week only and it never happened again, and the reason things happen sometimes, is when you get tired. The concentration you need when you fly, it's like a tightrope act. You've just got to focus the whole time. As soon as you put the helmet on you're focusing, so when you come back you're tired, you're hungry. When you start doing more than two hours and four hours and six hours, especially in the field, and you've got to do night work... you don't have the comfort of a nice air-conditioned bed to come to, you've just got to sleep in the field and that's when you sort of sometimes put your hand up and say, 'I am too tired to fly. I need a break or I need more time off.'

So the regiment gets flogged fairly badly, but it's just one of those things. There's not much you can do about it.

... I loved flying. I really enjoyed it, and my helmet, I really liked my helmet. I just really enjoyed the work, just being in the squadron. I used to get to work early. I loved wearing my flight-suit, being with the guys, going off and doing missions. I just really enjoyed flying 24/7, and especially when I got to do night-vision goggle work, you got a lot better at day-flying because your concentration at night was hyped up, more so than the day. You just become more aware of everything at night, so during the day, you're more aware, you become a better crewman. When we did the difficult stuff, like doing slope landings or doing a pinnacle landing where you basically bring the aircraft down and you've got to touchdown on the top of a rock formation with one wheel, using the hoist, doing external load work. I just enjoyed every aspect, I suppose, working with our customers like the infantry or the artillery, that sort of thing. When we did open days when the families would come in or the public would come in, I was always put with the Black Hawk to explain to people how things ran and stuff. So yeah, just every aspect, it was really good.

* * *

We'd been doing some lead-up training with the SAS for our biannual counter-terrorist exercise, and prior to the SAS we spent a week or two doing lead-up training, formation flying, doing time on target, doing assaults to buildings, that sort of thing, without the SAS, getting our calls down pat, and then when the SAS rock up we then started from scratch again and just work up and do it bit by bit and work up the training. On the day itself I remember just going to work, being a normal day. Everyone was quite relaxed and my crew . . . we were very slick at what we were doing. The crew coordination was excellent. We were a very high standard. We were reading each other's thoughts, we were reacting to everyone instantly, there were no problems whatsoever.

. . . We planned for the training mission that afternoon to do a practice run onto the target and everything went fairly well. A difficult target, because it was like a big open plain surrounded by trees and the targets were revetments for artillery pieces, so there was nothing that was really standing out that was a good reference point. So that made it hard, but still we got through okay and everything went according to plan. We then flew back to Townsville in the afternoon . . . had a final briefing and we got some hot box meals and then we refuelled the aircraft, flew back up to the high-range training area and we had dinner with the SAS, had a final briefing and at the last minute, we were actually sitting there turning and burning ready to go, they put on two additional SAS guys to act as snipers . . . you're sitting there with rotors turning, engines running and you're just waiting. Your rotors are turning and you're burning fuel. So it's like, let's kick the tyres and light the fires. So they put these two guys on at the last minute, which was a tragedy because they both died, and it was just a last-second thing. If they'd been left out of the aircraft they would've survived or maybe the accident wouldn't have happened at all. In fact the aircraft was that full that a guy by the name of Jonathan . . . was actually leaning against me 'cause we sit in a seat and they sit on the floor. His whole body was leaning against me the whole time and I met his parents later on and it was just really quite sad that I was the last point of contact for their son, and he was put on the aircraft at the last minute.

We took off and adopted the formation . . . We had three Black Hawks line abreast and Black 4 was behind us, so it was 1, 2, 3 and then we had Black 4 behind us and the sniper ships were on the outside . . . Went through our normal procedures, because as we approached the target we give the SAS guys a ten-minute call, so that way if they're using demolitions, say, if they've got to assault a building they've got to have demolitions to blow up the doors and that, they can then prepare the demolitions and prepare the weapons and load their weapons.

The cargo doors are opened and pulled back and locked into position and the arms or the FRAD are extended out of the aircraft. The FRAD is the fast roping and rappelling device . . . they're extended and locked out and checked. We then go through some more checks, and then we basically roll into attack formation and attack speed and we usually fly about 145 knots towards the target. We can't fly any faster than that because the cargo doors are back and that's the VNE, velocity not to be exceeded. When they're forward we can fly a lot faster.

As we were approaching the target we gave the two-minute call which means, 'Okay, we're close to the target now so get ready to deploy.' The SAS guys have got their ropes ready to go, the fast ropes which are quite large ropes and they're all coiled up like a snake.

They just kick them out and they just drop straight down and they deploy. It was at that stage that I noticed that Black 2 was closing in on us, and when we fly, we fly at a distance of two rotors from each other. So the rotor on the Black Hawk, the diameter is 53 feet 8 inches, so you're looking at basically 106 feet, 107 feet 4 inches. When you're flying along at just under 250, 300 kilometres an hour and you're only 107 feet apart there's not much room for error. I got Kel . . . to move to the left, move the aircraft to the left, because we were closing in on Black 2 or they were closing in on us. It looked like they were closing in on us from what I could tell. We got things settled in the formation, we settled up again. I called, 'thirty seconds,' which means, 'Okay, we're close to the target, about to deploy.' I scanned the formation three times to make sure. I was looking at the sniper aircraft and I was looking at Black 4 . . . and then I had to look forward to the target because I actually had to call the pilots into the target doing the heights to run distances below towards the target. When I looked forward I couldn't really see much because we were going that fast and I couldn't really get my head out far enough. So I just quickly put my head back to look through the cockpit windows, which is a practice I've done before and it's quite a common practice. A lot of other guys use it. Identified the target, and then I heard this grinding, screaming noise and I looked back and all I could see was sparks flying everywhere. I thought, 'This can't be good,' but it just happened in the blink of an eye. Next thing you know the aircraft was just flipped upside down and I could just feel this falling sensation and then this almighty bang, I suppose, for lack of a better word, and that was pretty much it. I don't remember anything after that.

. . . I do remember waking up briefly in ICU while they were cleaning up my face but that was about it. They had these little whistles they give you and when you suck on them you're actually taking in anaesthetic to make you feel pain-free. So they were giving me one of those on the way in, so they told me, when they were doing the medivac and that's all I remember. But it was later on, when I was in hospital I just had this dream one night that I'd been pulled out of the aircraft and these four guys are carrying me away and I started to stir and get really unsettled and everything and they put me down and it was like an outer-body [out-of-body] experience, and they came down and said, 'It's okay, you'll be fine.'

And I settled and then they picked me up and took me off to where the medics were and I did it again, and they said, 'No, no, you'll be fine, the medics are just there.'

And there was a medic by the name of Stevo...and he was actually a medic in 5 Aviation but he'd been transferred to the SAS and he looked after me and he said to me, 'Who are you, what's your name?'

Because it was pitch-black, there was aircraft on fire, there was ammunition going off, and he'd actually lost his trauma scissors so he couldn't actually cut my equipment off me, but I was renowned for having knives in my boots. I always had like a boot knife. He said, 'Who are you?'

I said, 'It's J.J. Fraser.'

He said, 'He always carries a boot knife.'

So sure enough there they were, so he pulled it off and cut all the equipment off me and bandaged me up and got me prepped for a medivac straight back to Townsville. I spoke to Stevo later on and asked him about that night and he said, 'Yeah, that's exactly what happened.'

...I was just medivaced back to Townsville and what they were doing was actually redlining the engines. Within the Black Hawk cockpit they don't actually work in numbers, they actually work in colours, so you've got green, yellow, red. Green's operational, yellow is like pay attention, red is like what the fuck are you doing? And basically from what I can tell they got approval to do it and they just pushed the engine to the max and redlined it all the way back to Townsville because there were guys dying as they were flying back and I remember talking to...our RSM at the time and he was at home and he heard the Black Hawks fly over his house and he said, 'That can't be good.'

... We lost eighteen guys that night. On my aircraft all my guys were killed except for one of the SAS guys ... he's in a wheelchair. And on the other aircraft I think they lost four guys, four or five, no, six guys, I think. We landed upside down in flames and nose down, which is just the worst way to go. They landed wheels down. If you can land wheels down in a Black Hawk your chances of survival, the percentage is raised dramatically. But upside down, no rotors, you're screwed. So that's why we lost the men. It was the damage that was caused, because as we collided, our rotors chewed through Black 2's side panel, through their fuel tank and their fuel spewed all over us, but because we lost our rotors we had no way to continue flying so we just flipped upside down, and also having the fuel flow onto the hot engines, that's going to ignite them straightaway. So yeah, we just didn't stand a chance, but because they landed wheels up and they weren't lucky to land wheels up, it was because of Captain Dave Burke and his flying skills and Lieutenant Simon Edwards that they landed wheels up. So he's a damn good pilot, but with my guys, well we didn't have the equipment to do it. We had no rotors. Superman couldn't have done it, so we just didn't stand a chance and that's why you had such a loss of life ... the other loadmaster, his five-point harness, which is the harness we attach ourselves with, basically it's a body harness. When you attach it to the roof, so if we're working at the back we don't fall out of the aircraft and if we do we're not going to fall a long way. He actually attached his harness to the floor and it was pretty loose, which is not a safety problem, it's just the way he liked it. I was attached to the roof and quite tight, and unfortunately when the aircraft hit the ground he was flung outside and was decapitated. As to the other guys I'm not too sure what happened to them. Yeah, it was just, don't know why.

... I'd been conscious for a couple of days but I didn't know. I was just so drugged up out of my eyeballs. I fractured my spine, my pelvis, my left knee, my right hip. I'd lost six litres of blood. My ribs were fractured. My face was like I'd been beaten up by Mike

Tyson, 'cause the night-vision goggles had been thrown back in my face or my helmet. I just wasn't aware of it.

... I was just putting myself back together bit by bit by bit... the physios basically said they'd never seen someone recover so fast with such bad injuries. It was just due to my fitness level and also my experience of weight training. I'd been training in the gym for about ten years and your muscles basically have a memory so they were able to re-establish themselves fairly well. Just with my spine and my pelvis and that sort of area, I'm still working on that at the moment. I've had a few problems with it so I'm just getting there. But basically I was able to get myself back to flying fitness. In fact I was able to pass the basic fitness assessments within the military, able to go for the runs and stuff. Did a couple of backpack marches, which I sort of paid for but I thought, 'I'll just suck it up and do it.'

... There was the Board of Inquiry which I had to attend for the accident, and probably one of the hardest things was meeting the families. When I was at Parkhaven Hospital I met Leah... who was Kel's fiancée at that time. They'd only just got engaged. In fact they weren't too far off getting married and I'd met her once or twice before, but not really had a good decent chat with her, and she came in. She came in with my psych, Marie... who was an army major, a fabulous lady, and we sat down and we started talking. She wanted to know exactly what happened so I took her from the very start of the accident and she was just in tears. She was very, very upset and then I sort of kicked into another gear and said, 'Okay,' and I started telling funny stories and when she left the room she had a smile on her face and she was laughing. So I told her some funny stories about Kel and she was there for three hours and I was pretty wasted, but then Leanne came in and she was Michael's girlfriend. She just appeared out of nowhere and she popped in to have a chat as well. I'm going, 'Oh God!' so I had a chat with her for an hour and a half or so, and then I slept pretty well for two days. But I think it was just important that the families found out what happened and they found out that their loved ones died without really feeling anything. When I met Kel's father it was like looking at a ghost. The similarities were just unbelievable, and I held it together the whole time he was there and we were talking, and when he left he said, 'Don't blame yourself.'

And that was hard to take. It was like, ooh, 'cause I did blame myself, that's the thing. I was the senior loadmaster on the lead aircraft and an accident's happened that wasn't my fault. It took me about four years to stop blaming myself, and to this day I still ask questions of why... I burst into tears. I just lost it. I held it the whole time and then when he said that it was just too much. I met John's wife. She was a very angry lady, just angry at the whole sort of thing and actually blamed me for the accident. She accused me of murder, but you know, she's just angry. So your husband's just been taken away, the father of your child's been killed and you've got to point your finger at someone and I copped it... So I was able to answer all those questions which I think gives them closure. It hurts, 'cause all the guys' parents you're talking to are dead and you're the only one left, and the other guy is a paraplegic, so you feel exceedingly guilty. You go through a lot of survivor guilt.

The inquiry was bullshit. Their reason for the accident was crap. I mean, they talked about, 'Captain Kelvin... was a junior pilot and his planning was poor.' Well, actually he was a senior pilot and he was specifically brought into the squadron because of his experience with counter-terrorist flying. So I don't know where they came up with that conclusion. And now at the moment we've got a case running against the makers of the night-vision goggles, to find that the night-vision goggles were at fault, not so much my crew. And the army has a habit, in fact the Defence Force has a habit, of always blaming the dead soldier. So because my crew's dead, they can't defend themselves, and I did my best to the Board of Inquiry, but yeah, they just seem to make up their own sort of results and they even ignored the testimony from the crew from Black 4 who said that Black 2 flew into us. They said, 'No, no, no, that can't happen.' They gave their reasons and it's like yeah, whatever... At the time I thought it was just an accident, that we've just flew into each other, that we've identified the same target and that's what we went for, but when it came out that they had their computer-generated sort of image of what happened, they said we banked right. My last memory was the aircraft was flying straight and level. I don't know where they got that from, and the thing is too, in formation flying, if Black 1 turns left, everyone turns left. It we turn right, everyone turns right. If we stop, we climb, everyone does what we do. So if we're turning right why the hell isn't Black 2 turning right? But my conclusion I thought was we've identified the same target but now it's come down to the night-vision goggles, and the Board of Inquiry seemed a bit of a farce actually.

* * *

I'm flat on my back in Parkhaven Private Hospital, fractured spine, fractured pelvis, post-traumatic stress disorder, scars, and the accident was in June and B Squadron commander came in and I said, 'I'll come back flying in September.'

I don't think I was even walking in September. So I had no idea that I was going to be there for that long, but I wanted to go back to flying. I didn't give it a second thought really.

... I just worked very hard at physio to do it and as far as I was concerned I was going back flying, and I remember the day I went for my first flight in a Black Hawk, was actually the regiment's anniversary ... and I flew in the lead aircraft with Tony Fraser. I wasn't current with the flying. I was qualified but I wasn't current, so an instructor flew with me, but it was just the best thing ever. I had a really good day and it was nice to fly ... We had all the Black Hawks and all the Chinooks up and a couple of Kiowas, and everyone was just standing around. I've walked out with my flight suit and my helmet and harness and everything else and people just didn't know I was going flying that day. They had no idea, and when they found out that I'd got back and I was clear to fly again as I passed my examination with the medical doctor, yeah, a lot of people were very proud of me and said that was a great thing. A few of the sergeants didn't even know in the regiment. They said, 'We actually had bets that you were gonna make it. We knew you would.'

It was hard. Like the day-flying was easy. Night-flying was very hard. It just threw me off, so they gave me some time, I said, 'Look, you know, I need some more time with this night stuff.'

But over that period of time the warning signs were there that I shouldn't be flying. I wasn't a danger to the crew. I wasn't doing anything stupid, but I had a couple of breakdowns and it just kept on coming back to plague me. But I worked hard; I got my night-vision goggle qualification back. I did it very well. I was very happy with it, but it did cause a lot of problems.

... When I flew, I flew safely and when I was tested I was tested harshly, which is a good thing because it's pointless going up there if I'm going to be a danger, if I can't do the job properly. They pushed me and in the training they flogged my arse, so when I actually went back for my flying tests I was able to pass with confidence and with ease, so to speak. It's not easy, but it's like the old sort of saying, 'train hard, fight easy'. I was able to do that. The fact that one of the instructors, Clyde Payne, who was a loadmaster instructor, prick of an instructor, great guy, but he pushes you to the limits and he had me out in the training area doing hoist after hoist after hoist, doing external load after external load and confined area after confined area, and this is all at night and had me lower an external load into a creek and maintain the distance from the rotors to the trees on the side of the creek and he gave me three missions in a row and really flogged me severely, but when I actually did the final handling test to get back my qualification with the regimental standards loadmaster, I actually found it easy because Clyde had pushed me so hard. So that was a good thing.

* * *

I think the family thought I was totally insane when I went to East Timor. 'What the fuck are you doing?' But once again, 'He's a big boy; he can make his own decisions.'

We got established. We were supposed to stay at the airport, but actually we went to the heliport which was good. It got us away from everybody else and that allows us to establish our own base and be a bit more comfortable. I think it was the second or third day we launched every Black Hawk we had mounted up with snipers from the commando units and from the SAS and basically flew around the city and made a lot of noise and said, 'We're in town, so don't fuck with us.' Then all the Black Hawks bar my aircraft and another one stayed on station and we just watched over the soldiers' backs on the ground and we had snipers on board with the new snipers' rifles they had, and cleared the city and you could actually see the militia leaving the city because they were burning everything on the way out, chicken shits that they are. So I think they were very good against children and women who can't defend themselves but when they came up against us they realised that they'd be copping an arse-kicking so they thought they'd just leave town.

... The support we got from the Australian community was fabulous and that's the sort of thing you want to see. Like we're paid a wage, but we're paid a wage to die and if I'd have died in East Timor I would've died with a smile on my face because this is the job I do and I'm dying for a cause that I believe in. So the support we had was fabulous. When people would write, strangers would write to us and send us parcels of lollies and stuff. In fact we had so much mail coming in from people sending us who didn't know us, just like, what is it? Adopt a soldier program, it was just ridiculous, just boxes and boxes of stuff. It was great, so we used to reply back and everything, but the support we got was fabulous. As usual we're treated like the political football by the politicians, but what do you expect? But in general the support from Australia was very, very good.

... I never really fitted back in. I never really got accepted again. Even though I went back to flying the guys were sort of, you know, they treated me well but I could just tell, there was just something there, especially on some of the deployments around the country we did I just got a feeling I just didn't fit back in again. Not much you can do about it. You don't go through something like that and everything's hunky-dory when you come back to work. So just one of those things. I tried very hard to fit back in and be part of the team. My bosses were happy with my performance, my troop sergeant was happy, but the guys, they were just a bit funny. A couple of guys were really good but in general the guys were just a little bit stand-offish and a bit iffy, a bit funny, but I flew with them. It really surprised me, some of the guys who I thought would really stand by me who normally said they would, didn't, and that was a bit disappointing. It's human nature, so—the ones who stood by me I expected them to, and they were there. The ones who didn't surprised me even more because I thought, 'I've flown with these guys, I've been on exercises, we've gone and had dinner, that sort of thing, and now when the chips are down where are they?'

They always say that the test of a true man is not when the times are good; it's when the times are bad. A bit disappointed in a few guys.

. . . I was actually sent home early from my second tour. I developed combat post-traumatic stress disorder. My post-traumatic stress disorder was in remission, but due to the incidents in Timor the body was just shutting me down because I wasn't stopping. I did a night mission which started at twelve o'clock midnight and we finished at seven o'clock the next morning and I just felt really tired afterwards and I was tired for two days straight. I couldn't get back on the horse, and my doctor was actually over in Timor. She was our medical doctor for the medivacs, and she decided that I had a virus and it was time for me to go home. I was due to go home anyway but I went home about five days early. So they flew me home and I actually had combat post-traumatic stress disorder or combat fatigue . . . and I had a couple of weeks off and in between tours I'd met a girlfriend and just started dating but things didn't go really well, but I went down to Melbourne to do some dunker training at East Sale, where you do the helicopter underwater escape training, the dunk, where they drop the dunker in the water and they spin it upside down and you've got to escape, and using some new equipment, your body armour, gas masks and helmets, that sort of thing and I remember feeling a couple of times in the last couple of runs I started to feel panicky. It was just a warning signal saying, 'Look, man, you've got to stop this crap, stop it.' But I came home and I got back on a Monday, Tuesday, went to work Thursday and I was feeling really stressed and wound up and very panicky and we were doing flight planning for weeks, counter-terrorist sort of stuff. On Friday afternoon I saw my psychotherapist . . . and man, I'm just not, I said, 'I'm really starting to lose the plot here. I'm just constantly stressed and not feeling good.'

And I saw him Sunday morning. We organised a session for Sunday morning and I just broke down and said, 'I can't do this anymore, I've had enough.'

I was just so stressed, I'm tired and I'm just really upset. I went back to my girlfriend, said, 'I've just quit flying. I can't do any more.'

It was really the worst day for me, but I rang up my boss, my immediate boss . . . told him. He said, 'Look, no one's going to hold it against you. We're amazed you got as far as you did.'

. . . I love flying. I live for it. If I'd died in the accident I would've died happy doing the job I love. If I'd been killed in East Timor, I would've died happy because I died doing something important. I was doing a job I loved and I was doing it to help other people. So it really tore me up. I think it was probably the hardest decision I've ever had to make, to really give away something I love so much was just very, very hard. I think because flying was actually killing me. It was slowly torturing my body. So what I loved was actually killing me. So a couple of days later it was like, that's actually really good because I know I don't have to worry about going back and do flying again. So it was sort of funny. I loved it but I had to stop because it was destroying me bit by bit.

* * *

Military Compensation is a joke. I don't know why they exist. They seem to go out of their way to take away everything that you've got. The way the system runs is poor. If you're given a Veterans' Affairs pension and you're given a lump sum payment from Military Compensation, but then deduct that from your pension, so they give with one hand and take with the other. I don't get that. It's not like the lump sum payouts are huge. The most you can get is $110 000. I got $70 000, not even that. I think I served my country fairly faithfully. I think I gave up a lot. It's got to the point now where I've actually had to engage my solicitors to deal with Military Compensation and we're fighting over a bed, of all things, and a whole range of other things, but it's just like they don't seem to care.

. . . It seems to be the politicians are very happy to be there when they send you off to war or to wherever they want you to go, but when it's time to pick up the pieces for the ones they break they're nowhere to be seen and when you've got to call in a solicitor to fight for what rightfully should be yours, that's pretty sad, so we're treated like crap. I've done group therapy classes at Toowong Private and you talk to the other veterans and they are treated exactly the same. You've got to fight for everything through Military Compensation and it's just like, why do we bother to have these guys? All they ever do is say no, so what's the point?

. . . You don't forget that sort of thing. It just doesn't go away. I generally have pretty good days but sometimes I have panic attacks and anxiety attacks and you just, I shut down or I lose focus. I get angry, frustrated, I get the shits. Panic attacks are the worst. They really drain you. You're just totally losing it. You're panicking, you're lost, you don't know what's going on. You're teary, you're upset. You're just sort of really out of control.

My way to deal with that, some people will go off and drink a carton of beer and grab a pizza or some guys will take drugs. I basically grab an ice breaker and have a really good hot shower, sit in air-conditioned comfort and watch *Friends*. That's my combat for it, or I'll go downstairs and have a work-out in the gym downstairs. So I talk to my girlfriend a lot. I talk to her about my pain levels and how things are going and she realises sometimes when the pain kicks in it gets fairly bad. I actually forget to take pain medication. It just shuts me down, I stop thinking, logic doesn't exist. So she reminds me, 'You need to take some pain medication, have something to eat, have a shower and go lie down, and put on *Friends* in the air-conditioning.'

So, especially things like when you have the other Black Hawk accident two months ago and you've got friends on board as well. When I went to see Michael's parents it's very hard. It actually stresses me a lot. I said I'd go back and see them. I just haven't seen them yet. I've had the 'flu and it's a pretty good excuse. I just don't like seeing them because I feel very guilty that I survived and their son didn't. But you have to deal with it. These are the cards I've been dealt with and so you move on. So I just try and make the best out of life.

NOEL 'PETER' MEDCALF

Infantry
Bougainville
World War II

The Depression was pretty hard times. You grew everything you needed to eat. You'd kill a bullock or sheep every now and again and share it with the neighbours and my brother and I trapped rabbits and foxes to earn pocket money. Wool was ninepence a pound and rabbit skins were ninepence a pound. And it was the era of the swag man. Everyday almost you'd get a swaggie come in and offer to cut wood, do a bit of gardening and he was always given a meal. We found out later they had a secret sign on the gatepost. Two stones on top of the gatepost said, 'You can always get a meal here.' Three stones said, 'These people are miserable.'

When I was about eight or nine the father had a bit of luck on a gold mine and we bought a property up north of Mudgee and moved up there . . . There was no myxomatosis so you called in the rabbiters, the professional rabbiters. They'd come along in an old truck or a wagon, usually about a dozen mangy looking hounds of various breeds, and they would set baits. Now on that particular property, to give you an idea of how bad the rabbit problem was, we had one paddock of about 180 acres and the first night they laid baits on bait lines, just a furrow with thistle root dipped in strychnine. The first morning they got 4800. The second morning they got 3900. The third morning I reckon they got over 1000 but when the take dropped to about 600 they let that go and went on to the next paddock. That's what it was like. My brother and I had a brilliant idea. Rabbit skins were ninepence a pound, five to a pound. We'd get up at five o'clock and throw a couple of bags over a packhorse and off on our horses and we'd go round the bait lines before they did and we'd get the hessian bags full of rabbits. Now, if you've ever skinned a hundred rabbits up behind the wool yards before breakfast and before you went to school you'll never look rabbit in the face again.

* * *

In early August 1944 they said to a dozen of us, 'Right, you're just turning nineteen. You're going to be shipping up to Canungra, to the Jungle Warfare School.'

That night the Japs broke out of the POW compound at Cowra. So next morning they paraded the battalion. Us twelve were set apart. And the rest of the battalion were sent down to Cowra to clean up the mess. They joined us about three or four week later and had some interesting stories to tell about the Japanese at Cowra. They said they were total fanatics. They said you could hold a gun on them and they'd throw up, as much as to say, you know, 'I'm a martyr, shoot me.' But you pick up a pick handle, boy they'd jump and start to obey the rules because a pick handle is a coolie instrument and there is no honour in being slugged with a coolie pick handle.

Canungra was a fascinating experience. In Bougainville I never struck anything physically tougher than Canungra. They taught you everything. All the instructors were old New Guinea veterans. They taught you all the weapons that the Americans used. All the weapons the Japanese used. All the weapons the English and the Dutch used. They taught you, even though you were riflemen in the infantry, they taught us enough to use in an emergency. Medium machine guns, even how to load and fire a 25-pounder artillery piece. They taught you all about tropical diseases, how to avoid them and think of all the young fellas in '42, '43, particularly around Buna, Gona where they lost a hundred per cent practically from scrub typhus and other tropical diseases. They even taught you how to load a packhorse, in case you needed to know. They taught you explosives, booby traps and all the time you are working with live ammunition and they're teaching you the tricks:

'Never go near a body on the track. No, don't you use the track. Let the Japs use the track. You go into the solid jungle and ambush the tracks. If they want to be stupid enough to keep using tracks, let them. Don't, if you see an Australian body, don't go near it. Go around it; see if it's booby trapped because they used to booby trap our dead and their dead.'

. . . We didn't know where we were being sent and it was a rumour it was either Borneo, Bougainville or possibly the Celebes. Malaya? Probably not, because the British Army hadn't got through from Burma that far yet. Then our brigadier, 'Mad Mick' Monaghan, was crazy as a two-bob watch. He let it slip one day. He was driving in his car and he'd given a couple of the boys a lift and they drove past a farmhouse covered in bougainvillea and he said 'You'll be seeing a lot of that where you're going.'

So much for the security of the brigadier. We left Brisbane in November, early November, on the *Cape Victory*, which is an American Victory ship. The farewelling crowd were two women and three dogs and I was seasick all the way to Torokina.

* * *

We hit the beach in this barge, fortunately unopposed. We formed a perimeter just off the beach. There was about a fifty-yard strip of jungle. You had the sand and then this tall jungle. The next morning we loaded up and followed this track and suddenly we stepped off dry ground and into knee-deep, and then waist-deep swamp. We were loaded down with ammunition and food. And it took until about three o'clock in the afternoon to get about a mile into the swamps. Later on the engineers slaved and put sort of split logs on the surface and they'd anchor them to the trees, so you'd have these two split logs side by side. We became very adept at getting over the Java River Highway, these two logs. The logs had become greasy with mud and if you slipped you probably went straight in up to your armpits. If you were carrying heavy loads you had to immediately get the load off the fella. And hope he'd got an arm over the log so you could get him out before he sank.

... We had the job of clearing the swamps. The swamps were a miserable place ... you were working mostly in foot-deep mud. You couldn't dig any fighting pits because even on a dry patch that was maybe eighteen inches above sea level you would strike water, so we used to throw up a few rotten logs in front of us and hope they'd stop a bullet, which we knew damn well they wouldn't. Anyway they put the perimeter down in the swamp and our job was to push down one of the only tracks in the swamp and the track used to disappear under the surface of the water and come up again and we'd been trained to infiltrate or surround whenever we struck problems ... we'd learnt long ago 'Don't attack fixed positions.' But in the swamps you couldn't encircle, you're liable to step off the track and sink up to your waist in mud. So the next six weeks were a case of like an angry bull bashing up that track after we struck them, and then a firefight.

... I remember the first time we lost three of our men up that track. Two were New Guinea veterans and one was a nineteen-year-old rifleman, like myself. But the tragedy was they'd walked onto a Japanese position and a man with a light machine gun got two of them and for the next half hour their lieutenant had to somehow think of a way to get them out and they lost another man trying to get them out and it must have been a pretty hard decision for Laurie. He said, nup, he wouldn't lose any more men. So, they backed off. They went up the next day ... and they'd been stripped totally of everything, clothing and so forth. So they had to bury them and they couldn't dig the graves more than about eighteen inches deep. I remember Perce Proctor, who was our company commander; one of the best officers I ever served under, Perce had trouble reading the burial service. Next morning, when we went up on the next patrol the three mounds of dark earth were a writhing mass of large white maggots and we had to pass that every day, on every patrol. It sort of gave you an inkling about what possible fate was in store ... it was unfortunate that we'd lost three good men, just the luck of the game. They'd run onto a Jap force and they didn't realise . . . But that could happen at any time unless you were incredibly careful. Or lucky. You closed your mind. You had to, because if you thought about it that was your possible future. So you closed your mind. If you didn't you'd probably drive yourself crazy. I don't think anyone did any differently to me. We just closed our minds. You'd see piles of dead. I've seen piles of Japanese dead, piled five feet high. You just closed your mind and did what you had to do.

* * *

The Americans took off and we moved down towards the Jaba [River] and onto the barge and began what was called 'The Battle of the Swamps'. It really wasn't a battle, it was just a stinking clearing, trying to clear small parties of Japanese troops out of the main trails, to get them out of the swamps and out of the way until we could get to the lowlands . . . it was a miserable place, but also fascinating. You'd be patrolling through the track and suddenly there'd be a tree practically covered with beautiful orchids. We were in parts of the swamp I don't think anyone had ever been before . . . everything was rotting. At night you'd be sitting in a very shallow fighting pit and everything is glowing with phosphorescence. You'd pick up little bits of stuff and spell your name and your initials out on the parapet. The next day when you'd look it was just dead twigs, dead leaves, nothing. One night I saw a ten-foot tree out in the clearing near the wire and it lit up with phosphorescence in a greenish glow. The whole tree just lit up. They had fireflies. You could catch them and put them on your watch and tell the time. The mosquitoes were fairly bad but there weren't that many leeches, which surprised me. But I guarantee there was everything else. They used to breed twelve-inch to fifteen-inch long centipedes, which were about two inches wide. They were the biggest I ever saw. We had one fellow bitten. He rolled over at night and it bit him. His ear disappeared in the swelling.

But mostly it was black water, black tree boles. The particular patrol we did once trying to find the village of Sisiruai where there was a report of Japanese. We never found it and we got lost in miles and miles of dreadful swamp. The whole swamp extended probably about twenty-odd miles and inland probably about fifteen, so it might take you all day to cover two miles. Mostly the ground underneath was anything from five feet up to one feet underwater, but there were little raised areas where you could put a camp down, put a perimeter down … It was black, black with decayed, well if you've seen decayed leaves, they normally turn creek water brown. This water was black and you could feel your way, but you might be up to your waist in almost liquid mud but you felt your way around and you could feel for tree roots and move through it. I can remember one day we were coming through the swamp and we stopped to have a rest. I sat on a log when coming through the surface of the black water was a Vickers machine gun, a green beret and a nose and it was this mate of mine, 'Junior' Morrow, he was a short fella. He said, 'Cop this Slim,' and gave me the gun. But it was a bit hard on the little short fellows.

… In that country, one or two men could hold the track. The first you ever knew normally was when they took a shot at you and you heard the shot go over your head. The ranges varied from twenty feet to twenty yards. At that short range a rifle shot has two explosions—the sonic crack as it goes over your head and then you hear the crack of the actual discharge. The timber and trees were mostly softwood. You could put a Bren gun blast through a tree two feet thick and it'd go clean through. They were full of sago palms and the Japanese in the swamps didn't have much. They were pretty badly off for food so they were felling the sago palms and scooping out the pip for crude soak and boiling that up. But the logs after a while had this dreadful latrine smell. The sago palms and the Japs themselves, they both smelled about the same.

It was about ninety degrees all the time and you sweated or you were desperate for salt. Once you came back to the beach, which usually took about three hours to get back to for supplies, you'd sit down for a rest and your greens would dry out and there was left a layer of salt. You could eat salt by the handful.

* * *

Our first officer, regrettably, after telling us all the wonderful things he was going to do to all these stinking Japs, a sniper fired twice over his head and he went home a nerve case. They called it, 'lack of moral fibre' with officers. If another rank does it they call it 'cowardice in the face of the enemy', but that's life. They gave us an officer, a very nice fella, a school teacher, totally devoted to the idea that the two-inch mortar was the last word in patrol equipment and he made our two mortar men carry it on all our patrols. Now a mortar fires a bomb up in the air but you never saw the sun, the jungle canopy was just like a roof and we were worried sick that bomb would go up, hit the tree limbs and explode over our heads, and one day it happened. He damn near killed us that fool. I remember my mate lying behind the log and the bomb landed on the other side of the log after it hit the trees and Fergie said, 'Somebody shoot that mad bastard in the arse, quick!'

So we put a stop to that.

We used to carry carrier pigeons because when the radios didn't work you'd have this little box on your belt with these stupid birds sticking their heads out of the holes going 'coo coo'. We had one fella got shot by a carrier pigeon. Which is most unusual. The string that held the lid on the box somehow got caught on the safety catch and trigger of the Owen gun he carried and he shot himself in the foot. I'll always remember him saying 'Shit, I'm shot!'.

* * *

Prowling through that heavy jungle down on the southern part of Bougainville if you found Japanese you'd sit and watch them. A mate of mine's patrol was out there and they saw four Japanese building a hut. So they sneaked off into the bush and waited and at first light in the morning they sneaked up to the hut and one of the boys, young Bobby Duncan—Bobby had eighteen kills to his credit—he sneaked up and peered in the doorway and here they are, the four of them all lying asleep. So he stepped in with his Owen and said 'Wakey, wakey.'

And ripped the burst right across the floor. The first three were okay but the fourth one took the last of the magazine through the stomach and dived through the wall and rolled down and disappeared into the scrub. Young Bobby was terribly upset. He said, 'What'd he have to go and do that for?'

I make the point that I suppose we did become very callous but it was hard to regard them as humans, and never, ever get taken prisoner.

We'd already heard some of the things that had happened in Singapore, Malaya, the Tol Plantation massacre in Rabaul, where the Japanese tied Australia wounded prisoners to trees and used them as bayonet practice. This was mentioned by the Japanese general commanding their 18th Army in Rabaul as a recommended procedure to 'blood' untried troops. So that wasn't a rumour, it actually happened, and we knew what was going to happen if we ever allowed ourselves to be captured. There were no Australian prisoners taken on Bougainville, not one. I suppose we may have taken twenty or thirty, although as the end of the war started to get nearer, a few more started to give up.

We had one interesting patrol over the river. Our idea at this time was to try and cause casualties. In other words, look for Japanese and really rip into them ... We hit a small party of Japanese, and made a certain amount of noise when suddenly we stopped for a rest and I looked back and my second scout was alongside of me and he suddenly aimed and here's this Jap, fifteen feet away. He was beautifully camouflaged with leaves but he forgot all about his great big, shiny, yellow, sweaty face. It shone like a lantern. Well, when we both hit him, it blew him over backwards. We put some grenades in behind him because I heard some more of them behind him and then we said, 'Right, we've gotta get out of here.'

And we had to cross a very fast flowing river and almost walked into a brand new, very large, Jap camp ... here's these big, brand new Japanese huts. They'd only been built, you could see, very recently. They were hidden from the air by the dense, tall trees. So our lieutenant said, 'Check 'em out and see if they're occupied.'

So the second scout and I had to go in the middle of this camp and sneak up to doorways and stick an arm and an armed gun muzzle around doorways and pray there was nobody there. It was empty. They were probably out looking for us, and they were the ones we'd had that brush with just across this small river. So we made a lot of noise and it started to rain and the officer said, 'Right let's get back down to the Mivo Ford where we can get back across and go home.'

I was still scouting on top of a slight ridge and I could see two huts, separate from the others, about thirty to forty yards away and I promptly tripped on a root and fell flat on my face and six Japs came out of their huts to see what the noise was. As I was getting up, the side of the Owen jammed up a root and I'm cursing and swearing. I finally got it free and there were shots firing and the Japs took off. One fella took off and he ran behind one of the huts and I managed to follow him with a burst and it was like a textbook exercise. The shots just ripped through the walls following him and he didn't come out the other side. So I claimed that one and they refused to let me have him.

It was raining like blazes and we went along this track, you couldn't move off the track because the scrub was too dense and about fifty yards further on I suddenly saw a log across the track and we'd been trained back in Canungra, don't step over a log on a track. That's where they love to put a machine gun and the first one who steps over they'll drop him and it's so much harder for the rest to try and get him out. It was a perfect trap and when I looked up and the rain had thinned a bit there is a pillbox, a beautiful big pillbox with rather ominous fire slits. So I called back to our lieutenant and said, 'Listen, I'm not going up there. There's a dirty big pillbox.' I said, 'If there are Japs in it we made a lot of noise.'

So we had with us an artillery signals group of three—a lieutenant and two signalmen. Most patrols we'd take the artillery signalmen with us. And this arty [artillery] lieut [lieutenant], said, 'Oh, let's do it over.'

Now anyone with half a brain never, ever did a pillbox over. You're asking for trouble. It usually had a machine gun in it and a clear fire path. Well, we tried to go round to the right, we couldn't. Tried to go round to the left and the river was ripping and roaring over the rocks. We couldn't cross the river. So it was a matter of, unfortunately, we'd probably have to do this pillbox over, and I got a funny feeling and tried to sneak round behind my lieutenant and my corporal said, 'Slim and I'll go.'

Someone will always volunteer you when you're under fire. Still, the artillery lieut said he'd come too. I remember I hated that bloke so much, if I didn't think the Japs would've heard it, I'd have cheerfully shot him in the foot.

It was raining enough to get close to the fire slit, about fifteen feet, and I passed my corporal a grenade and it stopped raining. I'm sure I saw something move behind that fire slit and he threw the grenade, four second fuse, and it bounced and sat in a little ginger palm right in front of the fire slit, fifteen feet from our faces, lethal to twenty-five yards. Well, all I could think about doing was leap out and dive backwards and wait for the crash. And I'm counting 'three, four, five, six . . . a dud.' And Bunny said, 'Quick!'

So we tore into the pillbox with Owens and put another grenade in and the artillery lieut's got a big gash on his forehead and Bunny said to him, 'Are you all right?'

And he said, 'Yes, but your mate's boot caught me as he dived backwards.'

And I suddenly felt a lot better. I remember Ferguson said to me, 'You know, nobody would volunteer to do this for a hundred quid.'

I said, 'We did, for six and bloody six a day.'

. . . One morning this fool colonel ordered our 15th Platoon back over the ford to hit that camp from the front, which is total stupidity, and my mate, Bob Minchin, I served with him right through the war, he come over when we're ready to go and they were putting black soot on their hands and faces, as we all did and he said, 'What's over there?'

And we explained to him about the pillbox. It was then we said, 'Why couldn't we have gone up the river and come in round the back?'

But, nup, the colonel demanded it. So they went over and the pillbox was occupied and they made a lot of noise cleaning and they got two out of the pillbox and of course that alerted the camp. Quite a solid fight started. The 21 Patrol, they lost one killed, one stretcher-case, five walking wounded and one missing, my mate, Bob Minchin. We could hear it. You could practically trace the course of the fight through the different sound of the different weapons, the heavy pounding of the Brens and the crackle of the Owens and that. When they came back they looked pretty well wrung out. They'd put the artillery in to give them a screen to help them and to get them back across the river. Of course, the problem was trying to get the wounded back across the river. The Japs that had woken up would have followed them and caught them out in the open water.

The next morning, about nine o'clock, B Company up the road, up Killen's Track, rang up and said, 'We got one of your blokes here, he just wandered in.'

It was my mate, Bob Minchin. What had happened, he'd heard the order to withdraw and he could see young 'Curly' Howell had been killed and several others wounded and he thought, you know, getting them back over the river, so he stayed, and tried to cover the crossing and the Japs realised the Australian patrol was pulling back and they started to get out of their fighting pits and Bob knocked off two or three of them. He was lying in an area of bracken about eighteen inches high and he turned the Owen on its side so the top magazine wouldn't show and he killed about three. They put two machine guns trying to find him. They thought he was behind a tree about fifteen yards away and 'Adolf'—he had a black moustache and a cowlick, we called him 'Adolf', said 'I was worried they were going to fell the tree on me.' He said 'There were chunks of wood and bark flying off it.'

Dead silence and gradually another Jap put his head over the parapet and then another and 'Adolf' waited until they were kneeling on the parapet and he knocked those two over as well...anyway, subsequently he spent the night deep in the scrub. Woke up to hear snoring. He'd spent the night on the edge of where these Japs had deserted the camp and settled in for the night. He'd spent the night on the edge of where they where. So at first light he measured back to the river, to get an idea of distance. And when he got in they sent him to the CO and they put the artillery on that position hoping they'd catch the Japanese. He got a Distinguished Conduct Medal.

In the same action, their stretcher-bearer was the scruffiest sort of type you ever saw, his name was Ron Vandersee. But he was one of those types whose pants legs were always out of his gaiters and dragging under the heels of his boots. His beret looked like a pudding cloth, so they called him 'The Wog'. Well, 'The Wog' came into his own in that fight. He crawled from one wounded to the other, fixing them up. He totally ignored the close-range heavy fire. One badly wounded fellow had dived behind a log with his rifle and was shot through both arms and 'The Wog' just sort of cheered them up. He said, 'You'll be right. You'll be perving on the nurses back in Torokina in two or three days.'

And he went back to the officer and said, 'We've got one dead, one stretcher-case and five walking wounded.'

So that was about a third of the patrol, so they pulled back. 'The Wog' got a Military Medal and his citation read that, '*He, without thought of his own safety had continually exposed himself to heavy enemy fire to look after the wounded.*' So, I reckon he deserved it. But that was a good example of the type of fighting you bought. It wasn't big. It didn't involve huge numbers but it was just as bloody.

We had one bloke that was shot in the backside, very embarrassing. Although, as Ferguson said, 'The number of fellows that got shot in the backside, because when you hit the ground that was the only bit that stuck up.'

'Scooter' Sullivan was a 15th Platoon corporal and every morning, or every hour on the hour you sent a three-man patrol around the perimeter, out in the scrub to make sure they weren't creeping out to do an attack and they were doing this security patrol and suddenly this Jap bobbed up and they shot at him and missed him and the Jap shot back and shot 'Scooter' in the backside. It was as though you took a butcher's knife and went 'Zip'. I always remember 'Bunny', my corporal, when 'Scooter' came in, he was cursing and swearing, and 'Bunny', he said, 'Don't worry mate, we'll write and tell your wife you got it from a broken beer bottle in a fight in that whorehouse in Brisbane.'

Humorous comedians again.

* * *

Around about early July, on the 9th of July 1945, the Jap general decided he would make one last major attack on the Australians along the Mivo River. He sent a Colonel Muda with the 13th Regiment and started to learn from our book, right round behind us to try and stop our supplies and ambush the Buin Road. He also had a Major Fukuda with a 23rd Regiment. Major Fukuda was told to attack the company perimeters of our battalion.

On the morning of the 9th of July—we always 'stood to' in our fighting pits at first light, and at dusk, 'cause that's when they tended to want to attack. And we're sitting in the pits, half-asleep, and the next minute there are two huge explosions from two hundred yards down the track in Don Company and a roar of gunfire. It was really heavy and a lot of it was whipping through the trees over our head to two hundred yards away. Fortunately for Don Company at the time all our three-inch mortars were in the Don Company perimeter. The three-inch mortar could throw out bombs to two thousand yards. It had a minimum range of ninety yards but that day the mortar lieut was saying to his team in the holes, 'Jack 'em up, higher and higher!'

He put down a six-mortar barrage on his own wire, which was fifty-five yards out. If he'd been a whisker out, the bombs would've dropped back on our own people. The Japanese slid two Bangalore torpedoes, that's ten-foot lengths of piping packed with explosives into the wire and set them off and that blew two gaps, and they rushed the two gaps. There were about eight hundred of them, Major Fukuda's 23rd Regiment. What they didn't know was everyone was in their fighting pits and three Bren guns cross-fired on each break.

ASE FOR
SLOOP | Arrived From
Britain Today
In Bride Ship

WENDY TREVOR joined the WAAF in World War II and met her husband, an Aussie air gunner, in London. She was one of many War Brides who left behind their country and all they knew to follow their husbands home. 'I remember I got my sailing orders with 24 hours to get myself demobilised from the air force and up to Liverpool … [where] we saw the little ship that we were coming out on, it was the *Nestor*.'

WALTER WALLACE (*above*) marching to parade with his platoon in 1940. 'Well, for me I suppose, I don't know if you call it patriotism or what, but I just felt you needed to be part of your country's defence. And at that time, war was coming on.'

PAUL COUVRET was a Prisoner of the Japanese during World War II. This is a post-war aerial shot of the camp he was in, in Nagasaki. 'It was mateship which helped you through, right through the prison camp.'

KEITH PAYNE served in the Infantry during the Korean War, Malayan Emergency, Indonesian Konfrontas: and was involved in Vietnam. Here he is (*right*) in Korea 'drinking' frozen coffee with a couple of mates. 'We weren't equipped very well in those days. We were still utilising World War II equipment, which didn't stand us in good stead in Korea … we were in 30 degrees below zero.'

KEITH PAYNE was awarded the Victoria Cross by Queen Elizabeth in 1970 for his actions in Vietnam.

JOHN FRASER pictured (*left*) at Kapooka Training Centre, Wagga Wagga and (*right*) on a 'hearts and minds' patrol with United Nations staff. 'I had no doubts. I didn't want to be a doctor or a lawyer or think of anything else. I just knew I wanted to be in the military.'

NOEL 'PETER' MEDCALF (*right*) joined up and was a member of the Infantry in Bougainville in World War II. 'We had the job of clearing the swamps. The swamps were a miserable place ... you were working mostly in foot-deep mud.'

Interned in Italy during World War II, ADELE MANCHOULAS had a promising career as a ballerina dashed by the war. Pictured with friends (*opposite page, top*) from the village of Oliveto Citra, Adele is second from the right. 'No matter how difficult things become, say to yourself, you will overcome … because you will … That's what I think … And believe in people.'

SALVATORE ANDALORO (*right*) has served in the Western Sahara and East Timor. 'The nature of the beast with intelligence corps is that you tend to be operating in much smaller units ... you tend to be extremely specialised.'

Until his death in June 2004, TED SMOUT was Australia's oldest World War I veteran. Pictured above (*left*) with mates in France, Ted spoke frankly about the impact of war on his life. ' … there's no way you could convey to the ordinary civilians the horrors that happened in war. No way. Indescribable.'

Too many lives have been lost in war, lives like those marked above in a war cemetery in France, their voices lost forever.

Well, then the furore and uproar died down, we had three tanks on our perimeter, Don Company had the mortars, so they came over to my section, 5 Section and said, 'Take a tank down and help them clean up.'

The infantry had to protect the tank. I think that was grossly unfair because with the motor of the tank you couldn't hear anything. You had to form a screen around it. But it was terribly vulnerable to an attack from the dense jungle on each side of the track and the track was really only not even as wide as this room. When we got down there a mate of mine who I trained with was sitting in his hole eating breakfast. The cook had cooked a two-course meal in the middle of a 'banzai' charge and I reckon he deserved a mention in dispatches and I said to 'Junior', 'Where's all the Pongs?'

We called them Pongs, as I said, because they stank. He said, 'Where do you think they are?'

And he pointed behind his parapet and there in each break in the wire the bodies were stacked that high, like flapjacks. There were bodies from both breaks coming further and closer to the front pits and even two had got through the front pits and had been killed by the troops in the second line ... they buried about forty-seven Japs with bulldozers that day. Two weeks later they knocked over a Japanese with an intelligence report from Major Fukuda back to base. Apparently Don Company had killed another fifty, 'cause they dragged their casualties away, and wounded another equal number. Major Fukuda said, *'Owing to regrettable, unforeseen circumstances 23rd Regiment is now no longer an effective fighting force.'*

So that sorted out Fukuda and his 23rd Regiment.

* * *

You're constantly smelling, listening and looking. A leaf would drift down, you'd see it. A little bird'd flick, you'd see it. You were looking into the trees, although the second scout was looking up to check their position, just in case they'd put a sniper up in the trees. You had to try and look at each side. But the whole patrol was looking each side. You were looking for signs of disturbed earth that might show a Japanese fighting pit, or their position or something. Mostly you were listening. Because strangely enough, the jungle on Bougainville was very quiet. Unlike what I've heard and what I've seen in the movies of say, the African rainforests, where you've got bird life, and all that. It was dead silence, so you did have a good chance of hearing if you kept on your toes. But if you got tired or careless, it was starting to get dangerous. They tried to change the point scout over every hour, because the strain was a bit too much.

. . . You could keep combat troops in action for about three months and then it starts to tell. I think towards the end my nerves were starting to go. There are some symptoms. You'd be out on patrol and something'd happen. Might be a sudden noise, a falling tree limb and you'd burn all over with a prickling burning itch and we thought it was prickly heat. But the doc said afterwards, no. It was the beginning of the breakdown of the nervous system. The next step would be scabies where the skin would react. But then they put us on vitamin B1 to counteract it. But that was the effect it has. If you stayed in too long, gradually it'd start to wear you down. It wasn't the actual fighting, that was only intermittent. You might go two-three days and there are no shots fired but then the next day you might be in the middle of a lot of action. It was the knowledge that every minute of every hour, it could happen. And you have to readjust your mental attitude to that.

There was a young chap, he was very religious. I think he'd been brought up by his parents and his church that the Lord would protect and when he realised that a copy of the New Testament was no protection against a Jap bullet he cracked up. We had another fella. Went off to rest camp and on the way back to battalion headquarters there were rumours that Colonel Muda's Japs were raiding Runai dropping ground, where the decoders used to drop our supplies from the kai [food] bombers and they'd come around picking up the dented cans of bully beef and that. So they grabbed Ronnie and a couple of other fellows to do a patrol to go out to Runai to try and see if they could find who these Japs were and do something about it. And Runai was huge, four hundred yards, that's a quarter of a mile long, cleared. And they saw some shapes over on the far side under the shade of trees and they said, 'Oh, the bloody Japs!'

And Ronnie said, 'I reckon I could get one.'

And they said, 'Oh, it's four hundred yards.'

He took a rest on the back of a tree, slipped the sights up and let jive and one of them flew over backwards. Ronnie shot a man named Morgan at four hundred yards clean through the head. The 42nd Battalion patrol was way off course and shouldn't have been there. They tried to keep it quiet but finally Ronnie heard about it. After that he was no good anymore, so they had to send him back.

* * *

On the spot we would vary something. If we thought the Japs were waking up to it we would vary it. One thing was we would bury a grenade in the middle of the track and break off a branch and let the branch lean with the butt of the branch just resting on the quarter of an inch of soil, that was the grenade lever, and you pulled the pin. The branch was holding the lever down. Now it's human nature, if a patrol came along, to kick the branch out of the way, Bang! So that was the type of thing you did. You were there to kill Japanese. Didn't matter how you did it. You did it as efficiently as you could. One that I never saw practised, but was taught in Canungra, was in that heat, a tin of bully beef, if it has a pinhole in it, it would go rotten in twenty-four hours. So you dose up a couple of tins and dropped them along the tracks. And they were desperate for meat, and they'd eat anything and we got a few with botulism. That's biological warfare that we practised ourselves . . . if we'd had strychnine or arsenic we could have used that.

. . . Bob Minchin's platoon was down behind the Japanese position and they found a clearing. On the far side of the clearing, quite a wide one, was what looked like a log block house, or something. And the officer said, 'We won't risk men trying to do anything with it.'

And the sig [signaller] said, 'Let me radio back and try and bring some guns down on it.'

So he radioed back and they brought in the first shell from the 25-pounder and it was spot on. It hit the logs and they flew everywhere. But out of the smoke and the flashes, suddenly came one lone, little Japanese, and he's coming like the clappers and everyone's saying, 'Quick, quick, get 'im, get 'im!'

So the sig's talking out 'Four guns, up fifty, fire!' and they hit. Smoke, fire, everything. And out of this mess, he's still going. By the end of the day they were stopped for a brew and 'Beetle-Brow' Bryson called over to Bob, 'You bunch of great big, bronzed Anzacs! All of you there and four great big, dirty 25-pounders and one poor little Jap and still you didn't get him.'

And Bob said, 'It did one thing. I bet it made him feel important.'

We had a guy, 'Commando' Anderson, he was called that because he was a very keen soldier. 'Commando' was on listening post every day outside the perimeter. We all took turns for an hour on listening post to try and stall any attack. 'Commando' goes out there hiding in the bushes and there twenty feet away is a Jap soldier. So 'Commando' flicked the safety catch, put the foresight on his shirt button and went '*whack*'. Well, the whole company stood to and 'Commando' came in, walked up to Perce, the OC, the boss, and said, 'One Pong, Sir. I flattened him.'

Perce said, 'One? One wouldn't be walking around by himself. You sure you weren't shooting at a bird or something?'

And 'Commando' was outraged he said, 'Of course not. I flattened him dead centre.'

So Perce said, 'Well done, son. Good. You did a good job. But you'd better go out and bury him.'

There's a stunned silence and 'Commando' said, 'What? Sir, I'm paid to flatten them, not play bloody undertaker.'

Perce said, 'Stop arguing. He'll stink the place out in twenty-four hours, go bury him.'

So 'Commando' trudged out with his shovel and his rifle and we hear '*dig-dig-dig*' and after a while 'Commando' came in and got a machete and we hear '*chop-chop-chop*'. When it's over he came out with his shovel and his machete and his rifle and somebody said, 'Did you strike some tree roots, mate?'

He said, 'No. I dug the hole too short. I had to make the bugger fit.'

Everyone sort of chuckled, but in that environment it wasn't that strange. Nobody thought anything about it.

* * *

If you walked onto a prepared position you'd cop it from the Nambus, their light machine guns, or their Juki, their heavier 'woodpeckers'. So the deal was to find their positions, pinpoint them but don't walk up against them. But that didn't always work . . . when we used armed gunners as forward scouts it gave you a definite edge. If you say, came on a track and there were three or four Japanese talking on it, a good Owen gunner could just write the lot off with one magazine. If you could get grenades in too. They didn't like our grenades 'cause they were lethal. So it would be very short, sharp. Probably the firing might last for ten seconds. There would be dead silence and terribly quiet and the old question, what do you do next? We'd instinctively try to encircle, as we were taught. If you saw a single Jap, okay you eliminate them. The day we took the Papuan Infantry with us to act as scouts we cut a Japanese phone line. Chop the phone, about twenty yards of it into pieces. And we're just moving in to ambush, because they send a party in to fix their phone line. Along came 'the party'. He was about four feet eleven. He had his little carbine and his pair of pliers and his roll of wire and the PIB [Papuan Infantry Battalion] shot him to rags in about three seconds. Everyone had a piece of the action. My mate 'Jive' was carrying the Bren that day and him and I tore up to get a part of the fun because it was all our way and it was all over by the time we got there. That was about the only time I ever saw a fella shot fifteen times through the face and head keep groaning, but he died while we searched him.

I never fired a shot in the swamps because I was on the tail end of the section on patrols. They didn't come up and attack our position. But later on, in the lowlands in that June, July and into August yes, we mixed it up pretty well. The first time was when Al Fuller and

I were scouting and we stopped for a rest. He turned around and saw this heavily camouflaged Jap about fifteen yards away and Al hit him in the pit of the stomach and I hit him in the shoulders. He just '*pfffttt*' blew over backwards. There were plenty of other times when you had a chance to fire.

If you knocked them over, you were elated. You felt ten feet tall. If your friends got him, that was a very different thing. But we didn't regard them as humans. If you managed to get a couple everyone would come in rejoicing. Our 13th Platoon once caught a platoon of Japs marching down a very distant track in threes. In the front rank was their camp comedian cracking jokes and all the other Japs 'ah, ha' thought it was great and the 13th Platoon leader shot the comedian through the chest at about twenty yards off and said, 'Laugh that off, you sod.'

The Brens fired down the track and the Japs jumped into the Bren fire. They got about eighteen to twenty out of that bunch of thirty.

... By the time we'd joined the army we'd heard the stories of their exploits. That was most of the war. Their own behaviour meant that people back home didn't regard them as human. The first time I ever thought of them as human beings was in Rabaul, after the war. There was a Japanese interpreter, who was a doctor and I was sitting ... reading a copy of *Pix Magazine* and there were some aerial photographs of Tokyo and the results of the fire-bombing. This Jap interpreter looked over my shoulder and said, 'Excuse me, Sir. When you're finished looking at the magazine can I have a look at the photos? My home was in Tokyo and I was wondering about my family.'

I had the most peculiar feeling. Suddenly, he was a human being. He was a doctor.

... But the worst part was losing mates and, of course, the business of having to bury them and such. It's, I suppose, like anyone who has a friend who's killed in front of them. Particularly with this chap who took my place. It took us about two hours to get us out, under fire, and back to where we thought the doc might be able to fix him up. But he bled to death internally and the doc said, 'There was nothing you could have done. There is nothing I can do. I can't operate on this.'

He was a nice fella, the doc. He was in charge of course of the stretcher-bearers and the medical team within the battalion. But one of them was telling us, one day the doc had had it. He was treating somebody, they'd brought a chap in, who'd been pretty badly hit and who'd died and the doc damn nearly blew his stack, according to Louie.

'They drag them in here, they're shot to ribbons and they look at me and say, "You can fix him up, Doc, can't you? He'll be right?" And he said, "What do they think I am? Jesus Christ? I can't even operate in this stinking mud pit."'

And Louie said, 'Look, they know that. But at least you give them a bit of hope.'

So that's what it was like.

I don't think we ever examined it mentally at all. It just happened. You probably wouldn't think about it after a while, after a couple of days, because other things would intervene. You never thought it would happen to you. A very funny thing. A couple of cases you'd find one of the boys would get very quiet or depressed and uncannily, within a day or so, he would be a casualty. I don't know about pre-sense. I don't believe in it actually but it used to puzzle you a bit and you were more or less, that was the lifestyle. You were a soldier, you were a combat soldier. That was part of the deal. Every hour of every day or night it could happen so you had to live with that. Now, if you thought about it too much you'd go crazy. So you didn't think about it too much, we'd crack jokes... a man's private life was sacrosanct. He might show you a picture of his wife or girlfriend. She could be about as ugly as a hat full of tarantulas but you always said how nice she looked. Things like that.

... Personal possessions were only just the clothes you wore. I was down to one shirt with a split up the back and a pair of boots and four pairs of socks. I had a couple of photos from home, of my girlfriend at the time. There were no plastics in those days so you had an oiled silk bag you could keep your personal items in. But they were starting to go mouldy. Anything leather would grow mould overnight. When your skin started to grow mould you were in trouble. That was the effect that the constant wet had on you. You tried to shave. That was one thing. The Americans let themselves go to pieces and grew beards and never changed their clothes or whatever. We were taught in Canungra, when you can you shave every day because it does make a difference . . . made you feel fresher, feel fitter. If you didn't shave you seemed to feel worse, you were tireder. And I think the Australian Army knew what it was talking about under those circumstances. It wasn't a matter of regimental appearance. It made you feel fitter.

Secondly every day, try and, even if you haven't got a clean shirt, take it off, wash it, wring it out and put it back on wet. Same with your socks, definitely your socks. Take your socks off, rinse them out and hang them out to dry. Change them, every day. Otherwise your feet will rot. That patrol that we did in the swamps where I spent one night hanging in a loop of vine, swinging up against a tree trunk, up to my hips in water. When I got back off that three-day patrol and I took my boots and socks off, the soles of my feet came off with my socks. So I thought, 'Hooray! I'll be able to go back.'

But 'Harpo the Herbalist' said you only go back if you're a battle casualty and have a temperature of 105. He gave me some cotton wool for my boots and said, 'You're fit for duty.'

. . . You jacked your bush bunk up. As the water on the floor of the sleeping bay rose you had to put a log under each end and jack it right up until your nose was nearly touching the overhead logs. If you felt your backside started to get cold one night you knew the water was starting to creep up under your canvas stretcher top. And you'd be lying there and something furry would crawl across your face and you'd be so tired you'd just brush it off and go back to sleep and the only ones who seemed to enjoy it were the mosquitoes . . . if you could find a banana frond then at least you can stop the rain from hitting your head. On patrol we were wearing green berets and you slept in it. It was pretty miserable.

* * *

The Japanese were going to retire to their big base in Buin, dig in and fight to the last man. Now on Buna, Gona and Sanananda trying to kill all the Japs cost hundreds and hundreds of casualties. I hate to think what would have happened had we been expected to take Buin by assault. It started to rain late in July, and it rained, and it rained. Our fighting pits filled up. Our sleeping bays, which were about seven feet by five . . . they were starting to fill up.

The last fight I was in occurred about the minute the atom bomb was dropped on Hiroshima: half-past eight on the Sunday morning, or Monday morning, of the 6th of August and south of our positions and perimeters where the Buin Road connected with Killen's Track there was a big area we called 'The Badlands'. That was where the major Japanese infiltration came in and for some weeks there'd been a Japanese Juki heavy machine gun firing whenever the patrols crossed the ford and he has to be somewhere on this bank where he could see the ford, so they got nine of us lined up and Perce said, 'You've got two hours. Find that bloody machine gun. Don't attack it. I don't want nine men trying to argue with a heavy machine gun. Pinpoint it and we'll turn the mortars on it.'

So 'Bunny', my corporal, came up and he said, 'You, down the back,' and I said, 'Why, why, what have I done wrong?' You know.

He said, 'Take a rest. Be drag man. You can watch the butterflies and criticise the rest of us.'

I think he realised it was starting to show a bit, the strain. When you start to have bad dreams and that. Anyway, grumbling, I went down the back and they used one of the two mortar men, a fella by the name of Bill Wallace to take my place. Now Bill had never scouted before which was probably not the right thing to do because my mate Ross Horton, 'Jive', he would have been better as a point scout. He and I'd become a pretty smooth working team together as scouts.

So off we took and we started to probe around heavy jungle down near the bank of the river across the road into these badlands and suddenly I hear from up front, if you're tail man on a nine-man patrol you don't see anything of the fight. It's only twenty yards ahead of you because they're spread out in front of you, seven or eight or nine yards apart and I heard two arms go off and a lot of shouting and they all came running back and somebody said something about 'woodpecker' so apparently they'd found the positioning and shot it up and we had with us a reinforcement sergeant who'd only been sent down to us two days before. He was hopelessly short on jungle craft and he'd been told by Perce, 'You do what Corporal Cumberford tells you to do.'

Bunny, my section corporal. This Bunny said, 'Right now we go home, we've found it.'

And this guy started to argue in a loud voice that, you know, 'Oh, I'm saying where we're going to go.'

They should've shot him in the foot. I was sure I heard some voices somewhere ahead of us. Anyway to cut the argument they said all right we'll go a bit further and Bill was leading them and he made the mistake of leading them across a clearing a little bit bigger than this room with a bit of a bank on the other side and a lot of bushes. And I was right back, I was the last man and I can suddenly remember seeing the whole patrol surrounded by white and grey flashes of smoke, and it's funny, I don't remember hearing them but they'd run onto a Japs' position and the Japs had thrown grenades. And the last grenade was one of ours that they'd captured, and our grenades were lethal. Theirs were a bit like firecrackers. The patrol did the right thing, as we'd been trained. You fire with everything you've got straight into them to shake them and then split and when the smoke lifted there's a body down on the other side and it was Bill Wallace.

That was the longest crawl I ever did across that clearing. But he'd been hit high in the thigh by one of the base plugs in one our grenades and that was about that big, and he was about fourteen stone. He was a big man and I wasn't about to get to my feet and try and drag him. And then there were a couple of shots came my way, so about the only thing I could do was pour fire into those bushes. They didn't like our Owen guns and the moment they started they kept their heads down. I had my Owen and seven full magazines and Bill's Owen. So I poured fire into those bushes and I'm trying to drag him and I'm saying, 'Try and help yourself, mate.'

And finally Bunny came down and we managed to drag him out of the clearing. The Brens started and we got him out under fire. Then we had to make a bush-stretcher and get him back. We got him back to Don Company after about an hour. We thought, 'Right. The doc will fix him.'

But we went back home to the C company perimeter and about an hour later, around midday, Bunny came over and he said, 'Bill died of loss of blood. Would the four of you like to go down to bury him because you're from Sydney, like he was.'

That was a miserable day too. They had the D Company graves, just low mounds with sapling markers hung with their meat tickets [ID tags] and I dug the grave for the other, the D Company boys had dug it and it was about a foot deep in water. So we carried Bill out, they'd wrapped him in blankets, and lowered him in it. And it rained. And the Padre came and said his words. One of the buglers played 'The Last Post', with a wad of rags into his bugle to keep it muffled. That was a bad day. That was the last action I was in.

* * *

After the atom bomb, they withdrew all patrols and told us to sit tight on the 12th of August. On the afternoon of the 15th of August the word came through that Japan had surrendered. One would have expected I suppose, under any other circumstances, particularly back home and in base areas, there'd be a lot of cheering and God-knows-what, as we've seen on film ever since. In our case, and it happened through every company perimeter of every platoon that was in action, there was dead silence. We just sat and it was a bit hard to grasp. It was a funny feeling. Then one of the tanks in the perimeter turned on the radio and managed to get Townsville and we heard the cheering crowds in Brisbane. Probably like that famous photo of that guy prancing down the street. But nobody said anything. After a few minutes somebody said, 'Turn that bloody thing off!'

It was as though we hated them for nakedly parading, which was wrong of us because they could feel joy and so forth. But it puzzled me for some time as to what was our attitude. I think our attitude was, that was a world away and we'd been more and more divorced from it. Plus, what we'd become. We weren't needed anymore. It sort of left you with a lost and uncertain feeling... Every afternoon in the army, the bugles blow a retreat on sundown and the retreat is blown in memory of our fallen. Of course there are no bugle calls while you're in action during the war, only back at base. But I heard later that the adjutant, back at battalion headquarters, said to the buglers... 'Get your horns out boys and let's hear it.'

That was the first time in months. But we were still sitting there talking about it. Suddenly, for the first time in months, the song of the bugles. It was quite uncanny. Most uncanny.

* * *

We stayed in the perimeter throughout August and up until early October. We built ourselves little humpies and so forth and roofed them with banana fronds and then they took us by truck, because the Buin Road was now navigable to road traffic. The engineers did a good job. They took us to Torokina and started the slow process of disbanding the combat units of Bougainville... Because shipping was a problem, to ship the troops home from Borneo, New Guinea, Bougainville etc. We were taken on the *Katoomba* to Rabaul to help look after the ninety thousand Jap prisoners in Rabaul, waiting our turn for repatriation... they were put to work building camps and so forth. See we were going to be relieved ourselves by fresh units from Australia and so the Japanese were building huts and digging latrines and all that type of thing.

It was interesting... Rabaul was destroyed totally and you'd want to go somewhere to see a mate in another unit so you'd walk out onto the road, the Japanese were driving their own work trucks, you'd stop the truck, kick the Jap officer out of the front seat, get in the front seat and go. You know what a crown seal is on a bottle of beer? Well, if you took, in those days, the cork liner out of it and pressed into your epaulet you could get a couple of those so you looked like an officer. The Japs were supposed to salute us anyway and we were under strict orders never to salute a Jap officer under any circumstances.

The ninety thousand Japanese there, they had dug ninety miles of tunnels into the hills around Rabaul. I saw a 200-ton coastal steamer ship running on rails into a vast cavern at water level off Simpson's Harbour. I saw machine shops that were fully fitted with machine lathes and everything, going into the mountain. Whole caverns full of aerial torpedoes and God-knows-what. It was an immense ant-heap of defence positioning. If [General] MacArthur or some idiot had thought to take Rabaul it would have taken tens of thousands of casualties. But I only was there over Christmas and on Christmas morning a lot of us from Bougainville ended up in hospital with malaria. We'd drank too much beer. We weren't used to it and the Atebrin, of course, didn't cure it, it only suppressed it. I went to hospital on Christmas morning and spent ten days there and it was after I got back they said, 'You're on no duties. We don't have an active convalescence depot but you can be acting hygiene sergeant and look after these Japs digging these latrines and such.'

I did that for a couple of weeks.

The army decided too, in Rabaul that everyone was bored, and these old Japanese transport horses were there, so they'd hold an official race meeting. Each unit would buy one of the horses, and have to supply a jockey and a trainer. The air force flew up from Townsville all the silks and the saddles and the harness. And they built a racetrack with a tote and a grandstand. Oh, it was beautifully done. The only thing was these horses were pretty far gone and they didn't think they'd last long if they made them run around in circles, so the racetrack was dead straight. Well, I reckon that was one of the funniest things. I wish I'd kept the program. It was sort of 'Shady Lady' by 'AWAS Mistake' out of something-or-other and a well-known Melbourne race caller and announcer was there. And all the natives on the other side of the track and the witchdoctors, Tul Tuls, Luluais were taking bets in trade tobacco. So the idea was you went along to the saddling paddock and picked your horse. So we thought this 'Shady Lady' was pretty good...we went up and put the rent on 'Shady Lady'.

Anyway the gun went. Two horses wouldn't run, one jumped the fence and the rest of the field's off and 'Shady Lady' leading by about three lengths and we thought, 'You bottler!' She got lonely and stopped and waited for the others. So finally, through some unfortunate neglect on the part of the jockey she got a nose in front and won. But you'd hear the public address system say, 'Fashions on the Lawn today, Ladies' and there'd be a digger in jungle greens escorting a Chinese girl, you know. It was a hilarious day, but a lot of fun.

* * *

They had a points system for discharge, depending on your age of enlistment, number of years service in Australia, number of years service overseas, whether you had dependants, or whatever. So a long-service AIF member of the 6th, 7th or 9th Division, he might have three or four hundred points, with two or three kids when he enlisted at, say, the age of twenty-five. I enlisted at eighteen, no dependants, and I only had 101 points. So, other nineteen-, or by then, twenty-year-olds, like me, would have had about the same. When they came around at the end of the war with a whole lot of things, 'Would you like a War Service Home? Would you like to continue your education under CRTS [Commonwealth Reconstruction Training Scheme]?' I ticked 'yes' to everything and after I came out of hospital, from malaria, in Rabaul, suddenly I was called into battalion headquarters and they said, 'You're going home.'

I said, 'Good heavens, why?'

Because at that time they were repatriating the 250-pointers and up, and my 101 was very insignificant and they said, 'Oh, it's something to do with Commonwealth Reconstruction Training Scheme, so you can finish your university course.'

They said, 'Look, I'll tell you what. We don't know much about this. How 'bout we just send you home and you can work this out?'

I said, 'Yeah, yeah, yeah!'

So I was out at the end of February when I'd been away, pretty well, eighteen months. And on the *Duntroon,* came home and we got off at Woolloomooloo and got on a double-decker bus and funny enough, I looked around and saw old people. I hadn't seen old people. I saw children. I hadn't seen children. And the women. The women all had high-pitched squeaky voices. We hadn't spoken to women in so long. Took us to Matraville depot, said, 'Here's your twelve-day leave pass, go.'

* * *

To be fair to the people back home they couldn't understand. How could you understand if you hadn't experienced it? We tried, when we got back home, to tell them. If they said, 'What was it like?' you tried to tell them but you could see the look in their eyes. They didn't understand it. You had to live it to understand it. I don't think I'd want it any other way, in a sense, because how would you want to inflict that on the people at large? I mean, the people in Germany and Russia and even the Blitz in England, the fire-bombing and the atom bombing of Japan, they experienced it but I realised our people didn't. On thinking, I would have preferred it if the government and the media back in Australia had tried to tell the people back here in Australia, and in subsequent years, more about it.

... The war made us grow up very fast, very fast. It taught us what was essential and what was frivolous. That's why it took me a couple of years and even now, one doesn't get overexcited about stupid uselessness. That's not important. The things that are important are the safety of yourself and your family. Your loved ones and their comfort, and it bred into you a sense of responsibility. You went away an eighteen-year-old kid and you came back a man, totally. I've seen men in their late twenties and I'm sorry but they're still adolescents. I've seen forty-year-old adolescents. They'd never grown up. That's one of the reasons you have so many broken marriages. A lot of the boys never grew up.

ADELE MANCHOULAS

Interned in Italy
World War II

M y parents were divorced when I was about three I suppose...
when they came out to Australia, before I was born, they decided
to have a cheese factory like in the area where my father came from,
which was Eboli. Close by there they have buffalos and they make
mozzarella cheese. It's far better made with buffalo milk than cow's
milk believe me. So they decided that that's what they would do.
Unfortunately my father didn't speak any English. I think if they had
stayed in Italy maybe the marriage would have worked. But out in
Australia with my father with no knowledge of English...! They
bought a property up on the Nepean, somewhere near Camden I
think. They bought out with them two Italian workers who made
cheese. And they made the very first mozzarella and those cheeses
in Sydney. But nobody had ever heard of them and they couldn't sell
them. So it foundered and little by little the marriage foundered too.

... One of my uncles died... and so my mother then inherited
the property, Blackdown. I remember it, little and all as I was, when
I first arrived there because it was a pretty rundown house and
everything... Bathurst was a nice, quiet country town. Clean, pretty,
cold in the winter, hot in the summer. I had always, from the time
I was two years old, had a pony and that as a little child was my
great passion. I really wanted to be able to ride on top of the pony,
stand on top of the pony and dance like a circus performer. I didn't

ever do that but I think I rode well. I entered the show several times. I had a rug of ribbons.

. . . I started my ballet training in Sydney in a studio up near the railway. My first teacher was Russian, Arnold Spearka. He was a ballet dancer and magnificent skater. He was not a great teacher, I have to say in retrospect. I didn't last long with Arnold Spearka and I found Leon Kellaway. Leon Kellaway taught and taught very well. A very good grounding. So the great teachers in Europe subsequently told me. Then the Ballet Russes visited in early 1937 and my teacher Leon Kellaway arranged for me and I think two other pupils of his to be given private lessons with Leon Voicakovski to see whether it was worth continuing. My mother said to him, 'Well, she's been learning for two years, we'll go to Paris tomorrow.'

And go to Olga Preobrazhenskaya [a Russian prima ballerina, famed as a teacher in France] tomorrow we did.

* * *

When we arrived in Paris, Mother had found a little hotel near the studios . . . and the first night we went out for dinner. I think she ordered mussels without realising what they were. She was having a little bit of trouble managing and a woman sitting at a table on her own, fairly close, a Madame Strauss, she said, 'Can I help you?' In very good English.

'Yes please.'

And she did. She was instrumental in helping us find the apartment; introducing us to a chemist and his two children and his wife who was mentally ill and in a hospital. So we became friends with the chemist and she also introduced us to another gentleman and his daughter, Monsieur Deharzay, and they altogether helped us a lot. Mother made friends very easily I have to say. She would talk to anyone and if she didn't speak the language she still made herself known.

. . . My mother thought that the French were inclined to be rude; too many dogs littering the pavement; hard business people, which I guess they are. I would say within two or three weeks of arriving in Paris I was on the bus on my own and an elderly English lady got into the bus, handed the bus conductor her fare and said, 'Rue de Roma silvu play.'

And I in my little corner shrank. And I thought, 'I am not going to talk like that.' And somebody said, 'Use a mirror. Get your tongue in the right place. And you will soon be saying it correctly.'

So it helped . . . once I found I could pass, my French was comprehensible and eventually nobody took any notice and just thought I was a little French girl.

. . . In Paris there was most of all a strong influence of Russians, White Russians. My teacher was Russian. I started learning Russian from a Russian engineer who was working on the Maginot line [this was a French defensive construction that was intended to protect against German aggression]. Very poor. He had little paper cuffs because he probably had a short-sleeve shirt and he had paper cuffs. A nice fellow, but yes I found the Russians fascinating. Absolutely fascinating . . . When my grandmother subsequently came over, they thought that because she wore a hat, I think, that she might have some money and be quite wealthy. So the studio sent around Prince Felix Yusupov. Prince Yusupov was the one responsible for the murder of Rasputin, and Prince Yusupov was living in Paris with his morganatic wife and needing money because she needed an operation. He came selling furs. The most beautiful sable furs and emeralds. My grandmother had her hands full of these beautiful Russian emeralds. And I can remember she said to Mother, 'What am I going to do with those? In Bathurst I can wear a fur, but I can't really do anything with all these beautiful emeralds.'

She probably could have had them for a song you know. So she ended up buying a most beautiful full-length Royal Russian sable. And it was only years later that it was cut into three. One for Mother, one for my aunt, one for me. Mine was a stole, virtually a cape, it needed to be relined and I took it into a furrier . . . He took one look at it and he said, 'Do you realise what you've got here?'

And I said, 'Yes, it's a sable.'

He said, 'No, it's a Royal Russian sable.'

I said, 'How do you tell the difference?'

He said, 'The tip of each hair is just off white. If you wear that to the Opera House, two or three people in the audience will know what you have, nobody else will, but *they* will.'

The Russians I found fascinating.

* * *

The Maginot line was going to save France. They weren't expecting the airborne threat to come over. Oh yes that was going to save France. I heard all the news but a lot of it went over the head of a thirteen year old . . . It didn't really affect me. What's this war? You know, a thirteen year old. But for me it was dancing, dancing, dancing. That was it. First of all classes and then private lessons twice a week. It was everything my dancing . . . I was informed by both my teachers, my Spanish dance teacher and Olga, my ballet teacher, that this competition that was held every year was coming up and I should enter for it. So I did.

I can remember my Spanish dance teacher saying, 'You remember, if you enter for this, you are no longer amateur, you are a professional.'

I said, 'That's fine by me.'

So Olga composed this beautiful dance, *La chasse l'alouette* which is the *Chase of the Swallow*. It's a piece from a Russian opera I believe, *Millions of Harlequins*. A funny name. But the music was beautiful. And she just choreographed it beautifully. The swallow comes on . . . flying hopefully on to the stage and feels hit as if a stone or something had hit it and she's wounded. And she drops to the ground and then she realises that she's not. She lifts her head and feels she's alive. And she feels her arms . . . through the whole body she's alive. And she gets up and she starts to dance for joy. It was lovely . . . and then I did also a dance composed by my Spanish dance teacher . . . They were both on the same evening as I remember, and I won the gold medal . . . I certainly did not expect to win. It was international. I mean there were students from various countries . . . that gold medal was to be a great open sesame for wherever else I wanted to dance.

Then the war came.

* * *

Everything was going beautifully. I had nothing but what I thought was stardom ahead of me until suddenly war was declared. We were actually in England, in Cambridge, the day that war was declared. We had gone there for a few days holiday. We were in church. It was a Sunday. So we raced back to Paris and then I guess it must have come over the air, people who were not essential, or foreign people, were asked to leave. Well, we could have gone to England. Mother thought, well that's going to be bombed, Germany might even take England, perish the thought, but Italy was neutral. So with that in mind ... see she wasn't psychic there. She thought well, we'll go down to Milan and see if you can dance at La Scala.

... It was touch and go at one stage, really truly. But it was hectic getting away from Paris. We left an apartment fully furnished, to a Russian princess, Madam Tududov, and we just took our clothes and departed. Caught a plane. Italy really was peaceful. We didn't notice any signs of preparations for war. Nobody was anti the English ... It wasn't until literally a few weeks later Italy actually joined the war with Germany ... it was like a tide of propaganda. It was suddenly like a tap was turned on.

* * *

The girls at La Scala had never heard of Australia. So it was really a totally unknown quantity ... I was every day at La Scala, and in the beginning everybody was happy and friendly, very friendly, great. The Italian teacher, the dance teacher, the girls. Even Beniamino Gigli [a famous Italian opera singer and film star] was singing there at the time and we used to call him Uncle Benumina. He used to come along and chuck us under the chin ... So they were all friendly and then ... the propaganda ... and I used to come home every night in tears because the dance teacher was really nasty.

... The moment Italy declared war on England, we were persona non grata really and likely to be spat on. I tell you, it was an overwhelming, horrid feeling if you spoke English in front of them. In a big city there was such a fascist feeling, great fascist feeling in the air. We were in Milan. My mother said it was a little bit like the fermentation caused by Il Duce [Benito Mussolini, Prime Minister of Italy] when he first came to power. She was in Italy then and she said the crowds that gathered in the squares were enormous and everyone shouting, 'Duce, Duce, Duce!' . . . So it was uncomfortable and that's why she thought, 'Okay, don't stay in a big city.'

She had been to see the American Consul, the British Consul, the French Consul, all to try and leave . . . we all had French identity cards and with a French identity card you went everywhere in France. And she thought if we go down to the border we could catch a little boat and row around and we would be on French soil. So we went down and we booked into a little *pensione* and forthwith she went down to the beach and started, as Mother was wont to do, to talk to some of the locals . . . And someone said, 'I can get you around in one of these little dinghies. If you haven't got much luggage. You might have to wade through water a bit.'

And Mother said, 'That's all right, so long as we're back in France.'

And she thought then we could catch a boat from Marseille or wherever. I don't know if it would have been any better. But the fact remains that we did go down there, we did this and it was all organised. This fellow was a sailor and he said he would come to the hotel, the *pensione*, at seven o'clock Tuesday evening or whatever it was.

'You be ready and I'll row you around.'

Well we waited seven o'clock, eight o'clock and by the time it was dark he came knocking at the door and said, 'I'm terribly sorry. Just this morning, they've put in motor torpedo boats with machine guns and big searchlights, so I'm not going to do it anymore.'

So we went back to Milan and that's when we went south. It was a bit scary.

. . . I wasn't told to leave La Scala. I left. My mother said, 'If you're so upset you can't go ahead like this.' Because it was day after day of being so upset. She just said, 'Don't go back anymore.'

And I didn't. And we just planned to leave. She said, 'I think if we disappear, virtually into the countryside, we may be forgotten.'

But I guess they had already noted us. I'm sure that under the circumstances if we couldn't leave Italy she did the best thing by going into the country, down the south. It's also possible that there was less anti-British feeling down south than there was up north. Yes, I'm sure. I mean people in the southern part of Italy and in the small towns particularly, they were really not worried about politics. The only thing that worried them was having their husbands or fathers away fighting.

* * *

We went to Eboli. My father was born on a property out of the town with a little cottage on it . . . actually the property belonged to my Italian grandfather . . . We were received very warmly but they had to be very careful. They had a huge house. They had something like thirty-six rooms, but we couldn't live with them because that would have been 'aiding the enemy'. Helping the enemy, even though we were family.

We were registered as internees within a matter of weeks of arriving there. So for the first two or three weeks we stayed in his house . . . but Mother felt, I'm sure, sensitive to his position and so she said we must move out so . . . he said that we could have the little cottage.

'I'll ask the people who are there if they've got somewhere else to go to.'

So we did . . . That little cottage was really . . . if we had been allowed to stay there instead of being shifted once the soldiers came down, life would have been much, much better there.

. . . There were at the front door of the cottage, glass panes, and the bottom two had been kicked out at some time or other and just replaced by thick plastic. Anyway they were opaque, and when we first moved in it was not clean and a lot of work had to be done there to get it clean. I remember Mother putting a pillowcase over her head and some old clothes and getting to work seriously as an Australian countrywoman would. And there was a knock at the door and it was the local priest. Mother opened the door and said, 'What can I do for you?'

'Oh,' he said, 'You are newcomers. I've come to bless the house.'

And Mother said, 'Yes, you well may because there's a curse on every animal that crawls.'

There were fleas, and what are those things, lice, and just about everything. He took off his hat and turned around and went. He thought, 'These infidels.'

She closed the door. Mother thought, 'Oh dear what have I done?' So she got down on her hands and knees and lifted the plastic to see if he had gone and she met his nose on the other side. He wanted to see what we were doing inside. Nothing ever occurred anymore. We were left in peace.

... When we were first interned in Eboli, the authorities said, 'Okay, you have to come and sign an Act of Presence every day. You can stay here for the moment in this little person's shack. You can't have a wireless.'

But we had a nice little wireless. And my mother said, 'Do you think, if I give the wireless to the family next door, that after the war they might give it back to me?'

'Oh yes, you can do that. Just don't have a wireless.'

By this time we were on very good terms with the peasants next door and she explained the situation. He said, 'Signora, I'll bring it back under cover of darkness.'

And he crept back with this wireless and my brother made a special timber box to house the wood for the fire and cooking, and the wireless was underneath that. Several times the fascist authorities came down and sat on the box with the wireless underneath... But we only put it on very low and mainly late at night so we could listen to this Colonel Stevens from England to get any news. Naturally the news we had in the Italian papers was propaganda plus... thank goodness for that little wireless... Stevens in one of his talks late at night used the expression 'catch as catch can'. The following morning, it was a Saturday, we went out and everybody was in the piazza. It was market day. And you could hear Italians everywhere saying, '*catcha capore*'. 'Catch as catch can', which was a dead giveaway. They had been listening to the English wireless too. That buoyed us up no end.

. . . We'd only been in Eboli . . . I don't know, two months and we were interned, and suddenly one day one of the peasants came calling on Mother and she said, 'Signora, there's an Englishman there wanting to talk to you.'

So Mother came out, and in fact it turned out that he was Dutch. A Mr Geharnne I think. And he was Saville Row . . . he spoke perfect English. No accent at all. And Mother said to him, 'What are you doing in a hole like this?'

And he said, 'They have interned me. Why? Because I have oil wells.'

And he said, 'I'm going to get even, I'm going to get even with them. But while I'm here I'm glad to know there's someone else I can talk to.'

He was very, very kind. He asked my brother to do a sculpture of him in clay for which he paid him handsomely knowing full well that he could never take it away with him. He had had an extraordinary life. He had been interned in Russia at some stage. I can't remember all of his life story. But he was fascinating. He said, 'I have friends in the American Embassy, a Mr Perkins. I'll see to it that you get mail through. You may not be able to get money but you'll get mail.'

And he did. He kept his word. Mr Perkins came down to see us. And we managed to get some Red Cross messages through that way. Oh yes. He was there for a couple of months at least I guess and buoyed us up considerably.

. . . You must remember I was a pretty empty-headed young girl who thought of ballet and music and . . . so we're down with the peasants? So we're down with the peasants. The only thing that worried me was that I couldn't dance. There was even not anywhere that I could have exercised. Once I accepted it, and I accept things fairly easily, once I accepted that we'd be there for a while, never dreaming that it would be three and a half years, I set about living the life we could with pleasure. Getting to know the peasants.

... We were notified by the authorities that a platoon of soldiers had come down and were camped on the outskirts of the town of Eboli and for fear that we may corrupt the soldiers we were going to be sent elsewhere. First of all they put us on a bus and sent us high up in the mountains to a place called Teggiano. Amazingly there was what they called an inn. There were two rooms and food provided of sorts. But it was never used. It was filthy beyond description. The first night there we spent getting rid of every crawling beastie. Everything was horrible about it I guess. But mostly the dirt. Dreadful. You can't imagine having bad food and little insects but by golly they sure provided it. So Mother just went to the local authorities there and said, 'I'll walk down the mountain. You can shoot me but I'm not staying here. And my children will follow.'

Well they ummed and erred a good deal but eventually they relented and said there was somewhere else they could send us. So a couple of days later they put us on the bus and after many hours travelling on a rickety old bus going round and round the mountains we arrived at Oliveto Citra.

* * *

Firstly there we just had a one room which was the overnight stay for the policeman who would come around once a fortnight for all the crime and murder and whatever. That was a room with a washbasin and a toilet and one bed. My brother and I slept on the floor in the beginning. Then the authorities realised that they had to provide something better than that. So they persuaded these peasants who weren't using these quarters most of the time to allow us to have two rooms on top. It left them the room below where the cooking would go on. So what we had in the two rooms above was a chimney. In front of the chimney was a hole that big. It would be about a foot high and about a foot wide. And you made your fire in front of it because you couldn't get it inside. You made your fire in front of it and you had a tripod and a cauldron. So you went out to the village square with your bucket or your jug to collect the water and you took it home and you put it on there and you cooked your pasta or any form of grass that was edible. And we ate a lot of grass. Dandelions... not too bad. So that was the main cooking arrangement. In the same room there was actually a baker's oven, a big one but you would have needed lots of timber to light it, and what could you have baked in it?

... Oliveto Citra was more difficult from the point of view of living in the sense that we were high up. It snowed in the winter. Our shoes were wearing out fast and that's when my brother invented the soles which he attached. He went to the local tip and he found some rope about that thick and he borrowed a hammer and some tacks, and tacked that round and round and round the sole of the shoe. And then on the top of that he cut from tins, from the top bits of tin also about this wide which he put over the top of the rope. And so it would cling to the mountain side as we were walking and the rope would last. So that was good. The heating, with snow on the ground in winter time... the cold, and our heating was a brazier. Do you know what that is? Quite a nice looking copper plate about so big with little charcoals in it. So you virtually almost sit on it to get any warmth. And we noticed that most of the women, because the place was mainly full of women and old men, they had marks, sort of black and red marks up and down their legs from being close to these braziers.

... We always stood out by our dress. We were never dressed like peasants. We had the clothes we had when we were first interned. Most peasants always wore a 'kerchief around their head. A scarf. Which we didn't. And Mother, both in Eboli and Oliveto Citra wore, as most Australian ladies did, particularly from the country, she wore a hat. And she was known in Oliveto Citra as *La Senora Carcopelo*... The Lady with the Hat. Mother said to us, 'Now it says in the Bible that you should go to the house of God to pray. I'll leave it up to you two. This is a Catholic church and we are Anglican, for what little difference there is. Not very much.'

She said, 'Shall we go to church on Sundays or shall we not?'

And we said, 'Yes we think we should.'

And so we did. Yes, it was a very wise decision. That integrated us better with the locals.

* * *

The only really unpleasant force if you like to use the word, was when we first arrived at Oliveto Citra. He was the power in the village. I think he was the mayor and fascist secretary all rolled into one. And he was pompous and very, very fascist and he thought, 'Ah, two women. I can get them to work in the house free. No payment.'

So once an abode had been found such as it was, and I must say that when we moved into the accommodation, and there was really no furniture... when we moved in, in the morning, by the end of that day, almost everybody in the village had provided us with something. Pillows, blankets, sheets, towels, a saucepan or two, a bucket. They got together... but this mayor cum fascist secretary, he said, 'I want you to come to my place. Be there at eight o'clock in the morning and you can clean and you can do the dishes. You can make the beds and you can also help my wife to make the pasta.'

And Mother said to us, 'We know we shouldn't be doing these things but he's such a power here that if we refuse he may send word to Salerno and invent something that wasn't true, and we could be put in gaol. Heaven knows what.'

So we started, Mother and I. My brother Bob was not required. We started doing all these things; cleaning the house and helping with the preparation of the food, but in the meantime we were talking to the other people all around the piazza and we told them the story. They were furious and we found that he had a very bad name and they hated him. Apparently he was behaving abominably to all... see they were nearly all women. So it was not long, maybe two months, and one morning we heard a commotion outside and we saw a crowd of women converging on the piazza with pitchforks and brooms and anything they could find and all going en masse to the little town hall where they picked up the ink pot, threw it at this man and said, 'Get out! *Via, Via!*'

So in fact he was removed and someone else came in his place who was quite amenable to us.

* * *

There was a family, a husband and wife and two small boys. The husband had been the taxi driver for the whole village and of course the government had taken away his car. So he had nothing more to do. And he came to see my mother and he said, 'If you are desperate for money, I will lend you some money. I have some put by. I know you're British and I can rely on the British, so I'm quite happy to lend you some money.'

Mother would not accept it but she surely appreciated it very much. One of his sons had had polio and was quite disabled with it and Mother had been a nurse and read the story of Sister Elizabeth Kenny [the Australian nurse, 1886–1952, who pioneered controversial polio treatments], I think she went to America. She said, 'I think massage can help.'

And so a couple of times a week she went to their house and spent quite a long time massaging this boy's limbs. When we went back after the war, he was walking unaided. Had a limp but was running a café, very successfully. And he said, 'God bless you!'

… We must have been there for at least a year and Rosetta from the chemist shop said, 'They've sent notice from Salerno (which was the closest big city) to say that people are coming round to give and demonstrate a permanent wave if anybody is interested.'

And I think quite a few of the peasants had never heard of it and were probably interested to have a permanent wave. So Mother said, 'That will be fun to watch.'

So the people duly arrived and they set themselves up in the one room of the little inn and in those days, in the very, very early days and probably it was no longer existing here, but there, the permanent-waving system, you were attached to some sort of big hood with little corkscrew things that went up into this hood and once you were attached and all your hair was caught up in these corkscrew things, they switched on the electricity for a few minutes and you were cooked. Anyway people were too frightened to come forward to have it done. Mother never being afraid of anything said, 'I'll give it a go.'

And they said, 'All right, if you want to be the first one we'll do it for you free.'

'Great,' said Mother.

So about eleven o'clock in the morning, she sits down in the chair and laboriously the hair is wound around these corkscrew things so she's all up like this. Can't hardly move. And they turn on the electricity and it goes off.

Now the electricity depended on these friends of ours all the way down in the valley where it took about three-quarters of an hour to walk down and another three-quarters of an hour to come back again. Nobody seemed to have heard of the telephone. Perhaps they didn't have one. But Mother was sitting there for hours while someone went all the way down there and told them to switch it on again and all the way back again, and they switched it on and for a few minutes . . . and it worked reasonably well. But the whole of the village was outside all looking in at this. It was the greatest peepshow ever. And then because of what had happened no one was keen to have it because it might go off again and they'd had have to sit there for all those hours. It was a bit of a fiasco. But to us it was very funny. Oh dear oh dear.

. . . We were given . . . that was by the lady next door, some sugar, and we sat and looked at that sugar for a few days because we hadn't seen any for ages. And Mother said, 'Suppose we borrow a donkey from somewhere and we go up and get the timber and we light this oven and make a sponge cake?'

How wonderful. So we borrowed a donkey and we went to get fuel. Also we had kept . . . every now and again we would be given an egg and so we had kept three eggs, just enough to make this. And if you had seen our three eager faces with the flames going up and this sponge cake rising and rising and then collapsing down to that. They call it in Italian *pane di Spagna* which is Spanish bread . . . well, it taught us how to make do with very little.

We had one very cold, wet winter in 1942. We couldn't go out. We had no raincoats. We had no umbrellas and it made it very difficult to go working for the peasants to get food in return. We had cornmeal and water and you would cook that up and it made a gruel. But even that with the weather turned mildew. But when you're hungry you eat anything.

... We made, with the help of the peasants, homemade pasta, and some of them had white flour, some didn't. If it was white flour it was great and it was beautiful pasta. We made bottles and bottles and bottles of tomato sauce, and they used mainly wine bottles or beer bottles with you know, that top with the rubber that you pull down. They would put them in a container and boil them. But they were beautiful tomatoes. Alas we don't seem to have the same tomatoes with the same flavour here. They grew their own basil so they had the flavour of that. Biscotti ... they taught us the use of biscotti. In other words, whoever had a baker's oven would make their bread about every three weeks. So they would make enough to last them. If they ran out they had what they called the biscotti, a loaf like the bread with an indentation about an inch and a half wide, just slightly done with a knife. And then left in the oven ... after all the bread was finished, it was left in the oven really overnight until they were quite hard. And then, when the bread was finished after two or three weeks, they would put this under running water and it became almost like fresh bread.

... Another personality in the village was Maria ... she had one eye the size of a big marble. It was a false eye. It was extraordinary and really made her look terrible. She said she could cure all ills. And we all had bad jaundice which really affects the liver very badly. We had jaundice. Bob had typhoid fever, and malaria. We all had malaria, bad malaria. And the only thing they cured us with was goats' milk. So this woman, she was old ... Maria the Witch. She came round and she said to Bob, 'Cut off your toenails and I will put them under the front door in the sand and in so many days you will be cured.'

Well we thought we had better do what we were told to do, but of course it didn't make any difference. He would have gotten over it anyway. But she went around the village curing people that way, like a witchdoctor. And people accepted her. Fortunately we had a proper doctor next door and he just said for things like malaria that they didn't have all the correct drugs. He said, 'Rest and goats' milk and eat very little and it will pass.'

And eventually we improved. The malaria came back to me in 1951 in the Bathurst Hospital.

* * *

When the newspapers carried the headlines that Australia was surrounded by the Japanese, we thought that was the most terrible news that could ever, ever reach us. My mother said, 'The Australians will fight to the death and there will be nothing left.'

And we had visions of not having any country, any home to come home to. It left us feeling really shocked, empty, awful. I think it's the only time that I as a young girl felt that I would go off my rocker. I felt like tearing my hair out by the roots. If it hadn't been for the broadcasts from the BBC at night, that saved us. Really. I do think a lot of them ... We were not afraid. It was more a sense of hopelessness. Will it ever end? Will we ever be home again? It must have been far worse for my mother, far, far worse.

... The local authorities told us that information had come through that we could be put on a special train if we so wished, to leave by such and such a date. They gave us very little notice I might add. I've sometimes wondered more about that, but I don't think it was an exchange of prisoners. I think it was simply ... this is how I feel: The Allies were about to land very shortly at Salerno beachhead and they knew the moment they did, the Germans ... would swoop down and of course they did. And so with the International Red Cross, I think they tried to get as many people out as they could ... but not my brother. My brother was of military age, so he would have to stay ... because he had an Italian passport. Because he was born there . . . My mother went through turmoil of indecisions about whether to leave him.

. . . It was just suffering on both sides. It was because of what he said that we went. Mother said, 'I can't bear to leave you behind.'

He said, 'I'll hide. Everybody knows me here now, we're all friends. I'll go higher up into the mountains where they have goatherds and the like, making cheese and so on. I'll go up there and I'll hide. Nobody ever comes up there if they have no reason to.'

That was his reasoning anyway. I believe he probably could have hidden almost anywhere. I don't think the Germans would have known that there was someone there of any interest I suppose. But in any case he said, 'With the Germans coming down, you'll either go back to a camp in Germany or far worse as women. You must leave.'

So we did.

. . . I don't think we ever quite recovered from that. It was never quite the same again. Because although we thought it wouldn't be long before he would join us, it was a long time before he did. And as far as he was concerned we were going into very troubled waters anyway. But it was his decision and he was old enough to decide. I'm glad he did in one way. He was quite all right as it turned out except for the brief moment he appeared out of the mountain side and shouted to the American soldiers . . . 'Hey!' . . . He went higher up into the mountains with a couple of the peasants and they were hiding because they knew the Germans were swarming around and when the Germans disappeared slowly and the Americans were then coming he thought, that's fine, we're liberated. So he jumped up and rushed down the side of the mountain calling out and waving his hands. And the Americans nearly shot him because they thought he was a spy.

* * *

It was a very interesting train load. People of many nationalities really . . . we had been told that we would get back to England. That's all we knew. We knew the train would take us up to the north of Italy which it did. We went up as far as Bologna. We spent one night in Bologna in quarters. Then back on the train across France, Spain and Portugal. Every station that we stopped at there was a row of German soldiers along the train, but in France, behind the German soldiers there were French ones making the V for victory sign and winking at us.

Eventually we arrived in Portugal and that was like a fairytale. Just like a fairytale. So we were put in what was then quite a nice spacious one- or two-star hotel, in a very fashionable suburb called Cascais … to be in Portugal, to be free even if we didn't have any money. The food! White bread and coffee … it was a very busy city with people from everywhere. I have no doubt it was a hot bed of spies.

… I wish I knew the name of the British Consul because the group … we were mainly women of course on the train, some of them went to see the Consul and said, 'Look we know perfectly well that when we get to England, there will be coupons for this and coupons for that and they will be short of everything and we won't be able to buy things. We need shoes and clothes.'

So the British Consul did the best he could which was to issue them with coupons so they could go and buy shoes and so on. They were going in two by two and when our turn came Mother and I … went in, sat down, were received very nicely by the British Consul and Mother looked at him in her funny way and she said, 'You know, you look exactly like a Miss McIntyre in the year 1920 something or other going between Adelaide and Perth.'

He said, 'That would have been my sister!'

And he described her and Mother said, 'That's who it was. We travelled all the way between Adelaide and Perth.'

So they chatted and chatted and after a while, he had a pair of pince-nez [reading glasses] and he looked over his pince-nez at my feet and he said, 'Now, dear, I presume you want a pair of Topi sandals don't you?'

And I was very fashion conscious at that time. And I said, 'Yes I would.'

And he put his hand in his pocket and he took out ten pounds sterling from his wallet and he said, 'Now dear, you go and buy yourself the nicest pair of Topi sandals that you can find.'

And I did and I've blessed him ever since and I wore them for years and years and I thought that was a lovely thing to do.

* * *

Every day we would receive notification. We were going, we weren't going, and we had to get ready and then when eventually the time came we took off late at night and all the windows were wooded in. It was a Dutch plane. When we arrived in England the Customs were very careful. One woman, she was . . . a singer. She had a lovely voice. She entertained us a few times in the hotel. While waiting for them to go through her affairs, she started to make up and she produced a lipstick and she was going through all this.

And the Customs Officer said, 'Just a moment, may I have the lipstick?'

He took the lipstick and turned it upside down and emptied out the other side and there was a diamond about this big.

Anyway we were hustled on and then we were searched. Nicely, but we were searched and then so to London. I think we were so tired, I don't remember the train trip. It's hazy. We were so tired. I just remember arriving at Paddington Station and Mother saying, 'There must be rooms near Paddington Station.'

And that's where we found rooms, at Paddington Station. Nice landlady and every time there was an air-raid alarm we went down into the cellar because the shelters on either side were too far. So Mother tried to contact the Bank of Australasia to find it had been bombed and because of that their records had been lost. They had no signature. So it was going to take weeks for any money from Australia. So she said, 'What am I going to do?'

They had lost her signature so we really had a problem. But there were two people in England who saved our lives. One was Bishop Crotty from Bathurst who was a very close family friend . . . Mother thought we'd go straight to St Pancras to see him. So off we went to St Pancras—flattened. Nothing there. And then we saw this little old lady walking across St Pancras Square and Mother said, 'I bet she's a local, she'll know.' So she said, 'Bishop Crotty?'

And she said, 'Yes, down at Hove. I can give you the address.'

So we contacted Bishop Crotty and darling Bishop Crotty lent us I think fifty pounds sterling which was a lot of money in those days. Mother also had a cousin, a distant cousin, Lady Abenger, who lived up in Scotland so she contacted her and she sent us some money until finally we received money from Australia.

We were in this boarding house for a few weeks and then Bishop Crotty came up to London and said, 'I can find you better accommodation. One of my young curates has a nice little flat near St Pancras Church. I'm sure for a nominal rent you will be able to have that.'

So that was fixed. We moved in there. In the meantime Mother went immediately to work close by in an American club, and then to the Boomerang Club. Everybody had to be actively engaged in the war effort, or entertaining the troops or whatever. So it was decided that I would go and apply to Sadler's Wells. I knew I hadn't done any dancing for two and a half years, but they might take that into consideration... so I went with what information I had, the gold medal and certificate. So yes they accepted me at Sadler's Wells in the classes. And I started very slowly and the teacher was Russian, with very little English and very little French. And so when I explained that I must go slowly, that I was very stiff, '*Nyet*'. He just took my leg and... what did he do? He tore a tendon in the groin and I collapsed in pain, went home, called the doctor and he said, 'I'm very sorry. That will take you quite a long time to get over that. There's nothing to do except rest.' He said, 'In peacetime you'd sue them, now you can't.'

So I was in bed for a short time and then I received notice that I was called up. Instead I applied for a job at the Foreign Office because of my languages, and so that was really the end of the ballet career. Even when I came back to Australia it was never the same again. So that was that.

* * *

On my day off from the Foreign Office I went to work at the Boomerang Club, serving luncheons and teas and coffee and so on, to our boys. And that was fun. I upset some scalding hot tea on a wing commander once, on his bald patch. Terrible. And then we saw so many come in wounded, scarred, sad, awful. But I became a member of the Overseas League and I went to dances at the Overseas League where I met Polish Air Force, French Air Force, Belgium Air Force, Americans by the millions and Australians, and I must say as a general rule, all the air forces were well behaved. The Americans too. Very polite. Very, very nice and thoughtful. Running late, ring you up, catch a taxi, yes. And I was spoilt. Totally spoilt. I had a lovely time. Dreadful isn't it? War time.

... In the building where we had our flat there was no cellar and we were far away from the closest air-raid shelters. Everybody in the building was told to go into the corridors, take their tin helmets, lie down and try and go to sleep and hope that the glass windows wouldn't be blown in. There was an Australian journalist in there, Keith Hooper, who worked for *The Truth*. He was in a flat on the floor above. And for the company he would come down with his tin hat and lie down beside Mother and me and chat until we went off to sleep. He was a funny guy. Good company. He really was very nice to a young girl. He took me sometimes to parties and on one night he brought some people home to his little flat and he let off a Verey [flare] cartridge and the smoke went everywhere. People came out. Silly Keith. [Before this, Keith Hooper had actually fought in the AIF at Bardia and Tobruk. He was captured by the Germans in Greece, became a POW, and escaped back to England at his sixth attempt.]

... My main job at the Foreign Office was going through the Italian newspapers picking out items of interest, or what I thought were items of interest and translating them into English. That was the main thing. Nothing very complicated. Never very complicated really. Translating... There were two of us working in the office, and we were approached by our immediate boss one night and he said, 'I have something to ask you two girls. There are some very high-ranking Chinese Air Force gentlemen here and they would like to go out for dinner to a Chinese restaurant and they've asked if some of the girls from the Foreign Office could accompany them.'

They were looking for some female company. She and I looked at each other . . . we didn't speak a word of Chinese. But he said, 'They speak some English and they've asked, so could you go?'

So we said, 'Well why not?' Nice meal.

And there were two girls and I think there were six Chinese, and one spoke just enough English. And another one, not enough English but he had a dictionary which was one inch by one inch. And every second or third word the thumb would go leafing through this tiny little dictionary. And he tried to tell us this funny story which went on and on. Oh dear. I remember my embarrassment. We had meatballs of some description. Goodness knows what the meat was . . . Anyway it went fine. The Foreign Office thanked us very much.

* * *

The war was still on. But we were allowed to return to Australia. We came out on a ship with the Duke and Duchess of Gloucester. Why we did and how we did is another thing I'd like to know . . . We spent the Christmas of '44/45 on board ship coming out and we went right up into the North Sea because the ship was obviously targeted by the Germans, and I know during the middle of the night we let off some depth charges which made the most frightful noise and terrified everybody. The Duchess of Gloucester spoke to everybody in the morning. She said, 'Now I think we're safe everybody. If you were wondering what the noise was, that was it.'

So a fairly uneventful trip. We had a concert on board and I danced for royalty. Funny. Then we came home . . . the very day that we got off the ship, we sat down on the wharf and ate bananas and passionfruit brought to us by friends and family.

. . . It was new again. Another new life. I started teaching Spanish dancing. I went back for ballet classes because I loved ballet and I went back to Leon Kellaway. He was much older too. He was very happy to see me. I shared some of my lessons with a young girl who went on to join the Australian Ballet and became one of its stars, Kathleen Gorham [dancer, 1932–83]... And I had a bit of fun too because I had missed three and a half years of growing up at a time when you're carefree and nothing matters. And so I went out a lot and had some fun, and then an acquaintance from New Caledonia came to stay with me and celebrated her twenty-first birthday and so I had a party and invited a French wool buyer. And at the last minute one of the number rang up to say... a German as a matter of fact, he couldn't come, he was going to Canberra. I said, 'Oh dear. I need a boy.'

So I rang the French wool buyer and he said, 'Don't you worry. I know just the man.'

And he brought along my [future] husband who told me that he had been told two months beforehand, 'There's going to be a great party, I'll see to it that you're invited.' So there you are.

* * *

In the beginning the only communication we had from my brother was from the American forces. An American padre kept on sending us messages. Then he came out in 1947... and it was extremely tearful on my part and my mother's part and our celebration at Romano's Restaurant in Sydney... But he didn't know what to do with himself. He thought that he would go back to Bathurst and perhaps manage the farm and do architecture by correspondence, which he finally did. He was okay. I mean he made plans for motels in Bathurst. He never became a top-notch architect and he was never cut out to go on the land. So later on he moved into town and started his own arts supplies. And he was quite happy with that because it gave him time to paint and draw, and he sculptured most beautifully I thought. He drew most beautifully.

... I can only say as I've repeated so often, one of the greatest blessings of human nature I think is that when you look back on suffering, and there were definitely very hard times, you think of the better times. So that now I remember the days of internment more happily than sadly. It's not that I forget the difficult moments, but I remember the kind people that we met and some of the happy times we had. How can you regret something over which you have no control? Yes I regret I wasn't able to become a prima ballerina. That mainly. But I had really no control over that from the day Italy came into the war. That was that . . . I can only say that reading, seeing films which I've subsequently seen, people that I've met, people who came out on the ship with my brother, a Polish doctor . . . our war was a picnic in comparison. So I have a lot to be thankful for. Ours was a picnic.

. . . No matter how difficult things can become, say to yourself, you will overcome them because you will. And then when you look back on them they're not nearly so bad as what you thought at the time. That's what I think. Make the most of what you have. In my case it included food and everything. We made the most of everything we could. And believe in people.

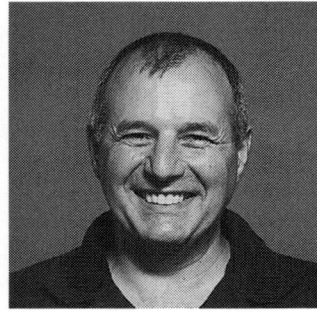

SALVATORE ANDALORO

Intelligence Corps
Western Sahara UN Mission
East Timor

My dad was easygoing, which is bizarre considering how strict he was and how hard working... but he had a genuine love of life I guess. He had been in the Italian Navy during the Second World War. He had been to places like Tobruk and he had seen some horrible things, and I think that might have coloured his outlook when he came out here. It was a lot easier out here, they came out in 1952. Dad came out in 1949 and then my mum and the brothers and sisters came out three years after. So I think having seen all of the hardships in Italy and Sicily and having been involved in the war, once he got here he tended to be a lot more easygoing as far as life went, but still maintaining the traditional values as far as the family went. And as I say, my mum was the strong one within the family. She laid down the law and he just beat it into them.

... I think Mum was the matriarch of the family, Sicilians are very much like the New Guinean people, they're very much a matriarchal family, the fellow thinks that he is in control and in front of his mates, 'Yeah just do what I tell you.' But it is the women in a Sicilian household that run it. Mum was more the guiding star, she was the one that forced him to put the deposit down on a house and she was the one that saved the money. My dad had an incredible love of life. He worked hard with the city council and on a Friday afternoon he would come home and I remember he would have his arms full of grocery shopping. And there would be fruit and bread and cheese and he would come home and open Mum's fridge up, pull out the vegetable crisper, upend it, fill it up with grapes and crush all of these grapes manually and make this really rough red. And he really liked his food. Used to watch him have huge amounts of spaghetti. So he had a huge love of life and Mum was the level-headed one, but he was also the enforcer. Like if anything went wrong Mum would just look at one of the kids and Dad would be after them.

... I still miss my dad. I go out to the cemetery and I have a bit of a chat. I miss the things that I didn't get to share with him, my service life and whatnot, he had a service background. I miss him taking me down to the Brisbane River to do crabbing which we used to do in those days down near the Grey Street Bridge, William Jolly Bridge there. I miss him taking me to the pub when I was twelve years old, he would get me a cherry soda and he would be there with his mates. I miss him taking me to work when he was a city council worker. Giving me a bottle of Coke and saying, 'Stand over there while we do this.' It is a long time ago but I still miss him.

... I remember having a pair of, to my eternal shame, those huge clodhopper shoes. Blue suede, they were blue suede shoes but they had a huge heel on them. Big glary shirts, which went really well with a little woggy boy like me because I had very thick curly hair and a dark, swarthy complexion. I didn't really fit into any of that because I was so short, so stocky and I wasn't really a John Travolta, it was only later that I lost a lot of weight; I lost twenty-five kilos. But fashion for me was always a problem because of colouring, stature. And to be honest I wasn't really into fashion, I went to a conservative school, Marist Brothers. Conservative family ... there wasn't a lot of girls in our street so you didn't have that natural competition amongst males to preen themselves, dress-up for girls. It was more jeans and footy shorts for me.

... Elvis Presley. He was my man; I still am an Elvis Presley fan which puts me at odds with a lot of other people ... I have got stuff there from the 1950s to the 1970s; each of those boxes is a decade ...

I have got original LPs in there that cost me I guess, two dollars fifty, three dollars, that are in mint condition. I have got everything. I have got movie music, Christmas music, his soul music, got everything. To me he was a consummate performer; it wasn't only one sort of music ... it was a very sad day when he died

... In the 1960s there were all of the standard jokes, 'How many gears has an Italian tank got?' 'One forward, and four reverse.' All of that sort of stuff.

'What's the shortest book in the world?' 'The Italian book of heroes.'

'Ah, you dago, you wog,' all of this.

I copped that every day. And because I was born here I went into denial very early. I used to say, 'Hang on, I was born here, I am Australian.'

And then I would go home and say, 'You bloody wogs, look what you have done, caused me all sorts of trouble.'

And I would get a backhand, 'Never forget your heritage, son.'

'Oh okay.'

So it was a cloud. And the Italians in North Africa, tens of thousands of them surrendering to very few Allied soldiers. So it took me a long time to come to grips with that and it was a shadow, but I know a lot more now. More background to what was going on.

* * *

We got on the bus to Melbourne in the morning in Brisbane. And our escort officer was a warrant officer that was resigning or discharging, this was his last job, and he was very easygoing all of the way down. We basically knew the rank structure and a warrant officer is up there as a soldier. And we thought, 'Oh this isn't so tough!'

And I remember on the way down the guys were sticking their heads out and yahooing at women and brown-eyeing cars, and I remember sitting there pretty quietly thinking, 'This army life is pretty good, look we have got a warrant officer he doesn't care, it can't be that hard.'

And we got down to Kapooka in the evening, about seven or eight o'clock. And the bus stopped and the air brakes hissed and the door opened and the screaming started. And there was yellow lines just outside the entrance to the bus and it was, 'Get out and put your toes on the line and do this and that!'

And they were still getting over the ride down . . . and the next morning it was even worse, it was six o'clock and people were screaming and yelling. And as we were walking from the initial accommodation block to another building it was like hazing at a university or something. All of the recruits that had been there for a while were all yahooing, or laughing at you, because you have all got long curly hair or moustaches or beards, whatever . . . and I think the first thing they did was all into the barbers, and it was like . . . *Biloxi Blues* or one of those movies, I remember three but there were probably more, barber's chairs, and they just sat you down and the old barber's clippers came out and *zzzt, zzzt*, two minutes and it was all over. You would go in like this and I can remember walking out, because I had sort of an Afro I guess, because I had long curly hair, and I remember going out and the guys were looking at me in shock, and some of them had shoulder-length hair and tears in their eyes. So that initial shearing of all of your hair, that is your first introduction to group mentality, because you all look the same after that. And then they did all of the administration side of it and then they started issuing gear, and I will always remember, I don't know if they still do it now but they did then, you could virtually turn up at Kapooka with the clothes you stood in and nothing else. They gave you a brown paper bag and in there was shaving gear and soap, toothpaste and toothbrushes, because guys came from all over Australia, they came from the country, the city, wealthy families, or poverty. So the system looked after you from the word go.

. . . My everlasting memory from Kapooka and it is the worst habit I have got, is scoffing my food. Unless I am talking to people and having a conversation I just stuff my food so quickly. We had a thousand recruits at Kapooka when I was there and you would come off the range for lunch and you would have fifteen minutes, and there would be a thousand blokes lined up. You would just rush through and if you happened to be midway or towards the end you would have five minutes before you were due outside and get ready for the next activity. So you would sit down and scoff your food, hot, cold it didn't matter, get it into you and get outside and get ready.

... I am a hundred kilos now; I was seventy-five kilos then. It was difficult to a degree but once you get into it, they build you up. The hardest thing for me was to climb the ropes. Everything else I managed to get through, that's where I learnt very quickly in army life you never do your best in the first physical test. Never push yourself to the extreme because when they repeat that test in two weeks time you had better do better or there will be trouble. That's what happened to me, I did my best on the first test and two weeks later I only bettered it by one or two push-ups and only did better in the run by a few seconds and, 'Not good enough Andaloro, you have been here for two weeks, you're bludging, you're coasting aren't you?'

So you always do enough to keep them happy in the first lot and then gradually improve. Never volunteer. Never tell people what sort of licences you have got, you just be the grey man. Be the grey man.

* * *

Back then in the 1970s drinking was the thing; it was part of our culture. That has changed completely now. Back then if you went out with the boys everybody drank beer or spirits and you all got rolling drunk and you did all sorts of things together. Nowadays young soldiers are more wont to drink a can of Coke... Personal space was very small in those days because you weren't expected to have a TV or stereo or record player, computers weren't around. It was basically just a bed, locker and your clothes locker whereas the young soldiers now they have individual rooms, they are all modulated, there is four individual rooms and a little common room. Every soldier has got his own stereo, a colour TV, a computer, a Game Boy or Xbox. Young soldiers will listen to hip hop, rap, American crap, just as soon as anybody outside would. That's been a big change too

I think, in that young soldiers, the Defence Force has always been a microcosm of what's going on outside. A little bit more conservative, but it has always been civilian people putting on a uniform, thinking the same way but still wanting to be part of society at large. So as Australian society has become more liberated and our thought processes have changed. That all flows into the Defence Force. And a young soldier now relates much more to people outside then I ever did as a soldier. When I was a soldier there was them and us, whereas now it is very much an us and us philosophy, which has got its good and bad points.

... Having served with lots and lots of girls and lots and lots of blokes, if a girl wants to become a member of the Special Air Service Regiment and she can perform all of the tasks and do all of the training and pass all of the courses, she should be allowed to have a go. If there is a problem with the blokes working with her then that's their problem... I think years ago it really was a problem because females were put on a pedestal, females were the child-bearers, they were the weaker sex, they were there to be nurtured and they weren't there to do a combat role. And there was a problem because if an artillery round or a mortar round or a tank round goes off near you, normally you're stripped bare, all of your clothes are stripped off, you might be dismembered or whatever. And there was a problem with blokes seeing a female in that situation because we were taught to respect and protect women and I think by and large that is still there, although not to the same degree. But all the girls I have seen, and I know for a fact that you can send them anywhere, and within their employment they will do as good a job wherever they are. So if a girl can do an infantryman's job and she is prepared to do a dump sitting next to a bloke and she is prepared to get in and have a common shower, not a segregated shower, and if she is prepared to do everything that is expected of an infantry soldier, good luck to her. But girls fart, swear, smoke, cuss better. Not the same as, better than blokes. Still a long way to go and it is not at the political level or the upper leadership level, it is at the digger level and it is the blokes being able to accept. They will accept girls working in the unit no problem at all, but it is still a long way to go before you will see a *Starship Troopers* type scenario where the girls are in sharing with the blokes, and that's what it has got to come down to. If girls want to have the opportunity to serve in all of these specialist units and specialist corps that's what they have to give up; all vestiges of being a female. You can still be feminine but you can't be female if that makes sense.

The downside of that is that that respect that I was talking about, that is by and large being lost. I found that some of the girls coming out of Kapooka, because they feel they have something to prove to the blokes, or they want to be tougher than the blokes, or whatever reason, they come out a lot harsher and a lot harder than a lot of the blokes. As soon as a girl starts swearing, particularly an army girl, because they swear better than blokes, they lose that respect. They might say, 'Yeah you're one of us.'

But they go away, 'She's a slut.'

Because of the way they talk, smoke, act. And all the girl is trying to do is be one of the boys, but you can't be one of the boys because you're not a boy. You can drink with them, laugh with them, go out with them, do what you want. But don't try to be a boy because you're not a boy, in that environment. I mean girls in civilian street swear and carry on I know, but don't try and be better than the boys, don't try and join the game of 'I am more macho than you', because you're not a bloke. Having said that I have seen the other side, wonderful people, females, do a wonderful job, better than the males. And not only in the clerical, medical or signals side, in intelligence, transport side. All sorts of areas. It all comes down to the individual nowadays.

* * *

Combat intelligence is basically where a commander has an information requirement, he says, 'I need to know this by this time.'

And it is up to you to use what we call the intelligence cycle, get the information or task sources and agencies, get the information, collate it, analyse it and make sure it gets to the commander in time.

Counter intelligence is identifying your opponent's capabilities and what he wants to know and then taking measures to stop him getting that information. And with that you're talking about espionage, terrorism, subversion, that sort of thing. I was trained in both of those areas. My first posting in intelligence corps was primarily combat intelligence with a task force or brigade in Townsville, and at that level at that stage I used to mark battle maps, collect information, maintain a battle log, that sort of stuff at a junior level. And get all of that together for the sergeant and the captain to do their analysis and they would do the briefings.

My preference if you can call it a preference, or my forte, is interrogation. I like interrogation, and it is not the beating or the slapping about that you see in the movies. How we're trained, and we are trained very strictly according to the Geneva Convention, this is when we're operating as Australian interrogators, it really is using your mind. And it's a mind game with whoever you're interrogating so I tended to move towards that.

It is a specialised course that we do at our school at Canungra. There is a little bit of psychology involved, we had a psychologist come along and explain about personality types and flaws and strengths. And then you're taught the various methods and techniques of interrogation. Whether it is going to be a harsh, abrasive interrogation or going to be a soft, appealing one, what you're trained to do initially is identify somebody's character traits. Whether they are an easygoing character, whether they are hyperactive, frightened, a mummy's boy, so you try and identify the character he is. And that would dictate the approach or the technique you take against that person. I say person because we do girls as well now which is good.

See I loved doing officers because officers, apart from my feelings towards them, they are trained to think logically, they can't help themselves. So what you would use against an officer would be a logical approach. You would attack him logically, you know, 'Why can't you tell me that? Why are you being an idiot? It's on your ID tag, your field notebook. Is that your shirt? Well it was in your pocket. What's your problem?'

And you can attack things logically. And with officers they like looking down their noses at diggers and we never wore rank, but even if they identify that you're a digger and in my case it was easy because I tended to be older than the general officer, they would try and outwit you, which was lovely because you want them to talk, you want them to put you down. To say something apart from number, name, rank, date of birth, 'I can't answer that, Sir.'

That's all they're supposed to say. But if they want to play little games with me, I used to love it, it was good.

... We used to conduct two types of training in the Australian Army. We used to conduct what was called resistance to interrogation training. That would be against our own people. And then we used to do training according to the Geneva Convention. Resistance to interrogation training was designed so that high-risk capture people such as Special Forces or submariners ... would have a benchmark of what to expect if they were captured, the sort of techniques and methods that would be used against them. What their requirements were under the Geneva Convention, what their rights were under the Geneva Convention, so that they would have an idea. The hardest thing for a soldier to do when he is captured is to sit there and say nothing, or become abusive because he doesn't know what to do. And we found that quite often the soldier that hadn't received our training went one of three ways; they would abuse the hell out of you, and suffer the consequences. We were enemy interrogators, acting as enemy interrogators, which meant different uniforms, the whole box and dice. We weren't Australians at all. They would abuse you, they wouldn't say a word or they would say too much. The guys that had had the training, they knew what the benchmark was and that's when it became a game between you and the person as to what you could extract ... and when we were training as Australian interrogators, it was designed to train us as to what our rights were as the capturing power but also what the Geneva Convention stated in certain circumstances.

So we played two roles, we played enemy interrogator and Australian interrogator, or trained as both. Of the two I prefer enemy interrogator because you can do so much more. When you're training as an Australian interrogator for real, for deployment overseas as I was in East Timor, you are really restricted as to what you can do. Very much so. Whereas when you are being trained as an enemy interrogator, even though you would never be employed in that role overseas, you can do a lot to our own people because that's what they would get... Special Forces people, particularly in the west, received much harsher training than people on the east coast did, than the general army did. I will say safety was never impinged, safety was always a priority and you could push to a certain barrier. On the east coast you could never touch anybody; you never beat them up or slap them around. Torturing people never works, because if you torture long enough they will tell you what they think you want them to say... torture and some of the older drugs don't work. You hear what you want to hear and with the drugs people just ramble. The newer drugs are better, but with the older drugs people would just ramble and you would have to pluck bits of information out of that. We were trained to use our minds I guess, that was the only way to do it. And you would augment that with captured equipment. So if you captured someone and he had a backpack or webbing or an officer's bag all of that would be gone through while you are talking to the bloke and then you would correlate information from both sides.

... Up until about 1994, resistance to interrogation training was very common. In fact that was my stock and trade for many years. After 1994 there were a few instances where a few people complained and it became extremely sensitive and political so they stopped enemy interrogation training for quite a few years. And to this day it is only conducted under very strict guidelines and only to very restricted units... So we would go to a unit in barracks for instance and we would give the Geneva Convention lessons and also resistance to interrogation theory. We would say, 'These are the type of methods and techniques that may be employed against you.' And then six or eight months later when that unit was out bush or on a course or whatever, we would bag the unit or an element of the unit. We would get them when they were tired or hungry, at their lowest physically and psychologically. Get them at that level...and even though in the back of their minds, particularly with the officers, they know what's going on, it is amazing how the military hierarchy kicks in. Where authoritarianism kicks in, where people will instinctively obey certain commands without you having to touch them. Once you get somebody to start talking or to inadvertently finger somebody else, it is like a floodgate. That logic kicks in, they think, 'Okay we will do this and this...'

And at the end of each exercise there would be a group debrief where the interrogation centre commander would get up and debrief everybody as a group and then there would be individual debriefs, you would take individuals aside and go through each session, each interrogation session and say,

'These are your strengths and weakness. You can improve here and you did really well here. This is where the Geneva Convention could have protected you.'

So each person would go away, no matter who they were, would go away with a bit of knowledge.

... There are various levels of interrogation and my level was purely and simply battlefield interrogation. Get the information, short-term information, and get it back as quickly as possible, that other stuff, I am not interested in that stuff, but you could use that against somebody if they weren't saying anything at all.

'Mate, it is here, Geneva Convention, I have highlighted it for you. I need to know where you were born, I need to know the name of your mum, your dad's name, you have got no ID card on you, no ID tags on you, it says here that we need to be provided with these items.' Which it does.

'I need to take your photo, I need your fingerprints, I need this information.'

And it is all information that you can use then.

'Oh you're from Victoria, mate? You follow Aussie Rules?' Blah, blah.

And you just go down the track, 'Oh you must have worked for Victoria Barracks, what were you doing there, mate?'

You can do it that way or you can yell at somebody or you can say, 'Mate, I am not real smart and if you don't tell me this basic information which is basic administration, they're going to kick my arse. I would like it if you can help me.'

And some of them look at you and think, you are an idiot. And they say, 'I was born in Victoria okay if that helps you at all.'

Because they think they're doing you a favour.

* * *

In 1991 my OC, my officer commanding came up to me and said, 'Sam, how would you like to go to the Western Sahara?'

And I didn't even know where the Western Sahara was, and the First Gulf War was arcing up and we were sending people there, and it didn't click west, east, so I thought he was asking me to go to the Gulf, so I said, 'Can I think about it overnight, Sir?'

'Yeah, of course you can.'

So I came home and grabbed the atlas, 'Oh it is over near Morocco, it is nowhere near Iraq.'

The UN Mission to the Western Sahara was to monitor a referendum. The Spanish had left Sahara in 1976 and the Mauritanians moved up from the south and the Moroccans moved down from the north to grab that area that had been a Spanish colony. The Mauritanians had to withdraw because they were too poor to maintain a military presence there. So the Moroccans took over the whole area. What the UN was there to do was to monitor a referendum between the ethnic Western Saharans, Berbers and Bedouins, that sort of thing, to see whether they wanted to have an autonomous country, stay with Morocco or a mixture of both. That was supposed to be a six-month mission in 1991, purely a monitoring mission.

... It was very frustrating as most United Nation operations are. Because they're made up of people from so many countries on the military side but on the political and bureaucrat side it is even worse. You might have a Third World country that is in charge of the mission which might be predominantly made up of Western countries who are used to doing things a certain way and corruption isn't such a big deal and efficiency is value. But you might have a Third World member who says, 'No we're going to do it this way.'

Which is money flowing into his or her pocket and they really don't care if the job gets done. A lot of UN missions are just cash cows for the countries that are represented. A lot of money goes through a mission, huge amount of money.

... Because we were under United Nations control we were very restricted as to what we could do anywhere. And I remember one time in Laayoune, which is where the force headquarters was, we were within a walled compound and I remember this fellow came running in, one of the locals came running in one day and he was yelling and screaming and he was terrified and he was followed by three or four Moroccan secret police in civilian clothes. And he ran into the headquarters building and he was begging for help, begging to be detained by the UN, he did not want to go outside that building, and these blokes just grabbed him and started to drag him off and the United Nations policeman, a uniformed policeman working for the United Nations, he sort of held them up for a few minutes while he talked to the head of the mission, both the civilian and military heads of the mission. And it turned out that the UN couldn't do anything under those particular circumstances. And that affected me because I knew what was going to happen to him. He was going to be taken away, tortured and either imprisoned or killed because he was one of the Polisario [Frente Popular de Liberación de Saguía el Hamra y Río de Oro—liberation movement]. That feeling of helplessness was double for me because firstly I was armed, I couldn't do anything even if I wanted to. And secondly knowing what was going to happen to him and just standing by, that's a horrible feeling. So when you work with the UN, that's usually the sort of thing that happens. They are very restricted as to what they can do. Particularly in a place like the Western Sahara, they're there at the King's, not his request but while he is patient enough to have them, if he doesn't want them then he will throw them out, so they are very sensitive...

there is a lot of criticism about the UN, but what a lot of people don't take into account is that it represents the vast majority of nations on earth and so it has got to please the vast majority of nations on earth and you can't do that. You can never do that. So even though they seem to fail in a lot of their missions, and they don't achieve anything and things go back to how they were, that's just the way it is. You can't please everybody and everybody wants to be pleased,

. . . Toward the end of our tour, Zac the regimental sergeant major said, 'Sam, let's grab a car and let's go through the outskirts of the place we're at and grab some video.'

And by this stage King Hassan [II] had started to stack the odds, in case there was a referendum, he started moving people down from Morocco so they could vote and rig everything. And there was a huge, so-called refugee camp near where we were and they were out of bounds. And we inadvertently took the wrong turn, you can imagine, it is like a maze a lot of their towns. We took the wrong turn and ended up in the middle of this refugee camp. And almost as soon as we stopped this Unimog, this army truck, pulled up and all of these armed soldiers got out and surrounded the vehicle, a couple of uniformed gendarmes got out and were eyeing us off and then the secret police came out. And it was like Casablanca, it was awful, ties were askew, stubble, cigarette hanging out, stunk to high heaven having been out with a camel or something. And he sort of leaned across and he started talking to us in French first because French was the common language, and then broken English and what he wanted was the video camera because Zac had been videoing this stuff while I had been driving. And Zac said, 'Piss off, mate, you're not getting it, it is my camera.'

And there was a bit of a stand-off, and this guy put his arm through to grab the camera and Zac said, 'Fuck off!'

And he wound the window up on this secret policeman's arm. And I am going, 'Zac, give him the camera, I don't care. Zac, give him the camera!'

They all went to instant, safety catches went off and weapons started to come off and this guy is spewing and everybody is getting very tense here.

'Zac, give him the camera!'

'No, piss off!'

So after about five minutes, this guy has dragged his arm out. He says, 'Come into the building, you two come here.'

'No mate, we're staying in the car. If you want to talk with us you come with us back to the compound, we have got interpreters back there, United Nations' interpreters, some of your guys there. You come and talk to us there. We are not getting out of the car.'

Fifteen minutes we sat there in the blazing Saharan sun. Everybody was getting twitchy. He went inside and made some phone calls and he sent us on our way, we were escorted out, a vehicle took us out. I thought that was the end of it. And then the next day the local government made formal complaint to the force commander who was a major general who booted my colonel up the bum, who booted us up the bum. Old Zac, he wasn't letting go of the camera for anything, and that's the typical Australian, 'Rack off, mate, it's mine.'

... The Moroccans by and large were very courteous, but stand-offish and uncooperative as much as they could be. To the extent, and we could never prove it, but we suspect, that they moved some mines onto tracks that they knew we were using. The Moroccans didn't want us there, we were only there under sufferance, and if they had to deal with us they were courteous but very uncooperative.

... One time I was on the Moroccan side and I had gone to a brigade headquarters to do something and we had been asked to stay for morning tea in the officers' mess and it was very nice, like being in Paris, patisseries came out and coffee in china cups and fans and air-conditioning. Very nice. The next day went onto the Polisario side and they said, 'Have mornos with us. Come and have a cup of tea, have a tea ceremony?'

'Okay.'

So I am looking around and there are no tents, no buildings, and I think okay, they're going to do it in the back of a vehicle. This door opens up and it is this huge boulder, this massive boulder with a door in it. And what they used to do, they would use explosives to hollow out these rocks to protect themselves from Moroccan aircraft. And I went in and it would have been three-quarters the size of this room, the boulder, and as high, and it had wooden shutter windows in it, a door, carpets, there were murals painted on the walls but they were patriotic Polisario murals. They brought out their crockery and it had the Polisario symbol and all of the rest of it and then they did their tea-pouring ceremony, three cups of tea, sweet, strong and bitter. Sweet for birth and then the strong cup of tea was for living life and having a good time and the bitter was for death. The old one knee up in the air, sipping tea with these guys, in a rock, where the day before I had been in air-conditioning. Eating in a Moroccan mess the food was okay, eating with the Polisario you would watch them pull out this haunch of camel which was all green and slimy because they didn't have air-conditioning and the camp cook would have his knife out scraping off all of the green and you would think, 'Oh, this is going to be nice.'

... We had very little information when we went over. A big part of my job was signalling Land Command in Sydney or JIO [Joint Intelligence Organisation] in Canberra trying to get information on the types of mines that were there, anti-personnel or anti-vehicle, and what we could do to try and protect ourselves. And it got down to the stage where the advice we were getting was, 'Sandbag the bottom of your vehicles; sit on your ballistic vests.'

Which wouldn't help you but that's all that came back. Finding out that there were a lot of Italian and Spanish mines there, which were plastic, which were hard to find. That was all part of my protection role for the force, I did a lot of communicating back with Australia.

... There was a lot of simmering stuff going on and we think they were starting to get spiteful by the end. And we also think they were telling us, 'You're not going into that area and if you do it is at your own risk.'

So we reckon that when we were going into those sensitive areas they were moving mines. Never proved it obviously and it is nothing that would ever get to an official stage but there were too many incidents going on. The Moroccans used to explain it away by saying, 'When you plant mines in sand it is like planting mines in an area that might become muddy like Cambodia, when you get rains and mud the minefields all move. And it is the same in the sand with dunes shifting and winds actually pick the mines up and move them around.'

It was just very strange that they were right in the vehicle tracks, and they were fairly firmly entrenched. And the vehicle that did go up, it hit an anti-tank and vehicle mine and thank God the guys had the good sense not to just jump out on either side because when you plant anti-tank mines you always plant anti-personnel mines which are much smaller just around them. So when crews and passengers disembark they jump onto the mines around that are a deliberately planted minefield. When you see that, you might expect half-a-dozen mines of one type to shift together but you don't expect one big mine and ten smaller mines to suddenly get up and move together.

. . . From a military perspective, from a soldier's perspective, we got really pissed-off at the chief finance officer and the chief executive officer who were both civilians, this is where the corruption started to come in. And this is where there is big money in UN missions; we got an allowance, we being the Australians and the others. We got an allowance of a hundred and ten dollars US a day, on top of our pay, that was the UN allowance for being there. We thought, 'Well, that's not too bad, a hundred and ten US a day.'

But it turned out that the UN said, 'Well you people in Laayoune because we're feeding you and accommodating you we're going to charge you sixty-five dollars US a day.'

Now we did our own sums and we could have got by on five dollars US a day. Accommodation and food, not a problem in the world, plus we had our own rations with us; the CO had brought over ration packs. So we figured probably fifty to fifty-five dollars was being skimmed off everybody in Laayoune, and then they hit the guys out in the field for forty-five dollars a day. And they were living in bombed-out buildings and they didn't have showers or toilets. They were living on ration packs from various countries, Polish ration packs, British ration packs, Americans. So all of this money was being withheld. And then to top it off in Smara, northern sector headquarters, the UN observers had been living in a small hotel there, and after three months the proprietor presented the northern sector commander, who was a French colonel, gendarme colonel, presented him with a US$90 000 bill. He said, 'What are you giving me this for?'

'Well you have been here three months and there are twenty people and you have eaten these meals, you owe me ninety thousand dollars.'

And the guy looked at it and said, 'I am not paying this. This has got to go back to Laayoune to the chief financial officer he will sort it out.'

The CFO who was either Algerian or Tunisian, I think he was Tunisian, he got the bill and he went straight back to the hotel proprietor and said, 'We are here as guests of King Hassan of Morocco, he has invited us here and he has said that he will provide hospitality, food accommodation whatever, we are not paying the bill.'

Those guys had been paying their sixty-five dollars or forty-five dollars a day back to Laayoune to cover this sort of thing so we started to think where is this money going? And I think we worked out on average US$250 000 a week was disappearing and it could only be going to two people. So there was the corruption side of it.

Trying to get vehicles from the United Nations compound was a nightmare because that was run by a Romanian or something. Getting on a UN helicopter was taking your life in your own hands. You would go out to the airfield and he would be there with the av gas, aviation gas, filling the tank and smoking away. And you get onto any Western military aircraft and there is a safety briefing, this is what you do if an alarm goes off and do your seatbelts up and if we crash do this and that. Not the UN aircraft. And no smoking on our aircraft, none at all. The loadmaster would be at the door smoking away; this is on an old Russian military helicopter, the HIP 8. Huge things they were, and there would be a fuel bladder inside to extend the range because they used to fly into Algeria as well. And you would look at the fuel bladder and you could smell all of the fumes, and there would be stains around the bottom of the bladder because they would take them in or out, and he would be standing at the door smoking, and you would say, 'G'day mate.' And he would grunt at you. He didn't speak English so he would grunt at you. And they would push you all in, overload the aircraft, helicopter or a fixed wing, it was interesting, it was scary a lot of the time . . . you would get onto the aircraft and the pilot and co-pilot would look back at you and there was stubble and clothes were half done up and the silliest grin and they would reek of alcohol and you would think, 'My God, what is going to happen?'

And this thing would go straight up in the air because they were powerful helicopters and then it would shake and wobble and go down in a dive, and you would think, 'We're going to die!'

And the pilot would look back and burst out laughing because he knew you were shit-scared. Oh dear. Good times.

Being an older soldier and going over with, on average they would have been nineteen, twenty, most of our guys. I thought, they're soft, younger generation, they haven't got all of the right gear so they won't get the job done, they will whinge and whine, because that's all they did on the way over there was whinge and whine. We got over there and once we had deployed all of the various people to the team sites particularly those first three months where we had crap gear, they did a fantastic job, they really did . . . it doesn't matter 2004 soldier, 1944 soldier, the same mentality. And because they were very much a can-do type group and they established communications and they ran the radio nets, initially there was animosity because apart from the Canadians who had a contingent and a Swiss medical unit, the bulk of the rest of the people were individual officers. You might have three or four Chinese spread through the area, a dozen Americans, some Russians and a lot of Italians. The team site leaders would normally be majors or lieutenant colonels and our senior rank out on the team sites might be a corporal, usually it was a signaller, a private, might be a corporal. So initially the officers—and you might have Italians, Russians, Nigerians, Venezuelans—the common language was English so it wasn't too bad, but you might have all of these different nationalities there who all had a different relationship with their soldiers in their countries. In most of the countries represented the soldiers didn't say boo, didn't have anything to do with the officers at all. Would bow and salute, scrape and all of the rest of it. Australians soldiers are not like that. So our blokes would set up the nets, and the colonel, and in one particular case it was the Italian colonel, would come along and he would pick up the radio and he would ring up the Italian major on another team site and they would natter away in Italian.

And this went on for a little while, they all did it, but the Italian is the one that sticks out. And the detachment commanders at the team sites got in touch with the Australian colonel and said, 'What do we do, Sir? They are tying up the net, it is a command net. It's a safety net, it is communication and they're using it like a telephone.'

And the colonel came back and said, 'You're the net control station.'

Which means he is the guy in charge of that radio. He said, 'Do what you have to do, it is a command net. It is what the force commander needs to operate so sort it out.'

So you had privates, signallers and corporals telling majors and colonels from countries where soldiers are in another universe, 'Fuck off, Sir, I have told you a hundred times it is a command net. You can't ring your wog mate up there and yap away. This is for communication between us and Laayoune and us and the patrol and us and other team sites. Piss off!'

This was right at the end when everybody's patience had been worn out. Our guys at the beginning were all, 'I am sorry, Sir, this is the radio network.'

The normal stuff, the normal respect and courtesy. And after a couple of weeks it was 'Piss off!'

And physically grab the radio handpiece from the guy's hand, slam it down and say, 'Go away, if you want to send a message to Laayoune or wherever, let me know, Sir, and I will do it for you.' Loved them.

* * *

September 27 we landed in East Timor, well arrived in East Timor... We went up on [HMAS] *Jervis Bay* which the navy had leased off the Tasmanian boat builders, that huge catamaran that runs between Tasmania and mainland Australia, been painted grey; it was in navy colours and all sorts of things. This thing does thirty-nine, forty knots out in the ocean. And I remember it chugging into Dili Harbour up to the wharves, and in the background, not on the horizon, within Dili itself there were flames, smoke, lots of noise. On the dock there was barbed wire everywhere. We had machine-gun posts at both ends of it and people had their helmets on, ballistics vests, webbing and they looked very serious. There were a few locals peering through the wire at the vessel as it came in. That's the sort of impression I got, with not just smoke, but flames. We got there a week after the first Australians went in, 3 Battalion; the airborne battalion had gone in the week before and secured the airfield so that Cosgrove and his group could come in. So we got there just a week after the first guys. And during that week and for the first two weeks we were there, as the Indonesian military vacated a building they would trash it, they would put faeces on the wall, throw papers everywhere, and in a lot of cases as they went out the back door they burnt the building or set it on fire as the Australians came in the front door. And I remember thinking, 'Oh, it is not very safe here.'

We had weapons, live ammunition, rules of engagement, because we had had training back in Australia on what we could and couldn't do. So it all sort of clicked that they weren't mucking around here. And once we got into Dili and saw the damage and the fear on people's faces. This would only be three or two and a half weeks after the massacres took place, all of the killings after the elections. And... 'Sixty Minutes'. Richard Carleton. He was over there during that election period and as the people were lining up to vote he was asking them, 'Who are you going to vote for?' and 'What are you going to vote for?'

And the militia and the Indonesian Special Forces were there and listening to everything. And I remember thinking at that time what a bastard, because these people would have been dragged away and killed if they were stupid enough to say anything. That's the kind of environment it was, the militia was still there, the Indonesians were still there. We weren't overly concerned about the Indonesian military, the ones we could identify, but we were concerned about Kopassus, the Indonesian Special Forces, they had been doing a lot of guerrilla warfare type stuff. So they were there but they weren't there in their uniforms and they were the ones that we were worried about. They were the most efficient killers and orchestrating a lot of stuff. I can say this because I am not in the army now. And it is common knowledge anyway; it has been in the press. The things that have remained with me are the noise, the smell and the fear on people's faces. I can still smell the smell right in the back of my nose. Not bodies, although there were bodies around, burning, stench all sorts of things.

When we first got over there, there was a lot of confusion and a lot of fear, not only from the locals, from everybody. My section, well we interviewers were operating from the airport, Comoro airport which was about six or seven kilometres from where INTERFET [International Force for East Timor] had its headquarters, we were on the outskirts. And when we first got there and started to set up our interviewing area, it was like chaos, the walls were all covered in faeces, not from the Indonesians and militia but the airport had been packed with thousands and thousands of people trying to get out or gain some sort of safety because the militia were hacking and slicing people to death all of the time. So we got there just as those people had been moved out, literally within hours of them moving out. And we came into the airport and it was horrific. The papers, the crap on the wall, blood, bloody bandages. So our first job was to clean that up. And not only us but everybody working out of the airport, the transport people, we had a mail section out there, medics, everyone got in there and we cleaned that up. And we operated out of the airport for two or three weeks I guess, and what we were doing there was interviewing detainees. People would be rounded up either by INTERFET forces out doing patrols and they would grab somebody that was carrying a weapon or had been fingered by the locals, 'He is militia.' 'He is Indonesian.'

All of those people would initially come to us and we would do more of a screening process than an interrogation process. We would find out who they were, what they were doing and go from there. If they were persons of security interest they would go over here, and if they were people of no interest to us they would go there, and if we weren't sure they would go here. We would work our way through.

Even though we are intelligence we are more a source. When you deal with that other stuff, that's called the intelligence cycle, that's the first thing that we do is get the information requirement and we task somebody to find out, we task the air force to send an F111 over to take photos of this area so we can find out. So as hum-inters [human intelligence gatherers], interviewers, interrogators. We were almost like a source in ourselves, our boss would get requirements from Cosgrove's headquarters, he would task us, find out X, Y, Z. We would do some collation there; some basic analysis and then we would feed it back to Cosgrove's headquarters because he had a fairly large intelligence staff there. So we were only one little cog in the wheel. We were passing information back to him but he was also getting information from the infantry units on the ground, from the Special Forces on the ground, from the UN political people that were there, we fed information into that big hub, and then they did all of that collecting, collating, analysis, dissemination.

The hardcore militia, there were three tiers of militia, tier one to tier three. The tier one militia had thrown their lot in with the Indonesians; they wanted East Timor to remain Indonesian. Tier two were thugs, murderers, rapists who would have done whatever they wanted to do anyway. Tier three, even though they were involved in murders, rapes and arson they had been forced into it. I had gone over there with very black-and-white views on the militia, and my views were, if you are militia you are bad, evil and you have been involved in all of these things against the East Timorese and we are going to deal with you whichever way we have to. But after interviewing so many of them, I did mainly tier two and three, the tier one blokes we just didn't get them. The Eurico Guterres [militia leader] people and those sorts of people, the head of Itara, we just didn't get them because they bolted into West Timor and Indonesia. And the people I dealt with, the tier two, were easy to identify because they were just thugs, criminals, but a lot of the tier three people, the low level people once I started talking to them, 'Well, I had to do it because they had a gun to my head,' or, 'They had a machete to my wife.' Or, 'They were going to rape my daughter.'

And my initial reaction was, 'Bullshit, mate, you don't just stab somebody to death or you don't shoot them if you don't want to.'

But then you get corroborating stories from other people, and they say, 'Yeah, I remember Jose Silverez, he had to do this, this and this.'

And this is from Fretilin, the East Timorese guerrilla organisation, and they said, 'Yeah, we know him and he had to do this and this.'

And my whole attitude changed then, I thought, 'Well it is not up to me to judge somebody that has had his family threatened.'

And they would have done it. They would have killed him on the spot and they would have raped his wife. They did all of those things. We saw evidence of it through the province. So that was a huge shock for me to know that people do that because they are forced to. I had led, not a sheltered life but a conservative life, there is right and wrong and people make decisions but it is not like that.

I think the main problem in Cosgrove's headquarters on the intelligence side, and I can't speak for any other area, was the pure volume of information coming in. And even though a reasonable number of people were in there, they were just under-resourced to sift through this information because there was so much coming in. In an average day we might send in twenty reports just from our tiny little section out at the airport. And then on top of that you have got counter-intelligence people, infantry reports, Special Forces people out on the ground. And all of this information would come back to the intelligence cell in his headquarters and there might be for argument's sake, ten or fifteen people, I don't know. And of those people half of them were officers so they were primarily involved in analysing and making sure the information got to Cosgrove. So you might have four or five people, because there were warrant officers and sergeants as well, four or five people sifting through all of this information keeping maps up to date, computer battle logs up to date which was even worse. And then on top of that, those five people had to operate twenty-four hours a day so you might have two on two off one sick or whatever. And when they were off they were doing gun piquets because we had security at night, we got very little sleep for the first two or three months because we had to maintain our own security.

. . . The first gun piquet I did at night, we didn't have any night-vision equipment at that stage, they came later. I remember we had our wire up, our barbed wire and stuff and our sandbags, and we were looking down the street through some open areas and they had a floodlight behind us. A big light behind us. And I remember thinking, 'What the bloody hell are these guys doing?'

Because I was silhouetted, and I couldn't see anything out there because this strong light was glaring behind me. And I am thinking, 'They have lit me up!' . . .

And you would look back every now and then and this thing would go 'zzt'. The only thing that made me feel a bit better was that there was a machine-gun post off to one side, and they were in the dark so if anything had happened they could have arced up, but we would have been the first to know what was going on. Little things like that were happening until they sorted themselves out.

. . . We didn't trust anyone we saw, including the kids and women. And they certainly didn't trust us because we were on heightened alert, we were very vigilant, we had our ballistic vests on, body armour on, helmet on all of the time, always kitted up. Rifles, grenade-launchers, the whole lot. And whenever we went anywhere in a vehicle there were always two vehicles and apart from the driver everybody else had their weapons pointing outwards. And you would have your weapon resting on the sill and as you were driving along if there was a group or somebody that looked suspicious you would track them with your weapon. And that is very disconcerting. If you're out there minding your own business, you're a local, and there are a half-a-dozen rifles tracking you because you're a bit dirtier than everybody else or you fit the profile of being a young, physically fit male. So there was little trust on either side but once the Indonesians started to pull out in the second and third week, and the locals saw truckloads of Indonesian soldiers going to the ports to embark on their vessels, lots of cheering, once the Indonesians left everything changed, there was cheering, lots of backslapping because they realised the Australians are here to stay.

I guess the first contact, contact being a firefight, that the Australian forces had was at a place called Suai, down in the south-east. What had happened was the militia had run an SAS roadblock, they had gone through, there had been a firefight and they had turned their vehicles around and bolted back down the road. And the SAS quick-reaction force had bolted after them. And in fact it was a very cleverly designed ambush because the SAS vehicles were ambushed and two of them were wounded, one in the throat and the other in the head. Anyway that all happened and I was in Dili and twelve detainees had been brought back by Black Hawks and some of them were wounded, and we had to go through the tactical questioning and then go into the other side of it. And three bodies came back with them. I don't know if you have been aware or know of the allegations that were made against the SAS soldier in East Timor for kicking dead bodies and bits and pieces, well this is all tied in with that. The bodies came back and they were laid out on the table and there was blood and bits and pieces still dripping out. That was a bit hard I guess that sort of thing. I didn't see it but one of my people had to go out and do some interpreting because he was a linguist, he was a soldier linguist, and he came across a ute that had I think thirteen bodies in the back, they had all been burnt and mangled or whatever. Other people went to a well where a large number of people had been murdered and thrown down the well.

I think what affected me a lot was I went down to Suai a few days later; they sent me down to do some work. And there was a cathedral that was three-quarters finished, and there was a smaller church and some church buildings. And it was a Sunday and they were having a mass and I didn't think much of it, but being Catholic I thought I would go along. And I think three weeks before they had had a mass on the Sunday and the Indonesians and militia had come along and thrown grenades in and shot people and stabbed people and all sorts of things. And there was evidence of that everywhere. There were expended rounds, but within the unfinished cathedral, I went in to have a look because it was an imposing building, there was blood everywhere, piles of rounds around. And talking to the people you found out what it was all about, and I remember I was talking to a group of people and a truck came down the road and they all looked up and they all stopped and were all shocked and it was a truck full of militia. And I don't know but I would imagine that some of them had been involved in the murders the weeks before. The priest had been tortured, had his arms hacked off, head hacked off. At Suai again I came across what was left of a body, it had been cut in half and it was decomposing. Yeah, that's enough.

It is not that we would lay ambushes, we would have aggressive patrolling. That's probably the best way to put it. And if they had come across the border and they were armed, we would challenge them, and if they didn't stop or they fired upon us it was into them and we did kill a few of them in the early stages, I think half a dozen or so were killed and photos were taken and all sorts of things and that's how the message got across. And we would have photos of the guys that had been killed and as part of my job when I was interviewing somebody, and it wasn't done as a threat or this could happen to you; it was done as a genuine, 'Do you know who this person was?'

And if the answer was yes.

'Well, what militia group did he belong to?'

And try to build the picture that way. That message got through that way, those people would say, 'I have just seen Ureko whoever and he is dead, he has got a big hole in the side of his head.'

And that message got across into West Timor, and the people that were worried about it were the tier one and two. Mainly the tier two, and the guys that had been forced into things, as soon as they got to the border they would just drop their weapons and anything military and scramble across the border and hope for the best. So by a few contacts in which some of them were killed, questioning people and showing the photos. The pamphlets, some of the pamphlets said, 'If you come across with your hands up, without a weapon, you will be treated fairly.'

And all of this sort of thing. Others would have the rifle with the big circle and cross, 'Don't come across, there will be trouble.'

There are ways and means. And then at the political level or the senior military levels they would have been liaising with people across the border as well. Cosgrove used to go down to the border a fair bit and he crossed into West Timor a few times to talk to his opposite number, the Indonesian general. They had face-to-face meetings. So it would have got across that way as well. And it was fair enough; they knew it, they were quite happy to kill us.

. . . I think one of the estimates was that there was something like a hundred and eighty thousand East Timorese had been forced into West Timor. And the bulk of them ended up in camps along the border. Atambua which was a fairly large town and then on the other side there was Batun and a few little places in between, a lot of them had been literally forced to cross and there were a lot of people that had been murdered out at sea. And their bodies were dumped overboard and murdered on the way down. Of those tens of thousands that were forced over, I guess there was a significant number that wanted to come back straightaway but there was also a large number in the first six months or so that were tossing up whether to come back. Some of the reasons they were hesitating were the propaganda, go back and they will kill you, regardless of whether you're militia or not, they will rape the women and kill you. A lot of the East Timorese had been public servants for the Indonesian Government because it was an Indonesian province so there was a bureaucracy in place and they had been told if you go back you will lose any pension rights you have. And some of these people had worked for twenty-five years at that stage . . . others got there and decided we will stay here for whatever reasons, but tens of thousands wanted to come back.

Our first mass screening was at Dili and the ship came from Kupang right down the bottom of West Timor and it was really a show thing. It really made me angry because this was the first one, the ship came in and it was pristine, it was a cargo passenger vessel and it was pristine, newly painted, white funnels and nice beige sides and all of the rest of it. Media was there, the world media was there, UN civilians were there in force and I had been tasked with setting up the screening lanes. And there were two thousand of these people on this vessel, and with screening what you do is that you set up lanes and you have people doing a basic security check and then people walk down the lane one at a time to a table and they get asked, and if everything is okay they go here and get on a truck and off they go, and if they are bad people they go here and get talked to or whatever. Two thousand people got off this thing almost at once because they had gangplanks everywhere, and they got off in family groups, so you might have mum, dad, grandma and five kids. And they all had baggage, masses of baggage . . . it just turned into a huge cluster, there were people everywhere. They were just a show thing for the media because over the next couple of weeks the real refugees started to come back. They would come back at night and the vessels they came back in were unseaworthy, rusty, and the people that came off the first time were all well dressed, well fed and I am sure that some Indonesian operatives came through as well because there were just too many of them. But the second lot, you could see that they had been in the camps, they were all thin, dirty, their clothes were all dirty, they had very little baggage, kids were crying and snotty noses and all of that sort of stuff, so we dealt with them.

The second time I went back to the border, the whole time I was there I worked on the border and I worked in an Australian battalion. And the battalion commander was fantastic, Colonel Moon. Brilliant man. He had been a company commander in Somalia and I think he had received a military medal, he had received a gallantry award . . . but he had been in charge of an infantry company so he knew what he was doing and as a battalion commander, as a colonel, he was just the best. Dead set, I would follow him to the ends of the earth. There are a lot of officers I wouldn't follow to the front door—well I might to see if they could find the front door, but he was so good, so cool, so good at his job . . . and I just felt confident, I felt safe. I felt safe with him, I didn't feel safe with the first battalion commander during the first tour, he was an idiot.

The other guy, who was also a good battalion commander I guess, but he would openly say, 'I want this sniper team put in here and we will draw them across the border and I want you to kill them.'

And that was his mentality; he just wanted kills, that body count thing. And sniper teams as much as anything else gather intelligence, because they have all of the gear, they have the long-range telescopes, the long-range video cameras, but they can be just as useful at gathering intelligence as they can at killing people. And he wanted to use his sniper teams, put them in a situation, artificially create a situation to draw the militia across so he could kill them and he would openly say this. And he is the idiot that had a company based at Batugade which is on the coast border town on the coast between West and East Timor and they went along to a church and ripped the cross off a church because they wanted to turn it into a local headquarters and they were blocking off streets, this is on the East Timor side. No hearts and minds at all, none at all. Catholic people see a cross being ripped off and get visions of Indonesians. So I didn't like working for him, he was dangerous as far as I was concerned.

We have got people on the border, Australians, and there was a New Zealand battalion on the border as well. We have got people down there that are actually doing what we want them to do and they are doing it in a no-nonsense manner. And achieving the mission, as opposed to a lot of other countries that would have gone down there, they would have stayed within the compound at Balibo and the two other areas and the gaps between the towns would have been porous and people could have flowed across backwards and forwards. So I think the UN was more than happy to have that Australian aggressiveness there. I guess I should qualify, it is not that the UN does not want to use Australian combat troops, I think that it is fully aware of what our capabilities are and it is aware that we don't put up with bullshit. Whereas most countries take the easy way, 'Well we don't want to upset them. We will just stay here in the compound.' Either because it is safer or because they are lazy, and they just want to get the money or whatever. Whereas Australian Defence Force, whether they are on a ship, a soldier, an airman whatever, they go somewhere and they go there for a reason.

Up until the early 1990s, the First Gulf War, it was pretty rare to be sent overseas unless you went to Vietnam or Korea wherever. So once we started sending people overseas in large numbers they tended to do the job they were sent to do and do it extremely well. So that's the reputation that they gained. But at the same time the UN, monitoring everything that is going on throughout the world could see, for argument's sake, and I am not picking on the Bangladeshi by any means, but the Bangladesh engineer battalion that they had in Dili, it built a gym and a sports centre for the UN in Dili. Instead of getting out into the country and rebuilding schools and roads and whatnot, that's what they wanted to do. The Pakistani engineers that we had down at Maliana it was almost like goading them out with a bayonet to get them out of their compound and they might lay a little bit of road base and then they would scurry back to their compound. Whereas Australians get out there, dominate that ground, do your job.

It really was a matter of the hard grind down on the border, if the guys weren't actually out on patrol, if the infantry weren't out on patrol they would be cleaning weapons or they would be doing other duties. And for us, my day might start at six o'clock and I would go through to eight, nine, ten o'clock at night because I would have to get a final report out. And there wasn't really a lot of time to relax as such. Second tour we had generators there so there were video machines, some of the guys had movies there that you could watch. Radios, we were able to pick up a radio station coming out of Ipswich of all places, Star FM I think it was, and they boomed through, they used to play 1970s and 1980s music. The guys had magazines; darts; cards; mobile phones, initially mobile phones were banned. But I think during the second tour they were still banned individually but there was a satellite phone that the guys could get onto once a week and phone home. But yeah, East Timor was pretty intense that way I guess. It was different in Dili, they had bars set up and they had movies every night. Towards the end of the second tour they had air-conditioned accommodation which really irked the guys on the border because everyone was getting the same allowance rate, whether you were in Dili or on the border. But the guys made their own fun.

... The nature of the beast with intelligence corps is that you tend to be operating in much smaller units, you tend to be extremely specialised in what you're doing, you tend to operate a lot with other units, other corps, so you are away from your own people and you tend to be standing out as an individual and people really don't know which way to take you because you're not infantry, armour or transport. So that mateship within intelligence corps is nowhere near as strong as it is in an infantry battalion or an armoured regiment. Even a transport unit. And that primarily because most int corps people are individuals, that's why they're int corps because they're probably no good as a rifleman or as a carrier driver. They tend to think for themselves and they tend to be a bit mouthy, they tend to say what they think, and they are quite happy to talk to a brigadier and say, at warrant officer level, 'Well, Sir, this is the information we have got and this is my analysis of it.'

I had no fear of senior officers, none at all; I got on well with senior officers because they recognise that. They can smell fear and there is always a lot of fear amongst junior officers and people of their own corps because everyone is trying to please them. Where my job was give him the information, if you don't know the information tell him you don't know and go and find out. And that's the attitude I had.

Within me it is the desire to win the information and win it any way you can. And there are two sides to me; in that role I am quite capable of being extremely sincere, I am quite capable of using religion, I am quite capable of using family ties. Whatever I can do within certain boundaries more than capable of using it and have used it and had to use it. Even in East Timor you couldn't touch people, an Australian interviewer particularly, couldn't touch them. So it was very much a case of having to use what was up here and devising strategies to get information. Because the militia that we captured and certain other people that we got, they were expecting to be beaten up, they were expecting to be tortured and knifed and all sorts of things because that's what *they* did, and when they came up against us and all we were doing was talking to them. Maybe yelling or other things but nothing too bad, they thought it was a big joke and so we had to devise other strategies ... And the dark side of me, that's in me I guess. Everybody has a core personality that nobody gets to except them. Personality is like an onion, layers, you present different personalities to different people, strangers, loved ones, friends, partners, but right in the centre there is you. And that's what we used to try and go for, that's where all your fears are, and all of your strengths as well, and if you know somebody's strengths you can work on them and defeat them.

* * *

My eyes are open a lot more now. And it's a natural thing I think, if people are really honest they will tell you that while you're in that cocoon your eyes are really blinkered to the reality and I have opinions now. I always had opinions but they were always pro-military or pro-government or whatever. Now I look at things and politically I am very cynical, I see things in a different way. I still have the greatest respect for everybody in the Australian Defence Force, past, present and future. But I don't agree with a lot of things that are going on.

The people that have gone to Iraq, I support them ten thousand per cent because they are service people just doing what they have been trained to do and doing what their government is telling them to do. However you feel about anything, whether it be Vietnam or Iraq, never ever take it out on soldiers or Defence Force people. They have no choice; they are just doing what they have to do.

It happens to be John Howard but it could have been Latham, it could have been Beazley, it could have been anybody. Such a cynical exercise, sending people into harm's way, for what reason? They couldn't give a rat's arse about Saddam Hussein killing ten million of his countrymen let alone what else was going on. Weapons of mass destruction, I must admit initially I thought, well he may have them, that's why they're going in. It is always easy in hindsight. I started to have doubts after the first week or two. And I think what really angers me is that Teflon Johnny has got away with it. Blair is under such scrutiny and even Bush now is twiddling his thumbs and saying, 'Well maybe we should find out what is going on.'

And he is the president of the most powerful country in the world! Teflon Johnny is just sailing through life, and I will tell you why. Because nobody has been hurt. No Australians have been killed. If you had five or ten or twenty Australians killed it would be a completely different story. And the British have had scores of people killed, the Americans have had hundreds killed and not one of ours had been killed. Lucky. I honestly think it is more luck than anything else, their rules over there would be very tight, very strict as to where they can go, have to go in a group, you're not going in that area, would be armed. And their security would be very tight. But having said that more lucky than anything else. If the insurgents, whatever you want to call them, are able to bring down a cargo plane at Baghdad airport, they could have put that rocket through the air control tower just as easily and that's where the Australians are. The ships, it is hard to get near a warship now because of what's happened with the Americans, but there is always ways to do things. He has just been very lucky. But I guess looking at it from a civilian point of view now and trying to understand why we went there I disagree with it. If ten years ago they had said, 'Saddam Hussein is skinning people alive and he is torturing and doing this and he has used chemical weapons on his own people, we need to get rid of him', I would have put my hand up and said, 'Let's do it, I fully support that.'

But it is the same with East Timor, the bastards waited from 1975 to 1999 before they did anything. Because it wasn't expedient, we didn't want to upset them. So it has got nothing to do with Saddam Hussein, nothing to do with the atrocities in there. I don't know about the oil, although I believe they are the second or third largest oil deposits in the world, I just don't think that we should be there. But I support our people that are there.

***

Well, take the First World War men, they came from the bush, they were good horsemen, good riflemen, excellent bushcraft, field craft because of what they were doing, so you could pick someone up like that, put a uniform on them, give them rudimentary training and push them off into a situation and they would perform very well, they would be self-sufficient, self-reliant, all of that sort of stuff. Same as the Second World War, you were able to pick up a lot of militia people and send them to New Guinea. And even though a lot of them were only eighteen or nineteen, a lot of them had come from the country so they were much harder, tougher people. It is ironic because your soldier nowadays is very well educated, extremely well educated and they have to be because of the equipment that we use now, the technology that is involved. Having said that, a soldier from 2004 has the same characteristics as a soldier from 1944 and I can only think it is back to that Australian psyche, our way of life, the way we are raised, our sense of humour, our attitude to jobs. You see a job, that's what's got to be done, let's get in and do it.

... We are a weird mob. My observation of Australians is that we would be one of the most apathetic peoples of the world: politics, economics, we don't care, someone else can do it. But having said that, when something has got to be done as a nation or as a Defence Force it is all hands in, and it is amazing. I was in Italy last year and I was so sad...nobody cares. Nobody cares about anything.

The toilet system is falling apart, the infrastructure is falling apart, the political situation is horrendous. And it has always been chaotic over there, but they have always had this love of life and if somebody needed something done they would band together. Not now. It is look after your family and the rest of the country can go to pot. Whereas I think we're different to that, when it comes to the crunch we do stand up as a Defence Force member, or a politician or a civilian whatever, we do take pride in being Australian and we do band together.

... I think what makes us so proficient in the Defence Forces is our leadership and our training. Not necessarily the gear that we have got, we have always made do with the gear that we have got ... because wherever you put Australian Defence Force personnel they always do an excellent job regardless. Their morale can be down in the dumps; they can be under-resourced or overtasked with a particular tasking sequence, but they always do an excellent job wherever we send them.

GARTH FITZGERALD

Black Hawk Loadmaster
East Timor
Gulf War II

I think the last sort of six months when I was in Margaret River I was starting to realise that it was going nowhere. I was taking it there faster and the nocturnal activities would carry over into the day and everything was becoming a blur and we weren't doing anything properly, from living to eating to staying in touch with family and friends. We were just out on our own in the bush, you know, down south surfing and collecting the dole and working for cash. We were making heaps of money but we had to have it to spend it as well and over a six-month period realising, 'I've got to do something. I can't keep doing this,' and you see people, when you get into certain circles, every circle, you see people that have been doing it for a while, no matter what it is and you just think, 'Do I want to end up like that?' . . . and I thought, 'Well,' you know, 'This army thing's pretty good.' I was interested in the aviation side and there's definitely no way known that drugs and drinking are going to be tolerated in the Defence Force and they're not, to a certain extent . . . that last six months down south I started to realise that I had to do something and the Defence Force or the army in particular was looking more and more inviting, given the stability that it offered and that I really needed to be honest, you know. It wasn't looking good, but I mean I made the right choice. I knew that it was going to be a huge culture shock and that I could end

up anywhere and nothing was certain and even though I enlisted . . .
you know, I might not pass. I might not be up to scratch and I could
end up anywhere, and I knew all that and I still went and did it
'cause I thought, 'Bugger it, I can run fast enough. I'll just keep
running.'

. . . Well I went to the recruiting office in Perth and the navy guy
bailed me up first, 'cause they just come at you, like the navy guy
comes at you, then the air force, 'cause they've got to get a quota I
guess, and then the navy guy came at me and I told him about
aviation and that I was keen on aviation and he's off on his spiel
about Sea Kings [helicopters] and all this sort of stuff and I think
he might have fired guns or watched a radar or something on a boat
somewhere, but he didn't really know that much and then the army
guy overheard him. He said, 'Aah. We've got all the helicopters,
come over here.'

And so I said, 'Yeah, no worries.'

So I trotted off into his little corner and he was really nice, you
know, 'cause they fool you at recruiting. They lie to you at recruiting,
arseholes, and he said, 'Yeah, yeah, no worries. We'll put you there,
mate.'

And so I signed on with the list saying I want to enlist . . . I went
up there, did my physical and my psych test one day and then the
next day I signed the dotted line and then two days after that I'm
on a plane to bloody Victoria, so it happened really quick for me.

* * *

When you get from the Wagga airport to Kapooka, you've got this
section commander up the front and he's just going, 'Yeah, g'day,
welcome to Wagga, welcome to Kapooka.'

And you're going, 'This ain't so bad. This is all good.'

But as soon as you drive through that front gate he fuckin' chucks
a different hat on, becomes a different person and just starts yelling
at you, you know, and you think, 'Holy shit, what's this?'

It's pretty crazy . . . I couldn't believe that he went from this placid
bloke up the front, eyes forward saying nothing and we were all

jibbery-jabbering and talking and being really loud in the back of the bus and he just stood up and went off like, 'Shut the fuck up! You're in the fuckin' army now. You do what I fuckin' say!'

And everyone's like, 'Oh, fuckin' shit!' I mean I've got hair down past my shoulders, so I'm like this fucking surfie hippie, going, 'What?' freaking out a bit, you know.

... There was heaps of bastardisation in my boarding school, more than in the military, yeah, but it wasn't as rough. When it happened in the military, it really happened and you knew that it had happened. If you messed up, you knew that you messed up and you wouldn't do it again, although it wasn't that bad when I was there either. I mean I'm not saying I agree with it, but you're going into a line of work where getting slapped around a bit is the least of your worries when you really have to start working, and you need to learn quick and that's the quickest way, well not bastardise, but to beat certain things into people. I don't agree with it, but it has its benefits and if people crack under that then maybe they shouldn't be there, you know. I nearly cracked. It was shit. A lot of people do, you know.

I think it offers so much, the military, and I took it for what I needed. I needed stability and security and that's why I would say I was doing it and at no stage did it even enter that I could be ending up in a war zone getting shot at, which is what happened, God damn it, but yeah. No I didn't at the time, and nor did I until it happened, until I got deployed because it's just a day at a time, you know, 'Where do I have to be tomorrow, what time do I have to be early for so that I'm not in trouble?'

That's all that you had, just day after day, you don't really think about it until you're over there, yeah, thinking, 'Shit, I didn't sign on for this eight years ago, what's going on?'

* * *

It was sort of a six-month course, three months ground school learning about the aircraft and how they work and the theory of flight and all that sort of stuff and then there's a weather component and then there's external load rigging, where you have to learn how to rig trucks and trailers and various other loads under sling under the helicopters which they do quite a bit. Then you start the flying phase and that's broken up into clearances, external loads and hoisting, or using the hoist, the winch and clearances, it's a pretty steep learning curve. You have to learn all the patter, which is just the talk, things you need to say to get a pilot to move the aircraft and how to not hit trees or obstacles, which failed me later. That's the hardest bit because it sounds easy but when the aircraft's coming in to land and you've got your head out the side and you're trying to take in this huge picture and then turn it into words so that the pilot can understand what you're seeing; and the whole time it's moving forward at a hundred ks an hour and getting lower and closer to everything and everything's coming at you and you get it eventually.

The next one is external loads where you go and actually pick up trucks or pick up litters or sort of pick up whatever loads and that's pretty cool, and fly around with them, yeah. It's pretty daunting for a trainee to be in control of a twenty million dollar aircraft with a tonne of equipment underneath it, so that sort of plays on your mind a bit. Then you start using the hoist, which is another whole kettle of fish because you're sort of in the doorway, hanging half out the door, you're attached obviously to a harness, to the aircraft, but you don't use the harness to restrain you in any way because you want freedom of movement, so it's a little bit of slack there, not too much or you will fall out of the aircraft and then you're trying to winch . . . It's almost three hundred feet of cable, so it's seventy metres. You're just winching away and the aircraft's seventy metres up in the air and it's just hard to maintain control when you're trying to get something with a base on it like this into a rock like this on top of a pinnacle and it's bloody hard because the pilot can't see. His hover reference is twenty kilometres away. It's another mountain. He's guessing. He doesn't know where the hell he is, and it just builds up and builds up but by the end of it, you know, as with all training, you master it.

* * *

We were down in Sydney for the Olympics, for lead-up training. 'A Squadron' is the Special Forces squadron and we were just down there supporting them. We were flying around all hierarchy and stuff and going to all the Olympic sites and dropping off whoever. We were just taxis basically, because we had free rein over Sydney . . . in Black Hawks. They basically cut off all the airspace prior to the Olympics and we were the only guys that had free rein which was gold when you could go cracking up the Hawkesbury River, all the way under the Harbour Bridge and out the Heads, chuck a big right, fang past Bondi and then back into the city. We had some good times. So we went and did some lead-up training for them and that's where I had an aircraft accident.

We were ground taxiing and we were at Williamtown Air Force Base just north of Newcastle and they're called the EOLSs which are explosive ordnance loading areas. They have these big walls and they park their jets in them and bomb them up, so that if a bomb drops and explodes it's not going to get the next aircraft, so they're pretty solid walls and we were just ground taxiing along and I was looking out, it's hard to explain, but when you're a loadmaster in a Black Hawk, my seat faces sideways and the two pilots sit here and they face north and so the loadmasters face east/west and I was just sitting there looking out my window leaning forward and I saw this wall coming and I gave him a verbal caution and he didn't respond and because I was a jube I just went, 'Oh well, I've told him. He knows it's there.'

And this fuckin' thing went straight past his window anyway, you know, 'How can he miss it?'

. . . And I've looked back out my window and the wall must have been about this far from the rotor tip, and the first bit of the rotors is just aluminium rotor tip cap, and it's just there to reduce the noise that the rotors make, so it's just nothing, and so when it started hitting the wall it just started going, '*Choong, choong, choong, choong, choong, choong, choong, choong*' and the pilot said, 'Fuck, what's that?'

And then the first titanium spar, which is the leading edge of the blade, which won't give, hit and sort of grabbed and tore chunks, huge chunks the size of footballs, out of this wall and there was a fuel truck parked at the other end of the wall and it's spitting football-sized bits of concrete and steel at this fuel truck and the guys are in the cabin getting covered in shrapnel, for want of a better word, and so they've reversed the truck and then one of the spars grabbed and didn't let go. So all the torque and power from the engines transferred back down the rotor blade, down through the rotor head into the engines, destroyed the engines and as a result the torque spun the tail of the aircraft round into the wall. We kept moving forward because we had momentum, and then we put . . . the tail rotor into the wall as well. And we were rocking and I remember, 'cause obviously, you know, it's only got three points, two wheels at the front and a wheel at the back and we started rocking and that's when I thought we were going to flip and die and I just remember seeing like bitumen, sun, bitumen, sun, screaming, people screaming . . . and they did an emergency shutdown and it all stopped turning and we got out and we ran away and it was leaking fuel and leaking hydraulic oil and shit everywhere and the firies came, the ambulance came.

. . . And they labelled me and I was the one to blame, and then we got to sweep up all the shit from our aircraft which was really, really depressing having to sweep that up and, you know, I was fucked. Because they did an emergency shutdown, they didn't turn the batteries off. They just basically pulled the fire extinguishers, chucked on the rotor blade and left the batteries on which wiped the black box because it repeats every half hour, so I had no evidence to back up my story that what I was telling them that, I gave him a verbal, he didn't answer and we were too close, we shouldn't have been there and all this sort of stuff, and so I basically had to fall on my sword and I went back to Townsville, went in front of all the aviation hierarchy from brigadiers to fuckin' lieutenants and other air crewman like myself. I had to get up and give this talk on my fuck-up, which was pretty bad. I didn't like that at all.

... Everyone walked away. There was a lot of bruised egos but everyone walked away, yeah, seatbelts and everything worked, so we were pretty lucky. If you had have been unrestrained in the back you would have probably fallen out and been crushed by the fuselage hitting the ground or something, so it would have been untidy for you. There was another crash... that the crash investigation team had to come over for, so that's when they let me off the hook because the boffins in Canberra worked the black box and got all the data back... justified everything I'd been telling them but it was too late by then. I was 'the guy that helped crash a Black Hawk', so that shit follows you round.

* * *

I went to Darwin and did some pre-deployment training at Darwin, some sort of cultural training about the East Timor people and what to expect over there and last-minute weapons handling and military law and red and yellow cards, and who you can and can't shoot, and stuff like that, and then we flew... to the border, to the West Timor/East Timor border to a town called Balibo, which is where those journalists got killed in 1975, those Australian journalists, so that was pretty interesting and we were on top of a hill, and from the top of our hill we could see Adembua which is in West Timor and there was Indonesian infantry there and we could only sort of see the buildings and the structures. We couldn't see people.

... We basically inserted and resupplied sections up to platoon strength of soldiers all along the border and in various observation posts, so that they could keep an eye on the Indonesians and more so the militia. The militia were the big problem over there... of a night-time, the militia would come back across the border, which in our sector was the river, and they would cross the river and move at night, at day if there was no one around, and we had to try and stop them, try and catch them, so we did a few quick reaction forces sort of thing. If some had been spotted, the infantry or the SAS would come running up and we'd launch in the aircraft to where they'd been seen and drop the boys in to try and catch them and they saw them a few times and they fired a few shots at them, but we never caught any, not while I was there anyway in the first rotation, but it was exciting nonetheless.

We were always being reminded just to be nice to [the Timorese], don't flash your money around when you go down to the markets, just take five bucks in your pocket and if you've got a photo of your wife and kids back home, take it and show them, to explain, 'This is my wife and kids,' point to their kids and point to your kids and stuff like that, so a bit of 'hearts and minds', but at the same time when you're doing it and sharing a bit of your life with a bit of their life, it's pretty good. I mean it's a good break from the shithole that is the next three months or six months for you. You've got to just treat them like people. Just because they're smaller and less well off and you don't speak the same language, doesn't mean they don't know what you're saying.

The sport was good, when we used to play soccer with them on Sunday afternoons after church and shit. I never got to play that, I played two games I think. It was too much for me. They're too quick. They're so fit, because they walk everywhere. They've got no cars. They have like these crazy Beamer [BMW] buses, feels like a Hi-ace [van], thirty-year-old Hi-ace that's got CDs all over the front windscreen that they've glued to the windscreen. I don't know why. They're just there and shit hanging off it and there's people on the roof. There's people hanging off the back and when they crash there's people, chaos, everywhere and we always used to see crashed cars everywhere, crashed trucks. But they're fit because they've got to carry everything and that was good fun playing sport with them and I think probably because Aussies love their sport and these guys, sport and religion are all they had and we got involved in both of those with them, we were always going to win a little bit with them and get on their good side.

The good thing about East Timor, there was lots of telephone and internet back home which was good and the mail was pretty regular. The biggest problem with the mail was that they couldn't find a plane big enough to fly it from Darwin to bloody Dili, so that's how much mail was coming into the country. They were filling up planes with it and it was getting banked up in Darwin but, because they put on the free mail and everyone's mum, aunty, grandma's sending them shoeboxes full of shit and so you can imagine, it doesn't take long, when there's couple of thousand soldiers overseas, to fill up a plane full of shoeboxes.

Just random people like schools, school kids, like classes of schools would write in from some hick town in the middle of Queensland. They'd just write, 'We think you're doing a great job,' and stuff like that and you'd get that and you think, 'Shit. No one even knows these people and they're writing to us.'... it was good to get mail from people you've never met before, just saying, 'Keep up the good work,' and I think that we went there to liberate someone that voted for their freedom, that was the big thing and everyone appreciated that, so yeah, everyone was happy.

There was a sat phone that you could use 24/7 which wasn't that good but it was still a phone, sort of had a break, a two-second lag in it but that was fine, and a laptop with internet access that was available 24/7 and then after six every day, every phone and every computer was free for all except for the ops, and the bosses and stuff. But there was a lot of laptops around that just got used for daily work and then after six, if they weren't being used for work you could go and jump on them and ring home or, punch out some emails, check yours. It was all good and they had obvious restrictions, you know, no porn, no death, no carnage, just emails and Interflora for sending flowers home, the normal stuff, so that was good. I remember thinking when I'm punching out my emails, 'Jeez. In the bad old days back in the First and Second World War and even Korea and Vietnam, guys must have just gone insane.'

Like you hit enter, boof, it's back in Townsville! I used to bitch to the missus because I didn't have my daily email, I'm like, 'Where the fuck?'

And then she goes, 'Sheezus! What about your grandad, he didn't get shit?'

And I'm like, 'You got me there.'

So yeah, big difference ... but we're brought up in this age, so doesn't matter what we're doing. We expect that, so if you take it away from us we're not going to be happy and so they provide it.

... Aeromedical Evacuation [AME], where we would go and pick up wounded or injured Australians or if they were bad enough, the local population, we would pick them up because there's a big hospital in Dili which was manned and run by the UN and they catered for everyone, and so we'd take them direct to Dili and that happened, especially on the first tour when guys were actively patrolling a lot of the time. They were always out for a few days at a time, go down with heat or suspected snake bites or knees, ankles, whatever, and things you do when you're humping around the bush at night-time with sixty kilos on your back and we'd go and we'd have an AME team which would be a couple of paramedics, a doctor and a nurse, and they would decide who went on the AME, depending on the severity of the case and we'd fly out there and nine times out of ten we couldn't land, so we'd winch down the paramedics and the doctor and then we'd piss off for ten or fifteen minutes and get out of the way, let them look after the patient. Then they'd radio us back up and we'd fly back overhead and winch the patient and the doctor and everyone back on board and he'd say, 'All right, we need to go to Dili.' Or, 'We need to go to Balibo.' And he'd impose maybe some height restrictions on us because his blood pressure was too low or too high and off we'd go.

I saw a couple of gunshot wounds, shrapnel from grenades. They were Australian guys. The local guy that I was lucky enough to cart back to Dili, he'd fallen off his donkey right next to this campfire that they'd set up in the middle of their village at the end of some rally, and the donkey got spooked by fireworks in the fire and ran through the fire, dragging old mate through it and then just continued bolting down the hill. They got some heinous roads with some big knobbly rocks sticking out of them, so old mate was barely recognisable when we got to him and that was pretty gory, but the one that shocked me the most was when we transported the Aussie that got shot in the back after a UD, or unauthorised discharge, from the guy behind him and very lucky to be alive. I mean, jeez, the rounds that we use and the Americans and the Poms use are not designed to kill you ... because they're so small and so fast and they're designed to tumble when they get into you, they're designed to wound you because it takes more people to look after a wounded person than if you kill him ... and I remember thinking, seeing him laying there just thinking, 'Shit, mate. That's pretty bad. You've been shot in the abdomen, you might not make it.'

And he's just laying there looking up. He felt no pain obviously because they banged him full of drugs but you could see he was thinking and he could see all of us thinking and everyone's thinking and he's freaking out and I mean he made it but that was a pretty big shock for me. We'd done heaps of practice ones back in Australia where, you know, 'Quick, someone's fallen; there's been a car crash here!'

And you'd get out there and there'd be some guy with tomato sauce and shit but to actually see it for real and you see blood on the aircraft floor and yeah, I mean it's pretty daunting and I thought, 'Shit, I hope this isn't going to happen every day.'

And it didn't because it's just an accident but certainly brings you back to earth ... I think the whole process from him getting shot to him being on the table in Darwin took all of about five hours, which is pretty bloody good really when you think about it, so yeah, pretty lucky guy. The ADF really looks after their casualties because we just don't have enough people just to let them pass away on you.

* * *

We got all sorts of new Gucci shit. We all got issued hand-held GPSs. We all got issued new uniforms and boots and cold weather gear and body armour and helmets and all our nuclear/biological suits and knives and all sorts of shit. They must have spent millions just suiting us up, backpacks to carry all the crap in and then we started getting handed out lists of what we should be taking, obviously all the new gear that we'd just got and stuff that we already had; and then about the start of February we started having these welfare briefs and that's the dead giveaway that you're about to go soon, because they start involving the family, getting them prepared for your departure, so we knew that we were going soon, or the guys that had been overseas before knew.

They gave us the date we were leaving... but we knew about a week before that it wouldn't be long because these two huge C5 Galaxies, which is the biggest freight cargo aircraft that the United States has, had landed in Townsville and you can't miss them 'cause they're so bloody loud... and we loaded the aircraft onto the Galaxies and my old man flew over from Perth because he started freaking out that I was going away. We knew that we were going to somewhere in the Middle East to fight in or against Iraq, and so he came over and the day we were leaving was all very teary-eyed, and everyone's hugging and kissing wives and kids goodbye and shit, and my fiancée and I had done it a few times with my Timor deployments, but not sort of off to a war, so it was pretty awkward. It was a strange feeling and then that was it. We took off out of Townsville and landed in Darwin and refuelled and then from there we went to Diego Garcia... and then from there we went and landed in Qatar, got some more fuel... and then we took off for our destination which was Jordan and we were at King Faisal air force base which is near Al Jafr, right smack in the middle of Jordan, between Amman and the coast.

So we got off there and it was freezing cold. It was the middle of the day and it was one degree and there was sandstorms blowing, so it was just a shit day and we were all in shock. We'd been briefed that the Americans would have all of our infrastructure set up for us, accommodation, showers, toilets, messes, all that sort of stuff and it just wasn't the case, so the aircrew were lucky. We got to move straight into our air-conditioned ATCO huts but all the ground crew and tradesmen and engineers and support staff had to live in tents for the first couple of weeks, which is pretty crap really, with the dust storms and all that that was going on, and there was thousands of Americans there and all their hardware. I've never seen so much military hardware in one place. They had more in that place than we've got in the Australian Defence Force... thousands of

Americans there, probably about fifteen hundred Poms and five hundred Aussies. The engineers went to putting the aircraft back together and getting them ready to fly and once they were back together we started our desert training, because there was nowhere really we could train for those sort of conditions other than there, so we had to wait for the winter to pass anyway before the war would start. So we started training and we kicked it off and we toured the American lines and all their aircraft and did the same with the British, and we did a lot of lessons on how to fight in a coalition with them and how dangerous it is for us to fight alongside the Americans and the British. They've fought alongside each other for a long time now and done a lot of operations together and they're set in their ways, which is good. They have a lot of routines and we just sort of had to slot in as best we could and try not to get in their way, that was the big thing, and there was all sorts of guidelines and rules that we had to make sure that we didn't get in their way.

We were there to support our Special Forces, co-located with the SAS and we...did a lot of aircraft famils [familiarisations] with those guys and learnt how to load and unload their vehicles, their long-range patrol vehicles and the like, and got ready for the war to start. Our job basically was to run supplies from where we were up the middle of Jordan to another air force base called H5 and then turn right and head towards the Iraq/Jordan border, to the Western Desert, which is where our Special Forces were based and we never crossed the border because we didn't have sufficient electronic warfare protection to be able to protect us against any surface to air missiles that the Iraqis had, so we never actually went into Iraq, which is good I thought. I didn't really want to go over the border and start getting shot at, more so by the Americans because they were shooting at everything.

... When we weren't flying, running 'ash and trash' up and around Jordan, for the first few weeks we'd just sort of hang around our own base and stayed in our rooms and read books and wrote letters, but then we started exploring around the air force base. It was a Jordanian Air Force base and it was a pretty shitty establishment but the Americans, jeez they know how to go to war. They had shops and a boozer and the best mess in town. They had recreation rooms with massive, three-metre TVs and shit and pool tables and table tennis. We started hanging out down there in our spare time and got to know a lot of them and became good friends with those guys, taught them a few Aussie card games and fleeced them of a lot of their hard-earned US dollars, drank a lot of their beer which we weren't allowed to do but we figured, 'What the hay, you never know.'

The first day [of the war] was pretty big. They pretty much launched about seventy-five per cent of the air force or the aircraft flew the first day . . . and basically they were going to hit all of the nodes, communication nodes. They were hitting all the coms [communications] points, so that they couldn't get any orders, because all orders come from Hussein and his generals, so all you'd have to do is take out the communication nodes around Baghdad and he can't tell his armies what to do. That's why it was over so quick, not only because of the firepower but because none of them were willing to make any decisions on their own, so a map of Iraq, up on the PowerPoint, and there was just red circles everywhere and that was what they were going to hit on the first day. Then the end of the second day, when they were briefing us about the previous day, I think they'd hit about eighty-five per cent of everything that they wanted to hit and that was mostly coms and radar dishes, all that sort of stuff that could impede aircraft movement over Iraq, a lot of missile sites. They hit a lot of missile sites . . . Day two and the PowerPoint come up again and all these red dots had turned blue because they'd been hit by the blue forces and they were gone, and then it was like that every night, not to that grand scale. Obviously it scaled down and the line would move up and down and as they overcome a town, it'd be an American flag there or a British flag there and there'd be the lone Aussie flag out in the Western Desert.

It was all CNN and BBC and stuff like that. There was TVs everywhere and we didn't have com, we didn't have internet or mail or phone back to Australia until the war had finished, so there was almost a two-month period where we didn't know what was going on back in Australia. The supply lines hadn't been set up or established well enough yet to handle the volume of mail, so we weren't getting any mail because they were still bringing over stores, so we didn't know what was going on back home, but just the sheer amount of coverage on the war was too much to take in and then we would get briefed about all this stuff and then the next day we would see it on the news, 'Oh yeah, that's that place we were told they were going to smash last night.'

It was just PowerPoint presentations of buildings and villages and towns that were going to get hit the next day and then the following night on CNN we'd see it all again after it'd been hit and you're just thinking, 'Shit,' you know, it was just, 'Why are you telling me all this? Just let me do my bit, I don't need to know all this!'

And it would go into detail about where the missiles were coming from, who was hitting it, what they were hitting it with, what expected casualties and all this sort of shit; and then the next night after it had happened you'd see it on the news and it was just a strange feeling.

[There] was only one time over there that I feared for my life, the whole crew did. We'd just been fitted out with a new electronic warfare protection system which was the best we had available to us and we were flying along the edge of a huge sandstorm and the radar that comes with this protection system, it talks to you and tells you what's happening and it gives you a left or right, then a clock ray direction, so it'll say, 'Left, nine o'clock,' and then it'll tell you what it is and what it's doing, so it'll give you a missile description and whether it's just sweeping you or tracking or it's launched, and we got the first warning which is just the sweeping warning. We got that for about five minutes and we thought, 'Well we're in Jordan, no one's going to shoot at us . . .'

And then it started saying, 'Tracking' which meant that they've locked onto us and if they wanted to they could launch and then that went on for a couple more minutes and we thought, 'Oh no, it's just someone painting us up, checking us out, seeing who we are.'

And then we sort of put it in the back of our minds as just this annoying noise and finally it said, you know, 'SA7' or, 'SA', can't remember what it was, 'Left, nine o'clock launch' and because there was this big dust storm only a few hundred metres out to our left . . . we knew that once the missile came through the dust storm we'd have no time at all to do anything . . . and so everyone basically started yelling, 'Fuckin' dive, dive!' and you basically want to get down as low as you can and hide behind the train, hide behind some hills or some trees or shit but if you've been to a desert you know there's fuck all of that around, so we just flew even lower, in a ten-tonne machine doing three hundred kilometres an hour, eight to ten metres off the ground, which is not kosher, and so that was scary enough as it was because you have very little depth perception when you're flying over the desert even in the day; it's just all yellow or white and nothing came of it and no missile came and we blew off the rest of the mission and everyone was just not saying anything the whole way back and we went back to our base, back to the air force base and we landed and everyone sort of got out and goes, 'Fuck!'

. . . Well, we were there to find weapons of mass destruction and apparently there's none there, so I've been told, and if that wasn't good enough then we were there because Hussein had gone back to killing Kurds and he was running black-market oil out of the country and he was impeding the no-go zones in the airspace, so theoretically that in itself was good enough to go back in there and kick him out, legally maybe, but the UN didn't sanction it, so obviously not, but we all accepted it. We thought, 'Oh right, he's got all these bombs and shit.'

And we'd trained for it as if he had an arsenal of them. We were always doing these gas-training drills and if you ever get the chance to do it, go and do some gas-training drills because it's really fucked and you just get a feeling for what it's like I guess, if you ever want your eyes to sting and your breathing to be all short and your lungs to burn, it's good fun, so we just took it for granted that he must have all this stuff if we're doing all this training, if we're getting anthrax inoculations and shit which is making people throw up and, you know, it's only good for British-made anthrax in the '50s. It's not good for the anthrax that he's got but, 'give it to me anyway'. So we all believed what we were being told and we all thought we were going to go and free the oppressed people of Iraq from this dictator, but after our little scare I just started thinking, 'Well, who's going to replace him? This Bush guy's just as bad.'

I mean he's imposing his will on the other side of the country where at least Hussein's just doing it in his own country. I've got a little bit cynical I will admit but I wasn't going around preaching it. I just sort of kept that shit to myself and the boys all thought it anyway.

[Bush] was just a goose. To us he was just a clown, mate, and it made us feel worse that Johnny had gone in with him. It's like, 'Well, it's the blind leading the blind, mate, come on, and why are we risking our lives for something that's just . . . ?' you know. Well yes he's not the nicest guy in the world and he's done a lot of bad things to a lot of bad people but it doesn't mean that I have to be over here risking my life when Australia's not being affected at all, you know. What's he going to do to us? Nothing!'

'Oh, but he's giving arms to the terrorists.'

Yeah, the terrorists you can't find in Afghanistan . . . and it just felt like they were chasing their tails and we were the ones doing the chasing for them and it just wasn't worth the risk and I think that was the clincher for me and a lot of other guys when we got back, to get out. 'No, enough's enough.' I mean a lot of guys don't stay career soldiers anymore because the entry levels for defence are a lot higher than they used to be, so they're getting educated people in the Defence Force and smart people know when they're being hosed over.

It was always interesting going into the American compound and seeing these young kids, they were seventeen, just armed to the teeth and all I had was a washing bag. I wanted to go and use the washing machines but I couldn't because my vehicle might be a threat and you're just like, 'Mate, come on, I'm going to do my laundry!'

But they're a different breed. They are so patriotic that I'm sure it brainwashes them all. Probably one in ten was capable of thinking for themselves and having an opinion other than what had been preached to them. I was more worried about getting shot in the American compound after the war than I was about driving around the base and running into Jordanians or something like that. I was just always cautious when I walked around there... They didn't come across as professional or as well-trained as us, and I think that's because of the way they are trained. They're all so specialised that for example, the guys that drive the trucks, that's all they do. If it gets a flat tyre they have to radio someone to come and change a tyre for them. If the dude on the gun gets shot, the truck driver can't stand up and start shooting the gun because he doesn't know how to use the gun. And each person's got a simple little job and that's it, whereas all of the Australians are diversified and can do a whole range of different jobs. Our average age is much higher than theirs. I guess their recruitment strategy's different than ours and they just suck these young kids off the street, like we do too but I think our entry level's a little bit higher than theirs. It has to be seen to be believed really, the difference... it's just crazy. Steve Irwin was the flavour of the month over there and shit, so we're all crocodile hunters driving Land Cruisers and shit, and they just don't know. That's just what they get fed on telly. History for them is American history, you know. They don't do any other history in school unless you specialise in it at college and shit like that, so they just don't know, which is fair enough... but the boys were always in your face about how good their air force is or how good their equipment is and how small and there's more bloody police in the NYPD than there is in the Australian Defence Force, which is true, just shit like that. They were always spruiking off, so we'd just take their money at cards and take their women. It was good.

* * *

I came home, had my Christmas holidays in May and June, found it hard to talk to friends and family because they were all of the opinion that we shouldn't have been there and like I'm trying to feel proud for what I'd done and I'd come back alive and none of my buddies got hurt, and you all think that what I was involved in was wrong. So that was really awkward and I mean it wasn't like Vietnam or anything, but it was still awkward nonetheless, and some of my family are really politically orientated and they get right into that shit and I mean they smash me with the questions about how I felt and, 'Do I think that,' you know, 'Killing innocent women and children?' I'm like, 'Hang on, I didn't kill anyone! Sure I helped, but I didn't pull the trigger or anything and I didn't get shot at, I'm home!' and so that was awkward.

[The WWII blokes] they did it so much harder than what we did. I mean we had so much contact with home. We were well supplied, well clothed, well fed. Information about what was going on around us was constant. We always knew what we were doing the next day, if not the next week and because of the contact we never felt isolated and there was always something for us to do. One of the first things that they would set up for us would be these rec tents or somewhere where you can go and get away from it all and stuff like that, and we weren't fighting for Australia. We were fighting, or peacekeeping, for someone else, and they were fighting for Australia and they fought a global war and we sort of peacekeeped in little pockets around here and there and Iraq, but I have the utmost respect for those guys. It must have been so tough for them compared to now, but they probably knew no different anyway. Life would have been tough back then anyway, I mean obviously war's a dangerous place to be at the best of times and I think the way we sort of fight and peacekeep is more clinical now. It's more precise, whereas they did everything on mass scale. You must have the maximum amount of firepower and people and they just went head to head and that must have been chaotic, and trying to keep the information and the supplies and everything up to that many people must have just been intense, and I can't imagine how hard it would have been not having that contact with home all the time and writing letters that would take months to get back to Australia and the same getting to them.

They had far greater issues than we encounter nowadays, you know. On the medical side of it, if they got injured, how long is it going to be before they're in the hospital? I mean for us it's a couple of hours at tops. For them it could have been a couple of days and that could be life or death. And the amount of people that went, hundreds of thousands of Australians went to war and just the huge scale. The whole country involved. One purpose and that was to win, to maintain our sovereignty and that's why they went and fought . . . it would have been huge to take that on and I've never felt that. It's always been peacekeeping and trying to find the enemy as opposed to, 'They're coming to get you,' and I mean the Middle East was just resupplying the good guys so that they can go and get the bad guys. We've never been on the back foot. I was never being pursued by an enemy like they were back then, like grandad was, and it must have been scary times for them, especially at his age, fifteen, sixteen, fighting the Japanese in PNG with a rifle that didn't fire a hundred per cent of the time and a first aid station that's a kilometre and a half away, but it'll take you two days to get there, up and down the mountains so no, it's hardly comparable, only on the death and destruction side I would say. Everything else is not comparable because they just did it so much harder than we did. With all the technology nowadays, it's so much easier to press a button . . . the guys that went and fought the Japanese, shit! They were coming for Australia! You certainly would have had motivation to keep fighting I think, whereas I think we lack that motivation, to a certain extent. We're all there to do our job and do it well and we did and Australians always do I think. I'm pretty proud that when we go somewhere we do a good job. I wouldn't put myself in the same league as those guys, no way. They're way, way above me.

It just frustrates me a bit I guess, that you get labelled. When we came back from East Timor, holy shit, couldn't put a foot wrong mate. I could have slept with the mayor's daughter and left her pregnant and I still would have been a champion because we freed the people of East Timor and everyone loved us. Jesus, go to Iraq, nearly get gassed and missiled and you're a baby-killer and it's like, 'Well we were just doing . . . what's the difference?'

510 • Voices of War

Yes, the outcome and why we were there but I mean the soldiers that you see now marching in front of you were doing the same job. They were in East Timor as they were in the Middle East. If they want to throw sticks and stones, go to Canberra, you know.

I'm still waiting on counselling for my second trip to Timor. They get to you when they get to you, mate, and they're never going to get to me 'cause I'm not there anymore, but there's not enough psych people in the Defence Force to cover the amount of deployments that we're on at the moment, and when you get units like the Special Forces and aviation and infantry that are constantly getting rotated overseas, you just get lost. It's too hard for them to catch up and it's not the psych corps fault or anyone's fault. It's just that there's not enough of them and we go overseas too much, or we go on exercise here too much, and we're just spread everywhere, that it's too hard for these people. We got a little tiny smidgen of counselling before we came home, nothing too much, it was a group session. Normally they get you by yourself and make sure you're not twitching and stuff when they say, 'Bang!' but they do a good job. I was very impressed after my first trip to East Timor because I wasn't having issues but I did have questions about, you know, how I was feeling and stuff like that and was it normal, and when they do get you, they do a marvellous job, they really do, and they're really personal and confident and they know what they're doing, and it's the same before you go with the welfare briefs, you know. They educate the family who, fifty per cent of the time knows nothing about the army except that's where Dad goes at seven-thirty and that's where he comes from at four, and so they do an excellent job. It's just they can't get to everyone.

It's made me a much better person. I went in, I had no direction and I was relatively clueless in the ways of the world and I came out the other end unscathed, a few football injuries and some free operations, but granted I'm ten years older almost than when I went in, but I'm a far more mature and self-aware person than I think I ever would have been had I not joined up and stayed in Perth with my friends, and I only have to go home every Christmas to justify that...

TED SMOUT
1898–2004

Stretcher-bearer
World War I

At school...we wore those high-peaked, straw, mushroom hats. They were known as mushroom hats with a very wide brim that carried the anti-fly string which you wrapped down around your neck. It was sheep country and the flies were very bad. They sort of attacked your eyes. I should have been born in Cunnamulla but there were no medical facilities, no hospital, the railway finished at Wyandra then, so my mother had to come to Brisbane for the birth.

We came down when I was seven years old to Brisbane...and my father was a Methodist, a churchman, but sort of a lay preacher. So I had a lot of religion pumped into me when I was young. Church on Sunday morning. My mother was the organist...and it was church in the morning at ten o'clock. Sunday school in the afternoon. Church again in the evening. So by the time I was sixteen I had a little bit too much religion. I was a very good churchgoer for many years after that. Those days on a Sunday, primitive Methodist people, and they don't believe in theatres, no dances. On Sunday they used to draw the blinds in the house. I remember the story told, I was walking along behind my father whistling and he said, 'Don't whistle! People will think you're happy.'

He was a bit too fond of the razor strap he used to belt us with. He used to use that fairly frequently. There were five in the family and though he had a reasonable government job he had to be careful financially. We couldn't have butter and jam on the bread. We could have butter or jam but not both. That was one of the rules at the time.

... There weren't any big departmental stores. You just bought at the local convenience store. Of course milk was delivered to your door and bread was delivered. There was a van selling butter and small goods, ham and lard and what have you. They came round to the house. The greengrocers came around with a van selling vegetables. A lot of shopping was done in the home. Vehicles coming around.

... I had a steel hoop which you used to trundle with a stick and another thing was a cat, which was a piece of broomstick handle that long, cut off at a point at each end. You used to put that down on the ground and then throw it up in the air and try and hit it while it was up in the air. And they were our toys. Later on we had a trolley made with kerosene tins—kerosene came in four-gallon tins—and there were two cases—wooden cases. So we got a set of wheels and made a trolley. We used to take that up the top of the hill and set off down the hill. Sit behind it and come back and pull it up the hill again. The gutters, the stormwater gutters, they were cement and they used to form a track and you could slide down those in your bare feet. But they were our toys—the hoop and the jack, so that compared to today, my great-grandchildren, I mean they've got everything. Bikes, mountain bikes, computers, the lot. But those days, a different story.

... The bus to school was horse-driven—a big coach with four horses and the driver used to have a very long whip that could reach the back of the bus—we used to jump on the back of the bus, back step, and some kid on the footpath would yell out, 'Whip behind!' and he'd lash round with his whip. You had to jump off the bus before the whip got you and then walk the rest of the way. They just got jealous you know, of anyone riding.

... You certainly were not brought up on the belief the world owed you a living. I mean discipline was quite strict. Children were spoken to when you spoke to them, before that they kept quiet. That was the story of the upbringing and training. Fairly strict.

* * *

We used to do cadet drill and we had the Lee Enfield rifles, 25/22 calibre. And we used to use that for shooting at the rifle range. There was a rifle range in Adelaide Street where the Shrine is now ... I was a fairly good shot as a youngster. And later on, of course, we had compulsory military training. So we had a .303 rifle and we used to shoot at the range up to six hundred yards. It was just part of the school curriculum. Learning discipline. I think that's a good one. There wasn't any thought of war. It wasn't thought of at the time. That came later.

... The main influence [to enlist] was the girls. I was fairly big for my age let alone presentable and girls used to hand you a white feather—meaning you were a coward, you know. The whole peer pressure. It was easier to enlist than to stay at home. The pressure was so heavy. Although I was a year ahead at school most of my mates had gone so I was kind of susceptible to this pressure which resulted in my enlistment at seventeen years of age. Put my age up. My father was quite happy about it but in those days you had to get your parents' consent as twenty-one was the age of consent. My father was quite happy about it but I had a great job persuading my mother to agree. Finally she did.

... In those days the Australian population was essentially British, not like later, when there were a lot of Greeks and later Italians. There were a few German settlers living up round the lower area but they returned quite a few of them as soon as the war broke out. They didn't give any trouble. But the population was essentially British and we looked on England as the Mother Country. We always spoke of England as the Mother Country. My father was a cockney. My mother was born in Australia but of English parents, so an English background and ninety per cent of the Australian population had a British background. Mostly English but some Scotch and Irish. So they were very much affiliated with Great Britain in the war and the AIF—the Australian Imperial Force was formed and you enlisted in the Australian Imperial Force which was attached to the British Army, under British generals who were floating the war on the Crimean War textbook. They were hopeless. We really never saw them at the front. They just put men up against positions, in front of machine guns, casualties very heavy. It wasn't until the Australian division of the army corps was put under General Monash, later Sir John Monash, that the Australian Army was able to do things.

... When the war broke out I went from the auditor's office straight into camp and of course, off to France for four years... I joined the army medical corps merely because some British general said mateship was bad for discipline. Mates have to be separated. Three of us had enlisted together and we wanted to stay together and they put us into separate units in the infantry. And the only way we could get together was to transfer. So we applied for the artillery but there were no vacancies and we were told there was a vacancy out in the medical corps, and that's the only reason we joined the medical corps. And the three of us went through the whole war together. One of them got the Military Medal at Passchendaele. We three survived. Mateship was one of the best things in the army, not the worst. It enabled you to survive.

... We were the last division to be formed under General Monash—the 3rd Division, and we were the only one with what was called a sanitary section. It's called the hygiene section now. It was a small unit of twenty-seven men and there were two health inspectors, qualified, a couple of car drivers because we had our own ambulance, a couple of plumbers, couple of carpenters and the others were general knowledge soldiers and my particular job was water testing. I was trained to test water and treat it because in France the farmhouses there were built like a 'U' and in the middle of the 'U' there was a huge cesspit about as big as this room or bigger. Everything went into it. And the well would only be fifty feet away from that so it was polluted, but of course the French children had it since they were babies. It didn't affect them but if our troops had drunk it, it would have killed them so we used to go forward and lock the well up, test the water and chlorinate it—make it fit for drinking. We weren't particularly popular but we did not lose one soldier in the whole of the war from drinking polluted water which was quite remarkable.

... In training we learnt first aid of course but I went to the Department of Bacteriology which was up in Wickham Terrace—that's where the headquarters were. Two-storey brick building and in the grounds they had just an ordinary-sized allotment... and they had a cow and the whole of its body was infected with smallpox. And they had a table with a galvanised trough running along the side. And they used to just get this cow alongside the table, put straps on him and then tilt the table up. He was belly up and they scraped it off his belly into this channel and that would drain down into a bucket and that was then treated, boiled and then broken down into smallpox vaccination. That was the smallpox and then the flu vaccines and other vaccines, they were done in test tubes. It was treated by boiling and then broken down to the right strength—so many parts to a pint of water and they became the vaccine for influenza, and that type of sickness. We made all of those.

... We had long trousers and putties, army boots, and a tunic. A tunic with the Australian badge on each collar and a colour patch on each arm. Our colour patch was like the shape of an egg, chocolate colour. That was the army medical corps colour patch. And the tunic had two breast pockets and two big side pockets and your trousers had pockets so you had plenty of pocket space. We had not only long trousers and putties but we had riding britches and leather leggings. We were a bit flash.

* * *

We went across on a troopship called the *Demosthenes*. It was a British ship that had twelve hundred men aboard—very crowded. The 41st Battalion, there was a cyclist corps and a legal corps and our unit, and the troopship colonel was Colonel Rankin of Rankin Collieries and he was a retired colonel. He just left everything to a Pommy sergeant major. He was the orderly room sergeant. He was very officious—universally hated—and bingo, then called housie, was illegal, because we had a housie game and we used to play this on deck and we were all up on deck in our shorts and we'd give warning if he was coming.

'Here he comes, here he comes!'

And he actually had an order put up on the noticeboard saying that any troops saying, 'Here he comes,' as he approached, anyone found guilty of that would be prosecuted. So when he came the next day, after he passed we said, 'There he goes, the bastard. There he goes, the bastard!'

So we still played housie.

... We left Sydney and went round to Perth where we formed a convoy with about six other troopships. We called into Durban for a day then we went round to Cape Town to refuel the steamships with coal. There were no cranes. Refuelling's done by an endless chain of kaffirs—niggers—and they had a soft basket which they carried on their shoulders, full of coal. Endless chain of them going up and they just tipped it into the hold of the ship. This was how it was loaded.

We went to shore every day and marched for exercise and we never broke ranks because we were told by the colonel... that the mayor of Cape Town was afraid of so many troops coming ashore that he didn't want us there, and the mayor heard about this and sent a note aboard that this wasn't true. They were waiting to welcome us. That was the signal for everyone to break ship which we did. We had a great time. You couldn't buy a drink—they insisted on paying for it. And eventually they rounded us up and they pulled the troopship out in the middle of the harbour, took us aboard in dinghies as we went up, to check our name and number... up to the prosecutors.

The prosecuting officer was Lieutenant Ash... and I was a second cousin... and we were manning the hospital, so I warned him... if we got field punishment we wouldn't be able to man the hospital and there were two or three serious cases there so he came and said, 'I'll just ask you some questions and you say "yes" to every question. Don't do anything, just say "yes".'

So the exam came and he said, 'Remember the day of breaking ship?'—'Yes.'

'You were standing there at the gangway'—'Yes.'

'And you were swept off your feet, found yourself ashore'—'Yes.'
'So you decided as you were ashore you might as well stay?'—'Yes.'
So we weren't fined. It was 'involuntary desertion'. We were
pardoned.

* * *

We got to England in late June [1916] and we were there until
November. At Lark Hill Camp, Salisbury Plains . . . a big army camp
with fibro-cement huts, holding about thirty to forty people in bunks
and Salisbury Plains was quite close to the city of Salisbury and
Stonehenge and we had a few months there. We were very fit physically.
We used to march every day about five miles . . . What pay we got
we used to spend on food because if you had tea at five o'clock then
by ten o'clock you were hungry again . . . We didn't have a great deal
of contact with civilians. And of course all the men were gone. Just
old men and women working in the munitions factories and what
have you . . . We did get around. We got to Stonehenge to see the big
stones and the cathedral.

. . . We went across to Le Havre which was down towards the
Spanish end of France. The Channel was much wider there and Le
Havre was a big city. The overnight camp there was quite a big
establishment. But it wasn't very well equipped. Bell tents and half
the sides were missing in the bell tents. Of course if people were just
there for one night they could tolerate that and the Irish guard
sergeant, if they were only there for one night, all they got was bully
beef and biscuits and he flogged the rations. He got away with it
because they left the next day but we were caught up there in isolation
because of mumps and we were there for three weeks. That was a
horse of another colour. He still kept flogging the rations and we
had no bread. We were getting biscuits, army biscuits, no fresh food,
till we complained about it and he was eventually charged and
dishonourably discharged and he got six months' gaol.

. . . On November 16 our first billet was in L'Ecole Professional
which was the technical college and we were billeted there and we
were quite comfortable really. We had our own stretcher-beds with

mattresses. And the town of Armentières was still functioning as a town. There was nothing there except old ladies and old men. All the young females were gone to work in factories and the hotels used to be around the town square and they used to close down at eight o'clock at night. The town square was cobblestones. One night a plane came over and dropped a bomb on the cobblestone pavement, shrapnel, several wounded. We had to go out and bring them in.

Otherwise it was a quiet sector. The trenches there were well maintained over the years by both sides as a kind of a training ground for trench warfare . . . you'd go round there and do seven to ten days in the trenches . . . and that particular section of the Western Front was shared by both sides as a kind of training area . . . with a no-man's-land between them. Shells coming over and machine-gun fire about every half-hour and they'd have raids at night—just the same as happened later on. That was training. Practically every commissioned officer had a Military Cross because he'd be sent on a raid at night and if he came back alive, he'd get the Military Cross . . . The Germans were very methodical. They used to raid right on the half-hour tick. They were all allowed fifty rounds and when they were gone you could just walk across quite safely.

I saw my first casualty there. His name was Purdey. He was six foot one tall. He was a fatalist. You know, 'If I'm going to be killed, I'll be killed.'

And killed he was. Because he wouldn't duck in the trenches because he reckoned you know, he'd be immune, and he was shot by a sniper right through the head. And that was my first casualty. I had to bring him out. He was dead. His name was Purdey. He was a champion chess player in New South Wales. Didn't do him any good in the trenches.

. . . [There was a] huge difference between English units and the Scots units and [the Australians]. The Scots soldiers were more like Australians but the Pommy, see anyone who went to what they call a Public School which was a private school, automatically got a commission. Not a question of his capacity. If he went to a Public School, he got a commission. So the strong caste system—the upper class and the lower class—and the ordinary Tommy [English soldier] was the lower class and if the officer was lost, the NCO didn't know what to do. There was nobody to take over. Whereas in the Australian Army, and the Scots Army, there was always somebody—officer was killed, somebody would step in—sergeant or private, somebody would step in and take charge. There was always somebody to take responsibility . . . the poor old Tommy, they all sat around . . . He was just taught to obey orders and not ask questions. They were just cannon fodder . . . the infantry was just cannon fodder put up against impregnable positions, facing machine guns. Casualties were terrible.

* * *

[The trenches] were badly infected with lice—body lice—and rats as big as cats. All the trenches—and some of them had six inches of water in the foot of them with duckboards to walk on, and the common illness was trench feet. If you got your feet wet, they'd be frozen. Suffer from trench feet and then they'd have to be amputated. Perhaps toes or sometimes the whole foot.

. . . [The Germans] could be a hundred yards away in some cases, some cases further, but the nearest would be a hundred yards and we never occupied the front-line trench, we occupied the reserve trench. From the front line there was a trench coming back up to the reserve trench. And there'd be spots where the roof was protected and it'd be open but we'd be in one of these areas . . . and that's where we were on duty at the dressings-table or in the reserve trenches. We had a little table with a primus stove, hessian round it and we used to light the primus stove to warm all our feet. Played cards or whatever. Filled in the time doing nothing . . . I learnt to play bridge there.

. . . A typical day—you'd go to one of the camps and go round and check and you'd find they were short of latrines and you'd order a pit to be dug and our carpenters built the seats and put them there and then the plumbers built grease traps. You establish grease traps and the kitchen and generally ensure that sanitation was reasonable . . . Prior to that they'd be stooling all around the camp. That was our job daily and then at night we used to go into the township, the town square. The establishments used to go till eight o'clock at night. French beer two francs a glass, which was a penny. We were able to drink the French beer. For two francs a glass it was cheap enough. That filled in quite a while we were there. Coldest winter in forty years. Really cold.

... But even if you got away from the front you were still subjected to shellfire and more bombing, you were never completely free of this. It was an incessant pressure you know. It never stopped. There was never any respite ... one time we went right back about twelve miles behind the line to a fairly big town called Poperinge [Belgium] and the Germans came over and they started bombing at eight o'clock, when the hotels or establishments around the town square were closing down and the soldiers were all coming out, they came and dropped bombs on the town square. Casualties were quite heavy. We were called out to bring them in and then they came over right on top, every half-hour till three o'clock in the morning. Right on the dot of half-hour. So of course eventually our searchlighters knew they were coming, so the searchlights would pick them up. Anti-aircraft guns would start firing at them. And they dropped their bombs.

We were in a brick house next to a big building which was the overnight billet for British officers going on leave to England and this was their target and we heard this huge bomb drop ... almost on top of us, and it didn't detonate, didn't explode. And we went over the next morning and it had come through the tile roof of this building—there was no ceiling—and that couldn't detonate it. It landed on the big French bed—those high beds. A British officer was staying there overnight, broke both his legs, and fell off onto the floor beside him and didn't explode. We went out in the morning and here was this 200-pound shell with fins put on it as a tailpiece and used as a bomb. The artillery people came and took it away and detonated it. So he was a bit unlucky. He got the fright of his life—instead of going on leave he had his legs broken.

* * *

[The ambulances were] all Fords. They were all black. Black Fords—the car went for about forty years. And you drained the water out of the radiator in the evenings otherwise it would have frozen and broken the radiator. And then in the morning you used to jack one back wheel up, because then you'd start the car in gear. No electric starter. Magneto ignition. So a gang of men would line up and they'd crank until she fired ... the gear box got its oil from the sump in the Fords in those days, so you lit a primus stove and put it under the sump to unfreeze the oil and then once that motor started it never stopped all day 'cause if you stopped it, it'd freeze up again. And then that night you'd drain it and the next morning that was repeated. That was the procedure. The car idled all day. It was that cold.

... [The field-dressing station was] just the bare floor and a table—operating table in the middle of it and stretchers all round the place. The Germans were over there and there were British round here just lying on the stretchers waiting to be treated. Brought in by the ambulance. You might have up to a hundred stretchers round the floor with soldiers waiting to be treated. You'd get different coloured labels according to where they had to go. Whether to a base hospital or, if they were lucky enough, to England. But the wounds were dressed, bleeding was stopped, sufficient to tide them over for a week or so ... the ones who were least wounded made the most noise. Chap who'd had his toe shot off would be yelling blue murder. The ones who were seriously injured were semi-conscious. Never heard from them.

... You had your regimental first-aid people that would just put a pad on and temporarily stop the bleeding. They'd be brought by the army stretcher-bearer to pick-up point and then the army medical corps stretcher-bearers would pick them up there—mostly on duckboards because of the mud—and bring them to a pick-up point. They'd be put in an ambulance and taken to the field-resting station by the ambulance. About a kilometre behind the line. That was the procedure. We'd either be manning the field-dressing station, helping the surgeons or we'd take our turn at stretcher-bearing. Do a bit of each.

. . . It wasn't very pleasant with shelling going on all the time and some of the shells came uncomfortably close. Quite a few of them didn't detonate; the ground was so muddy that it was too soft to detonate some of the shells. But the trouble was you couldn't get off the duckboard because you'd go up to your knees in mud. You couldn't move. Had to stay on the duckboard and if part of the duckboard was shot away you had to wait for the pioneer crowd [engineers] to come up and lay another duckboard down before you could move. You had to walk on the duckboard and there'd be wounded men, you could see them but you couldn't do anything for them. Couldn't get to them . . . you could see them calling out to you but you couldn't do anything for them. You couldn't get off the duckboards. You'd be up over your knees in mud. Just leave them there to die. You couldn't do anything else. Pretty terrible. But you could do nothing about it. You were fully occupied bringing out the men that you could bring out without having to be concerned about the ones that you couldn't . . . the shells didn't recognise the Red Cross which you had on your arm. Didn't make any difference to them. Oh yes we had casualties in the medical corps. Nintey-nine per cent of casualties were in the infantry of course, but there were casualties.

. . . The worst was Passchendaele. We were looking after a field-dressing station there and stretcher-bearing to it. We had our own ambulance and I worked seventy-two hours with very little sleep. Just lie on the floor of the dressing-station and they'd run you over with their feet going out for stretcher-bearers. You had to get out then for the stretcher-bearing. That was on for three days. Seventy-two hours with very little sleep. You had to be young to take that. The casualties were horrific. Horrific. The chloroform—they just stuck a thing over their face and poured the chloroform on to put them out. No question. As for a cardiogram or monitoring, that was unthought of. The doctors manning that dressing-station would learn more surgery in a week than they would have in years. Some of the wounds were terrible. Arms blown off and one British major had both his legs blown off. He died from loss of blood before we could save him. The British big gun came and they established it about a hundred yards away from our dressings table. We remonstrated but it made no difference, then a German spotting plane came over and directed the German artillery and the first shell landed on the trench side of the field station and the second one spot on. It blew both this major's legs off. But they were guilty of that kind of thing. Like the Germans. You'd see a church with a big red cross on the roof be stacked with small arms ammunition. We were guilty of the same type of thing.

You didn't exactly become callous but you were dispassionate about it. You kind of just treated them, not so much as individuals, just as human beings and the casualties—just became immune to it. That's all there was about it ... it was really bad. Passchendaele was terrible ... men being put up against impregnable positions, just being slaughtered by the German generals. Terrible.

* * *

The Americans were very conscious of their manpower. You know, they'd use vast amounts of artillery shelling before they went in. Whereas the British were inclined to be a bit careful with that. Then of course, they fed their troops so well. When they arrived they had these civilian tan shoes, pug-nose shoes and of course they were hopeless. They pulled them off and made a huge mountain of them and gave them the Australian waterproof boots, you know. So I pinched a pair of shoes, put them away and when I went off to Paris on leave some months later I had these beautiful tan shoes. Amazing. They had a khaki wool shirt and trousers with epaulettes with two pockets—beautiful.

You used to come out of the trenches and you were riddled with lice, you'd strip off your underwear and chuck it in and go in the steam bath. You'd be given new underclothing. Well the steam would kill the lice but it doesn't kill the eggs. So the armpits were riddled with eggs. Used to light a cigarette or small cigar and go *'pssst'* and explode them. Then you'd put the clothing back on. We'd go to the public baths on Tuesday, put all your clothes in and you'd get new underclothing and then on the Thursday the clothes that you put in on Tuesday came out on Thursday. So the Yanks went on Tuesday with these beautiful shirts and passed them in. We all went for baths on Thursday and we got these Yankee shirts and they got our grey flannels. They weren't happy about that. But I got this Yankee shirt with two breast pockets and epaulettes and when I went off to leave with the jacket under my tunic and the tie and I had leather leggings— part of the uniform and these fancy shoes, I was really Beau Brummel.

* * *

In April 1918 the Germans broke through the advance. They could have gone straight through to Paris in trucks because there was nobody left. The British Army lost all their guns, even their rifles but they stopped to consolidate and the Australian Army shifted down from Belgium to the front and far beyond, and we used to attack every night. The Germans thought we were strong and we were. So that gave us from April till August to build up, which, with American supply, built up unbelievably. On August 8th the advance at Villers Bretonneux, the field guns were almost touching each other. Aeroplanes, you name it, they had everything. Terrific. So the British advance was quite as successful as the Germans. They went right through and we finished up in the north in an army hospital and of course that was a champagne district, so the courtyard of the hospital was a big bed of strawberry plants and they were big plants, big leaves. But round every plant was a bottle of champagne so we had a good supply. The officers wondered where we were getting it from. It was a well-kept secret. But then the advance went from there and was quite successful.

The Armistice, we were back a fair way from the front in a rest camp in a little village called Fouquohertnesle . . . there was one hotel we used to drink in and that night the hotel owner just threw the place open—free drinks for all. So we spent the whole night there and the next day I decided I'd go to Paris which I did—AWL [Absent Without Leave]—so I got on the train and got to Paris and I had ten days there before I was picked up by a British MP sergeant, put on the train back to the unit and the OC [Officer Commanding] asked me if I'd been picked up, said, 'I'll have to charge you, otherwise I'm in trouble.'

I said 'Yes.'

So he put me up and fined me fourteen days pay which I thought was a bit silly because the war was over but it was worth it.

I had a great time in Paris because I was skilled in French. I'd learnt French at college, so I was quite good at it—a second language. I had a pretty good supply of French money because in the advance on April 18 we struck a group of German prisoners coming back unarmed and we'd just made a pot of morning tea, so we boiled the billy and gave them tea and some cigarettes and the officer, he had a pocket in the tail of his tunic and he pulled out—he'd drawn the company pay, so he handed me this wad of German notes. So when we got back to the village bank I went and cashed half of it in French money, kept half of it in case Germany won the war, so when I went off to Paris I had a few thousand francs in French money.

... I booked into a hotel, The Rue Calais, about two hundred yards from the Folies Bergère. Just to go to the Folies Bergère. Had a great time. Really enjoyed it... They had a huge tricolour and at the end of the programme this flag came down to cover the whole ceiling and they played 'La Marseillaise'. Everyone got up and sang it, including me, and I was the only Australian soldier there... all the froggies there were going 'Viva Australia!'. So I had some good times... because I had plenty of French money and the girls were quite accommodating, so generally speaking you could really enjoy yourself. You didn't always finish up back in the hotel either. They'd have a flat or something. Spend the night with them. I was young and active.

When we went back [to France] in 1998 they took us out to the Folies in the morning. We met the director. He gave us a book on the Folies Bergère. I went up and had a look at the stage. We didn't go to the show there because it was a men's stripping show. We didn't go to that.

***

I was discharged on the 8th September 1919... the great disappointment to me was when I left the auditor's office, I was promised that my seniority would be preserved. There wasn't any other returned men in our office and they were completely unforgiving if you absented yourself. Settling back in an office after war service is very difficult. Sometimes I'd just throw the pen at the wall and have to go out and walk around town and I'd be put on the mat for this. And I was quite unhappy in the office. Pay was lousy because we were professional officers—we had no union. So the ordinary clerks had outstripped us salary-wise so the salary was pretty poor and they hadn't reserved my seniority. They hadn't done it. There were four men ahead of me. There should have been none because the one ahead of me was killed ... I had no intention of staying and while I was there I had a complete breakdown, delayed action from shell shock ... I think it's the pressure of trying to settle back into office work. That was partly it and the dissatisfaction of the job.

... I went out on the property outside of Cunnamulla, spent three months there, got my physical health back became quite fit physically ... but still mentally I was a bit troubled. Well, I'd burst out in tears. You know, no control at all ... I finished up working as an unpaid jackaroo. I did everything. Shearing, and lamb-marking, biting his tail with your teeth, droving, did everything. So after three months were up I was as fit as a fiddle physically but still mentally in trouble. A long way back.

... I went teetotal when I got back, for twelve months. Deliberately, to break off any association with any—you see most of them got back before me because I was in London for six months so when I got back everyone I knew was back here and the first thing was 'Come and have a drink.' I'm not drinking. I did that as a matter of principle for a year so I could cut adrift from most of these coves. A few of them were all right in army life but they were on different sides in civilian life so I wanted to make a complete break. I went teetotal for a year, which was a good thing ... a few particular friends, but apart from those I wanted to cut adrift from anything connected with the war. It was a kind of revulsion. A reaction and I wanted to get back into civilian life without any attachments to any ex-army groups at all. So I didn't join the RSL, I didn't join any group of men who met annually at functions. I kept completely away from it for many years. Many years later I joined the league. That was a deliberate policy. It's my way of getting back into civilian life.

I remember one time I left the old office and I was secretary of a public company—probably the youngest secretary of a public company in Australia I think, but I had my own private secretary and one of my old mates, he hit the grog. He used to finish up sleeping in parks. He used to come up regularly and I'd give him some money. And this lass said, 'Why would you bother with him?'

And I said 'But for the grace of God, that would be me.'

. . . There was no free medical treatment. Doctors were expensive. You only went once to find they knew nothing about shell shock. Couldn't do anything for you. I just gave it away . . . and set myself a course of six months. There were two things—I considered any man who could get up and sing socially deserved a VC and anyone who could get up with a strange girl for a dance, so I learnt singing and dancing. I went to Leonard Francis who conducted the Apollo Club which is still going—he was the leader before the war—to learn singing and took up dancing and after some months I was quite comfortable doing this so I went to Francis and told him I was throwing it in and he said, 'Oh you've got a voice—it's developing. You want to keep going.'

So I told him I really wasn't considering singing and he said 'Why did you come to me?'

And I said 'You wouldn't understand if I told you.'

So that was that. I learnt dancing too and I was comfortable with that. So I got on top of the two things that I was afraid of and it taught me a good lesson because right through my business career I never had a hard basket. I always tackle a tough job first. Six months was a good training for later life.

* * *

If a shell was coming towards you or past you there's a big scream. Whereas a bomb landing was like a steaming noise of a train . . . but the shells would scream and if you could hear it you knew you were all right—means you were still alive. And if one landed quite close, it exploded before you heard the sound of the fire. The shell travelled faster than sound. The sound of it being fired came after it arrived which is quite interesting. Memory plays strange things... I'd gone in to receive the Citizen of the Year Award and we went out on King George Square afterwards for a flag-raising ceremony. My daughter was with me and they fired a twelve-gun salute from South Bank and the first shot I went to dive for the ground. My daughter caught me and every shot that was fired it was like I was having a fit. And that was 1988 I think.

... We go to the schools before Anzac Day and talk to the classes and answer questions... What is noticeable today is the school children are being taught Australian history. When I went to school we were taught about all the British wars—nothing about Australia but the school children today are being taught Australian and these children have got a surprising knowledge about the war. The questions they ask about the war are quite intelligent. It's interesting.

... I still dream occasionally. Wake up at night and realise, 'Oh, I'm in bed.' Just occasionally but not much now. I think there's a subconscious way of putting it in the background. And you never talk about it 'cause there's nobody to talk to about it. All the diggers are dead and anyone else wouldn't understand. I mean there's no way you could convey to the ordinary civilians the horrors that happened in the war. No way. Indescribable.

INDEX

Abdiel (HMS) 316
Aberdeen, bombing of 111
Aboriginal people 59, 61
  Cherbourg settlement 59, 61
  trackers 264
Aeromedical Evacuation (AME) 499
Albatross leader 45
Americans
  Iraq 487, 502, 506–7
  Japan 365–6
  London 450
  Vietnam 148, 157–9, 213–4,
    338–9
Andaloro, Salvatore 454–89
Anderson, 'Commando' 418
Anderson, Jack 307, 311
Anzac Day 277, 528
ao dai 155
Aquitania 322
Archerfield Aerodrome 103, 105
Argus (HMS) 112, 113
armoured personnel carriers 205
Ash, Lieutenant 516
Australian Defence Force 486–9
  bastardisation 492

Cambodia 376–83
contact with home 497–8, 508
East Timor 386, 387, 396–8, 463,
  474–86, 496–500, 509
females serving in 459–60
Helicopter School 383
peacekeeping missions 484
recruitment 491
training 492–4
Australian Imperial Force (AIF) - WWI
  3rd Division 514
  41st Battalion 515
  British generals 513
Australian Imperial Force (AIF) -
  WWII
  15th Battalion 316
  2/4th Battalion 244
  2/28th Battalion 13
  24th Battalion 307
  43rd Battalion 316
  6th Division, Tobruk 303, 305
  discharge points system 428
  Gaza camp 7
  Mount Isa to Darwin road 66
  reception for POWs 24

Australian Women's Land Army 135
Austria
  Hungarian refugees in 34–7
  POWs working in 20
Azuma Maru 358

Bacskai, Arpad 'Paddy' 29–54
Balibo 496
Barlow, Buck 182, 183
Battle of Britain 108, 110, 221, 278
Battle of Milne Bay 118–24
Battle of Moresby 118
Battle of New Guinea 117
Battle of Sunda Strait 161
Battle of the Swamps 406
Benevolence (USS) 187, 188
Benghazi 17
  The Palms POW camp 17
Berchtesgaden 32, 237
Bet Het 345
Black Hawks 375, 378, 383–95,
  479, 494–6
  collision during training 390–5
  East Timor 386, 387, 479, 496
  Williamtown accident 494–6
Blair, Tony 487
Boomerang Club, London 281, 449,
  450
Borneo 195–9, 202
Bosnia 88–91
Bougainville 66, 70, 404–28
The Brisbane Line 67
Brussels 24
Bryson, 'Beetle-Brow' 418
Budapast 29
Buin 423
Buna 403, 423
Burke, Captain Dave 392
Burma Railway 167–70
Bush, George W 487, 506
Bushell, Roger 227, 234

butterfly catching 324
butterfly mines 381

Cambodia 376–83, 470
Cameron, Norman 260–77
Campbell, Ken 324
Canungra Jungle Training Centre
  201–2, 265, 403–4, 461
Cape Town 516
Cape Victory 404
Carleton, Richard 474
Castle Lager Mitteberg Eins 34
Castleton 110
Changi POW camp 26
Cherbourg Aboriginal settlement 59,
  61
Churchill, Winston 25, 111, 237
Citizens Military Force (CMF) 66,
  104
City of Mexico 244
Clarke, Nolly 109
Claymore mines 201, 216
Clement, Jack 343
combat intelligence 460–1
Commonwealth Reconstruction
  Training Scheme 428
concentration camps 33
Cornish, Dr Geoff 220–41
Cosgrove, General Peter 93, 474,
  476–8, 481
counter intelligence 461
counter-terrorist exercises 386,
  388–90
  Black Hawk collision 390–5
Couvret, Nell 367
Couvret, Paul 355–71
Cowra breakout 403
Creswell, Dick 130
Crotty, Bishop 448, 449

D-Day 280
Da Lat 137
Da Nang 350
Daly, Sir Thomas 337
Dat Do 207
Defence Force Discipline Act 83
Dellwo, Gerry 343, 348, 349, 350
delousing 24
Delp, Lowen 234
Demosthenes 515
The Depression 1, 56, 103, 260, 402
Dili 474, 479, 482, 484, 485, 499
dog handler 262–73
Donkin, Ted 312
Drouer, Captain 169
Duke and Duchess of Gloucester
    258, 451
Duncan, Bobby 408
Duncan, Vic 185, 187
Duntroon 429
Dutch East Indies 355
Dyaks 196, 199

Eagle, Betty 66
East Timor 92–7, 386, 387, 396–8,
    463, 474–86, 496–500, 509
Eboli 430, 436–8, 440
Edwards, Lt Simon 392
Eisenmonger, Bill 70, 71, 76
El Alamein 8–17, 317–22, 327
elastic shortage 67
electric shock treatment 27
Emperor Hirohito 184
England 108–17
    airforce training 108
    Lark Hill Camp 517
    London 116, 278–81, 448
    reception for AIF POWs 24

Finschhafen 323
Fitzgerald, Garth 490–510

Foreign Office, London 449–51
Fouquohertnesle 524
Francis, Leonard 527
Fraser, John 372–401
Fraser, Tony 395
Fremantle 286
French Foreign Legion 377
Fretilin 477
Fukuda, Major 414, 415

Gaza AIF camp 7
Geharnne, Mr 438
Geneva Convention 461–4
German machine guns 10
Gestapo 230–3
Gigli, Beniamino 434
Gona 403, 423
Gorham, Kathleen 452
Gould, Arthur 'Nat' 103–34
Gowrie House 24
Graz 20
Gruppingnano PG57 18
Gulf War II 500–7
    veterans, treatment of 509

Hall, Charles 234, 236
Hasluck, Paul 136
Hawker DeHavilland 131
Hay, General 351
Higgins, Jimmy 230
Hino, Sergeant 179, 187
Hirohito, Emperor 184
Hiroshima
    atomic bomb 423
    Mayors for Peace conference 370
Hitler, Adolf 104, 105, 220, 221
HMAS *Jervis Bay* 474
HMAS *Perth* 161, 162, 164
HMAS *Tobruk* 100
HMS *Abdiel* 316
HMS *Argus* 112, 113

HMS *Indomitable* 129
Holland 221–6
Hollywood Hospital, Perth 26–8
Hooper, Keith 450
Horton, Ross 423
Houston (USS) 161, 164
Howard, John 487, 506
Howell, 'Curly' 412
Hungary
  occupation of 29
  refugees from 31–40
Hurricanes 107, 108, 111–17
Hussein, Saddam 487, 488, 503,
  505, 506

Ibans 196, 199
Indomitable (HMS) 129
Indonesian Special Forces 475
insulin shock treatment 27
Intelligence Corps 460–5
  East Timor 463, 474–86
INTERFET 92–7, 475, 476
International Committee of the Red
  Cross (ICRC)
  East Timor 94
  Yugoslavia 88–91
interrogation 461–5
Iraq War 487, 500–7
  veterans, treatment of 509
Italy
  capitulation 19
  declaration of war on England 434
  Gruppingnano PG57 18
  internment in 436–45
  La Scala 434, 435

Jaba River 406
Japan
  Australian POWs 164–88, 357–71
  surrender 184, 425

Japanese POWs
  Cowra breakout 403
  Rabaul 426–8
Java 356
  POW camp 164–7
Jeffery, Michael 337
Jervis Bay (HMAS) 474
Johnson, Major Frank 351
Joint Intelligence Operation (JIO)
  469
Jordan 501–7
Judge Advocate Generals 82

Kama Ninami Shipyard 358
Kapooka 372–3, 457, 460, 491
Katoomba 426
Katyusha rockets 30
Kellaway, Leon 431, 452
Kenna, Marj 255–9
Kenna, Ted (VC) 242–59
Kenny, Sister Elizabeth 442
Khmer Rouge 376, 380
King Hassan of Morocco 467, 471
Kingaroy air force camp 68, 118
Kittyhawks 118–25
Kokoda Trail 119, 249
Kokutai 324
Korean War 332–9

La Scala 434, 435
Laayoune 466, 470, 471, 474
Lake Victoria 125
Lark Hill Camp, Salisbury Plains 517
Latham, Kev 343, 344, 348
Laverack Barracks 218
Le Havre 517
lice 519, 523
Livingstone 126
Lloyd, Colonel RDF 351
London 116, 278–81, 448
Long Green 204–6

Macassar 357
MacDonald, George 21–4
McGovern, Frank 161–90
McGrath, Frank 172
Mae West (life jacket) 162
Maginot Line 432, 433
Major, Pat 177
malaria 41, 118, 167, 324, 428, 445
Malayan Emergency 40–2, 195–9
Manchoulas, Adele 430–53
Mayors for Peace conference 370
Medcalf, Noel 'Peter' 402–29
Menzies, Robert 6, 104
Messerschmitts 191, 222
Mildura Fighter School 124–6
Military Compensation 399–400
Mills, Keith 176, 177, 180
Milne Bay 70, 118–24
Minchin, Bob 411, 412, 417, 418
mines
    butterfly mines 381
    Cambodia 381, 470
    Claymore mines 201, 216
    Vietnam 201, 216
    Western Sahara 469–70
Mivo River 414
Mobile Strike Force 343–50
Monaghan, 'Mad Mick' 404
Monash, General John 514
Montagnards 138–9, 342–50
    Mobile Strike Force 343–50
Montennuis, Norman 233, 234
Moon, Colonel 483
Morocco 465–74
Mount Isa to Darwin road 66
mouse plague 295
Muda, Colonel 414, 416
Munro, Stuart 123
Murgon army camp 68
Murmansk 113
Mussolini, Benito 435

Nagasaki
    atomic bomb 179, 359–62
    Mayors for Peace conference 370
    POWs working in 358–69
Nauru 97–102
Nestor 285
New Guinea, 72, 75, 117–24,
    245–54, 323–5, 488
    Battle of Moresby 118
    Battle of the Swamps 406
    Bougainville 66, 70, 404–28
    Milne Bay 70, 118–24
    Rabaul 409, 426–8
    Salamaua 70, 71
    Shaggy Ridge campaign 70
    Wewak 246–9
nicknames 374–5
North Sea 109, 111, 280
North Vietnamese Army 156, 158,
    342, 344, 345
Northam Migrant Camp 38–40
Nui Dat 44, 200
Nui Dinh 214

O'Brien, Col 311
Oliveto Citra 439–45
Operation Lismore 267–9
operations law training 82
Orana 221
Oriana (SS) 192
Overseas League, London 282, 450
Oxbridge 280

Palestine 7, 322
    Gaza AIF camp 7
Palmer, Mike 181, 186
The Palms, Benghazi 17
panic attacks 400
Paris 431–4, 523–5
Parker, Bush 231
Parker, Don 311

Parker, Reggie 268
Parker, Roy 307, 309
Parkes, Jerry 173
Passchendaele 522
Patton, General 238
Payne, Clyde 396
Payne, Flo 340, 341, 354
Payne, Keith (VC) 329–54
Pearl Harbor 65, 66, 117
Pearson, Sandy 352
Perkins, Mr 438
Perth (HMAS) 161, 162, 164
petrol rationing 69
pillbox 410–2
Portugal 447
post-conflict counselling 91
post-traumatic stress disorder 398
Powell, Dave 224, 226
PowerPoint presentations (Iraq) 503, 504
Preobrazhenskaya, Olga 431, 433
Prince Felix Yusupov 432
Princess Margaret 25
prisoners of war
   abuse of 93
   Austria 20
   Burma Railway 167–70
   Changi 26
   disease 165–6
   East Timor 92–5
   escape 21–4, 227, 234–6
   execution of escapees 235
   Gruppingnano PG57 18
   Holland 221–6
   Japan 175–88, 358–69
   Java 164–7, 367
   Macassar 357
   Nagasaki 358–69
   The Palms, Benghazi 17
   psychological effects 28, 94, 189–90

   reception for AIF POWs in England 24
   shipped to Japan 171–5
   Stalag Luft 1 226
   Stalag Luft 3 226, 232
   Yokohama 175–84
Proctor, Perce 405, 418, 423, 424
Project Concern 136–43
psychological aspects 10, 26–8, 91, 132–4, 245, 302, 321, 324–8, 526–8
   interrogation 461
   operations law training 82
   panic attacks 400
   post-conflict counselling 91
   post-traumatic stress disorder 398
   POWs 28, 94, 189–90
   R&R 52–3
   shell shock 32, 324–5, 526
   survivor guilt 394
   track crossing drill 52
   Vietnam vets 53–4, 160, 218–9, 271–7
   WWI vets 526–8
Puckapunyal 332

Queen Elizabeth II 25

Rabaul 409, 426–8
Rankin, Colonel 515
Rankin, Dr 256
Rasputin 432
Red Cross
   messages 438
   Missing Persons Bureau 367
   parcels 368
Redbank staging camp 75
refugees
   Hungary, from 31–40
   Nauru 97–102
   Northam Migrant Camp 38–40

repatriation 428
Commonwealth Reconstruction
Training Scheme 428
psychological aspects 26–8
Richards, Rowley 175
Ritchie, Frank 174
Roma, Queensland 287–99
Rose, General Michael 379
Roser, Iris 135–59
Royal Air Force (RAF)
17 Squadron 110, 115
134 Squadron 116
short service commission 220
Royal Australian Air Force (RAAF)
128
3 Squadron 111
75 Squadron 118
76 Squadron 118, 123
Kingaroy camp 68, 118
Royal Australian Navy Volunteer
Reserve 128
Squadron 801 128
Royal Australian Regiment (RAR)
195
1st Battalion 199
2nd Battalion 332
7th Battalion 273
RSL 526, 527
refusal to join 526
treatment of Vietnam vets 53–4
Ruin Ridge 13
Runai 416
Russia 111–14
Russians in Paris 432

Sadler's Wells 449
Saigon 136, 144, 170
Salamaua 70, 71
The Salient 307, 308
Salvation Army 119, 324

SAS
Black Hawks 386, 387, 479
counter-terrorist exercises 386,
388–90
East Timor 474–86
females serving in 459–60
Gulf War 502
Malayan Emergency 40–2
Vietnam 43–51
Scheyville Officer Training Unit 340
Schofield navy base 128
Schwartz, Reg 136
Scullion, Sister, 254, 256, 258
Seafires 129
Seeley, Barry 191–219
Sentanella, Mr 192
shell shock 32, 324–5, 526
Simpson, Ray 352
Smith, Commodore Mike 97
Smout, Ted 511–28
Somalia, Canadians in 92
Somdong Maru 164
South Vietnamese Army 158, 350
Spearka, Arnold 431
Spitfires 116, 117, 124
SS *Oriana* 192
Stalag Luft 1 226
Stalag Luft 3 226, 232
Stalin, Josef 111, 237
Status of Force Agreement 83
Staubo, Jan 238–40
Stevens, Colonel 437
stretcher-bearing 521–3
Suai 479, 480
Suez Canal 8, 192
Sullivan, 'Scooter' 413, 414
Sunda Strait 161
survivor guilt 394
Sutton Bridge 108, 109
Sydney Olympics 238, 494

Tampa refugees, 97
Tean, Father 148–9
Teggiano 439
Tet offensive 136, 151, 342
Thieu, President 144
Tobruk 304–16, 450, 454
Tobruk (HMAS) 100
Tol plantation massacre, Rabaul 409
Toohey, Dulcie 55–76
Toovey, Patrick 1–28
Townsville 82, 218, 254, 384, 391,
  461
track crossing drill 52
Truman, Harry 237
Truscott, Bluey 123
Tududov, Madam 434
Turnbull, Peter 120, 123

Udine 18
UN peacekeeping missions
  Western Sahara 465–74
USS *Benevolence* 187, 188
USS *Houston* 161, 164

Vandersee, Ron 413
Varley, Brigadier 174
VE Day 284
Victoria Cross 250, 258, 351–3
Viet Cong 43–8, 140–3, 153, 157,
  158, 203, 208, 216, 267
Vietnam War 43–54, 136–59,
  199–219, 261–74, 341–52, 487
  A Company 268, 269
  Agent Orange 212–3
  ambushes 335, 344
  Americans 148, 157–9, 213–4,
    338–9
  dog handler 265–73
  Free Fire Zones 214
  Long Green 204–6
  Mobile Strike Force 343–50

Nui Dat 44, 200
Nui Dinh 214
Operation Lismore 267–9
orphanages 144–51
Project Concern 136–43
rules of engagement 213
Tet offensive 136, 151, 342
veterans, treatment of 53–4, 160,
  218–9, 275–7
Vietnamese people's view 208–11
Vung Tau 267, 271, 351
Vietnamese women 155–6
Villers Bretonneux 524
Voicakovski, Leon 431
Vung Tau 267, 271, 351

WAAF 279
  11 Group Fighter Command 279
Wallace, Bill 423, 424, 425
Wallace, Walter 302–28
war brides 72, 283–301
Warfe, Peter 77–102
water testing 514
West Timor 481, 482, 496
Western Sahara 465–74
Westwood, Ian 92
Wewak 246–9
Whitehead, Lieutenant 252
Windmill Theatre 281–2
Wirraways 105, 106, 107, 124
Wirui Mission 251
Wondai army camp 68
World War I 488, 513–28
  Armistice 524
  internment of Germans in
    Australia 63
  pressure to enlist 513
  stretcher-bearing 521–3
  trenches 519
  Villers Bretonneux 524

water testing 514
Western Front 518
World War II
    Australian life during 65–76,
        283–301
    Battle of Britain 108, 110, 221,
        278
    Bougainville 66, 70, 404–28
    El Alamein 8–17, 317–22
    German descendants in Australia
        62–3
    internment in Italy 436–45
    Japanese POW camps 164–87

military training for Australians
    65, 193
modern war compared 508–9
New Guinea, 72, 75, 117–24,
    245–54, 323–5, 488
Pearl Harbour 65, 66, 117
refugees 31–40
Tobruk 304–16

Yokohama
    bombing of 178–84
    POW camp 175–8
Yusupov, Prince Felix 432

CREDITS

The Australians at War Film Archive

Produced by:
MULLION CREEK PRODUCTIONS PTY LTD

Project Director:
MICHAEL CAULFIELD

Producer:
LIZ BUTLER

Consultant Historians:
PROFESSOR JOAN BEAUMONT
DR MICHAEL McKERNAN
DR JOHN REEVE
DR RICHARD REID
DR PETER STANLEY
DR ALAN STEPHENS

PRODUCTION TEAM:

Production Supervisor:
KYLIE FLEMING

Production Managers:
BRYONY KING
ANNELLA POWELL
TRACEY SHARP

Production Coordinators:
TANIA HORNE
ANNELLA POWELL
TRACEY SHARP
WENDY TRUELOVE
CORINA YIANNOUKAS

Production Accountant:
JOHN RUSSELL

Production Assistants:
LISA CAMILLERI
LEAH GIBSON
JOANNE MARTIN
LUCY WATERER
LOUISE WHALLEY
KRISTY WILSON

Researchers:
BRETT BARLOW
PHILLIPA CANNON
VICKI ESLICK
SARAH GURICH
BRADLEY HAMMOND
ANGELA HAMMOND
SERENA PORGES
BRONWYN REED
ELIZABETH HALLORAN RICHARDS

Dubbing Officers:
BARRY ELVERD
KIEREN ROBISON

Senior Supervising Transcription Editors:
DIANNE BRAMICH
MICHAEL CAULFIELD
MICHELE CUNNINGHAM
DR WAYNE GEERLING

Supervising Transcription Editors:
DIANNE BRAMICH
KEN BURSLEM
KIT CANDLIN
MICHELE CUNNINGHAM
CATHERINE DYSON
CHRISTOPHER ELEY
KATE HABGOOD
RON HARPER
CHRISTOPHER HOUGHTON
CHRISTOPHER KEATING
HILARY McGEACHY
MYLES McMULLEN
JEANETTE RIMMER
JOHN ROBBINS
JOANNE STEWART
CRAIG TIBBITTS
LEONARD HARRY WISE

Transcription Editors:
GEMMA BATTERSBY
KATE BATTERSBY
DALE BLAIR

PHILLIP BRADLEY
DIANNE BRAMICH
KEN BURSLEM
COLIN CAIRNES
KIT CANDLIN
MICHELE CUNNINGHAM
KIRSTY DE GARIS
CATHERINE DYSON
LUCINDA EDSELIUS
DARREN ELDER
CHRISTOPHER ELEY
ROD FAULKNER
KATE HABGOOD
MAT HARDY
RON HARPER
ROSALIND HEARDER
CHRISTOPHER HOUGHTON
DR JUDITH JEFFERY
CHRISTOPHER KEATING
JOHN KERR
MATTHEW LIBBIS
CHRISTOPHER LINKE
IAN MACKAY
HILARY McGEACHY
MYLES McMULLEN
JAMES MORRIS
LOUISE PASCALE
TRISH PATON
CATHY PRYOR
JEANETTE RIMMER
JOHN ROBBINS
KATHY SPORT
JOANNE STEWART
VANESSA STUART
CRAIG TIBBITTS
JOSH WADDELL
ALAN WILSON
LEONARD HARRY WISE

Camera Training Consultants:
PETER COLEMAN
KATHRYN MILLISS

Transcribers:
SUE BARTIMOTE
MATTHEW BIENEK
ELLA BOWMAN
MARJORY BRADLEY
ALISON BRUCE
ALISON BURGE
HELEN CARVER
MELISSA CAULFIELD
BARBARA DADD
AMANDA DRAKE
KRISTINA GOTTSCHALL
ANGELA GRAY
GRAHAM JOHNS
SHARON JOHNSON
CLAIRE JONES
KERRY KLEMENS
DAVID MARTIN
DARRYL MASON
RACHEL MEEHAN
FRANCES MILLER
LOUISE MUDDLE
KIM O'DONNELL
JESSICA RICHARDS
KAREN SIMS
KATE SMITH
MARYANNE SMITH
MONICA STEFFAN
JUSTINE WILLIAMS

Additional Transcription Services
CLEVER TYPES
THE LAST DRAFT PTY LTD

Website Design and Database Consultants:
HYRO LIMITED

Logo Design:
GEORGIE HAWKE

INTERVIEWING TEAM:

The Archive interviews were conducted by two-person teams in every state and territory of Australia. Each team interviewed in 'tours' of eight weeks, filming three hundred hours of material per team, per tour. The number next to each name is the number of tours each interviewer completed.

Interviewers:
JULIAN ARGUS – 3.5
MARTIN BALL – 1
REBECCA BARRY – 2
MICHAEL BENNETT – 3
DENISE BLAZEK – 3.5
COLIN CAIRNES – 4
ELLEN CARPENTER – 2
LOUISE CHARMAN – 1
KIRSTY DE GARIS – 1
SERGEI DE SILVA-RANASINGHE – 5
SIMON DIKKENBERG – 2
CATHERINE DYSON – 4
CHRISTOPHER ELEY – 5
KEIRNAN FITZPATRICK – 4
ISABEL FOX – 2
ROSEMARY FRANCIS – 1
KYLIE GREY – 1.5
ZELDA GRIMSHAW – 1
MATTHEW HARDY – 2
NAOMI HOMEL – 3
CHRISTOPHER HOUGHTON – 3.5
IANTO KELLY – 2
SEAN KENNEDY – 1.5
STELLA KINSELLA – 2
ANNIE LETCH – 1
DAVID LEVELL – 1
DENE MASON – 1
CLAIRE McCARTHY – 1
NICOLE McCUAIG – 2
MYLES McMULLEN – 2

COLIN MOWBRAY - 2
KRISTEN MURRAY - 1
PATRICK NOLAN - 1
KAREN NOBES - 1
ROBERT NUGENT - 2.5
LOUISE PASCALE - 2
HEATHER PHILLIPS - 2.5
CATHY PRYOR - 2
SOPHIE RELF - 1
SUE ROBERTS - 1
CHRISTOPHER SALISBURY - 1
GRAHAM SHIRLEY - 2
KATHY SPORT - 5
VANESSA STUART - 2
MICHELLE WARNER - 2
KYLIE WASHINGTON-BROOK - 1.5
JOHN WELDON - 1
PETER WELMAN - 3

PHOTOGRAPHIC ACKNOWLEDGEMENTS

Thank you to all those included in *Voices of War* for allowing the reproduction of their personal photographs in the book: Salvatore Andaloro; Arpad 'Paddy' Bacskai; Norman Cameron; Dr Geoff Cornish; Paul Couvret; Garth Fitzgerald; John Fraser; Arthur 'Nat' Gould; Ted Kenna, VC; Adele Manchoulas; Frank McGovern; Noel 'Peter' Medcalf; Keith Payne, VC; Iris Roser; Barry Seeley; Ted Smout; Dulcie Toohey; Patrick Toovey; Wendy Trevor; Walter Wallace; Peter Warfe.

Thank you also to the Department of Veterans' Affairs and the Australian War Memorial for the following images: AWM A03962, AWM PO4713720, AWM PO4222005, EPI DVA5, AWM P0003733, AWM E00109, AWM H11576, AWM JK0140, AWM GIL670483VN, AWM 013757, AWM P1735033, AWM E01220.

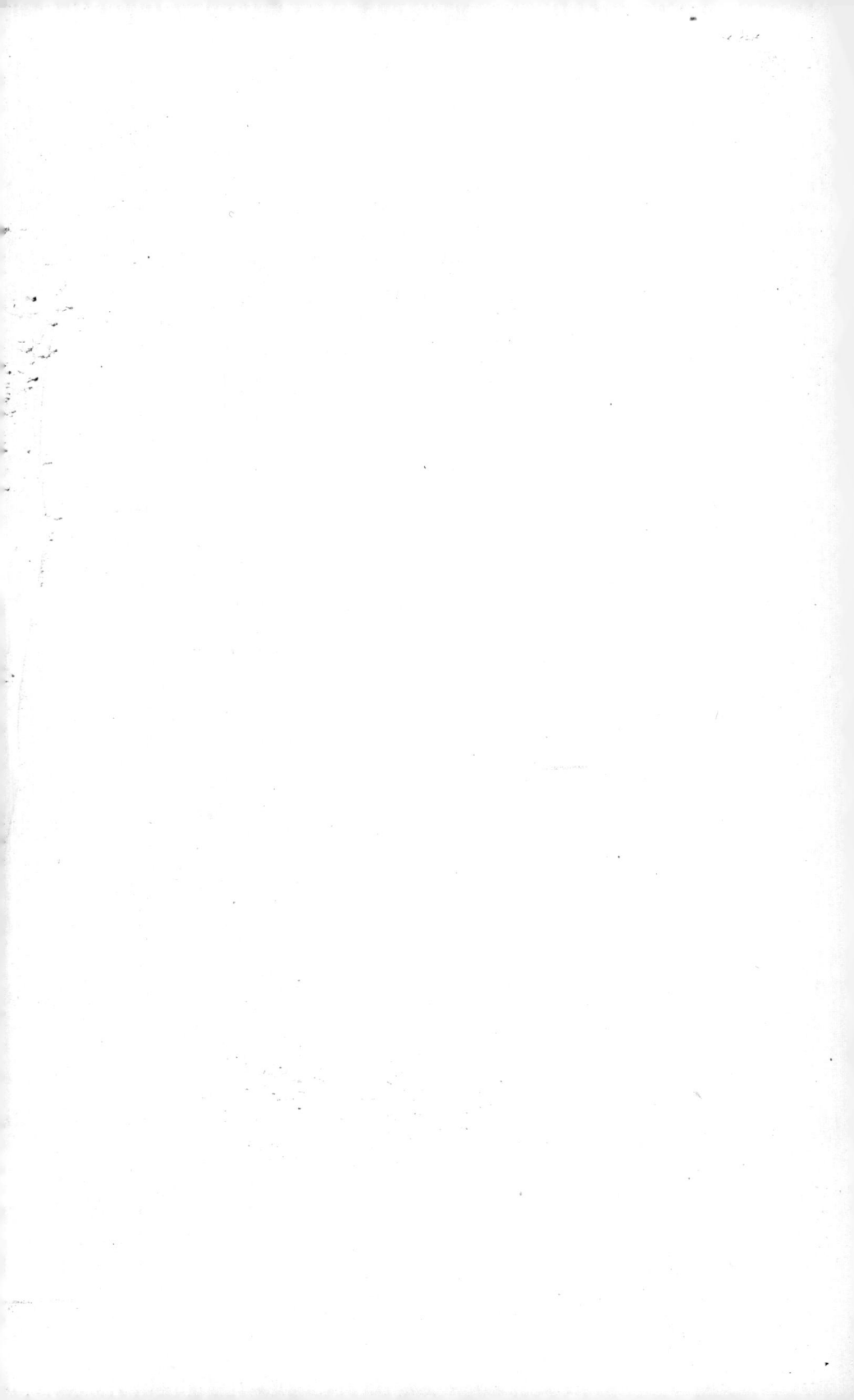